The Social Visions
of the Hebrew Bible

Thanks to the publishers who have allowed me to adapt
previously published material:

"Death and Endurance: Reassessing the Literary Structure and Theology of
Psalm 49," Journal for the Study of the Old Testament 69 (1996): 19–27.
With permission of Sheffield Academic Press.

"How Ought We to Think About Poverty?—Re-thinking the Diversity
of the Hebrew Bible," Irish Theological Quarterly 60/4 (1994): 280-86.
Used with permission.

"Divine Silence and Speech in the Book of Job," Interpretation 48
(July 1994): 229–38. Used with permission.

"Is a Palestinian Theology of Liberation Possible," Anglican Theological
Review 74/2 (1992): 133–43. Used with permission.

"Poverty in the Social World of the Wise," Journal for the Study of the Old
Testament 37 (1987): 61–78. With permission of Sheffield Academic Press.

The Social Visions
of the
Hebrew Bible

A Theological Introduction

J. David Pleins

Westminster John Knox Press
Louisville, Kentucky

Scripture quotations, unless otherwise indicated, are from *The TANAKH:
The New JPS Translation According to the Traditional Hebrew Text.* Copyright
© 1985 by the Jewish Publication Society. Used by permission.

Book design by Sharon Adams
Cover design by Night & Day Design

First edition
Published by Westminster John Knox Press
Louisville, Kentucky

This book is printed on acid-free paper that meets the
American National Standards Institute Z39.48 standard. ∞

PRINTED IN THE UNITED STATES OF AMERICA

00 01 02 03 04 05 06 07 08 09 — 10 9 8 7 6 5 4 3 2 1

Library of Congress Cataloging-in-Publication Data
Pleins, J. David
The social visions of the Hebrew Bible : a theological introduction /
J. David Pleins.
p. cm.
Includes bibliographical references and index.
ISBN 0-664-22175-0 (alk. paper)
1. Sociology, Biblical. 2. Bible. O.T.—Criticism, interpretation, etc. I. Title.

BS 1199.S6 P54 2000
221.6—dc21   00-040810

Contents

Preface

"What light can we get on the troubles of the great capitalistic republic of the West from men who tended sheep in Judea or meddled in the petty politics of the Semitic tribes?" With these words, the great purveyor of the social gospel, Walter Rauschenbusch, opened his influential *Christianity and the Social Crisis*, raising questions about the enduring legacy of the Bible's social ethics.

Of course, from the vantage point of twenty-first century biblical scholarship, this "light" has been scattered through the prism of a host of sociohistorical methods and postmodern readings. The "capitalistic republic" has been replaced by global markets. The "West" has been deconstructed as an ideological landscape, and scrutinized by "north-south" political realities. Feminist analysis has exposed the patriarchal bias favoring the "men" of that culture, and opened to us the rhetorical world of the women who are missing from Rauschenbusch's equation. The "sheep" and the "petty politics" of the Bible have been read against the institutional and cultural backdrop of the Syro-Palestinian and ancient Near Eastern archaeological record. For the sociologist, talk of sheep nomadism oversimplifies the cultural picture. To the liberation theologian, "petty politics" grossly mischaracterizes the systemic oppression experienced by the poor of that day. Even the "tribes" have been reassessed by turning to the pages of the anthropologist's field notebook. With so much recast or up for grabs, one may wonder what, if anything, remains of Rauschenbusch's question.

While perhaps less clear in his day, it is certainly now apparent to the student of literary criticism that our encounter with the past is very much an encounter with ourselves. While I am perhaps less skeptical about the value of historical methods than some of my colleagues, I am also aware that the Hebrew Bible raises key questions about the nature and shape of communal life that continue to speak to the challenges of living in our troubled and divided global village. In a sense, in the Bible's struggles we will see our own. In its wrestling with divergent theological perspectives and diverse ritual practices, we can hear our own civic debates. In its people's struggle for survival, autonomy, and liberation, we can see enduring political aspirations. In its conflicting voices, we find encouragement to add to its provoking of the conscience of the postmodern polis.

That the past is not simply a mirror, however, will become apparent in the pages that follow. The Hebrew Bible is too rooted in its particularities to be easily driven to universalities. The road of ancient Israel's historical experience is loaded with far too many obstacles, wrong turns, detours, and cul-de-sacs to yield a singular "grand narrative" that can speak to successive political epochs, whether theirs or our own. Thus, to the extent that we are able, we should be prepared to encounter unique perspectives concerning the construction of a community's social ethics, perspectives that can augment or even undermine our own thinking on these pressing matters. We should be prepared, in other words, to enter fully into a conversation that has been going on for some time now.

The explorations of this book would not have been possible without the commitment and support of a number of individuals who deserve thanks in this moment. There are my dedicated research assistants who have valiantly braved my illegible scrawl, excessive bibliographic demands, and a host of computer glitches to see this project through to the end: Kimberly Miller, Lulu Santana, Paul Marchione, Grãine O'Leary, and Giuliana Chion. I offer thanks as well to several colleagues who waded through some very rough draft chapters to lend their comments and bring clarity to this work: John C. Endres (Jesuit School of Theology at Berkeley); Gary A. Herion (Hartwick College); J. Clinton McCann (Eden Theological Seminary); and William C. Spohn (Santa Clara University). I am only too well aware of the gaps that remain in this book, but I am ever so grateful for their assistance in areas beyond my own competence. I have been blessed with strong institutional support for my work, in particular through Santa Clara University Research Grants and funding from our Bannan Institute for Jesuit Education. As always, a word of thanks goes to Don Dodson, who works behind the scenes for much of this funding; likewise to our department chair, Denise Carmody, whose unstinting support smoothed the way for the completion of this work and who facilitated a semester's teaching at the Jesuit School of Theology in Berkeley, a stay that allowed serious rethinking of a number of chapters in this book. I extend similar words of appreciation to our previous chair, James W. Reites, S.J. Thanks, likewise, to our administrative assistant Vicky Gonzalez, whose timely assistance salvaged some much-damaged computer data. A word of enduring gratitude to George Pickering (University of Detroit), who initially encouraged this project and who warned me that it would take this long. Thanks also to the adventurers at Westminster John Knox Press. Certainly, Carey Newman, Vicki Hochstedler, Don Parker-Burgard, Linda Webster, and the team behind the scenes are to be thanked for their absolutely solid commitment to this project and for their willingness to give me the space to say what I felt needed to be said about these complex issues. Finally, where words alone will not do, a word of thanks to my wife Teresa, who has given so much to see that I have had the time to think and to write.

One procedural note: Verse numberings follow the traditional Hebrew text, with the English verse equivalents indicated in parentheses (or brackets where appropriate).

This book is dedicated to the memories of two fine students who have graced our department only to leave the light of this world much too soon, Joanne Brennan and Victoria Waters.

J. David Pleins
Feast of St. Francis of Assisi

Abbreviations

AB	Anchor Bible
ABD	*Anchor Bible Dictionary*
ANET	*Ancient Near Eastern Texts*, 3d ed., J. B. Pritchard, ed., Princeton, 1969
AOAT	Alter Orient und Altes Testament
BA	*Biblical Archaeologist*
BASOR	*Bulletin of the American Schools of Oriental Research*
BAR	*Biblical Archaeology Review*
BEATA	Beiträge zur Erforschung des Alten Testaments und des Antiken
BK	Biblischer Kommentar
BZAW	Beihefte zur *Zeitschrift für die alttestamentliche Wissenschaft*
CBQ	*Catholic Biblical Quarterly*
DBSUP	*Dictionnaire de la Bible, Supplément*
EvTh	*Evangelische Theologie*
HUCA	*Hebrew Union College Annual*
IBS	*Irish Biblical Studies*
IEJ	*Israel Exploration Journal*
Int	*Interpretation*
JAOS	*Journal of the American Oriental Society*
JBL	*Journal of Biblical Literature*
JCS	*Journal of Cuneiform Studies*
JEA	*Journal of Egyptian Archaeology*
JESHO	*Journal of the Economic and Social History of the Orient*
JNES	*Journal of Near Eastern Studies*
JPS	*The TANAKH: The New JPS Translation According to the Traditional Hebrew Text*
JQR	*Jewish Quarterly Review*
JSOT	*Journal for the Study of the Old Testament*
MthSt	*Method and Theory in the Study of Religion*
NIV	New International Version
NLB	New Living Bible

OBO	Orbis biblicus et orientalis
OrAnt	*Oriens antiquus*
OTS	*Oudtestamentische Studiën*
PTMS	Pittsburgh Theological Monograph Series
RB	*Revue biblique*
RHPhR	*Revue d'histoire et de philosophie religieuses*
RSV	Revised Standard Version
SBLDS	Society of Biblical Literature Dissertation Series
SJT	*Scottish Journal of Theology*
TDOT	*Theological Dictionary of the Old Testament*, ed. G. R. Botterweck, H. Ringgren (English translation of *Theologisches Wörterbuch zum Alten Testament*)
THAT	*Theologisches Handwörterbuch zum Alten Testament*
UBL	*Ugaritisch-biblische Literatur*
UF	*Ugarit-Forschungen*
VT	*Vetus Testamentum*
VTS	Vetus Testamentum, Supplements
WMANT	Wissenschaftliche Monographien zum Alten und Neuen Testament
ZAW	*Zeitschrift für die alttestamentliche Wissenschaft*
ZDPV	*Zeitschrift des deutschen Palästina-Vereins*

Introduction

Chapter 1

Literature and Location

Reading the Bible is not enough. To understand the social vision of the
Hebrew Bible, it is essential that we study the contours of the biblical writers'
world. How do the various institutions, social structures, and values of that
realm we term "ancient Israel" intersect with the literary compilation we label
"the Hebrew Bible"? In what ways have changing historical and material conditions played their part in shaping and recasting the ethical dilemmas, and
hence the political and theological perspectives, that emerged during the
centuries-long development of this complex tradition? Since we have in view
here the advances held out to us by a plethora of social-scientific approaches
to the Hebrew Bible, we can frame our concern more pointedly by asking in
sociological and historical terms how we ought to characterize the various
conflicts regarding social justice questions that we witness in the ancient
Israelite literary traditions. It is these conflicts that drive the production of the
biblical text. A successful analysis of the social ethics of the Hebrew Bible will
make sense out of the divergent views concerning social justice and poverty

3

found in the Hebrew Bible. In this chapter, we will search for ways to place the ethical perspectives of the Hebrew Bible into an intelligible social context, reviewing several significant classic and contemporary sociological constructs operant in the field of biblical studies. The perspectives we encounter here, both from the history of biblical scholarship and from current trends in biblical research, will guide our reading of biblical legal, narrative, prophetic, wisdom, and other writings. The questions we raise in this chapter will outline for us the historical, sociological, and theological issues we must tackle as we engage the Hebrew Bible's rich and varied contribution to the enduring challenge of creating a more just world.

Jeremiah: A Case Study

The hermeneutical and exegetical obstacles we face in characterizing the social ethics of the Hebrew Bible are illustrated by the seemingly straightforward case of Jeremiah denouncing the king for grossly underpaying the laborers at royal construction projects. By examining the key text cited below and by working through several lines of attack, we will come to see not only the complexities that abound in locating the text in its sociohistorical context but also the manifold theological possibilities available to communities that seek to use such texts as resources for thinking about social ethics.

On the surface, at least, the passage selected from Jeremiah would seem to be rather transparent:

> Ha! he who builds his house with unfairness
> And his upper chambers with injustice,
> Who makes his fellow man work without pay
> And does not give him his wages,
> Who thinks: I will build me a vast palace
> With spacious upper chambers,
> Provided with windows,
> Paneled in cedar,
> Painted with vermilion!
> Do you think you are more a king
> Because you compete in cedar?
> Your father ate and drank
> And dispensed justice and equity—
> Then all went well with him.
> He upheld the rights of the poor and needy—
> Then all was well.
> That is truly heeding Me
>   — declares the LORD
> But your eyes and your mind are only
> On ill-gotten gains,

On shedding the blood of the innocent,
On committing fraud and violence.
Assuredly, thus said the LORD concerning Jehoiakim son of
Josiah, king of Judah:
They shall not mourn for him,
"Ah, brother! Ah, sister!"
They shall not mourn for him,
"Ah, lord! Ah, his majesty!"
He shall have the burial of an ass,
Dragged out and left lying
Outside the gates of Jerusalem.

Jer. 22:13–19

On closer examination, however, this text gives way to a number of difficulties in interpretation, asking us to distill the prophet's "social ethics." Here we shall underscore three challenges of interpretation: institutions, social location, and editorial history.

Rereading the text, we realize that in order to understand this passage on the level of institutions, we are required to know something about ancient Israel's socioeconomic structures. Standing in the background to such a text is a political system of monarchic authority and an economic system that permitted the state to rely on forced labor to carry out its construction projects (cf. 1 Kings 5:27–32 [13–18]; 9:15–22; 12:1–7). To study this aspect of the biblical world requires a clear historical teardown of the institutions and social structures of ancient Near Eastern society, variously termed the "dimorphic society," with its symbiotic connection between urban and nomadic lifestyles, the "palace-temple complex," where these two major institutions serve as the locus of ancient social life, or the "Asiatic mode of production," referring to the feudal nature of the division of land and labor.[1] To what extent, one may wonder, do sociological structures of this kind govern the economic relationships and ills presumed by the text?

While such an analysis is critical to our task, it is rendered difficult precisely because records from ancient Israel apart from the Bible are sparse indeed. Even the *lmlk* seals ("belonging to the king") stamped on over a thousand jars, with their obvious royal connections, remain enigmatic as to distribution and purpose.[2] Likewise, various Hebrew ostraca (pottery shards with writing) from places in Judea such as Arad, Lachish, Wadi Murabbaat, and Yavneh-Yam hint at economic practices and royal political structures that might illuminate our text, if only these economic texts and letters had been written in a more detailed fashion.[3] Yet so much more remains unattested by the few written records that have survived from ancient Judah. To fill out our picture, we must rely on the far more plentiful written records from the wider ancient Near East; yet this data is often centuries removed from the biblical context and imprecise in terms of its fit with the biblical record. With due caution, we will want to press such evidence to flesh out the institutional setting and processes presupposed by the biblical materials.[4] If, for example, K. W. Whitelam is correct to say that "the centrality of the judicial responsibilities of the king throughout extant ancient Near Eastern literature from the various state archives points to its importance in the control and management of social and political tensions endemic to such societies," then appeals by the prophet to the king may serve less to challenge existing monarchic structures than to reinforce royal ideals and practices.[5] With care, the historical record can enable us to read the text against the institutional backdrop and economic arrangements of the text's social world.[6]

The preceding considerations suggest that in order to set this text firmly in its social context we also have to ask questions about the social locations of the various actors within Israel's society and in the biblical text. In the case of the Jeremiah passage, we need to ask about the social status of the prophet in relation to the king. However, depending on where we place the prophet in his social world, we will hear the prophet's denunciation in staggeringly different ways. Our understanding of the text changes radically if we think that Jeremiah's talk is that of a peasant farmer, an educated religious functionary, a dissident poet, or a provincial landowner at odds with the elite residents in the capital city.[7] To say that the prophet denounces social injustice is not enough; we must also understand, to whatever extent possible, the social setting out of which the prophet's words arise. To be sure, much of this work will remain terribly speculative, but we will thereby avoid postulating unnecessary dichotomies, such as prophet versus priest, where such dichotomies may not have been sociological realities but simply devices of rhetoric.[8] To confuse rhetoric and sociology, in this sense, has led to many distorted views regarding ideological and values conflicts in ancient Israel. Furthermore, to import a modern agenda about what it means to be prophetic into a starkly different ancient context serves to muddy the waters concerning how to make use of the Bible in contemporary discussions of social ethics. Gauging the place of the prophet in the ancient environment is a difficult but ultimately theologically instructive task.

Questions about societal institutions and social location help us to understand the fabric, tensions, and power relations at work in ancient Israelite society. As we shall see, these questions apply not only to the institutions and actors we find in the texts but also to the very editing and transmission of the biblical text. A careful review of the social ethics of the Hebrew Bible must also take seriously the impact of the communities that produced and preserved these texts. The Torah and the prophetic literature, in particular, have passed through successive editorial grids that have stamped the received tradition with alternate, if not at times contrary, ideological and ethical perspectives. In the case of Jeremiah, we find ourselves asking several questions: Is this harsh social critique original to Jeremiah? Is the prophet echoing a more ancient tradition about social justice? How has the transmission and collection process created new images of the prophet as a voice in the community? To fail to account for the diachronic dimension is to fail to grapple with the text in a historically credible fashion. We do not find theological validity only in material that we can ferret out and isolate, such as, for example, an "eighth-century Isaiah" or the "historical Jeremiah." Such whittling tends to leave us with precious little "original" material and distorts our use of the evidence historically and theologically. Likewise, there is a loss in not grappling with the later often dramatically significant recasting of the tradition. The Jeremiah passage in question has become amalgamated with a number of royal pronouncements. These texts in turn have been swept up in a much larger document that has constructed an image of a prophet who is a seer of visions, a preacher of parables, and a tragic sufferer who spins songs of lament. In the process, the justice message of the text has become part of a broader presentation of the prophetic voice, a presentation that anchors itself only partially in a strident prophetic social critique. Thus, by carefully observing the shaping of the text over time, whether in terms of its "origins," stages of transmission, or in its "final" canonical form, we enrich our theological repertoire for the discussion of ethics. In the process, we discover that the passage from Jeremiah constitutes one frame in a tableau of oracles gathered by a dislocated community that found it necessary to attach itself to an idealized portrait of the "prophet" during a time in which this community sought to pursue its own postexilic interests. Allowing neither end of the diachronic scheme to gain a privileged position, we can hold the chronological layers in tension as a fruitful ground for contemporary theological discourse. In the book of Jeremiah, then, we find a multidimensional work, far more theologically complex than any search for the "original" Jeremiah would suggest. The transmitted tradition has become the place for a highly textured ethics project.

Our case study of this provocative passage in Jeremiah has driven home some valuable lessons: (1) As we learn to read the biblical texts within their social matrices (i.e., the institutions, actors, and editorial communities of the Hebrew Bible), we will find traditional readings and interpretations of the text challenged and frequently undermined. (2) We also learn that any contemporary attempt to claim these texts for our time will be complicated by our historical and theological observations. (3) Nevertheless, a probing sociological analysis of the biblical text that pays attention to the material conditions out of which these texts arose will produce insights into biblical social thought that can only enhance current discussions regarding how the Bible can be engaged when seeking to develop a contemporary theological ethic.

As a result of our study, we will have the tools to develop a more sophisticated appropriation of the biblical text for discussions of social ethics, both in the Bible's world and in our own.

Ethics and the Social-Scientific Analysis of the Hebrew Bible: Historical Perspectives on the Discipline

The trend to do sociological study, or, as it might be termed today, social-scientific analysis, of the Bible is one that has emerged progressively over the course of the last hundred years.[9] When New Testament scholar Shailer Mathews of the University of Chicago coined the term "biblical sociology" in 1895, he was giving expression to the increasing realization of many scholars that the social teachings of the Bible needed to be studied in light of the developments in the field of sociology taking place throughout the nineteenth century.[10] Techniques and questions in the social sciences have been refined since that time, but Mathews's call to consider the ethics of the Bible in light of the Bible's social world remains a vital task. There is no doubt that theological ethics can benefit from an interaction with the questions and possible interpretative schemes that arise from a consideration of the social world of the biblical text.

There is no need to rehearse the entire history of the sociological study of the Bible here, but as we consider these developments, we should bear in mind that the sociological understanding of the text has changed significantly since the late nineteenth century.[11] Consider, for example, the varying scholarly assessments of prophecy. According to many nineteenth-century biblical critics, the prophets were "great innovators and the real founders of the spiritual religion of Israel," namely, "ethical monotheism."[12] A major shift in assessing the prophets took place in the mid-twentieth century when scholars "focused their attention upon the persons of the prophets" in an effort to "describe the inner religious development of the prophets."[13] The shift in interest from the prophet as ethical innovator to the prophet as inspired seer was in large measure displaced throughout the 1950s, '60s, and '70s by a focus on the prophetic writings themselves through form criticism. This meant that scholars increasingly came to be concerned with "the prior history of ideas and literary forms employed by the prophets" and in the "redactional adaptation and expansion of these ideas and forms by those who created the canonical books."[14]

The latter decades of the twentieth century witnessed boom times for a reinvigorated social-scientific study of the Hebrew Bible. In particular, there was a renewed effort at applying anthropological models to the study of biblical texts. The nineteenth and early twentieth-century studies of W. Robertson Smith and J. G. Frazer, for example, find counterparts in the more recent writings of M. Douglas on the decoding of ritual norms, T. Overholt on the

cross-cultural analysis of prophecy, J. W. Rogerson on the "primitive mentality" and other classic anthropological categories, and H. Eilberg-Schwartz on
the "primitive"—procreation, circumcision, menstruation, impurity, and the
body.[15] These forays have raised the ante on the usefulness of the anthropological method for biblical research. Appropriating this material for a reassessment of the biblical approaches to social ethics is really in its infancy, but the
social-scientific groundwork has already been established.

In this segment of our study, we will look at several classic sociological evaluations of the biblical text. Again, this is not a comprehensive review of the
history of the sociological study of the Bible.[16] Our concern here is to consider
what these writers have to say insofar as their use of sociology enables us to
place biblical social ethics into its social world. After looking at several efforts
of earlier scholars, whose legacies continue to frame the way biblical scholars
consider these issues, we will briefly consider how more recent social-scientific
research on the Hebrew Bible impacts the study of biblical social ethics.

Law in a Sociological Matrix (Max Weber)

In the early part of the twentieth century, the famous German sociologist
Max Weber reread the biblical text as a sociologist. His reading, although
dated in many respects, remains instructive for us.[17] When Weber looked at
the Bible's law codes, for example, he did not simply summarize the laws;
rather, he sought to understand the social relationships and economic conditions that such laws presuppose. How, in other words, does the biblical legal
tradition reflect ancient social institutions and structures?

Weber, best known for his book *Ancient Judaism*, also took up the biblical
material in the course of his discussion entitled *The Agrarian Sociology of
Ancient Civilizations*.[18] The Bible of ancient Israel, he maintained, should not
be read in the abstract; it must be seen as a text reflecting its agrarian background. The laws regarding oxen (Ex. 21:28–37 [21:28–22:1]), for example,
are laws about a "work animal."[19] This economic fact tells Weber a great deal,
namely, that Israel's law codes are not nomadic laws: "One can no longer maintain that even the oldest code (Exodus 19ff) is a product of a 'primitive' society of peasants still untouched by urban influences and money economy."[20]

While more recent studies regarding the dimorphic shape of ancient
Israelite society (i.e., the intimate urban-nomadic symbiosis of the ancient
Near East) would seem to downplay or even contradict Weber's view of biblical law, the archaeological corrective provided by Stager and others regarding
early Israel provides us with a plausible *village* community locus for at least
some of Israel's oldest laws (see chapter 2).[21] Yet even though we may prefer to
think of ancient Israel as a "trimorphic" society, with a continuum that runs

the gamut from urban residents to village dwellers to those who practice trans-humance, early on Weber was pointing us toward a fruitful way to read biblical law in its sociological matrix. His approach urges us to keep in mind the dynamics of a society built around farming villages and an expanding urban population as we assess the nature and scope of the Hebrew Bible's laws.

Thus, when Weber considered the laws regarding the prohibition against the taking of interest, he did not blithely assume that these were simple protections for the poor.[22] In scrutinizing the laws, Weber asked who was responsible for such laws, what were the guiding interests framing such laws, and what were the possible deleterious effects of such laws on ancient Israelite society. In the background, he sees a variety of conflicting groups: the monarchy, military families, the temple priesthood in Jerusalem, rural priests, rural gentry, peasants.[23] More specifically, Weber treats the laws in Deuteronomy as the fruit of a vigorous and successful effort on the part of the Jerusalem priesthood to influence state policy under King Josiah (cf. 2 Kings 22:1–23:30):

> One result of this new order was the promulgation in 622 B.C.E. of the Law of Moses, that is *Deuteronomy*. Henceforth the monarch of Judah must be a 'legitimate,' of the line of David. . . . The Temple in Jerusalem is designated as the only place where the cult may be celebrated, while the priests of rural areas are deprived of their function and reduced to the status of dependents of the priestly families of Jerusalem.[24]

If the laws related to the taking of interest are indeed born out of this particular conflict, and this is admittedly debatable, the biblical interpreter would nonetheless have to ask if the social ethics of the text function to support specific power arrangements in ancient Israelite society. This latter insight is key, suggesting that such texts both emerge out of social conflicts and at times serve to mediate them. This consideration, in turn, raises the question as to whether or not the injunction actually served to assist the poor in ancient Israel. Such is the line of thought Weber followed when he argued that "the interests of the Temple priesthood conflicted with those of the peasantry and . . . the rural gentry."[25] Law codes, in other words, do not drop from the sky; rather, they serve as one group's attempt to enter the conflictual arena of society's power-holders and gain some advantage in that arena.

Discerning the probable social factors behind the shaping of the biblical legal materials is frequently speculative, especially given our distance in time. Weber, for example, imagined that the limitations placed on the rich concerning the taking of interest probably served "to give a monopoly of the business of lending on interest to metics [resident alien merchants] and perhaps also . . . to the Temple."[26] However, regardless of the final analysis, it is clear that a sociological approach to the biblical legal materials forces us to reassess the purposes behind Israel's legal tradition and to consider the social function of ancient Israel's law codes. Weber teaches us that the social vision of the text can fruitfully be read in light of the social arrangements and conflicts that drove this vision. Biblical law codes, on Weber's scheme, are misunderstood if they are seen simply as protections for the poor; rather, these codes function as protections for the "mass of free men against the consequences of social differentiation in wealth and power."[27]

To be fair to Weber, we should observe that he does not reduce the religious dimension to the economic. Peter Berger, referring to what he terms Weber's "anti-Marxian theme," writes, "Weber was concerned to demonstrate that religious ideas have a historical efficacy of their own and cannot simply be understood as a 'reflection' or even 'function' of some underlying social process."[28] For Weber, religious ideas and ethics can and do drive economic processes and shape social institutions. Key for our present discussion is the insight that the religious ideas and social visions of a particular group are invariably distorted when abstracted out of the attending social context.

Prophetic Social Teaching in a Sociohistorical Context (W. B. Bizzell)

By the time 1916 rolled around, enough scholarly work had been done on the sociology of religion in general and on biblical sociology in particular that W. B. Bizzell, an analyst of farm tenantry and agrarianism in the United States in the late nineteenth and early twentieth centuries, was able to declare in his book, *The Social Teachings of the Jewish Prophets: A Study in Biblical Sociology*, that "we are in the midst of a *renaissance* in the study of the Old Testament scriptures."[29] Significantly, he was able to make these claims *before* Weber published his well-known series of articles in the *Archiv für Sozialwissenschaft und Sozialforschung* (1917–1919) that later constituted his well-known work, *Ancient Judaism*.

Bizzell argued that "it would be impossible to understand the meaning of the social program of a Jewish prophet without taking into account the conditions that produced it."[30] This means that the biblical sociologist is necessarily dependent on good historical work. The danger in the biblical sociology method, of course, is that a sociological analysis of the Hebrew Bible might rest on a weak or flawed historical assessment of the text. Bizzell's consideration serves as an important caveat for those interested in biblical social ethics: Careful historical and sociological work is the prerequisite to a sociological study that seeks to interact with the prophetic social vision as a *material* production. Thus, one important background sociohistorical factor for Bizzell is the biography of the prophet. He explains the differences between Isaiah and Micah, for example, on the basis of their social backgrounds: "The former [Isaiah] was a man of the city, and probably of princely blood, while the latter [Micah] was of humble origin and a man of the soil."[31] While other considerations will generate alternate analyses of the social locations of the Hebrew prophets (see chapters 6–9), Bizzell was right to sense varied backgrounds and historical connections in the prophetic texts.

For Bizzell, sociology is not only useful in placing the prophets in context, but the method also sensitizes us to the social message of the prophets. Bizzell argued, for example, that the prophets do not simply make random pronouncements about social injustices. Rather, the prophets have comprehensive social programs. Thus, Bizzell could claim: "The moral program of Amos may be said to comprehend two great classes of social wrongs: (1) *International crimes against humanity*; (2) *national social wrongs*."[32] Bizzell explains the subsequent variations in prophetic social visions by saying that, diachronically, "the social situation that confronted the prophets in successive eras made their social programs differ widely."[33] As we shall see, Bizzell is quite correct to suggest that the prophets and the prophetic texts differ with one another in their "social programs," reflecting changes in historical moments in ancient Israel's past. However, we may need to go further than Bizzell to inquire regarding the extent to which the prophets and the prophetic texts also *conflict* with one another on such matters. The very notion of a unified "prophetic tradition" is a terribly problematic concept, and our sensitivity to differences of social visions between and among the prophetic texts will open up significant avenues of biblical social thought.

Finally, Bizzell's interest in biblical sociology was not only guided by an interest in the study of society and religion, but also by the more practical belief that "the content of the prophetic literature is rich in suggestiveness and social teaching for an age like our own."[34] This interest in contemporary issues undoubtedly explains why biblical sociology bears such strong affinities to the social gospel movement (see chapter 6) and why in more recent decades the social-scientific study of the Bible has gone hand in hand with liberation thinking.[35] The prophetic literature, in other words, provides fruitful terrain for a sociohistorical characterization of prophetic social criticism.

Rereading the Values Crisis in Biblical Narrative (Antonin Causse)

While Causse's writings have been overshadowed by those of Weber, his reading of biblical narrative and his reconstruction of early Israelite history explore in detail the values and structures of the nomadic and village communities as they were affected by the encroaching power of the monarchy. In Causse's analysis, the clash between the urban elite and the nomadic settlers shook the foundations of the latter's patriarchal organization and tribal kin ties.[36]

Causse believed that this tainting of the nomadic ways initially occurred as the Israelites came into contact with the lifestyles and beliefs of Canaanite urban civilization, transforming the desert YHWH into an agricultural Baal.[37] Causse argued further that the urban-based social reorganization which took place under the Israelite monarchy, a monarchy patterned after Canaanite forms, brought about the displacement of ethnic and kin group by geographic districts, leading to the replacement of the patriarchal aristocracy by a court aristocracy. The process intensified, according to Causse, under the Omride dynasty, during which the society's "increased secularization," namely, its use of force to enact policy as seen in the story of Ahab's ruthless taking of Naboth's vineyard (1 Kings 21), demonstrated how far the monarchy had moved away from the community's deepest religious commitments and desert roots.[38]

The concurrent centralization of the religion in the hands of the society's elite undermined familial-based religious rites, a jarring restructuring that saw communal land ownership give way to associations based on territory, urban life, and a concern for wealth.[39] In the process of adaptation to urban values, YHWH was further transformed from the god of the dispersed tribes into the lord of the land and the master of the state.[40] The building of the temple by Solomon signaled that the religion of YHWH could no longer be considered the property of the rural community.[41] The mountain dwellers and their ancient traditions were left to be exploited by those in power.[42]

Causse believed that the biblical narratives attest that the desert tribes and later the peasant villages of Israel sought refuge in a conservative reaction against royal civilization in an effort to protect their way of life.[43] The peasants' reaction as evidenced throughout the biblical narratives took several forms: (1) continuation of nomadic life and preservation of nomadic values (e.g., the Rechabites); (2) abstention from the pleasures of civilization (the Nazirites); (3) continuation of the ancient cult (the Levites); (4) the collection of mountain traditions that elevate the values of the older patriarchal society against those of the urban community (the Yahwist source); (5) rejection of the religion of the monarchy in favor of the religion of the ancestors; and (6) the promulgation of the view that the land belongs to the entire community of tribal dwellers.[44]

According to Causse, the biblical narrative traditions preserve these varied reactions to shifting economic and institutional forces with the advent and development of the monarchy in ancient Israel. In the book of Genesis, Causse finds a nomadic disdain for sedentary life in the story of the cursing of the soil (chap. 3).[45] Where Cain is rejected (chap. 4), proving that Canaanite civilization is considered a proud human effort, and where Babylon is seen as folly-filled (chap. 11), the Yahwist writer by contrast elevates Abraham as the perfect nomad, free of the impurities of royal society. The narratives devoted to the monarchy's inception, according to Causse, preserve traditions of YHWH's hostility with David and with the possibility of the construction of the temple under David. On Causse's analysis, these narratives are symptomatic of the populist, peasant, and nomadic sources of opposition to the monarchy from its start.[46]

For Causse, the prophets drew on the ancient desert and tribal traditions to critique both the aristocracy and the peasants.[47] The prophetic figures, in other words, begin to move in a different direction than the biblical narrative sources in terms of social thought and criticism. Prophetic social analysis, arising from figures such as Elijah, the "man of the desert," stood in vigorous opposition to pagan values, thereby preserving the nomadic critique.[48] However, with the eighth-century prophets (such as Amos, Hosea, and Isaiah), the prophetic voice, still steeped in desert values, turned against the peasantry, critiquing their cult of the dead and worship at the high places.[49] Such a critique, innovative in its own way, amounted to an attack on basic elements of the peasant familial and social structure in tribal Israel. Causse sees in the prophetic critique a deeper grounding for the community, namely, in the notion that the society's relation to YHWH is to be based neither on ethnic ties nor ritual practices, but on a just way of life.[50] Thus, Causse maintained that the prophetic contribution to Israelite religious thought lay in its elevation of an ethical critique that operated independently from the interests of both the ruling elite and the peasantry. Unexpectedly, however, this critique only made matters worse by intensifying the crisis in values between the rural, peasant, and urban populations. Causse suggests that a compromise was needed to avert a collapse in Israel's value structures, a compromise he finds in the Deuteronomic reforms, which he ascribes to the work of prophets in the school of Isaiah.[51]

Causse's studies alert us to the value systems and structures operant in the biblical narrative materials. As we consider such texts in chapters 3–5, we will find that there are indeed powerful social visions at work in the various pentateuchal sources (see also below). Likewise, Causse's suspicion that prophetic thinking offers alternatives to the narrative materials will at times be born out by our investigations.

Who Speaks for the Poor? (Louis Wallis)

This same practical concern for applying the results of a sociological study of the Bible to the pressing social problems of the day that we found in Bizzell's work also motivated the work of another early biblical sociologist, Louis Wallis.[52] The "great social awakening" in the nineteenth and early twentieth-century Christian world brought it into "a new attitude with reference to the Bible," Wallis remarks.[53] Sociology of religion, the study of the social problems in the past, and a concern for social justice in contemporary society all converged in the writings of the turn-of-the-century biblical sociologists.[54] Although Wallis's work, like that of Causse, has been overshadowed by that of Weber,[55] his work on ancient Israel actually appeared before Weber's and merits consideration here.

Wallis maintained that developments in biblical thought were driven by the contact and conflict of two divergent ethnic groups and value systems, namely, the "civilized" system of the ruling, urban-dwelling Amorites (Canaanites) and the "primitive clan" ethic of the highland village dwellers known as the Hebrews, who had recently invaded Canaan.[56] Even with the rise of the Hebrew monarchy and the spread of the worship of YHWH, Wallis maintains that the values of the settlers remained confined to "the more backward and remote classes,"[57] whereas the monarchy's version of Yahwism represented an adaptation of previous Amorite urban religious practices and ideas that focused on Baal worship.[58] For Wallis, the struggle over matters of justice in ancient Israel represented a struggle that had its roots in a contrast between urban and nomadic values; it was a struggle that became institutionalized in the form of class divisions after the Israelites had settled in Canaan, and, in particular, with the establishment of the monarchy.

Who then speaks for the poor? When Wallis tries to place prophetic social criticism into this social matrix, he argues that the canonical prophets, his "insurgent prophets," carried on the ancient village values.[59] The prophets were, therefore, not innovators, but functioned as the representatives of the peasantry and their ancestral nomadic traditions, championing resistance against the monarchy.[60] For Wallis, prophetic social criticism represented a religious articulation of the socioeconomic struggle that had far older and deeper roots in the population.[61] We might also note that for Wallis the prophetic critique was not conceived of as a comprehensive social program in the way that Bizzell believed. For Wallis, prophetic social criticism can be placed in its social matrix, but this does not mean that the prophets understood injustice in structural terms. The prophets simply believed that "all the troubles of the world arise from the bad will of certain individuals—chiefly rich persons."[62] Against these persons the prophets voiced their protest. While Wallis's view differs markedly from the contention that the prophets are concerned with systems of oppression, he does open for us the question of who speaks for the oppressed in the Bible and today.[63] Are the "insurgent prophets" of the Bible and our times the sole advocates for the poor? Are the other biblical traditions unable to articulate voices that speak for justice?

Social Forces, Institutions, and Values: A Legacy of Questions

These four classic sociological statements are sufficient to illustrate the variety of fruitful possibilities that open up to us when a sociological analysis is applied to the biblical text to illumine its social ethics. These writers raise critical questions about the biblical text and about the relationship between biblical ethics and the structures of ancient Israelite society. Their efforts yield valuable perspectives from which we can begin our look into the social ethics of the Hebrew Bible. Weber alerts us to the sociological matrix of biblical law, helping us to see law as a product and mediator of social conflict. Bizzell encourages us to locate prophetic social teaching in its sociohistorical context, grounding sociological analysis in sound historical investigation. Causse suggests that we observe the values tendencies at work in the biblical narrative materials. Wallis raises the issue of class divisions in the Bible and pushes to the front the question of who speaks for the poor in ancient Israel. Taken together, these interpreters, using sociological tools and asking institutional questions, seek to understand and characterize the social forces, institutions, and values that worked to shape the biblical record in all its complexity. Certainly our classic theorists are incorrect in many ways and their analyses need to be updated with reference to more recent historical, archaeological, and social-scientific research into the biblical text (see below). Nevertheless, these pioneering writers are formidable thinkers who deserve our admiration and attention for articulating the basic issues that remain before us in this present book.

Toward an Integrated Social Reading: Current Perspectives

Since the mid-1970s, we have witnessed a marked resurgence in the social-scientific study of the biblical text. The gap between the late 1930s and the mid-1970s is considerable, and we should note what developments stand in between, insofar as these affect our current study. It must be admitted that the early biblical sociology theories had their limitations, not only in terms of their sophistication as sociological theories, but also in terms of the lack of hard evidence, apart from the biblical text itself, to confirm whatever theories were imposed on the text.[64] Sasson points out that these "classic" theories also suffered from the fact that they knowingly or unknowingly imposed modern political perspectives and biases onto the ancient text. Sasson suggests, for example, that Wallis's writing retrojects into the past "(neo)-Jeffersonian ideals," finding "evidence in the biblical texts for ideals espoused by Henry George: inalienability of land, individual autonomy, and social justice."[65]

The danger of retrojecting one's own values and biases into the past during the execution of a sociological study of the biblical text is a continual methodological cul-de-sac.[66] The ideal is to draw on social-scientific methods to enable us to understand better how the social ethics of the Hebrew Bible fits into its social matrix. But we must be careful not to force the text to fit our sociological theories or modern political biases. We should not necessarily expect, for example, any or all strands of the biblical tradition to be "demo-cratic" or "liberationist," and if we do find the whole corpus to be so oriented, we can probably rest assured that our analysis has gone severely wrong at some point. When we come to see our own image in the biblical mirror, we have not come closer to an understanding of the biblical world as an investigatable datum. If Causse can characterize peasant movements of the Bible as a "con-servative reaction," we ought to at least be cautious about finding "progres-sive" forces everywhere in the biblical text. How, then, can we move forward?

Admittedly, these methodological challenges do not make the contempo-rary theological use of the text any easier or politically convenient. Yet there are no shortcuts around a sound historical and social-scientific reading of the ethics of the Hebrew Bible against the backdrop of its own social world as the necessary prelude to the modern appropriation of the text.[67] Fortunately, we can be greatly assisted in our endeavors by drawing on more recent analytic and methodological developments to construct an integrated theological-materialist reading of the biblical record. In this section of this chapter, we shall underscore the key role that archaeology as a discipline must play in our analysis. Having noted the important strengths but also limitations of the archaeological approach, we shall also explore the renewed role of social-scientific analysis in the study of the Bible, establish the critical value of fem-inist and liberation readings of the biblical text, and accent the importance of postmodern methods of exegesis in biblical analysis, in particular rhetorical criticism, structuralist analysis, and deconstruction. We will then turn to con-sider the continuing place of source criticism for our study of the social visions of the Hebrew Bible.

Archaeology as an Anchor

While it is true that a disenchantment with sociological methods led to something of an impasse among biblical scholars, we should not forget that during the 1920s and 1930s major archaeological discoveries were made both inside ancient Palestine and throughout the ancient Near East, creating the expectation that the biblical materials could now be directly understood "against their environment."[68] Scholarly attention turned to the study of ancient Near Eastern historical and cultural documents that were mined for comparative data to illuminate (or "prove the accuracy of") the biblical text. The impact of these discoveries on biblical studies has been considerable, even if many today are understandably much more skeptical about using ancient Near Eastern texts to demonstrate the veracity of the Bible than they may have been in the pioneering years of archaeological discovery.[69] Nevertheless, no modern sociological or anthropological study of biblical law, prophecy in

Israelite society, cult and ritual in the Bible, Israelite education, and the like, could hope to proceed successfully without recourse to comparative ancient Near Eastern materials and the material remains of ancient Palestine.[70]

However, while no serious modern study of biblical ethics can succeed without attempting to blend sociological, archaeological, and comparative Near Eastern approaches to the biblical text, the challenges faced in this regard are enormous. In part, this results from the fact that we are bringing together disciplines that, as Dever has so long and cogently argued, have different agendas and speak different languages.[71] Whereas biblical scholars have as their preserve philology, exegesis, and theology, the Syro-Palestinian archaeologist works as a secular researcher, using social-scientific tools and models to explore the material remains and records unearthed from the region in question. While separate, Dever does think that a "true dialogue between mature, autonomous disciplines" is possible and essential if we are to make progress in our understanding of the history of the religion(s) of ancient Israel.[72]

From the archaeological side, we have a record that does not simply supplement the biblical accounts but more often challenges the picture the Bible paints of religious possibilities, norms, and practices in ancient Israel. Thus, Dever consistently and repeatedly points to the extant nude female figurines, funerary remains, cultic worship installations (*bāmôt*), cult stands, and Asherah inscriptions to indicate that archaeology outstrips the Bible when it comes to presenting us an accurate and detailed picture of lived religious practice on the part of women and indeed the masses in ancient Israel.[73] The diverse picture of Yahwism that emerges bears greater resemblance to its parent Canaanite religion—the worship of Asherah, Molech, the sun, and the like—than it does to the monotheistic tendencies and the ideological blinders of the Hebrew Bible.[74] Thus, as we read and dissect the Hebrew Bible, we must do so cognizant of the larger and more complex material reality out of which these texts have emerged and to which they are reacting.

While Dever is correct to point out that the Hebrew Bible contains historical information that accurately reflects the preexilic period, indicating that the overall biblical tradition reflects, conveys, and builds upon the elite state religion and attendant movements of that time, he does underplay the significance of the final redaction of the texts for the shaping of the presentation of any historical data in the Hebrew Bible that might emanate from the period prior to the exile.[75] As students of the text, we will want to proceed with caution, distinguishing between what might be early from what might be late, as we attempt to characterize developments in Israelite ethics discussions, debates, and practices.[76] Yet we will also remain aware of the heavy influence the final postexilic shaping has had on the stories, oracles, laws, indeed the visions of social ethics presented in the Hebrew Bible.[77] This is not to descend into "nihilism" or to "retreat from history" as Dever seems to think, although his strictures against Davies are well taken.[78] Rather, it is to acknowledge that our study of the Hebrew Bible is a study of that portion of the religion of ancient Israel that is preserved in the Bible, and is not a comprehensive portrait of all religious life in ancient Israel.

Yet neither is Israelite religion as depicted by archaeology the total story. The Hebrew Bible preserves a wide-ranging and ample record that can be mined for great insight into the religious, philosophical, and ethical debates in ancient Israel over the course of its pre- and postexilic existence, albeit among Israel's "*literati*."[79] While to Dever the stones may speak volumes regarding the history of Israelite religion, in particular in its popular form, the fact is that it is notoriously difficult to write a history of Israelite religion from the archaeological record that can take into account the extensive and diverse materials of the Hebrew Bible.[80] Furthermore, Dever's efforts to "segregate theology" and his suggestion that theology is "unproductive when it comes to understanding ancient Israel on its own terms" not only undercuts the very dialogue he claims is needed between text scholars and archaeologists but also distorts the genuine contribution theology, grounded firmly in a social-scientific approach, can make to the reconstruction of major aspects of the history of Israelite religion and social thought.[81]

A Social-Scientific Framework

Given these provisos, where does the contemporary discussion stand with respect to the use of the social sciences for biblical research?[82] A reading of any of the more recent social-scientific forays into the biblical text will reveal that these writers seek to take advantage of (1) advances in sociological theory, (2) an increase in our knowledge of the ancient world, and (3) a more sophisticated understanding of the interface between theory and text.[83] Malina, for example, cogently defends the view that a judicious use of cross-culturally based and historically oriented models of society deriving from the social sciences can be invaluable in our quest to understand texts that emanate from an ancient and alien culture.[84] More recent discussions emphasize the necessity of using anthropological categories such as honor and shame, kinship patterns, in-group and out-group boundaries, patron-client relations, and social location as ways to jar loose the false assumptions biblical readers invariably bring to the text. A cross-cultural hermeneutic assists in more rigorously ferreting out a credible understanding of the text within its own cultural semiotics of symbol and conduct.[85] We must bear in mind that ancient Israel is a culture that not only uses familiar terms such as "justice," but also the less familiar "holiness" and what for many moderns is the completely foreign "pure/ impure," all in reference to what we would call "social ethics." Thus, we find that the biblical world is poles apart from our enlightenment world of rights. Where North Americans might speak of "rights," the biblical world seems to know only duties and upright actions.

While the theological appropriation of these cultural divergences can be challenging, a fuller social-scientific reading of the biblical texts can work to enrich the range of possibilities behind that appropriation.[86] Thus, although it is the case that biblical studies lacks the data to produce statistical studies (what Malina refers to as "sociological 'number crunching'"), nevertheless, this "does not preclude using social science models for determining with some high degree of probability how meanings were imposed on people in the past and what those meanings might be."[87] The social sciences can enable us to more clearly see in biblical ethics lived social realities, meaningful social interactions, signposts in various social worlds, and discourses reflective of struggles for social power. Hence, the ways that the social sciences will be tapped in biblical interpretation are as varied as the social parameters of the ancient Israelite materials and the subdisciplines of the larger field. Studies such as Overholt's on prophecy,[88] Rogerson's on segmentary lineage societies,[89] or Coote and Whitelam's on the emergence of early Israel[90] all seek to take cross-cultural and/or comparative systemic factors into account in developing a view of the social world of ancient Israel. Yet for all the advances that have been made in recent years, the goal of these efforts, constituted as social-scientific explorations of the biblical text and world, is much akin to the aims of our "classic" theorists discussed above. As Long so aptly states, the "social scientific study of ancient Israel seeks to grasp typical patterns of relationship stopped in time, the clearer to see their systemic structure and social functions."[91]

The social-scientific study of the Bible is not necessarily reductionistic, devoid of any concern for questions of ethics and values.[92] Rather, in a well-rounded scheme, social values can come under scrutiny, not being allowed to "drop from the sky" to command assent without philosophic justification, theological force, or historical connectedness. A successful social-scientific analysis of the Hebrew Bible's ethics presses below the Bible's ethical statements to ascertain the "social roots" of the text's ideas, asking, for example, "what group gained in status by not only believing but promulgating that idea?"[93] Even further, we will seek to know how those values in turn shaped ancient Israelite society and the longer-lived tradition.[94] In bridging between sociological analysis and ethics, it is the task of the contemporary biblical interpreter to ensure that historical models and sociological theories are employed to clarify the nature and character of biblical social ethics in the context of its social world both as an integrative as well as a generative force. As Long states, "social scientific study of ancient Israel at the very least underscores the social nexus of religious claims and theological truth."[95]

Such an analysis of the Bible makes it clear, as we shall see, that on matters of social justice, the tradition does not present us with one simple vision. There are many voices and many diverging perspectives. From a social-scientific viewpoint we discover that we will only make progress toward a post-modern understanding of biblical social ethics to the extent that we begin to openly and honestly grapple with the Hebrew Bible as an anthology of theological diversity, radical political dissent, and conservative resurgence. We will not see a genuine advance regarding the use of scripture in contemporary theological ethics until we resolve to enter and engage the political and social conflicts that have indelibly stamped the biblical text. When we have grasped fully the sense that no single theology commands universal assent throughout the whole of the biblical text, we will be free to enter the modern political arena with a healthy and open awareness of the role of the Bible and its limitations for use in contemporary debates over matters of social injustice and oppression. An integrated, sociologically informed, theological-materialist reading of the biblical text, vigorously pursued, will serve as the productive ground for bringing the Hebrew Bible into current theological debates over social ethics.

We have much to learn from the fact that rabbinic interpretation over the centuries, and Jewish tradition as a whole, has been reluctant to subscribe to the Christian effort to produce one "biblical theology," as if one such overarching perspective could possibly be produced.[96] In fact, the conflictual character of the legal debates of the rabbinic Mishnah and Talmud is far truer to the parent biblical documents than the Christian penchant for systematic theology. As Levenson incisively states,

> The effort to construct a systematic, harmonious theological statement out of the unsystematic and polydox materials in the Hebrew Bible fits Christianity better than Judaism because systematic theology in general is more prominent and more at home in the church than in the *bet midrash* (study house) and the synagogue.[97]

The rabbis long ago realized that the Hebrew Bible opens the door to debate and diversity of opinion. Without Levenson's sensibility, we fail to find a biblical theology that both faces the text squarely and meets the changing needs of postbiblical society, whether we mean by this second temple Israel or the contemporary world. In the Hebrew Bible we encounter texts that refuse to give only one view about the poor or about social injustice and its causes. When we sweep aside our impressionistic uses of the biblical text, we confront a document that forces us, by its very diversity of perspectives, to reassess our own views about oppression and political exploitation. To put it simply, the Bible never leaves the reader out of the theological debate. Modern interpreters are urged not merely to examine ancient Israel's diverging views about the social order, as if the debate has ended. On the contrary, in this encounter with ancient views about God and social justice, we are compelled by the biblical text to reexamine our own participation in the structures of injustice that shape our own world.

New ways to analyze the Bible, situated consciously amid contemporary efforts at social transformation, are helping us to hear these voices of biblical diversity. Liberation and feminist theological analyses, in particular, ask us to develop our theology in light of the concrete conflictual character of the biblical text and biblical society. P. Bird captures the spirit of the project well:

> While interpreters such as Phyllis Trible, Mieke Bal, Cheryl Exum, and Esther Fuchs represent differing aims and approaches to the patriarchal text, they share a common reader orientation that invokes response to their retold tales: celebration for unsung triumphs, mourning and rage for unlamented victims and unnamed crimes. These literary-constructive readings present the mothers and daughters of ancient Israel as sisters "heard into speech" by modern feminist interpretation.[98]

Writers in Third World and other marginalized contexts, in particular Latin America, South Africa, and Palestine, have fostered insightful ways to read the biblical text, breaking new ground regarding the Bible's emphasis on concrete human suffering, the question of the marginalization of women in the Bible, and the continuing tragedy of oppression justified in the name of God (see especially chapter 4).[99] These sociologically rooted, rhetorically informed readings of the text make it apparent that the various biblical writers were not speaking about worship and community in the abstract, but were quite often concerned to address very real issues that confronted their society, whether because of domestic crises or as a result of foreign domination. It is not merely quaint, therefore, to know that the Bible arises out of an agriculturally based society; for a compelling theological analysis of the Bible's social ethics, it is imperative to understand the ways ancient Israel's land ownership and distribution may have functioned to oppress large sectors of ancient Israelite society. Only in this way will we, for example, grasp the strength of the prophetic social critique or discern the weakness in ancient Israel's gleaning laws.

To sum up: Social-scientific, feminist, and liberation readings assist in the reconstruction of the plausible sociopolitical matrices for the biblical materials by taking up the challenge of a historical and critical exegesis while exposing the ideological underpinnings of the text through revised reconstructions of the text's social moorings and transmission.[100] By this type of analysis we can enter the social world of the biblical authors. We can begin to see the contexts of the struggles of women, day laborers, and the poor in ancient Israel. The recovery of these ancient marginalized voices has enabled us to more fully appreciate the depth and scope of the biblical debates over justice in society.

Texts in Conflict: The Integral Character of Rhetorical and Postmodern Exegesis

Sociologically based theologies do more than give us a refined picture of the economic system and political structures of the ancient world. When we press the text sociologically, we also see that the Hebrew Bible's diversity of theological and social thought, its rhetoric, is inextricably linked to the conflictual character of the concrete political institutions and social structures that shaped ancient Israelite society.[101] Conflicting texts emerge from conflictual social contexts. To understand ancient Israel sociologically is not only to understand its various institutions, but also to understand, as reflected in the literature, how those institutions and structures were in collision and competition. A sociologically based reading of the text enables us to place the Hebrew Bible's diversity of social thought into a context of historical and social conflict. We can even begin to understand why certain voices play down or avoid treating poverty as a structured injustice of the social system. Rhetorical criticism and other forms of postmodern exegesis enable us to watch those voices at work in the biblical text.

Rhetorical criticism, structuralist analysis, and poststructural exegesis have begun to help us understand the literary conventions and discourses the biblical writers tap and fall victim to as they convey their views on matters of society and justice. *Rhetorical criticism* represents an ahistorical look at texts as such.[102] Rather than seeking to go "behind" the text in terms of its historical background, social world, or history of transmission, rhetorical criticism observes the language of the text. Rhetorical criticism lingers over repetitious phrasing, key word development, plays on words, the characterization of persons, and the use of the narrative voice or dialogue in the text, often with a view to underscoring the ideological drift of the material under investigation. Such close readings seek to leave no narrational or linguistic stone unturned as the inner resonances of the text are exposed to inspection. *Structuralist analysis* works to unpack the underlying patterns and structures that govern a text.[103] This method has been used rather effectively in the study of mythology, where repeated patterns can most readily be discerned within and between mythic tales.[104] Structuralism, in relation to literature, is particularly interested in isolating the binary oppositions in texts, from simple oppositions such as heaven/earth and light/darkness to seemingly higher-level wrestlings over life/death or nature/culture. Structuralism is not limited to the study of literary works or oral traditions but has also been applied by anthropologists to the study of social institutions and ritual practices, seeing in these institutions and practices symbol systems that encode cultural patterning, in particular categories such as pure/impure.[105] Structuralism, in essence, brings forward the "grammar" of myth and society. *Post-structuralist criticism or deconstruction*, dissatisfied with the mathematical certainties of structuralism, explores the ambiguities and slippage in language that occur even as texts seek to create ordered realities, hierarchical power structures, and homogeneous human experiences.[106] Deconstruction uncovers what ancient imperial texts and even so-called modern "Enlightenment" productions, with their grand narratives of heroes and states shaping the destiny of humanity, work to conceal: Texts do not have singular meanings, but through interconnectedness and infinite regression slide between meanings and layers of meaning, thereby allowing the text to betray itself.[107] Where a text might seek to privilege one ideology over another, one group against another, or one set of terms above another, by contrast deconstruction, "relativizes the authority attributed to them [i.e., texts], and makes it evident that much of the power that is felt to lie in texts is really the power of their sanctioning community."[108]

We can enter the Bible's conflicted diversity from these methodological vantage points, observing the text's language as it embodies contrasting ideologies and contending cultural norms. The variety of the Bible's genres of discourse impresses on us the need for closer analysis of the biblical texts in terms of their diverse and competing social visions. Overlooking the range and textures of the materials, biblical theologians have frequently spoken about topics such as poverty and injustice as if all genres deal rather uniformly with the same social realities and speak with the same voice. All literature, and biblical literature in particular, is a concrete expression of human ideas and ideals, serving as embodiments of social status and power.[109] Abstracting the biblical texts from their social and political context defeats our effort to uncover the role of these writings in ancient Israel's social justice debate. While we might fall prey to a bland systematization of the biblical record, we are continually challenged by a polyvalent biblical literature that is rooted in concrete social contexts, changing historical moments, and communal struggles. By employing postmodern methods, we encounter a variety of voices in the Hebrew Bible that seek to persuade and critique, mollify and challenge, instruct and dissuade. In this collision of rhetorics, our theological work begins.

Kerygma and Justice: The Continuing Role of Source Analysis

Since this present study makes a great deal of use of a more traditional source analysis for the pentateuchal traditions, a word or two is in order about this method of analysis. Clearly biblical scholarship is in an uproar regarding the formation of the Hebrew Bible. The older efforts to divide the Torah into four

major sources—J (Yahwist), E (Elohist), D (Deuteronomy), and P (Priestly)—
together with an overarching editor or redactor, has fallen on hard times in various quarters.[110] Carr frames the issue well:

> The field of pentateuchal studies has often served as a bellwether for
> the broader field of Hebrew studies. Therefore, it should be no sur-
> prise that the methodological confusion of contemporary biblical
> studies might be reflected with particular intensity in study of the Pen-
> tateuch. Not only do biblical scholars not agree on many aspects of the
> formation of the Pentateuch, but many disagree about whether one
> can say anything reliable on that subject or what difference it would
> make if we could.[111]

As Carr sees it, there are two major areas of disagreement: First, some are
asking questions of chronology, geographical distribution, and textual spread.
Are the sources to be dated so cleanly, with J in the tenth through ninth centuries B.C.E., E in the ninth century, D in the seventh century, and P in the
exilic or more likely postexilic period? Is J a Judaean source, E a northern
source, D a code connected with the Jerusalem of the time of King Josiah (c.
640–609 B.C.E.), and P a Jerusalem temple document? How far do J, E, D, or
P extend in the Torah? Is Deuteronomy to be read as the introduction to an
extended history running from Joshua to 2 Kings, a so-called Deuteronomic
History (DH)? Do any of the sources other than D impact the stories from
Joshua to 2 Kings? Does one source know about another? Does one source
consciously react to or expand on another? Are there even sources at all?

The second area of disagreement involves other scholars, who are asking
questions of literary and rhetorical nature, finding either unity or complexity in
the text. Some argue for unity in the Torah, treating the splitting of the text into
a variety of sources as implausible and subjective. By contrast, there are some
who are aware of the text's complexities, but sense that the assured recovery of
coherent earlier phases behind the text is an illusory endeavor. In either case, for
such scholars, literary archaeology is not a substitute for dealing with the Torah
in its final and received compilation. Carr's piece merits our attention as he
warns us about the difficulties of traversing the source-critical waters today.

In the end, however, attempts to dismantle the Documentary Theory seem
not to be compelling. We have to bear in mind that this theory arises out of
well-grounded suspicions that the Torah was composed over a long period of
time and stems from various hands. There are oddities of language, duplica-
tions of episodes, contradictions of subject matter, repeated revelations of the
divine name, and the like, which call for some sort of explanation along the
lines proposed by the Documentary Theory.[112] From the simple observation
that Moses did not write about his death in Deuteronomy 34 (or speak of his

own humbleness in Num. 12:3), to the understanding that the two creation stories in Genesis 1 and 2–4 do not stem from the same author, to the fact that the divine name comes to be revealed in different ways in apparently different sources (Ex. 3:13–15 = E; Ex. 6:2 = P; with J using the divine name from the start), to the dovetailing of two very different flood stories in the present single story, to the even more complex observations about the composite and supplementary character of so many Torah narratives, we must conclude that not only different writers but different theological schools of thought have come to be amalgamated in the Torah as it stands today.[113] To be sure, we need not think simplistically that four originally distinct sources were combined at some time well into the second temple period. One could argue, for example, that materials attributed to P may not have stood as an independent source but may well represent an expansion of the available J and E traditions. Yet regardless of whether or not we call J, E, D, and P "sources," "tradents," or "traditions" (and I intermingle all these designations in this study), the fact of the matter is that in large measure we can discern in these labels competing theological voices that have contributed uniquely to the ongoing discussion of ethical praxis in ancient Israel.

Like many, however, I do have my own considerations regarding the dates of these tradents. I am far less convinced of the antiquity of these sources, or major aspects of them, than other interpreters. Thus, in light of the inevitable controversies that attend such discussions, it seems best to outline here the framework that will govern this study of the social visions of the Hebrew Bible. Specific documentation and arguments will be offered in chapters 2–5. Several considerations, however, merit attention here.

> *Deuteronomy and the Deuteronomic History:* I treat the Deuteronomic Law Code (chaps. 12–26) as the product of the Judaean royal court, from either the reign of Hezekiah (715–687 B.C.E.) or, more likely, Josiah (640–609 B.C.E.). As for the Deuteronomic History (here abbreviated as DH, i.e., Joshua, Judges, 1–2 Samuel, and 1–2 Kings), based as it is, in part at least, on ancient royal annals, it undoubtedly went through several phases of development, with perhaps an initial edition supporting Josiah's reforms and a full-scale work refocusing royalist efforts in the wake of the exilic disaster (Jehoiakin's circle) and during the period immediately thereafter. I will also suggest that there was a priestly redaction of some of the DH materials.

> *The J source:* Here I will treat J (the Yahwist) as a postexilic product that has built itself upon DH, invoking a "promise of land" motif for the returnees from exile, furthering royalist and nostalgic tendencies in the population guided by specific ritual interests. The theological stamp of exile is plain in J, regardless of any ancient patriarchal traditions that may be enshrined therein.

The E source: I will argue here that E (the Elohist) is a genuine and distinctive source. In part, E is certainly reflective of many of the ancient epic traditions of early Israel and its monarchy, traditions on the order of the ancient myths known from Ugarit. However, like J, these materials have been severely refracted in light of postexilic debates about religious praxis, communal values, and equitable social structures. E, with its Mosaic tendencies and "fear of God" theology, falls in line with theological motifs fostered by Haggai. It is possible that J has edited and hence responded to E, although the linkages here are not always clear.

The P source: Unlike those who posit that P (the Priestly writer[s]) has preexilic roots, I will agree with those who find P thoroughly at home in the age of the postexilic priestly commonwealth. P is not a unified stream, however, since the Holiness Code (Leviticus 17–26) would seem to culminate these efforts. In this source, the authority of a particular priestly circle is paramount, but this stream also exhibits a profound and inclusive social vision.

Genesis–Kings: The large amalgam of Genesis–Kings is to be credited to P or to other late Persian-early Hellenistic period efforts aimed at codifying and elaborating the traditions and social teachings of Israel and Judah.

In this book, then, I will treat these sources in large measure as products of movements in the early postexilic period, so much so that attempts at recovering the previous layers behind the texts will be considered problematic at best.[114] This is not to say that there are no clearly identifiable preexilic texts present in the Hebrew Bible. Poetic texts such as Exodus 15, Deuteronomy 33, and Judges 5 attest to an ancient epic tradition behind the Hebrew Bible.[115] Likewise, "accurate" annalistic materials stand behind many segments of 1–2 Kings, although even here, in the absence of corroborating data, we often have no way of knowing precisely where these early materials leave off and where the final shaping of the experience of exile has produced an archaizing of the data.[116] Neither is this to say that we have not recovered substantial material remains from a living and breathing Israel and Judah of the preexilic eras (see above).[117] Yet the needs and anxieties of the postexilic age have so colored the presentation of most texts that any effort to peel away this lens leaves little that derives with certainty from prior periods. Thus, while there are Abrahamic traditions that reflect the epic tales of an earlier age, as we know from the tales of childless patriarchs from Late Bronze Age Ugarit, the "promise motif" has obviously been stamped by the exilic experience of separation from the land and a desire to return to it (see chapters 3 and 5). The attendant sources, whether J, E, or P, appear to be so infused with exilic survival issues that it is difficult to place the sources with confidence far back into the monarchic period as is so often done.

While these considerations may seem negative to some, we can see in the various sources vibrant theologies and social-ethical discussions that give evidence of a vigorous debate in ancient Israel concerning the nature of society, the place of ritual in the construction of a just people, and the relation of the divine to these very human projects. On that score, the studies of R. B. Coote, W. Brueggemann, and H. W. Wolff have taught us to think of the sources as vital programs of thought and action, not simply as the dissected remains of an antique cadaver.[118] Brueggemann and Wolff, in particular, see in the sources four *kerygmas*, or theological messages: Blessing will come to the world through Israel (J); fear and obey God (E); in repentance there is hope (DH); and be fruitful and multiply (P). Building on these crucial insights, we will tackle these diverse theological programs in terms of their social ethics dimensions in chapters 3–6. Far from being a method to be dispensed with, even as we take into account the synchronic dimensions of the final form of Genesis–Kings, attentiveness to source analysis can produce insight into the varied perspectives regarding poverty and justice in these materials. In and between the sources, in other words, reside the compelling and competing social visions of a large portion of the scriptural canon.

The Art of Reading Struggle-Ridden Texts

From whatever vantage point we now approach the biblical text, we can clearly see that conflict is foundational to the biblical text. The biblical writers quite often diverge in their views, and this gives rise to significant differences in opinion and analysis within the biblical text. Theirs too was an age of pluralism, although their pluralism and philosophical diversity have often been obscured by our need to systematize and bring the Bible under a uniform ideological umbrella, whether we are conservatives or liberals, moral majority advocates or liberation activists. The biblical age was an era in which universalist views of God and nationalist views of God stood in competition, sometimes even within the same book of the Bible.[119] The Bible as a whole and even individual texts go in various directions at once. These are indeed what I. Mosala, the South African liberation writer terms, "struggle-ridden texts."[120] The discord of voices is both the refreshing challenge of the Hebrew Bible and its thorn in our side.

While this kind of theological analysis will shake up the oversimplified uses of the Bible found not only in fundamentalist but even in radical circles, there is a strong need to rediscover the biblical diversity that shatters contemporary efforts to make the sacred text conform to narrowly construed political programs and agendas built on flawed views of ancient Israel and its writings. Biblical Israel saw a number of "faiths" and "civic creeds" jostle for room as the community pursued (or evaded) the demands of justice.[121] That was the world of their ethical discourse. Major blocks of biblical material from a variety of authors—the prophets, the wise, the legal writers, the historians, and the hymnists—are all vying for attention, offering differing and at times radically conflicting approaches to the social questions of their day. Not only do these major blocks offer diverging outlooks, there are also differences within each camp. It is no longer possible to speak of one prophetic or one wisdom viewpoint. We cannot leaf through the Bible, hoping to find a unified directive on questions of peace, justice, family, or economics.

Of course, the discovery of such diversity inside sacred scripture can be disconcerting and frightening. I believe, however, that these elements of dialogue, debate, and diversity are the ground for a vital contemporary biblical social ethics. This is not to suggest, as some may, that the recovery of the fact of biblical diversity is an end in itself. Such an attitude might only represent ambiguity and confusion about one's own principles or even indicate an unwillingness to engage the pressing social concerns of our day. But neither is conflict to be feared. Conflict can breed clarity of purpose and direction. Conflict can be the first move toward a viable social vision. Conflict can be the sign that not all are really interested in seeing justice done to the poor, regardless of what their rhetoric may seem on the surface to be saying.

Once we have unearthed the conflictual nature of the voices, we will be in a better position to evaluate their contribution to ancient Israel's ongoing debate over its social ethics and the demands of the Divine Sovereign regarding poverty in society. Once we have heard the contributions of the competing biblical voices, we will be ready to develop a modern theological discourse about social ethics, one that is unafraid to engage the conflicts of our present moment in history. The struggles of the oppressed, of women, of those whose lands and homes are confiscated—all these will become part of our discourse and of our struggle. In the chapters that follow, I ask the reader to hear the diverging voices of the biblical text as they speak to matters of social justice and poverty.

As we proceed, we will deal with all of the major traditions of the Hebrew Canon, though not entirely in the canonical order, nor in the order that the texts seem to date themselves. In large measure, the book's divisions do follow the classic Jewish arrangement of the canon into the tripartite structure of Torah (Pentateuch/Five Books of Moses), the Prophets (narrative of the kings of Israel and Judah and the canonical prophetic literature), and the Writings. Thus, in chapters 2–4 we will take up Torah laws and Torah narratives, in chapters 6–9 we will discuss the canonical prophetic texts, and in chapters 10–12 we will deal with such key elements from the Writings as the Psalms, Song of Songs, Lamentations, and the wisdom texts of Job and Qohelet (Ecclesiastes). Yet in two significant ways our study will depart from the Jewish canonical ordering. The books of Joshua–2 Kings and 1–2 Chronicles will be set alongside the Torah's narratives to bring out more fully the diverging ethical perspectives that appear in extended biblical narratives. Likewise, some key narrative texts among the Writings, namely Ezra, Nehemiah, Esther, Ruth, and Daniel, will be brought together, both to highlight additional issues of ethics in biblical Hebrew narrative and to accent key moments in the overall historical development of the canon of scripture during the Persian (539–332 B.C.E.) and Hellenistic (332–63 B.C.E.) time periods. In this way, it is hoped that this book will be of use both to those who wish to follow the general contours of the Hebrew canon and to those whose interests lie in the overall historical development of the biblical materials. The theological study of the social visions of the Hebrew Bible is, after all, both a textual as well as a historical endeavor.

Notes

1. One should not underestimate the problems encountered when seeking to label the land ownership relationships and production arrangements of ancient Israel across its several phases of development. The phrase, "Asiatic mode of production," poses particular difficulties insofar as scholars disagree over what Marx meant by the phrase and its relation to other stages of production, and where the phrase might be used too loosely to cover aspects that Marx would have linked into his "ancient" and "feudal" modes. In any event, the content of our labels must be guided by the biblical and ancient Near Eastern data and not imprecise phrasing about communal village and despotic land ownership. See the debates in T. Brook, ed., *The Asiatic Mode of Production in China* (Armonk, N.Y.: M. E. Sharp, 1989). The notion of the palace-temple complex or the "great organizations" is set against the general phenomenon of urbanism in A. L. Oppenheim, *Ancient Mesopotamia: Portrait of a Dead Civilization*, revised edition completed by E. Reiner (Chicago: University of Chicago Press, 1977), chap. 2. Among his numerous studies on the dimorphic society, see M. Rowton, "Enclosed Nomadism," *JESHO* 17 (1974): 1–30.
2. See, e.g., H. D. Lance, "Stamps, Royal Jar Handle," *ABD* 6: 184–85.
3. For representative texts, see J. C. L. Gibson, *Textbook of Syrian Semitic Inscriptions*, vol. 1, *Hebrew and Moabite Inscriptions* (Oxford: Clarendon Press, 1971), chap. 3.
4. The archaeological optimism of K. A. Kitchen, *Ancient Orient and Old Testament* (Downer's Grove, Ill.: InterVarsity Press, 1966) and *The Bible in Its World: The Bible and Archaeology Today* (Downer's Grove, Ill.: InterVarsity Press, 1978), is roundly countered by the sort of questions raised, for example, by J. Van Seters, *Abraham in History and Tradition* (New Haven, Conn.: Yale University Press, 1975). The "fit" between the archaeological data and the biblical material is often one of "flavor" and less of factual corroboration.
5. K. W. Whitelam, "Israelite Kingship: The Royal Ideology and Its Opponents," in *The World of Ancient Israel: Sociological, Anthropological, and Political Perspectives* ed. R. E. Clements (Cambridge: Cambridge University Press, 1989), 131–32.
6. Clements, *World of Ancient Israel*, offers a number of studies concerning the social world of the biblical materials. Particularly relevant here are Whitelam's study of kingship in ancient Israel (chap. 6) and Carroll's on prophecy in ancient Israelite society (chap. 10).

7. See, e.g., M. A. Cohen, "The Prophets as Revolutionaries: A Sociopolitical Analysis," *BAR* 5/3 (1979): 12–19. Cohen uses a social-scientific approach to characterize the preexilic prophets as in some sense revolutionary figures with a sizable following. Contrast E. Jacob, "Les prophètes bibliques sont-ils des révolutionnaires ou des conservateurs?" *Christianisme Social* (Paris) 71 (1963): 287–97, who finds conservative elements in the long-term institutional connections of prophecy, connections that date back to the texts at Mari, and in the lack of a truly revolutionary oratory in the prophetic writings. For Jacob, the prophetic "revolution" consists in radically drawing the people as a whole back to God. See also D. L. Smith, "Jeremiah as Prophet of Nonviolent Resistance," *JSOT* 43 (1989): 95–107.

8. R. P. Carroll, "Prophecy and Society" in Clements, *World of Ancient Israel*, 203–25, offers appropriate warnings about the speculative dangers of reconstructing the ancient prophetic world, although his points of extreme skepticism would seem to be unwarranted.

9. See R. R. Wilson, *Sociological Approaches to the Old Testament* (Philadelphia: Fortress Press, 1984), 1–29.

10. S. Mathews, "The Old and New Testament Student," *Biblical World* 5 (1895): 3. A profile of Mathews's methodology and thought is provided by K. Cauthen, *The Impact of American Religious Liberalism* (New York: Harper & Row, 1962), 147–68. A discussion of the Chicago School and Mathews's role in it can be found in J. C. Rylaarsdam, "Introduction: The Chicago School—And After," in *Transitions in Biblical Scholarship*, ed. J. C. Rylaarsdam (Chicago: University of Chicago Press, 1968), 1–16.

11. Wilson, *Sociological Approaches to the Old Testament*, chap. 2.

12. J. A. Dearman, "Hebrew Prophecy and Social Criticism: Some Observations for Perspective," *Perspectives in Religious Studies* 9 (1982): 131–43, esp. 132.

13. J. M. Ward, "The Eclipse of the Prophet in Contemporary Prophetic Studies," *Union Seminary Quarterly Review* 42 (1988): 97; cf. Dearman, "Hebrew Prophecy and Social Criticism," 133. The possible inner, psychological dimensions of prophecy achieved something of a summation in J. Lindblom, *Prophecy in Ancient Israel* (Philadelphia: Fortress Press, 1962).

14. Ibid., 99; cf. Dearman, "Hebrew Prophecy and Social Criticism," 133.

15. See especially W. Johnstone, *William Robertson Smith: Essays in Reassessment* (Sheffield: Sheffield Academic Press, 1995); M. Douglas, *Purity and Danger* (New York: Praeger Publishers, 1966), chap. 3; idem, *Implicit Meanings: Essays in Anthropology* (London: Routledge & Kegan Paul, 1975), chap. 16; J. W. Rogerson, *Anthropology and the Old Testament* (Sheffield: JSOT Press, 1984); H. Eilberg-Schwartz, *The Savage in Judaism* (Bloomington, Ind.: Indiana University Press, 1990), esp. chaps. 6–8; idem, "The Problem of the Body for the People of the Book" in *People of the Body: Jews and Judaism from an Embodied Perspective*, ed. H. Eilberg-Schwartz, (Albany: State University of New York Press, 1992), 17–46; T.W. Overholt, *Channels of Prophecy: The Social Dynamics of Prophetic Activity* (Minneapolis: Fortress Press, 1989).

16. For a general orientation with some specific application see also N. K. Gottwald, "Sociology of Ancient Israel," *ABD* 6:79–89.

17. A useful discussion of Weber in the context of Marx and Durkheim is offered by A. D. H. Mayes, "Sociology and the Old Testament," in Clements, *World of Ancient Israel*, 39–63.

18. M. Weber, *Ancient Judaism*, trans. H. H. Gerth and D. Martindale (New York: Free Press, 1952).

19. M. Weber, *The Agrarian Sociology of Ancient Civilizations*, trans. R. I. Frank (1909; 1924; reprint, London: NLB, 1976), 134.

20. Ibid.

21. L. Stager, "The Archaeology of the Family in Ancient Israel," *BASOR* 260 (1985): 1-35. See also F. S. Frick, "Ecology, Agriculture and Patterns of Settlement," in Clements, *World of Ancient Israel*, chap. 4, whose study of the Iron I highland settlements in Palestine seeks to understand the dynamics of both regional interconnectedness and fracture that not only permitted tribal survival but also induced the rise of the early chiefdoms under Saul and David. The difficulty with so many of these studies that focus on Iron I phenomena is that texts such as Joshua, Judges, and 1 Samuel are treated as quasi-anthropological reports on the time period. Iron I settlement patterns and subsequent state formation *may* underlie the biblical memory of the region's past, but we should also be aware of the stylized tendencies of the literature and the filters created by the production of these texts at a date far removed from the Iron I period. Cf. D. Jobling, "Feminism and 'Mode of Production' in Ancient Israel: Search for a Method," in *The Bible and the Politics of Exegesis: Essays in Honor of Norman K. Gottwald on His Sixty-Fifth Birthday*, ed. D. Jobling et al. (Cleveland: Pilgrim Press, 1991), 229–51, 246–47. Likewise, the effort to describe premonarchic Israel as a "segmentary society" will falter to the extent that sociological and anthropological theorizing is allowed to sit too loosely next to the biblical record. See the survey of this discussion in J. D. Martin, "Israel as a Tribal Society," in Clements, *World of Ancient Israel*, chap. 5.

22. Contrast Weber, *Ancient Judaism*, 61–74, where he modifies his views considerably. There he argues that the prohibition against the taking of interest, "is the source of the distinction between in-group and out-group morality for Jewry. The prohibition against the taking of interest from in-group members derives primarily from the old ethic of brotherliness of the neighborhood organization with its duty of interest-less aid in time of need" (64). Weber's attempt to analyze the laws in terms of ethnic contrasts is less convincing than his earlier analysis considered here where the focus is on social institutions and competing social interests.

23. Weber, *Agrarian Sociology*, 139–43.

24. Ibid., 141.

25. Ibid., 142.

26. Ibid., 142–143.

27. Ibid., 136.

28. P. L. Berger, "Charisma and Religious Innovation: The Social Location of Israelite Prophecy," *American Sociological Review* 28 (1963): 949; cf. Weber, *Agrarian Sociology*, 136.

29. W. B. Bizzell, *The Social Teachings of the Jewish Prophets: A Study in Biblical Sociology* (Boston: Sherman, French & Co., 1916), i; cf. 2–4. Cf. L. Wallis, *Sociological Study of the Bible* (Chicago: University of Chicago Press, 1912), 299–301.

30. Ibid., ii.

31. Ibid., 107. In many ways, Bizzell's views anticipate more recent discussions on the possible rural background of Micah; cf. H. W. Wolff, "Micah the Moreshite—The Prophet and His Background," trans. C. Weber, in *Israelite Wisdom: Theological and Literary Essays in Honor of Samuel Terrien*, ed. J. G. Gammie et al. (Missoula, Mont.: Scholars Press, 1978), 77–84; *Micah the Prophet*, trans. R. D. Gehrke (Philadelphia: Fortress Press, 1981).

32. Ibid., 65.
33. Ibid., 9.
34. Ibid., i.
35. See W. B. Bizzell, *The Green Rising: An Historical Survey of Agrarianism, with Special Reference to the Organized Efforts of the Farmers of the United States to Improve Their Economic and Social Status* (New York: Macmillan, 1926). There Bizzell situates the "agrarian protests" of Micah and Isaiah among the first such protests in history, whereupon he discusses subsequent agrarian movements down through the centuries in Europe and the Americas to his own day (15).
36. S. T. Kimbrough, *Israelite Religion in Sociological Perspective: The Work of Antonin Causse* (Wiesbaden: Otto Harrassowitz, 1978), 2, 128.
37. A. Causse, *Les "Pauvres," d'Israel* (Paris: Istra, 1922), 11–12; idem, *Du Groupe Ethnique à la Communauté Religieuse* (Paris: Félix Alcan, 1937), 32, 40.
38. Causse, *"Pauvres," d'Israel,* 28–31; Causse, *Groupe Ethnique,* 47–53, 63–66.
39. Causse, *"Pauvres," d'Israel,* 15–17, 28–34.
40. Ibid., 33.
41. Ibid., 33–34.
42. Causse, *Groupe Ethnique,* 65–66.
43. Causse, *"Pauvres," d'Israel,* 11; see also Causse, *Groupe Ethnique,* 38–40.
44. Ibid., 17, 45–49; Causse, *Groupe Ethnique,* 72–75.
45. Ibid., 46–47; Causse, *Groupe Ethnique,* 72–73.
46. Ibid., 35; Causse, *Groupe Ethnique,* 62.
47. Ibid., 35, 62, 75.
48. Ibid., 41–42; Causse, *Groupe Ethnique,* 66–67, 71.
49. Causse, *Groupe Ethnique,* 97.
50. Ibid., 102.
51. Ibid., 115.
52. L. Wallis, *The Struggle for Justice* (Chicago: University of Chicago Press, 1916) offers a popularization of his views. His study *God and the Social Process: A Study in Hebrew History* (Chicago: University of Chicago Press, 1935) further elaborates views discussed here.
53. Wallis, *Sociological Study,* 6; cf. 3.
54. Ibid., xxxi.
55. Cf. L. Epsztein, *Social Justice in the Ancient Near East and the People of the Bible,* trans. J. Bowden (London: SCM Press, 1986), 97.
56. Wallis, like many other scholars of his time, sought Israel's origins in the nomads of the Arabian desert (Wallis, *Sociological Study,* 39). Sharp criticisms of this line of thought have been offered by G. E. Mendenhall, "The Hebrew Conquest of Canaan," *Biblical Archeology* 17 (1962): 50–76; J. T. Luke, *Pastoralism and Politics in the Mari Period* (Ph. D. diss., University of Michigan, 1965); and N. K. Gottwald, *The Tribes of Yahweh: A Sociology of the Religion of Liberated Israel, 1250–1050 BCE* (Maryknoll, N.Y.: Orbis Books, 1979), 435–63. Contrast the recent efforts to reintroduce the nomadic factor into the discussion by R. B. Coote and K. W. Whitelam, *The Emergence of Early Israel in Historical Perspective* (Sheffield: Almond Press, 1987), 94–111. The fact that Wallis's analysis has in time come to be undermined by both archaeological and anthropological research ought to warn us against analyzing ideological conflicts too closely in light of specific sociological analyses of the biblical material. We should also keep in mind that values are fluid and cross economic and social lines: Neither peasants nor urban dwellers are uniform in their outlooks, and this leads to tremendous conflicts in matters of social ethics.

57. Wallis, *Sociological Study*, 90.
58. Ibid., 134. Consider the rather similar analysis of R. Wilson, "Ethics in Conflict: Sociological Aspects of Ancient Israelite Ethics," *Text and Tradition: The Hebrew Bible and Folklore*, ed. S. Niditch (Atlanta: Scholars Press, 1990), 193–205. Using more recent methodology, Wilson argues that the rise of a monarchic state would work to transform a lineage-based legal system, thereby creating a potential source of conflict between the state and traditional norms.
59. Wallis, *Sociological Study*, xxviii.
60. Ibid., 141, 150, 195.
61. Ibid., 150, 173–78.
62. Ibid., 163.
63. Cf., e.g., J. D. Miranda, *Communism in the Bible*, trans. R. R. Barr (Maryknoll, N. Y.: Orbis Books, 1982), 33.
64. Cf. Wilson, *Sociological Approaches*, 25.
65. J. M. Sasson, "On Choosing Models for Recreating Israelite Pre-Monarchic History," *JSOT* 21 (1981): 11–12.
66. Liberation theologians warn that the greatest danger in this regard rests in the fact that our readings of the biblical text, even sophisticated sociological readings, can serve to undergird reactionary and oppressive responses to modern efforts at liberation and social change; cf. I. J. Mosala, *Biblical Hermeneutics and Black Theology in South Africa* (Grand Rapids: Wm. B. Eerdmans Publishing Co., 1989), 43–66, 107. Our historical interpretation of the biblical text needs to take seriously Mosala's view that "a black theology of liberation necessarily realises that both the Bible and theology are themselves *arenas* of social conflict. Neither the Bible nor theological discourse is 'above' social structures and conflict. They are cultural and political products, which reflect the socio-cultural struggles of the societies that produced them" (108). The conflictual nature of biblical social ethics will be explored in chapter 7. Liberation approaches to the Hebrew Bible will be discussed in chapter 3.
67. Mosala, *Biblical Hermeneutics and Black Theology*, 55–66, offers firm strictures against a weak sociological method that speaks in a limited way about ancient social phenomena but fails to grapple with macrosocial realities of class and ideological division both in the ancient world and modern times.
68. Cf. Sasson, "On Choosing Models," 14; and G. E. Wright, *The Old Testament against Its Environment*, Studies in Biblical Theology 2 (London: SCM Press, 1950).
69. Cf., e.g., J. Van Seters, *Abraham in History and Traditon*. On the material remains from ancient Palestine, see, e.g., A. Ben-Tor, ed., *The Archaeology of Ancient Israel* (New Haven Conn.: Yale University Press, 1992); O. Keel, *Gods, Goddesses, and Images of God in Ancient Israel* (Minneapolis: Fortress Press, 1998); T. Levy, *The Archaeology of Society in the Holy Land* (New York: Facts on File, 1995); and A. Mazar, *Archaeology of the Land of the Bible: 10,000–586 B.C.E.* (New York: Double-day, 1990). With respect to the reconstruction of Israelite religion, see J. S. Holladay, "Religion in Israel and Judah under the Monarchy: An Explicitly Archaeological Approach,"*Ancient Israelite Religion* in: *Essays in Honor of Frank Moore Cross*, ed. P.D. Miller, P. D. Hanson, and S. D. McBride, (Philadelphia: Fortress Press, 249–99); and W. G. Dever, "The Contribution of Archaeology to the Study of Canaanite and Early Israelite Religion," in ibid., 209–47.
70. Cf. R. R. Wilson, *Prophecy and Society in Ancient Israel* (Philadelphia: Fortress Press, 1980), 89–134.

71. Of his many studies, his two-part series conveniently summarizes his views and serves as a guide to his previous works: W. G. Dever, "'Will the Real Israel Stand Up?' Part I: Archaeology and Israelite Historiography," *BASOR* 297 (1995): 61–80; and "'Will the Real Israel Stand Up?' Part II: Archaeology and the Religions of Ancient Israel," *BASOR* 298 (1995): 37–58.

72. Dever, "'Will the Real Israel Stand Up?' Part II, 39; cf. Dever, "'Will the Real Israel Stand Up?' Part I," 73–74.

73. Ibid., 44–51.

74. Ibid., 40–43.

75. Dever, "'Will the Real Israel Stand Up?' Part I," 71–72.

76. The analysis of Carol Meyers, *Discovering Eve: Ancient Israelite Women in Context* (New York: Oxford, University Press, 1988), which builds on a number of previous studies, gets into trouble on precisely this point. Whereas her archaeological analysis regarding women in premonarchic Israel is insightful, her reading of the biblical text conflates later monarchic and postexilic materials with the social conditions of a much earlier time (see, e.g., p. 120). Jobling offers a useful critique in "Feminism and 'Mode of Production,'" 243–47.

77. See L. K. Handy, "Biblical Bronze Age Memories: The Abraham Cycle as Usable Past," *Biblical Research* 42 (1997): 43–57. Handy argues that the biblical text imagines an age in which Egypt is restricted to the Nile, the Mesopotamians exert little influence on Canaan, and in Canaan only YHWH is known or acknowledged as God. These "memories" have little to do with the Bronze Age and everything to do with the Judaean political aspirations at the time of Haggai and Zechariah, according to Handy.

78. Dever, "'Will the Real Israel Stand Up?' Part I," 67–69.

79. Ibid., 73.

80. Ibid., 63, 65.

81. Ibid., 73–74. For other cautions about ignoring or skirting the biblical texts when constructing an archaeological reading of Israel's history, see J. M. Miller, "Is It Possible to Write a History of Israel without Relying on the Hebrew Bible?" in *The Fabric of History: Text, Artifact and Israel's Past*, ed., D. V. Edelman (Sheffield: JSOT Press, 1991), 93–102.

82. Cf. N. K. Gottwald and F. S. Frick, "The Social World of Ancient Israel," *SBL 1975 Seminar Papers* 1 (1976): 165–178; J. Elliott, *What Is Social-Scientific Criticism?* (Minneapolis: Fortress Press, 1993); and F. S. Frick, *The Formation of the State in Ancient Israel: A Survey of Models and Theories*, Social World of Biblical Antiquity Series 4 (Sheffield: Almond Press, 1985).

83. For a general survey and evaluation see Elliott, *What Is Social-Scientific Criticism?*

84. B. J. Malina, "The Social Sciences and Biblical Interpretation," *Int.* 37 (1982): 229–42. Among his many books, perhaps the essential starting point is *Christian Origins and Cultural Anthropology: Practical Models for Biblical Interpretation* (Atlanta: John Knox Press, 1986).

85. See, e.g., V. H. Matthews and D. C. Benjamin, *Social World of Ancient Israel* (Peabody, Mass.: Hendrickson Publishers, 1993).

86. The call specifically to explore the "moral world" of the Hebrew Bible in social-scientific terms despite the challenges and limitations is resoundingly issued in Wilson, "Ethics in Conflict." Wilson's analysis uncovers three major components to the "moral world" of the Hebrew Bible (adopting Meeks's term), namely, customary norms for behavior, law as a tribal and state institution, and prophecy as both a support for traditional norms as well as a disruptive social force.

87. Malina, "Social Sciences and Biblical Interpretation," 238.
88. T. W. Overholt, "Prophecy: The Problem of Cross-Cultural Comparison," *Semeia* 21 (1982): 55–78; and *Channels of Prophecy: The Social Dynamics of Prophetic Activity* (Minneapolis: Fortress Press, 1989).
89. J.W. Rogerson, "Was Early Israel a Segmentary Society?" *JSOT* 36 (1986): 17–26; cf. D. Fiensy, "Using the Nuer Culture of Africa in Understanding the Old Testament: An Evaluation," *JSOT* 38 (1987): 73–83. Rogerson offers a useful discussion of the anthropological approach in Clements, *World of Ancient Israel*, chap. 2.
90. Coote and Whitelam, *Emergence of Early Israel*.
91. B. O. Long, "The Social World of Ancient Israel," *Int.* 37 (1982): 244.
92. Vigilance is required, however, if we hope not to strangle a study of values by reducing all considerations to economic or political factors. See G. A. Herion, "The Impact of Modern and Social Science Assumptions on the Reconstruction of Israelite History," *JSOT* 34 (1986): 3–33.
93. Long, "Social World of Ancient Israel," 246; cf. Malina, "Social Sciences and Biblical Interpretation," 237; Herion, "Impact of Modern and Social Science Assumptions," 19–21.
94. On the religious mode as a determinative factor, see M. Heirich, "Cultural Breakthroughs," *American Behavioral Scientist* 19 (1976): 685–702.
95. Long, "Social World of Ancient Israel," 255.
96. Levenson keenly observes that efforts to produce a biblical theology have largely overtly or tacitly worked to undermine Jewish religion, bearing a harsh, even anti-Semitic stamp. See J. Levenson, *The Hebrew Bible, the Old Testament, and Historical Criticism* (Louisville, Ky.: Westminster/John Knox Press, 1993), esp. chap. 2.
97. Levenson, *Hebrew Bible*, 51.
98. P. A. Bird, *Missing Persons and Mistaken Identities* (Minneapolis: Fortress Press, 1997), 65–66. She notes the following works: M. Bal, *Lethal Love: Feminist Literary Readings of Biblical Love Stories* (Bloomington, Ind.: Indiana University Press, 1987); idem, *Death and Dissymmetry: The Politics of Coherence in the Book of Judges* (Chicago: University of Chicago Press, 1988); C. Exum, "You Shall Let Every Daughter Live: A Study of Ex. 1:8–2:10," *The Bible and Feminist Hermeneutics*, ed. M. Tolbert (Chico, Calif.: Scholars Press, 1983), 63–82; E. Fuchs, "The Literary Characterization of Mothers and Sexual Politics in the Hebrew Bible," in *Feminist Perspectives on Biblical Scholarship*, ed. A. Y. Collins (Chico, Calif.: Scholars Press, 1985), 117–36; P. Trible, *God and the Rhetoric of Sexuality* (Philadelphia: Fortress Press, 1978); and idem, *Texts of Terror: Literary and Feminist Readings of Biblical Narratives* (Philadelphia: Fortress Press, 1984). One should also add L. M. Russell, ed., *Feminist Interpretation of the Bible* (Philadelphia: Westminster Press, 1985); and E. Fuchs, "Who Is Hiding the Truth?: Deceptive Women and Biblical Androcentrism," in Collins, *Feminist Perspectives*, 137–44.
99. See especially E. Tamez, *Bible of the Oppressed*, trans. from the Spanish by M. J. O'Connell (Maryknoll, N.Y.: Orbis Books, 1982).
100. Such a model is worked out in detail by E. Schüssler Fiorenza, *In Memory of Her: A Feminist Theological Reconstruction of Christian Origins* (New York: Crossroad, 1984), introduction and chap. 1. See also the considerations of M. Fander, "Historical-Critical Methods," in *Searching the Scriptures*, vol. 1, *A Feminist Introduction*, ed. E. Schüssler Fiorenza, (New York: Crossroad, 1993), 205–24.
101. See Mosala, *Biblical Hermeneutics and Black Theology*, 29.
102. A fine example of this method that also offers a probing feminist analysis of several narratives in which women are depicted as victims of violence is Trible, *Texts*

of Terror. Her *Rhetorical Criticism: Context, Method, and the Book of Jonah* (Minneapolis: Fortress Press, 1994) offers an extended discussion of the methodology, indicating that the many postmodern reading strategies tend to dovetail as biblical scholars analyze the biblical materials.

103. On the study of structuralism in relation to biblical studies, see D. Patte, *What Is Structural Exegesis?* (Philadelphia: Fortress Press, 1976).

104. See, e.g., C. Lévi-Strauss, "The Structural Study of Myth," in *Structural Anthropology* (New York: Doubleday, 1967), 202–28. For insightful and provocative applications of this method to the Bible, see E. Leach, *Genesis as Myth and Other Essays* (London: Jonathan Cape, 1969).

105. See Douglas, *Purity and Danger.*

106. A useful guide to postmodern methods in relation to the Bible can be found in E. A. Castelli et al., eds., *The Postmodern Bible* (New Haven, Conn.: Yale University Press, 1995). For a critique, see R. P. Carroll, "Poststructural Approaches: New Historicism and Postmodernism," in *The Cambridge Companion to Biblical Interpretation*, ed. H. Barton (Cambridge: Cambridge University Press, 1998), chap. 4.

107. On the role and collapse of metanarratives or grand narratives as justifications for knowledge and political thought, see J. Lyotard, *The Postmodern Condition: A Report on Knowledge* (Minneapolis: University of Minnesota Press, 1984), 31–41.

108. D. J. A. Clines and J. C. Exum, "The New Literary Criticism," *The New Literary Criticism and the Hebrew Bible* (Valley Forge, Pa.: Trinity Press International, 1993), 20.

109. See T. Eagleton, *Criticism and Ideology* (London: Verso, 1978).

110. A strong popular defense of the standard hypothesis, with an argument for an earlier dating for P, is presented by R. E. Friedman, *Who Wrote the Bible?* (San Francisco: HarperCollins, 1997). His appendix contains a chart with a suggested distribution of the various sources. In the main, I follow Friedman's determinations concerning the spread of the sources, although I disagree radically regarding the ordering and the resultant dating of the sources and their additional redactions.

111. D. M. Carr, "Controversy and Convergence in Recent Studies of the Formation of the Pentateuch," *Religious Studies Review* 23/1 (1997): 22–31.

112. Thus, K. A. Kitchen, *Ancient Orient and Old Testament* (Downers Grove, Ill.: InterVarsity Press, 1966), 116–21, hardly does justice to the complexities of the Torah when he suggests that the differences are akin to the combination of a poetic and prose account in the Karnak Poetical Stela of Amun.

113. Many of these considerations are clearly lined out by Friedman, *Who Wrote the Bible?* That the Babylonian Talmud suggests that Moses wrote Deuteronomy 34 while crying at God's dictation is a sign that some sort of explanation was required to explain the odd situation of Moses writing about his own death (b. Kodashim Menachoth 30a). On the other hand, that the text itself tells us, "Never again did there arise in Israel a prophet like Moses" (Deut. 34:10), clearly indicates that this evaluation must come from long after that figure's time and not from Joshua's hand as other rabbinic traditions might claim (b. Baba Bathra 14b). To be fair to the evidence, the statement of Moses' humility in Num. 12:3 does find parallel in the early eighth-century B.C.E. inscription of Zakir, king of Aram, who boasts, "A pious man [*hh*] was I, and Baalshamayn [delivered] me." In the book of Numbers the claim is made by the narrator, not Moses as speaker. The inscriptional context might indicate that the claim for Moses reflects both his piety and his royal-like character. For the entire text of this inscription see J. C. L. Gibson, *Textbook of*

Syrian Semitic Inscriptions, vol. 2, *Aramaic Inscriptions including Inscriptions in the Dialect of Zenjirli* (Oxford: Clarendon Press, 1975), 9.

114. The works of T. L. Thompson, *The Historicity of the Patriarchal Narratives: The Quest for the Historical Abraham*, BZAW 133 (New York: Walter de Gruyter, 1974) and J. Van Seters, *Abraham in History and Tradition*, have in different ways set off a firestorm of controversy in this regard. Thompson raises questions about the supposed archaeological links between the narrative and the Bronze Age material record, while Van Seters undermines the confident assertions that the customs and practices of the narratives reflect Bronze Age patterns. While alternative readings are possible, they are not entirely compelling. See, e.g., J. J. Bimson, "Archaeological Data and the Dating of the Patriarchs," in *Essays on the Patriarchal Narratives*, ed. A. R. Millard and D. J. Wiseman (Winona Lake, Ind.: Eisenbrauns, 1983), 59–92; and M. J. Selman, "Comparative Customs and the Patriarchal Age," 93–138 in the same volume.

115. For commentary on Exodus 15 and Deuteronomy 33, see F. M. Cross and D. N. Freedman, *Studies in Ancient Yahwistic Poetry* (Grand Rapids: Wm. B. Eerdmans Publishing Co., 1975), chaps. 2, 4.

116. An effective use of the comparative chronicalistic materials from ancient Mesopotamia appears in M. Cogan and H. Tadmor, *II Kings: A New Translation with Introduction and Commentary* (New York: Doubleday, 1988). See especially their discussion on pp. 3–7. They observe that the Deuteronomic project combined the synchronistic style known from Assyria, pulling together ancient records from now lost sources, while also subsuming that data to the larger Deuteronomic view.

117. To the previous discussion of Dever we should also add here W. G. Dever, "Archaeology, Ideology, and the Quest for an 'Ancient' or 'Biblical' Israel," *Near Eastern Archaeology* 61/1 (1998): 39–52; and A. Biran and J. Naveh, "An Aramaic Stele Fragment from Tel Dan," *IEJ* 43 (1993): 81–98.

118. See R. B. Coote, *In Defense of Revolution: The Elohist History* (Minneapolis: Fortress Press, 1991); and R. B. Coote and R. D. Ord, *In the Beginning: Creation and the Priestly History* (Minneapolis: Fortress Press, 1991). See also W. Brueggemann and H. W. Wolff, *The Vitality of Old Testament Traditions*, 2d ed. (Atlanta: John Knox Press, 1975).

119. See, e.g., N. S. Ateek, *Justice, and Only Justice: A Palestinian Theology of Liberation* (Maryknoll: Orbis Books, 1989).

120. Mosala, *Biblical Hermeneutics and Black Theology*, 27.

121. I have adapted Anderson and Pickering's contention that the civil rights era witnessed "American creeds in competition." See A. B. Anderson and G. W. Pickering, *Confronting the Color Line: The Broken Promise of the Civil Rights Movement in Chicago* (Athens, Ga.: University of Georgia Press, 1986), 389–410.

Law

Chapter 2

Law and Justice

אגדה

The Pentateuch

As a totality, the first five books of the Hebrew Bible, the Torah or Pentateuch, provide later tradition with the two great modes of theological discourse that are the cornerstones of Jewish social thought and practice, *aggadah* and *halakhah*. *Aggadah* embraces story as reflected in the narrative strands of the Pentateuch, a body of literature that we will take up in chapters three and four under the rubric of the historian. By contrast, *halakhah* embraces that side of the Torah that is concerned with the formulation of legal decisions and the construction of a just commonwealth under the divine sovereign. Of course, a clean separation of *aggadah* from *halakhah* is at best artificial, at least insofar as the Torah tradition is concerned, where narrative carries forward the competing agendas of the law codes and ritual texts. Indeed, the biblical predecessors to the rabbis came to understand that the revelation at Sinai had to be expressed both in terms of exodus stories and covenant laws to ground social ideals and practices into the deepest reservoirs of ancient Israelite thought. In this, the biblical and later rabbinic traditions recognized the value of

41

intertwining two seemingly disparate modes of discourse, story and law, thereby dovetailing literary streams that remained rather distinct in other ancient Near Eastern contexts.[1]

Nevertheless, from the point of view of the editorial history of the Pentateuch, it makes a great deal of sense to dissect and study separately the *halakhic* and *aggadic* component parts of the Torah. Prior to their compilation in our received Torah, the legal materials were marked by divergent editorial histories that are reflective of extensive and provocative encounters with this voice over the centuries in ancient Israel. By engaging these legal texts directly we go to the heart of several key "justice projects" at work in the biblical tradition, allowing us to ask from a variety of biblical perspectives how the biblical legal and ritual traditions speak to the changing demands of the justice equation. Thus, while many today turn to the Hebrew prophets for their model of social critique and change, the biblical record joins its Mesopotamian neighbors in insisting that the voice of law, what Kaiser terms the "center of the Hebrew Bible," is the primary institutional framework for constructing a society that embodies social ideals.[2] The priority given law in the Torah encourages us to consider this area first in our survey of the Hebrew scriptures.

How shall we proceed in this chapter? To put those projects in their cultural setting, we begin this chapter with a discussion of ancient Near Eastern law. We then turn our attention to the one text that readily comes to mind when readers think of biblical law, namely, the Ten Commandments. However, societies cannot live on principles alone, and so we will explore, in order, three major traditions that sought to speak to the plight of the disenfranchised in ancient Israel: the Exodus Covenant Code, the law code of Deuteronomy, and the legislation of the Priestly (P) source (for a brief discussion of source analysis see chapter 1). Here we shall find evidence of a vigorous debate over how precisely to remedy the structural ills of society. Then, after briefly considering the place of this vast body of legal material in the context of the still larger biblical tradition, we shall conclude this chapter with a reassessment of the relation of the Hebrew prophets to that covenant and legal tradition.

Texts in Context: Frameworks for Biblical Law

The fashioning of law codes, whether for practical, religious, or propagandistic purposes, was a time-honored tradition within the monarchic houses of the ancient Near East. Codes from several centuries remain extant from the archives of the Assyrian and Babylonian kings, such as those of Ur-Nammu (c. 2100 B.C.E.), Lipit-Ishtar (c. 1934–1924 B.C.E.), Eshnunna (c. 1850 B.C.E.), and Hammurabi (c. 1792–1750 B.C.E.), as well as the Hittite Laws (c. 1650 B.C.E.), the Middle Assyrian Laws (prior to 1100 B.C.E.), and the

Neo-Babylonian Laws (c. 700 B.C.E.).[3] The most famous of these codes is that of Hammurabi of Babylon.

Although the extant codes are numerous, we are not in a position to say precisely why these codes were collected. At the practical level, as with the collections of omens, undoubtedly collections of laws functioned to educate judges and served as reference works in preparation for the rendering of legal decisions. Yet can this mundane use seriously be said to lie behind the creation of monuments set out to display such codes? At the very least, the codes also served the religious purpose of informing the gods that the justice they desired had been realized in the laws of the society as contained in the codes. These texts may have been for "the gods' eyes only."[4] Furthermore, the codes probably served the propagandistic or ideological function of undergirding the institution of the monarchy as the final arbiter in matters of public law and social justice. The promulgation of a law code served to underscore the legitimacy and power of the central authority.

The scope and emphasis of ancient Near Eastern law included such recurring topics as bodily injuries, slave laws, property matters, adultery and other sexual excesses, family and marriage law, and theft. Dangerous animals, in particular goring oxen, are frequently at issue in early times, as reflected in the codes of Lipit-Ishtar, Eshnunna, and Hammurabi.[5] A look at the outline of the subject matter of the 282 provisions of the Hammurabi Code is instructive:

1–5:	Trials
6–13:	Theft and lost property
14:	Kidnapping
15–20:	Slavery
21–25:	Theft
26–39:	Military
40–65:	Land use
66–107:	Borrowing and lending
108–111:	Wine-sellers
112:	Goods and transport
113–119:	Debts and debt-slavery
120–126:	Storage of goods
127–194:	Family law, including marriage, sexuality, and inheritance
195–214:	Damages, including fights and miscarriages
215–240:	The trades—doctors, branders, builders, and boatmen
241–256:	Oxen
257–274:	Laborers and shepherds
275–277:	Hiring boats
278–82:	Slaves

While similar subjects are covered in the pentateuchal law codes, a comparison between biblical legal materials and Mesopotamian laws must not mislead the interpreter.[6] Biblical law is not reducible to a narrowly construed "civil law." Biblical law, unlike other Near Eastern codes, regularly blends ritual and social obligations.[7] Neither the Ten Commandments, the Covenant Code, the Priestly texts, nor the Deuteronomic code try hermetically to seal off the one sort of law from the other. Ancient Israel's approach to the legislation of norms and practices, therefore, does not draw sharp lines between laws concerning the religious rite (purity, sacrifice, holiness, vows) and social laws devoted to community (family, property, inheritance, refuge, and the poor). While our emphasis in this study will be on certain aspects of the latter, we will nonetheless examine the social legislation within the total matrix provided by the wider body of laws as each strand of the tradition seeks to come to terms with all aspects of ancient Israelite life. By reading the pentateuchal texts against their ancient Near Eastern counterparts, we discover that the social visions spawned by Israel's variegated legal traditions are inextricably intertwined with the liturgical programs of the tradents. The biblical authors and compilers discovered the necessity for nurturing the religious and symbolic ground beneath the social embodiment of justice ideals. In other words, social well-being is not simply a product of royal or judicial fiat but finds its deepest roots in the community's worship response to Israel's divine sovereign. The Near Eastern context draws our attention not only to Israel's firm and unique ideological commitments in this regard, but also the particular place of the poor in that ritual-law equation. For, as Lohfink observes, whereas ancient Near Eastern rulers claimed to service the disenfranchised, Israel's ritual and social legislation actually addressed their situation in a concerted and straightforward fashion.[8]

Culturally speaking, therefore, the tradition of law code collection played a significant role in the self-definition of ancient Israelite religion, as Israel sought to situate itself amid the empires and petty kingdoms of the ancient Near East. At the heart of the Torah is the making of laws to be enacted in the land of the promise. Various major codes and other legal texts have made their way into the Pentateuch: the Covenant Code of Exodus 20–23; the Deuteronomic legislation of Deuteronomy 12–26; various priestly regulations in Leviticus, especially those of the Holiness Code found in Leviticus 17–26; and a number of important priestly legislative texts imbedded in the narrative of Numbers. Our focus on the treatment of the disenfranchised in ancient Israel takes us into each of these great compilations of law found in the Torah. Each block of tradition makes its contribution to the ongoing Israelite discussion regarding the legal dimensions of their social vision. We begin our study, however, with a major focus of biblical lawmaking, the Ten Commandments.

The Ten Commandments: Creating a Principled Society

The Babylonian Talmud tells the following story:

> Rab Judah said in the name of Rab [a teacher in the third century C.E.]:
> "When Moses ascended on high, he found the Holy One, blessed be
> God, engaged in affixing scribal flourishes to the letters of the Torah.
> Moses said, 'Lord of the Universe, who is it that holds back your
> hand?' The Holy One answered, 'There will arise a man, at the end of
> many generations, Akiba ben Joseph is his name, who is ready to lec-
> ture upon every little letter mark, making piles and piles of laws.' 'Lord
> of the Universe,' said Moses, 'Let me see him!' The Holy One replied,
> 'Turn around.'
>
> Moses went and sat down behind eight rows [of students]. Not
> being able to follow their arguments, Moses grew ill at ease, but when
> they came to a certain subject and the disciples said to their teacher,
> 'Rabbi, how do you know this?' and their teacher replied, 'It is a law
> given unto Moses at Sinai,' suddenly Moses began to feel much better.
>
> Thereupon, Moses turned to the Holy One, blessed be God, and
> said, 'Lord of the Universe, here you have such a teacher and you
> choose to give the Torah through me?' The Holy One replied, 'Quiet!
> This is my idea.'
>
> Then Moses said, 'Lord of the Universe, you have shown me this
> man's Torah, so show me his reward.' 'Turn around,' said God. So
> Moses turned around and saw them weighing out the teacher's flesh at
> the market-stalls [a sign of his death as a martyr during Hadrian's per-
> secution]. 'Lord of the Universe,' cried Moses, 'such Torah, and such
> a reward?' The Holy One replied, 'Quiet! This is my idea.'[9]

This imaginative tale seeks to resolve a key dilemma facing the biblical and
Jewish lawmaking tradition, namely, how to connect later transformations and
developments in that tradition with the earliest manifestations in the Hebrew
Bible. Cleverly, Moses is turned into the muse of law. The construct of Moses
as lawgiver has shaped the tradition such that in one sense all the laws go back
to Moses. Of course, for the historian this tantalizing ideological maneuver
obscures a vital aspect of the tradition, leaving us uncertain about the origins
of basic texts such as the Ten Commandments, the Covenant Code in Exodus,
the Deuteronomic legislation, the Holiness Code, and the various laws in
Numbers. Thus, although there is generally little doubt among biblical scholars that the Ten Commandments (Ex. 20:1–14; Deut. 5:6–18 [6–21]) constitute an ancient part of the biblical legal tradition, whether or not any of these
prescriptions go back to a historical Moses remains an open question. Moreover, while each of the strands, J, E, D, and P, value Moses as the "patron saint"
of law and the recipient of a number of commandment lists, very different

formulations of principles are thought to stem from this hoary forebear of the tradition. We consider in this section several versions and permutations of the so-called Ten Commandments.

What are we to make of the Ten Commandments as presented in the related, though slightly divergent, texts found in Exodus 20 and Deuteronomy 5?[10] More specifically, by what principles is the community to operate according to E, JE, and D? In the sphere of worship and ritual, there are to be no other gods than YHWH, no sculptured images, no swearing falsely by the name of that divine sovereign, and a day of rest is to be devoted to that sovereign's honor (the latter provision underwent several expansions by P). That the Ten Commandments are not solely a part of some sort of religious reform movement is indicated by the second half of the list, which is devoted to matters of familial relationships, social interaction, and, most importantly, property matters. This latter part of the Ten Commandments is rather inclusive: honoring of parents, not murdering, not committing adultery, not stealing, not bearing false witness in a trial, and not coveting a fellow citizen's property (including his wife and slaves).[11] One can hardly escape the impression that the Ten Commandments represent a distillation of the essence of ancient Israel's faith and community ethic.[12]

The Ten Commandments take the form of a series of prohibitions. What value does this relatively simple framework have over the more time-honored law code format? Clearly E, who appears initially to incorporate the Ten Commandments into a wider narrative framework by adapting a now lost ancient version of the Decalogue, as well as the Deuteronomic tradent, who expanded the fuller JE version of the Ten Commandments by invoking the Exodus enslavement motif (Deut. 5:15), both valued apodictic law (the command form) as the principle framework for the encounter between the people and their God.[13] The command rhetoric does differ rather markedly from the casuistic (or case law) format in the Bible, found in particular in the Covenant Code of Exodus and in Deuteronomy 12–26, though here and there the apodictic rhetoric has had an impact on the formulation of some biblical laws. Nonetheless, the distinction between the Ten Commandments in their apodictic form and the standard case law style is noteworthy. We may well wonder what the Ten Commandments accomplish that the law codes do not.

A clue is provided by another branch of the ancient Near Eastern legal corpus, namely, the ancient treaties. Mendenhall in particular has noted the striking similarities between the shape and character of ancient Near Eastern treaties and the form in which the essentials of the biblical covenant are couched. These treaties and their biblical counterparts share key elements such as (1) the preamble regarding the identity of the sovereign, (2) the statement of the historical background to the treaty, (3) the stipulations, (4) the curse and blessing clauses, and (5) the words of ceremonial institution.[14] By analogy, for Mendenhall and others, the Ten Commandments have an imperative force akin to an ancient vassal treaty. From the point of view of the ancients, then, the Ten Commandments were not laws in the strict sense of the term, if we mean by "law" an injunction that takes up a particular legal case, such as a murder, evaluating that case in terms of attendant circumstances and punishments. The Ten Commandments, or as they are termed in Hebrew, the Ten Words, in contrast to the body of case law, are rather bare bones. For the most part, the prohibitions are given without spelling out precisely how they are to be enacted or what sort of sanctions are to befall the lawbreaker except in the most general of terms. Yet in the treaty format, the Ten Commandments are striking. Since case law in the ancient Near East, in any event, is certainly far older than any possible version of Israel's Ten Commandments, we must assume that the simplicity of the Ten Commandments' structure and the resultant expansiveness of their content arise from deliberate design. The rhetorical form adopted mattered a great deal. As an adaptation of the ancient treaty scheme, the resultant literary form of the Ten Commandments sparked a cultural and ideological force that was far greater than their few words might imply.

Fundamental to this formulation of the Ten Commandments is the view that Israel's Lord is to command the sort of respect that ancient Near Eastern treaties reserved for earthly rulers.[15] A monarch such as Assyrian ruler Esarhaddon (680–669 B.C.E.) affords us a fine example of this mentality in a treaty in which he is at pains to ensure that the vassal accept the divinely sanctioned succession of the crown prince Ashurbanipal.[16] Everything in the Assyrian treaty is geared toward ensuring that the vassal understands that any sign of defection against Esarhaddon or his designated crown prince will be punished through divine retribution. Notably, the Ten Commandments, as formulated and presented by both E and D, restricted the role of an earthly monarch and reserved social authority to God, to the landowners (by implication from the accent on property protections), and to the Levitical leadership (as imaged by Moses throughout E and D).

Why have the Ten Commandments been made party to the emergent law codes and narratives of the Torah? Perhaps one might be right in suggesting that this is a northern phenomenon, namely, landowners in Israel over against the Judaean establishment. Yet other texts will suggest that the landowners even in Judah sought such leverage against Jerusalem, as evidenced, for example, in Josiah's backing by the "people of the land" (2 Kings 21:24).[17] We may never recover the regional context of these disputes that have come to us enshrined in Israel's magna carta, yet the Ten Commandments are clear that both ritual and social aspects of life required sound *communal* governance and ought not be left to the whims of a particular power holder.[18] Israel's Lord is presented as both the ultimate giver and mediator of the covenant. The people as a whole are the vassals. Unlike ancient Near Eastern treaties where the gods grant the laws and the earthly kings dispense divine justice, the Ten Commandments, as presented by E and D, impose on each and every member of the community, through its elders (E) or later its judges and judicial officers (D), the duty of fostering the workings of a just society.[19]

We might arguably see in these formulations of the Ten Commandments the makings of a subtle critique of monarchy and an attempt to limit its powers.[20] Such an understanding of social authority and political power would be consistent with what we know elsewhere about both E and DH, where the prophetic voice is commandeered by the landed elite to press its agenda against the royal house (see chapter 3). In these trajectories, the image of Moses as prophetic lawgiver acts as a leveraging point against royal encroachments in various aspects of life. It comes as no surprise, then, that interpreters like R. Friedman have suggested that E and DH have a common wellspring of inspiration, for they also display a strikingly similar approach to the commandments and law in general, presenting the makings of a formidable program of restrictions against an unbridled monarchy. Additional attempts to circumscribe royal authority in the context of property matters appear in the blessing and curse lists that follow upon D's law code (see especially Deut. 28:36–37). The critique gains momentum in the DH when Samuel offers several pointed observations concerning the dangers of the monarchic system (1 Sam. 8:10–18).[21]

While we might never recover the precise circumstances behind the adoption of the Ten Commandments' rhetorical structure and diffuse content, we certainly can say that the conjunction of the Ten Commandments with the case laws found in the Covenant Code and Deuteronomy achieves a remarkable effect: Israel's legal system, at least for E and D, is established to carry forward the *people's* response to their covenant obligations at Sinai. Unlike elsewhere in the ancient Near East, where law was a royal prerogative, in the Israel of E and D, each and every member of the community has a religious, moral, and social duty toward the nation's deity.[22] The Ten Commandments are integral to this political process. Thus, long before the so-called individual retribution theme found in Ezekiel, to which we shall return in our discussion of that text, we find in the use of the singular "you" in the commands a radically egalitarian form of address—egalitarian, that is, with respect to the entire male landowning class. Law for E and D, as catalyzed by their versions of the Ten Commandments, is in a restricted but key sense a *communal* political enterprise.

While some may want to see in the E and D presentations of the Ten Commandments the basic ethical foundation for any civilized community, the fact that J and P offer altogether different lists (as well as their own additions to the Ten Commandments) should serve as a red flag to indicate that the Ten Commandments are more than a cache of ethical principles. Principles they are, but principles that undergird the particular sort of social arrangements and political structures congenial to the framers of this side of the tradition. The power of this formulation of the basic commandments is recognized insofar as later narrators had these tablets destroyed and Moses reascend the mountain in order for J's version and P's version to gain any credence in the mix.

J's own unique contribution is markedly different than the Ten Commandments (Ex. 34:10–28). The passage's reach encompasses numerous specifics in the ritual life of ancient Israel—namely festivals such as the Feast of Unleavened Bread, the Feast of Weeks, and the Feast of Passover, in addition to the Sabbath rest, molten images (reflected also in J's expansion to the Ten Commandments in Ex. 20:4–5 and Deut. 5:8–9), livestock redemption, and first fruits of the soil.[23] Yet this ritual emphasis, as pervasive as it is in this passage, ought not to cause us to lose sight of the leading concern for J, namely, the danger of making covenants with the surrounding pagans or of worshiping as they do. The major concern in J's postexilic reconstruction program is the problem of the pagans, or the failure of the community to counter the dangers posed by the encroachment of "foreign" peoples who must be driven out. J's ritual program functions to create a hedge against these religious opponents. We shall return to this matter when we consider the laws in the book of Numbers, where we shall find that, far from simply erecting a barrier against foreigners, J is attempting to counter opponents within the Israelite community.

P's commandment list, which Morgenstern terms "the very heart of the Holiness Code," breaks new ground (Lev. 19:1–18).[24] Grounded neither in the escape from Egypt (E), nor in sheer obedience (D), nor in acts of divine conquest (J), the P writers predicate *holiness* as the ground of the commandments and their observance. Far from being simply a ritual program, as some might visualize for the priestly writers, the P tradition presents a set of religious and social principles that offer a clear challenge to the Ten Commandments of E and D. Reverence for YHWH and a concern for sacrifices mark the first part of P's list, but greater attention is shown to matters of social justice than in E or D's Ten Commandments, the latter rather misleadingly termed the "ethical decalogue." P's sweep includes theft, swearing falsely, fraud, laborer's wages, the physically disabled, murder, and vengeance. While P's list urges blind justice with respect to both the rich and the poor (19:15), that very same list enjoins harvest provisions for the "poor and the stranger" (19:9–10). P's inclusive vision, encompassing the laborer, the physically disabled, and the hungry poor, is rather remarkable when compared to the other lists. This statement of P's vision, however, does remain consistent with the theme sounded elsewhere in P, namely that the priestly group, the keepers of "holiness," as it were, has a social vision that draws together all members of society, from the least to the greatest. It is for this reason that we should be reluctant to give over to E, D, or the prophetic voice the ethical concerns of ancient Israel. P's voice and vision afford a potent challenge, in part because P moves well beyond the rather limited (though not insignificant) provisions for the poor and the debt slaves that are given in the Covenant Code and Deuteronomy. That P consciously adapts the Ten Commandments is a strong sign that P's program has been styled as a credible response to the vision reflected in the Ten Commandments.

To sum up: Treated as the patron of the legal tradition, the figure of Moses is connected to several key passages that in essence offer summations of the principle prohibitions that undergird each of the source traditions in the Pentateuch. Undoubtedly based on a now lost primitive formulation, the current canonical commandment lists reflect both the source traditions of the Pentateuch as well as a variety of redactional moments in the transmission of biblical law. The lists in Exodus 20 and Deuteronomy 5 both serve as bold endorsements of the law codes to which they are connected. The Ten Commandments amalgamate sacred and secular concerns, weaving an expansive communal structure and social ethic. The apodictic or command form, while not unique in the larger ancient Near Eastern legal tradition, nevertheless stands out as a distinctive literary device that, much as an ancient Near Eastern treaty, constitutes an imaginative and persuasive force in the body politic of ancient Israel, reserving social authority to God and restricting the powers of earthly sovereigns as a result. The canonical linking of the Ten Commandments to the law codes has the effect of making the legal system an extension of the community's Exodus freedom traditions, presumably a linkage fostered by the landed gentry over against an unrestricted exercise of royal legal prerogatives. J's list places far greater emphasis on the ongoing ritual life of the community, creating boundary lines in communal disputes in which J is engaged. P's list is predicated on an entirely different basis than in the other traditions. For P, holiness is the ground for a far grander social agenda than that conceived by the traditional Ten Commandments. In fact, the P source's social vision, as expressed in its formulation of commandments, is the most far-reaching and inclusive of the various commandment lists.

The Exodus Covenant Code: Protecting the Disenfranchised

Both pride of place and apparent antiquity single out the small code given in Exodus 21–23. We do not know the precise date of its original formulation or the specific phases of development, but as it now stands the Covenant Code is set out as the first "commentary" on the Ten Commandments as given in Exodus 20.[25] Since the Covenant Code deals with matters that are typical of the various legal documents known from Mesopotamia, there is no need to think that the Covenant Code was originally produced in relation to the Ten Commandments. Indeed, this is doubtful. Moreover, some (such as Phillips) would argue that the Ten Commandments are a summary of Israel's more ancient criminal law.[26] Yet in their current canonical configuration, the Ten Commandments and the Covenant Code have been drawn together as a preliminary contract and an expansive set of stipulations. In essence, the current structuring of the Exodus legal materials represents an attempt socially and ritually to embody the Ten Commandments, while viewing the Ten Commandments as the fundamental datum of Israelite thought. By this juxtaposition, the Elohist tradition, whether consciously or not, has built within itself a powerful mechanism for taking into account the changing social conditions, economic formations, and political arrangements of succeeding generations. Each generation's legal and social system is to be measured by a higher standard, namely, the Ten Commandments. Justice toward the poor is, at least in the text's latest redaction, central to the Covenant Code's commentary.

The scope and content of the Covenant Code is akin to the ancient Near Eastern law codes noted earlier in this chapter, though with additional ritual components:[27]

21:1–11:	Debt-slavery
21:12–27:	Capital crimes and fighting (with special emphasis on miscarriage)
21:28–36:	Oxen
21:37–22:5 [6]:	Theft and damages
22:6–12 [7–13]:	Safekeeping
22:13–14 [14–15]:	Borrowing
22:15–19 [16–20]:	Sexuality, sorceress, sacrifices
22:20–26 [21–27]:	The poor and lending
22:27–30 [28–31]:	Respect for chieftains and other ritual duties
23:1–3:	Trials
23:4–5:	Oxen
23:6–10:	The poor
23:11–19:	Sabbath and other festivals

Integral to the Covenant Code, and unique when compared to Near Eastern law codes, are a variety of protections for the poor. The alien, widow, and orphan are supported (22:20–23 [21–24]). The Code stipulates the absolute legal obligation to protect the poor (23:6–8; cf. Deut. 24:17). Lending procedures toward the poor are regulated (22:24–26 [25–27]; cf. Deut. 24:10–13, 17), and the kidnapping and selling of persons is prohibited (21:16; cf. Deut. 24:7).[28]

While terms other than "poor" are used of the disenfranchised in the Covenant Code, a study of the specific references to poverty and their contexts alerts us to the social justice vision of the code. The words *'ĕbyôn, dal,* and *'ānî* are the terms for "poor" adopted by the Covenant Code.[29] These terms identify ancient Israel's disenfranchised, and one section of the Covenant Code devotes itself specifically to their plight. This segment treats, in turn, the resident alien (22:20 [21]), the widow and orphan (22:21–23 [22–24]), the oppressed *'ānî* (22:24 [25]), and the neighbor whose garment has been pledged (22:25–26 [26–27]). In each case, the mistreatment of these persons is condemned.

For the resident alien, the prohibition against oppression was based on the tradition of the Israelites' enslavement in Egypt. The text states: "You shall not wrong a stranger or oppress him, for you were strangers in the land of Egypt" (22:20 [21]). Already, this legal tradition draws on the covenant narrative to frame a theological and historical motivation for conduct toward the poor, constructing an explicit *theology of obligation*. The prohibition against abusing the widow, orphan, *'ānî*, and neighbor is joined with the notice that should these people be mistreated and they cry out to God, their cry would not go unheeded.

Significantly, the only mention of the *'ānî* in the Covenant Code is found in v. 25(24). Since the *'ānî* were the "economically oppressed," they were not to be charged interest. It is perhaps noteworthy that the term *'ānî* is juxtaposed here to *'ammî*, "my people," and it appears that *'ānî* further explicates the term *'ammî*. We might observe in passing that while the text of Micah curiously does not use any of the Hebrew terms for "poor," the text does make use of the more general term *'ammî* when discussing exploitation (Micah 2:9; 3:3; cf. Isa. 3:15). This connection between the prophetic text and the Covenant Code undoubtedly should not be pressed too far, but it seems useful to observe that such a use of *'ammî* is shared with the Covenant Code, although in Exodus the scope of *'ammî* is clarified by the addition of *'ānî*. This and other considerations may suggest that Micah is carrying forward a village tradition of covenant that is akin to the Covenant Code tradition. Perhaps the prophet was aware of this legal tradition and is appropriating it, or is even mocking it, as a villager protesting the failure of the urban-based legal tradition. We will return to the vexed question of the relation of the prophets to the covenant tradition at the end of this chapter.

The thrust of the Covenant Code is not simply toward individuals or classes of persons but also to social structures and communal practices. In other words, the attempt was made in the early legal tradition to institutionalize some of these concerns, a development that can be seen in the practices of gleaning and the sabbatical year. Those who do not have enough food are permitted to glean from the crops of others (23:11; cf. Lev. 19:9–10; 23:22; Deut. 24:19–22; Ruth 2). During the land's time of rest the *'ĕbyôn* was still permitted

to gather from this land any food that was needed (23:11). Clearly the *'ĕbyôn*
is one who does not even have the means to be self-sufficient, and might be
termed a "beggar."[30] As one who is forced to gather food simply to stay alive,
the normal regulations for land use were suspended. Life mattered more than
law.[31] Furthermore, in the sabbatical or seventh year, slaves were to be released
(21:2–6; cf. Deut. 15:1–2, 12–18), and farmlands were to be left fallow (23:10;
cf. Lev. 25:1–7, 20–22).[32] The seventh year here seems not to involve a universal release of slaves every seven years, but more simply to refer to the seventh year of a particular person's service. Likewise, it is possible that land relief
occurred by rotation, such that in any given year only designated segments
would lie fallow and not the entire region all at once.[33] It will be left to
Deuteronomy to universalize and regularize the practice.[34]

Injured slaves became the beneficiaries of a rather noteworthy interpretation of the *lex talionis*, or "eye for eye" provision of the legal tradition. This
general provision, invoked in various pentateuchal sources, works to ensure
that punishment and compensation are not excessive but are meted out with
the specifics of the case in view (cf. 21:23–25; Lev. 24:19–20; Deut. 19:21).[35]
According to the Covenant Code, when a slave owner strikes a slave who in
turn loses either an eye or a tooth, the slave is to gain his or her freedom.[36]
This application of the *lex talionis* represents a classic case where general principles come to embody a more institutionalized framework that speaks to the
concrete situation of the disenfranchised. As we cull together these various
institutional practices, we may justifiably suspect that they may have fallen
short of their intended goal. Yet one cannot help but be impressed with the
range of provisions that were made to cushion the blows engendered by a life
filled with want.[37]

While some might want to push the code back to the early Davidic period,
the development of the Israelite and Judaean monarchies, in particular the
Omride period and after, saw increased pressures on the small landholders
throughout the region (see chapter 4).[38] The Covenant Code might more
plausibly be read against this background as a *social charter* designed to regulate a state of affairs in which the members of the small farming communities
of the tribal federation had begun to suffer severe dislocation and sought in
law a framework for exacting justice for their constituency. The Covenant
Code would represent a negotiated settlement between the village elders and
the royal house, regardless of which group actually promulgated the Code.[39]

By framing the poverty question as both a matter of persons and structures,
and by invoking laws to regulate these circumstances, the Covenant Code far
surpasses its ancient Near Eastern counterparts. Justice for the poor became
self-consciously both a civil and religious matter in ancient Israel. As such, the
social praxis of justice making comes under scrutiny in the code.

Two of the references to the poor in the Covenant Code appear in a context concerned with legal processes in a passage that McKay terms a "decalogue for the administration of justice in the city gate."[40] The importance of impartial judgment is stressed in Ex. 23:2–3 where it is enjoined that one not show deference to either the *rabbîm*, "the mighty," or the *dal*, "poor." One might take this text to mean that neither the powerful nor the weak are to be favored because of their condition or status when judgments are made in legal disputes. Alternatively, Kennedy suggests that the prohibition is against favoring one who was formerly a person of modest means and not abjectly poor.[41]

Regardless, even the Covenant Code understands that impartiality does not mean, in practice, to favor the rich, as is so often the case in the modern world. The "decalogue for the administration of justice in the city gate" warns not to "subvert the rights of your needy [*'ebyôn*] in their disputes" (23:6). There follow further prohibitions against false charges and bribes (23:7–8). Here the emphasis is on the active maintenance of justice with regard to the disenfranchised. Even the poorest are to be protected in the Israelite community. With the Covenant Code, attentiveness to those living on the underside of the monarchy's economic developments becomes a sacred social duty.

To sum up: This concretization of a concern for the poor and the effort to institutionalize remedies stands at the heart of the Covenant Code. With the exodus event as motivation, the tradition will ever after link exodus and justice, even if different streams of the tradition will debate the nature and scope of that justice in daily practice. Nevertheless, the conjoining of the Covenant Code with the Ten Commandments ensured that the Ten Commandments would be heard as part and parcel of a social movement that acted on behalf of Israel's disenfranchised. If our surmising is correct, we can go further to state that the ancient village federation found in such laws and commandments a mechanism for consolidating their position over against an encroaching monarchic elite. On the level of civil legislation, they understood each other's language. The code must not be read in the abstract. Law functions as a key factor in the negotiation of the balance of power between city and village in a burgeoning monarchic commonwealth.

From Exodus to Deuteronomy:
A Developing Tradition of Legal Ethics

Although Deuteronomy stands last in the Torah, this arrangement of the Pentateuch is misleading with respect to the intimate relation between Deuteronomy and the Covenant Code. As a legal code, Deuteronomy 12—26 covers ground similar to Exodus, raising our suspicions and justifying a closer inspection of the two blocks of biblical texts in relation to one another. Indeed, if we follow Levinson's analysis, the Deuteronomic Code not only adopts the Covenant Code but profoundly *subverts* the Covenant Code with an agenda of its own making.[42] As Levinson crisply characterizes the relation between the Deuteronomic Code and the Covenant Code: "Imitation becomes the sincerest form of encroachment."[43]

A comparison between the laws in Deuteronomy and those in the Covenant Code of Exodus reveals a striking degree of overlap in terms of content. The following is organized following the order of material as found in Deuteronomy:

Exodus	*Deuteronomy*	
23:12	5:13–14	Sabbath
23:13	6:13	Worshiping God alone
20:19–23	12:1–28	False gods and altars
22:19	12:29–13:19 (18)	Worshiping other gods
22:30	14:21a	Eating animals who die in the wild
23:19b	14:21b	Not boiling a goat in its mother's milk
23:10–11a	15:1–11	Role of every seventh year
21:2–11	15:12–18	Treatment of Hebrew slaves
22:28b–29 (29b–30)	15:19–23	Consecrating male firstlings
23:14–19	16:1–17	Feast days
23:2–3, 6–8	16:18–20	Judging fairly
22:19 (20)	17:2–7	Worshiping other gods
22:17 (18)	18:10b–11	Sorcery
21:12–4	19:1–13	Killing unintentionally—place to go
23:1, 2b	19:15–21	False testimony
21:15, 17	21:18–21	Disobedient sons
23:4–5	22:1–4	Observing wandering animals
22:15–16 (16–17)	22:28–29	Seducing a virgin
22:24 (25)	3:20–1 (19–20)	Extracting interest on a loan
21:16	24:7	Kidnapping
22:25–26 (27)	24:10–13	Taking and returning pledges
22:20–21 (22); 23:9	24:17–18	Strangers, orphans, widows
23:11	24:19–21	Gleanings
22:28 (29); 23:19a	26:1–11	First fruits

A careful study of the language and contents of both texts would seem to suggest that the Covenant Code in Exodus, at least in large measure, was written first.[44] This leads us to a key observation: Whatever else we might say about any changes that occur in Deuteronomy, there is a strong degree of conscious overlap in content between the two collections of laws. In other words, Deuteronomy seeks to stand squarely in the streambed carved out by the rushing waters of the Covenant Code. Deuteronomy represents a legal tradition self-consciously in the making.

As part of this rather deliberate activity, Deuteronomy rearranges the materials of the Covenant Code in a startlingly different fashion and in complete disregard to any organizational principles that may have been at work in the Covenant Code. In fact, the Deuteronomist betrays the organizing principle of this project. As Kaufman perceptively observes, Deuteronomy structures its law code in light of the Ten Commandments.[45] In other words, the framework of Deuteronomy 12—26 patterns itself after the general subjects raised by each of the Ten Commandments following the precise sequential ordering of the commandments:[46]

Exodus 20		*Deuteronomy*
2–6:	no other gods; no idols	12:1–28
7:	taking God's name in vain	12:29–14:27
8–11:	Sabbath day	14:28–16:17
12:	honor father and mother	16:18–18:22
13:	manslaughter/murder	19:1–22:8
13:	adultery	22:9–23:19
13:	stealing	23:20–24:7 (23:19–24:7)
13:	false witness	24:8–25:4
14a:	neighbor's wife	25:5–12
14b:	neighbor's property	25:13–16

As such, this pattern displaced the structure of the Exodus Code. The overall net effect is remarkable: Whereas Exodus 21—23 became a "commentary" on the Ten Commandments simply by its juxtaposition to them, Deuteronomy 12—26, which is structured topically to follow the order of the Ten Commandments, became a veritable commentary on both the Ten Commandments and the entire Exodus Covenant Code as the legal tradition adapted to speak to the changing questions and needs of a developing community.

However, it is also clear that not all of the material of the Covenant Code has been taken over by Deuteronomy. The following indicates the areas of omission from Exodus:

Altar	20:24–26	Altar of earth enjoined
Quarrels	21:18–27	Quarrels and injuries
Oxen	21:28–32	Ox goring
	21:33–34	Ox falls in cistern
	21:35–36	Ox injuries
	21:37 (22:1)	Stealing oxen
Theft	22:1-3 (2–4)	Housebreaking, theft
Fire	22:4–15 (5–6)	Vineyard, fire accidents
Safekeeping	22:6–8 (7–9)	Safekeeping article stolen
	22:9–12 (10–13)	Safekeeping of animals
	22:13–14 (14–15)	Borrowing animals, and their injury

Poverty	22:22–23 (23–24)	God hears their cry (clause has shifted contexts in Deut. 24:15)
Curses	22:27 (28)	Do not revile God or curse a prince
Sacrifice	23:18	Blood and fat prohibited in sacrifice

Furthermore, beyond Deuteronomy's deletions from the Exodus material, there are also significant additions to the collection in Deuteronomy:

Pagan Worship	12:29–31	Prohibits inquiring into how the nations Israel dispossessed worshiped other gods
	14:1–20	Avoid pagan mourning rites; clean and unclean animals
	16:21–22	Sacred poles and pillars
Tithe/Levites	14:22–29	Tithe; care for Levites
	17:1	Do not sacrifice defective animals
Authority Figures	17:8–13	Judges
	17:14–20	Kings (possibly linked to Ex. 22:27 [28])
	18:1–8	Levites
Abominations In Worship	18:9	Abominations of the land
	18:12–21	Abominations, soothsayers, prophets
Landmarks	19:14	Removal of landmarks
Warfare	20:1–4	Courage in time of war
	20:5–8	Exemptions from military service
	20:9	Role of military officers
	20:10–18	Negotiations and spoils
	20:19–20	Trees of a city under siege
Dead Bodies	21:1-9	Expiation for unsolved murder
	21:22–23	Executed criminal's body (reference moved up for clarity)
Women	21:10–14	Female captives
	21:15–17	Co-wives and their sons' inheritance
Mixtures	22:5	Mixed dress
	22:6–7	Birds
	22:8	Parapet
	22:9–11	Mixed seeds, animals, cloth
	22:12	Wearing twisted cords
Sexual Matters	22:13	Virginity, accusation
	22:23–24	Illicit affair in the city (betrothed woman)
	22:25-27	Rape in the countryside (betrothed woman)
	23:1 (22:30)	Not to marry father's wife
Community Identity and Cleanliness	23:2–9 (1-8)	Limitations on community membership

	23:10–15 (9–14)	Cleanliness in the camp
	23:16–17 (15–16)	Escaped slave
	23:18–19 (17–18)	Temple prostitution
Marriage	24:1–4	Divorce writ
	24:5	Military exemption for marriage
Various	24:6	Prohibition on types of debt
Determinations		pledges
	24:8–9	Leprosy (notice about Miriam)
	24:14–15	Paying wages
	24:16	Each bears own guilt
	25:1–3	Punishment procedures
	25:4	Not to muzzle ox
	25:5–10	Levirate marriage
	25:11–2	Woman seizes man's genitals
	25:13–6	Weights and measures
	25:17–19	Blot out memory of Amalek
	26:12–15	Tithe and Levites

While it is the case that the content of the ancient Near Eastern law codes is rather unpredictable and they do at times differ considerably from one another, one might think that the differences between the Covenant Code and Deuteronomy are simply products of happenstance. However, chance alone cannot be decisive in the case of Deuteronomy, for Deuteronomy's overlap with the Covenant Code is so extensive that we must posit that the additions and subtractions were deliberate, reflecting the changing interests of the period in which Deuteronomy was framed.

Several key items stand out as the two codes are compared. In terms of subtractions, the omission of the oxen issue may result from a shift from a village focus in the Covenant Code to an overwhelmingly urban focus in Deuteronomy. Likewise, the omission of the Covenant Code's call for earthen altars probably reflects the centralizing tendencies and worship prohibitions of Deuteronomy. The additions to the Exodus material are no less revealing. We should note, in particular, the concern for authority figures in society as well as the extensive material related to the conduct of war. Concerning the warfare materials, Rofé insightfully draws attention to the "decidedly humane" character of several passages, in particular with regard to the dangers of the "destruction of nature" in war (Deut. 20:19–20), matters of "private and public negligence in the camp" (Deut. 23:10–14 [9–13]), and "cruelty toward a civilian population . . . especially women" (Deut. 20:11, 14; 21:10-14). Rofé is correct to note, however, that a later editor's incorporation of the "total ban," wherein the complete destruction of the enemy is stipulated (Deut. 20:15–18), "nullified the tolerant and humane spirit that imbued the original series" of laws on conduct in war.[47] Among the other additions to the Exodus material, the propertied interests of Deuteronomy are drawn to our attention in the text's reference to the removal of landmarks. Marriage and sexuality come under considerable scrutiny, all betraying the urban locus of these laws. We might also note the concern to delimit community membership.

Despite these differences in content and orientation, the poor continue to have a place in the revisionist project of Deuteronomy.[48] Deuteronomy 15 is concerned with the practice of the remission of debts (šĕmiṭṭâ) during the sabbatical year. The promise is made that there will be no 'ebyôn, "poor," in the land because YHWH will cause the land to prosper (vv. 4–6). This idealized conception had to come to grips, however, with the realities of poverty and indebtedness (vv. 7–11). So Deuteronomy, like Exodus 23:11, offers instructions on the care of the 'ebyôn (a term used six times in Deuteronomy 15) during the sabbatical year.

This link between the term 'ebyôn and the sabbatical year in both Exodus and Deuteronomy can hardly be coincidental, and one begins to suspect that Deuteronomy is not simply expanding on Exodus but restating, reformulating, and regularizing the practice for a later period. In Exodus, the provision was simply that the 'ebyôn could glean. In Deuteronomy 15, however, the people are required to lend freely to the 'ebyôn (v. 11 adds 'ānî, "oppressed"), even as the sabbatical year approaches (v. 15:9). It appears that the farm village setting of Ex. 23:3 is adjusted to suit the needs of an urban society where the lending of a variety of goods would be more appropriate.[49]

Deuteronomy 24:10–22 is also concerned with the treatment of the disenfranchised. The issues enumerated here include pledges (vv. 10–13), the payment of wages (vv. 14–15), the protection of the orphan and the widow (vv. 17–18), and gleaning rights for the stranger, orphan, and widow in the fields, olive groves, and vineyards (vv. 19–22). As for the 'ānî, one of the topics under scrutiny is the pledged garment. The passage states that a garment taken in pledge from the 'ānî must be returned before sundown (vv. 10–12). Both the 'ebyôn and 'ānî are the subject of wage payments in vv.14–15. In v.14 'ānî (twice) and 'ebyôn (once) function as adjectives modifying śākîr, "wage laborer." This reference helps to clarify the specifically economic status of the 'ebyôn and 'ānî. Such people live from hand to mouth, struggling daily to survive. Since this person is an 'ebyôn, the wages must be paid every day (v. 15).

The detailed correspondences between Ex. 22:24–26 (25–27) and Deut. 24:10–15 are striking. In addition to 'ānî as a shared term, several other terms or phrases are shared. Both use rē'eh, "neighbor, countryman" (Ex. 22:25 [26]; Deut. 24:10). Both limit the activity of the acceptance of a pledge until the time when the sun goes down (Ex. 22:25 [26]; Deut. 24:12). Both speak of (śalmâ, "garments" (Ex. 22:25 [26]; Deut. 24:13).

Of course, the differences between the passages are just as striking. In Exodus one is not to act like a moneylender (nošeh) toward the borrower by

charging interest (Ex. 22:24 [25]). In the parallel text in Deuteronomy, lending is permitted (note the use of *nsh* in Deut. 24:11), but with the proviso that
one accept the pledge out of doors and not enter the dwelling of the borrower
(Deut. 24:10–11). The basis for returning the garment differs between the
texts. In Exodus the speaker warns that the poor will cry out "to me," namely,
God, and God will respond to the injustice (Ex. 22:26 [27]). However, in
Deuteronomy the motivation is more positive. There it is said that upon the
return of the pledged garment the borrower will bless the lender "before the
LORD your God" (Deut. 24:13). Yet the notion of crying out to YHWH is
found in Deuteronomy as well (Deut. 24:14–15; cf. Ex. 22:26 [27]).

This latter fact probably indicates that Deut. 24:14–15 should be read
together with Deut. 24:10–13, and the entire block treated as an expansion on
Ex. 22:24–26 (25–27). In this analysis, the reference to *'ānî* in Deut. 24:14–15
serves to specify further the *'ānî* of v. 12, which was originally picked up from
Ex. 22:24. In Deut. 24:14–15 the term *'ānî* becomes the characterization of a day
laborer (*śākîr*). Again the sun's setting is mentioned, this time in reference to the
payment of wages before sundown (v. 13). The worker's wages are said to be necessary for survival (v. 15), much as the garment is said to be so needed in the
Covenant Code (Ex. 22:26 [27]). The motivation for payment is that the poor
might cry out and be heard by YHWH if payment is not made (Deut. 24:15).

The differences notwithstanding, the overall impression one obtains from
this comparison is that the passage in Deuteronomy is consciously expanded
from the text of the Covenant Code. Deuteronomy 24 appears to form an
adaptive commentary on the Exodus 22 material, much as Deuteronomy 15
appears to have done for the relevant material in Exodus 23.[50]

We cannot be sure of the precise social and political forces that combined
to forge the revisions of Deuteronomy, but on the surface at least it appears
that Deuteronomy reflects an urban environment, a shift away from the
clearer agrarian background of the Covenant Code. More speculatively, we
may also surmise that Deuteronomy's format as an Assyrian-styled vassal
treaty means either that Israel's landed gentry or, less likely, the royal house,
gave shape to the text.[51] Whichever of these scenarios we select, the social legislation of Deuteronomy would appear to mirror efforts on the part of a faction within Israel's elite to wrest control of the state away from Assyrian
overlords by asserting national independence. Both the courts of Hezekiah
and Josiah have been the scholarly suggestion for the context of the compilation of Deuteronomy, but the deeper political significance of this document as
a text of gentry-backed rebellion has often been overlooked.[52] In this historical context, the reading of Deuteronomy in the public square would have the
effect of rendering any other treaty with the Assyrians inoperative. Loyalty to
Judah and YHWH would be one and the same thing.[53] Such loyalty would be

tantamount to rebellion, at least the sort of resistance we find tacitly ascribed to Josiah as he maneuvered largely independent of Assyrian control (1 Kings 22:8–23:30). The Deuteronomic Historian who incorporated this legislation into the larger Deuteronomic History seems to have understood this implicitly: The failure to give singular loyalty to YHWH brought disaster to Israel's monarchic houses. By implication, the question of justice to the poor served as at least a litmus test for measuring the failings of these monarchs. As we shall see in chapter 3, however, the poverty question is at best a minor issue in DH.

Toward a Priestly Social Vision

The Priestly legal materials of the Torah are wide ranging and reflective of complex developments.[54] Of course, major strains of Priestly writing are found dispersed amid the narratives and genealogies collected in Genesis, where the picture of YHWH as the tempered lawgiver stands as a profound theological construct that shapes the Priestly narratives of the Creation, the Flood, and other tales. Yet throughout Exodus, Leviticus, and Numbers we see the full scope of the Priestly legislative program. The peoples' exodus of Exodus 1–19 soon becomes the Priestly program of tabernacle construction and ritual reorganization of Exodus–Numbers. In making this observation, we should not succumb to the view, so characteristic of nineteenth and early twentieth-century biblical analysis, that since the Priestly program was simply one of ritual and hierarchy, it was therefore inferior to the socially minded legislation of Deuteronomy or the ethical pronouncements of the prophets. Today the line between prophets, lawmakers, and priests is not so clear as it once may have seemed. Research in recent years suggests that a complicated set of interactions occurred between prophets and priests in ancient Israel. Both the separation and the links between prophecy and cult, a fluid sociological and theological line, must be kept in mind when assessing ostensibly Priestly and prophetic materials. The book of Ezekiel is a more obvious case, but other prophetic texts subtly bear a Priestly and cultic stamp as well. Thus, as we turn to the more generally acknowledged Priestly materials, we today recognize in them an equally profound voice at work in the shaping of Israel's total social vision. To be sure, the mode of Priestly expression has its own distinctive rhetorical features, theological leanings, and political emphases. Nevertheless, we should look for a Priestly social vision that is part and parcel of its interest in ritual and purity.

The Priestly program was an alternative to the collapsed royal project of Israel's monarchic period. While we must recognize the antiquity of many of the Priestly texts, it is difficult to shake the impression, continued to be held by many scholars today, that the Priestly material in its current formulation appears to represent the fruits of a political program inaugurated in the second temple era. Arguably, the crystallization point in the compilation of the final version of the Priestly torah must certainly be the period of renewal after the years of sabbatical required for the land to rest from its folly.[55] This is the implication of the curse segment of Lev. 26:27–35:

> But if, despite this, you disobey Me and remain hostile to Me, I will act against you in wrathful hostility; I, for My part, will discipline you sevenfold for your sins. You shall eat the flesh of your sons and the flesh of your daughters. I will destroy your cult places and cut down your incense stands, and I will heap your carcasses upon your lifeless fetishes.
>
> I will spurn you. I will lay your cities in ruin and make your sanctuaries desolate, and I will not savor your pleasing odors. I will make the land desolate, so that your enemies who settle in it shall be appalled by it. And you I will scatter among the nations, and I will unsheath the sword against you. Your land shall become a desolation and your cities a ruin.
>
> Then shall the land make up for its sabbath years throughout the time that it is desolate and you are in the land of your enemies; then shall the land rest and make up for its sabbath years. Throughout the time that it is desolate, it shall observe the rest that it did not observe in your sabbath years while you were dwelling upon it.

The period of exile is fully realized in 2 Chron. 36:21, where the "rest" is defined as seventy years. What else can Leviticus have in mind but the exile to Babylon? At the very least, then, we must consider the ritual and social legislation of Leviticus and Numbers to be the quasi-utopian vision of a priestly cadre vying for control of the land after the lapsed and spent monarchic debacle. The Priestly vision is comprehensive in scope, embracing shrine, community, household, and the disenfranchised. Like a grand liberation army of the Persian king, the *degel* troops of YHWH (i.e., those carrying their "banners") are envisioned marching forth from their exile to reconquer the land of promise for the purified worship of God (Numbers 1, 2, and 10). The text fosters a Priestly agenda that could remain viable under the auspices of the Persian overlords (see chapter 6). In this section, we consider the broader character and impact of this social legislation.

Purity, Holiness, and the Priestly Configuration of Social Justice: Leviticus 11—15

Following a major discussion of Israel's ritual sacrificial system (Leviticus 1—10), the next section of Leviticus (chaps. 11—15) is devoted to a series of rules concerning ritual uncleanness and purification procedures.[56] These chapters embrace such subjects as prohibited foods (11:1–23, 41–47), impurity from dead animals as a contagion (11:24–40), impurities associated with childbirth (12:1–8), skin diseases (13:1–14:32), impurity of buildings (14:33–57), and male and female genital discharges (15:1–33).

The operative word in these passages is "impurity" (ṭāmê).[57] Whether addressed to Moses and Aaron (11:1; 13:1; 14:33; 15:1) or to Moses alone (12:1; 14:1), these chapters identify impure states or classify items that can render one ritually impure. While P initially gave the command to "Be fertile and increase, fill the earth and master it" (Gen. 1:28), only the purity and ritual chapters of Leviticus navigate the treacherous waters toward making that dominion a reality.

From the Priestly viewpoint, various interactions with that world pose problems of purity. In part, the issue is the danger of external impurity entering a person. The animal kingdom poses a twofold threat, either through the ingestion of anomalous creatures (land, sea, and air) or through contact with dead animals (chap. 11). However, the greater problem resides in what emerges from within a person to flow into the external world. Birthing children into that world creates an impure state both for the mother as well as for the male or female child, though the birth of the female doubles the impurities caused thereby (chap. 12). Furthermore, sundry points of inner/outer contact with that world pose grave dangers, in particular skin diseases (chap. 13) and by extension contagions festering in one's domicile (chap. 14), or places where the body's inner fluids cross into the outer sphere in the form of male genital discharges, semen, a woman's menstrual flow, and other female fluid flows (chap. 15). Here we should also add reference to Leviticus 5, which focuses on the equivalent danger posed by impure speech, the emergence of inner thoughts into the external sphere where God resides.

These troublesome boundary crossings find their rectification in the careful work of the priest, who closely inspects each situation, performs purification rites, offers up sacrifices on behalf of the afflicted, oversees periods of quarantines for people and their houses, and issues lasting instructions for the community (e.g., Lev. 15:31). The priest is, after all, the stable connection between a volatile community and the ever more terrifying divine dwelling place, the tent of meeting. As this community and the divine intersect, the priest mediates the attendant worldly disorders to create an ordered universe and a people fit for worship (cf. Num. 5:1–3). In this way, the Genesis command to dominate the earth finds a mirror and model in Israel's ritual governance of itself.

One could well argue that the social effects of the regulations of these chapters, whether practiced fully in actuality or in the main advocated ideologically, would serve to create a communal nexus in which priestly technical education came to govern the social order. This structure shifted power and profit (in the form of sacrifices) to the priesthood while effectively isolating women to the domestic sphere.[58] To be sure, this marginalizing process had its variables, both for women and for the infirm, insofar as various forms of compensation to the divine priests could effectively remediate the social estrangements engendered by cultic impurity. Yet the purity regulations would have a powerful structuring effect, leaving sectors of the populace "cared for" but still marginalized. The priests were, after all, the patrons, while those under their oversight constituted their clients. Thus, by being the keepers of difference, this priestly group became the guardians of a particular order, both social and moral. By setting the corporeal boundary lines, they also defined the cultural bonds of the community.[59]

To which communities and locales this vision appealed in ancient Israel is difficult to say. That Priestly thinking appears to function as one of the dominant ideologies in the biblical tradition over a long period might lead us to conclude that the Priestly vision exerted sizable influence in the history of the people. This would not be surprising, either for Israel or other parts of the ancient Near East. Likewise, this sociological dominance accords well with Eagleton's observation that "successful ideologies must be more than imposed illusions, and for all their inconsistencies must communicate to their subjects a version of social reality which is real and recognizable enough not to be simply rejected out of hand."[60] Priestly legislation, therefore, represents a definition of priestly dominance, with its exertion toward hegemony in the life of ancient Israel. To quote M. Douglas, "whenever a people are aware of encroachment and danger, dietary rules controlling what goes into the body would serve as a vivid analogy of the corpus of their cultural categories at risk."[61] This legislative social construction offered a concrete and viable embodiment of priestly social ideals in the light of which "prophetic" ramblings may have seemed like deranged and detached pronouncements. We should not, therefore, underestimate the social viability of the Priestly voice, especially in a climate of modern interpreters who prefer to invoke only prophetically linked "liberation" voices.

We can sense something of the parameters of P's thinking about social justice by examining the vocabulary of poverty in these passages. The variable between rich and poor surfaces as a mitigating factor in Leviticus 14. The text of Leviticus omits any reference to the *'ĕbyôn*, but unlike Deuteronomy it does make use of *dal* in addition to *'ānî*. In Lev. 14:21 the *dal* is permitted to offer less in the ritual for cleansing of a skin disease, a permission which stands in sharp contrast to Ex. 30:15 where no allowance was made for the *dal* over against the rich in the census offering.[62] P makes similar allowances for the poorer woman who has born a child and must make the requisite purification offering (Lev. 12:8).

While due allowance is made for the poor man or woman, and thus the disorder posed by that state is remedied, the Priestly legislation recognizes that poverty is not so simply overcome. Yet the very making of such provisions tacitly acknowledges the need to institutionalize the norms of justice. Although such verbiage may at times simply represent propagandistic pronouncements, the Priestly contribution to Israel's debate about justice appears to recognize the harsher realities of the life of the poor. In so doing, P joins the other constituencies of the legal tradition, whether the village, urban, and monarchic traditions represented elsewhere in the Torah and prophetic traditions, to suggest that there is a concrete measure to God's holiness, namely, the ritual system's own treatment of those who are poor.

By the same token, the remedial practices promulgated by these chapters of Leviticus effectively serve to further enforce particular social configurations: priests versus laity (the tribes), men versus women, villagers versus the urban environment, and rich versus poor. However, in terms of overarching rhetoric, the continuum between village farms and the temple or shrines (Leviticus 1—10) was undergirded by a common vision that the exodus God is at root a *holy* deity who demands a rigorous purity praxis, which was to dominate both home and shrine (Lev. 11:44–45; 15:31). Of course, when priests mediate this "holiness," they are the philosophical architects and legislators of the social order. Thus, the priests, and not the poor, are ultimately the focus of P's legal materials: The larger Priestly vision and social praxis are not framed around the poor as such. Nevertheless, this stream of legal thought and ritual practice does remain cognizant of the status of the poor, treating their situation not as an impure state but as a condition that requires a tempering of the "fees" exacted when seeking reconciliation with the holy God. Baldly stated, the hierarchy is reinforced through the cooperation and the tending of those in need. This outlook is indicative of a dominant social vision that has profoundly shaped the final commitments of the Torah tradition.

Addressing Concrete Needs: The Bold Social Program of the Holiness Code

More fruitful for our purposes are those chapters scholars commonly term the Holiness Code (Leviticus 17—26), a block of material that decisively extends and at times diverges from the Priestly legislation found elsewhere in Leviticus.[63] Following chap. 16, which details the purification of the tabernacle for the Day of Atonement ceremony, the Holiness Code adumbrates a broad range of worship and social obligations. Here the Priestly legislation concerning the poor finds its place within this web of ritual, sexual, communal, and familial legislation. To do justice to the complexity of this particular contribution to Priestly social thought, we must examine the poverty materials of this segment of Leviticus against the backdrop of a more general discussion of the Holiness Code itself.

The Code begins by emphasizing the one central altar and the importance of blood in the ritual process (17:1–16). As with chaps.11—15, the Holiness Code legitimates itself by accenting the holy deity. Likewise, the exodus event is tapped to underscore this primary allegiance to the holy (18:1–5; cf. 20:7–8; 22:31–33). Specifically, the social agenda of the Holiness Code reinforces the regulation of communal life around the central priestly shrine as mediated by the official priesthood.[64] Thus, the exodus tradition plays a social maintenance function through the interpretations and ritual practices of a priesthood in whose hands social power resides. To the extent that the poor are embraced by and actively embrace this vision of holiness, they are functionaries in an all-encompassing hierarchical commonwealth. The priests have established themselves as the champions of YHWH's poor, a posture that would be consistent with their role both during the time of the monarchy as well as during their postexilic bid for power.

The Holiness Code details a series of regulations concerning incest and other sexual relations (Lev. 18:6–23; cf. chap. 20; Deut. 27:20–23). The lines of permitted sexual intercourse among relatives is clearly delineated, and disgrace functions as the social mechanism to make operant the Priestly injunctions. According to Priestly thinking, the sacred in ancient Israelite society was mediated within the family household by means of a tightly protected family structure and by clearly defined patterns of marriage. Here Priestly notions of purity serve as the sufficient ideological ground to create the necessary social glue to bind together households within villages. Even in the physical absence of a priest, the social mechanisms thereby established would lend credence to their authority.

Yet there is an issue here that runs deeper than simple social solidarity or social control. P's architectural plans for society are calculated to ensure that Israel *retains the land*. The Priestly writers interpret the conquest of the promised land by Joshua as the "spewing out" of the native inhabitants because of their sexual defilement of the place (18:24–30). From the postexilic situation of the Code, what we have here is a philosophical and ideological effort designed to create a holy society that might escape the sort of judgment encountered in the exile to Babylon. As we shall see later, the Priestly message is akin to that of Ezekiel; yet there is a greater specificity in the Priestly attempt to encapsulate precisely the sort of economic conditions and legal practices that should prevail in such a just society.

We observe something of this specificity in relation to the poor in Leviticus 19. As noted earlier, this chapter bears the tone of the Ten Commandments, overlapping it in a number of matters. However, there is no apparent systematic arrangement of the various injunctions covered in this chapter; only the recurrent terse phrase, "I am the LORD," serves as a binding agent to the chapter. Statements about worship and ritual are intermingled with sexual concerns. The Sabbath receives particular attention in two places (vv. 3, 30). Idol worship and peace offerings stand in sharp contrast (vv. 4–8). Blood and divination are noted (vv. 26, 31; cf. 20:6, 27). Sidelocks, beards, and other bodily marks are regulated to achieve ritual holiness (vv. 27–28). This chapter's emphasis on right worship, and in particular on holiness, is further underscored by its insistence and its conclusion that the ground of the Priestly social ethic is the exodus God (vv. 3, 34, esp. 36b–37; cf. 11:45).

Where are the disenfranchised in the vision of chapter 19? If not the ground or the sole parameter of the Priestly discussion as we found in our discussion of Leviticus 11—15, certainly the poor and oppressed serve as one of the major categories of this legislation. The laborer's wages are to be paid on the day of service and not retained overnight (v. 13). We found a similar concern addressed in Deuteronomy 15 as the legal tradition came to cope with the shift to an urban context. Likewise, in the commonwealth of God envisioned by the Priestly writers, the wage laborer receives just treatment. Yet the context is no longer the urban one of Deuteronomy but that of the uprooted and replanted members of postexilic society. Thus, Leviticus 19 is hardly a carbon copy of Deuteronomy 15. The Priestly writers broaden the understanding of the disenfranchised to include the physically disabled and, presumably, the senior citizens of the society (v. 14). To be sure, the standard concern for honoring father and mother is retained in this legislation (v. 3; cf. 20:9).[65] Nonetheless, this broader inclusion of the disabled enables the Holiness Code to move beyond simple cliche toward greater realism with respect to the reality of community building. The express concern for the physically disabled is noteworthy in Leviticus, although we must also observe that physical disabilities are elsewhere treated as deformities that severely limit participation in the principle works of worship (cf. 21:17).

Likewise, there is great ambivalence about foreigners in the Holiness Code, at times bordering on antipathy (18:24–30; 24:10–16). Nevertheless, in chap. 19, respectful treatment of foreign workers and residents is clearly enjoined, an injunction that bears the same weight as the text's call for just weights and measures in the passage that immediately follows:

> When a stranger resides with you in your land, you shall not wrong him. The stranger who resides with you shall be to you as one of your citizens; you shall love him as yourself, for you were strangers in the land of Egypt: I the LORD am your God.

> You shall not falsify measures of length, weight, or capacity. You shall have an honest balance, honest weights, an honest *ephah*, and an honest *hin*.
>
> I the LORD am your God who freed you from the land of Egypt. (Lev. 19:33–36)

We might observe in passing that this concern for just weights and measures is shared with the wisdom tradition as exemplified by Proverbs. Note, however, how much more concrete and all-embracing is the Priestly vision regarding the disenfranchised than the vision and attitude of Proverbs. Chapter 19's generous attitude toward the resident alien stands in tension, however, with the sharp distinction made between the foreign slaves whom one may possess permanently and the Israelite slaves who are to be redeemed when at all possible (25:44–55). Most moderns will find this aspect distasteful, but we should not overlook the degree to which certain categories of marginalized individuals did factor into the Priestly program.

It would seem that a woman's status as slave served to justify the lack of severity with which inappropriate sexual relations with such a woman was treated (19:20–22). Payment of an indemnity is permitted to compensate the owner for the loss of value as a virgin.[66] Daughters, on the other hand, are to be protected from prostitution (v. 29). Clearly, a woman's value as a commodity, whether as slave to her owner or as marriageable property for her father, stands as one of the dominant governing factors determining the woman's role in the Priestly economy. As the lines for sexual intercourse are sharply drawn, women's role in the commonwealth is conservatively established, with dominant familial power in the hands of fathers and husbands, and with dominant political power in the hands of the male, tribally based priesthood (cf. 18:16–20; 20:10–21). Indeed, daughters in priestly families fare better than others in the social structure (21:9). Here is the key problematic for the contemporary interpreter, for there is no escaping the fact that the Priestly vision is built on the conscious domination of women as a group, though such is the case throughout much of biblical literature.[67]

When we speak of the disenfranchised, the poor receive considerable attention in chapter 19 and in the rest of the Holiness Code. Curiously, Leviticus 19 differs from Exodus and Deuteronomy in its use of the term *'ānî* . In Lev. 19:9–10, it is the *'ānî* who receives the benefits of gleaning food from the fields and vineyards. Similarly, the *'ānî* is again granted gleaning privileges in Lev. 23:22. The term *'ānî* is not used in such a context in either Exodus or Deuteronomy. It would seem that the severe state of oppression denoted by the term *'ānî* has garnered the attention of the Priestly writer. Furthermore, in matters of votive offerings, provision *is* made for a distinction between rich and poor, though this injunction stands outside of the Holiness Code proper (27:1–8). These cases represent a consistent Priestly view in which poverty serves as the ground for the assessment of the duties and needs of the poor.

By contrast, Lev. 19:15 reflects the view that neither the *dal* nor the rich were to be favored when rendering legal judgments. This statement bears clear similarities to Ex. 23:3 where *dal* is used to the same effect. In fact, both texts use the verb *hdr*, "to favor" (Ex. 23:3 concerning *dal*, Lev. 19:15 concerning *gādôl*). From the uses of *dal* in Leviticus it appears that the Priestly text draws on the Covenant Code for its inspiration and adheres to a standard that must have been very ancient in the biblical legal tradition. This standard, however, does not prevent the Priestly writers from developing their own "option for the poor" when it came to matters of food and worship, as we have seen.

Perhaps it is this attentiveness to concrete social need and want that stands behind the bold and visionary program of social reform advocated by chap. 25. The Priestly document culminates the cycle of seven Sabbath years (or forty-nine years) with a year of jubilee (25:8–55).[68] At this time the land was to lie fallow, debt slaves were released, and, most importantly, property that families were forced to sell since the time of the previous jubilee was to return to the original owners. This program of social reform is part and parcel of the ideological engine that drove the priestly machine of ritual reform. For if, as I suggest, the Holiness Code is the platform of the postexilic priestly commonwealth, much as 4QMMT was for the Qumran community, then the elaborate discussion of the priesthood (chap. 21), offerings (chap. 22), and festivals (chap. 23) represents a rejuvenated liturgical program and ritual structure enshrined as the goal and the constitution for Israel's survival after the exile.[69] In adopting such a program, the Priestly writers appear to have tapped the long-lived ancient Near Eastern royal practice of making proclamations of freedom, either upon accession to the throne or during a reign (the *mīšarum* and *andurārum* edicts).[70] In these proclamations, a broad range of social remedies were instituted: cancellation of specific taxes and debts, release of debt slaves, restoration of families and property, exemption from forced labor, offering protection to widows and orphans, pardon for criminals, and release from military service. The edicts, as Weinfeld characterizes them, represented an attempt on the part of the king, "to show favor to his people by protecting them and lightening their burden, or to reward his subjects who benefitted him."[71]

The Priestly writers have boldly taken up the monarchic mantle, promising to deliver concrete social change on the order experienced throughout the centuries in the ancient Near East. Leviticus, therefore, was not designed as some nostalgic tour book of Israel's Mosaic-Aaronic heritage, but as a programmatic and even utopian platform for its future. There is, of course, the danger here that the category of poverty is simply being scavenged and exploited by the priests for its political value, much as the Akkadian *andurārum* pronouncements undoubtedly were.[72] Nevertheless, we must credit the Priestly writers with proffering a postexilic program that did not rely on the kingship for its inspiration or driving force, as the Deuteronomic and Isaianic writers were inclined to do.

Much as the Jewish community had to reconstitute itself after 70 C.E., choosing to do so around the formation of the Mishnaic code and thereby surviving catastrophe (as J. Neusner has forcefully argued), the community of the Levitical writers faced the postexilic drama by drawing up legislation for a postexilic world (cf. 26:14–46).[73] In that world, the poor, women, the aged, the stranger, and even the environment itself were the focal points of Priestly legal discussion. For these writers, the success of the reconstruction after the exile was a direct function of the care with which the disenfranchised were treated economically, socially, and legally.

It is a mistake to assume that the Priestly writers were more deficient in this regard or less conscious of social ethics than Israel's prophetic voices. Certainly there is a prophetic/priestly split that informs much of the biblical text, functioning as a convenient rhetorical tool in the prophetic voice; nevertheless, there are also blurred lines (as with Ezekiel and Joel) and serious degrees of overlap in terms of issues surrounding the poor in Israel's community. We should not confuse prophetic rhetoric with social reality, which is always far more complex. If we fault the Priestly writers for their lack of complete universalism in their social vision, we could also fault the prophets for a similar myopia. Indeed, the entire biblical text evidences Israel's wrestling with the tension created by affirming YHWH as both the Lord of Israel and the Lord of all.[74] In the end, all sides of the early biblical tradition agree that Israel is the Lord's light amid nations. Neither the priestly nor the prophetic voice has cornered the market on either cultural exclusivism or theological universalism.

Within the general limits of the Holiness Code, then, there does appear a broad social vision that attempts to concretely address the situation of the urban and village poor in ancient Israel as part of a larger social enterprise of rebuilding the languishing commonwealth. Those today who so loosely champion the prophetic texts would do well to remember that it was the priestly tradition that saved Judaism from almost certain extinction as a political and national entity both in the land and in exile. In fact, as we shall see in chapter 4, if the prophets played a role in the postexilic reconstruction, it was in energizing the priestly program of return to the land, rebuilding the temple, and restoring the commonwealth!

Law and Authority in Numbers: The Force
behind the Priestly Codes

The book of Numbers situates a variety of legislative sections within the extensive narratives of the tribal wanderings out of the Sinai, to Kadesh, and beyond to the plains of Moab. These legal and ritual texts carry forward the spirit and vision of the Priestly writers. In particular, these texts regulate civil grievances (5:5–10), adultery and suspicions of adultery (5:11–31), the nazirite vow made by men or women (6:1–21), defilement by corpses (9:6–13), success in war (10:9–10), sacrificial offerings (15:1–31; 28:1–29:39), Sabbath work (15:32–36), the red heifer offering (19:1–22), female inheritance rights (27:1–11), laws regarding vows (30:1–17 [29:40–30:16]), and laws on manslaughter and murder (35:9–34).

Although widely divergent in content, these legal materials are united by more than their presence in the narrative of Israel's march to the promised land. Throughout the Priestly narratives in Numbers, the Aaronic priestly sacrificial system undergirds, frames, and enforces the social arrangements implied by these rituals and legal texts.[75] In the priestly commonwealth, the tent of meeting has become the locus of social and tribal identity (1—4; 10:13–28; 13:1–6; 26:1–65; 32:1–36:13), the mechanism of the transfer of wealth (chap. 7), as well as the legitimator of Aaronic priestly ascendancy over the Levites (chap. 8), indeed over all who are in the land, including the "stranger" (9:14; cf. 15:14–16).

The priestly program is seen to be the genesis and fulfillment of Israel's territorial destiny. Narrative, in other words, is put to the service of legislation, as is consistently done throughout P (see chap. 3). In other words, for P, Israel's march from Mesopotamia to Egypt to the promised land is to give rise to a society governed by a ritual structure rather than a royal house. Whatever P's preexilic roots, this vision would hold powerful sway over various constituencies in the postexilic restoration period.[76] This Aaronic ascendancy and authority structure offers a socially viable alternative to the purely Mosaic/ prophetic tendencies of E, where legal authority is vested in a rigorously policed prophetic group that finds social power extended to a select number of "elders and officers of the people" (11:10–20). The pro-prophetic, anti-Aaronic polemic by E reached its height in a stinging rebuke of Aaron and more explicitly Miriam in chap. 12. P's version suggests a more comprehensive structuring of legal and social authority.

The Aaronic response also served to undermine the pro-Mosaic tendencies of J (cf. 14:5–10, 26–29 = P; 14:11–25, 39–45 = J). In chap. 14, P's Moses and Aaron are instrumental to the prospect of successfully taking the "exceedingly good land" (v. 14:7), whereas J's emphasis remains on the need for prophetic/

Mosaic intercession to avert YHWH's justifiable anger at a recalcitrant people (vv. 11–19). Yet for both J and P the net effect of the wilderness exile and punishment is to defer to a later generation the opportunity to settle the promised land (vv. 20–25 = J; 26–35 = P).

J, E, and P, in other words, present alternate programs for reclaiming the land and for structuring authority in the community in the postexilic era. Yet the disputes engaged by P go well beyond the priestly versus prophetic conflict to include intrapriestly matters. J and E's Mosaic/prophetic emphasis does not mean these strands were devoid of ritual programs. Such matters became points of dispute. While specific rituals, sacrifices, and holidays were all undoubtedly at issue, all strands agree that what is ultimately at stake is who controls and influences the ritual structure and hence the production of ethical norms and principles in the community. Numbers 16, which incorporates J's account of the rebellion of Korah and others against Moses, has been couched by P in terms of a rebellion against both Moses and Aaron. P makes it clear that the dispute is over priestly prerogatives: "Is it not enough for you that the God of Israel has set you apart from the community of Israel and given you access to Him, to perform the duties of the LORD's Tabernacle and to minister to the community and serve them?" (v. 9). The contrast between J and P with regard to the shunning of the opponents is strikingly indicative of P's and J's divergent orientations toward social authority. Whereas J has Moses and the elders physically separate from the rebels (vv. 25–26), P has the moment *ritualized* by Moses and Aaron at the tent of meeting (vv. 16–19). The P narrative's vision of ritual as a mechanism for shaping the hierarchical structure of the priestly commonweath's social fabric could not be depicted in more vivid a fashion than in P's trial scene, where the rebels appear before Aaron carrying incense in 250 fire pans (vv. 17). Surprisingly, J's prophetic emphasis on Moses as miracle worker appears to outdo even P, for the fate of the rebels is for them to be swallowed up by Sheol itself (vv. 27b-32a)! P's ending might seem weaker than J's insofar as the 250 incense carriers are not swallowed up but only consumed by a fire from YHWH, but, ironically, it is a fire that completes the permanent ritualization of *Aaronic* authority (16:35–17:27). P's accent on this ritualized authority is signaled both by the reuse of the 250 firepans as "plating for the altar" (17:3 [16:38]) and by the sprouting of the staff of Aaron (17:23 [17:8]).

Thus, while the dangers of rebellion beset both the community and the priesthood at every turn (e.g., 20:2–13), P's narrative legitimizes the Aaronic structure and sacrificial system as the sole means for removing the guilt of that rebellion (chap. 18). By contrast, E seeks to envision prophetic magic (in the form of serpents) to serve as the sign of legitimation behind whatever ritual system it might support (21:4–9). E develops this magical dimension further with respect to the pagan prophet Balaam (22:2–24:25). Presumably E sees in the prophetic voice the only viable mechanism for mediating the people's crisis over land, political power, and worship.

Likewise, in contrast to P's concern for an authority structure grounded in a highly specialized sacrificial system, J posits communal regional failures, in particular the difficulties negotiating territorial agreements and concessions vis-à-vis neighboring powers, to be key to the community's long-term survival (20:14–21; 21:21–35). Furthermore, J links the community's troubles to the paganizing taint of foreign women, again accenting the need for the community to sort out its relations with surrounding peoples (25:1–5). Clearly J is interested in developing an ethnically unique ritual system. J's divergence from P would seem to be more in terms of a perceived failure of the priestly program to protect the landed interests of J's audience.

While both J and P raise the disturbing matter of sacral violence as they line out their plan of attack, J frames the issue less in terms of the "Moabite women" than as concern over defection to the deity Baal-Peor. For J, in other words, the punishment is meted out against the "men who attached themselves to Baal-Peor" (25:5). P explicitly ritualizes the pagan threat by having Phinehas, one of the Aaronids, murder the offending Midianite woman, treating the execution of both the man and the woman as a divinely authorized act (25:8).[77] No doubt P's scene of ritually sanctioned retribution echoes and repackages E's description of the Levitical "revolutionary purge" of the idolatrous offenders who raise up the golden calf, leading the community astray (Ex. 32:26–28). There E posits equivocation on the part of Aaron, whereas in Numbers P sustains the Aaronids by having them institutionalize sacral slaughter. For P, neither E's prophetic magic nor J's admission of communal failings could be considered the sufficient ground for the erection of a totally new society. What was required by P was a priestly vanguard willing to take the risks and exercise the force necessary to whip a reluctant people into shape as a viable congregation of God.[78]

The reference to the pagan women in this connection raises the question of the place of women generally in the authority structure of the priestly commonwealth. As we conclude our discussion of the Priestly legislation, we would do well to keep in mind that the seemingly egalitarian beginnings of the P narrative in Genesis 1, where male and female are created together, have not given way to an egalitarian commonwealth. Feminist attempts to "retrieve" anything more than a male-dominated hierarchicalism from P's creation story would seem to have misconstrued the nature of the text in its sociohistorical context.[79] While it is true that Zelophehad's daughters are accorded inheritance rights in the absence of a male heir (Num. 27:1–11), the primacy of male inheritance is thereby protected and reinforced. Likewise, while latitude is given to women not to be bound by vows in cases where either their fathers or husbands object, the principle of male predominance in the family structure is more than subtly ensured within the religious framework (Num. 30:1–17 [29:40–30:16]). In any event, the overall trajectory in P suggests that legal power and ritual authority in the official cultus are given over to males in the priestly system. Reading together the legislation in Numbers and P's creation story, we come to see that P's agenda for women rests in the idea of a structured cosmology that distributes social power and roles according to status, gender, and relationship. To say that humankind is male and female is to say that the female requires male supervision. Moreover, to say that the act of creation involves a sacred day of rest is to say that the overseers of that day, namely the Aaronids, exercise divine authority over all men and women. It will be left to the Deuteronomic History to posit a relatively more expansive role for women in ancient Israelite social thought (see chapter 3).[80]

Law Codes and the Traditioning Process

When examining the Israelite record, we should be careful to distinguish between the historical development and the religious functioning of these texts. The narrative materials make clear that the king of Jerusalem was the final arbiter of Israelite law in cooperation with regional judges. The narratives specifically note the role of King David (2 Sam. 15:1–6) and King Jehoshaphat (2 Chron. 20:4–11) in the legal sphere, crediting the latter with the reform of ancient Israel's legal structure. Sociohistorically, the Torah's law collections undoubtedly functioned at some level in the maintenance of the palace-temple social complex.

Yet we must also pay careful attention to the traditioning of the codes. In ancient Israel, unlike Sumer, Babylon, and Assyria, the amalgamation of law codes within the larger narrative scheme of Israel's descent to Egypt, exodus from Egypt, and trek to the land of the promise, subsumed the law codes to the far grander religious and social project of the second temple community under the constraints of the power of the Persian rulers. Whatever role various conceptions of Moses may have played in the Israelite tradition prior to the exile, throughout the early postexilic period this priestly-prophetic figure was reworked to shore up competing claims to political authority.[81] Ironically, though much later in the wake of the destruction of 70 C.E., the complete collapse of the priesthood would open the door to the reappropriation of the Mosaic legal tradition by the rabbinic teachers of the Mishnaic period.[82]

As we examine the social legislation of the Pentateuch, we must bear in mind this distinction between the sociohistorical functioning of the codes during the time of the monarchy and their traditioning within the Torah as a product of the second temple period's renaissance in religious thought and practice. At times we may not be in a position to render a definitive judgment regarding the matter of the precise dating of the composition and editing of these texts. Scholarly disputes over the historical development of the biblical text have reemerged, as the writings of Whybray and Van Seters firmly attest.[83] Yet in broad measure, the biblical legal record does afford us some key diachronic considerations as well as indications of sociological contexts for the composition and transmission of these texts. We will take up the narrative embodiment of these competing legal traditions in chapters 3–6.

Prophets and Covenant: A Reassessment

How did the prophets relate to this body of legal material? Since, as we have seen, the Ten Commandments, the Covenant Code, Deuteronomy, and the Priestly legal materials all stem from different periods in biblical history, with the dating of these materials still the subject of vigorous debate, the question of the prophetic relation to the legal materials must be posed in different ways. On the one hand, the Covenant Code is generally regarded as antedating the books of the prophets and suggests a possible source for prophetic concerns for the poor. On the other hand, Deuteronomy is thought to represent a reformist text that received its final form during the reign of Josiah (although some of its content may have roots in earlier periods). This text may bear traces of prophetic influence. In examining the relation between prophecy and covenant, we need to consider both the prophetic use of inherited traditions as well as the possible impact of the prophets on the Deuteronomic reforms.

In a general way, it can be said that covenant traditions sparked the imagination of the prophets. The most dominant images the prophets adapt and rework from the nation's early "history" are those of the exodus and the wilderness wanderings. The exodus image was called upon by the prophets as a means to affirm the continued presence of YHWH among the people of Israel, no matter how hard their condition might become.[84] Images of YHWH's protection of the ancestors in the wilderness provided comfort to succeeding generations through the voice of the prophets.[85]

However, the prophets' relation to the covenant and legal traditions is more tenuous than this picture implies.[86] Certainly there is a role for the giving of the covenant in the prophetic texts (cf. Isa. 42:6; 49:8; Jer. 11:3-4; Ezek. 16:7–8). Yet the individual actors behind these events—Moses, Aaron, and others—are given scant attention in the prophetic literature, appearing only occasionally (cf. Isa. 63:11-12; Jer. 15:1; Micah 6:1–5; Mal. 3:22 [4:4]). More surprisingly, the narrative of the events of the conquest of Canaan, the figure of Joshua, and the notion of the promise of land play virtually no role in the prophetic literature (cf. Amos 2:9–12; Jer. 2:7). Certainly the idea of a special relation between YHWH and Israel is vital to the thinking of the prophets. Yet the prophets appear to focus on one aspect of the covenant relationship, namely, the dire consequences of violating it.[87] Thus, while even the notion of a "new covenant" comes to play a role in the prophetic tradition, the nuanced idea of covenant and law as portrayed in the Pentateuch exerts far less influence than one might imagine in the course of the development of the prophetic literature.[88]

How then are we to account for the fact that the term covenant (*bĕrît*) is found numerous times in the prophetic literature, although the term "is a rare word in their speeches"?[89] Let us look at the book of Jeremiah. Observe how the term "covenant" never appears in the prophet's oracles. This confirms suspicions we shall explore later which suggest that the prophet's own original and rather strident social justice critique has been filtered through a lens (which we would term Deuteronomic) that stylizes Jeremiah as a "prophet" who supports and sustains a Mosaic-like covenant of obedience, a covenant birthed in the exodus experience and revisited after the calamitous era of the prophet Jeremiah (cf. Jeremiah 11). The bulk of the covenant references in Jeremiah are clustered in chaps. 31–34, where the "new covenant" motif carries forward a program that was aimed at renewing the "covenant with your fathers" from the exodus period (Jer. 34:13). Whatever the intent of these chapters, it is clear that the *prose* narrative materials of Jeremiah diverge rather sharply from the message and agenda of the more ancient prophetic oracles. The prophet's voice comes to be shaped by an editorial layer that is heavily invested in the image of a prophet who preaches the new covenant. Insofar as this is the case, the prose prophet resembles the prophetic narratives found in the Deuteronomic History (see further chapter 3).

Stated baldly, therefore, the fact that covenant traditions play a shaping role on the prophetic writings does not mean that the prophets sat with scroll in hand and quoted their favorite texts from the Torah.[90] To be sure, fragments of the Ten Commandments can be discerned in Hosea (3:1; 4:1–2, 12:10 [9]; 13:4), Amos (3:1–2), and Jeremiah (7:9), but even here Weiss is compelled to conclude that "we find that there are no more than slight traces of the Decalogue in prophetic literature, that these traces are not always entirely clear, and that they are confined to three of the prophetic books in all."[91] Greenberg also notes that "the main prophetic themes are absent from the Decalogue: saving the oppressed from the hand of the oppressor, aiding the poor, executing justice at the gate, etc."[92] Scholars who wish to see the covenant at work in the thinking of the prophets have had difficulties tying this general orientation of the prophets to the specifics of the covenant as found in the present collection of materials in the Pentateuch. Often this means, as Hillers points out, that covenant is considered a late notion which exercised no role on the earlier prophetic tradition.[93] However, this is not necessarily the case. One solution to this dilemma has been offered in two interrelated ways. In the first place, some suggest that the many threats of judgment the prophets make against Israel should be seen as prophetic invocations of treaty curses.[94] Others suggest that the problem is solved with reference to a literary form said to be found in the prophetic writings, namely, the covenant lawsuit (see especially Micah 6:1–8).[95]

Clements is highly critical of both of these solutions which attempt to link the prophets to specific notions of covenant. Concerning treaty curses he writes,

> What we lack is any evidence which can demonstrate that the woes threatened by the prophets have been drawn directly from a specific tradition of covenant curses, and not more generally from a knowledge of the ills and misfortunes of life in the ancient world, which also find illustration in the curses of the treaties as well as more generally in curse formulae.[96]

While this criticism is well taken, it should be pointed out that treaty curses were known and utilized theologically in Israel (Deut. 27:15–26; 28:15–68) and provide the most plausible context for the prophetic threats, even if one cannot absolutely demonstrate that covenant curses supply the singular background to the prophetic attacks. It is the broken relationship with Israel's divine sovereign that is at issue for the prophets. Clements is likewise critical of the covenant lawsuit analysis:

> We do not need to call upon the existence of the treaty form in Israel, nor on borrowings from the form and content of imperial letters accusing vassals of having broken their treaty obligations, in order to explain the prophetic portrayal of a lawsuit between YHWH and Israel. Neither, in fact, is there any need to reconstruct the pattern of a special cultic "covenant lawsuit," since the material that is claimed to show this simply shows the adoption into cultic poetry of widely used legal imagery.[97]

Although the lawsuit may be a legal image as Clements says, it seems that he has overlooked the link between the lawsuit and the covenant tradition. The lawsuit concerns the response of the people to the benevolent deeds of YHWH as sovereign. The very crime under consideration is the violation of the relationship established through the covenant between the people and YHWH as the divine sovereign. Israel had broken its relationship with YHWH and had to suffer the consequences of such an action. Such a conception is covenant thinking in its simplest form. The genius of the lawsuit pattern is that legal imagery has been adapted to the covenant and covenant-curse context. To dismiss the covenant background behind the lawsuit is to pull the rug out from under the image.

Still, the role of the covenant tradition in the prophetic literature remains problematic. Perhaps further clues can be gleaned if we ask how the prophetic writings may relate to the pentateuchal legal materials on poverty. In general, one can say that, as with the Ten Commandments, the prophetic observations about the poor unevenly overlap with the pentateuchal laws concerning the poor. There is no talk of gleaning or of protections for the poor during the sabbatical year in the prophetic texts (Jeremiah 34 concerns the jubilee year). Neither is any concern shown in the prophetic writings over allowances for the poor in ritual matters. The taking of interest is rarely a concern in the prophets, and what examples are found in the prophetic materials are either unclearly related to the pentateuchal legislation (Amos 5:11, if this has to do with interest at all) or else find their inspiration apart from the terms for poor (Ezek. 18:17; cf. Lev. 25:36). Finally, little connection can be posited for the material concerning wage payments (Deut. 24:13; Jer. 22:13–4). For those who wish to dip only into the prophets for their contemporary social protest, this comparison should make it quite clear that the prophets do not constitute the exclusive preserve of constructive social programs in the biblical tradition. Indeed, the major drawback to adopting a so-called prophetic critique, as is so popular in some circles today, is that the prophetic literature often fails to advocate the kinds of concrete mechanisms that would be necessary for the alleviation of poverty in society. Each of the bodies of Torah legislation examined in this chapter goes far beyond the prophetic literature in this regard.

Firmer ground for comparison between the prophets and the Pentateuch is discernible in the texts that concern legal justice for the poor and the matter of pledged garments. The relevant prophetic texts are found in First Isaiah and Amos. In Isaiah 5 the prophet pronounces a series of woes against the power elite, those who enjoy a life of luxury at the expense of others. In the last woe of the section, Isaiah condemns those who "vindicate him who is in the wrong in return for a bribe, and withhold vindication from him who is in the right" (v. 5:23). This could be more literally translated: "the ones who pronounce the guilty to be innocent because of a bribe [*šoḥad*]; and they remove the innocence of the innocent." This inversion of right and wrong picks up a thought developed in v. 5:20. This text has possible affinities to Ex. 23:6–9, in which the concern is also that of legal justice. This Exodus passage mentions the injustice of declaring the guilty to be just, and follows this up with a statement prohibiting the acceptance of bribes (*šoḥad*).

Similarly, texts in Amos seem to bear a relation to the passage in Exodus 23. Amos 5:12 speaks of hostility (*ṣrr*) toward the innocent (*ṣaddîq*), the acceptance of bribes (here *koper*), and injustice against the poor (*wĕ'ebyônîm baššaʿar ḥiṭṭû*). The text in Exodus uses the same root (*nṭh*) in the Hiphil with *mišpāt*, "judgment, justice, legal pronouncement," in relation to the *'ebyôn*, speaks of the slaying of the *ṣaddîq* (an obvious act of hostility comparable to *ṣrr* in Amos 5:12), and prohibits the acceptance of bribes. The connections between the Pentateuch and the prophets Isaiah and Amos on this point are striking and require some explanation (see below).

Further, in Amos the issue of pledged garments is raised. This concern is found both in Exodus (22:15–26 [16–27]) and Deuteronomy (24:12–13). Amos 2:8 speaks about garments (*beged*) taken in pledge upon which the unjust people lie next to altars. Exodus 22:25 (26) speaks of pledged garments (here *śalmâ*) and uses the same verb (*ḥbl*) as in Amos (contrast Deut. 24:12–13, which replaces this with the noun *'ăboṭ*). The discrepancy between the terms for garment (*beged* in Amos and *śalmâ* in Exodus) might seem to speak against a connection between the two texts were it not for the fact that both texts depict these garments functioning as items upon which one can lie down (Ex. 22:26 [27]; Amos 2:8).

The correspondence between Ex. 22:25–26 and Amos 2:8 is perhaps not as strong as that for Amos 5:12 and Isaiah 5:23, and yet it seems one must postulate more than Dion's explanation that Amos resembles the Covenant Code simply because the texts are treating a similar topic.[98] Following upon McKay's argument that in Ex. 23:1–3 and 6–8 we have material that regulates legal practices in the city gate, one might suggest that Amos was a village elder (not a prophet; cf. Amos 7:14) who was trained in the ways of the Covenant Code, a text whose traditions, as has been noted above, are rural/village as opposed to urban in their orientation.[99] Unfortunately, this suggestion remains speculative. It is even less certain what one might conclude about Isaiah in this regard.

One issue that should be addressed here is the possible impact of the prophets on the Deuteronomic reforms. The analysis given earlier leads one to suspect that with respect to questions of poverty the text of Deuteronomy is simply reworking the material inherited from the Covenant Code. No new issues are raised, and certainly the broad range of topics found in the prophetic literature do not make their way into the Deuteronomic legislation. Deuteronomy in this respect appears to be a conscious adaptation of the past, updated to be sure, but nevertheless out of touch with many of the gross injustices with which the prophets were concerned.

These considerations leave us in an ambiguous position with regard to the prophetic relation to the Torah. While there is some link between the Covenant Code and a few passages in the eighth-century prophets, most of the prophetic discourse on the poor lacks specific roots in the old legal traditions, in many cases ranging far beyond it.[100] It seems as if the prophets may have understood covenant obligations in a more general sense: the demands of YHWH entailed the pursuit of justice, a pursuit in which the nation has failed. This perspective was inherited from early times, as seen in the Covenant Code. It is the demand for justice toward the poor that became for the prophets one of the pivotal aspects of the nation's relation to YHWH, the negligence of which was a violation of the covenant, and led to the collapse of the covenant relationship. Such was Zechariah's understanding of the prophetic legacy: "Thus said the LORD of Hosts: Execute true justice; deal loyally and compassionately with one another. Do not defraud the widow, the orphan, the stranger, and the poor; and do not plot evil against one another" (Zech. 7:9–10). In spirit, both the prophets and lawmakers would agree on this principle. In actual practice, the social vision and praxis engendered thereby could differ in significant ways. While the prophets may not have cornered the market on ethical discourse in ancient Israel, neither was it the case that the legal tradition was as comprehensive as the sources might lead us to believe.

To sum up our findings in this chapter: With roots that are not easy to reconstruct, the biblical legal materials nonetheless are clearly reflective of the long-lived Mesopotamian legal traditions. Through various commandment lists, however, the various strains of the Pentateuch sharpen the focus of biblical legal thought by creating an underlayer of "principles" that govern and measure the work of lawmaking. While the Covenant Code undoubtedly has an independent history apart from the Ten Commandments in Exodus 20, the juxtaposition of list and code foster mechanisms by which biblical law can remain open to the changing conditions of social life while still remaining true to the demands of the exodus God. This vision is realized most straightforwardly in Deuteronomy, where the laws rework significantly the Covenant Code, yet remain committed to the Ten Commandments as the framework for the expression of law. The codes of Exodus and Deuteronomy incorporate major segments that concern the situation of the weaker elements of society, namely, debt slaves and the poor. Thus, in practical terms, the codes outstrip the commandments by seeking to institutionalize avenues of assistance for those who would otherwise suffer from poverty and various forms of social injustice. While the specifics of the commandments do not call for such social practices, it is clear that the biblical writers have come to see these provisions for the poor as an outgrowth of the nation's submission to the exodus God. If, as suggested here, the Covenant Code represents a negotiated arrangement between the royal house and (smaller) landholders outside the capital city, then we have in this code evidence of the dangers represented by the growing economic influence and social power of the monarchy, perhaps early in its history. Likewise, the legal material in Deuteronomy would represent a rather conscious attempt, at a much later date, to further regulate and cope with changing socioeconomic conditions and political constraints in relation to the royal house. The developments in Deuteronomy probably reflect the sentiments of Josiah's supporters.

The Priestly legal materials bring a rather complex ritual program to bear on the shaping of the priestly commonwealth after the exile. The parameters of such a community are established through a variety of provisions regarding "purity" and divine "holiness." These conceptions undergird Priestly legislation, which encompasses sexual, communal, and familial matters. While there is no denying the marginalization of women in this scheme, even in the case of Genesis 1, the Priestly legislation offers an almost utopian commitment to the rectification of the plight of the poor, as the Priestly writers work to secure the Aaronic hold on power in the commonwealth. Finally, the prophetic writings stand in a rather ambiguous relation to the legal traditions of the Pentateuch. In many ways it appears that the prophets find little rooting in the traditions embodied in the Torah, a reality that allows them to bring to light injustices left unaddressed in the Bible's legal traditions.

Notes

1. See H. Huffmon, "The Exodus, Sinai, and the Credo," *CBQ* 27 (1965): 101–113.
2. O. Kaiser, "The Law as Center of the Hebrew Bible," *Sha 'arei Talmon: Studies in the Bible, Qumran, and the Ancient Near East Presented to Shemaryahu Talmon*, ed. M. Fishbane and E. Jov (Winona Lake, Ind.: Eisenbrauns, 1992), 93–103. While Kaiser's arguments are of an uneven quality, he does demarcate the extent to which Torah/Law plays the key role in the structuring of biblical thought.
3. Now conveniently collected in M. T. Roth, *Law Collections from Mesopotamia and Asia Minor* (Atlanta: Scholars Press, 1995).
4. See A. L. Oppenheim, *Ancient Mesopotamia: Portrait of a Dead Civilization*, rev. ed. (Chicago: University of Chicago Press, 1977), 158, 231–32. See also J. J. Finkelstein, "Ammiṣaduqa's Edict and the Babylonian 'Law Codes,'" *JCS* 15 (1961): 103.
5. For an invaluable discussion of the Hammurabi Code and its interconnections with biblical law, see H. J. Boecker, *Law and the Administration of Justice in the Old Testament and the Ancient East* (Minneapolis: Augsburg, 1980), chap. 4.
6. On the complexities, see S. Greengus, "Some Issues Relating to the Comparability of Laws and the Coherence of the Legal Tradition," in *Theory and Method in Biblical and Cuneiform Law: Revision, Interpolation and Development*, ed. B. M. Levinson (Sheffield: Sheffield Academic Press, 1994), 60–87. For Greengus, both an oral legal tradition behind ancient law codes as well as editorial updatings within the biblical materials play decisive roles in kindling and reshaping the Covenant Code.
7. This is not meant to imply that there was a lack of ritual texts in Mesopotamia. On the contrary, texts devoted to ritual practice abound. See, e.g., G. van Driel, *The Cult of Aššur* (Assen: Van Gorcum, 1969) and J. R. Paul, *Mesopotamian Ritual Texts and the Concept of the Sacred in Mesopotamia* (Ph.D. diss., University of California, Los Angeles, 1992). In the course of her discussion of various examples of the Marduk-Ea dialogue context for incantations that are joined to

purification rituals or exorcisms (esp. pp. 174–86, 284–90), Paul suggests that the "dialogue is used here not as a means of transmitting the instructions for the ritual, but as a way of validating the ritual by describing the gods' involvement in it" (180). Although it is also clear from this study that the dialogue evolves in its function over time, the link between a dialogue-narrative and a ritual might suggest that for ancient Israel its narratives work to service the ritual by describing God's involvement (to paraphrase Paul). Of course, whereas the gods perform rituals in Mesopotamian culture, Paul is correct to point out that the Hebrew Bible's God leaves this task to Moses and Aaron (193). Hence their importance to the biblical narratives of the various schools.

8. Lohfink, "Poverty in the Laws of the Ancient Near East and the Bible," *Theological Studies* 52 (1991): 34–50.

9. Babylonian Talmud, *Menachot* 29b, my translation.

10. On their variations, see M. Greenberg, "The Decalogue Tradition Critically Examined," in *The Ten Commandments in History and Tradition*, ed. B. Segel, and G. Levi (Jerusalem: Magnes Press, 1990), 83–119, 91–96.

11. Such a mix of familial, social, and property matters is likewise integral to the undoubtedly ancient list of the twelve curses found appended in the "enforcement section" to D's law code (Deut. 27:11–26).

12. They are hardly the sort of strict summary of Israel's criminal law that Phillips claims, however. See A. Phillips, *Ancient Israel's Criminal Law: A New Approach to the Decalogue* (Oxford: Basil Blackwell Publisher, 1970).

13. While Alt's attempts to make the Ten Commandments into a type of law unique to ancient Israel are not convincing, his discussion of the fundamental differences between apodictic and casuistic law remains insightful. See A. Alt, *Essays on Old Testament History and Religion*, trans. R. A. Wilson (Garden City, N. Y.: Doubleday, 1968), 103–71. To be sure, Mesopotamian codes do incorporate apodictic elements. Nevertheless, these instances are dwarfed by the preponderance of the casuistic form. See, e.g., R. Westbrook, "What Is the Covenant Code," in *Theology and Method in Biblical and Cuneiform Law: Revision, Interpolation and Development*, ed. B. M. Levinson (Sheffield: Sheffield Academic Press, 1994), 15–36, esp. 29. Scholarly discussions on the origins of the Decalogue have been divided. For an overview of earlier positions, see A. S. Kapelrud, "Some Recent Points of View on the Time and Origin of the Decalogue," *Studia Theologia* 18 (1964): 81–90. Most would argue for the Decalogue's antiquity, but Kapelrud's attempt to link the Decalogue to Hittite treaties confuses form with date. The Decalogue may very well reflect the treaty form, but this hardly confirms a late second millennium B.C.E. date. It is more likely that the Hittite treaty form has simply remained fossilized in the collective memories of what were once outlying districts of their empire. On the development of the Decalogue in relation to the documentary sources, I follow especially A. Lemaire, "Le Décalogue: Essai d'histoire de la rédaction," in *Mélanges bibliques et orientaux en l'honneur de M. Henri Cazelles*, ed. A. Caquot and M. Delcor (Neukirchen-Vluyn: Neukirchener Verlag, 1981), 259–95. For a contrasting view, see A. D. H. Mayes, "Deuteronomy 5 and the Decalogue," *Proceedings of the Irish Biblical Association* 4 (1980): 68–83. D. Patrick, *Old Testament Law* (Atlanta: John Knox Press, 1985), chap. 3, offers useful comments both on the possible Elohist origins of the Ten Commandments and Alt's categories. E. Gerstenberger, *Wesen und Herkunft des "Apodiktischen Rechts"* (Neukirchen-Vluyn: Neukirchener Verlag, 1965), attempts to locate the command form of the Ten Commandments in a clan ethos rather than the treaty tradition. While superficially compelling, it would seem that the linguistic forms

utilized in the wisdom texts do not bear out Gerstenberger's analysis. See the argument of J. Bright, "The Apodictic Prohibition: Some Observations," *JBL* 92 (1973): 185–204. In so arguing, Gerstenberger not only fails to take into account the royal and elite character of Israelite wisdom literature, but more importantly for our purposes, seriously obscures the rather obvious formal similarities between the Ten Commandments and the treaty structure. See G. E. Mendenhall and G. A. Herion, "Covenant," *ABD* 1:1179–1202.

14. Mendenhall and Herion, "Covenant." However, I am less inclined to see the presence of "blessings" in both Hittite and biblical texts as proof that the biblical texts stem directly from the Late Bronze Age. I suggest that this element has survived in a fossilized way from those times insofar as Syro-Palestine remained stamped with vestiges of Hittite influence. Somehow this feature remained alive in Syro-Palestinian political parlance and was only later resurrected in the biblical texts of the Israelite and Judaean monarchic age. Many of the Hittite texts are available in G. Beckman, *Hittite Diplomatic Texts* (Atlanta: Scholars Press, 1996). Relevant Mesopotamian texts can be found in S. Parpola and K. Watanabe, *Neo-Assyrian Treaties and Loyalty Oaths* (Helsinki: Helsinki University Press, 1988). Key also for comparative purposes is the eighth-century B.C.E. treaty in Old Aramaic from Sefire. See J. A. Fitzmyer, *The Aramaic Inscriptions of Sefire* (Rome: Pontifical Biblical Institute, 1967).

15. For a convenient and comprehensive statement of the topic see Mendenhall and Herion, "Covenant."

16. Parpola and Watanabe, *Neo-Assyrian Treaties*, 28–58.

17. Admittedly, complexities abound here. See the review by J. P. Healey, "Am Ha'arez," *ABD* 1:168–69.

18. P may very well be responsible for the expansion of the Sabbath commandment, but P is hardly the only tradent interested in ritual matters.

19. B. M. Levinson, *Deuteronomy and the Hermeneutics of Legal Innovation* (New York: Oxford University Press, 1997). Where Levinson sees the movement from the Covenant Code to the Deuteronomic Code to be away from the clan system to a royal stucture, I would argue that Deuteronomy represents a compromise negotiated between the clans and a monarch whom the clans found they could influence to a great degree. Levinson appears to miss the point of the Deuteronomic History, namely, the creation of an image of Josiah that is consonant with an imagined past of Deuteronomy, measuring the positive character of Josiah's reforms and his sympathies for the people against the successes and failures of past monarchs, especially with regard to the execution of just laws and the satisfaction of right worship. DH and Deuteronomy are hardly in contradiction here. See Levinson, 139–43.

20. The correlative use of *nāśî'*, "prince," in Ex. 22:27 (28) by E would seem to bear out this critical approach to the monarchy, despite Phillips's attempts to see behind this phrasing a Davidic original which used *melek*, "king" (Phillips, *Ancient Israel's Criminal Law*, 160). It is hard to know what to make of Levinson's distinction between Deuteronomy and the Deuteronomic History on the matter of king and cult. For Levinson, the code splits king and cult, whereas DH joins them enthusiastically (Levinson, *Deuteronomy and the Hermeneutics*, 95). Yet the Deuteronomic Code appears to be largely reflective of Josiah's cultic reform. I would argue that this code and DH represent a continuity on this score, which in the case of the Deuteronomic Code represents an intimate connection between the monarchy and a landowning cadre who sought a new cultic consensus that was anti-Assyrian. In the process, the elder system is not entirely displaced but *replaced* with

"royal appointees" who would doubtless come from the ranks of the landed supporters backing Josiah. The reform does not displace all the clan elders but only those unsympathetic to Josiah! Nonetheless, the code in Deuteronomy reflects the negotiated settlement between the landed classes and the monarchy and did not constitute a unilateral move on the part of Josiah. DH furthers these themes in the postexilic context by fostering some rather nostalgic royalist aspirations, undoubtedly among the descendants of the crowd of now-former landholders.

21. On the links between E and DH, see R. E. Friedman, *Who Wrote the Bible?* (New York: Summit Books, 1987), 128–30, where he localizes the traditions in the Shilonite priesthood, the origins of the prophet Jeremiah.

22. One need not resort to Phillips's schema, which pushes the Ten Commandments back chronologically to a Mosaic-period Hittite model and then presents the Covenant Code as the product of the newly formed Davidic state. See Phillips, *Ancient Israel's Criminal Law*, chaps. 1 and 14.

23. Whether this emphasis is reflective of Hezekiah's reforms as Phillips contends is far from clear. Also, his view that J's material does not constitute a ritual decalogue would seem to be wide of the mark. See Phillips, *Ancient Israel's Criminal Law*, chap. 16.

24. J. Morgenstern, "The Decalogue of the Holiness Code," *HUCA* 26 (1955): 1. While one may quibble with Morgenstern's dissection of Leviticus 19 and his linking of the text to the dedication of the second temple, his review does make plain the interconnectedness of the chapter to other Decalogue materials. For comparison, see M. Weinfeld, "The Decalogue: Its Significance, Uniqueness, and Place in Israel's Tradition," in *Religion and Law: Biblical-Judaic and Islamic Perspectives*, ed. E. B. Firmage, B. G. Weiss, and J. W. Welch (Winona Lake, Ind.: Eisenbrauns, 1990), esp. 3–47, esp. 8–21. Whether the Decalogue proper constitutes the focus of an ancient and long-lived festival of covenant renewal is difficult to say, especially insofar as updates to the Decalogue seemed to have been in vogue. See also Weinfeld's related study, "The Uniqueness of the Decalogue and Its Place in Jewish Tradition," in B. Segel, ed., *Ten Commandments in History*, 1–44. The arguments in this regard devolve, in part, on a reading of Psalm 81. See also A. Lemaire, "Décalogue," 263–64.

25. On the development of the Covenant Code, see the wide-ranging discussions in Levinson, ed., *Theory and Method*. Phillips, *Ancient Israel's Criminal Law*, 158, for example, considers the extent of the original code to be Ex. 21:1–22:19, 27–29; 23:10–19. However, since the Deuteronomic Code's reworking of the Covenant Code also rewords material found in Phillips's gapped sections, it would seem that the Covenant Code either included such sections initially or added them well before the Deuteronomic Code's formulation. While the Covenant Code's editorial history is difficult to penetrate, one must disagree with R. Westbrook, "What Is the Covenant Code?" in Levinson, ed. *Theory and Method*, 15–36, who argues that the Covenant Code is "a coherent text comprising clear and consistent laws" (36).

26. Phillips, *Ancient Israel's Criminal Law*.

27. J. Milgrom, *Leviticus 1–16* (New York: Doubleday, 1991), 24, rightly points out that in the ancient Near East, ritual and ethical matters were frequently mixed. Our point here simply speaks to the difference between ancient Near Eastern *law codes* and the biblical law codes, as noted also by L. Grabbe, *Leviticus* (Sheffield: JSOT Press, 1993), 26. Regarding the mix between ancient Near Eastern ritual and ethics, Milgrom points to the able studies of W. G. Lambert, "Morals in Ancient Mesopotamia," *Ex Oriente Lux* 5 (1959): 184–96; and K. van der Toorn, *Sin and Sanction in Israel and Mesopotamia* (Assen: Van Gorcum, 1985).

28. Phillips's attempt to restrict the Ten Commandments' prohibition against "stealing" to merely "kidnapping" confuses the Covenant Code's discussion with that of the more general prohibition in the Ten Commandments. Phillips's view is governed by his overall effort to read the Ten Commandments as criminal law, which accents person rather than property. His view would seem to be forced on the Ten Commandments rather than derived from them. See Phillips, *Ancient Israel's Criminal Law*, 10.

29. The occurrences of terms used for poor in the pentateuchal materials are:

'ĕbyôn	dal	'ānî	'ānāw	maḥsor
Ex. 23:6	Ex. 23:3	Ex. 22:24 (25)	Num. 12:3	Deut. 15:8
Ex. 23:11	Ex. 30:15	Lev. 19:10		
Deut. 15:4	Lev. 14:21	Lev. 23:22		
Deut. 15:7 (2)	Lev. 19:15	Deut. 15:11		
Deut. 15:9		Deut. 24:12		
Deut. 15:11 (2)		Deut. 24:14		
Deut. 24:14		Deut. 24:15		

30. See P. Humbert, "Le mot biblique *ebyon*," *Revue d'histoire et de littérature religieuses*, (Paris) 32 (1952): 1–6.

31. Lest anyone think that this is merely a later Christian distinction that of necessity denegrates law, see U. Simon, "Territory and Morality from a Religious Zionist Perspective," in *Voices from Jerusalem: Jews and Christians Reflect on the Holy Land* (New York: Paulist Press, 1992), 107–17.

32. For a full discussion, see G. C. Chirichigno, *Debt-Slavery in Israel and the Ancient Near East* (Sheffield: JSOT Press, 1993).

33. See N. P. Lemche, "The Manumission of Slaves—the Fallow Year—the Sabbatical Year—the Jobel Year," *VT* 26 (1976): 38–59, esp. 42–43.

34. L. L. Grabbe, "Maccabean Chronology: 167–164 or 168–165 BCE," *JBL* 110 (1991): 59–74 argues that the evidence from the later second temple period and after indicates that there indeed was a regularized, universal sabbatical year.

35. The principle is implied in various other passages, including Gen. 9:6; Ex. 21:12, 36; Lev. 24:18, 21; and Deut. 19:19. For a fuller discussion, see H. B. Huffmon, "Lex Talionis," *ABD* 4:321–22.

36. Note that the *lex talionis* provision does not necessitate the owner's eye or tooth loss. Rather, this principle dictates the *limits* of punishment. Appropriate compensation appears to have been a common occurrence. See Patrick, *Old Testament Law*, 76–77.

37. E. W. Davies, *Prophecy and Ethics: Isaiah and the Ethical Traditions of Israel*, JSOT Supplement Series 16 (Sheffield: JSOT Press, 1981), 72–75; F. Dijkema, "Le Fond des Prophéties d'Amos," *Oudtestamentische Studiën* 2 (1943): 25–26, 28.

38. Phillips, *Ancient Israel's Criminal Law*, chaps. 1 and 14.

39. Lohfink, "Poverty in the Laws," 40, sees the Covenant Code to be reflective of the "administering of law in a rural area where there was neither city nor king."

40. J. W. McKay, "Exodus XXIII 1–3, 6–8: A Decalogue for the Administration of Justice in the City Gate," *VT* 21 (1971): 311–25.

41. J. Kennedy, *Studies in Hebrew Synonyms* (London: Williams & Norgate, 1898). While Kennedy's suggestion is possible, it would seem that the juxtaposition of *dal* to *rabbîm* would more naturally favor the former interpretation. Mentioning the two groupings together creates an all-encompassing designation indicating that economic status is not to bias legal decision making. If this interpretation proves

correct, one must still reckon with the fact that *dal* does not appear to indicate dire poverty, but simply "having less." Nonetheless, the call for unbiased judgments could actually work to the advantage of the poorer elements of the populace, who undoubtedly faced dislocation from legal enactments that went against them without due cause. Elsewhere, in Ex. 30:15, outside of the Covenant Code, the term *dal* is found once. There the context is that of a census, and the stipulation is given for the *dal* to pay a half shekel as part of an offering to God. The amount was to be precisely the same for the rich. Again, this text offers additional support for the view that the *dal* was a person who possessed at least some property, though certainly in a reduced form. In any event, the reference remains consistent with the Covenant Code insofar as it holds that the *dal* is not to be given preferential treatment. All of these judgments stand in contrast to P's provision in Lev. 19:15, where those characterized as *dal* are permitted a reduction in offering because of the harder economic situation in which they were found. As we shall see, P's social vision will turn out to be more all-embracing than the Covenant Code.

42. Levinson, *Deuteronomy and the Hermeneutics*, 94.

43. Ibid., 150.

44. See ibid., 11–13, for reference to recent debates regarding the relation between the codes. See also Lohfink, "Poverty in the Laws," 39, and his article, "Gibt es eine deuteronomistische Bearbeitung im Bundesbuch?" in *Pentateuchal and Deuteronomistic Studies* (Louvain: Leuven University Press, 1990), 91–113. Lohfink sees "no evidence of a Deuteronomic reworking" of the Covenant Code.

45. S. A. Kaufman, "The Structure of the Deuteronomic Law," *Maarav* 1 (1979): 105–58.

46. The chart is based on Kaufman's article.

47. A. Rofé, "The Laws of Warfare in the Book of Deuteronomy: Their Origins, Intent and Positivity," in *The Pentateuch*, ed. J. W. Rogerson (Sheffield: Sheffield Academic Press, 1996), 128–49, esp. 147. For a nuanced study of the "ban" (*ḥerem*), see R. D. Nelson, "*Ḥerem* and the Deuteronomic Social Conscience," in *Deuteronomy and Deuteronomic Literature: Festschrift C. H. W. Brekelmans*, ed. M. Vervenne and J. Just (Louvain: Leuven University Press, 1997), 39–54, who views the concept as a "culture map category" reflective of an "in-group" social ethic. P. C. Craigie, *The Problem of War in the Old Testament* (Grand Rapids: Wm. B. Eerdmans Publishing Co, 1978), offers insight into the problems involved when attempting to appropriate such texts in contemporary discussions. Craigie is certainly correct to observe the Hebrew Bible's bitter realism about war. The difficulty comes in knowing when to affirm that "God has participated in warfare towards the ends of both judgment and redemption" as Craigie confidently asserts based only on parts of the Hebrew canon (chap. 9).

48. The terms *'ebyôn* and *'ānî* occur in Deuteronomy, but are restricted to chaps. 15 and 24. Lohfink, "Poverty in the Laws," 43–47, argues that Deuteronomy distinguishes between the poor, on the one hand, and the stranger, orphan, and widow on the other. In fact, a close reading will show that Deuteronomy has taken its lead from the Covenant Code but has added numerous other references to the stranger, orphan, and widow. Deuteronomy 24, however, makes it clear that Deuteronomy certainly understood the poor, stranger, orphan, and widow to stand together among the disenfranchised. Curiously, the term *dal* does not occur at all in these passages. For those scholars who wish to see links between Deuteronomy and the wisdom tradition, this stands as a severe hurdle to be overcome, for neither *rāš* nor *dal*, the preferred terms for the poor in Proverbs, appear in the book of Deuteron-

omy. See W. McKane, *Prophets and Wise Men* (Naperville, Ill.: Alec R. Allenson, 1965), 107–108.

49. Cf. H. E. von Waldow, "Social Responsibility and Social Structure in Early Israel," *CBQ* 32 (1970): 198. The Deuteronomist's agrarian to urban shift is rather deliberate and hardly reflective of forgetfulness as Lemche suggests. See Lemche, "Manumission of Slaves," 45.

50. Parallel law codes in Exodus and Deuteronomy (adapted from Patrick, *Old Testament Law*, with additional observations):

Ex. 20:19–23	Deut. 12:1–28	False gods and altars
Ex. 21:2–11	Deut.15:12–18	Treatment of Hebrew slaves
Ex. 21:12–14	Deut. 19:1–13	Killing unintentionally—place to go
Ex. 21:15, 17	Deut. 21:18–21	Disobedient sons
Ex. 21:16	Deut. 24:7	Kidnapping
Ex. 22:15–16 (16–17)	Deut. 22:28–29	Seducing a virgin
Ex. 22:17 (18)	Deut. 18:10b–11	Sorcery
Ex. 22:19 (20)	Deut. 13:1–19 (12:32–13:18; 17:2–7)	Worshiping other gods
Ex. 22:20–21 (21–22)	Deut. 24:17–18	Strangers, orphans, widows
Ex. 22:24 (25)	Deut. 23:20–21 (19–20)	Extracting interest on a loan
Ex. 22:25–26 (26–27)	Deut. 24:10–13	Taking and returning pledges
Ex. 22:28 (29)	Deut. 26:1–11	First fruits
Ex. 22:28b–29 (29b–30)	Deut. 15:19–23	Consecrating male firstlings
Ex. 22:30 (31)	Deut. 14:21a	Eating animals who die in the wild
Ex. 23:1, 2b	Deut. 19:15–21	False testimony
Ex. 23:2–3	Deut. 16:18–20	Judging fairly
Ex. 23:4–5	Deut. 22:1–4	Observing wandering animals
Ex. 23:6–8	Deut. 16:18–20	Judging fairly
Ex. 23:9	Deut. 24:17–18	Strangers, orphans, widows
Ex. 23:10–11a	Deut. 15:1–11	Role of every seventh year
Ex. 23:11b	Deut. 24:19–21	Gleanings
Ex. 23:12	Deut. 5:13–14	Sabbath
Ex. 23:13	Deut. 6:13	Worshiping God alone
Ex. 23:14–19	Deut. 16:1–17	Feast days
Ex. 23:19a	Deut. 26:1–11	First fruits
Ex. 23:19b	Deut. 14:21b	Not boiling goat in its mother's milk

51. A sensible overview and analysis is provided by M. Weinfeld, *Deuteronomy and the Deuteronomic School* (Oxford: Clarendon Press, 1972), chaps. 2–3.

52. Levinson's otherwise remarkable study, for example, leaves the social location of the forces behind the Deuteronomic Code and the Deuteronomic History rather obscure. See Levinson, *Deuteronomy and the Hermeneutics*.

53. It would seem that monotheism arose as a product of Israel's program of resistance to its polytheistic overlords. Commandeering the treaty language of the colonizer who demanded sole loyalty, the colonized project that singular loyalty on its own divine field as a response.

54. For compelling arguments in favor of viewing the P materials as a distinct source that has been fleshed out by J materials, see A. F. Campbell, "The Priestly Text: Redaction or Source?" in *Biblische Theologie und gesellschaftlicher Wandel: für Norbert Lohfink SJ*, ed. G. Braulik et al. (Freiburg in Breisgau: Herder, 1993), 32–47.

55. See B. A. Levine, "The Epilogue to the Holiness Code: A Priestly Statement on the Destiny of Israel," in *Judaic Perspectives on Ancient Israel*, ed. J. Neusner, B. A. Levine, and E. S. Frerichs (Philadelphia: Fortress Press, 1987), 9–34.

56. One might add for completeness Leviticus 5, which treats impure speech. Generally what we say about chaps. 11–15 applies equally to this chapter.

57. On the nature of pollution, see M. Douglas, *Implicit Meanings: Essays in Anthropology* (London: Routledge and Kegan Paul, 1975), chap. 3.

58. The Ezra and Nehemiah texts note the presence of female singers in the community, although in what capacity is unclear (Ezra 2:65; Neh. 7:67). The Chronicler references the presence of female temple singers during the reign of David, though perhaps this represents a retrojection of some modest second temple practice (1 Chron. 25:5). However, this is not the testimony or the direction of P. Moreover, the one text that gives a liturgical singing role to women shows no further interest in public roles for women. P. Bird, *Missing Persons and Mistaken Identities: Women and Gender in Ancient Israel* (Minneapolis: Fortress Press, 1997), observes, "This service, performed both by males and females, was in any case clearly auxiliary to the main cultic office" (42).

59. Cf. M. Douglas, *Implicit Meanings*, chap. 16.

60. T. Eagleton, *Ideology: An Introduction* (London: Verso, 1991), 15.

61. Douglas, *Implicit Meanings*, 272.

62. Curiously, both references to the poor in the Pentateuch that concern ritual matters use the term *dal* (Lev. 14:21; Ex. 30:15). As observed earlier, it is this evidence from Leviticus that suggests the *dal* is not one who suffers *abject* poverty, since the person so designated was able to offer up a number of goods, though not able to contribute the kinds of offerings the rich could afford. Furthermore, Fabry rightly notes that since *dal* is not mentioned in the biblical text in relation to the sabbatical year, the jubilee, or gleaning, this probably indicates that "the *dal* was not numbered among the dependents who have no property." See H. J. Fabry, "dal," *TDOT*: 3:219. Such a consideration lends additional support to the thesis that the term *dal* denotes a condition which is not as harsh as that marked by either *'ānî* or *'ĕbyôn*, although certainly there would have been overlap between the terms.

63. The complexities of the growth of the Holiness Code as well as its chronological and ideological relation to Leviticus 1—16 is much debated. For convenient discussions see Grabbe, *Leviticus*, chap. 1; and H. T. C. Sun, "Holiness Code," *ABD* 3:254–57. C. R. Smith, "The Literary Structure of Leviticus," *JSOT* 70 (1996): 17–32, argues for the overall architectural integrity of the law-narrative alternation found in Leviticus. While the Holiness Code is integrated into a coherent frame, Smith does not account for the differences in the legal sections in Leviticus that would indicate that the Holiness Code functions as an independent unit. H. Cholewinski, *Heiligkeitsgesetz und Deuteronomium: Eine vergleichende Studie* (Rome: Biblical Institute Press, 1976), believes that the Holiness Code is an amalgamated corrective to an earlier version of P (his P$_p$), which contained the laws now gathered in chaps. 20-22. His dissection of the Holiness Code into a number of major phases of development and additional minor redactors, while attractive for countering Smith's claim that there is a rhetorical and theological unity to Leviticus, is unfortunately far too detailed and complex to accept. Both Cholewinski, as well as G. Bettenzoli, "Deuteronomium und Heiligkeitsgesetz," *VT* 34 (1984): 385–98, posit links between Deuteronomy and the Holiness Code such that the Code is construed to be largely an extension and updating of the laws in Deuteronomy. Bettenzoli also detects influence in the opposite direction in some of the social laws of Deuteron-

omy. However, these "links" seem in my judgment to be superficial connections by subject matter rather than true, conscious responses between the writers and redactors of Deuteronomy and the Holiness Code. Levine, "Epilogue to the Holiness Code," argues that rather than thinking Leviticus 26 presents a Priestly response to Deuteronomy 28, the two passages are only linked by their common treaty background. Furthermore, one can hardly accept Cholewinski's view that the Holiness Code reflects a priestly contingent amid the Deuteronomic school.

64. Haran sees P as a reformist text, though he places the work well within the Hezekiah time frame. See M. Haran, *Temples and Temple Service in Ancient Israel: An Inquiry into Biblical Cult Phenomena and the Historical Setting of the Priestly School* (Winona Lake, Ind.: Eisenbrauns, 1985), chap. 7.

65. Such a vision is akin to Deut. 21:18–21, expanding on the same commandment.

66. B. A. Levine, *Leviticus*, Jewish Publication Society Torah Commentary Series (Philadelphia: Jewish Publication Society, 1989), 131.

67. The distinction between a more sympathetic view of the poor and a lack of consciousness about women spurred E. Tamez to initiate her edited work, *Against Machismo* (Yorktown Heights, N. Y.: Meyer-Stone Books, 1987).

68. Lohfink, *"Poverty in the Laws,"* 48–49, observes, "With the short life expectancy of that time, most Israelite victims of poverty would never see a year of Jubilee." Yet one must imagine that those who promulgated the Code thought this program was meant for their day and not some distant future.

69. See L. H. Schiffman, *Reclaiming the Dead Sea Scrolls: The History of Judaism, the Background of Christianity, the Lost Library of Qumran* (New York: Doubleday, 1995), chap. 5. See also J. A. Fager, *Land Tenure and the Biblical Jubilee: Uncovering Hebrew Ethics through the Sociology of Knowledge* (Sheffield: JSOT Press, 1993), chap. 4; and J. Maier, "Self- Definition, Prestige, and Status of Priests towards the End of the Second Temple Period," *Biblical Theology Bulletin* 23 (1993): 139–50.

70. See, e.g., R. B. Coote and D. R. Ord, *In the Beginning: Creation and the Priestly History* (Minneapolis: Fortress Press, 1991), chap. 11.

71. M. Weinfeld, *Social Justice in Ancient Israel and in the Ancient Near East* (Jerusalem: Magnes Press, 1995), 77. For an assessment, see J. J. Finkelstein, "Ammiṣaduqa's Edict," 91–104; and for a strident critique of the use of this material for interpreting biblical texts, see N. P. Lemche, *"Andurārum* and *mīšarum:* Comments on the Problem of Social Edicts and Their Application in the Ancient Near East," *JNES* 38 (1979): 11–22. Chapters 4 and 8 in Weinfeld's book offer a compelling and balanced assessment.

72. See Weinfeld, *Social Justice in Ancient Israel,* 78; cf. J. H. Hamilton, *Social Justice and Deuteronomy: The Case of Deuteronomy 15* (Atlanta: Scholars Press, 1992), chap. 2.

73. J. Neusner, *Ancient Israel after Catastrophe: The Religious View of the Mishnah* (Charlottesville, Va.: University of Virginia Press, 1983). See also D. Sperber, "Social Legislation in Jerusalem during the Latter Part of the Second Temple Period," *Journal for the Study of Judaism* 6 (1975): 86–95.

74. See N. Ateek, *Justice, and Only Justice: A Palestinian Theology of Liberation* (Maryknoll, N. Y.: Orbis Books, 1989), chap. 4. See also the discussion in chapter 4 below.

75. J. Blenkinsopp, "An Assessment of the Alleged Pre-Exilic Date of the Priestly Material in the Pentateuch," *ZAW* 108 (1996): 495–518, repeatedly wonders why the Aaronids are omitted from other non-P sources if P is preexilic as some claim. The Aaronid emphasis would seem to be a key feature of the priestly postexilic authority structure.

76. Milgrom, *Leviticus 1—16*, 3–34, offers arguments in favor of a preexilic dating for both P materials and the Holiness Code, with the P materials predating the time of Hezekiah, and the Holiness Code reflecting the fall of the Northern Kingdom. His views are based, in part, on the linguistic analyses of A. Hurvitz, which come under critical scrutiny in Levine, *Leviticus*. Blenkinsopp, *"Alleged Pre-Exilic Date,"* offers a wide-ranging and rather devastating critique of various attempts to date P to the preexilic period.

77. Phinehas later serves as the official priestly representative on the successful campaign against the Midianites, indicating the importance of the Midianite strand for the P narrative. as opposed to the "Moabite" framework of J's analysis of the Baal-Peor incident (Numbers 31).

78. On the notion of purges and the vanguard see M. Walzer, *Exodus and Revolution* (New York: Basic Books), 59–61, 102–3.

79. P. Trible, *God and the Rhetoric of Sexuality* (Philadelphia: Fortress Press, 1978) offers a comprehensive feminist analysis and reinterpretation. See, in particular, chap. 1. For a profoundly incisive critique, see D. J. A. Clines, *What Does Eve Do to Help? And Other Readerly Questions to the Old Testament* (Sheffield: JSOT Press, 1990), chap. 1.

80. M. I. Gruber, "Women in the Cult according to the Priestly Code," in *Judaic Perspectives on Ancient Israel*, ed. J. Neusner, B. A. Levine, and E. S. Freichs (Philadelphia: Fortress Press, 1987), 35–48, tries to read the record more positively, arguing from the fact of women's participation in the cultus that their situation was not as dire as critics of P imagine. However, even Gruber is forced to admit that for P, "men and women were less than equal participants in the cult of ancient Israel" (39–40). What Gruber misses is the more substantive observation that women were not power holders in the ancient Israelite cultic structure envisioned by P.

81. Moses is the Jewish equivalent of the Egyptian reformist and Persian collaborator Udjahorresne. See chapter 6 below.

82. Neusner, *Ancient Israel after Catastrophe.*

83. R. N. Whybray, *The Making of the Pentateuch: A Methodological Study*, JSOT Supplement Series 53 (Sheffield: JSOT Press, 1987); J. Van Seters, *Abraham in History and Tradition* (New Haven, Conn.: Yale University Press, 1975); idem, *In Search of History: Historiography in the Ancient World and the Origins of Biblical History* (New Haven, Conn.: Yale University Press, 1983); idem., *Prologue to History: The Yahwist as Historian in Genesis* (Louisville, Ky. Westminster/John Knox Press, 1992); idem., *The Life of Moses* (Louisville, Ky.: Westminster John Knox Press, 1994).

84. Cf. Isa. 10:26; 11:15–16; 43:16–17; 44:27; 63:7–14; Jer. 2:6; 3:15–17, 19; 16:14–15; 23:7–8; 32:20–23; Ezekiel 20; Hos. 11:1; 12:10, 13–14 (12:9, 12–13); Amos 4:10; 9:7; Micah 6:4; 7:15; Hag. 2:3–5.

85. Cf. Isa. 4:5–6; 48:16–21; Jer. 2:2, 6; 7:21–26; Ezekiel 20; Hos. 2:16–17 (14–15); 9:10; 13:5–8; Amos 5:21–25.

86. Cf. H. B. Huffmon, "The Exodus, Sinai and the Credo," *CBQ* 27 (1965): 101–113.

87. Cf., e.g., Isa. 24:5; 33:8; Jer. 11:8; 22:8–9; Ezek. 16:59; Hos. 6:7; 8:1–2; Mal. 2:10.

88. Cf. Jer. 31:31–32; 32:40; 50:5; Ezek. 16:59–63; 34:25; 37:26; Hos. 2:20 (18).

89. D. J. McCarthy, *Old Testament Covenant: A Survey of Current Opinion* (Oxford: Basil Blackwell Publisher, 1972), 39.

90. See, however, R. Friedman, *Who Wrote the Bible?* (New York: Summit Books, 1987), chaps. 9 and 12, where he offers a number of considerations in favor of the view that P is older than Deuteronomy and Jeremiah, and is quoted by the latter texts. I have not been convinced by his arguments.

91. M. Weiss, "The Decalogue in Prophetic Literature," in *The Ten Commandments in History and Tradition*, ed. B. Segal and G. Levi (Jerusalem: Magnes Press, 1990), 81.
92. Greenberg, "Decalogue Tradition," 111.
93. D. R. Hillers, *Covenant: The History of a Biblical Idea* (Baltimore: Johns Hopkins University Press, 1969), 120.
94. Cf., R. E. Clements, *Prophecy and Tradition* (Oxford: Basil Blackwell Publisher, 1975), 15-17; Hillers, *Covenant*, 131-140; and McCarthy, *Old Testament Covenant*, 39-40.
95. Cf. e.g., M. O. Boyle, "The Covenant Lawsuit of the Prophet Amos: III 1–IV 13," *VT* 21 (1971): 338–362; Clements, *Prophecy and Tradition*, 17–20; and Hillers, *Covenant*, 124–131. See also Isa.1:2–3, 10–20; Jer. 2:4–13; Amos 3:1–4:13; Micah 6:1–5 (8); Deuteronomy 32; Psalm 50.
96. Clements, *Prophecy and Tradition*, 16.
97. Ibid., 20.
98. Cf. P. E. Dion, "Le message moral du prophète Amos s'inspirait-il du 'droit de l'alliance'?" *Science et Esprit* 27 (1975): 18-19. Note that Dion omits discussion of Amos 5:12.
99. McKay, "Exodus XXIII 1–3, 6–8."
100. Cf., e.g., Davies, *Prophecy and Ethics*, 115; and Dion, "Le message moral," 27–30.

Narrative

Chapter 3

The Grand Narratives

Genesis–Kings, Chronicles

Source Analysis and the Social Justice Question: Evaluating the Pentateuch and the Deuteronomic History

The Social Vision of the Deuteronomic History
    Kingship in the Deuteronomic History: The Limits of Power
    Prophetic Acts of Power: Shamanism as Politics
    Players and Pawns: Women in the Deuteronomic History

Social Ethics in the Narrative Torah: Ideological Uses of the Stories of the Ancestors in J, E, and P
    Nomadic Values or Nationalist Imagination?
    Social Ethics in J: A God of Blessing in Exile
    Toward National Unity: Reading E's Social Ethics
    Reading P: An Ordered Commonwealth

Voices in Competition: Looking at Genesis–Kings as a Total Entity

Reinventing the Social Question: 1–2 Chronicles as Creative Vision and Radical Rebuttal

Myth as Social Charter: The Narrative Mediation of Ancient Israel's Social Ethics

We turn now from the *halakhic*, or legal, component of the Torah to that side of the tradition, both in the Torah and beyond, that is rooted in *aggadah*, or narrative. While the lawmaking tradition was clearly taken up with matters of social obligation, justice, and the treatment of the disenfranchised, the "grand narratives" of the Hebrew Bible present us with a situation that is difficult to assess. One critical observation might cause us to proceed no further with these writings in relation to our social ethics discussion: Rarely, and then only in the poetic inserts, does the historical literature make use of the many Hebrew words for "poor" and "poverty" that are common in the rest of the Hebrew Bible. In this regard, the historical literature bears little connection to the legal, prophetic, and wisdom traditions of ancient Israel. The poor, in other words, are not the object of the ethical wrestlings of the historical sections of the Hebrew Bible. This fact alone is astonishing and ought to at least force us to pause before we all too quickly apply this material, even the book of Exodus, to modern projects aimed at liberating the poor. Whatever else is going on in the narrative literature, the politics and ideology of this material would, at least at the outset, appear to be moving in a decidedly different direction than other segments of the Hebrew Bible.

Yet it is clear to any reader of biblical narrative that institutional questions and sociopolitical issues abound in this literature, particularly questions of royal, tribal, and priestly authority. Strident perspectives on politics, power, and the construction of an ideal society form an ideological matrix that infuses the narrative literature with a rhetoric that compels readers to find in these texts competing voices vying for influence over, if not control of, the fate of the postexilic community.

Under the rubric of historical literature we shall take up a number of major texts, namely, the Deuteronomic History (DH); the J, E, and P sources of the Torah; and the works of the Chronicler. Beginning with DH, we will focus, in particular, on the question of kingship, the view of prophetic acts of power that undergirds the work, and DH's presentation of women as players and pawns in the nation's past. Turning to J, E, and P, after a discussion of whether or not "nomadic values" stand behind these traditions, we shall study, in turn, J's political and social ideology concerning communal survival, E's understanding of wealth, property disputes, and tribal relations, and P's all-embracing program for communal and ritual restoration. We will then take up the larger question of characterizing the competing social visions of Genesis–Kings. Turning to 1-2 Chronicles, we will consider this work as one that contains a creative social vision that radically challenges Genesis–Kings. The chapter will conclude with a discussion of the implication that myth serves as the narrative mediation of the Hebrew Bible's social ethics. At the risk of seeming to cut the heart out of these narratives, we will discuss the exodus event in the next chapter, although in so doing we will not only gain a greater appreciation for other significant issues taken up in these narratives, but we will also be in a better position to assess the role of the exodus story in the biblical tradition. We will also reserve discussion of several isolated texts such as Ruth, Esther, Daniel, Ezra, and Nehemiah for chapter 5, rounding out our examination of biblical narrative materials.

To label the material discussed in this chapter as historical clearly prejudices our reading, and perhaps it would be better simply to label this material *narrative*—as opposed to law, wisdom, prophecy, or hymnody. Yet in calling this writing historical we are suggesting that no matter how they read the past, Israel's chroniclers undoubtedly incorporated material from the national archives, ancient epic materials, and venerable religious lore as they developed their theological assessment of Israel's past and its exilic predicament. The present, in other words, is being read with a view to the ongoing relationship between God and God's people. Through the making of "historical" narratives, Israel and its many ancestors become the vehicle for the social ethics discourse that governed the political imaginations of various segments of Judah's postexilic community.

Source Analysis and the Social Justice Question: Evaluating the Pentateuch and the Deuteronomic History

To enter into the discussion of the editorial history of the Pentateuch and of DH (i.e., Deuteronomy through Kings) is, admittedly, to traverse a minefield of scholarly discussion. The ante has been raised in more recent years, where source analysis has either been subsumed to canonical questions or where the older consensus regarding J, E, D, and P has been called into question (see chapter 1).[1] As to the question of canon, it is clear that the final shape of the texts and the respective locations of chapters, laws, and stories, deserve critical attention.[2] Yet in the process we should not overlook the contribution each stage of the tradition's development makes to the growing theological dialogue that the Hebrew Bible represents.[3] We will find that each stage, to the extent these are recoverable, functions as a springboard and a stepping-stone in the development of the ethics of the Hebrew canon.

Hence, a characterization of the various combined theologies or voices of Genesis–Kings remains essential to a complete study of the social ethics of the Hebrew Bible. P's refined God of ritual law and community is hardly comparable to J's autocratic deity of blessing. Nor does E's God of fearful obedience bear the same demeanor as these other portraits of God in the Pentateuch. Perhaps canonical criticism could underscore the need to avoid hastily dismissing one image of God in favor of another. In this regard, such a methodology can be helpful. However, the failure to appreciate the competing conceptions of deity that have been amalgamated in Genesis–Kings represents a serious distortion that can cloud our appropriation of the vital character of the historical development of ancient Israelite religion.

Regarding criticisms of the J, E, D, and P consensus, as raised especially by the noteworthy efforts of scholars such as Rendtorff and Whybray (who have posed substantive questions about source analysis itself), we must insist that classic documentary analysis or source criticism contains an inner logic that is not thoroughly circular in character (see chapter 1).[4] The narrative contradictions and theological complexities of the Torah demand that we posit some sort of webbed editorial history for the whole of the Pentateuch. This is not to say that by default we must adhere to J, E, D, and P, since no better hypothesis has appeared on the scene. Yet neither should we have to reinvent the entire history of biblical scholarship over the last one hundred and fifty years. The source theory is not vaporous!

To this end, we shall try to separate four critical matters as we conduct an evaluation of Genesis–Kings: (1) the identification of a source or editor, (2) the dating of the source or editing, (3) the question of the historicity or the historical accuracy of the source, and (4) the adaptation of the source as it becomes reformulated within larger and later editorial frames. While questions about one area tend to bleed into the others in much of the criticism of the Documentary Theory and of reappraisals of DH, these distinctions are useful when seeking to understand the social vision of particular narrative strands both in terms of a text's theological tendencies as well as its place in the overall history of the development of ancient Israel's ethical traditions. By keeping these very different dimensions of the problem in mind as we explore Genesis–Kings, we will come to place the competing theological voices of the narratives into plausible historical contexts, thereby illuminating the social ethics debates that dominated the ancient Israelite community. It was these vigorous debates over social institutions and ethics that led both to the production of the various sources, such as J, E, D, and P, as well as to the final amalgam of traditions that we now possess as Genesis–Kings.

The Social Vision of the Deuteronomic History

Since the time of Noth's pathbreaking study, scholars have looked on the books of Deuteronomy, Joshua, Judges, 1–2 Samuel, and 1–2 Kings as a relatively continuous and coherent theological project. As Noth himself so aptly states,

> Dtr. did not write his history to provide entertainment in hours of leisure or to satisfy a curiosity about national history, but intended it to teach the true meaning of the history of Israel from the occupation to the destruction of the old order. The meaning which he discovered was that God was recognizably at work in this history, continuously meeting the accelerating moral decline with warnings and punishments and, finally, when these proved fruitless, with total annihilation.[5]

While many quibble over the nature of this project and would reject Noth's rather gloomy characterization, arguing in favor of more positive dimensions to DH, most would agree that DH as a whole develops a significant and far-reaching theological construction for coming to grips with Judah's experience of destruction at the hands of the Babylonians.[6] Yet in the elements of its theological critique of Judah's disaster, DH fleshes out a vision of the nature and purpose of one of the major social institutions of the ancient Near East, the rule of kings. DH is more than simply an assessment of good and bad rulers; we find in this work a powerful social vision that raises probing questions about the use and abuse of political power, the place of Torah obedience in monarchic rule, and the roles of prophetic criticism and prophetic engagement with the established rulers.

In what follows, we will develop the view that a postexilic author has adapted royal chronicles and poetic epic lore (and perhaps a first edition of DH under Josiah) to produce an assessment of the demise of Israel and Judah, an assessment in which Hezekiah and Josiah are pitched as reformist heroes. In other words, this exilic DH (what some treat as the revised edition of the Josianic work) was rooted in the landed gentry circles that had backed Josiah's reforms (see chapter 2) and who wished to recover the royalist past of Judah, circles that presumably gathered around Jehoiakin in exile and later around Zerubbabel (see chapter 5). It certainly makes good sense to think that a particular view of the Levites and of prophets was integral to this initial redaction of DH, although it also seems clear that cycles of stories of prophets such as Elijah and Elisha must have floated free of DH prior to their incorporation into the latter work. Moreover, there are signs of a priestly redaction of DH, in particular in Joshua, a redaction that draws DH together with the final form of the Genesis—Kings complex. This latter redaction subsumes DH's monarchic criticisms to the priestly project of a nonmonarchic postexilic commonwealth.

Kingship in the Deuteronomic History: The Limits of Power

Clearly, a focus on the institution of kingship drives the entire work of DH, in either of its presumed editions, whether under Josiah or, as the work now stands, from the exile. Deuteronomy, Joshua, Judges, 1–2 Samuel, and 1–2 Kings all wrestle with the notion of the wielding of power in the commonwealth of YHWH in one way or another. Deuteronomy as a law code par excellence frames the issue of power and authority:

> If, after you have entered the land that the LORD your God has assigned to you, and taken possession of it and settled in it, you decide, "I will set a king over me, as do all the nations about me," you shall be free to set a king over yourself, one chosen by the LORD your God. Be sure to set as king over yourself one of your own people; you must not set a foreigner over you, one who is not your kinsman. Moreover, he shall not keep many horses or send people back to Egypt to add to his horses, since the LORD has warned you, "You must not go back that way again." And he shall not have many wives, lest his heart go astray; nor shall he amass silver and gold to excess.

> When he is seated on his royal throne, he shall have a copy of this Teaching written for him on a scroll by the levitical priests. Let it remain with him and let him read in it all his life, so that he may learn to revere the LORD his God, to observe faithfully every word of this Teaching as well as these laws. Thus he will not act haughtily toward his fellows or deviate from the Instruction to the right or to the left, to the end that he and his descendants may reign long in the midst of Israel. (Deut. 17:14–20)

The indication is already made in Deuteronomy 1–10, through the narrative voice of the prophet Moses, that love of YHWH will need to be paramount. In ancient Near Eastern terms, reverence and love have political overtones that are lost on modern readers.[7] Such language, however, goes to the core political problem at work in DH, namely, whether to love YHWH or go the way of the nations. In other words, Deuteronomy frames its theological concerns and social vision in terms of a _covenant obedience_ that has strong political overtones. As we shall see, this emphasis surfaces especially at critical junctures in the course of DH. In the book of Deuteronomy, the charge concerning Joshua is constructed around obedience to the Torah and the threat of expulsion for disobedience (Deut. 1:34–40; 3:18–29). Moses' final speeches drive home this same choice (Deut. 31:1–29; 32:44–47). The rest of DH is a working out of this political theology. Thus, operating against the backdrop of specific ideas of prophecy, human governance, Levitical authority, covenant obedience, and divine presence as presented in the book of Deuteronomy, the Deuteronomic History, running as it does from the establishment in the land of Canaan of a kingless community in the books of Joshua and Judges, to the initial installation of kings Saul, David, and Solomon in 1–2 Samuel and 1 Kings, down to the fall of the kingdoms of Israel and Judah in 2 Kings, offers a breathtaking theological and "historical" assessment of political power and civil authority in ancient Israel and Judah.

The book of Joshua presents one side of the coin. Here we find the worth of a capable and successful military leader. The spying out of Jericho and its conquest (chaps. 2–6), the conquest of Ai (chaps. 7–8), together with the treaty with the Gibeonites (chap. 9) and various other regional conquests (chaps. 10–12), present the lightening military successes of Joshua against the failure of a collapsing Canaanite royal political structure. These victories set the stage for the allotment of tribal lands (chaps. 13–19), lists that most likely reflect conditions during the time of the Judaean monarchy. In other words, by developing a "history" of Judah that takes as its lead a divinely ordained conquest as a seal of approval, the writers of DH are able to grant to the community, who once enjoyed the collapsed monarchy's land holdings, a continuing claim to the land.

As the book now stands, however, this land claim is supplemented by a number of ritual and legal issues that make it clear that Joshua has come to be marked by a Priestly redaction of its materials and hence an altering of its social vision. This expanded redaction furthers, for example, matters raised in the P source of the Pentateuch, namely, the question of cities of refuge (Joshua 20; 21:13–40; Numbers 35), the practice of circumcision (Joshua 5; cf. Genesis 17; etc., with no reference at all in Deuteronomy), the eating of manna (Joshua 5; cf. Exodus 16; Numbers 11), the property rights of Zelophehad's daughters (Josh. 17:3–6; cf. Num. 27:1–11), the extensive territorial regulation of the Levitical clans (Joshua 21; cf. Gen. 46:11; Numbers 1—10), the incident of apostasy at Baal-Peor (Josh. 22:16–20; cf. Numbers 25), and the integral role of Aaron (Joshua 21, 24). Shearing away this Priestly redaction, reflected also in the references to Balaam (cf. Numbers 21—24) and the concern for "alien gods" found in Joshua 24 (cf. Gen. 35:2–5; Judg. 11:15–16; 1 Sam. 7:3–4), we find a more basic layer to Joshua, which invoked the conquests and tribal land allotments solely to underscore Torah obedience (Joshua 1, 8, 23). This latter focus is consistent with other segments of the initial layer of the book of Joshua, which, like many other parts of DH, is concerned with the "ark of the covenant" (cf. Joshua 3, 4, 6, 8), a point of contrast with P, which focuses on the "ark of the testimony (*'ēdût*)" and the tabernacle. It was this Torah obedience layer that carried forward the postexilic royalist political project, a movement that tied itself by this language to the reforms of Hezekiah (2 Kings 17) and Josiah (2 Kings 22—23). It is this layer, likewise, that presents the possibility of a positive cultic role for monarchy, provided Torah obedience serves as a hedge against monarchic political and cultic abuses. King Manasseh's downfall, for example, is predicated on his Torah disobedience (2 Kings 21). In this layer of DH, shorn of its later Priestly expansions, we seem to find the Levitical teaching emphasis that was eventually subsumed by the priestly postexilic restoration project.

If the book of Joshua exhibits an intrusive Priestly layer, then DH has been augmented by a view that downplays monarchic Torah obedience, elevating instead the danger of worshiping "alien gods" (Josh. 24:23). Consistent with the priestly postexilic reconstruction project, this latter view thoroughly undermines monarchic claims in favor of the priestly governance of the commonwealth and oversight of ritual affairs. The Priestly redaction of DH introduces a great irony in the history of the Hebrew Bible's developing social vision regarding political power. Rather unwittingly, the royalist movement that produced DH created the very document that ultimately portrayed the monarchy to be bad for the community's health. Thus, although DH in its initial conception had philosophic underpinnings that permitted a cautious embrace of the monarchy on the basis of the possibility of Torah obedience, the final form of DH began to pull apart at the seams, leaving the priestly alternative as the only viable voice in the postexilic community. In other words, the problematic view of political power in DH paved the way for the viability of a Jerusalem-based priestly "tabernacle" (temple) project (Josh. 22:29). This theological transformation of the book of Joshua in the larger amalgam of Genesis–Kings finds a historical analogue insofar as the postexilic royalist ambitions of Haggai and Zechariah, prime backers of Zerubbabel, yield to the civil and ritual reforms of Nehemiah and Ezra (see chapter 5).

Following upon dual notices of Joshua's death in Judges 1—2 and a conquest account in those same chapters, a staggered and inconclusive incursion that differs markedly from the sweeping tales of conquest recounted in the book of Joshua, the book of Judges presents stories and brief references to a series of twelve noteworthy leaders, or thirteen if one includes the figure of Samuel, who guided the community in the era before the monarchy.[8] These leaders, the so-called "judges" (*šōpēṭ*), are theologically "deliverers" and anthropologically an "embryonic chieftaincy," sent by YHWH to act as the human agents of YHWH's desire to liberate God's people from their oppressors (Judg. 2:16–19).[9] Since this oppression is viewed as a divine punishment for apostasy, the liberator's deeds mitigate the continued divine wrath that has been meted out because of the people's forsaking of the exodus God and their embracing of Baal and Ashtoreth (Judg. 2:10b–15). Thus, however ancient the separate and original stories of the deliverers may be, their compilation in the initial layer of Judges has been done with a view toward making theological claims about institutional leadership in the community of YHWH. The community of YHWH is one that can prosper and even survive for a time without centralized bureaucratic authority. In particular, Othniel (Judg. 3:7–11), Ehud (3:12–30), Shamgar (3:31), Deborah (chaps. 4—5), Gideon (chaps. 6—8), and Samson (chaps. 13—16) are presented as having provided successful communal protection against threats posed by Aram-naharaim, Moab, Philistia, Canaan, and Midian.

Yet there is a deeper threat that Judges faces through its presentation of the deliverers. While the book acknowledges the relative successes of divinely appointed deliverers, it also faces the fact that internal conflicts among the people of YHWH were so great that even this system might have to give way to some other form of leadership. Thus, while the worship of the Baalim certainly created fractures in the community (Judg. 2:11; 3:7; 8:33; 10:6, 10), the greater danger lay in the temptation on the part of many to seek a king-like ruler, one not appointed by God, to lead the community against its foes. This is the sad lesson from the writer's point of view of the story of Abimelech, whom the people of Shechem and Beth-millo had installed as king (chap. 9). His brutal slaying of seventy brothers and his marshalling of a militia funded by the people spoke to everything that was excessive in monarchic rule. Likewise, Jephthah, established as "commander and chief" (11:11), gained military victory against the Ammonites through a despicable act that bore out his reputation as an illegitimate outsider (11:1–3), namely, the sacrifice of his own daughter (10:6–12:7). In a similar manner, for the Greeks, Agamemnon's sacrifice of his daughter Iphigenia, which permitted the launching of the Trojan War, became an occasion for the Greek playwrights Aeschylus and Euripides to think through issues of human leadership and divine governance.[10] Abimelech and Jephthah stand in marked contrast to Gideon, who rejects kingship to accent the rule of God (8:22–23).

These brushes with monarchy in Judges, sandwiched as they are in the context of stories of divinely appointed deliverers, offer the reader food for thought in terms of the nature of human governance in the community of God. On the surface, Judges would seem to prefer a charismatic set of deliverers. Yet read more closely, the text is actually making a subtle argument in favor of the selection of a human king by the divine sovereign. This ambivalent commitment to an earthly monarch will infuse DH throughout with a surprisingly realistic assessment of the abuses of apostate kingship, while at the same time holding out hope that a divinely chosen line might provide the community with the institutional framework, political savvy, and theological roots necessary to ensure Judah's survival, not only over the monarchic centuries but also after the exile. Certainly the royalist aspirations of the postexilic period have imposed their stamp on the shaping of DH. In some sense, DH is in a philosophical corner, trying to remain invested in an institution that failed the people of Israel and Judah so miserably. However, DH seems to argue that the catalyst for a successful monarchy is provided by inspired individuals such as the deliverers in Joshua and Judges or the prophetic voices of 1–2 Samuel and 1–2 Kings (see below). These figures, and not the Jerusalem priestly crowd, provide those who aspire to monarchy a theological platform for their endeavors.

To be fair, there are ritual interests in Judges, but these interests concern the rights and protections of the Levites (unlike the delimitation they receive in the Priestly redaction of Joshua discussed above), a priestly group that in Judges appears to be dispersed throughout the land, perhaps reflecting its historical disenfranchisement by the central priestly authorities in Jerusalem. In Judges, however, the dangers of an unprotected Levitical clan are made clear in the story of the kidnaping of the Levite who is taken away to tend a sculptured image among the Danites (chaps. 17—18) and in the story of the rape of the Levite's concubine (chaps. 19—21). The former event left the community deeper in theological chaos, and the latter plunged the community into civil war. These events, concerned as they are with the Levitical priesthood, are a sign that for DH a religious structure that lacks monarchic oversight is a source of not merely bad doctrinal views but, more importantly, of tribal fracturing and unrest. The world of Judges is ultimately one in which there is conscious recognition that there is no king (18:1; 19:1; 21:25), where people do what is right in their own eyes (17:6; 21:25), and where Torah is absent (the word does not appear in Judges at all). For the Levitical priests, with their Deuteronomic law code and according to the Torah they proclaim, the lack of a strong, spiritually committed monarch is a dangerous situation.[11]

Despite DH's growing argument in favor of monarchy, DH also offers a frank and well-honed critique of monarchy, as we see in the books of 1–2 Samuel. First Samuel 8 presents us with a bitter denunciation of kingship by the prophet/judge Samuel:

> Samuel reported all the words of the LORD to the people, who were asking him for a king. He said, "This will be the practice of the king who will rule over you: He will take your sons and appoint them as his charioteers and horsemen, and they will serve as outrunners for his chariots. He will appoint them as his chiefs of thousands and of fifties; or they will have to plow his fields, reap his harvest, and make his weapons and the equipment for his chariots. He will take your daughters as perfumers, cooks, and bakers. He will seize your choice fields, vineyards, and olive groves, and give them to his courtiers. He will take a tenth part of your grain and vintage and give it to his eunuchs and courtiers. He will take your male and female slaves, your choice young men, and your asses, and put them to work for him. He will take a tenth part of your flocks, and you shall become his slaves. The day will come when you cry out because of the king whom you yourselves have chosen; and the LORD will not answer you on that day." (1 Sam. 8:10–18).

In this passage, DH actively challenges what are perceived as abuses of state authority. Key here is Samuel's critique of the royal taxation system and the monarchy's labor practices. The monarchy was instituted nonetheless (8:22).

Although Saul was successfully anointed by Samuel as king and demonstrated his military prowess against the Ammonites (chaps. 9–11), Samuel challenged Saul's judgment on two occasions. In the first instance, when Saul faced a formidable Philistine force and found that Samuel was delayed in coming, he sought to calm his warriors' fears by offering a burnt offering in Samuel's absence (chap. 13). In the subsequent case, Saul had taken the Amalekite king Agag captive, not killing him as he ought (chap. 15). Likewise, the warriors had taken sheep and cattle as spoil, again not totally destroying them as they had been ordered by Samuel. The cumulative effect of Saul's disobedience was clear to Samuel: God rejects Saul as king. Saul's desperate efforts to retain control of the throne in order to pass it on to Jonathan only served to drive Jonathan deeper into David's camp. The rather complex narratives consumed with David's presence in Saul's court and flight from Saul (chaps. 16—26), including the competition between Michal, Saul's daughter, and Jonathan for David's "love" (contrast 18:20 with 20:17; cf. 18:1–4; 19:1) can be read as an attempt to paint David as the true "son" and heir to his "father" Saul.[12] Highlighted throughout is the tension between obedience and disobedience. Criticism of Saul's rule rests precisely in his disobedience. Support for David, even in his darkest moments, seems to rest on a belief in his ultimate obedience to God, insofar as he did not kill Saul when he had ample opportunity (chaps. 24, 26). Saul's suicide sums up his disobedience and rejection as king (chap. 31).

DH goes further to document monarchic abuses of power, detailing fully the potentially chaotic nature of the monarchy under David and his immediate family.[13] Thus, even the best of times are viewed with scrutiny by DH. The successful installation of David to the throne of all Israel does not come about without intrigue in the Davidic court by Joab, David's commander, nor without the murder of rivals from Saul's entourage such as Abner and Ish-bosheth, who had been made king (2 Samuel 2—4). While control of the ark of the covenant, the conquest of Jerusalem, the defeat of a number of enemies, and the generous support of Mephibosheth, Jonathan's son (chaps. 5—9), would seem to speak favorably of David's political and religious acumen, DH incorporates a significant look at the sordid deeds of the king and the king's family. Thus, splayed out for all to see are David's affair with Bathsheba and his murder of her husband Uriah, his son Amnon's rape of his half sister Tamar, the murder of Amnon by his half brother Absalom in revenge for Tamar's rape, Absalom's rebellion and attempt to take the throne for himself, and David's humiliating flight from the capital city (chaps. 11—19). Yet tales of the Davidic family's disunity are not without purpose, for on several occasions prophetic rebukes such as those of Nathan (chap. 12), Shimei (16:5–13), and later Gad (chap. 24) work to redirect the conscience of this monarch who is open to the prophetic voice (see further below on the prophets in DH). Thus, David remains on the throne and after Absalom's death (chap. 18) is restored to his Jerusalem palace from which he launches a number of successful military campaigns (chaps. 19—23). The prophet's critique, and hence DH's critique, has the effect of producing a ruler who is committed to the sort of reign sanctioned by God.

As we turn to 1 Kings, we find a continued critique of monarchic rule. This critique finds expression in the profound contradictions of Solomon's reign. Prior to the building of the temple, Solomon is noted for loving the Lord but still allowing the shrines to dot the countryside. Of course, even the author admits that this was during a time when the central shrine had not yet been built (3:2–3). By implication, however, every subsequent reign can be assessed in terms of those religious practices that destabilize the temple of YHWH in Jerusalem. Even Solomon is not above criticism in this regard, for later in life, under the influence of the many wives and concubines he is credited with having collected through the conclusion of foreign alliances, Solomon himself promoted the worship of neighboring deities such as Ashtoreth, Chemosh, and Milcom (11:1–13, 29–39). In this way, DH introduces an evaluative scheme that will be employed with great regularity as the text assesses the reigns of the kings of Israel and Judah. The danger of such royal failures in worship stands at the heart of the political analysis of DH. That danger will result in the destruction of Israel and Judah, but it manifests itself initially in the tearing of the kingdom away from Rehoboam, Solomon's immediate successor, who blatantly disregarded the northerners' contempt for Solomon's program of forced labor (9:15–22; cf. 5:27–32 [13–18]). In addition, a subtheme is introduced that suggests that although the hazards for the kings of Judah will be great, YHWH will continue to demonstrate a commitment to Judah out of loyalty to David (11:29–39). This difficult message regarding the royals would not be lost on DH's exilic readers. The message seems designed not simply to throw everything over to the priestly camp, as the final amalgam of Genesis–Kings will do, but to raise red flags for the reformist crowd that backed the Davidic line after the exile.

The Northern Kingdom appears to be off to a divinely sanctioned start, yet the same standards apply to both kingdoms in DH's analysis. Thus, the founder of the Northern Kingdom, Jeroboam I, finds his alternative altar building denounced by a prophet (13:1–10), who predicts that Josiah will one day rise up to exact the Lord's vengeance. Likewise, when Jeroboam has his wife seek out the prophet Ahijah at Shiloh to provide a cure for his ailing son, the prophet reiterates the impending doom of his line (14:6–16). This doom is thought to be fulfilled in Baasha's defeat of Jeroboam's heir Nadab (15:25–30). Framed in this way, DH makes clear that the political leadership that does not follow the reformist path of a Hezekiah or a Josiah (see below) cannot hope to succeed after the exile. This path, which includes a rigorous application of the Deuteronomic code from Josiah's time as well as a forthright attack on pagan ritual, is the only alternative to degradation and destruction. DH, in other words, has found an effective tool not only for critiquing the past but also for charting a direction toward a postexilic royalist future by means of this critique.

Yet we should be careful not to think that DH limited its critique to purely ritual matters. As we have already noted, the callousness with which Solomon approached his building programs with the extensive use of redistricting and forced labor cost his successor Rehoboam dearly. Likewise, DH has Elijah criticize Ahab not only for his worship of the Baalim (18:16–19) but also for his release of the conquered king Ben-Hadad (20:35–43) and for his murder of Naboth to secure the man's property (21:17–24). Although the king's wife, Jezebel, is portrayed as the mastermind behind the murder, the prophet holds the king squarely accountable.[14] For DH, the critique of the monarchy through the prophetic voice is at one and the same time religious, political, economic, and moral. Similarly, Elisha's critique carries similar weight. Criticism might be directed against a king such as Ahaziah, who seeks healing from another god (2 Kings 1), or his critique might open the eyes of a king who thinks that God is unable to deliver Samaria from the clutches of Aram (2 Kings 6:24–7:20). In either case, such prophetic criticism makes clear the power of God in all spheres of royal life, whether governance, ritual, health, or war.

The failure to rely on the power of God reaches a key juncture for Judah during the reign of Ahaz. This king is noted for the ritual deviation of consigning his son to the fire (2 Kings 16:3) and for bribing the Assyrian king into supporting Judah against Aram and Israel by paying him off with temple treasures (16:5–9). These excesses, together with the account of Assyria's destruction of Samaria, provide DH with the occasion to offer an extensive statement that provides the theological justification for the Assyrian invasion and the fall of the Northern Kingdom. All the key elements are there: the worship of other gods, the breaking of the Torah commandments, the worship of the calves, the worship of the host of heaven and of Baal, child sacrifice, the failure to heed the prophetic warnings, and the following of Jeroboam I's ritual practices (chap. 17).[15] DH accents the arrogance of the people of Israel by having the Assyrian king send an "orthodox" priest to teach their exiles the way of God. The priest fails in the attempt. This rather gloomy assessment of the kings of Israel and the justification for the destruction of Samaria sets the stage for DH's evaluation of Judah's decline and fall, for the errors of Ahaz and others in the north are mirrored in the folly of Manasseh, who willfully reverses the reforms of Hezekiah (chap. 21). The Babylonian exile is predicted and even Josiah's reforms will not carry the day when his heirs and successors chart their own rebellious paths. Clearly for DH, the path of reform is the only worthy path. Yet it is also clear that this path is fraught with great danger.

DH's critique of kingship, however, does not constitute the rejection of *all* kings, for DH had to come to grips with the people's heavy investment in a royal past. Thus, DH also presents us with a strong affirmation of a covenanted, *conditional* kingship (2 Samuel 7). The conditionality of God's relationship to early Israel's social institutions was indicated when God removed the priesthood from Eli's sons (1 Sam. 2:12–36) and when the Philistines captured the ark of the covenant (1 Sam. 4:11). By the same token, since the Lord is committed to Israel, the ark is returned and the Lord takes heed of the plight of the people by sending Saul as ruler and deliverer (1 Sam.

7:3–4; 9:16). The conditional character of the monarchy at its inception is indicated on several occasions by Samuel who lines out the "rules" of the game and indicates that the king must obey God's commands or face being "swept away" (10:25; 12:14–15, 20–25). Nonetheless, God's commitment to the people overrides Saul's errors to such an extent that though Saul loses the kingship, God seeks out David, who has the right heart for the job (13:8–14; 15:8–31; 16:7). The text accents a respect for the institution of kingship despite the ills of the reigning monarch by having David not take Saul's life when he has the opportunity, despite Saul's relentless pursuit of David (chaps. 24–26). Thus, we are not surprised to find David being pointed by God toward Hebron as the central place of his initial rule over Judah (2 Sam. 2:1). Likewise, David's victory over Jerusalem and his palace building are all seen as the Lord's doing (2 Sam. 5:11–12). When we arrive then at the major statement of divine commitment to a conditional kingship in 2 Samuel 7, all the ideological parameters and pieces are in place for DH both to sustain a royalist view but also to approach the continued life of the monarchy after the exile with a critical eye. Second Samuel 7 sums up ideas and motifs about kingship that are lurking everywhere in DH: freedom from enemies, an enduring role line, offspring on the throne, a temple, Israel as a unique nation, the commitment of the exodus God, and the promise of military victories. The promise is so powerful that in the generation after David, despite all of Solomon's shortcomings, Solomon himself is depicted for a time as the divinely anointed heir (1 Kings 1), the pious and wise ruler (chaps. 3–5) who ruthlessly dispatches David's enemies with religious zeal (chap. 2) and who builds God's earthly dwelling (chaps. 6–7). This dwelling, a symbol of the royal care for the ark of the covenant, is to be a source of comfort even in times of national disaster (chap. 8). Even the conditional promise could be a source of comfort insofar as each generation understood that it bore the burden of renewing that covenant and learned the lessons of the disasters of the past. If Jeroboam I had the chance at an eternal dynasty, surely the returning exiles had a better chance then he (11:29–39). If Jehu's utter destruction of Ahab's descendants could work to his advantage despite his continued support for the calf worship at Bethel and Dan (2 Kings 10:29–31), how much more could the "orthodox" returnees from exile (i.e., those backing the royalist project of DH) hope to succeed against the forces arrayed against their endeavors. Such messages could hardly be lost on the postexilic readers who might wish to resurrect a king to rebuild the fallen temple and restore the old glories of Judah. Theirs was a generation that badly needed to hear that God had relented in times past, as when God stayed the angel's hand who brought pestilence as a punishment for David's census of the people (2 Samuel 24). Yet the lesson of the conditional covenant was more than simply a respite from divine wrath. The past, as conceived by DH, had seen real gains by kings who were faithful even for a time. In this regard, DH pinned its postexilic hopes on the examples supplied by Hezekiah and Josiah.

Hezekiah is noted for doing "what was pleasing to the LORD just as his father David had done" (2 Kings 18:3). His singular devotion to the Mosaic commandments is evidenced by his destruction of various shrines and pillars (18:1–8). However, his rebellion against Assyria comes at a price, with the subsequent invasion putting Hezekiah's loyalties to the test. He is reported to have bought the Assyrian ruler's cooperation by means of precious objects and metals that included the temple's silver and its doors and doorposts laden with gold (18:14–16). The Assyrian army commander even claims that the Judaeans could hardly be relying on YHWH, for was it not YHWH's shrines that Hezekiah had destroyed to favor Jerusalem (18:19–25)? Yet under the prophet Isaiah's inducement, Hezekiah's prayer, echoing Solomon's appeal to God's wisdom and power, seeks divine favor in the form of the departure of the looming Assyrians (19:14–19). The divine response is favorable, thousands of soldiers are suddenly cut down by a divine messenger, and the remainder of the army is forced to retreat (19:20–37). However, Hezekiah soon falls ill and, though he is cured through divine support, the king unwittingly shows the royal treasures to some Babylonian messengers, a deed which leads to the prophet's announcement that the treasures will one day be hauled off to Babylon (20:1–19).

Josiah, whose rise to power is attributed to the politically potent nationalistic force of the "people of the land"[16] (2 Kings 21:24), is also likened to David in devotion (22:2). This attitude initially translates into financial support for the work of the temple (22:4–7). However, the finding of a scroll in the temple (presumably a version of the book of Deuteronomy) leads Josiah to anguish over the society's failure to carry forward the worship of YHWH in an exclusive manner (22:11–20). When the prophetess Huldah confirms both the potential for divine wrath but also mercy because of Josiah's compliant heart (22:14–20), Josiah renews the covenant with God by reading the scroll publicly and assenting along with the people to the terms of the covenant (23:1–3). Josiah is then credited with a more systematic purging than conducted by Hezekiah of proscribed worship practices (23:4–7). The king is also said to have destroyed a variety of shrines, some presumably of YHWH located outside of Jerusalem, and to have brought various demoted priests to Jerusalem to live (23:8–14). DH's political interests are clear here, for in this destruction Josiah was undermining the worship life of the old Northern Kingdom's territories and invoking Passover in Jerusalem as the national ritual activity (23:15–25). In this, Josiah is DH's royal ritual hero, fulfilling the Torah's teaching in a fashion unparalleled in Judah's history from the time of the judges to his day (23:21, 24–25). The author must have been perplexed to have to admit that despite these commitments and gains, the evils of King Manasseh could not be expunged without the destruction of the temple and the expulsion of the people from Jerusalem and Judah (23:26–27). In that sense, DH is unrealistically romantic, rooting itself in a vision of royal power and divine support that history itself could not sustain.

Thus, in its vision for social renewal, DH does hold out an emphasis on the ark of the covenant and the temple, that is, on the centralization of worship in Jerusalem under royal auspices. However, the Priestly interest in the tent of meeting is almost entirely absent. Whatever the genesis or dating of the P program might be, it would seem obvious that DH and P represent different wings of the ancient Israelite political and religious spectrum. In being lumped together as Genesis–Kings (i.e., Torah and History), we miss this ideological volatility that shaped the debates in the exilic period and the era of the restoration (see chapter 5). The combination of the two streams results either from ignorance of the preceding debates or, more likely, represents the deliberate coopting of one program by the other tradition. Thus, while both DH and P share an interest in a central shrine, they differ dramatically over who should run the state's religious apparatus and over the nature of priestly authority in the commonwealth.[17] Thus, for DH, the prophetic voice could remove Eli's sons from priestly authority, holding out hope for the rise of a faithful and enduring priesthood (1 Sam. 2:27–36). Likewise, David's transfer of the ark of the covenant to Jerusalem indicates that the cultic balance lay with royal oversight (2 Samuel 6). God's subsequent promise puts the construction of the divine house firmly in David's and Solomon's hands, following a pattern of royal cultic commitment cultivated throughout the ancient Near East (2 Samuel 7).[18] That Judah's own priestly elite might seek to construct a commonwealth without the royalists must have seemed treasonous to particular sectors of the restoration community, a veritable abandonment of the social vision adhered to for centuries by the royal house vis-à-vis the now destroyed Solomonic temple. Fortunately for the long-term endurance of the tradition, the priestly cadre, as enshrined in P, realized the terrible liability that a failed monarchy represented to a community that needed secure structures in order to have a chance for survival in a tenuous era.

To sum up: There is enough material throughout DH for us to appreciate the sort of ideological fence DH wished to construct around any restored monarchy in ancient Israel. Whoever the writers are that are responsible for DH, they are heavily invested in a recovery of the kingship as a useful institution—perhaps to counter priestly power. Yet at the same time, the institution will no longer be permitted to ride roughshod over the concerns of the community. Presumably those behind the composition and compilation of the initial edition(s) of DH (i.e., the Josianic edition [if such there was] and the exilic DH [before any Priestly redaction]) were situated among the landed gentry of ancient Israel, those for whom, under the right conditions, monarchy could be a useful institution, especially against an encroaching temple establishment of the sort envisioned by P (see further below). We require further study of DH's characterization of the prophetic voice to see how these texts come to frame this tradent's unique social agenda.

Prophetic Acts of Power: Shamanism as Politics

Whatever the social vision of DH is, we are not presented with a wholesale rejection of kingship, but a kingship that is guided and tempered by various ideological limitations and theological underpinnings. Integral to the construction of this social vision in DH is the mediation of prophetic voices, who can institute the Lord's "rules" for the monarchy and hold kings to the divine sovereign's commands (1 Sam. 10:25; cf. 12:14–15). Prophetic presence and proclamation abounds in DH. In fact, DH's prophetic voices would seem to be the rhetorical successors to DH's references of Levites in Joshua, Judges, and 1–2 Samuel. We first consider here the prophetic voices that are key to DH's theological project. We then turn to explore, through the Elijah and Elisha texts, the integral role that the anthropological phenomenon of shamanism appears to play in the overall fashioning of DH's social vision.

Many prophets litter DH's record, offering a variety of interventions in monarchic politics: The seer Samuel guides the inception of kingship under Saul (1 Samuel 8—12), while Nathan critiques David's abuse of power (2 Samuel 12) and actively intervenes in the transition from David to Solomon (1 Kings 1:1–40). Shemaiah guides the rending of the monarchy into two (1 Kings 12:1–24; 13:22–24). A nameless "man of God" denounces Jeroboam's altar building (1 Kings 13:1–10). Ahijah offers denunciations of both houses (11:1–40; 12:25–13:32; 14:1–8). Jehu condemns Ba'asha (16:1–4, 7). Micaiah speaks up against Ahab's efforts to recover territory from Aram (22:1–38). A "man of God" announces support for Ahab against the arrogant Ben-Hadad, king of Aram (20:13–14, 22, 28). Elijah denounces Ahab (chaps. 17–21), offers a pronouncement against Ahaziah (2 Kings 3:4–27), and encourages Jehu's uprising (2 Kings 9:1–27; 30:10–31). Jonah offers inducement for Jeroboam II's territorial successes (2 Kings 14:23–25). Isaiah speaks to the Assyrian invasion (2 Kings 18:13–19:37; 20:1–19) and against Manasseh (21:10–15). Huldah offers a stern affirmation of the finding of the law materials during the reign of Josiah (22:14–20).

The portrayal of these prophetic interventions into the political life of Israel and Judah are shaped by DH's distinctive view of the role of a prophet in relation to the bureaucratic apparatus. In so observing, we will not want to confuse DH's notion of the prophetic with impressions we might glean from the earlier layers of the canonical prophets. Overall it would seem, for DH at least, that the monarchy got into trouble to the extent that it ignored or disregarded the prophetic voice. The repeated negative evaluations of so many of the kings of Israel and Judah drives home this point throughout the work. DH becomes the arbiter of a renewal of the prophetic voice as a part of its overall program for Israel's recovery after the exile, the disastrous note on which DH ends.

If not the voice of the canonical prophets, what sort of prophetic voice is at work in DH? One clue is provided for us by the preponderance of the phrase, *îš hā-ĕlohîm,* "man of God," throughout DH, especially in 1–2 Kings. This phrase appears roughly eighty times in the Hebrew Bible, seventy times in DH alone.[19] When we consider that six of the occurrences outside of DH appear as replications in 1–2 Chronicles, we find only five uses of the phrase elsewhere in the Hebrew Bible, referencing Moses, David, and a certain Igdaliah (Jer. 35:4; Ps. 90:1 [title]; Ezra 3:2; Neh. 12:24, 36). The phrase is never used in the canonical prophetic literature as a designation for any of the canonical prophets. Clearly it would seem that if we could unlock this elusive phrase we would have a handle on the kind of prophetic voice that has become rhetorically valuable to DH's program.

It is useful to note that a number of named figures are labeled "man of God." In particular, DH uses the designation with reference to Moses (Deut. 33:1; Josh. 14:6; cf. Ps. 90:1 [title]; Ezra 3:2; 1 Chron. 23:14; 2 Chron. 30:16), Samuel (1 Sam. 9:6–10), Elijah (1 Kings 17:18, 24; 2 Kings 1:9–13), Elisha (2 Kings 4:7–13, 16), and Shemaiah (1 Kings 12:22; 2 Chron. 11:2).[20] In addition, several otherwise unnamed figures bear this designation (1 Sam. 2:27; 1 Kings 13:1–31; 1 Kings 20:28; 2 Kings 23:16–17).[21] Following Bratsiotis, we might note a number of characteristics of the "man of God" as portrayed by DH, namely that such a person brings divine messages, is also labeled a prophet (*nābî'*), has disciples who follow in his stead, is acknowledged as a holy figure, works miracles, and can deliver physically toxic curses.[22] These patterns are most evident in DH's presentation of the stories of Elijah and Elisha.

Elijah is credited with six acts of power: (1) he is fed by ravens (1 Kings 17:1–5); (2) he supplies a widow with a miraculous jar of flour and jug of oil, and raises her dead son (17:7–24); (3) he defeats prophets of Baal at Mount Carmel by calling down fire from heaven (18:1–46); (4) he is fed by God and receives a theophany (19:1–18); (5) he calls fire down on soldiers (2 Kings 1:1–18); and (6) he is taken to heaven in a whirlwind (2:1–12).

Extending his master's legacy, to Elisha are ascribed twelve acts of power: (1) he parts the water of the Jordan River (2 Kings 2:13–18); (2) he cleanses ("heals") the brackish spring (2:19–22); (3) he punishes the taunting children who are thereupon "mangled" by two she-bears (2:23–25); (4) the widow's jar miraculously produces oil to pay off debts (4:1–7); (5) he raises the dead son of the woman of Shunem (4:8–37); (6) he purifies the poisoned stew (4:38–41); (7) he feeds one hundred people (4:42–44); (8) he heals Naaman (5:1–19); (9) he miraculously knows that his assistant Gehazi sought payment from Naaman for Elisha's healing work (5:20–27); (10) he retrieves a lost axe head (6:1–7); (11) he blinds a Syrian raiding party (6:8–23); and (12) his bones revive a dead man (13:20–21).

Since DH's perspective on prophecy cannot simply be fleshed out with reference to the canonical prophetic texts, we might ask if social-scientific analysis can provide insight into DH's choices and perspectives on prophecy. The general anthropological work by Overholt is instructive here, as well as Overholt's and I. M. Lewis's specific reflections on shamanism.[23] Lewis and others draw a distinction between spirit possession and spirit medianship, with the latter being the purview of the shaman. Lewis defines the shaman as "an *shaman* inspired prophet and healer, a charismatic religious figure with the power to control the spirits, usually by incarnating them."[24] While this phenomenon is based on far-flung examples from Siberia, Central Asia, among Native Americans and Eskimos, and throughout the world, one must wonder if the reluctance to apply the term shaman to the biblical materials results from a bias in favor of keeping the picture of the prophets restricted to that of rational ethical innovators (cf. 1 Sam. 19:18–24). Yet the portraits of Elijah and Elisha in 1–2 Kings present these figures as persons who engage the mystical and "irrational" with a view toward at least in part exerting influence over the shaping of social and political institutions. Both Elijah and Elisha are credited with interventions in the political life of Israel and Judah.[25] Elijah, sometime after his profound theophany (1 Kings 19), is found courageously denouncing Ahab over the incident concerning Naboth's vineyard (21:1–29). Elisha, induced by music (a common inducement of trances among shamans), encourages King Jehoshaphat and his coalition to face Moab, for victory is assured by God (2 Kings 3).[26] Elisha also has a hand in Hazael's succession (8:7–15), Jehu's rebellion (9:1–10), and Joash's victory over Aram (13:14–19).

Both the stories of power and the tales of political intervention set the tone for the prophetic voices of Elijah and Elisha in DH. The extensive reliance on the stories of power, however, would seem to indicate DH's keen interest in a particular style of prophecy that became rhetorically useful as DH constructed its proposals regarding a revived but conditional monarchy.[27] DH, in other words, taps tales of shaman-like men of power who work miracles, cure illness, resuscitate the dead, and control the weather, putting these prophetic stories to work for very different purposes than the original prophetic story-cycle would have served.

We are left with asking why DH found it possible—even necessary—to conjoin such a form of prophecy with its own national program. For whom would this lore have had persuasive appeal? We, of course, cannot discount the possibility that these prophetic "stories of power" once stood as an independent unit or source that has now been incorporated into DH. Yet this voice's centrality would seem to indicate that DH was fashioned at its inception around an amalgamation of (1) Judaean court annals concerning the kings of Israel and Judah, (2) ancient epic texts perhaps from an early cycle of tales, as in Judges 5 and 1 Sam. 1:19–27, and (3) lore regarding prophets/shamans such as Elijah and Elisha. The combination of annals and legendary material created a powerful theological tool in the hands of DH for evaluating the ill-fated monarchy's demise. The shaman's voice, on the periphery of the social loop of the palace-temple complex, offers DH a vantage point from which to guide a critical reevaluation of the monarchic institution.[28] Thus, Moses and his kindred successors are drawn into DH's social vision, while Aaron and his priestly heirs tend to remain outside of DH's political and social framework. We can imagine that the priestly group came to terms with DH complex only with great difficulty.

Concretely, then, the postexilic nostalgia for a prophetic movement, as evidenced also by the compilation of the highly redacted canonical prophetic texts, has been transmuted by a concern on the part of DH to use the prophetic voice as a *rhetorical device* to recapture the center of the exilic and postexilic debate. In this, we can hardly think of DH as an isolated figure, as Noth seems to imagine (see above). Rather, DH must have played an integral role in the stirrings of a movement to rebuild the temple in Jerusalem and to restore the Davidic dynasty. The books of Haggai and Zechariah show us the practical outworkings of such a position. While it is true that the Persians most likely worked to thwart such an effort, the fact remains that throughout the second temple period there would have been those for whom the monarchic option was the only viable political configuration appropriate for the people of Israel, whatever drawbacks there might be to such a setup. A resurrection of the prophetic voice was useful to DH's ends. The mysterious disappearance of Zerubbabel from the pages of Judah's history would seem to have spelled the death knell for this movement, though its resurgence in the Maccabean period would indicate a submersion of the tendency rather than its outright disappearance (cf. Hag. 2:1–7).

The portrayal of prophetic figures in DH warns us not to confuse the gentry's "prophetic" voice with the subterranean layers of the canonical prophetic texts. Everywhere the canonical prophetic writings betray later editorial hands that have brought them more closely into line with DH's efforts. Yet since these editings have not turned those texts into writings by "men of God," DH's picture has not entirely obscured the preexilic layers of these texts. This state of affairs leaves open the possibility that we can successfully recover something of a preexilic prophetic tradition that stands in contrast to DH's own shamanistic idealization of the tradition. One outstanding difference between DH and the earlier layers of the canonical prophetic materials that ought to command our attention here is the fact that the Hebrew terms for poverty, so common to the canonical prophets, are almost entirely absent from the entire DH. If we observe that such terms appear only in Deuteronomy 15 and 24 (i.e., the older law code), in poetry of extraneous origins (1 Sam. 2:8; 2 Sam. 22:28), or with altered meanings (Judg. 6:15; 2 Sam. 3:1; 2 Kings 24:14; 25:12), then we must be stunned by the complete lack of interest shown by DH in the poverty question as such. When DH critically appraises ancient Israel's economic and political structures, its "prophets" are not talking as the canonical prophets did in defense of the exploited poor and landless. Rather, DH's criticisms tend to center on *specific* abuses of royal power, not the calling into question of the monarchic institution as such or the highlighting of the situation of the underclasses. Remarkably, Samuel's critique of kingship (1 Samuel 8), Solomon's use of forced labor (1 Kings 5:27–32 [13–18]; 9:15–22; 12:1–7), and Ahab's taking of Naboth's vineyard (1 Kings 21) are all narrated without invoking the vocabulary of poverty so important to the prophets, Psalms, Proverbs, Job, and the lawmakers. Clearly DH has adapted the prophetic voice for its own brand of social criticism. DH's protection of landholdings would seem to be consistent with a landed gentry position. Elijah does not stand up for the poor as an Amos or a Micah might have done. The divergent social analysis of the biblical "historians" and the canonical prophets could hardly be more striking.[29] The social ethics of DH is predicated rather on the triad of land, covenant fidelity, and monarchic political authority. These three intersecting interests constitute the underpinnings of DH's view and offer a point of departure for both the critique of past failures and the clearing of a ground for future renewal.

Players and Pawns: Women in the Deuteronomic History

From Rahab the prostitute, who hides the Israelite spies and thereby permits the ultimate fall of Jericho (Joshua 2; 6:17, 22–24), to Huldah the prophetess, who confirms the finding of God's law, thereby striking fear into the heart of King Josiah (2 Kings 22:14–20), DH presents an array of women who are integral players and pawns in DH's royalist project. A study of some of these figures is essential to our understanding of the social vision of DH, which is built in light of women who are victims of tragedy, who are dangerous figures, who confirm the power of God, who mark out males who have political authority, and who are, at times, major actors in DH's monarchic drama.

A number of women are portrayed as victims of tragic or even brutal circumstances. Most notorious are the tragedies in the book of Judges, texts that Trible insists be read in memoriam.[30] Jephthah's daughter becomes a victim of her father's flippant vow that he will sacrifice whatever comes out of his door first if he can just gain a military victory over the Ammonites (Judg. 11:29–31). Needless to say, after the victory, his daughter appears. While he is torn up over this mistake, she nobly resigns herself to her fate, much as a number of female figures in Euripides' plays do to at least preserve their dignity in a patriarchal system that has gone awry. Worse still is the tale of the Levite's concubine who is horribly raped, a deed that leads to civil war among the tribes (chaps. 19—20). The victimization is compounded when the tribes arrange for the offending Benjaminites to take their replacement wives from the women of Shiloh who were out tending their vineyards (chap. 21). These tales would seem to be in DH to demonstrate the evils of life without a centralized shrine or a single dominant political authority.

Stories of victimization arise as well in 1–2 Samuel and 2 Kings. Hannah's barrenness provides an occasion for DH to point out the obtuseness of the priest Eli, but more importantly, the rectification of her situation by birthing Samuel also supplies a new direction for the priesthood and ultimately the establishment of the conditional kingship (1 Samuel 1–2). Out of tragedy hope can arise, at least where an obedient priesthood and kingship are concerned, according to DH. The wife of the slain priest Phinehas gives birth to Ichabod, whose very name indicates the loss of the glory of the ark of the covenant when captured by the Philistines (1 Sam. 4:19–22). While Saul's daughter Michal is a victim, in part, of her own infatuation for David, both Saul's callous use of her as a political pawn to contain David, as well as David's ultimate dislike for her, seals her fate as a victim of the larger forces at work in the narrative of David's rise to power (1 Samuel 18–19, 25:44; 2 Sam. 3:13–16; 6:16–23). The story of the rape of Tamar by David's son Amnon, and later the exacting of revenge by her brother Absalom, a son of David by another wife, forms a sad commentary on the course of David's reign (2 Samuel 13). Next, Rizpah, one of Saul's widows, finds that two of her sons are among the seven sacrificed in revenge for Saul's attack on the Gibeonites. In her grief she would not bury the bodies, an act accomplished by David's intervention (2 Samuel 21). Finally, the account of the women who eat a child to deal with the famine during the war between Samaria and Aram (2 Kings 6:24–30) and the reference to Menahem's battle that includes the ripping open of the bellies of pregnant women (2 Kings 15:16) are highly poignant moments in a work that all too often glorifies the wars of the Lord.

Women in DH are frequently portrayed as dangerous foreigners. While it would seem that Samson is to be credited with a wandering libido, the text

comes to focus on Delilah as the duplicitous figure who sought the ruin of
Samson (Judges 14—16). Overall, the text accents his sexual escapades as
opportunities for YHWH to bring down the Philistines (Judg. 14:1–5), yet the
notorious character of the foreign woman is a motif that is integral to the success of the story. The most blatant case of detrimental foreign feminine influence occurs under Solomon, who is said to be led into the worship of the
neighboring gods Ashtoreth, Milcom, and Chemosh as a result of his contacts
with his many wives obtained through foreign alliances (1 Kings 11:1–8). Certainly the most notorious of the females of foreign extraction in DH is Jezebel,
the wife of King Ahab. She is accused of promoting the worship of Baal in
Israel (1 Kings 16:31), killing off the Lord's prophets (1 Kings 19:1), urging
Ahab to kill Naboth to steal his property and of actually arranging Naboth's
murder (1 Kings 21). The last of the more notorious figures is Athaliah (a
daughter of either Omri or Ahab according to 2 Kings 8:18, 26), the queen
mother who reigned after Ahaziah. She is depicted as attempting to kill off the
royal line, an act that leaves only Joash alive to curry supporters from the
crowd that successfully resists Athaliah (2 Kings 11:1–3). When a conspiracy
among court figures and priestly leaders leads to her assassination, the texts
details the covenant renewal and ritual reforms that ensue (2 Kings 11:17–20).
The demise of dangerous foreign women is healthy for ritual reforms and for
the establishment of royal power under God, according to DH.

Frequently women confirm the actions and power of God. We have already
alluded to the role played by Huldah's affirmations in the finding of the scroll
of the law that launches Josiah's reforms. Yet Huldah is not alone in the role
that she plays in DH. While functioning as a more negative figure, the woman
who conjures spirits at En-Dor quite powerfully calls forth a Samuel who
speaks directly to the reasons why God removed the kingship from Saul (1
Sam. 28:7–25). David's first two wives are victims of an Amalekite raid, though
their recovery comes via a counterattack that has divine approval (1 Sam.
30:1–6, 17–20). Their presence in the story serves rhetorically to highlight
David's moral capital under God at a time when it was not obvious that he
would succeed in establishing his rule. On a more grandiose scale, the arrival
of the queen of Sheba's entourage and her many questions placed to Solomon
serve to affirm his status as a wise and wealthy ruler chosen by YHWH
(1 Kings 10). The story of the miraculous supplying of the widow of
Zarephath with flour and oil seems designed in large measure as a way of confirming Elijah's status as a "man of God" (1 Kings 17). Likewise, the stories of
Elisha's aiding of the debt-ridden woman by supplying her with miraculous oil
(2 Kings 4:1–7) and the raising of the woman of Shunem's dead son both would
seem to function to affirm Elisha's divinely granted powers (2 Kings 4:8–37;
cf. 2 Kings 8:1–6).

There are various women whose presence serves to indicate a male figure's hold on power or claims to political authority. Thus, Caleb gives his daughter Achsah away as a prize to the one who captures the town of Kiriath-sepher, though at least she has the fortitude to demand property from Caleb to enhance her status (Judg. 1:12–15). Concubines play a key role in the demarcating of political power in DH. Saul's concubine Rizpah becomes a political volleyball in the hands of rivals Ishbosheth and Abner (2 Sam. 3:6–11). Similarly, the concubines David left behind to tend the palace when he fled Jerusalem during his son Absalom's rebellion are commandeered by Absalom, who has intercourse with them to lay claim to his father's throne. When the rebellion collapses, David simply leaves the women secluded and untouched in his palace (2 Samuel 15—20). Women function as signs of male power in other ways. Very simply, Solomon's acquisition of Pharaoh's daughter is presented as a product of their political alliance (1 Kings 3:1; cf. 7:8, 9:16, 24). Of course, the reverse can also be the case, where a woman can serve as the occasion for DH to indicate a *loss* of power. The virgin supplied to David near the end of his life, Abishag the Shunammite, far from energizing his rule, becomes rhetorically symptomatic of not only his decline in vigor but also his loss of political control (1 Kings 1:1–4). Later, after Adonijah's bid for the kingship has been thwarted by Bathsheba's and Solomon's maneuverings, Adonijah has the gall to request from Bathsheba this same Abishag to be his wife, an act that Solomon understands to be tantamount to usurping the throne (1 Kings 2). A female figure, likewise, serves to indicate a loss of power when Jeroboam's wife approaches Ahijah the prophet in secret at her husband's behest to seek a cure for their ailing son, only to be told in no uncertain terms of God's anger at Jeroboam's apostate regime (1 Kings 14).

Despite the negative portrayal of women in DH, there are some circumstances where a characterization of women as key or major players in the political game finds its way into the overall DH project. Most notable in the military sphere are the figures of Deborah and Jael. Both are integral to an early tribal victory that is lauded in one of the most ancient texts in the Hebrew Bible, the poetic Judges 5, which has a prose counterpart in Judges 4. Likewise, a woman is credited with dropping a millstone on Abimelech's head during a siege, although in his dying moments he insists that his arms-bearer kill him so that he does not go down in infamy as having been killed by a woman (Judg. 9:53–54). Similarly, the "wise woman" of Tekoa cleverly averts the raiding of her town by seeing to it that the head of the enemy that David's commander Joab sought was tossed in a timely fashion over the town wall to the eager warriors below (2 Sam. 20:16–22). Certainly Abigail, who diverts David's wrath away from her foolish husband Nabal after he chose not to assist David with desperately needed provisions, is one of the more memorable female players in

DH's scheme.[31] Her words confirm David's mandate from God (1 Sam. 25:28–31, 39), while David's marriage to Abigail after Nabal's death comes as something of a reward for her successful tempering of his anger, a noble character feature that saves David at a number of junctures in the narrative. Perhaps the major female player in DH is Bathsheba. Her successful manipulation, along with the prophet Nathan, of her aging and decrepit husband King David ensures that her own son Solomon beat out the rightful heir Adonijah for control of the throne upon David's death (1 Kings 1–2).

To sum up: While DH is constructed around the doings of male heroes, royal figures, warriors, courtiers, priests, prophets, and rivals, there is nonetheless an integral role for female figures in the fleshing out of DH's ideology of kingship and postexilic royalist agenda. Thus, the successes and failures of the kingship in Israel and Judah are measured by women's lives lived out as tragedies in the face of brutal abuses of male social power. The commitments of the leadership, both royal and priestly, to the national program are refined to the extent that foreign influences, framed in terms of a feminine paganism, are defeated by ritual reforms and a royalist ideology that adheres to the rigors of Yahwism. Women join DH's plan of action when they confirm that power is with YHWH's Judah even in moments of uncertainty and duress. Everywhere women can serve as signs of male claims to political authority, and loss of that authority. At times for DH, women can push the program forward, such as a Deborah, Jael, Abigail, or those many nameless "wise women" who are clever enough to side with the right cause in the hour of struggle. To be sure, women in central leadership positions are potentially a disaster, as evidenced by Jezebel and Athaliah. Hence, here DH's program reveals itself to be thoroughly an "androcentric theater," such as Ackerman finds in Judges.[32] Yet throughout DH we find many women who are more than mere stagehands in the rise and shaping of the monarchy. Presumably, the text envisions that there are other Rahabs and Huldahs, strong women with insight and commitment, who will stand up for the social vision advocated in DH for Judah, as the community, both women and men, seek to find a way to rebuild after the exile.

Social Ethics in the Narrative Torah: Ideological Uses of the Stories of the Ancestors in J, E, and P

The books of Genesis to Numbers present us with a wide array of narratives that carry forward the competing social visions of the traditions that have come together to form this portion of the Torah. These conflicting social visions establish ideological matrices that combine theological constructs such as covenant, blessing, fear of God, and purity, with pressing concerns about national survival, interaction with foreigners, the establishment of material security, the construction of a viable leadership, and the fostering of a ritual program for Judah's exiles. At this intersection of ancient symbols and the crushing challenges of building for the future, we meet a set of voices that offer differing insights and conflicting perspectives concerning how the past shall be taken into Judah's seemingly uncertain, yet at times strangely promising, future. By encountering these divergent voices, we are taken inside the thicket of the exilic and postexilic political forest. By drawing on source analysis, we will unfold the scaffolding of several powerful narrative structures that were built on the quaking ground of Babylonian invasion and Persian triumph. These voices—J, E, and P—will offer alternate social visions to that of the failed royalist project of DH. These additional voices will, step by step, create social visions that will ultimately yield to the construction of a priestly commonwealth on this side of the exilic divide. The past has not been entirely lost but has been thoroughly adapted to the deep questions raised by exilic dislocation and postexilic revival. By engaging these social visions, we will find some potent answers to those disturbing questions. In this segment of our chapter, then, we will consider the social visions of J, E, and P in turn. We begin, however, with one historically problematic aspect of these narratives, namely, the issue of their "nomadic" character.

Nomadic Values or Nationalist Imagination?

As we observed in chapter 1, in their sociological studies of biblical social ethics in the late nineteenth and early twentieth centuries, Causse and Wallis invoked the nomadic dimensions of the pentateuchal stories as a means to understand various later cultural and political developments such as the fabric of peasant life in monarchic Israel, thereby explaining the values clashes found both in the society and its literature. The Genesis narratives in particular were read as historical treatments reflective of Israel's nomadic past, in which the virtues of hospitality, the structure of male-headed households, and the harshness of wandering all factored into the equation of a tribal social ethic. Yet historical problems remain and the question arises of whether or not the ancient values of Israel's nomadic past are truly preserved in the text. Our answer to this question will greatly affect the sort of social ethics we will find in these narratives.

Wallis and Causse, like many other scholars of their time, sought Israel's origins in the nomads of the Arabian desert.[33] However, in more recent years, sharp criticisms of this view of nomadism have been offered by Mendenhall, Luke, and Gottwald.[34] Mendenhall made it clear that the Arabian desert was no engine that produced hordes of hostile nomads that either settled to become great civilizations or who constantly loomed with threats to destroy all of urban society. Luke and Gottwald, likewise, have greatly assisted us in seeing that any nomadic analysis of the ancient Near East ought to counter the common (but mistaken) view that such nomads simply wandered aimlessly. Transhumance represents a specific eco-niche. Nomads are adjuncts to urban society, living in a dependent relationship to a socioeconomic structure that vastly overpowers any political aspirations they may harbor.[35] Hence, Alt's position, which maintained that peaceful nomads gradually infiltrated the ancient Israelite countryside to eventually arise as an independent force, could only be partially correct in terms of sociological analysis.[36] The formation of outlying peasant villages might also be posited as an outgrowth from or even a breakdown of the urban structures that dominated Late Bronze Age Canaan. Coote and Whitelam may indeed be correct in saying that we must be careful not to throw out the nomadic dimension altogether.[37] Yet it is the peasant-urban dynamic, rather than a nomadic-urban interchange, that more clearly reflects the archaeological, historical, and biblical picture as we know it. Root-less nomadism as an explanatory model for the social processes of the ancient world and behind the Bible's development grossly oversimplifies matters, however much pastoral life may have factored into the dominant peasant-urban social system of ancient Israel.

There is a lesson here, however, even for those who subscribe to the peasant-urban model. The fact that Causse's and Wallis's analyses came to be undermined by later archaeological, anthropological, and sociological research ought to warn us against too readily reading the apparent ideological and theological conflicts of the Bible in light of unexamined or uncorroborated sociological analyses of the biblical material. As Herion makes clear, there is great fluidity in sociological analysis that must temper our hermeneutical labors.[38] There is, likewise, no substitute for sound comparisons between the biblical data and the extant ancient Near Eastern written remains. Furthermore, our historical reconstructions must remain cognizant of the fact that neither peasants nor urban dwellers are uniform in their outlooks. We should be open to historical and textual analysis leading us to the recovery of tremendous conflicts in matters of social ethics *within* camps and not simply between social actors.

Yet we can take this discussion an important step further. The works of Redford, Thompson, and Van Seters have raised serious doubts about the antiquity of the patriarchal narratives from which the study of these texts have never recovered. Redford made it clear that the Joseph story's so-called Egyptian ambiance was either simply mistaken or reflective of late period developments.[39] Thompson cogently demonstrated that the known archaeological record of the Bronze Age simply does not accord with the view of Canaan given in the patriarchal travels, but fits with the realities experienced by those living in Iron Age Canaan.[40] Van Seters strongly championed the view that the many customs long used by scholars to "confirm" that the patriarchal stories must stem from the Middle Bronze Age either (1) did not fit with that time period, (2) could be used to argue for any time period, or (3) fit better with the Neo-Babylonian era.[41] Attempts by Kitchen, Mendenhall, Millard, and Selman, in particular, have not convincingly eradicated the strong suspicion that the patriarchal narratives bear, in large measure, the stamp of the monarchic period, if not simply the exilic and postexilic eras.[42] This is not to say that there are no elements of great antiquity in the patriarchal narratives, but it seems clear that the texts as a whole reflect the tensions and concerns of the later periods. Read in this light, the texts most fully illuminate for us the ideological disputes and conflicting social values of the monarchic period as these are taken up and recast by the exilic community. The patriarchal narratives do not, in other words, present us with the thinking of nomads from the Middle or Late Bronze Age. Thus, we must read the narratives of Genesis as a defense of agendas that undoubtedly have aspirations of a return to the land of Judah, are concerned with the fight for national survival, and harbor the hope of a return to national political prominence, however much that power is tempered and subsumed to Judah's domination by foreign potentates. The expressed values, such as hospitality and male-headed households, then, are hardly the markers only of nomadic society, but reflect, in this case, the values of a genteel class poised for its rightful restoration to power in a "promised land."

Social Ethics in J: A God of Blessing in Exile

To what sort of social ethics does J move its hearers? J's interest is not primarily in law, so we must evaluate the corpus in a broader fashion to discern its method and orientation. Yet narratives, particularly the sort we find in the Torah, embody specific beliefs and practices that enable us to discern the sort of social values and communal structures J envisioned for the restored Judaean commonwealth. The legends of the patriarchs and Moses become the carriers of ideological perspectives that betray a consistent interest on the part of J to galvanize a movement among the exile's survivors.

Theologically, J's social ethic is grounded in the blessing-curse construct. In the primeval history (Genesis 1—11), the curse enters to destroy the man's nurturing relationship to the garden and leads to the expulsion of the couple from the garden (chaps. 2—3). The curse brings the wandering of exile. Likewise, Cain's crime leads to his wandering (4:11). Yet where there is curse, there can also be blessing for the ground (5:29). Noah becomes an instrument of blessing, opening the way for the sort of sacrifice useful to J by which the Lord is appeased (8:20–22). Even Noah himself comes to embody both blessing and curse, when in his drunkenness he passes the curse to Canaan and the blessing to Shem (9:24–27). The exilic scattering in the tower of Babel story rounds out the theme of the primeval history (chap. 11) and paves the way for the announcement of the promise to Abram in terms of land, progeny, and blessing (12:1–3).[43] However, even the Abram pronouncement is prefaced by reference to the situation of barrenness in the Chaldean town of Ur, an obvious and anachronistic reference to Judah's condition of exile in Babylon (11:28–30). The promise marches forward in J through Jacob (27:20–29, 28:10–16). The foreign seer Balaam cannot reverse the bless-curse scheme as Balak, king of Moab, desires (22:6, 18; 24:3–9).

To be sure, threats abound. The Lord tries to make it clear to Abraham that judgment is meted out fairly (18:20–33), which one may have questioned in light of the flood story and the Babel judgment. Onan's failure to secure his brother's line shows another sort of threat at work (38:8–11). Likewise, Judah's actions in relation to Tamar reinforce the need for lines of heirs as a way to fulfill the divine promise (chap. 38).

For this promise to move forward in J, certain social conditions must be obtained, particularly for women. Clearly women pose a danger to the process, as seen from Eve's role in the garden story, for she becomes the human source for the curse (Genesis 3). Though created from the man (2:18–25), her success at childbirth is circumscribed by a male-dominant familial structure (3:16). Later in J, this threat translates into the barrenness motif. The first mention of Sarai, for example, thrusts this issue into view (11:29–30). Her laughter makes the danger a woman poses even more striking (18:12). The same motif dominates the Leah-Rachel rivalry (chaps. 29—30).

The barrenness motif is not the only factor that complicates J's obsession with the succession of heirs. Concubinage creates problems for Abram (16:1–14), though the system itself drives the narrative. Other dangers include the foreign woman, Potiphar's wife, who threatens to sap Joseph's vigor (chap. 39). Finally, intermarriage with Moabite women spells danger for J in the incident at Baal-Peor, where pagan worship slips into the community (Numbers 25). References to these additional dangers help to frame J's focus on the need for the community to procreate "children of the promise" as an act of resistance to the assimilationist temptations of exile.

This concern for delineating the boundary between the community of YHWH and the foreigner is repeatedly encountered in J. When Lot is among foreigners, there is a danger (Gen. 19:4–11). Isaac is not to obtain a wife from among the Canaanites (Gen. 24:3, 37). The story of the rape of Dinah by the Shechemites reinforces this perception of the other (Genesis 34). The story of the blotting out of Amalek serves a similar function (Ex. 17:8–16).

Yet if the community is beset by the dangers of harsh treatment by foreigners, are they to sit back and take it? Hardly, according to J. A people in exile can pursue its own interests and do so with success. Here we can see J's social ethic at work in a positive way, a communal ethic for survival amid exile. Both Abram in Egypt and Isaac among the Philistines found that caution among the foreigners, especially with regard to one's wife, could bring wealth and protection (Gen. 12:10–20; 26:6–18). Joseph's success in his exile (Genesis 39 and 41) reversed his kin's misfortunes such that Pharaoh promised them "the best of all the land of Egypt" (Gen. 45:20). Even the story of Jacob's prosperity finds a place here, with the difference that his successes occurred among kin, although still in a context that was outside of the promised land (Gen. 30:25–43). The ethic at work here encourages circumspect behavior in exile as a key to communal success and survival.

Unfortunately, there is a grave danger here that J acutely recognized: Obvious communal advancement can provoke the envy of the host peoples. In a more general fashion, this is the story of all immigrant communities who wish to remain intact and visible in a foreign political context. Thus, J elevates the warning signs as well. Joseph's successes get him noticed by Potiphar's wife (Gen. 39:6–8) and count for nothing when a new pharaoh arises (Ex. 1:8). In the latter case, the Egyptians are said to fear Israel's power (Ex. 1:9). Thus, while success in the foreign courts is possible, the prudent exile will know how to anticipate reversals in political fortunes. Like Jacob, one might also need to know when it is time to leave (Genesis 31).

For all that, J finds in wealth a virtue and a joy. Abram was rich in livestock, silver, and gold (Gen. 13:2). His servant is able to brag about this wealth as he seeks a wife for Isaac (24:35). The wealth's passing from Abraham to Isaac is mentioned by J (25:5). And, as we have noted, the successes of Jacob (30:25–43) and Joseph (chap. 39) are sources of inspiration for J.

The struggle for survival and the hope of success in exile are not the only values pursued by J. In J we also find the workings of a political economy. The economy has its focus on the promised land. For J it is vital to know that the patriarch Abram moved through the land staking out claims, as it were, by building a series of shrines (Gen. 12:6–9). Indeed, Abram is brought out of Ur of the Chaldeans for the express purpose of possessing the land (15:7–18). The divine pronouncement is solemnized through a covenantal sacrificial ritual. J sums this view up best by stating, "the LORD has granted us ample space to increase in the land" (26:22). Yet it is also clear in J that all are not committed to the project of a return from exile. In Numbers, the question becomes whether to capture the rich promised land or to return to Egypt (13:17–14:1; cf. 11:1–9).

In J's political economy, very specific social mechanisms create a cohesive society. We have already noted that the man dominates the woman (who functions as a childbearer), a social fact symbolized by Adam's naming of Eve (Gen. 3:14–21). In a context of hospitality, Abram oversees, Sarai bakes, and the servant slaughters the calf (18:6–8). Socially she is excluded from the visit since she is "in the tent" (18:9). Yet beyond the male dominated household, we do see other social mechanisms at work in J's communal arrangement of power. A distinctive system of judicial authority constructed around prominent elders assists Moses in lawmaking (Num. 11:10–17). Likewise, the voice of inspired prophecy is given room, as evidenced in the Eldad and Medad story (Num. 11:26–30). Those who opposed this voice found themselves rebuked in turn. Of course, prophetic authority and inspiration constitute a potential source of volatility in the social system, and challenges to this authority were inevitable. The assertion of a female voice and a priestly voice, Miriam and Aaron, against the Mosaic ground of prophetic tradition is roundly countered by J (Numbers 12). The subsequent challenge offered by Dathan and Abiram highlights J's emphasis on Moses' ethical leadership as the ground for true prophetic authority (Num. 16:12–5).

The text of J stands poles apart from P on matters of communal judicial and political authority, weighing in favor of a tribal confederacy. In fact, J's hope for a viable political future seems to rest on the restoration of the tribal system of rule. Thus, a concern for the very real danger of kin strife and intramural discord stand at the heart of J's political rhetoric. There must be no factionalism between kin groups (Gen. 13:8–13). The strife among Joseph's brothers threatens to destroy the tribal system (Gen. 37:3–28). Yet in that same narrative, J holds out hope of a renewal of the old kin-based, tribal confederacy.

J also harbors territorial ambitions beyond Judah and Israel's borders. YHWH's ability to exert prophetic authority over Balaam (Num. 23:31–35) is matched by a pronouncement concerning Israel's prospects at politically dominating the lands of Moab and Edom (Num. 24:15–18). Jacob's reconciliation with Esau amounts to the same thing, although the text's note of fear toward Esau probably reflects the historical experience of Judah's violent treatment at the hands of the Edomites during the time of the Babylonian incursions (Gen. 32:3–13 [2–12]). The hope for J appears to rest in the possibility of treaties of friendship with one-time enemies (cf. Gen. 26:26–33).

To sum up: J's political and social ideology is that of a community bent on struggling to survive exile. The project of restoration may have already begun, or at least with J those discussions are well underway. The community's twofold task is to procreate and provide blessing, even as the curse looms large in the world. The community's pursuit of these communal and political ends

[margin note: J summary]

must be such that even a reluctant, embittered Pharaoh will in the end beg for that blessing from Israel (Ex. 12:32). While J's lore may be rooted in the ancient Judaean traditions, it is also clear that these traditions have been adapted in a vital way to the needs and demands of Judah's exilic disruption.

Toward National Unity: Reading E's Social Ethics

While it is universally acknowledged that the notion of "fear of God" infuses E with its confident spirit, what is increasingly less clear are the concrete social circumstances that led to the production of these materials.[44] Many would argue for an early monarchic and northern orientation of the E material. Certainly its focus on shrines at a variety of locales might serve as warrant for this belief, perhaps reflective of very ancient epic traditions from earlier centuries. Yet I will argue that E, far from being an early monarchic document, is actually the product of the first phases of the return from exile. Thus, if we move beyond E's emphasis on "fear" to look at its sociopolitical dimensions, especially with regard to its emphases on foreigners and wealth, we will find a trajectory in the Torah that is committed to rebuilding the community under the aegis of an imperial administration that has imposed itself on Palestine after the exile, namely, the Persian royal court. E is to be localized in the decades prior to the advent of a Nehemiah or the arrival of an Ezra on the scene (see chapter 5).

As we take into account the major themes of E's social ethics agenda, we will find E's formulation of the covenant, what Noth terms E's "brief programmatic view of the entire pentateuchal narrative":[45]

> And He said to Abram, "Know well that your offspring shall be strangers in a land not theirs, and they shall be enslaved and oppressed four hundred years; but I will execute judgment on the nation they shall serve, and in the end they shall go free with great wealth. As for you,
>
> > You shall go to your fathers in peace;
> > You shall be buried at a ripe old age.
>
> And they shall return here in the fourth generation, for the iniquity of the Amorites is not yet complete. (Gen. 15:13–16)

The writer recognizes the fact of an exilic-styled oppression. The context of this oppression is a foreign environment where the people will endure conflictual conditions for a lengthy period of time. Yet E's focus is not on the oppression itself so much as on the movement out of oppression, a liberation that comes not only through a change in geography but also by way of the acquisition of "great wealth." The end of E's fundamental statement on covenant provides the assurance that this process will surely come to pass. E's program breathes newfound confidence into a foreign context, undoubtedly the situation of Cyrus's original program of political liberation for those who showed loyalty to this noble "pharaoh."

Notably, E follows up this proclamation regarding exile with passages that nuance the function of the exilic circumstance for the molding of the community. What does the experience of exile accomplish according to E? E's Joseph story would seem to pave the way for the Isaianic notion that exile is a time of penalty, which the brothers must publicly acknowledge as part of their atonement for their intertribal rivalries (Gen. 42:21). In the larger scheme, as we shall see in Isaiah, dislocation becomes a time to test the people as a way to prove their integrity (Gen. 42:18, 31–34). Clearly for E, exile is no longer the sheer punishment that it may have been to the earlier prophets. Elements of renewal abound in E, as also come to mark numerous prophetic texts in their latest editorial adaptations. Likewise, E represents a coherent advance on the rather gloomy estimate given in the DH. E, in this regard, is much more a theological precursor to the more expansive emphasis on compassion found in the Chronicler's volumes. E's own analysis sees in the exilic community those forces that preserve life, a sentiment epitomized elsewhere in E in the story of the midwives' resistance to Pharaoh's orders to destroy the newborn Hebrew males (Gen. 45:5b–6; cf. Ex. 1:15–21). In other words, the committed remnant will provide a critical theological voice that can galvanize the community, propelling the people into an era of renewal beyond survival (cf. Gen. 50:20–21).

So how does exile, the foreign context, function in E's sociopolitical vision? In preserving a remnant, exile quite literally provides material security for the people. Joseph's presence in Egypt offers the community the physical means for survival (Gen. 45:11–12). Indeed, much like Jeremiah's call to seek the peace of Babylon and therein find prosperity (Jeremiah 29), E's confidence lies in fearlessly going to Egypt since Israel's greatness lies there (Gen. 47:5–6; cf. 41:48). The promises of return from Egypt are not entirely predicated on escape but on bringing out of Egypt those possessions and skills that come by means of raw involvement in imperial administrations run by evenhanded rulers, such as a pharaoh who is open to Israel's communal distress (cf. Gen. 47:5–6; 48:21; 50:24).

Since E is far less interested in land claims than in honing tools for negotiating the terrain of foreign rule (Gen. 33:19–20), we might examine E passages on foreigners to see what stance E suggests in relation to the exilic and postexilic powers. In particular, E expects foreign rulers to honor the people of God, as seen, for example, in Abimelech's honoring of Abraham when he recognizes Abraham's "prophetic" status and is restrained from sinning against Sarah (Gen. 20:1–16). This honoring of Abraham, which incidentally occurs by means of the *granting of possessions* (20:14), underscores the mutual advantage foreigners and Israelites can have in political interaction. But stories about permitted interactions also lay emphasis on Israel's communal uniqueness by highlighting the urgency of avoiding intermarriage, that is, at least in the giving away of Israelite women into foreign hands.

The positive character of E's advocacy for Israelite involvement in imperial politics is driven home most candidly in E's rendition of the Joseph story. From the portrayal of Joseph in these passages, it is hard to see E as anything other than an independent source in its own right. In E, Joseph is not wrongly imprisoned on a charge of moral violation, as he is in J. Instead, he is in the service of the captain of the guard. This singular service is presented in encouraging terms, with Joseph's role as advisor and interpreter of dreams functioning as keys to his social advancement (Gen. 40:2–23; 41:1–48). The anticipation of E regarding the future success of Israel is predicated, in part, on the writer's view that God "fixes" times of prosperity and famine, a fact that Pharaoh acknowledges in selecting Joseph as supervisor (41:37–48). This positive appraisal of the political process will come as a surprise to those who focus, in one way or another, on the Exodus text alone, seeking a political philosophy that calls for liberation from *all* Pharaohs. It is clear that E has no such intentions. In E's analysis, turning to Egypt for assistance, as Jacob does, can be much more than an evil necessity. Such an act can be a way of acknowledging God as a player who shapes the course of imperial history, provided the people position themselves adequately, like Joseph, to ride the tides of positive political change (42:1–7). Whatever we make of the exodus story, our estimate must by tempered by the knowledge that for E, at least, Joseph could boast about being honored in Egypt (45:8–9, 13).

What, then, is E's view of the exodus story and how does this understanding factor into E's political leanings? E's narrative accents noncollaboration with bad or recalcitrant rulers. E lays particular emphasis on the role women must play in securing the nation's survival in the most tumultuous of times.[46] However, E is far less concerned with resistance to overlords and far more interested in how Israel ought to deal with traditional foes in Palestine who might threaten the rebuilding process. Perhaps too self-consciously, E has God rather anachronistically lead the people *around* the Philistines, noting that fear of open conflict might lead the people to back down (Ex. 13:17–18). Whatever resources are available to E, the posture seems to be driven by a sense of internal military weakness, a situation that forces reliance on negotiation and imperial graciousness to achieve national success. More straightforwardly, Edom and Sihon are presented as foes, reflecting either the experience of the monarchic period or of the war of Nebuchadnezzar on Jerusalem (Num. 20:14–21; 21:21–31; cf. Obadiah; Psalm 137). In this context, and in light of the finds of Balaam texts from Transjordan (see chapter 6), the consternation of Balak at Balaam's refusal to curse Israel from Moabite territory is, from an ancient Israelite point of view at least, a theologically creative twist on the prophetic traditions of Israel's neighbors (Numbers 22—23).

A number of E passages focus on the acquisition of wealth as an integral element to E's vision of survival. If E highlights this issue in its version of the covenant, how does the element of possessions also factor into the larger narrative? In part, as we have already noted, possessions are the product, at times, of successful interactions with foreigners who learn to honor Israel, as in the case of Abimelech's treatment of Abraham and Pharaoh's reliance on Joseph (Gen. 20:1–16, esp. 14; 40:2–23; 41:1–48). Property disputes, however, form the locus of the Jacob-Laban narrative. Here the shift draws our attention to intra-kin conflict as a threat to the survival of a community in exile. This element is most dramatically portrayed when Jacob, who succeeds as a result of hard-won labors in a foreign geographic environment, finds himself cheated of his wages by his own kin, Laban (Gen. 31:2–13). This unjust treatment seems to earn Jacob the right, according to E, to demand his people's return home (31:13). One group may remain behind in exile, but E is clearly on the side of those who, while they have prospered in exile, nevertheless sense a lingering injustice that can only be set aright through return to the homeland. Possessions, therefore, do not become an end in themselves for E; rather, possessions are to be put to work for the project of return.

Yet E's awareness of intra-kin and intertribal conflict refines the philosophy of wealth and the understanding of power at work in this text. We see, for example, an accusation against rivals in the community, when Jacob blisteringly denounces Laban for having forced him into the position of being sent away "empty-handed," straits mitigated by the God who saw Jacob's "affliction" and acted (31:36b–42). This divine rebuke of Laban appears indicative of serious rifting in the community over the project of development in exile and its relation to any program of return. E, likewise, is open to staking out a claim to property in exile and acting in noncooperation against community members who would treat E's group as if they were foreigners, much as Leah and Rachel see their position vis-à-vis Laban (31:14–16). Yet Jacob's firm commitment not to take wives outside of the community, however splintered this community may have been, is surely a sign that E saw the future of Israel to be in the hands of the writer's surviving remnant (Gen. 31:43–55). This posture is driven home most eloquently in what is perhaps E's most significant passage on possessions, namely, Jacob's offer to Esau of wealth gained in exile (32:13 [12]). In making this offer, Jacob solidifies the remnant's role as the instrumental political faction for the restoration of Israel in the form of a viable national entity and for the strengthening of Israel's posture in relation to the outlying communities in that region. Esau's acceptance of this future represents the height of E's political fantasy (33:11). Whether Israel's neighbors saw the return of Judah's exiles in this fashion is another matter entirely.

Whether E represents a northern movement or not, its related ritual program is certainly not focused on a restoration of a central shrine. Rather than seeing this as indicative of a northern locale, one might argue that E's ritual program is reflective of a populist movement that could reach into any geographic setting. In this sense, E may simply represent an assertion of the landed gentry, displaced by the exile, over and against the aspirations of forces tied, however nostalgically, to a restoration of monarchic and priestly power, most specifically in Jerusalem (as represented by DH). In part, E's concern is to have God oversee and regulate the activities at local shrines, not to obliterate them in a fever of centralization. Thus, God orders Jacob to build an altar shrine at Bethel (35:1). Jacob's shrines represent ancient stone pillars that served to denote divine presence in a place (33:14; 35:20). E has some investment in worship at places of God's choosing (22:9; Ex. 3:12). Yet E's program is hardly tied to the sort of ritual minutiae championed by P. For E, ritual demarcates those who have committed themselves to God over against those who have ritually removed themselves from the liturgical practices and ideology of their kin, namely, those who appear to have assimilated to pagan ways. This separation is brought out most starkly when Jacob's household puts away rival gods (35: 2–4). E's view of ritual is tied overtly to the program for possessions envisioned in the narrative when Jacob vows, "If God remains with me, if He protects me on this journey that I am making, and gives me bread to eat and clothing to wear, and if I return safe to my father's house—the LORD shall be my God" (28:20–21).

E's God is not the focus of ritual questions but of matters of communal survival. God sustains the community through the people's acquisition of the basics, such as bread and clothes. E rallies followers, not around a centralized temple program but by means of a program of possessions that alone could give returnees the security they needed to successfully sustain the endeavors of reconstruction. E's efforts are geared at success in the short term in relation to the imperial powers and in the long run in relation to rival factions in the community, presumably movements reflected in the earlier DH and the later P.

If E represents an alternative movement among the returning exiles, what sort of leadership does E envision? With no ties to the priestly or palatial centralization movements, E must envision a radically different leadership structure. E comes down decisively in favor of a charismatic, prophetic leadership, a type of prophecy not entirely unlike the shaman of DH. Moses, the recipient of God's law, is claimed as the capstone of the Abraham, Isaac, and Jacob tradition. Such a figure can advocate concessions from tough-minded rulers when the transitions from life in exile to life beyond exile must be effected (Ex. 3:4b–12).

Needless to say, E understood the very real opposition encountered when elevating prophetic norms and tribally based institutions. Certainly E's portrayal of Jethro, the tribal figure, and Aaron, the priestly figure, deferring to Moses is yet another sign of the rather fantastic ambitions harbored by E (Ex. 14:11–12; 17:3; 18:12). Yet out of the tribal mix, in sentiments that are put in Jethro's mouth, comes a fairly decentralized form of leadership that respects the rule of law when based, of course, on the "fear of God" and on proper instruction (Ex. 18:19–26; cf. 24:9–11). E would seem to pave the way for the Torah to embrace, not the extensive ritual legislation of P, but the incorporation of the Ten Commandments and law codes that appear to have arisen out of tribal efforts to contain the coercive powers of the monarchy as it had encroached on the villages and outlying urban centers (cf. Exodus 20—23; Deuteronomy 12—26). Such are the laws E would seem to have Moses receive from God on the mountain (Ex. 19:16–19). E views with suspicion those efforts aimed at putting Aaron at the center of a ritually based political program. Indeed, for E, it is Aaron who leads a paganized rebellion against Moses (Ex. 32:1b–4a, 21–24). Beyond these considerations concerning leadership, we only obtain vague hints from E regarding the internal structuring of the tribal community, in particular E's acceptance of the traditional patriarchal social structure in which common legal norms regulate the status of wives and cowives (Gen. 21:10, 12). God is the rubber stamp for traditional patterns of marriage and inheritance rights in E.

So how do we account for E's views? A careful attempt to come to grips with E, both in terms of its ideological orientation and its historical context, has been offered by Coote.[47] Coote maintains that E was a distinctive reediting of J, but that E never stood alone as an independent source that was wedded to J, as is the more standard scholarly view.[48] In other words, for Coote, there never was an E source that ran parallel to J in terms of basic format and content. Rather, Coote constructively argues that E represents a deliberate supplementation of J, designed to stamp J with the concerns of the secessionist dynast Jeroboam I (c. 922–901 B.C.E.). Although Coote himself does not posit this analogy, the reshaping of J by E would seem to be on the order of the recasting of the Pentateuch by the Samaritan community to reflect their interest in Mount Gerizim as opposed to Jerusalem. Thus, Coote's theory is not without precedent in the ancient Palestinian environment.

In Coote's analysis, the recasting of J by E functions to highlight Jeroboam I's concern for an heir, for Joseph as a tribal exemplar, and for a vigorous cultic life outside of Jerusalem. It would seem that much of the anxiety expressed in the Pentateuch over the fate of succession found in the stories of Abimelech, Hagar, Isaac, Rachel and Bilhah, Laban, and throughout the Joseph narrative reflects a distinctive E stamp. Whether this factor results from Jeroboam I's desire for an heir is perhaps plausible but appears to be a less compelling part of his thesis. Indeed, Coote's understanding of the political motivations and ideological anxieties of E are far less problematic than his more circumstantial arguments for specific links to Jeroboam I. One would have to account compellingly for the reception of a similar theme into other portions of Judah's court literature preserved in the Bible, for the Judaean court certainly had no lack of concern about successful dynastic succession. We might argue, therefore, that one does not require Jeroboam I's anxiety to explain the subterranean discomfort of vast tracks of biblical historical narrative. Moreover, the exilic distress over survival would seem to offer the most plausible context for E's program. Further, we must also not discount the possibility that the Judaean chroniclers have deliberately heightened the secessionist problems of the North to accent their ideological commitment to the view that a failure to heed Judaean Yahwism was tantamount to rebellion and that only a reassertion of southern Yahwism could help the North succeed as well.

Thus, while we might dispute with Coote over the time period of E, we would agree that E is consistent with an attempt to exert authority over the northern territories. The older monarchic period struggle between monarchic authority and village autonomy that lingers in J gives way in E to a bureaucratized religious and legal system that exerts itself over the larger populace, ironically paving the way for the priestly authority claimed by P. From E we find, as Coote correctly discerns, an embrace of the northern cults, with El as god of conquest and productivity, with menhirs and oil in ritual, with altar sacrifice (though a shunning of child sacrifice), with shrines for pilgrimage, and with incubation rites inspired by an interest in dream theophanies. But is this embrace simply indicative of E's attempt to stamp the J tradition with Jeroboam I's "revolutionary spirituality" as Coote contends? Are we to see in the E additions to the Joseph narratives simply a Jeroboam who descends to Egypt and returns to save the people? Is the Covenant Code really Jeroboam's attempt to rise above a Solomon or a Rehoboam? Or is the inclusion of this code (adapted by E, but not composed by E) within the narratives of the emerging Pentateuch a postexilic effort to reclaim ancient legal traditions as normative guideposts for politics of the postexilic community?

What sort of revitalized community does E envision? Clearly E's community is not to be seen as simply a "monopoly of force," to use Mendenhall's phrase, as the monarchy was when the old legal code could stand on its own apart from narrative texts. The narrative equivalent of this monarchic monopoly is most certainly J's exodus deity who sends plagues as a way to exert authority vis-à-vis Egypt. E's ideology is replete with its own sort of fear; after all, in E there are towns without fear of God (Gen. 20:11) and ancestors such as Abraham and Joseph who prove their fear of God (Gen. 22:12; 42:18). In addition, it is E's Pharaoh who seeks the babies' deaths that is countered by the midwives' fear of God (Ex. 1:17, 21), and it is E who adds thunder to Moses' Mount Sinai ascent, filling the people with the appropriate fear of God (Ex. 20:18–20).[49] Yet for E, the legal system must be wise and organized, persuasively adhered to and not arbitrarily enjoined, as the Jethro insertions forcefully and self-consciously argue, drawing out the necessary social justice implications of fearing God (Ex. 18:21).

Thus, the postexilic community of E, as a community of narrative, finds its deepest aspirations not in the monarchic imposition of law by force but in the rekindling of the patriarchal and matriarchal traditions of survival that undergird and provide rationale for a community of law, as represented by the inclusion of the Covenant Code in the story of the ancestral escape from Egypt. J's God of plague power was not persuasive. E's God was feared precisely because a failure to fear would put the whole community ethos and legal system into jeopardy. Is this not the practical import of Neh. 5:1–19 and 7:2, for whose author the "fear of God" as motivation for the legal system most clearly parallels E?[50] Put most baldly, departure from Babylon to rebuild Jerusalem required an obedient commitment to law. But more importantly, it required a compelling commitment to the preservation of the ancestral stories that might again catapult the Judaean community back onto the world stage, a theologically charged playground where the divine will effects its intentions for the people of the promise.

In this analysis, E, wittingly or not, paved the way for Ezra's reforms and for the assertion of P's claims and authority. The image of the wise Jethro and the prophetic lawmaker Moses must have charged the renewal attempted by Ezra. Though certainly by Ezra's time the images of Samuel the reluctant king maker, Josiah the ritual reformer and nationalist, Abraham the ancestor of the promise, and Solomon the idolatrous ruler must have joined Jethro and Moses as theological tools of persuasion (cf. Neh. 1:7; 8:1–18; 9:6–37; 13:1, 23–30). Admittedly, from the confused state of the Ezra-Nehemiah amalgam, we cannot be entirely certain about what materials belong to the time of the reform and which portions might actually belong to a late Persian-early Hellenistic effort to codify and preserve some rather stylized memory of that period of renewal (see chapter 5). Certainly the books of Ezra and Nehemiah cannot be treated as historicist mirrors of the times, as some scholars would apparently do. Garbini is right to raise questions about the problematic aspects of Ezra, which "had remarkably confused ideas about the historical period in which his narrative is set," even if we cannot accept Garbini's far too late, early second century B.C.E. dating of the text.[51] Thus, while the books of Ezra and Nehemiah do not take us into the reform period in a direct literalist manner, they do help us engage the impact of reforms conducted in light of the overtures and groundwork initiated by E, Haggai, and Zechariah, which the books of Nehemiah and Ezra certainly build upon, with the hope of uniting all of Israel under the umbrella of Mosaic law.

Thus, the Covenant Code, which is very old, finds a placement in penta-teuchal narratives of the exodus that owe nothing to Jeroboam's anxious rev-olution but that owe everything to the postexilic will to survive as a community built around law and the proper worship of God. Perhaps E's penchant for 'ĕlōhîm is reflective of the postexilic dis-ease with J's YHWH terminology, a feature that parallels the large so-called Elohistic block of postexilic psalms. That the *Priestly* postexilic materials use YHWH may, therefore, have less to do with chronology than with social location and ideological commitments, wherein the Priestly writers stand closer to the sacred than the more "secular" scribes penning the E emendations. Indeed, the fashion appears to move from 'ĕlōhîm back to YHWH, if the straightforward move, for example, from Psalm 67 to 115 is to be preferred over Beyerlin's attempt to read Psalm 67 as origi-nally a YHWH text.[52] In any case, we must leave open the possibility that the shifting uses of divine names in the Pentateuch is indicative of the postexilic ideological battlegrounds in Judah rather than simply markers in a study of the diachronic development of pentateuchal sources.

To sum up: E, then, would evidence the bold strokes in a theological argu-ment that makes God not only the God of Jerusalem but also a God who encompasses the shrines and peoples of the northern territories, locales that Nehemiah's and Ezra's reforms so desperately wished to embrace as they forged their new consensus in Israelite religion. Admittedly, this is a far cry from Coote's predication that E depends on Jeroboam I's secessionist revolu-tion. Indeed, the Joseph narratives, far from paralleling Jeroboam's experience as Coote maintains, actually stand Jeroboam on his head. In DH we find Jer-oboam returning with the specific and (to the DH) horrifying effect of dis-uniting the populace, just as the pharaoh who did not know Joseph sought to contain and destroy the people. E's story of Joseph, if it can be read against DH, has the effect of saying politically and ideologically that Jeroboam's way cannot be the way of Israel if the people hope to survive. Survival only comes when all are united as brothers of the promise. Is this unity to be provided by the North? Hardly. E's Joseph story and E's other narratives subtly embrace the North through the promises given to the house of David and the people of Judah. It would seem to be the job of E's narratives in the Torah to persuade the community to hold this theological stance toward its history and its future. E's God, therefore, is the God of the survival of both Israel and Judah.

Reading P: An Ordered Commonwealth

P's extensive system of priestly ritual authority is predicated on a surpris-ingly narrow construal of the idea of covenant. P's covenant changes an Abram to Abraham, a Sarai to Sarah, a Jacob to Israel, and even an Elohim to YHWH

(Gen. 17:6–8, 17; 35:9–12; Ex. 6:2–9). The Priestly covenant thoroughly lays claim to the monarchic heritage, for each patriarchal/matriarchal name change involves the pronouncement that kings will emerge as their descendants. Of course, the Priestly project thoroughly circumscribes any royalist agenda with a hedge of priestly controlled ritual. There could be no independent monarch in the priestly commonwealth.

Consistently the character of Moses is turned into the founder, architect, and engine behind the *Priestly* program. While Moses plays "God" to Pharaoh, and Aaron is the prophet (Ex. 7:1), nonetheless Israel obeys *both* Moses and Aaron (Ex. 12:28). There are those who rebel, yet P continues to assert the authority of both. (Ex. 16:2–6, 9–35; cf. Numbers 11). By contrast, the E materials in this segment have only Mosaic (prophetic) authority in view (Ex. 16:4–5; cf. 14:31b = J). The P source goes further—its treatment of the narrative on rebellion accents its ritual program and highlights the Sabbath as solemn rest (Ex. 16:22–27). Later, while it is Moses who sets up the tabernacle (Ex. 40:17–25, 28–29, 33), the famed prophet must also bow to Aaron by vesting Aaron with authority over the ritual apparatus (Lev. 8:7ff.). We also see the clear subordination of the royal-prophetic to the priestly in the final scenes of P, which concern the deaths of Aaron and Moses. Aaron's authority transfers directly to his son Eleazar (Num. 20:25–26). Moses' authority likewise transfers, although not to a son but to an assistant, namely, Joshua (Num. 27:15–23). More importantly, the text emphasizes that this conferral of "royal"-prophetic authority to Joshua was done *in the presence of Eleazar*, who was the one to intercede to YHWH on Joshua's behalf.

P, therefore, represents the assertion of priestly authority in the face of undoubted rival claims concerning the scope and conferral of royal and prophetic powers. Other stories of rebellion drive home the impression that P uses the Mosaic image as its own to assert its claims. Thus, the rebellion after the spies give their report on the prospects of life in the promised land is defined as a rebellion against both Moses and Aaron (Num. 14:1–10). Again, the rebellion concerning the lack of water while in the wilderness is presumed to be against both Moses and Aaron (Num. 20:2–12). Beneath the P narratives runs a clear undercurrent of concern over the dominance of the priestly voice in public life. The narratives are constructed to bolster these claims against the grim opposition of rival claimants.

For its part, the social order the P source conceives is one in which priestly power and ritual is exerted on a permanent basis. The lamb sacrifice of Passover becomes a perpetual ordinance (Exodus 12). The priestly rules are, likewise, a perpetual ordinance to be sustained by the Israelites (Ex. 28:43; 29:28). The exodus faith, in P's thought, is to be realized in a regular process of offerings through all generations (Ex. 29:42–46). This is a social hierarchy that puts central religious authority in the hands of a bloodline priesthood (Ex. 20:25–26). Aaron and sons are to tend the tabernacle's lamp perpetually (Ex. 27:20; cf. Ex. 28:1–5).

In such a scheme, the general populace is envisioned as adopting the attitude of active supporters. All are said to willingly obey, readily bringing their offerings to the construction of this tabernacle project (Ex. 35:20), which one might take to be an obvious reference to the reconstruction and maintenance of the postexilic temple. Both men and women come with offerings (Ex. 35:22–27, 29). P's apparent anxiety over the potential failure to restrict women seems to be indicated by the abundance of reference to the support of women in this project. In fact, the references to women's support outnumber the references to the support given by the men.

This is not to say that there is a lack of reference to males in P. Elsewhere the genealogical material is largely given over to tracing male descent lines (e.g., Gen. 5:3–32), even where daughters might occasionally be mentioned. The only mothers who get real attention in P are Leah and Rachel (Gen. 35:22–26), though even here the ultimate focus is on the male-dominated tribal system. The book of Numbers offers us a full picture. The camps of P's imaginary followers are arranged as bodies of troops, namely, the picked and numbered males of the populace (Numbers 1–2). A spin-off layer of priests emerges, the Levites, a group that is distinct tribally in Israel and functions to support Aaron and his sons (Num. 3:14ff.; 8:18). This nexus of Aaron and sons, Levites, and numbered men all march forward as a unified army under the cloud that is God (Num. 9:15–23). The women, one presumes, have vaporized in P's utopian enthusiasm. YHWH's central tent of meeting is the command center for a priestly-led offensive to wrest the promised land from the grip of the pagan giants. Internal rebellion alone thwarts this endeavor (Numbers 14, 20).

In the Priestly program, it is apparent that woman's true function is procreation. Whether P emerged in the land of exile or after the return—the latter being the more likely view—the offensive at reestablishing the community's foothold in the promised land could not move forward without children. P holds out the promise that Sarah will have a son (Gen. 17:19). In this version Sarah has no role beyond that of reproduction. It is in this version that *Abraham* laughs (17:27), unlike the J story where Sarah laughs and even speaks (18:9–15). P's emphasis on multiplying and filling the earth carries forward this emphasis on the social role of women in P's program (1:27–30; 8:17; 9:1, 7; 48:3–4; Ex. 1:7). In this case, P's creation account in Genesis 1 can hardly be construed as an egalitarian statement regarding the essential equality of male and female. Genesis 1 must be read in light of *all* that P says about women, where cooperation with and subjection to socially dominant males is seen to be integral to P's program and to Israel's survival.[53]

The threat, of course, to P's success comes from the problem of intermarriages. Thus, Esau is paraded as the bad example for his marriages to Canaanite women (Gen. 28:6–9). Such practices force Jacob and Esau to separate (28:6–8). Thus, while the patriarchs buy segments of Hittite land (23:1–20; 49:1a, 30–32; 50:12–13), Rebekah grows weary of Hittite women and fears that Isaac might marry one (27:46).

P, thus, frames its program around a system of authority that requires the active support of both men and women to aggressively preserve the community against detracting forces. Is this a program for life in exile or life after the return? There are arguments in favor of both. There is certainly a keen sense in P that God remembers the people in the land of their suffering (Ex. 1:13–14; 2:23–25; 6:5–7). Precursors of this exodus memory are said to go back to God's remembering of Noah amid the floods and storms (Gen. 8:1; 9:15). Yet it is the simpler details of the narrative, such as the sheer confidence by which Terah seems to move Abram, Lot, and Sarai out of Ur of the Chaldeans that gives one pause to wonder if P is decidedly more than a program for group preservation in exile. Abraham, too, boldly buys land (Gen. 23:1–20). There is confidence in a covenant that will yield land and kings (Gen. 17:5–8). Such a confidence marks P's discussions of the land, as covenant promises and blessings are handed down from patriarch to patriarch (Gen. 28:4; 35:12; 48:3–6; Ex. 6:4, 8). This taking of the land is at the heart of the covenant to Abraham, Isaac, and Jacob. Whereas the passages about rebellion in the wilderness may serve to acknowledge that not all wanted to leave exile, other texts indicate that an entirely different project is afoot among a revitalized priestly contingent, probably already reestablished in Palestine. Presumably, P dates from the time of its successful assertion of control, for the strife between the brothers that is so much the focus of J's version of the Joseph story is nowhere apparent in P. Likewise, Lot and Abram separate without strife (cf. Gen. 13:6, 11, 12). P is taken up with counterrebellions against priestly authority, not with intratribal struggles.

To sum up: This, then, is the narrative setting of the Priestly social legislation discussed earlier in chapter 2. Whatever advances one may postulate regarding the Holiness Code (Leviticus 17–26), the Code nevertheless situates itself roundly amid the social ideals and power arrangements envisioned by the P narrative materials. In these narratives, the priestly commonwealth, driven by a hierarchy sustained by the male household heads, the tribal groups, and the procreative women, emerges as a formidable project, comprehensive in scope and structure. While it is possible that the Holiness Code has been written as a corrective to some of the ideas contained in P, it is nevertheless the case that this Code presupposes the hierarchical apparatus and ritual schema promulgated in the larger body of P texts. We do not find outside of the Code talk of the jubilee year, for example, yet the hierarchical and Priestly social order envisioned throughout the Holiness Code has as its bedrock the P narrative materials strewn throughout Genesis–Numbers. The P narratives and the Holiness Code together establish a comprehensive Priestly program that could hold its own against rival claimants who cloaked their alternative efforts in terms of royal or prophetic ideals. P does not appear to be seeking to embrace these other elements so much as to command them. In the end, P would seem to have been a most successful project, laying claim to all the ancient traditions that preceded by adapting Mosaic, covenantal, temple, royal, and previous Priestly materials for the movement's own designs.

Voices in Competition: Looking at Genesis–Kings as a Total Entity

Can we pull together the foregoing discussion to characterize the various trends operant in Genesis–Kings? As we step back to look at Genesis–Kings as a total amalgam, what does each of the major lines of tradition contribute to the overall tensions at work in the composite work? In characterizing each strand, we encounter one part of the larger dialogue that has been set in motion by the rise and ultimately the collision of these competing voices. By setting the various tradents side by side, we begin to see more plainly the parameters of this debate. In other words, as these trajectories intersect, converge, and diverge, we gain a sense for the underlying values and perspectives that weave together this larger work even as it explodes in a kaleidoscopic array of reconfigurations of those values and root traditions. Theologically we are left with the necessity of listening to each of the voices at work in the composite final work. In part, this necessity is forced on us because the final shape of the tradition insists that each voice has made its own unique contribution. Moreover, we find that in heeding the variety of voices rather than siding with any particular subgrouping, we preserve more than a nuanced understanding of the questions faced in ancient Israelite social thought. We also engage the significant and varied values constructs that proved viable for the renewal of that tradition after the brutalities of war and the experience of harsh dislocation. To not lose this variety is one of the most valuable discoveries we might make of the social legacy of Genesis–Kings (see chapter 13).

What question can the exilic edition of DH have in mind other than the destruction of the kingdom of Judah? While we did not find in DH an earlier edition that goes back with certainty to the time of Josiah, we did discover hints that DH had an initial "Torah instruction" edition that has been merged with a later Priestly "anti-foreign god" layer.[54] Perhaps this Torah-obedience layer undergirded Josiah's reforms, though clearly the exilic edition of DH finds it useful to continue invoking this teaching as the community sought to navigate the turbulent waters of the exile. Certainly some of the accurate historical information of Kings goes back to court chronicles preserved from Josiah's court, if not earlier, but this hardly explains the direction and thrust of the exilic DH. It would seem that the exilic DH has in mind the sort of question that Noth initially identified, namely, why Judah was destroyed and, perhaps, as Wolff argues, how to recover a connection to the God of compassion in the condition of exile.[55] It is likely that the book of Deuteronomy contains a Josianic law code. To be fair, this Deuteronomic Code, which sounds for all the world like an Assyrian vassal treaty, could have emerged anytime during the Assyrian domination of the region, although one might suspect that the Deuteronomic Code, which makes YHWH the sole sovereign, was the text undergirding Josiah's moves versus Assyrian domination. But this is only a suspicion and cannot be proved. In any event, regardless of any supposed Josianic edition of DH, what we see in the exilic DH is a document composed during a time of national reassessment and political crisis. This document has taken earlier court chronicles, legal materials, and theological speculations about the monarchy, creating a major literary work that refocuses the old monarchic vision of power and politics in light of the nation's calamitous fall. We might, therefore, characterize the exilic DH as the document concerning the people of the broken covenant.[56]

The next significant postexilic document would seem to be J. It is hard to see how this source could, in its developed form, go all the way back to the royal court of David and Solomon as so many have postulated. It is true that the childless patriarch motif is quite old in Canaanite literature, but the theme of the return to the promised land from exile seems to dominate the intellectual probings of the J corpus. Moreover, the theme of survival against all odds amid foreigners and wanderings shapes episode after episode in J. Can this be anything other than an exilic issue? Further, the people's vocation in J, to be a blessing to and among the nations, is hardly different in substance from Second Isaiah's proclamation that a rebuilt Israel will be a light to the nations. Again, J's theme would appear to be a postexilic theological concern. The J source, stamped as it is with Mesopotamian myths of origins, appears to be a postexilic attempt to recover traditions of patriarchal promise and the Davidic dynastic claims on the part of a community that still entertains dynastic ambitions of the sort known from the texts of Haggai and Zechariah. No doubt the linkage between Abraham and David is very old, but such a consideration hardly accounts for the usage of this link in the J context, which for all the world looks like an answer to exilic dilemmas of the sort raised by the letter to the community in Babylon attributed to Jeremiah (Jeremiah 29). The exilic context demanded wrestling with the sorts of issues engaged by J. Survival required the unambiguous affirmations made by J. We might characterize J as the document concerning a royal people who are a blessing for all nations.

I have argued elsewhere that the quartet structuring scheme of Saul + David + Solomon + Divided Kingdom arose first by way of DH and that this scheme pressed the editorial contours of the Torah into the Abraham + Isaac + Jacob + Joseph narrative arrangement.[57] Viewed on this scale, Genesis would seem to counterbalance the curse critique developed by the DH. The J material in its initial form (now partially lost) offered the compiler a way beyond curse, specifically through the motif of blessing that actually has its roots in DH's theological mindset, which opened the door to the blessing-curse mode of analysis of Israel's experience of destruction.[58] This is not to say that all of J was composed out of thin air during the postexilic period. Indeed, some of its traditions are clearly of the sort that would have had their home in the monarchy. Yet J is attempting to reassert that very belief system in the face of DH's rather scathing indictment of the nation. In this sense, J itself is recoverable only as a postexilic source that has been mediated through the final shaping of the Genesis-Kings compiler. In other words, some segment of the postexilic community, which wished to reclaim a royalist heritage for its own purposes, found in J an appropriate response to DH that extended the latter's focus in a more positive direction.

The E source we now find wedded to J in the Pentateuch appears to represent an attempt to update J in relation to the sort of resistance to reform encountered by those returning from exile, as reflected elsewhere in the biblical text, namely, in Third Isaiah, Nehemiah, Ezra, and Malachi. In part, E reflects the notion that going into exile can, in the end, be beneficial, provided the community's powerbrokers know how to navigate within the imperial system and learn how to manage the tribal neighbors among whom the exiles and the returnees may find themselves. The patriarchal stories, and the Joseph story in particular with its dreams, go a long way toward reinforcing this message. Certainly this is the same context as Esther, Ruth, and the earliest stages of the Daniel tradition, the latter work which in its more developed form responded much more vigorously to the problem of foreign domination over Israel in the Hellenistic period. E is still at the stage where the wielding of bureaucratic power is a virtue, as the idealized pictures of Nehemiah and Ezra also indicate. But E has met resistance and seeks through the power of persuasive stories to inculcate a fear of God that will undergird a community of law, of the sort found in the Covenant Code in Exodus 20—23. This is not to say that the Covenant Code is postexilic. Indeed, the Code once must have stood alone as an ancient document, as we have already seen (chapter 2). But its current use results from the sort of efforts idealized in Nehemiah and Ezra to cultivate a community that feared God and honored the law. Thus, the broad message of J to the world, the message couched in the form of international blessing, has given way to the message of E, a message that has become bogged down in the difficulties of asserting Jerusalemite authority over the northern territories, however much E tried to embrace the northern shrines, myths, and rituals. Unlike others who see in the northern elements of the E narratives evidence for an ancient northern provenance for E, I maintain that these elements represent late, southern, rhetorical devices for *embracing* the northern territories of Israel. E is, therefore, to be characterized as the document (or redaction) concerning an expansive people who fear God. E fails in its attempt to curry favor with the North but does succeed in paving the way for P.

In this analysis, P stands last in this sequence. The basic elements of the story, from the creation, through the patriarchs, to the stay in Egypt, reception of the law, and the conquest of the land, down to the monarchy and its destruction, were already present. Far from being the organizer of this history, P represents an update, albeit a significant one, of that basic scheme. P emerges at a time when the temple has been reestablished and priestly authority has been seriously reasserted. One might well see the traditional figure of Ezra behind this effort at editing and supplementation. Ezra could not be responsible for the Covenant Code or the Deuteronomic legislation. Yet the tradition is well aware that significant work remained that transpired during his era. P goes a long way toward reclaiming the centrality of the cult in the land. This is clearly an issue that is at work in Leviticus and probably is behind much of the tabernacle mysticism found in the text. The P document (which incorporates JE) is to be characterized as the document concerning the people who cleanse the land. Final authority rests in the hands of the priests. The compilers of P seem to have that authority well in hand. For P, the attempt of the early returnees from exile to reassert royal claims has failed, and counter movements based on prophetic ideals such as in DH have not gained a politically successful following. What remains is for the priestly leadership, under the watchful eye of the Persian authorities and their designates, to ritually cleanse the people and the land. This is hardly the decadent task that Wellhausen left to the priests.[59] Indeed, P's "God of law" appears much more refined and noble than the autocratic figure in J. While, again, canonical criticism might caution us not to choose here, it would seem helpful to take seriously P's social vision, which roots itself in the reasoning power of a God of law who creates the universe by divine decree and who carefully outlines the duties of the community. Of course, sociologically these texts have the effect of sustaining a system of ritual built around ritual specialists—a system that is heavily dependent on education and interpretation. Such is the dilemma when the community moves away from the open shrine system alluded to in J and E, which was not tolerated at all in DH. Yet it would seem that whereas DH's system of forced centralization around the royal temple had effectively cut off the laity from real access to the sacred, P's system restores access to the laity not envisioned by DH. DH offers little for the community to cling to in order to survive beyond the catastrophe apart from hopes in a royal revival; J extends promises of blessing; E offers utopian fantasies for reclaiming the North; whereas P provides the community with a way of restoring its ritual and mythic heritage after the catastrophe.

The stability of P's system ought to create in us a renewed appreciation of P as well as of Chronicles, which was compiled while inhaling the vapors of the stability created by P. Indeed, the environment created by P enabled the Chronicler to discover in Judah's history a God who is more compassionate than the one envisioned by DH. At long last, the message proclaimed by J and Second Isaiah was finally realized in the Chronicler's reassessment of the course of Judah's history (see below). It is the same message urged upon us from a careful study of the final shape of the Psalter. DH cast a dark shadow over Judah's estimate of itself, perhaps defensibly so, in the initial period of the exile. But the renewal carved out by J, E, and P created the space for an entirely different "historical outlook" to appear in Israel via Chronicles, the Psalms, and several postexilic prophetic texts.

What might we conclude about matters of social justice as they emerge in Genesis-Kings? The curious difference in discourse choices between the narrative writers and other parts of the biblical tradition is remarkable. The historical narratives, even Exodus, are not interested in developing the sort of analysis that would have been at home in the legal, prophetic, or wisdom traditions. This is not to say that the historical writers were unfamiliar with the terms for *poor* in their language. To cite but one of several illustrative examples, in Gen. 41:19 the term *dal* is used to describe the emaciated condition of the cows in Pharaoh's dream, a word that elsewhere, in the legal, prophetic, and wisdom traditions, is used to detail the situation of the economically poor and politically oppressed. Yet for the historian, while the word may be useful to describe "thin" cows, the poor as such are not an analytic category worthy of theological reflection. Hence, although such words are known to the narrative writers, they are not used in a manner comparable to the social analysis found in other parts of the Hebrew Bible, in particular, the legal and prophetic materials. This observation raises some difficult questions for the liberation reading of the pentateuchal narratives and DH, even the book of Exodus, which is at least dealing with a clear-cut case of oppression.

We move to a broader set of observations. The penchant for communal and ritual law, while old, plausibly resurfaces in the second temple period as the appropriate bedfellow to the ancestral stories, for, as in the later rabbinic synthesis, story supplies the persuasive category behind a popular acceptance not only of the law codes but also of the authority of the lawmakers and interpreters. The postexilic period took the legends of old that had once sustained the monarchy and transmuted them into stories that would continue to nourish and sustain the authority of the postexilic leaders and provide the community with the ritual apparatus to ensure conformity to the community's long-term needs. In this period, story and law, *aggadah* and *halakhah*, are wed in ways not found elsewhere in the ancient Near East. Hence, Nehemiah and Ezra become the prototypical lawmakers in the chronicalistic mind, surpassed only by Moses. Myth and law blend in a new cultural synthesis.

Prophecy too has finally been subsumed to law. Story has embraced both prophecy and law. Incipiently, and most fully in the later rabbinic age, communal theological authority moves from prophets and (after 70 C.E.) priests to rest fully in the hands of the legal interpreter and the storyteller. This broad trend in the development of Judaism is hardly the deadening of religion, as critics of Wellhausen's scheme frequently observe; to the contrary, the historic processes of the Persian epoch unleashed a new combination of elements that would take the old themes and practices of monarchic Yahwism and reconfigure them to survive in and beyond Babylon to become shaping forces in the new consensus that emerged under the Persian banner of Nehemiah and Ezra. Wellhausen and others in the nineteenth century were wrong to cast the history as a shift from prophetic insight to priestly negligence, for the effective shift to the postexilic consensus was to be most fully effected within the constraints and confines of priestly educational and legal commitments.

Reinventing the Social Question:
1–2 Chronicles as Creative Vision and Radical Rebuttal

History writing is invariably an ideological act. Nowhere is this more clear in the biblical tradition than in a comparison between Chronicles and Samuel–Kings. Of course, at one level Chronicles is a reprise of Samuel–Kings. There is no doubt that the Chronicler had access to a version of Samuel–Kings and altered it to suit the Chronicler's purposes.[60] However, for far too long, Chronicles languished as scholars viewed it as a tendentious work that offered no new insights into the early history of Israel. Yet if we remember Brueggemann's statement that "History in Israel is a very particular linguistic practice which is a vehicle for a specific conversation about social power and social possibility,"[61] Chronicles offers more than a truncated Samuel–Kings; Chronicles represents a creative alternate vision and radical challenge to the views of power and ethics engendered by Samuel–Kings.

By noting what is omitted by Chronicles, we see that a deliberate portrait of the ancient monarchies is under construction. Some might consider the Chronicler's presentation simply to be a sanitized version of the past, since any of the more notorious episodes from David and Solomon's time have been expunged. But is this all the Chronicler is up to? By cutting and pasting, the Chronicler also places the accent on a series of ritually minded, reformist kings—David, Solomon, Asa, Jehoshaphat, Joash, Hezekiah, and Josiah.[62] Even Manasseh, the worst king according to DH, finds a role in terms of repentance and ritual reform (2 Chron. 33)! The idea of the king functioning as ritual specialist, sympathizer, and supporter dominates the Chronicler's landscape.

Perhaps this thrust reflects royalist tendencies, although such a view seems unlikely. If the writing stems from the Persian epoch, which seems probable, then we have a text that is the product of a priestly program that finds comfort and support in a royal house.[63] A subtle clue is perhaps provided by the text's culmination with Cyrus, who closes Chronicles as the final torchbearer of a train that extends from David to Josiah (2 Chron. 36:22). Herein is a powerful statement on the part of the Chronicler about royal politics in YHWH's economy: If the community tends the (rebuilt) temple, then the God of compassion shall rule from Jerusalem. The famous Cyrus cylinder, reflecting Cyrus's propagandistic religious triumphalism, breathes the same atmosphere. I have elsewhere termed 1–2 Chronicles a "historiography of hope," a set of writings that stand in marked contrast to the gloomy review found in the Deuteronomic History.[64] Where DH was obsessed with the transfer of power and with the sordid demise of the monarchy (i.e., on "blessing and curse"), Chronicles' focus is on atonement beyond national guilt.[65] Chronicles sees in Judah the hope for a renewal of God's compassion. Historically this hope for a renewal has its roots in the ancient throne and in a "hope for a future renewal of the throne of David."[66] But as Williamson argues, the Chronicler's program opens out to a much broader future of hope:

> The Chronicler's doctrine of retribution and repentance thus becomes another of his ways of demonstrating the openness of the future. . . . His general policy is to demonstrate from a retelling of the people's history that there is no barrier from that quarter [i.e., from the nation's past] to the hopes for a restoration of one people united under one king around one temple.[67]

If we understand that the Chronicler's program is consistent with the effort at restoring the temple's ritual under Persian auspices, then we have grasped the accent of the record. Nowhere is the hope of national unity more apparent than in the Chronicler's addition of a letter purportedly sent by Hezekiah to those who remained in Samaria after the Assyrian invasion:

> The couriers went out with the letters from the king and his officers through all Israel and Judah, by order of the king, proclaiming, "O you

Israelites! Return to the LORD God of your fathers, Abraham, Isaac, and Israel, and He will return to the remnant of you who escaped from the hand of the kings of Assyria. Do not be like your fathers and brothers who trespassed against the LORD God of their fathers and He turned them into a horror, as you see. Now do not be stiffnecked like your fathers; submit yourselves to the LORD and come to His sanctuary, which He consecrated forever, and serve the LORD your God so that His anger may turn back from you. If you return to the LORD, your brothers and children will be regarded with compassion by their captors, and will return to this land; for the LORD your God is gracious and merciful; He will not turn His face from you if you return to Him."

As the couriers passed from town to town in the land of Ephraim and Manasseh till they reached Zebulun, they were laughed at and mocked. Some of the people of Asher and Manasseh and Zebulun, however, were contrite, and came to Jerusalem. (2 Chron. 30:6–11)

Unlike DH, which treats the invasion as yet another example of divine intervention and retribution, the Chronicler deliberately shifts the focus away from concrete judgment by not describing the invasion itself. In so restructuring the narrative and by the addition of alternative material, the Chronicler places great emphasis on a renewal of God's compassion in light of the people's obedience.[68]

To sum up: In this all-too-brief evaluation of Chronicles, we find another strong social vision cast in the form of a review of Judah's past traditions. Fortunately, we possess the groundwork upon which Chronicles has erected its vision, namely, D. H. Set side by side we can see not only the constructed nature of DH but we also glimpse the purposiveness of the assessment provided by the Chronicler. This review makes it clear that the Chronicler seeks more than simply a rehearsal of the known traditions. Rather, Chronicles stands as a creative alternative to DH's ideas regarding the monarchy, ritual reforms on the part of monarchs, the place of God's compassion in Judah's history, and the hope that can be held out to all the region's inhabitants, both in Samaria as well as Judah. Thus, unlike DH, which rests on the curse, or J, which roots itself in blessing, or E, which cultivates "fear" of God, or P, which seeks a cleansing of the land, the Chronicler sets divine compassion as the lynchpin of its hopeful social vision.

Myth as Social Charter:
The Narrative Mediation of Ancient Israel's Social Ethics

The relation the biblical text has to lived history is hotly debated, but most agree that the effort to connect the two is not without helpful results. Even Dever, who has rightly sought for textual scholars and archaeologists to work separately so as not to confuse these very different analytic projects, more recently has argued that historical methods can engage the biblical texts in an illuminating fashion (see chapter 1). Yet when it comes to specifics, the past century has seen the pendulum swing this way and that with no certainty in sight. The gamut spans from Wellhausen's comprehensive reconstructions of the development of biblical literature, Alt's nomadic sociological reconfigurations, Albright's archaeological positivism, Thompson and Van Seters's historical skepticism, Davies' radical minimalism, and scores of other reconstructions. In one way or another, numerous scholars have tried to place the text in an intelligible historical framework of one sort or another. However, since the question of the Bible's historicity versus its possible mythic and legendary character can pose great difficulties for the contemporary interpreter who wishes to draw on the biblical text as a resource for discussions of social ethics, we must take seriously the problems posed here and seek to develop, at least in a preliminary way, some estimation of precisely how to assess ethics that are mediated to us via the narrative form.

On the one hand, apart from the most radical minimalists, most will agree that Genesis–Kings and other narrative materials contain material that can be correlated with the archaeological and chronistic records of the ancient Near East, with the soundest materials appearing in 1–2 Kings. Clearly some in the exilic and postexilic periods would seem to have had access to annalistic materials from the court of Judah that resemble the types of royal records found in the archives of many Mesopotamian kingdoms.[69] While the latter trace mostly secular events—in particular, acts of war—nevertheless, religious matters can attract the chronicler's attention, as in the notices regarding the lack of Akitu festivals (New Year's) during the reign of Nabonidus.[70] In the more immediate environs, a mid-ninth-century B.C.E. Moabite inscription devoted to King Mesha's act of resistance to Israelite hegemony offers a theological reading of these events, attributing past subjugation to the national god Chemosh's anger, and victory to Chemosh's support.[71] Likewise, the Bible's writers saw in their monarchic annals an essential ground for continuing theological reflection. Here the "past," however inaccurately remembered, provided the language and lessons, both on an individual and national level, that might offer clues as to how the community might rechart its path into the future. The programs of J, E, D, and P are historical programs insofar as the community's efforts are directed toward bringing into their history a successful reconfiguration of the inherited symbol system. This is not a mere replication of the past but a revitalization of the present through a confrontation between lived experience and the diverse "memories" of the culture.

Nonetheless, the consternation of the contemporary interpreter is compounded by the inextricable combination of history, annal, and myth in

Genesis–Kings, with so many narratives framed in terms of classic mythological scenes and structures. The problematic efforts to archaeologically situate the tales of Joshua's conquests within a historical frame have long made apparent the dangers of treating such texts as archival transcripts of actual events.[72] The same can be said for so much of the Genesis–Kings record. Yet this is not an entirely unrewarding determination. Positively speaking, we may say that regardless of how much information of a historical character is present in the biblical narratives, that record is mediated to us via the mode of myth, saga, and legend.[73] By myth, we mean more than the typical comparison of ancient creation and flood stories to the Bible. These are useful linkages, but hardly exhaust the comparative work that is possible.[74] Indeed, restricting our view to such stories can actually leave us in the dark about the nature of much of the biblical narrative. For Genesis–Kings, for example, one would need to consider a broad range of background and comparative materials, such as the following texts and traditions: (1) the *Hittite myth of Appu*, the story of a childless, rich man who is promised a son, and whose sons become rivals; (2) the *Babylonian creation epic*, the story of conflict with the sea goddess, the building of a temple, and the praise of the victorious Marduk, to which one would also compare the Ugaritic tale of Baal's battle with the sea god, Yam; (3) the *Keret epic*, the Ugaritic story of a childless monarch who establishes an heir, suffers illness, and faces rebellion in old age; (4) the *Gilgamesh epic*, especially in its reference to a monarch who loses a devoted companion, faces death, and goes on a journey into foreign lands to gain wisdom; (5) the so-called *Hadad Inscription of Panammu I*, a divine grant of rule to Panammu I, with a conditional throne accorded to his heirs; (6) various *Hittite myths* of the disappearing god; (7) *Lament texts* over the destruction of cities; and (8) the *Erra epic*, the Akkadian story of the devastation wrought by the war god Erra (Nergal) during a time of weakness in which the averting of destruction leads to the restoration of the scattered people of Akkad.[75]

One might already suspect that these texts, among a host of others, display Near Eastern themes and motifs that have obvious parallels in Genesis–Kings. This is not to say that the biblical writers knew these specific stories and "plagiarized" them. Yet it seems clear that such widespread and time-honored lore about the gods and mortals has *somehow* impacted the thought, literature, and hence the social ethics of the biblical narrative materials, much as many of these tales left their imprint on the later Greco-Roman literary traditions. In other words, the Hebrew Bible has filtered its history and its ethics through a mythic screen. Following the ancient Near Eastern texts referenced above, biblical mythic mediation includes childless patriarchs [1]; YHWH's mythic battle to slay Pharaoh and build a shrine [2]; a royal epic concerning King David, who loses his companion Jonathan, faces succession problems, rebellion, and illness in old age [3,4]; a divine charter to David that makes the monarchy conditional on the obedience of his heirs [5]; a God who disappears over time [6];[76] divine punishment of bad kings and the destruction of cities [7]; and a wandering people of exile who are restored to their lands [8]. The so-called historical narratives of the Bible are heavily infused with traditional themes found throughout the ancient Near East.

The presence of what we moderns label myth and legend in the biblical text complicates our evaluation of the texts not only as historical records but also as resources for discussions of contemporary ethics. The mythic mediation also urges us to cautiously situate the ethics of the narratives into specific sociopolitical contexts, which generate such narratives in the first place. If the Near East is any guide, royal and priestly contexts are fundamental for the construction of such narrative traditions. At some level, the biblical narratives must be largely products of intra-elite rivalries with little or no connection to the lived realities of far-flung peasants in the countryside. In other words, the biblical myths and legends do not stand in isolation from the political and religious institutions that generated such texts and that found legitimation in them. Such stories charter and sanction cultural values and social institutions at the deepest levels.[77]

If the scope, nature, thrust, and parameters of much of Genesis–Kings is hardly unique to its world, we must still ask if we find any significant contributions and perspectives, particularly concerning social justice questions, that nevertheless stand out in the biblical narratives. As we move to survey the larger landscape of biblical narrative, do we see sociopolitical tendencies and even solutions that might engage the contemporary reader regardless of whether or not the narratives are labeled either history or myth? A number of points do stand out. The Joseph story's concern for brotherly unity certainly may reflect a Judaean concern for tribal and political unity. The exodus story's emphasis on bricks and enslavement, while not meant as a symbol of a divine "option" for the lowest caste, nevertheless is symbolic of a divine commitment to a politically weaker entity, Israel, which faced Assyrian, Babylonian, and Persian domination during the periods under consideration here (see chapter 4). While the conquest narratives of Joshua and Judges in some ways are no different than the conquest annals of the Assyrian imperialists, the Joshua–Judges texts strike an eternal bond between the people of Israel and the land of Israel. This land is the place where the construction of a community of the covenant takes place, a community of law and justice. Thus, whereas Hammurabi might hand down laws and Sennacherib might conquer territory, it is the people of Israel themselves who become the vehicle for Israel's justice imagination. Certainly, the chronicle of the Israel-Judah rivalry has something of a parallel in the so-called Synchronistic History, which charts the shifting relations of a praiseworthy Assyria and a criminal Babylonia.[78] Likewise, the Jerusalem temple's disheartening destruction has thematic precursors in Sumerian texts regarding the destruction of cities and related communal laments (see chapter 10). Nevertheless, DH's attempt to assess the Israelite and Judaean dynasties in their onward march to collapse reflects a unique assessment of the weakness of monarchy as a viable political institution. Likewise, the narrative's prophetic impatience with monarchy, running from Moses, through Samuel, down to Micaiah, Elijah, Elisha, and Isaiah, gives evidence of a persistent layer in Genesis–Kings that at the very least seeks limitations on the shape and charge of the monarchy. Of course, for the narrators, the questions of the monarchy and temple remain the focus of the discussion.

Even a cursory discussion of how myth and history are fused in our literature enables us to begin to isolate the essential parameters of the historian's ethics, opening up new insights regarding the unique contributions to social thought that are made through the mediation of myth. Without anxiously seeking to extract the historical from the mythical, a futile enterprise in any event, we are apprised of the dominant concerns these texts harbor regarding divine action, law, land, royal power, prophetic critique, and exile, as each of these elements factor into the web of the biblical narrator's estimation of salvation history.[79] While not eschewing source analysis—indeed, we have derived so much from it—we can readily begin to see that excavating the mythic substructures of our sources can open us to a firmer grasp of the issues of power and politics that were key to the various narrators' theological outlooks and agendas. The closer we come to this mode of expression, without seeking to sift the historical wheat from the mythic chaff, the sooner we can more lucidly characterize the ethical perspectives raised and addressed with narrative literature.

To conclude this chapter: A study of the vocabulary for poverty in the narrative literature of the Hebrew Bible starkly reveals that, unlike the rest of the Hebrew Bible, the issue of social justice for the poor hardly appears as a priority agenda item for Israel's narrative tradents as immortalized for us in the pentateuchal sources and the Deuteronomic History. If poverty and injustice are not the focus of these historians, then what is? As we have seen in this chapter, it would seem that theological centerpieces for much of the social ethics of the historical writers are the broader matters of (1) the land, (2) the family and procreation, (3) political power and leadership, (4) national sin, (5) proper worship and priestly authority, and (6) the nation's survival. Whether singularly or in combination, these are the governing analytic categories for social ethics in this vast literature. This is not the rhetoric of the prophets, the wise, or the legal tradition, as we have seen and shall see. Certainly there are strong indications of resistance movements behind the narrative texts, but these are movements from within the landed gentry and other powerholders vying for political space and authority against the encroachments from foreign powers, whether that of Babylon or Persia. In the biblical narrative literature, then, we have discovered unique and competing social visions that provoked debate in the biblical world and propelled the nation well beyond its exilic dislocation into a theologically rich restoration of the commonwealth.

Notes

1. See, e.g., R. N. Whybray, *The Making of the Pentateuch: A Methodological Study* (Sheffield: JSOT Press, 1987).
2. This point is adumbrated most articulately for the Hebrew Bible by B. S. Childs, *Introduction to the Old Testament as Scripture* (Philadelphia: Fortress Press, 1979).
3. See S. Boorer, "The Importance of a Diachronic Approach: The Case of Genesis–Kings," *CBQ* 51 (1989): 195–208.
4. R. Rendtorff, *The Problem with the Process of Transmission in the Pentateuch*, trans. J. J. Scullion, JSOT Supplement Series 89 (Sheffield: JSOT Press, 1990); and Whybray, *Making of the Pentateuch*.
5. M. Noth, *The Deuteronomistic History*, 2d ed., JSOT Supplement Series 15 (Sheffield: JSOT Press, 1992), 134.
6. Contrast W. Brueggemann and H. W. Wolff, *The Vitality of Old Testament Traditions*, 2d ed. (Atlanta: John Knox Press, 1982), chap. 5, where Wolff offers a more positive characterization of the message of the Deuteronomic History. Note that many, following Cross, would argue that there are two redactions to DH, one at the time of Josiah and the other with the exile. For this and other redactional schemes, see S. L. McKenzie, "Deuteronomistic History," *ABD* 2:160–68. See also F. M. Cross, *Canaanite Myth and Hebrew Epic: Essays in the History of the Religion of Israel* (Cambridge, Mass. Harvard University Press, 1973), chap. 10, who argues that the first edition of DH was concerned with the "sin of Jeroboam" and God's commitment to David, themes that Cross terms "the platform of the Josianic reform" (284), whereas the second edition, updated in the exile, interjects notices here and there that "threaten defeat and captivity" (287) while at the same time cultivating an awareness that YHWH will not ultimately forget the people. A comprehensive review of monarchic cultic abuses is not without precedent in the ancient Near East, as attached in the so-called Weidner Chronicle. See B. T. Arnold, "The Weidner Chronicle and the Idea of History in Israel and Mesopotamia," in *Faith, Tradition, and History: Old Testament Historiography in Its Near Eastern Context*, ed. A. R. Millard et al. (Winona Lake: Eisenbrauns, 1994), 129–48.
7. W. Moran, "The ANE Background of the Love of God in Deuteronomy," *CBQ* 24 (1963): 77–87.
8. The twelve are as follows: Othniel (3:7–11), Ehud (3:12–30), Shamgar (3:31), Deborah (4:1–5:31), Gideon (6:1–8:35), Tola (10:1–2), Jair (10:3–5), Jephthah (11:1–12:7), Ibzan (12:8–10), Elon (12:11–12), Abdon (12:13–15), Samson (13:1–16:31).
9. See, e.g., J. W. Flanagan, "Chiefs in Israel," *JSOT* 20 (1981): 47–73, esp. 50; and F. S. Frick, *The Formation of the State in Ancient Israel* (Sheffield: Almond Press, 1985), chap. 3. W. Brueggemann, "Social Criticism and Social Vision in the Deuteronomic Formula of the Judges," in *Die Botschaft und die Boten: Festschrift für Hans Walter Wolff zum 70. Geburtstag*, ed. J. Jeremias and L. Perlitt (Neukirchen–

Vluyn: Neukirchener Verlag, 1981), 101–114, sees in the deliverance stories a creative tension that joins the "deed-consequence" scheme known from Proverbs together with a liberating demand for justice.

10. Aeschylus in *Agamemnon* and Euripides in *Iphigenia in Aulus*.

11. For an alternate view of the latter part of Judges, see W. J. Dumbrell, "'In Those Days There Was No King in Israel; Every Man Did What Was Right in His Own Eyes': The Purpose of the Book of Judges Reconsidered," *JSOT* 25 (1983): 23–33.

12. See J. D. Pleins, "Murderous Fathers, Manipulative Mothers, and Rivalrous Siblings: Rethinking the Architecture of Genesis–Kings," in *Fortunate the Eyes That See: Essays in Honor of David Noel Freedman*, ed. A. B. Beck et al. (Grand Rapids, Wm. B. Eerdmans Publishing Co.), 1231–36.

13. Flanagan, "Chiefs in Israel," offers a reading that is anthropologically illuminating but assumes a historicity and antiquity for these tales that is rather difficult to accept.

14. A. Rofé, "The Vineyard of Naboth: The Origin and Message of the Story," *VT* 38 (1988): 89–103, offers a different approach, arguing that certain linguistic phenomena secure a fifth or fourth century B.C.E. date for the passage in question. In this connection, Rofé contends that 1 Kings 21 represents a later impugning of Jezebel that has transformed an earlier tale, reflected in 2 Kings 9:21–26, in which Ahab is solely to blame for the Naboth affair. For Rofé, the Naboth story of 1 Kings 21 finds its historical counterpart in disputes over land confiscation and intermarriage in the period of Nehemiah.

15. B. Becking, "From Apostasy to Destruction: A Josianic View of the Fall of Samaria (2 Kings 17, 21–23), in *Deuteronomy and Deuteronomic Literature: Festschrift C. H. W. Brekelmans*, ed. M. Vervenne and J. Lust (Louvain: Leuven University Press, 1997), 279–97, charts two stages here, with 2 Kings 17:21–23 serving as the Josianic analysis and 2 Kings 17:7–20 offering a postexilic assessment.

16. T. Ishida, "'The People of the Land' and the Political Crises in Judah," *Annual of the Japanese Biblical Institute* 1 (1975): 23–38, offers a clear and insightful analysis of this phrase.

17. See M. Haran, *Temples and Temple-Service in Ancient Israel: An Inquiry into Biblical Cult Phenomena and the Historical Setting of the Priestly School* (Winona Lake, Ind. Eisenbrauns, 1985), chap. 4.

18. On the links between the biblical presentation of "divine grants" and the ancient Near Eastern practices related to royal grants see M. Weinfeld, "The Covenant of Grant in the Old Testament and in the Ancient Near East," *JAOS* 90 (1970): 184–203. Weinfeld sees ancient Mesopotamian and Hittite roots to biblical expressions in regard to divine grants to Abraham and to David.

19. N. P. Bratsiotis, "*îsh*," *TDOT*, 222–35.

20. Bratsiotis, "*îsh*," 233–34.

21. Ibid., 234.

22. Ibid., 235.

23. See, in particular, T. W. Overholt, *Cultural Anthropology and the Old Testament* (Minneapolis: Fortress Press), chap 2.

24. I. M. Lewis, *Religion in Context: Cults and Charisma* (Cambridge: Cambridge University Press, 1986), 88.

25. Clearly, DH has set these stories in a sharply framed political context. Whether or not these stories were once part of the fabric of Jehu's rebellion, as Todd claims, is far from clear. See J. A. Todd, "The Pre-Deuteronomistic Elijah Cycle," *Elijah and Elisha in Socioliterary Perspective*, ed. R. B. Coote (Atlanta: Scholars Press, 1992), 1–35.

26. Overholt, *Cultural Anthropology*, 48.
27. Contrast B. O. Long, "The Social Setting for Prophetic Miracle Stories," *Semeia* 3 (1975): 46–63, who sees these stories functioning more simply as defenses for prophecy in an era of increased skepticism with regard to that institution.
28. While the parallels are certainly inexact, the Russian Orthodox encounter with the shamanism of the Aleut and Alutiiq peoples of Alaska in the late eighteenth and nineteenth centuries provides cogent examples of the incorporation, integration, and embrace of an ecstatic folk religion, leaving an indelible Orthodox imprint on the village cultures of the region. See S. A. Mousalimas, *The Transition from Shaminism to Russian Orthodoxy in Alaska* (Providence: Berghahn Books, 1995). Needless to say, the shamanism that was swept up into the Orthodox orbit was tempered in ways reminiscent of DH's use and transformation of the prophetic-shamanistic voice for very different sociopolitical ends.
29. Whatever the ideological roots or political aims of DH, the philosophy and theology it develops is strikingly different from that of the prophets, psalms, and wisdom materials. Of course, we can generalize this situation to the rest of the Torah, which also shows a similar lack, leading us to observe that in Hebrew narrative, the "historians" have little regard for poverty as a measure of political importance.
30. P. Trible, *Texts of Terror: Literary-Feminist Readings of Biblical Narratives* (Philadelphia: Fortress Press, 1984), esp. chaps. 3 and 4.
31. Contrast A. Berlin, *Poetics and Interpretation of Biblical Narrative* (Sheffield: Almond Press, 1983), chap. 2, who treats Abigail and Nabal as simply "exaggerated stereotypes." Berlin's other characterizations of female figures in the David narrative would seem to be more on target.
32. S. Ackerman, *Warrior, Dancer, Seductress, Queen: Women in Judges and Biblical Israel* (New York: Doubleday, 1998), 1.
33. See., e.g., L. Wallis, *Sociological Study of the Bible* (Chicago: University of Chicago Press, 1912), 39.
34. G. E. Mendenhall, "The Hebrew Conquest of Canaan," *Biblical Archeology* 17 (1962): 50–76; J. T. Luke, *Pastoralism and Politics in the Mari Period* (Ph.D. diss., University of Michigan, 1965); and N. K. Gottwald, *The Tribes of Yahweh: A Sociology of the Religion of Liberated Israel, 1250–1050 B.C.E.* (Maryknoll, N. Y.: Orbis Books, 1979), 435–63.
35. On nomadism, see references given in chap. 1.
36. A. Alt, *Essays on Old Testament History and Religion*, trans. R. A. Wilson (Garden City, N. Y.: Doubleday, 1967).
37. R. B. Coote and K. W. Whitelam, *The Emergence of Early Israel in Historical Perspective* (Sheffield: Almond Press, 1987), 94–111.
38. G. A. Herion, "The Impact of Modern and Social Science Assumptions on the Reconstruction of Israelite History," *JSOT* 34 (1986): 3–33.
39. D. B. Redford, *A Study of the Biblical Story of Joseph (Genesis 37–50)*, Supplements to Vetus Testamentum 30 (Leiden: E. J. Brill, 1970).
40. T. Thompson, *The History of the Patriarchal Narratives: The Quest for the Historical Abraham*, BZAW 133 (Berlin and New York: Walter de Gruyter, 1974).
41. J. Van Seters, *Abraham in History and Tradition* (New Haven, Conn.: Yale University Press, 1975).
42. K. A. Kitchen, *Ancient Orient and Old Testament* (Downers Grove, Ill.: InterVarsity Press, 1966); idem, *The Bible in Its World: The Bible and Archaeology Today* (Downers Grove, Ill.: InterVarsity Press, 1977); G. E. Mendenhall, "The Nature and Purpose of the Abraham Narrative," in *Ancient Israelite Religion: Essays in Honor of*

Frank Moore Cross, ed. P. D. Miller, P. D. Hanson, and S. D. McBride (Philadelphia: Fortress Press, 1987), 337–356; A. R. Millard, "Methods of Studying the Patriarchal Narratives as Ancient Texts," in *Essay on the Patriarchal Narratives*, ed. A. R. Millard and D. J. Wiseman (Winona Lake, Ind.: Eisenbrauns, 1983), 35–51; M. J. Selman, "Comparative Customs and the Patriarchal Age," in ibid., 91–137.

43. For a full study, see D. J. A. Clines, *The Theme of the Pentateuch* (Sheffield: JSOT Press, 1978).

44. See Brueggemann and Wolff in *Old Testament Traditions*, chap. 4. Fear in E can be found in Gen. 15:1; 20:8; 20:11; 22:12; 28:17; 31:42, 53; 35:5, 17; 50:19–21; Ex. 1:17; 18:21; 20:20. Fear in E occurs under four rubrics: (1) fear of God, (2) fear that there is no fear of God in a place, (3) the fear or dread of Israel that falls on enemy peoples, and (4) fear regarding communal survival.

45. M. Noth, *A History of Pentateuchal Traditions*, trans. B. W. Anderson (Englewood Cliffs, N. J.: Prentice-Hall, 1972), 236.

46. See, e.g., J. C. Exum, "'Mother in Israel': A Familiar Figure Reconsidered," in *Feminist Interpretation of the Bible*, ed. L. M. Russell (Philadelphia: Westminster Press, 1985), 73–85.

47. R. B. Coote, *In Defense of Revolution: The Elohist History* (Minneapolis: Fortress Press, 1991).

48. This point is defended by Wolff in Brueggemann and Wolff, *Old Testament Traditions*, 67–82.

49. For a fuller treatment, see Brueggemann and Wolff, *Old Testament Traditions*, 70–75.

50. Coote notes Nehemiah 5, but does not draw from this the historical conclusions that I see between E and Nehemiah's reforms. See Coote, *In Defense of Revolution*, 123–124.

51. G. Garbini, *History and Ideology in Ancient Israel*, trans. J. Bowden (New York: Crossroad, 1988), 151–58.

52. W. Beyerlin, *Im Licht der Traditionen: Psalm LXVII und CXV, Ein Entwicklungszusammenhang* (Leiden: E. J. Brill, 1992).

53. Cf. P. Trible, *God and the Rhetoric of Sexuality* (Philadelphia: Fortress Press, 1978), chap. 1.

54. S. McKenzie, "The Trouble with Kings: The Composition of the Book of Kings in the Deuteronomistic History," *VTS* 42 (Leiden: E. J. Brill, 1991), surveys the various approaches and argues for stages of redactional development. See also R. D. Nelson, "The Double Redaction of the Deuteronomistic History," JSOT Supplement 18 (Sheffield: JSOT Press, 1981).

55. Brueggemann and Wolff, *Old Testament Traditions*, 83–100. Accurate historical information in Chronicles, for example, concerning Shishak, hardly guides us to the date of the compilation of the Chronicler's work. The positions of Noth and Wolff are not altogether irreconcilable to the extent that Noth may have believed.

56. For J, E, D, and P, this section loosely adapts the kerygmatic approach and messages discussed in Brueggemann and Wolff, *Old Testament Traditions*..

57. Pleins, "Murderous Fathers"; cf. G. Hölscher, *Geschichtsschreibung in Israel* (Lund: C. W. K. Gleerup, 1952), 20–32, as quoted in Brueggemann and Wolff, *Old Testament Traditions*, 42–43. Hölscher was trying to find J's extensions down into the DH material.

58. Thus, unlike R. E. Friedman, *The Hidden Book in the Bible* (San Francisco: HarperSan Francisco, 1998), who roughly views J and DH, or an underlying core, to be a single work that can be extracted from the current Genesis–Kings amalgam, I

would argue that J represents a rather deliberate supplement to DH that works to counter the perspectives of the latter.

59. J. Wellhausen, *Prolegomena to the History of Ancient Israel* (New York: Meridian Library, 1957.)
60. See S. L. McKenzie, *The Chronicler's Use of the Deuteronomistic History*, Harvard Semitic Monographs 33 (Atlanta: Scholars Press, 1985).
61. W. Brueggemann, *Abiding Astonishment: Psalms, Modernity, and the Making of History* (Louisville: Westminster/John Knox Press, 1991), 28.
62. See, e.g., J. D. Newsome, "Toward a New Understanding of the Chronicler and His Purposes," *JBL* 94 (1975): 201–17; and F. L. Moriarty, "The Chronicler's Account of Hezekiah's Reform," *CBQ* 27 (1965): 399–406.
63. H. V. Van Rooy, "Prophet and Society in the Persian Period according to Chronicles," *Second Temple Studies*, vol. 2, *Temple and Community in the Persian Period*, ed. T. C. Eskenazi and K. H. Richards (Sheffield: Sheffield Academic Press, 1994), 163–79, argues by contrast that Chronicles provides prophetic support for the postexilic Levitical hierarchy in its ideological struggle against the apocalypticists.
64. J. D. Pleins, *Psalms: Songs of Tragedy, Hope, and Justice* (Maryknoll, N.Y.: Orbis Books, 1993), 151.
65. See W. Johnstone, "Guilt and Atonement: The Theme of 1 and 2 Chronicles," in *A Word in Season: Essays in Honor of William McKane*, ed. J. D. Martin and P. R. Davies, JSOT Supplement Series 42 (Sheffield: JSOT Press, 1986), 113–38.
66. M. Noth, *The Chronicler's History*, trans. H. G. M. Williamson with an introduction, JSOT Supplement Series 50 (Sheffield: JSOT Press, 1987), 105; cf. H. G. M. Williamson, "Eschatology in Chronicles," *Tyndale Bulletin* 28 (1977): 115–54.
67. H. G. M. Williamson, *1 and 2 Chronicles* (Grand Rapids: Wm. B. Eerdmans Publishing Co., 1982), 33.
68. Cf. H. G. M. Williamson, *Israel in the Books of Chronicles* (Cambridge: Cambridge University Press, 1977), 66–67.
69. The ability to correlate material in 1–2 Kings with Assyrian records, for example, would not be possible were it not the case that genuine and relatively historically accurate Judaean annals serve as the partial ground of DH. See J. K. Kuan, *Neo-Assyrian Historical Inscriptions and Syria-Palestine: Israelite/Judean-Tyrian-Damascene Political and Commercial Relations in the Ninth–Eighth Centuries BCE* (Hong Kong: Alliance Bible Seminary, 1995).
70. A. K. Grayson, *Assyrian and Babylonian Chronicles* (Locust Valley, N.Y.: J. J. Augustin, 1975), 104–7.
71. For text, translation, and extensive analysis, see A. Dearman, *Studies in the Mesha Inscription and Moab* (Atlanta: Scholars Press, 1989).
72. For a useful review, see N. P. Lemche, *Early Israel: Anthropological and Historical Studies on the Israelite Society before the Monarchy* (Leiden: E. J. Brill, 1985), esp. chaps. 1, 2, and 7; also W. G. Dever, "Israel, History of (Archaeology and the Israelite 'Conquest')," *ABD* 3: 545–58.
73. For a succinct but comprehensive review, see R. A. Oden, "Myth and Mythology," *ABD* 4: 946–56; and idem, "Myth in the OT," *ABD* 4: 956–60.
74. Consider B. Batto, *Slaying the Dragon: Mythmaking in the Biblical Tradition* (Louisville, Ky.: Westminster/John Knox Press, 1992).
75. For the Appu myth, see H. A. Hoffner, *Hittite Myths* (Atlanta: Scholars Press, 1990), pp. 63–65; see 14–37 for various myths concerning gods who disappear. For the Hadad Inscription see J. C. L. Gibson, *Textbook of Syrian Semitic Inscriptions*, Vol. 2, *Aramaic Inscriptions including Inscriptions in the Dialect of Zenjirli* (Oxford:

Clarendon Press, 1975), 60–76. For convenient translations of the other texts consult *ANET*.

76. On the theological and philosophic significance of God's progressive absence, see R. E. Friedman, *The Disappearance of God: A Divine Mystery* (Boston: Little, Brown & Co., 1995).

77. This idea has been developed in mythic analysis in particular by B. Malinowski. See, e.g., B. Malinowski, "The Role of Myth in Life," *Psyche* 24 (1926): 29–39.

78. See A. K. Grayson, *Assyrian and Babylonian Chronicles* (Locust Valley, N.Y.: J. J. Augustin, 1975), 51–56, 157–70, who dubs the "Synchronistic History" a clear example of "bias in writing history" (51).

79. Contrast, e.g., R. Bultmann, "The New Testament and Mythology," in *The New Testament and Mythology, and Other Basic Writings*, ed. by S. M. Ogden (Philadelphia: Fortress Press, 1984), whose program of demythologization made the texts palatable for the modern person without taking seriously the embedded character of the values in the thought forms and literary structures of the time. It would seem that the task is not so much to demythologize the Bible as it is to *re*mythologize the interpreter's rationalistic framework.

Chapter 4

Political Deliverance

Exodus

The Exodus Story: Hearing the Slaves' Outcry

Social Liberation: Gutiérrez on Exodus

Toward an Alternative Liberation Reading of Exodus: A Palestinian
Christian Approach

Exodus in Its Historical and Canonical Context: Cosmic Miracles and
Monarchic Rule

In modern contexts of oppression, the ancient story of the God who leads
slaves out of the harshness of oppression toward the promised land has had the
power to capture the political imagination. It was this story that inspired Rev.
Martin Luther King Jr. to assuredly declare,

> Looking back, we see the forces of segregation dying on the
> seashore. . . . Evil in the form of injustice and exploitation shall not
> survive forever. A Red Sea passage in history ultimately brings the
> forces of goodness to victory, and the closing of the same waters marks
> the doom and destruction of the forces of evil.[1]

For liberation theologians one of the key biblical symbols of liberation has
been the exodus story. In Latin America, the exodus story has functioned as a
resource and guide for the church's involvement in the task of human liberation.[2] According to Gustavo Gutiérrez, the exodus story is paradigmatic, calling one to reread the entire Bible and to construct a contemporary theology
from this creative vantage point. Gutiérrez, for example, sees in the exodus the
creative power of YHWH operant in history, bringing about the political liberation of the people: "The liberation of Israel is a political action. It is the
breaking away from a situation of despoliation and misery and the beginning
of the construction of a just and fraternal society."[3]

Others have followed Gutiérrez's lead. The pervasive appeal of the exodus
theme as a ground for liberation action is evidenced by its impact on Christian

discourse in the South African context. Here too the exodus has become a charged political symbol undergirding the quest for political transformation and social justice. For Allan Boesak, YHWH of the exodus is a liberator:

> Nothing is more central to the Old Testament proclamation than the message of liberation . . . In the Old Testament, the Exodus, that liberating deed par excellence, is the object of the confession of Israel.[4]

In the exodus event, Boesak sees "not a myth, but the opening up of history in which God's liberating act was revealed to his people."[5] The transition Boesak makes between this ancient text and the modern day is clear and straightforward:

> Yahweh's liberation is not an isolated happening, a kind of flash-in-the-pan that is here one day and gone the next. It is a movement through history wherein Yahweh has proven himself to be the Liberator.[6]

By this simple hermeneutical move, Boesak seeks to bind the ancient text to contemporary situations of injustice. For those involved in the process of liberation today, the Exodus text has become a locus for examining the justice question, exposing the spiritual parameters of the struggle for release from oppression.

This chapter, then, continues our review of the social visions of the biblical narrative literature. However, given the central nature of the Exodus text in contemporary discussions of the Hebrew Bible's social ethics, this story deserves its own separate discussion. Thus, in this chapter, after a review of the basic story, we will consider the liberation reading of the book of Exodus, especially as construed by the Peruvian theologian Gustavo Gutiérrez and the Palestinian liberation thinker Naim Ateek. While we will glean benefits from the insights of these liberation writers, a sociohistorical reading will raise significant questions concerning the liberation analysis of Exodus, leading to an alternative appropriation of this potent tale in the contemporary justice debate.

The Exodus Story: Hearing the Slaves' Outcry

Setting aside for the moment a consideration of the possible underlying sources to Exodus (J, E, and P), the total tale addresses a wide array of political and social issues. The consistency of the book in this regard led Steffens to depict Moses as a "labor agitator." He even described the account of the conflict between Moses and Pharaoh as one that "follows the course of a typical revolution."[7] While Steffens's comments may be somewhat wide of the mark, there is much in this narrative that captures our political imagination, not merely for the forcefulness with which the book speaks to the condition of enslavement but also the clarity with which the text exposes intransigent political power.

Exodus opens in a political climate that has changed drastically from the end of Genesis. The patriarch Joseph has died, a new pharaoh has risen to power, and the few Israelites who went down to Egypt have become a numerous lot (Ex. 1:1–8). Much as the gods in the Mesopotamian myth of Atrahasis seek to destroy a burgeoning human population through disease, drought, famine, and finally flood, the pharaoh of the book of Exodus actively seeks to curtail the growing Israelite menace, first through increased forced labor and then by killing off the newborn children (1:8–14).[8] The text is careful to accent the oppressiveness of the labor conditions of the Israelites, using verbs such as '*nh*, "to oppress," and *mrr*, "to make bitter," to starkly characterize their plight. If the Atrahasis story-pattern can serve as our guide, however, we have every reason to suspect that the evil plan of Egypt's god-king will be thwarted through the work of a divinely designated deliverer. For like Atrahasis, Moses will preserve the people, though through a different sort of watery passage.

To anticipate this deliverance, the text sets out as heroes the Hebrew midwives. We are specifically told their names, Shiphrah and Puah, unlike the pharaoh who remains nameless (1:15). When they are found to have directly disobeyed Pharaoh's orders, they are brought before him and are called on to explain their actions (1:18). They actively deceive the king by claiming that Hebrew women give birth so fast that the children are born before the midwives arrive for the delivery (1:19).[9] Their success in this confrontation with Pharaoh most certainly foreshadows the course of the rest of the book.[10]

The text's anticipation of a deliverer is reinforced by the folkloric character of the next scene, wherein the Levite mother of Moses hides her newly born son only to have him found by Pharaoh's own daughter, who then raises him in the pharaonic court (chap. 2). Tales of children who are hidden only later to rise to power are numerous in the ancient world. Typically, as in the cases of Sargon of Akkad and Cyrus the Persian, royal overtones and questions of political legitimacy are transparent.[11] Bearing this literary background in mind, we see that the text has rhetorically fitted Moses not only to be a savior of humanity (Israel) against the gods (Pharaoh) but also to be a political deliverer of royal proportions.

The question of legitimacy, so crucial to many hero birth stories, takes a curious twist when Moses murders an Egyptian who was beating up a Hebrew (2:11). The matter of Moses' authority comes straight from the lips of a Hebrew slave: "Who made you chief and ruler over us?" (2:14). Moses, a product of the Egyptian elite, could hardly rely solely on familial or ancestral solidarity with this fellow Hebrew. Consequently, he is forced to flee to a place where he unexpectedly gains the skills and credentials to lead the people to freedom. As soon as he arrives in Midian, Moses plays the role of deliverer, driving the bandit shepherds away from the well, thereby rescuing the woman who would soon become his wife (Ex. 2:16–20). In his exile, which was not unlike ancient Judah's banishment from its land, Moses then marries Zipporah and he names their son Gershom, which is explained as "I have been a stranger in a foreign land" (2:21). In this exile, the God who hears the cries of those who are in bondage appears to Moses, thereby fitting him with the spiritual legitimacy that Moses was lacking in Egypt (3:1–6). By extension, of course, these chapters play a positive role for Judah's own exiles in Babylon who were putting these tales of exile, political legitimacy, spiritual authority, and cultural deliverance into their final form.

Repeatedly the text emphasizes that God has heard the outcry of the slaves who are in bondage (2:23–25; 3:7). The facts of that oppression are detailed in several places in chaps. 1–3, making it clear that "forced labor" (1:11, 14), burdensome "taskmasters" (1:11, 3:7), "bondage" (2:23), their suffering "plight" ('ônî; 3:7), and "misery" ('ônî; 3:17) were the salient features of their oppression. Thus, when the divine appears to Moses (3:1–6), this theophany is to be viewed not simply as a revelation of cosmic mysteries but as the commissioning of Moses to carry out YHWH's work of deliverance from a concrete situation of political and economic degradation (3:7–10). Again, we are familiar with this literary pattern from the Mesopotamian flood stories, wherein the earthly heroes Atrahasis and Utnapishtim receive special announcements that reflect their commissioning for the task of deliverance.[12] The appearance of the god Enki/Ea to the flood hero is as mysterious as that of YHWH to Moses, rhetorically indicating that although Pharaoh may seem to have the upper hand, in point of fact his evil will would be thwarted. This victory, like the situation of oppression, is to involve concrete elements. The text likewise repeatedly emphasizes that (1) the Israelites will make distinctive economic and political gains with the defeat of Pharaoh (3:8, 17), and (2) they will be free to establish a ritual apparatus that will function to offer sacrifices to YHWH (3:12, 18, 21–22). These are realized later in the story and the text consciously links the exodus escape to both the enrichment of the Israelites and their newfound ability to worship God as God desires (see below). In other words, the economic, political, and ritual purposiveness of the exodus event is key to the theology of divine action implied by the total story in Exodus and in its several strands.

From these initial chapters, it is also clear that Pharaoh will not give up without a fight. The first chapter explains Pharaoh's action as both a product of ignorance and fear, ignorance of the good that Joseph has done (1:8) and fear that the Israelites, being so numerous, will join in a coalition against Egypt that would supply a formidable opposition to the empire's hold on the region and the peoples therein (1:9–10). The unavoidable character of this battle between Pharaoh and YHWH supplies much of the drama throughout the next several chapters. Thus, once Moses is supplied with his divine commission (3:13–15 = E), magical powers (4:1–9), and an assistant—namely, Aaron the Levite, who can offer up powerful speeches that clearly proclaim the demands of YHWH for YHWH's people (4:10–17)—the stage is set for Moses to be the one "playing the role of God" (4:16). In part, these powers and abilities God gives Moses are designed to break the chains of pharaonic power (4:21–23), but they are also designed to evoke belief on the part of the Israelites. This "belief" is not merely of a doctrinal sort. Rather, Moses has gained these powers precisely to convince the people that God has indeed "taken note" of their "plight" (4:30). This recognition on the part of the people leads directly to their response in which "they bowed low in homage" (4:31). In other words, their worship comes as a response to the divine initiative on behalf of the people's suffering. Put more simply, the work of politics ought to evoke a spiritual commitment.

As the conflict between YHWH and Pharaoh plays out over the next several chapters of Exodus, many of the themes we have discussed reemerge. Continually Moses and Aaron issue their demands in the form of a call to worship their God (5:1–3). Pharaoh's harsh response clarifies and heightens what we already know about the Israelites' plight. Consequently, the workload and the oppression increase (5:6–18). The battle between Pharaoh and YHWH takes the concrete form of brick making quotas and charges of laziness (5:13, 14, 17–18). Also, a theme that would seem to have been submerged with the Israelites' profession of belief (4:31) reemerges as their situation becomes more and more bitter, namely, the questioning of the authority of Moses by the Israelites (5:20–23). This leads to the recommissioning of Moses (6:2–13 = P), with the difference here that the people fail to acknowledge Moses or his God (6:9). In these ways, themes that were established in the first four chapters continue to emerge, shaping the apparent forward movement of the text even as the situation of the Israelites and then of the Egyptians gets continually worse. This latter fact is driven by yet another theme hinted at in the first four chapters, namely, that YHWH is out to demonstrate a "greater power" than that of Pharaoh (3:19; cf. 6:1; 7:3–5).

This demonstration of power initially takes the form of magic. Moses, acting in the "role of God to Pharaoh" (7:1), to pick up on yet another theme of the first four chapters (cf. 4:16), performs God's wonders before pharaonic court magicians who imitate his every move (7:8–13). Thus, even though Aaron's rod-turned-snake swallows those of the courtiers, Pharaoh acts as predicted, his "heart stiffened and he did not heed them" (7:12–13; cf. 3:19–20; 4:21–23). The theme of magic is carried forward in the stories of the first two plagues, water to blood (7:14–24) and frogs (7:25–8:11 [8:1–15]). In this way, the text rhetorically outlines the character of the conflict between God and Pharaoh. The conflict is over who commands the forces of nature. At some level Pharaoh does have power, otherwise there would be no explanation for the political and economic force that he wields. Yet his hold is based on low-level powers over nature and is rooted in sheer stubbornness.

However, as the next plagues emerge, namely, lice and insects (8:12–20 [8:16–24]), it is also clear that Pharaoh's powers are no match for the hand of YHWH, regardless of how stubborn Pharaoh might be. These plagues work to affirm that God takes sides against the tyrant, favoring God's own people (8:19 [23]). Thus, the text portrays God's struggle with Pharaoh not simply as God's defense of God's own name or honor, but as an integral response to God's witnessing of the suffering of God's own people. In other words, God is not acting merely to show God's superior power, but to free God's people, hence the repeated demand from Moses: "Thus says the LORD: Let My people go that they may worship Me" (8:16 [20]; cf. 7:16; 7:26 [8:1]).

At this point, the plague sequence would seem to have left behind the justice and oppression question, favoring almost exclusively the demand to free the people for the worship of YHWH. The matter of worship is the focus of Pharaoh's ineffective attempts at forging a cheap compromise, as if the matter were merely religious in scope (8:21–25 [8:25–29]; 9:27–28; 10:8–11, 16–17, 24–29). Yet we can see that at each step, YHWH's distinction between the Egyptians and the Israelites has the very concrete result of protecting the property, possessions, and personhood of the Israelites. Thus, the plague on all sorts of livestock occurs such that the property of the Israelites is unharmed (9:1–7). The Egyptians and their animals alone suffer the plague of boils, making us aware that the sufferings of the Israelites initially detailed in Exodus have been displaced onto the Egyptians (9:8–12). This distinction between the persons and the property of the Egyptians and the Israelites continues in the plague of hail, which kills off all persons and animals of the Egyptians who were out-of-doors but falls nowhere in the region inhabited by the Israelites (9:13–26). The Israelites are depicted as having been ghettoized in Goshen by the Egyptians, but now that the tables have turned, the locale in which the Israelites were once victimized has become a safe haven from God's acts of power against Egypt. Thus, as the Egyptian landscape is furthered damaged by the plague of locusts (10:1–20) and the land is enshrouded in darkness (10:21–23), we see that YHWH's demonstration of power has political and property implications for Pharaoh and the Egyptians. The oppressor has been made quite literally to be oppressed amid all his possessions. We are not surprised, then, to find that the narrative has let the final "property" matter, the death of the firstborn (11:1–10; 12:29–32), blend quite naturally with the concrete freeing of the Israelites to enjoy the taking of the possessions of the Egyptians (11:2–3; 12:33–36). Whereas Pharaoh wished to narrow the conflict to worship rights and privileges, the God of Israel linked the freedom to worship with the freedom to be a people with adequate material goods.

With these developments, the story of the final defeat of Pharaoh at the sea and the escape of the Israelites might seem rather anticlimactic (chaps. 14—15). Yet the text is quite consciously working to resolve the oppression issue, putting onto the lips of Pharaoh these words of political and economic regret: "What is this we have done, releasing Israel from our service?" (14:5). Though the theme of the Israelites' opposition to Moses reemerges here, their questions have the rhetorical effect of sharpening the purposiveness of YHWH's deeds in relation to people of Israel. In asking, "What have you done to us, taking us out of Egypt?" (14:11), the people's questioning highlights the fact that God's display of power is more than show, it marks the toppling of the one power that would thwart Israel's emergence as a viable political, economic, and ritual community. Indeed, as long as Pharaoh is in power, it would seem that the people would be tempted to find nourishment in him rather than in the God who defeats such Pharaohs at the sea and supplies food and drink for those in need (14:15–17:7).

But the God of the exodus wishes to do more than provide temporary relief for God's people. To truly realize the exodus trajectory, the text points toward the ultimate purpose of such a freeing: The community must find a way to structure itself ritually and legally so that an enduring community might function in the wilderness and beyond. Thus, the narrative places Moses back with his father-in-law Jethro, in that situation of "exile," although this time with the recognition that God has performed a liberating action, a deed reflected in the name of the second son of Moses and Zipporah, Eliezer, whose name is explained as, "The God of my father was my help, and He delivered me from the sword of Pharaoh" (18:4). In that wilderness place, Moses learns to construct a system of governance (18:13–27), obtains the laws necessary to govern a complex community (chaps. 19–23), and learns the procedures required for worshiping the exodus God (chaps. 24–31; 34–40). These latter chapters of Exodus are the full realization of Israel's release from Egyptian service. The Israelites themselves are to be put to the service of God's community as shaped by God's laws. Their property is to be put to the service of God's sanctuary as defined by God's directives (25:1–8).

That this service must be performed with care and vigilance is indicated by the incident with the golden calf. There Aaron and the crowd present the golden calf as being the exodus God (32:4). In other words, the text no longer has to distinguish between Egypt and Israel but between Israelite and Israelite. Chapters 32—34 wrestle with the reality that some are with the program and some are not. Ought these Israelites who are faithless to be destroyed or are they to be tolerated? Does their presence jeopardize the success of the entire enterprise? This book, so full of promise for the future of the Israelites who had been freed from the clutches of the Egyptians, takes up the rather sobering issue of internal resistance to the cause of God. The exodus will lead to real material gains. The people will have their "land flowing with milk and honey" (33:3) but the promise of settling in that land runs the risk of being thwarted by the very people whom God has freed from captivity. The links with the challenges and concerns of those who sought to reconstruct Israel after the Babylonian exile are rather transparent (see chapter 5). Escaping Egypt (or Babylon) is only the first step toward building a new and just society. The program could not be fully realized until the leadership and the people as a whole committed themselves wholeheartedly to the cause of the "impassioned God" (34:14).

Social Liberation: Gutiérrez on Exodus

Since most would agree that Gutiérrez is one of the leading speakers for the liberation theology movement, I would like to follow more carefully his arguments with a view toward a renewed understanding of the place of the historical within discussions of biblical social ethics. In particular, we must critically assess Gutiérrez's theological method and emphases, his approach to the biblical text, his findings on social justice in relation to the story of Exodus, and his elaborations with respect to prophetic social criticism.[13]

Gutiérrez operates within a consciously Christian framework. And yet his theological analysis does not begin with a survey of traditional Christian doctrine. Neither is he content with previous theological discussions regarding the "social problem."[14] The intent of his theology of liberation is to restructure the theological task within a nontraditional framework, especially by adopting the vantage point of modern social-scientific analysis. The liberationist approach to the study of the biblical text stands at the crosscurrents of two different streams. Gutiérrez's endeavors combine the surge of interest in social justice matters in the Latin American context with the burgeoning efforts to apply analyses derived from the social sciences to the study of the biblical text. Though there is a recognizable change in analytic methods and emphases (such as in the reliance on Marxist economic theory and the emphasis on total revolutionary social transformation), the approach taken by liberation theologians bears close affinities to the other positions examined in chapter 1 in that they share a desire to read the social justice materials in the Bible within a sociohistorical framework. This formulation of analytic categories together with a distinct emphasis on the poor, (i.e., doing theology "from the underside") constitutes what Frostin has described as the "episte-mological 'break' in third world theologies."[15]

From the outset it is clear that Gutiérrez's theology of liberation is con-structed in response to the concrete circumstances of Latin American life. As he says in his introduction to *A Theology of Liberation*: "This book is an attempt at reflection, based on the Gospel and the experiences of men and women committed to the process of liberation in the oppressed and exploited land of Latin America."[16] Critical awareness of the political situation in Latin Amer-ica is foundational to Gutiérrez's theological analysis. For Gutiérrez, "human action" is "the point of departure of all reflection."[17] Gutiérrez is attempting to build a theology that will reflect on the historical praxis of people in Latin America, a theology that serves to aid the process of revolutionary social trans-formation in that region.[18]

An interest in the process of liberation profoundly shapes the manner in which Gutiérrez interprets the biblical text. Liberation for modern people, says Gutiérrez, is a "process of transformation" designed to "satisfy the most fundamental human aspirations—liberty, dignity, the possibility of personal fulfillment for all."[19] It is a movement that seeks to attack the basic problems of society, "and among them the deepest is economic, social, political and cul-tural dependence of some countries upon others . . . of some social classes over others."[20] The process of liberation is analyzed by Gutiérrez within definite social categories and affords a contrast to the spiritualized solutions proffered by traditional theology. For Gutiérrez, only a radical break from the status quo, that is, a profound transformation of the private property system, access to power of the exploited class, and a social revolution that breaks this depend-ence, can create the conditions for the development of a new society, a social-ist society.[21]

For Gutiérrez, when liberation is conceived in concrete social and political terms, the social dimension becomes an essential component of theological reflection. Social liberation comes about in relation to the oppressive struc-tures that human sin creates. To Gutiérrez, both sin and liberation are best understood in social as opposed to personal terms, even if there is "a personal or collective will responsible" for oppressive structures.[22] As Gutiérrez observes, "An unjust situation does not happen by chance; it is not something branded by a fatal destiny: there is human responsibility behind it."[23] Gutiér-rez claims this perspective is shared by the Hebrew prophets.[24] Since the social order is out of balance because of human sin, it is the task of theology to be concerned with the social dimension of human sin in seeking to transform this world. The story of Exodus presupposes oppressive conditions that have been brought about by corrupt political tyranny.

Gutiérrez's emphasis on the concept of liberation is reflected in how he approaches the biblical materials, especially with regard to the theme of social justice. Gutiérrez finds a number of events that reveal the God of the Bible to be one who works for liberation in the midst of the concrete processes of history. To be sure, as a Catholic theologian, Gutiérrez understands the measure of this history to be Christ. Thus, he conceives of history as a "Christo-finalized" process, which is to say that what "underlies all human existence" is "the salvific action of God," particularly as seen in Christ.[25] However, this process finds its roots and definition in the key moments of the Hebrew scriptures: (1) the act of creation, (2) the exodus experience, and (3) the prophetic understanding of the future. All of these events are taken by Gutiérrez to be important paradigmatic examples of the liberation theme in the Hebrew scriptures.

Gutiérrez contends that the act of creation is the first step in the process of salvation or, as he would term it, liberation. He claims that

> the Bible does not deal with creation in order to satisfy philosophic concerns regarding the origin of the world. Its point of view is quite another. Biblical faith is, above all, faith in a God who reveals himself through historical events, a God who saves in history.[26]

The God who creates the world order continues to shape this order through acts designed to bring about human freedom and liberation. Gutiérrez contends that we must not neglect the understanding of God that is to be derived from a biblical theology of creation that intimately connects the divine will to divine action in history.

For Gutiérrez, the pivotal event in the liberation process for the Israelite writers was the exodus from Egypt.[27] The exodus event reveals God to be concerned with the oppressive political plight of the people of Israel. Elsewhere in the Bible, Egypt is likened to the mythical creature Rahab, whom YHWH has to overcome in order to bring cosmos out of chaos (Isa. 51:9–10; 30:7; Ps. 87:4).[28] Yet Gutiérrez maintains that while mythic language may be used to describe YHWH's creative and liberating acts, YHWH's actions take place within the concrete framework of human history, in this case the slave barracks of Egypt. The creative power of YHWH operates in history to bring about the political liberation of the people.

Extending his understanding of Exodus to the continued work of concrete political action, Gutiérrez finds the prophetic materials of the Bible to be fundamental to understanding the biblical view of future liberation. The prophetic eschatology is oriented to a future that is bound up with a concern for present historical realities.[29] The prophetic vision of YHWH's "kingdom of peace" is for Gutiérrez an outgrowth of the "establishment of justice."[30]

However, Gutiérrez does distance himself from a thoroughly "realized eschatology" when he writes,

> We refer to the prophets' concern for the present, for the historical vicissitudes which they witness. Because of this concern the object of their hope is very proximate. But this "closeness" does not exclude an action of YHWH at the end of history.[31]

Nevertheless, for Gutiérrez the prophets herald a new act of YHWH in history through which a just order will be established. This new order is not simply an outgrowth of the old oppressive political order, rather, it represents a definitive "break with the past."[32] And herein lies the link between the God of the exodus and the God of the prophets. In both cases, YHWH is characterized as one who removes the existing ruling structures in order to establish a more just political and economic system.[33] The exodus experience offers a profound cultural memory, which gives credence to the prophetic hope that a new social order will be instituted.

Gutiérrez is not only concerned to define what constitutes the parameters of liberation, he is also concerned to determine who are the agents of liberation. Here his direction is again supplied by a consideration of the secular process of liberation. Gutiérrez contends that "the social praxis of contemporary man has begun to reach maturity. It is the behavior of man ever more conscious of being an active subject of history."[34] The key to the process of transforming the world order is not simply that oppressed peoples aspire to be liberated, but that they are in fact entering the stage of history and taking their own destinies in hand.[35] Gutiérrez writes that "in order for this liberation to be authentic and complete, it has to be undertaken by the oppressed people themselves."[36] The agent of liberation in Latin America is the Latin American who "is taking hold of the reins of his historical initiative and perceiving himself as master of his own destiny."[37] And for Gutiérrez, this refers in particular to the poor peasants who seek liberation.

When applied to the biblical record, Gutiérrez's notion of agency takes on a curious twist. On the face of it, the biblical narrative of the exodus would seem to speak for YHWH as the sole agent of liberation. In the tradition, it is YHWH who is acclaimed as the God who brought Israel out of enslavement in Egypt (cf., e.g., Ex. 20:1). However, for Gutiérrez, an event such as the exodus is not simply a bare act of God, but it involves elements in which the people are at work shaping their own destiny: "the Exodus is the long march towards the promised land in which Israel can establish a society free from misery and alienation."[38] By emphasizing the human element in the exodus story, Gutiérrez can claim that the exodus experience represents the "'desacralization' of social praxis which from that time on will be the work of man. By working, transforming the world, breaking out of servitude, building a just society, and assuming his destiny in history, man forges himself."[39] Hence, in Gutiérrez's view the Exodus material reflects human political activity intended to undermine a contemporary social system in order to erect more just social arrangements.

Of course, the validity of Gutiérrez's analysis regarding human agency in the story of Exodus can be questioned. He derives a view that affirms human acts of political revolution from a text that depicts liberation as an act of YHWH. The biblical record even emphasizes that the participants in the exodus group were notable for their continued complaints, disobedience, and desire to return to Egypt. This is hardly what one might term a "people's revolution." To be sure, the resistance of the midwives and the continued confrontations between Moses and Pharaoh appear integral to the movement of the overall book. Yet it would seem that Gutiérrez has read perspectives supplied by modern revolutionary struggles back into the biblical text, imposing notions of popular resistance on a text that only knows of a "God who acts."[40]

However, there is another aspect of Gutiérrez's thinking that is crucial for developing an understanding of his approach to the exodus story and other biblical materials, namely, his belief that the process of liberation involves conflict on many different levels. In the first place, Gutiérrez maintains that the "political arena is necessarily conflictual."[41] The process of "building . . . a just society means the confrontation—in which different kinds of violence are present—between groups with different interests and opinions."[42] Conflict and confrontation are treated as the driving forces of the liberation of the human community.

First and foremost, Gutiérrez conceives the struggle for liberation to be a political struggle. It is a struggle that seeks the establishment of new social and economic arrangements that obviate private ownership of capital in favor of "the social ownership of the means of production."[43] In Gutiérrez's terms, "the Latin American peoples will not emerge from their present status except by means of a profound transformation, a social revolution, which will radically and qualitatively change the conditions in which they now live."[44] Closely bound to this political struggle is "a confrontation between social classes."[45] Gutiérrez conceives of the social order as being divided into social classes and structures, which tends toward the oppression of the populace to the benefit of the elite sectors of society.[46] In Gutiérrez's words, "the class struggle is a fact, and neutrality in this matter is impossible."[47] The conflict between these groups, the struggle for liberation, means a struggle for release "from oppressive structures which hinder man from living with dignity and assuming his own destiny."[48] The very nature of the divisions in society bring "confrontations, struggles, violence."[49] On this score, the exodus story speaks volumes regarding the violence and political intransigence that attends most attempts to restructure oppressive social orders, what Brueggemann terms the "royal consciousness."[50]

Yet another important source of conflict is found on the religious and ideological level. Gutiérrez recognizes a radical division in the religious communities of Latin America between those who use religious values to maintain the repressive political order and those who develop their values through engagement in the revolutionary struggle, a split reflected in the book of Exodus in the conflict between the gods of Egypt and Israel's God. In other words, with regard to social conflicts, the God of the Bible is on the side of the poor. As a general principle, Gutiérrez observes that "to love Yahweh is to do justice to the poor and oppressed."[51] And this justice reaches into the concrete structures of society, molding them into an order in which the rights of the poor are defended.[52] The critique leveled by the prophets against members of their society is twofold, according to Gutiérrez. In the first place, the prophets raised the concern that just relationships be established in society, especially that the disenfranchised members of society find protection from oppression.[53] Secondly, the prophets leveled their criticism against the forms of religious expression that held sway in their society, namely, "purely external worship."[54] But prophetic religious criticism is not treated by Gutiérrez as separable from the prophetic concern for just social relationships; rather, concern for a just society flows from a concern for appropriate religious values. The prophets understood that true worship of YHWH will not rely on formal structures and ritual but will give expression to YHWH's concern for the poor and oppressed.[55] The prophetic critique of external worship is but one aspect of the general prophetic critique of the social apparatus, a critique grounded in particular religious beliefs and commitments.

Toward an Alternative Liberation Reading of Exodus: A Palestinian Christian Approach

When Argentinean liberation theologian José Severino Croatto links the exodus as liberation paradigm to the promise to Abraham and the "existence of Israel as a people on its land," he actually brings together those matters that complicate a Palestinian appropriation of the text as a liberation document.[56] The Palestinian case highlights the major hermeneutical problems that the exodus as a political liberation construct must squarely face if one wishes to build a truly liberating theological methodology that avoids the pitfalls of the oversimplification of the use of scripture in the contemporary context.

What for Latin Americans and South Africans is an easy leap from ancient texts to modern situations of oppression is impossible in the Palestinian context, where biblical traditions and categories heavily infuse the political vocabulary of the oppressor.[57] Confronting this "political abuse" of the Bible, Palestinian Christian theologian Naim Ateek sharply defines the Palestinian theological problematic: "How can the Old Testament be the Word of God in light of the Palestinian Christians' experience with its use to support Zionism?"[58] How is one to work theologically with the Bible in such a context? Of particular difficulty to Palestinians are the biblical accounts of the conquest of the peoples of Canaan.[59] While no liberation theologian has ever treated the Joshua conquest narratives as significant to the grounding of liberation theology (preferring instead the Exodus text), a few reactionary voices in Israel have invoked these passages to justify the expulsion of Palestinians.[60] In this climate, Ateek argues, Palestinian Christians require a liberation hermeneutic that will directly tackle biblical texts stamped by conquest and domination. Ateek is convinced that if Palestinians hope to continue to take the biblical texts seriously, they must not simply take refuge in "allegorizing" or "spiritualizing" them.[61] Ateek's method involves both a modern and ancient component: The Palestinian liberation hermeneutic must not overlook those modern uses of the text that bring about exploitation and domination. Moreover, this hermeneutic must confront the liberating and oppressive tendencies inherent in the text itself for its own historic moment.

Ateek's proposed hermeneutic takes seriously the notion that a human understanding of the transcendent has undergone a number of developments. He sees the biblical text marked by remnants of both "primitive" and more "mature" ways of thinking. Fortunately, Ateek's analysis does not fall into the trap of positing a simple evolutionary scheme of historical development, as if Israel's religion progressed from more simple to more complex (or more ethical) notions. He suggests that both exclusive/nationalist and inclusive/universalist trajectories infuse the biblical text:

> The Bible is a record of the dynamic, sometimes severe, tension between nationalist and universalist conceptions of the deity. For Palestinian Christians, this theme is one of the most fundamental theological issues.[62]

Even Second Isaiah, who is credited with great insight into the "universal and inclusive nature of God," could also speak in a rather nationalistic mode.[63] A contemporary use of the Bible must grapple with both of these trajectories at work in the various streams of the biblical tradition.[64] Ateek argues that there is an increasing interest in universalism among the biblical writers that has the effect of subverting the more exclusivist tendencies of the biblical tradition.[65]

For Ateek, this universalist trajectory is the opening toward a constructive Palestinian Christian engagement with the Hebrew Bible. However, since the biblical tradition is also marked by nationalistic or even militaristic tendencies,

Palestinian Christians are forced to treat these texts with a great deal of caution, especially when using them in relation to their context of theological reflection.[66] One is reminded of Elisabeth Schüssler Fiorenza's "feminist critical hermeneutics of suspicion," which "places a warning label on all biblical texts: *Caution! Could be dangerous to your health and survival.*"[67] Ateek's critical approach to the text, likewise, finds a counterpart in the work of the South African writer I. J. Mosala, who suggests that since the biblical text has been used "to justify the colonial dispossession of blacks by whites," this ought to tell us "that not all the Bible is on the side of human rights or of oppressed and exploited people."[68] For Mosala, a critical appropriation of the biblical text demands that the interpreter remain cognizant of the fact that the "finished textual products are . . . still cast in hegemonic codes."[69] Again, the oppressive tendencies of the text for its own historical moment constitute the fodder for a probing modern theological and liberation analysis.

Bearing in mind Mosala's critical caveat, liberation interpretations of the text should avoid swiftly moving from an apparently liberating story in Exodus to modern contexts of oppression, at least without a prior critical evaluation of the oppressive codes inherent within the biblical text itself. This evaluation would look at the text as a production of social and political conditions demarcated by oppression. Fiorenza, Mosala, and Ateek are directing us toward a much more sophisticated hermeneutical approach to the biblical text than sometimes occurs in liberation circles, where the biblical texts (the prophets and the exodus story in particular) are automatically seen as liberating.

To sum up: For Ateek, a critical hermeneutics of biblical nationalism/universalism is the necessary counterpoint to modern-day nationalistic uses and abuses of the biblical tradition. The Palestinian case, as well as Mosala's critique and Fiorenza's cautionary statements, makes it quite clear that liberation critics must reexamine the relative ease by which they often move from exodus and promised land to present-day political realities.[70] A more decisive hermeneutic is warranted: If the Hebrew Bible is infused with a primitive, developing, or stridently nationalistic view of God, then one needs to be cautious about using the exodus, conquest, or even prophetic texts when addressing modern sociopolitical situations. The "liberating" agenda we moderns hope to find in the text may actually cause us to overlook its unliberating aspects.

Exodus in Its Historical and Canonical Context: Cosmic Miracles and Monarchic Rule

In the ancient context, the exodus story bears a striking resemblance to the cosmic battle myths known especially from the Babylonian and Canaanite traditions.[71] The most elaborate of these is the Babylonian creation epic, a text that lauds the triumph of Babylon's Marduk over the sea goddess Tiamat and her minions. Marduk's victory also leads to his creation of the Babylonian temple complex and the fashioning of humans out of the blood of Qingu, Tiamat's fallen commander.[72] The myth's royal connections were highlighted by the reading of the epic during the Babylonian New Year festival in the month of Nisan.[73] The biblical rendition witnesses the Israelite national god's victory over Pharaoh at the sea, which gives way to the building of the wilderness tent shrine and the creation of a covenant people.

The mythic origins and the obvious royal associations of the battle myth complicate a modern liberation appropriation of the story of Exodus. On the one hand, one might simply argue that the text was functionally equivalent for the Israelites. In other words, the combat myth of YHWH propped up the monarchy in much the same way that the Marduk/Aššur myth ran tandem to the Mesopotamian political apparatus. On the other hand, the specifically Israelite claim to the potency of their particular national god ran counter to the claims of the Mesopotamians. In imitating the combat myth of the Mesopotamians, the ancient Israelites also distanced themselves from the imperial powers, staking out their own theological claim. This was dangerous for a tiny nation to do in opposition to the major powers, but whether we would call this "liberation" is problematic, unless we define that liberation in terms of a decolonizing process. As we begin to read the exodus story sociohistorically, we will find ourselves asking if the final canonical version of the text or any of its constituent parts (the J, E, or P traditions) are "liberating." Certainly our discussion earlier in this chapter ought to make it clear that we should not expect these texts to be *automatically* so. Several considerations emerge here.

On the level of vocabulary, the Exodus narratives never use the terms for "poor" common throughout the writings of the law, prophets, or wisdom. This is a curious situation that deserves some explanation, particularly in light of Ateek's and Mosala's reservations about the Exodus text. However concrete the suffering of the slaves in Egypt may have been, the author(s) of the Exodus narratives are not entertaining the sort of social justice discussion that we find in the other parts of the Hebrew Bible. The specific and alternate word used, 'ônî, if it has any currency, is limited to Genesis, Exodus, Job, Psalms, and Lamentations. Quite commonly, the situation of the 'ônî is suffering that can be observed, in particular, that which gains the attention of God. The suffering in Egypt was just such a situation that required divine action from above to bring an end to the people's affliction. The political dimension is couched in terms of the miraculous. There is a nationalist focus, to be sure, but of the sort found in the Second and Third Isaiah materials, where political liberation transforms the language of oppression, and where divine action through a higher power, namely, Cyrus the Persian, is the paramount mechanism behind national renewal.

If the writers of Exodus self-selected an alternate vocabulary, could this not be symptomatic of an ideological agenda that runs counter to other parts of the Hebrew Bible? In the narrative materials, Israel's "liberation" is secured so that Israel might gain the land, worship its God, and rule itself if no favorable pharaoh will aid in their quest for survival. The text of Exodus offers a nationalist, monarchic, hierarchical agenda. The triumph over Pharaoh, who is emblematic of any number of possible conquering nations that strode regularly through Canaan, represents the monarchic political aspirations of the ancient Judaean dynasts as readapted into the political programs of J, E, and P. There is a kind of liberation here, but not the sort that is usually envisioned in liberation theology treatments of Exodus.

That the text is compatible with monarchic ambitions and hierarchical tendencies should be seen from its context, wherein the Israelite's situation of suffering is engendered by the pharaoh who did not know Joseph. A critical reading of the Joseph story (as discussed in chapter 3) shows us that there were writers in Israel, undoubtedly remnants of the royal court, who nurtured the virtues of administrative advancement, aristocratic power, and royal privilege. The Joseph-Exodus complex by its very nature represents a domestic program of national liberation, but it is a program that also ensures the continued rule of a tribal, monarchic, or sacerdotal elite that has literally justified its theological existence via the Exodus narrative. To blithely use this material for the purposes of the liberation of the poor today might actually frustrate the ideological tendencies of the text, placing liberation thinking in theologically shallow waters. That DH could, likewise, root itself in this narrative tradition, with both Moses and Josiah as heroes, ought to make us pause and reassess the royalist and even imperialist dimensions of this "liberation" narrative.

Such are the considerations that emerge at the macrolevel when we discuss the final form of the Exodus text. Yet there is the possibility that the component parts of the text—namely, the J, E, P traditions, and the Deuteronomic version of Deuteronomy, might evidence varying degrees of concrete "liberation." E and P are particularly interested in the people's material situation of suffering in Egypt under the pharaoh (1:8–12 = E; 1:13–14 = P). J, and to a much lesser extent P, focuses on the interaction and negotiations between Moses and Pharaoh.

Yet at the level of source analysis, there are also divergent political perspectives of the exodus displayed by these sources. E's interest in law, as evidenced in the Covenant Code, is connected with E's concrete awareness of the suffering of the ancient Israelites. Once such an awareness is realized, E's response manifests itself in the sort of social legislation envisioned by the

Code. By contrast, J understands politics not so much in terms of liberation from slavery but as a (successful) nationalist, political confrontation between Israel's God and Pharaoh's military might. P's approach is grounded further in a combination of these strands, namely, an awareness of suffering and a national confrontation with the powers, leading to the establishment of a tabernacle/temple worship complex under priestly authority.

If we peel apart the layers, we might argue for the sort of ideological splintering and tempering that Mosala finds operant in the development of the Micah tradition (see chapter 9). For Mosala, the latest theological layer of Micah is one of "domination and control."[74] The middle layer is riddled with ambiguous, generalized statements about poverty and justice, reflecting the fact that this layer is "largely the product of a scribe or scribes who are at the service of a ruling elite."[75] According to Mosala, the initial layer of Micah is that which is specific and trenchant in its structural analysis of the causes of poverty and oppression in ancient Israelite society.[76] While not wanting to press too far a comparison between Mosala's analysis and this one of Exodus, still Mosala's approach is instructive for the dissection of the Exodus text. Ideologically speaking, the E layer of Exodus is critical in its awareness of the affliction of the Israelites, leading to a productive and concrete approach to the situation of the poor in terms of lawmaking. J's tempered concreteness lends an opportunity to present an exodus story that is in line with the royalist ambitions of the Joseph story. Of course, E is also interested in the Joseph-Pharaoh complex, and so we must not divide too sharply between J and E on matters of monarchic or tribal politics. Perhaps we have here only the difference between a more inclusive monarchic or tribal design, represented by E, and a more baldly nationalistic project, represented by J. If the later tradition of 2 Chron. 19:4–11 concerning Jehoshaphat's judicial reforms carries any weight, perhaps we have here the sort of postexilic vision that could have produced E. The locus of the production of J remains even less clear. In any case, we would still not be justified in reading Exodus as some sort of political tract for the oppressed masses. If Mosala is right about the "hegemonic codes" of the Bible, then we would well proceed cautiously in the cases of both E and J. As for P, it is clear that a new ideological and material situation has emerged in which both an interest in concrete suffering and national politics function as the focus of the construction of a priestly political complex.

Therefore, regardless of which tradent one chooses, the exodus story and the Torah as a whole are "liberating" to the extent that one finds elite-based nationalist movements liberating. Where critics find hierarchical, pseudomonarchic, and priestly power structures distasteful, however, they will find the Exodus text increasingly problematic for liberation analysis. A sociohistorical reading leads us to the view that the book of Exodus is hardly as incompatible with monarchic or hierarchical ambitions as liberation theologians seem to imply. The writers of Exodus are scrupulous in avoiding any linkage between the oppressed of the exodus and the poor in their own society. Whereas the legal tradition addresses concretely their situation, the wisdom writers muse about it, and the prophets at times protest against it, the narrative writers have not directed their programs to end the suffering of the oppressed underclass as such.

So if Exodus is not the manifesto of the ancient poor in their struggle against their oppressors, what is it for us moderns? Exodus is the mythic recasting of Israel's national resistance to foreign domination. Exodus is replete with the political aims of the dominant class, not society's lowest echelons. In its various layers, the text represents the self-assertion of ancient Israel's priestly, monarchic, and tribal hopefuls. It undergirds the quest for national survival that plagued Israel for centuries. Exodus does not in the end encourage internal social revolution of the sort envisioned by liberation writers.[77] The poor as such are not being elevated out of their condition to wrest control from the ruling elite.

This reading of Exodus is made clearer by considering the juxtaposition of the end of Genesis and the beginning of Exodus. If we read only Exodus, we have merely the wicked pharaoh to think about. But we must bear in mind that Joseph's pharaoh was ultimately kind and sensible (Gen. 41:41–57; 47:1–6). The contrast between the pharaohs of Genesis and Exodus tells us that there is room for good monarchic, priestly, and tribal hierarchies in the estimation of the various narrators. In this sense, the exodus story is as far removed from a classless society as the rest of the biblical narrative materials are. God may indeed be on the side of the exploited, but the dominant code of the final form of the Exodus text implies that God is more specifically on the side of a crushed nation that is seeking, either through priests, kings, or tribal leaders, to move out from under the yoke of foreign domination (or at least to manipulate the foreign powers) to pursue the nationalistic aims of its ruling elite. This may not necessarily be good news for the poor, who, by giving assent to the theology that God is the Exodus liberator, may wind up being crushed and exploited by the drive for national independence in God's name.

Certainly the historical origins of the Exodus enthusiasm are clouded in mystery. Too much of the J, E, and P presentations are stamped by the later concerns for release from exile and the struggles over leadership in the community of reconstruction. Yet Exodus 15 and Judges 5 provide us an ancient set of poetic, epic-styled texts, which would seem to indicate something of the antiquity of the commitment to a warrior God who brings relief from national subjugation at the hands of enemy powers.[78] What context do we have for Israel's ancient epic tales of deliverance? Recognizing the mythical character of the Exodus narrative, one might nevertheless suggest that the early Israelites enshrined in this archaic poetry the eventual collapse of Egyptian political domination in Canaan after the long-lived reign of Rameses II (1279–1212 B.C.E.), in particular during the reigns of Rameses III (1198–1166 B.C.E.) and his successors.[79] The Egyptian garrison presence and hold on Canaan is well known from the archaeological record. Extant monuments make it clear that this Egyptian presence had been of a military character.[80] The collapse of this empire's hold on its vassal states must have appeared as something of a miracle to those who long endured Egyptian subjugation. One might imagine this as the very real historical experience behind the ancient Israelite celebration of the defeat of pharaonic domination. If so, the book of Exodus reflects not simply a deep yearning for the possibility of political self-determination but also the memory of the concrete realization of that reality, if only for a time. For the ancients, this freedom was experienced as a divine gift, deserving not only of annual renewal and celebration but also continued struggle and commitment. *nice*

Notes

1. M. L. King Jr., *Strength to Love* (Philadelphia: Fortress Press, 1963), 82.
2. See J. Alfaro, "God Protects and Liberates the Poor—O.T.," in *Option for the Poor: Challenge to the Rich Countries*, ed. L. Boff and V. Elizondo (Edinburgh: T. & T. Clark, 1986, 27–35.
3. G. Gutiérrez, *A Theology of Liberation: History, Politics, and Salvation* (Maryknoll, N.Y.: Orbis Books, 1973), 155.
4. A. A. Boesak, *Farewell to Innocence: A Socio-Ethical Study on Black Theology and Black Power* (Maryknoll, N. Y.: Orbis Books, 1977), 17.
5. Ibid., 18.
6. Ibid., 20.
7. L. Steffens, *Moses in Red: The Revolt of Israel as a Typical Revolution* (Philadelphia: Dorrance & Co., 1926), 21, 63.
8. For the Atrahasis story, see S. Dalley, *Myths from Mesopotamia: Creation, The Flood, Gilgamesh, and Others* (Oxford: Oxford University Press, 1989), 1–38.
9. I do not see their resistance to Pharaoh as any less active than that of Moses' mother, as Exum claims. See J. C. Exum, "'Mother in Israel': A Familiar Figure Reconsidered," in *Feminist Interpretation of the Bible*, ed. L. M. Russsell (Philadelphia: Westminster Press, 1985), 73–85, esp. 80.
10. On other aspects of literary foreshadowing in Exodus see M. Fishbane, *Text and Texture: Close Readings of Selected Biblical Texts* (New York: Schocken Books, 1979), chap. 4.
11. See B. Lewis, *The Sargon Legend: A Study of the Akkadian Text and the Tale of the Hero Who Was Exposed at Birth* (Cambridge: American Schools of Oriental Research, 1980), esp. chap. 5 where he surveys the numerous occurrences of this story in the ancient world.
12. Cf. Dalley, *Myths from Mesopotamia*, 29–30 (Atrahasis), 110 (Utnapishtim in the Gilgamesh epic).
13. We will reserve a discussion of Gutiérrez on the book of Job for chapter 12. In some ways, his interactions with Job nuance the more straightforward investment in the liberation ideology of his earlier writings under examination here.

14. Gutiérrez, *Theology of Liberation*, 64.
15. P. Frostin, "The Hermeneutics of the Poor—The Epistemological 'Break' in Third World Theologies," *Studia Theologica* 39 (1985): 127–50; cf. J. Armstrong, *From the Underside: Evangelism from a Third World Vantage Point* (Maryknoll, N. Y.: Orbis Books, 1981.)
16. Gutiérrez, *Theology of Liberation*, ix.
17. Ibid., 9.
18. Ibid., 10, 15.
19. Ibid., 21.
20. Ibid., 26.
21. Ibid., 26–27.
22. Ibid., 35.
23. Ibid., 175.
24. Ibid.
25. Ibid., 153.
26. Ibid., 154.
27. Ibid., 155.
28. Ibid., Gutiérrez now also adds important considerations from his reading of the book of Job. See chapter 12.
29. Ibid., 162.
30. Ibid., 167.
31. Ibid., 163.
32. Ibid.
33. Ibid.
34. Ibid., 45.
35. Ibid., 36, 68.
36. Ibid., 91.
37. Ibid., 68.
38. Ibid., 157.
39. Ibid., 159.
40. This view was developed by G. E. Wright, *God Who Acts: Biblical Theology as Recital* (London: SCM Press, 1952).
41. Gutiérrez, *Theology of Liberation*, 48.
42. Ibid.
43. Ibid., 111.
44. Ibid., 88.
45. Ibid., 174.
46. Ibid., 272–73.
47. Ibid., 273.
48. Ibid., 174.
49. Ibid., 273.
50. W. Brueggermann, *The Prophetic Imagination* (Philadelphia: Fortress Press, 1978), chap. 2.
51. Gutiérrez, *Theology of Liberation*, 194.
52. Ibid., 195.
53. Ibid.
54. Ibid., 192.
55. Ibid., 195–96.
56. J. S. Croatto, *Exodus: A Hermeneutics of Freedom*, trans. S. Attanasio (Maryknoll, N. Y. Books, 1981), 15–16. Similar connections are made in Alfaro, "God Protects and Liberates."

57. On the relationship between Zionist nationalism and the Jewish religious heritage, see S. Deshen, "The Social Foundation of Israeli Judaism," in *The Social Foundations of Judaism*, ed. C. Goldscheider and J. Neusner (Englewood Cliffs, N.J.: Prentice-Hall, 1990), 212–39; and G. Aran, "From Religious Zionism to Zionist Religion," 259–81 in the same volume. See also C. S. Liebman and E. Don-Yehia, *Civil Religion in Israel: Traditional Judaism and Political Culture in the Jewish State* (Berkeley and Los Angeles: University of California Press, 1983).

58. N. S. Ateek, *Justice, and Only Justice: A Palestinian Theology of Liberation* (Maryknoll, N. Y.: Orbis Books, 1989), 78.

59. This dilemma is recognized by Rabbi Jeremy Milgrom, son of the eminent Jacob Milgrom, in his statement "Don't Close Off This Small Opening towards Peace," reprinted in *Captive Corpses* (Jerusalem: B'Tselem, 1999). Noting the command to annihilate Amelek, Milgrom writes that "the ferocity of sanctioned, even commanded, warfare described in the Deuteronomy passages in the Bible cannot possibly serve as a blanket permission for a beleaguered society to use every means at its disposal to gain an advantage and/or demoralize the enemy" (pp. 29–30). That these texts pose dilemmas for the modern situation is not only recognized by Ateek but also Jewish thinkers of various schools of thought. See, e.g., M. H. Ellis, *Toward a Jewish Theology of Liberation: The Uprising and the Future*, 2d ed. (Maryknoll, N.Y.: Orbis Books, 1991); idem, *Beyond Innocence and Redemption: Confronting the Holocaust and Israeli Power* (San Francisco: Harper & Row, 1990); Y. Landau, "*Oz v'Shalom*: A Moment Interview," *Moment* 11 (1986): 25–30, 44–46; idem, "Blessing Both Jew and Palestinian: A Religious Zionist View," *Christian Century* 106 (1989): 1196–99; and D. Burrell and Y. Landau, eds., *Voices from Jerusalem: Jews and Christians Reflect on the Holy Land* (New York: Paulist Press, 1992). Some important insights can also be found in D. Hartman, *Conflicting Visions: Spiritual Possibilities of Modern Israel* (New York: Schocken Books, 1990), 225–42.

60. Ateek, *Justice, and Only Justice*, 84–85. For studies in Jewish fundamentalism, see J. S. Lustick, *For the Lord and the Land: Jewish Fundamentalism in Israel* (New York: Council on Foreign Relations, 1988); and E. Sprinzak, *The Ascendance of Israel's Radical Right* (New York: Oxford University Press, 1991).

61. Ateek, *Justice, and Only Justice*, 78.

62. Ibid., 92.

63. Ibid., 96.

64. Ibid., 92–100.

65. Ibid., 92–93; cf. 79–81.

66. Ateek's critical analysis of the stories of the fall of Jericho (Joshua 6) and Naboth's vineyard (1 Kings 21) is quite instructive (83, 86–89). In the former story of utter destruction, we have a case where the picture of God is deemed "inadequate and incomplete" by Ateek. In the latter story, even though it is concerned with social justice, Ateek suggests that its emphasis on "justice without mercy" renders the text's vision of God incomplete in significant ways. We must go beyond both texts. Other liberation writers might lift up the Naboth text as a proof of God's concern for justice, overlooking the text's failure to teach justice *with* mercy.

67. E. Schüssler Fiorenza, "The Will to Choose or to Reject: Continuing Our Critical Work," in Russell, ed., *Feminist Interpretation of the Bible*, 131.

68. I. J. Mosala, *Biblical Hermeneutics and Black Theology in South Africa* (Grand Rapids: Wm. B. Eerdmans Publishing Co., 1989), 30. See also chapter 1.

69. Ibid., 10.

70. On the land question in the biblical tradition, see W. D. Davies, *The Gospel and the Land: Early Christianity and Jewish Territorial Doctrine* (Berkeley and Los Angeles:

University of California, 1974); and idem, *The Territorial Dimension of Judaism*, rev. ed. (Philadelphia: Fortress Press, 1991). This edition of Davies' classic statement contains an important chapter on the modern dispute over the land. Davies' updated views in many ways parallel Ateek's observations about the topic of land.

71. See B. F. Batto, *Slaying the Dragon: Mythmaking in the Biblical Tradition* (Louisville, Ky.: Westminster/John Knox Press, 1992), chap. 4.

72. See, e.g., S. Dalley, *Myths from Mesopotamia*, 228-277.

73. See J. A. Black, "The New Year Ceremonies in Ancient Babylon: 'Taking Bel by the Hand' and a Cultic Picnic," *Religion* 11 (1981): 39-59; and K. van der Toorn, "The Babylonian New Year Festival: New Insights from the Cuneiform Texts and Their Bearing on Old Testament Study," in *Congress Volume: Leuven, 1989*, ed. J. A. Emerton (Leiden: E. J. Brill, 1991), 331–44. Black situates the ceremony in the context of an enthronement festival. Van der Toorn examines the linkage between the *akitu* festival and an Israelite autumnal festival.

74. Mosala, *Biblical Hermeneutics*, 134.

75. Ibid., 141.

76. Ibid., 146-49.

77. This analysis runs counter to the claims, for example, of N. Gottwald, *The Tribes of Yahweh: A Sociology of the Religion of Liberated Israel 1250-1050 B.C.E.* (Maryknoll, N.Y.: Orbis Books, 1979), chap. 22.

78. F. M. Cross and D. N. Freedman, *Studies in Ancient Yahwistic Poetry*, 2d ed. (Grand Rapids: Wm. B. Eerdmans Publishing Co., 1997), chaps. 1–2. See also P. C. Craigie, *The Problem of War in the Old Testament* (Grand Rapids: Wm. B. Eerdmans Publishing Co., 1978), chap. 3.

79. On the character of Egyptian rule during this period, see D. B. Redford, *Egypt, Canaan, and Israel in Ancient Times* (Princeton, N.J.: Princeton University Press, 1992), chap. 11.

80. For the text of the stelae of Seti I and Rameses II at Beth-shan, see A. Rowe, "The Two Royal Stelae of Beth-Shan," *Museum Journal* 20 (1929): 89–98. In both stelae the kings proclaim military victories, with Seti boasting conquests over several towns in the Canaanite locale. In one segment of the Rameses stele, the king also declares himself to be the protector of the widow, poor, and afflicted.

Chapter 5

To Build a Just Society

Ezra, Nehemiah, Esther, Ruth, Daniel

Ezra-Nehemiah in a Sociohistorical Frame: Problems of Interpretation

Nehemiah: A Foundation of Justice

Ezra: Law, Reform, and Tradition

Esther: The Politics of Folly and the Price of Commitment

Ruth: Aggadah Nourishes Halakhah

Daniel: Toward a Postimperial Political Vision

As diverse as the narrative materials in Ezra-Nehemiah, Esther, Ruth, and Daniel may be in terms of content—with Nehemiah focused on rebuilding, Ezra consumed with lawmaking, Daniel laced with visions, Esther not even mentioning God, and Ruth pointing the way for *halakhah* ("law"), these works share more than a formal link as tales and novellas of the Persian-Hellenistic age. Whether the figures are depicted as emissaries of a foreign power (Ezra-Nehemiah), or inside the courts of those kings (Daniel, Esther), or as a foreigner finding a home (Ruth), each of these works tells fairly coherent stories of heroic figures who defy great odds to keep alive the Jewish community and its traditions. In this unity of theological purpose, these works shed light on the mood of the tradition-bearers well into the second temple period. Indeed, the work of Daniel, though it includes older tales of a wise sage, finds itself on the cusp of a new era, the reassertion of royal prerogatives of the Maccabean period. Seeking communal preservation, these works exhibit marked attitudes toward political power and a decisive commitment to a national ethic that must have been rhetorically persuasive to those who came to identify their struggles with the rather idealized portraits of Nehemiah, Ezra, Esther, Ruth, and Daniel. After a brief discussion of several issues raised when trying to place Ezra and Nehemiah into a historical framework, we will look at these five books in turn.

Ezra-Nehemiah in a Sociohistorical Frame:
Problems of Interpretation

Artifactual evidence such as the recovery of the cylinder inscription of the Persian ruler Cyrus the Great (550–530 B.C.E.) would seem to provide the plausible material for reconstructing in a straightforward fashion the historical background to the books of Ezra and Nehemiah. Cyrus's edict, stamped by what Bright terms a "moderate general policy" designed to "allow subject peoples as far as possible to enjoy cultural autonomy within the framework of the empire," announced the triumph of Cyrus over Babylon.[1] In the extant record, Cyrus portrays himself as the beloved of Marduk, the Babylonian deity, a true devotee who restores ruined sanctuaries and returns displaced populations to their former homes.[2] It would seem here that we have a historical counterpart to the Jewish restoration proclamations found in Ezra 1:2–4 and 6:3–5.[3]

In light of such textual considerations, Bright, among others, offers a rather uncomplicated reading of the postexilic restoration sequence. The first movement, under Sheshbazzar in 538 B.C.E., witnesses the restoration of the temple vessels to Jerusalem and possibly the laying of the foundation of the new temple (cf. Ezra 5:14–16). Bright then posits a second return group, the "major return of exiles" in the years 538–522 B.C.E. under Zerubbabel of the Davidic house, who succeeds Sheshbazzar as governor.[4] Finally, there is the period of the completion of the temple (520–515 B.C.E.) during the reign of Darius I, a period that harbors messianic stirrings around Zerubbabel, as reflected in the books of Haggai and Zechariah.[5] In the subsequent century, Nehemiah after 445 B.C.E. and Ezra after 428 B.C.E. or 398 B.C.E. conduct missions to finalize this process. These deeds are recorded in their "memoirs," i.e., sections of their books that have been filled out with other material by the Chronicler.[6]

Such a reconstruction, as sharp and appealing as it is in its overall outlines, fails to do justice either to the complexities of the historical reconstruction of the period or to the problematic dimensions of the transmission history of the books of Ezra and Nehemiah. It is true that clear insights into the economics of the period, Persian foreign policy and administration, and the effects of Persian expansion can be gleaned from a variety of textual sources: from Persepolis, the "Persepolis treasury texts" and the "Persepolis fortification texts"; from Babylonia, the Murašu business archive and the Nabonidus Chronicle; and from Egypt, the business and legal documents of the Jewish colony at Elephantine after 495 B.C.E.[7] Likewise, important information regarding events and reigns for the period can be garnered from the rather extensive Greco-Roman sources, such as Herodotus (fifth century B.C.E.), Thucydides (fifth century B.C.E.), Xenophon (fourth century B.C.E.), Diodorus Siculus (first century B.C.E.), Josephus (first century C.E.), and Plutarch (first–second century C.E.), with additional insights from the fragmented sources that have survived in quotations from Ctesias (fourth century B.C.E.), Berossus (third century B.C.E.), and Pompeius Trogus (first century C.E.).[8] As one can imagine, these pre-Hellenistic, Hellenistic, and Roman period records vary in quality and content, being distorted not only by inaccuracies, but also by the biases and agendas of their writers, who frequently have a defense of Greek or Roman politics in the foreground.[9]

The archaeological record provides us with several key insights into the socioeconomic and political processes at work in Persian Palestine, creating the stage for the Ezra-Nehemiah drama, namely, the establishment of the Persian province of Yehud.[10] This province, which does not appear to have been formally established as a separate entity until the latter half of the fifth century B.C.E., was a territory whose "boundaries were far more limited than those of the kingdom of Judah, and even more important, with the exception of the cultic dimension, the new province adapted itself in everyday life to its environment."[11] Stern points out that this small province harbored larger ambitions, as reflected in the use of *pym* and *ayin* weights, rosette symbols, the archaic Hebrew script—all features symptomatic of a desire to recover the bygone days of the Judaean monarchy.[12] Likewise, the lack of cultic figurines would suggest a strong commitment to the religious ideals reflected in the reforms of Ezra and Nehemiah.[13] In other words, the archaeology indirectly attests to the royalist aspirations and priestly reform tendencies of the period among the elite in Yehud.

However, even if the extrabiblical texts and archaeological remains were unproblematic in scope and interpretation, we would be no closer to placing the books of Ezra and Nehemiah into a precise context, if for no other reason than the fact that these books are not clear regarding which kings and dates are intended for Ezra or Nehemiah. Persian expansionism and imperial policy required collaborators and military retrenchment in Egypt, Ionia, Judah and elsewhere throughout all Achaemenid reigns, so transitions in rule may not be a good guide for locating Ezra and Nehemiah in time.[14] Widengren has carefully outlined the options available to us:[15] (1) Ezra precedes Nehemiah, arriving in 458 B.C.E., early in the reign of Artaxerxes I (465–424 B.C.E.); (2) Ezra follows Nehemiah in 398 B.C.E. under Artaxerxes II (405/4–359/58 B.C.E.); (3) Ezra and Nehemiah overlap, with Ezra arriving late in the reign of Artaxerxes I; (4) Ezra precedes Nehemiah, following Cross's complex argument based on haplographies in the list of the priestly line.

Of course, these positions can place us in wildly different chronological frames. If Ezra and Nehemiah do overlap, one cannot but feel that this fact is rather strangely portrayed in Ezra-Nehemiah, where the figures are brought together in imprecise and clumsy ways. In what follows, we will follow option 2 that Nehemiah preceded Ezra. I will argue further that not only do the original "memoirs" of Ezra and Nehemiah stem from different points in the restoration process, but they were also restructured and edited according to ideological and editorial interests later in the Persian period, to be finalized as "novellas" in the Hellenistic age.[16] Insofar as the social ethics of these works is concerned, therefore, we find sentiments and perspectives connected with political and social movements that transcend the precise historical moment to which we would date either Nehemiah or Ezra.

Nehemiah: A Foundation of Justice

The final form of the book of Nehemiah represents a complex amalgam of texts, reflective of several phases of the second temple period. Yet, whether focused on building walls, making laws, prescribing rituals, or warding off opponents of all sorts, it is clear that the writers and editors of this work shared, if not a common set of ethical guidelines, at least the collective conviction that the moral life of the community was determinative for a successful reconstruction process.

The final form of Nehemiah, however, admits of a number of problematic interpretive issues, not the least of which is the relation between Ezra and Nehemiah. It would seem that the ground form of each book was some sort of official report or dedicatory document issued by or on behalf of each protagonist to indicate that his work for the Persian overlord had been successfully accomplished. Such a mission under Persian imperial auspices is not unknown, as evidenced by the legal codification project of Udjahorresne in Egypt at the behest of Darius I, and undoubtedly various reports and communiques could underlie the original strata of both Ezra and Nehemiah.[17] Indeed, as von Rad observed, such texts are akin to temple inscriptions of the period from Egypt, wherein an official's deeds would find a final, first-person encomium.[18] Very soon, however, this "memoir," which Williamson suggests focused on wall building (Nehemiah 1—2; 4—6; 7:1–5; 12:31–43; 13:4–31), passed into editorial hands that expanded and supplemented the text with archival material, with the effect that the work came to focus on the temple and the law.[19] Of course, this latter set of expansions incorporates the figure of Ezra into a text not originally tied to the famous priest-scribe, creating serious complications for modern interpreters who remain baffled concerning the historical relationship (if any) between Nehemiah and Ezra. Indeed, it is not at all clear that their careers even overlapped (see above). If only for convenience' sake, we will deal with Nehemiah's work first, under the assumption that wall building preceded law giving.

The Nehemiah report or memoir, the ground stratum of the book of Nehemiah, was likely restricted to an account of the rebuilding of the walls of Jerusalem and intramural communal disputes as occurred some time during the fifth century B.C.E.[20] While the confession of sin detailed in Neh. 1:4–11 would seem to be intrusive, bearing a connection to the covenant renewal ceremony of chapters 9—10, the memoir as such, to use Williamson's phrase, concerns the charge issued by the Persian royal house instructing Nehemiah to return to Judah to rebuild the ruined walls of Jerusalem.

The memoir would have presented Nehemiah as a royally charged figure, on a par with Themistocles, devoted to justice and dedicated to the rebuilding of the city's walls.[21] The Nehemiah of the initial phase was a reformist or activist who censured the local Judaean nobles and prefects—*internal* opponents—for communal injustices (chap. 5), much as did Udjahorresne,[22] prominent collaborator and chief physician under the Persian conqueror of Egypt Cambyses (530–522 B.C.E.), and Darius I (521–486 B.C.E.), who brought legal reforms to Egypt.[23] The people dedicated themselves to the task (Neh. 2:18; cf. 3:38 [4:6]), but became their own enemies as social injustices proliferated. Their successful resolution of the crisis as a community results in a successful completion of their building program.

In this phase of the book of Nehemiah, the question of social justice is raised rather directly and extensively (chap. 5). There the complaints concern injustices within the community. Sizable numbers of people involved in Nehemiah's program have had to sell off homes, vineyards, and fields not only to pay off the royal taxes but also to simply acquire food to live (5:1–5). Nehemiah takes up their cause, censuring the "nobles" (*ḥôrîm*) and "officials" (*sĕgānîm*), groups regularly appealed to elsewhere in the memoir (cf. 4:8, 13 [14, 19]; 13:11, 17). Nehemiah's anger results in a group protest that takes the form of a moral/theological appeal:

> It angered me very much to hear their outcry and these complaints. After pondering the matter carefully, I censured the nobles and the prefects, saying, "Are you pressing claims on loans made to your brothers?" Then I raised a large crowd against them and said to them, "We have done our best to buy back our Jewish brothers who were sold to the nations; will you now sell your brothers so that they must be sold [back] to us?" They kept silent, for they found nothing to answer. So I continued, "What you are doing is not right. You ought to act in a God-fearing way so as not to give our enemies, the nations, room to reproach us. I, my brothers, and my servants also have claims of money and grain against them; let us now abandon those claims! Give back at once their fields, their vineyards, their olive trees, and their homes, and [abandon] the claims for the hundred pieces of silver, the grain, the wine, and the oil that you have been pressing against them!" (5:6–11)

This abandoning of claims and canceling of debts certainly bears a striking resemblance to the provisions in the Torah for debt canceling and release (as discussed in chapter 2 above), but the text of Nehemiah makes no explicit connections here, unlike the overt references to the Mosaic law found in the expanded sections of Nehemiah concerning Ezra's work (e.g., 8:13–18). The abandoning of debt claims, however, is a powerful invocation of the structural understanding of injustice found elsewhere in the biblical tradition. The narrative takes the description of the turmoil one step further by depicting Nehemiah and his agents to be free of corrupt taxation practices. Like the judge Samuel, Nehemiah did not abuse his royally sanctioned duties or office (1 Samuel 8; 12). This aspect of the initial stage of the memoir, together with its theological overtones calling on God to "remember" Nehemiah for good or his non-Judaean foes for evil (3:36–37 [4:4–5]; 5:19; 6:14; 13:31), constitutes a prayer that is meant more to evoke a divine hearing than it is to serve simply as an official report by Nehemiah to the Persian royal court.[24]

There are, however, other issues at work in the final form of the book of Nehemiah. The book, as it now stands, accomplishes the wall building not only against internal opponents but also in the face of two major obstacles: (1) the opposition of various foes, namely, Sanballat, Tobiah, Geshem, Noadiah, and their allies (i.e., various Ammonites and Ashdodites), and (2) the difficulties organizing the community of exile returnees into a viable force for reconstruction, moral purpose, and ritual action. It would seem that in these various texts that concern foreign foes and ritual dangers we have a revision of the original memoir. This expanded memoir represents a composite document that, much like the book of Daniel, the Joseph story, or even Esther, portrays an Israelite hero acting in a responsible way with royal powers to benefit his people, doing so in the context of powerful external opponents and for great moral and ritual purposes.[25] The memoir, in this revised edition, presents a Nehemiah who acts to bring the Sabbath practice and other laws of God into fruition (chap. 13).[26] The expulsion of the foreigners is key to this phase of the memoir (13:29–31).

Reading the external foes and ritual passages as intrusive layers, we find that the expanded memoir transforms Nehemiah from a wall builder and a justice advocate into a moral figure in conflict. Opponents such as Sanballat, Tobiah, and Geshem (i.e., non-Judaean foes and rival Jewish families) threaten to thwart the rebuilding program, and only through Nehemiah's strong stand does the program succeed. The social justice aspects of this phase of the memoir incorporate but also mark a shift away from the issues of chap. 5 (the memoir in its initial conception) to place greater emphasis on ritual matters, namely, support for the priestly structure, the Sabbath observance, and mixed marriages. How did this shift in emphasis occur?

While the details will never be entirely clear, we must see in the expansion and shifting of emphasis in Nehemiah something of the same historical process that led to the second giving of the law in Exodus, for precisely the same shift in emphasis occurs from the more pragmatic justice concerns of Exodus 20—23 toward the ritual focus of Exodus 34. The memoir in its initial "activist" phase is true to Exodus 20—23, whereas the ritual memoir is truer to Exodus 34. This transformation of the tradition is credited to the mission of Ezra, a patently intrusive layer in the book of Nehemiah. In the book's final form, Nehemiah becomes the defender of the Ezra program, just as Exodus 20—23 gives way to J's ritual vision in Exodus 34. Frankly, one would be hard pressed to imagine that the reformist refashioning of the pentateuchal traditions of Israel, with the narrative storyline recounted in Nehemiah 9, would have had no impact on the social justice considerations of the final form of the book of Nehemiah. Yet by merging Ezra into Nehemiah's story, the tradition's handlers ensured this would be the case. The original Nehemiah may have been a royal functionary in an architectural program who enacted reforms in civil law, but with the intrusion of the Ezra material and other additions Nehemiah becomes the one who, against named foes, literally laid the foundations for a priestly commonwealth.

Of course, this final form of the Nehemiah figure is a late Persian/early Hellenistic period composite. Yet theologically this construct is a powerful springboard for social analysis and reflection. The fractures created by foreign domination at this time would have elevated the issue of national preservation and religious autonomy in new ways. Stories such as that of the composite figure of Nehemiah would alert the community to its need to stand together both in terms of social justice and in terms of religious identity. Those who would sever the two, as if the exodus story itself could split apart its commitment to the oppressed (Exodus 1—23) and to worship (Exodus 34—40), will not have understood the comprehensive program envisioned by the theological masterbuilders of the second temple period. Yes, Ezra is intrusive in Nehemiah and Exodus 34 is intrusive to the exodus story, but the amalgam proved decisive for preserving the Jewish community in the face of very real foreign opponents into the Hellenistic period and beyond.

The power of the final phase of the book of Nehemiah rests in its sense of a structured polis. Where chap. 5 relied, as did the prophets of old, on attempts to persuade the nobility to do justice, the final phase of Nehemiah, like P in Leviticus, knows that social and ritual restructuring matters. Hence, this phase of Nehemiah holds out a consistent and comprehensive social hierarchy of district heads, priests, Levites, and provincial governors as an effective governance scheme (cf. 3:1–32; 7:6–72; 10:1–30 [9:38–10:29]; 11:1–24; 12:1–26).[27] Similarly, the temple is accorded its share of priestly figures, singers, and servants.

We have observed this tendency to structure a priestly commonwealth as *the* answer to the plight of the hungry and exploited in P. It would seem that we have in the Ezra intrusion into Nehemiah the locus, if not the impetus, for this vision in the second temple period. We are not surprised to see this phase taking up the plight of the oppressed by incorporating Nehemiah 5, but we are also not surprised to find in the expansion of the text the broader set of structures erected by the priestly group of Ezra's time and later. The rhetoric of the final layering is designed not simply to recount the past but to persuade Jews of the Hellenistic period to hold fast to the priestly commonwealth as the answer and antidote to foreign foes and assimilation. Nehemiah the activist is the stuff of prophecy, but Nehemiah the foe fighter and commonwealth builder provides the ground upon which a priestly administered community could finally find rejuvenation.

Ezra: Law, Reform, and Tradition

The intrusion of the Ezra layer into the book of Nehemiah has several effects. The rebuilding under Zerubbabel, with its failed royal messianism, and later under Nehemiah, with his architectural and civil law focus, becomes a *theological process*. National rebuilding and even monarchic aspirations from the time of Sheshbazzar and Zerubbabel, the latter as evidenced also in the books of Haggai and Zechariah, give way to the priestly interest not only in the temple construction project but also in putting priestly rather than native royal authority at the heart of the reconstruction movement. In other words, Nehemiah yields to Ezra much as J's ritual vision in Exodus 34 ultimately gives way to P's Aaron. In the process, the royalist tendencies of other groups are pushed aside in favor of increased collaboration with the Persian authorities.

We observe then that the rehearsal of covenant history given in Nehemiah 9 serves an analogous function to that of Ezra 1—6. Both passages invoke history as the ground for the legislative program of Ezra and for the people's continued participation in that program.[28] In so doing, Nehemiah 9 and Ezra 1—6 reshape the past for the reader: Nehemiah 9 presents the pentateuchal sources and DH in miniature, attesting that it is in this period that the Genesis–Kings amalgam is being brought to completion, for that is when such literary and theological codes were operant and cogent. This great story of Israel's past is trumped only by Ezra 1—6, which roots itself in imperial claims and official correspondence:

> Thus said King Cyrus of Persia: The LORD God of Heaven has given me all the kingdoms of the earth and has charged me with building Him a house in Jerusalem, which is in Judah. Anyone of you of all His

people—may his God be with him, and let him go up to Jerusalem that is in Judah and build the House of the LORD God of Israel, the God that is in Jerusalem, and all who stay behind, wherever he may be living, let the people of his place assist him with silver, gold, goods, and livestock, besides the freewill offering to the House of God that is in Jerusalem." (Ezra 1:2–4)

Did the Persian royal house back the priestly commonwealth's program? It is historically hard to say. The letters certainly look authentic when measured linguistically against imperial Aramaic. Likewise, Ezra 1—6 is consistent with the release proclaimed by the Cyrus cylinder:

He [i.e., the god Marduk] scanned and looked (through) all the countries, searching for a righteous ruler willing to lead him. . . . (Then) he pronounced the name Cyrus, king of Anshan, declared him (lit.: pronounced [his] name) to be(come) the ruler of all the world . . . Marduk ordered him to march against his city Babylon. . . . Without any battle, he made him enter his town Babylon, sparing Babylon any calamity. . . . I returned to (these) sacred cities on the other side of the Tigris, the sanctuaries of which have been ruins for a long time, the images which (used) to live therein and established for them permanent sanctuaries. I (also) gathered all their (former) inhabitants and returned (to them) their habitiations. . . .[29]

Similarly, the *Demotic Chronicle* attests to legal and religious reforms in Egypt under the impetus of Darius I (521–486 B.C.E.) following the pattern of cultic restoration attributed to Udjahorresne, the Egyptian figure under Cambyses and Darius I discussed earlier.[30] While Ezra builds on all that precedes, it is also clear that various letters and other Aramaic sections of Ezra would seem to carry some degree of historical validity (4:8–6:18, 7:12–26). We might go so far as to say that the substance of the material in Ezra 1—6 is not to be doubted.[31]

However, in terms of vision and activity, chaps. 1—6 seek to take the community far beyond the rebuilding programs we find in Haggai, Zechariah, or in the early phase of the Nehemiah memoir. We might readily argue that the Aramaic sections of Ezra have roots in official records and memoranda but the *reuse* of these materials in Ezra 1—6 is consistent with Nehemiah 9: The past of divine chosenness and royal support is invoked to sustain a program of ritual reform that emerges *after* the time of temple rebuilding under Haggai-Zechariah or the wall rebuilding program of the activist-architect Nehemiah of the early phase of the book of Nehemiah. The focus on ritual implements is one sign of this temple agenda (Ezra 1:5–11). Likewise, the list of temple personnel in Ezra 2 (repeated in Nehemiah 7) reflects this emphasis. The text extols the founding of the temple as a *community* project (Ezra 3:10–13).[32] Yet this project does not operate on its own, but with a priestly figure (not a governmental agent) at the helm, namely, the venerable Ezra. The Ezra "memoir" found in Ezra 7—10 and in the dislodged segment of Nehemiah 8 (and possibly Nehemiah 9—10) presents Ezra as the principle priestly/scribal/Aaronic architect of the renewal of the Torah of Moses in the reconstructed Judaean community, with Nehemiah playing a supportive, Mosaic role.

Several questions emerge: Who is this Ezra who is connected to this appeal to the divine and royal pasts? Who is this figure who is given a prominent place alongside the ritual making, foe fighting Nehemiah of the expanded Nehemiah memoir? We may not be able to answer such questions definitively, but we can say that the *image* of Ezra was integral to the particular program of social and ritual reform key both to the Ezra memoir and to the final phases of Ezra-Nehemiah, much as Aaron was to P's refashioning of the Moses tradition.[33] However, while currently imbedded in the context of linkage to the Nehemiah program, it would seem that the Ezra memoir once stood alone as a first person narrative account of Ezra, similar to the Nehemiah memoir discussed above. While the phases of development are not clear, the most straightforward explanation of the current textual amalgam would suggest that the Chronicler or some other redactor revised the initial Ezra memoir into third-person form and created the Ezra-Nehemiah composite, with Nehemiah 8 dislodged from the original Ezra memoir. Nehemiah 9—10 would seem to be integral to the portrait of Ezra, yet scholars remain divided over this section's integrity in relation to Nehemiah 8. This distinction between an independent Ezra memoir and the canonical Ezra-Nehemiah is key, for, as we shall see, the social agendas of the Ezra memoir and its composite redaction are not exactly the same.

In any event, the portrait of the Ezra memoir and its composite redaction has come to govern our understanding of the reform period. Anticipation of the need for Ezra's reform is carefully framed by the structuring of Ezra 1—6, which portrays Ezra's foes in terms different than Nehemiah's opponents. Ezra's foes use appropriate diplomatic channels and correspondence to effect their cause, correspondence filled with vituperation and recrimination not unlike the appeals known from the Canaanite letters to Pharaoh Akhenaten (Ezra 4:6–16).[34] The opponents Ezra faces are *within* the Judaean community and leadership, not outsiders as in the expanded version of the Nehemiah memoir.[35] The redactor places Ezra in a prime position, for the Persian royal house has decreed that no internal opposition shall prevail (Ezra 6:1–12). Persian rule through appointees is attested by the Udjahorresne inscription (discussed above) and the later Herodotus, but, as Graf argues, the appointee system was not always one of imposition, as Herodotus implies, but involved considerable extraction from the existing families and power bases in the regions the Persians attempted to control.[36] Particular native individuals or families would retain control to the extent that "the tyrant and his kinsmen cooperated with Persian rule."[37] Yet on a number of occasions, Darius I acted on behalf of slain or ousted dynasts' heirs, restoring them to power against local usurpers. When read in this manner, Persian support for a Nehemiah or an Ezra would have been perceived as the backing of legitimate claimants to authority.[38] It is no wonder then that Ezra-Nehemiah is at pains not only to document imperial decrees but also to establish the genealogical claims of the restoration program. Likewise, it would seem that the governorships of Shesh-bazzar and Zerubbabel over Judah would follow the pattern of Persian support for local dynasts, in this case that of the Davidides.[39] However, since it would appear that Sanballat, Tobiah, Geshem, and their successors owed their authority to Persian support, it is quite understandable that Nehemiah (and later Ezra) would have worked to deflect their collective criticisms directed at Nehemiah or his supporters.[40] Yet there is a shift between the times of Zerub-babel and Nehemiah, in that Nehemiah in no way represents the extension of the royal Judaean house. Graf is probably correct to surmise that Nehemiah's commission stems from reorganization necessitated by Judaean involvement in the rebellions of Babylon and Egypt under Xerxes.[41] Support for the earlier Judaean temple reconstruction project as a nativist movement, by contrast, would parallel Darius I's efforts in Egypt to restore temples as a way to secure his own legitimacy over the land.[42] By the time Ezra is on the scene (post-Nehemiah), this is all history, but the lessons learned permit yet another exter-nal (albeit nativist) appointee to reassert the exiles' claims over the Judaean territory and temple. In the context of the times, therefore, Ezra's moral force capitalizes on the edges of the interface between fracturing indigenous move-ments and an imperial center that desires to maximize its legitimacy and which, as under Xerxes, might resort to more forceful means to assert its hold over the populace.

Chapter 5 of Ezra structures into the account *prophetic* support for the building program (5:1–2; cf. 6:14). In other words, Ezra's reforms rely far less on moral suasion, as in the earlier activist phase of the Nehemiah memoir, and far more on official approval and divine approval. The early Nehemiah dis-plays the power of the office, whereas Ezra 1—6 displays the power of tradi-tion, even before the figure of Ezra appears on the scene! Moreover, the situation for Ezra is entirely different. Where Nehemiah finds a city in *physi-cal* ruins, Ezra finds it in *moral* ruins:

> When this was over, the officers approached me, saying, "The people of Israel and the priests and Levites have not separated themselves

from the peoples of the land whose abhorrent practices are like those of the Canaanites, the Hittites, the Perizzites, the Jebusites, the Ammonites, the Moabites, the Egyptians, and the Amorites. They have taken their daughters as wives for themselves and for their sons, so that the holy seed has become intermingled with the peoples of the land; and it is the officers and prefects who have taken the lead in this trespass." (Ezra 9:1–2).

One might not have anticipated this development from the content of chaps. 7—8, which present us with an Ezra of towering proportions, a man with a lengthy pedigree, abundant supplies, and a vast entourage. His three-day wait and fast at the river near Ahava before journeying to Jerusalem is a pregnant moment (8:15–34).[43] Ezra is the new Moses, readying the community for passage into the promised land. He is also Joshua *redivivus*, pausing with the troops before entering the land to do battle. The entire group reaches the temple in Jerusalem, and by the end of chap. 8 all seems well. However, they find the situation to be as awful as it was in the time of the judges, with paganism rife and intermarriage an ever-present danger (9:3–15). Like the Egyptian envoy Udjahorresne under the Persian ruler Cambyses, Ezra is charged to "regulate Judah and Jerusalem according to the law of your God" (Ezra 7:14).[44] This vision of the Ezra text is consonant with the ritual reformist layer of Nehemiah, betraying the hand of the same redactor and indicating that the conflict over leadership and over questions of identity had not subsided well into the Hellenistic period, the era during which the Ezra-Nehemiah composite must have developed.

We can still discern in Ezra earlier phases of the history. No doubt official decrees enabled the temple to be rebuilt fairly early in the Persian period. No doubt too an official on the order of a Nehemiah must have been empowered to rebuild Jerusalem's walls and enact civil reforms. Yet we should see in Ezra an effort on the part of some in the Persian or Hellenistic period either to seize singular control of the temple or to ward off foreign influence, or both. Building the temple is no longer the rallying cry, but remaining consecrated and dedicated to this worship system is paramount to the composite Ezra-Nehemiah text.[45] The choice is starkly depicted as either assimilation or insularity in a world that only tolerates a different sort of pluralism. This tension has come to stamp other parts of the biblical record, such as the isolationist wanderings of the Genesis patriarchs or the assimilationist aggravations of the Judges text. These cross-biblical connections ought not to surprise us, for this is the period during which the Torah and DH took their final shape. Since traditions live and breathe to the extent that they are recast in light of the pitched battles of succeeding eras, the issues of the Ezra-Nehemiah amalgam are the overt side of concerns that are only thinly veiled in other parts of the biblical tradition. Thus, the Persian and Hellenistic periods saw not only covenant renewal but the hammering out of a new version of that covenant with Moses. Ezra and Nehemiah, in other words, became literary banners in that priestly cause.

At a later point, intermarriage became the cause célèbre (Ezra 9—10; cf. Neh. 13:23–28). Ezra 9, built with historical reminiscences akin to Nehemiah 9, invokes the sordid history of the Israelite and Judaean monarchies as the ground for a moment of collective confession (Ezra 9:7–9).[46] This covenant renewal is to be a *liturgical* renewal and not a new jubilee as the activist Nehemiah phase would have enjoined. Yet it is a liturgical renewal that envisions profound consequences for families structured around marriages to those perceived to be outsiders (9:10–14), namely, the expulsion of the foreign women (10:3). Thus, the problem which was imagined to have lingered from the times of the judges, and which supposedly strapped even the wise Solomon, became the postexilic rhetorical rallying cry in a program of national preservation against Persian and Hellenistic expansionism. Of course, this issue is central really only to Ezra's redactors, and not simply the "point at which Ezra overstepped his commission," as Blenkinsopp contends.[47] The issue does not go back to the initial phase of the Ezra memoir, which, to judge from the "I" sections of the book of Ezra, presents an Ezra who was not caught up with the question of mixed marriages but with a successful transfer of ritual goods and offerings to the temple in Jerusalem, i.e., with priestly authority. The issue, however, became pervasive in the latest phases of biblical historiography, as its presence in the final phases of Genesis–Kings would seem to attest. The issue of intermarriage, likewise, consumes the social imagination of Malachi (see chapter 9).

Esther: The Politics of Folly and the Price of Commitment

The very first verse of the Masoretic text of Esther gives us the context and immediately poses the problem: "It happened in the days of Ahasuerus—that Ahasuerus who reigned over a hundred and twenty-seven provinces from India to Nubia." We are presented a Persian setting for an absolutely unhistorical work, a work that adopts an "archivist or annalistic style" only to "lampoon the pretensions of the Persian government."[48] Ahasuerus is hardly the Xerxes (486–465 B.C.E.) of history. The heroes play their parts on the imaginative stage of a romanticized past, however much those tragic tones still resonated in the hearts of Jews living in dispersion. Yet in a way this work is no less historical than some parts of Herodotus that are given over to speeches and deeds of heroes and rulers—allowing Herodotus to think through issues of power, governance, and freedom—where even Persian nobles debate the tenets of democracy (Herodotus 3:80–82).[49] If all of the particulars are not neat and tidy, still Herodotus's "researches" profited the educated Greek reader at a more profound philosophic level. So it is that the writer of Esther uses characters both sublime and sinister to wrestle with similar issues of national identity, political powerlessness, and heroic resistance, with (in good Hellenistic fashion) the barbarous Persian as an ideological foil. [50]

The first two chapters play off two beautiful women, one against the another. Queen Vashti, at a sumptuous royal banquet designed to put the glory of Persia on display, refuses to "display her beauty," presumably preferring to remain at the banquet she was holding for the women (1:9–12). We find Vashti upholding codes of conduct appropriate not only to a patriarchial social structure but also a society built within the strictures of honor/shame categories. The two code structures clash when she disobeys her husband in order to preserve her "sense of shame."[51] To make matters worse, the court advisors stack the legal deck against Vashti by issuing a decree banishing her from the king's presence, thereby sending the stern message that "every man should wield authority in his own home and speak the language of his own people" (1:16–22).

Esther, the adoptive daughter of Mordecai (2:2, 7, 12), is thrust into this perilous situation by the whim of the king and his advisors, who require a suitable replacement (2:3–4). Ironically, the court advisors, through their banishment of Vashti, have created an opportunity for a Jewess to aid her exiled people, provided she learns to work inside the complexities of a pagan world in which royal edicts carry forward brutal, ill-conceived policies, and in which minority protections are gained only through calculated appeals and actions (3:12–14; 8:7–8).[52]

Much like Joseph and Daniel, however, Esther manages to take her fortuitous rise to the top and turn it to her people's advantage (chap. 7).[53] When Haman, who embodies crass political opportunism at its worst, tries to bring down Mordecai, who represents the open loyalty of a conscientious subject within the limits of his Jewish practice (2:21–23; 3:1–4; 6:1–11), Esther is able to use her position to extricate Mordecai from certain disaster and expose Haman's viciousness.[54] In so doing, Esther moves effectively, if only momentarily, beyond the woman's sphere toward public acts that sustain her people.[55] The combination of Esther and Mordecai is particularly profound insofar as Esther's youthful energies are channeled into ensuring the success of the community as measured by the fate of its elders (4:14). In this way, the book presents us with a statement of Hellenistic Jewish heroism at its best.

Feminist critics will undoubtedly be divided about this portrayal of Esther. Some may wish to point to Esther as a positive figure. They may argue that Esther, like the midwives in Exodus or like Deborah, though being a woman in a patriarchal world, nevertheless provides an example of a biblical woman who exercises *public* power and influence.[56] However, others, such as Fuchs, will argue that Esther hardly offers us a female type different than the norm:

> Deceptiveness is a common characteristic of women in the Hebrew Bible. It is a motif that runs through most narratives involving women, both condemnatory and laudatory ones. From Eve to Esther, from Rebekah to Ruth, the characterization of women presents deceptiveness as an almost inescapable feature of femininity.[57]

Does Esther not use cunning and manipulation to press her interests? Is she not reliant upon deception to finally champion her cause (2:10, 20; 5:4)? If so, then she is much like other female figures in the Bible, for whether they are notable or notorious, biblical women are nevertheless restricted by the patriarchal structures of the society and the patriarchal interests of the text. As such they are forced to uphold particular values through doing what comes "naturally," namely, deception. This is hardly a positive portrayal of women! An even harsher portrayal of women as dangerous deceivers is further provided by Zeresh, Haman's wife, who recommends impaling Mordecai (5:14). As Klein observes, "It is implicitly shameful that a man rely on his wife for advice about public matters; thus the narrative shames Haman even as it displays his pride."[58]

Fuchs's analysis of the portrayal of women in the Hebrew Bible, however, does not capture the complexities of the Esther figure. By means of these complexities, Esther ultimately succeeds where Vashti failed. She can be beautiful, even be on public display (2:15), but she also is a heroine to the populace (8:17), shows obedience in her family (2:20; 4:14), and brings honor to her husband (the king), even though she also acts contrary to the law (4:11–17). That the writer has the king turn Esther into Queen Esther (2:17) is hardly an accident. Rather, we see in her deeds, not simply her beauty but the true definition of her character. While Esther plays the edges of the patriarchal world, her elevation leads to acts of justice by the king, remission of debts, and grants of gifts (2:18). Fuchs's analysis obscures the very real dangers that diaspora women encountered as they sought to remain loyal to family and community in the face of the pressures of either dispersion or Hellenism. So while it is true that the patriarchal shape of the book of Esther is fairly transparent—it is Mordecai, after all, who gains public power and military authority in the end (9:4–5; 10:3)—there is an ennobling aspect to this book when one observes that the biblical writers portray women to be active agents of Jewish resistance and freedom (9:29–32).[59] When we compare this state of gender affairs to the portraits of resistance in Herodotus, we find a striking contrast, for in the Greek mind it is *men* who defend Greek freedom against the Persian threat. It is true that for Euripides there are heroic women who sacrifice their lives in a solitary act for the good of the polis. However, for the writer of Esther, while war plays a role (8:11; 9:1–15) and one's life may be on the line (3:13; 4:11–14), resistance is a life-long pursuit waged by both women and men against the persistent structures of pagan power, law, rule, and presence.

We must be careful not to reduce the book of Esther to a tale about the "great heroes of the faith." In writing about it, one would be remiss not to take into account the Purim connection, which is so vital to the final section of the canonical text (9:16–19, 24–32).[60] Indeed, the book is at pains to regulate and coordinate calendric differences found in the population with respect to this festival. Likewise, the book addresses differences with regard to urban/countryside practices. Here we sense the grander design of this fictive project. Esther is heroic not merely insofar as she helps preserve the community as a living organism but, more importantly, as she submits her energies to a ritual program that unifies that community. Her service is akin to Miriam's commemoration of YHWH's exodus triumph (Ex. 15:20–21) or the service of the women in Exodus who contribute to the tabernacle's construction and maintenance (Ex. 35:22–26; 38:8; cf. 1 Sam. 2:22).[61] In other words, the story of Esther is a story of commitment not simply to a cause but also to a cult. Yet Esther, like the P source, does not divorce cult and ethics. Like P, the writer of Esther understands that cultic celebration creates communal consequences. As the story of Esther's heroism and Mordecai's steadfastness lives on in this solemn commemoration and festive celebration of Purim, the community finds this an occasion for the continued necessity of sustaining and supporting the poor (9:22). The emphasis on Purim focuses the justice message of the book, namely, that community, cult, and conduct are one.

Ruth: Aggadah Nourishes Halakhah

The charming narrative of Ruth, the story of a Moabitess who comes into the Israelite fold, while not overtly a social ethics work, is nevertheless replete with overtones that reinforce specific values and modes of conduct adumbrated more dryly in the legal portions of the Pentateuch. Ruth, at one level, could be termed a tract in defense of specific justice norms, a common function of many a folktale.[62] However, the oftentimes loose interface between the "legalities" of the Ruth narrative and the more specific and detailed laws of the Pentateuch probably justifies Levine's assertion that the writer's "purpose was to extol the spirit rather than the letter of Israelite law."[63]

Thus, we see that the laws regarding gleaning serve as a pretext and framework governing the inner logic of the narrative. Boaz, the influential relative of Naomi, soon permits Ruth to glean behind "my girls" (2:8). Yet, as Sasson observes of this initial encounter between the pair,

> By assuring her that his men have been instructed not to interfere with her, Boaz in reality is permitting little more than the customs of glean- ing required of him. Boaz does, however, grant Ruth a privilege that might not have been expected: he allows her to share the water that his workers have drawn from the wells. But to repeat: Boaz's first speech to the Moabites shows him exceeding the "correct" behavior expected of a *gibbor hayil* ['a man of substance'] by very little indeed.[64]

Boaz's general reluctance to assist Ruth is tempered by his realization that she has virtually joined the people of Israel, and so he offers the blessing of the God of Israel's sheltering wings (2:11–12). This text profoundly presents the implicit recognition that law must be driven by a covenant motivation or a motivation that the community has together shared in the exodus experience of freedom from economic oppression. The law codes understood the social necessity for grounding the treatment of the poor and the resident aliens in a set of broader communal obligations to YHWH. The story of Ruth, con- sciously or not, plays off the distinction between law as such and law guided by a communal commitment to a sense of shared justice. The latter brings unexpected rewards and success to an initially hesitant Boaz.

It is true that the precise connections between the story of Ruth and the levirate laws of Deuteronomy 25 (cf. Genesis 38; Leviticus 18, 20) are not entirely exact or clear. Yet the phrase in Ruth 4:5 is plain enough to indicate that norms similar to the levirate laws are being invoked as a rhetorical device to secure the triadic bond between Boaz as *gô'ēl*, "redeemer," Ruth as wife, and the estate of the deceased.[65] Certainly the woman does not find an independ- ent "liberation" anywhere in the text. Rather, the story reinforces the woman's role in heightening a *man's* commitment to the laws of Israel. In other words, it is Boaz's commitment to something deeper that makes the transaction of marriage, like the institution of gleaning, something more than a bland legal requirement.

Ruth's posture in the ancient patriarchal context is all the more powerful in that her insistence to secure an heir in such a community becomes the frame- work for defining the proper role of a woman, even a woman of foreign extrac- tion, in relation to the governing norms of the male-dominated community. The writer's interest in female protagonists may be remarkable, but for all that, Ruth is hardly a feminist heroine, however bold her initiatives might be to ensure survival.[66] In the story, her measure of social worth is calculated in terms of the strength of her insistence on a marriage to a figure such as Boaz (3:6–13).

Her social status, as Sasson notes, is underscored by the use of the term *qanah*, "purchase" (4:10).[67]

Daniel: Toward a Postimperial Political Vision

The book of Daniel looks at the life of the exiles from the edges, both of time and of the interface of divergent cultural practices. As with Ezra, Nehemiah, and Esther, we find Daniel and his colleagues on the move as observant Jews within the imperial realms of the diaspora, exerting political power and religious influence far beyond the imaginings of preexilic Israelites. Yet by situating Daniel's dreams and dilemmas squarely within the frame of Nebuchadnezzar's conquest of Jerusalem (Daniel 1:1–5), the writer indicates that a Jewish postexilic theology must answer to the earlier histories such as DH and 1–2 Chronicles, works that end where Daniel picks up, namely, with the fact of dispersion (DH) and the realities of reconstruction (1–2 Chronicles). Far from acquiescing to despair, Daniel offers a potent view of the exercise of Jewish political power in terms of a prophetic theology of loyalty and resistance. This loyalty to one's national tradition and a deep commitment to resist foreign domination comes to fruition in the Maccabean revolt, but the seeds for these attitudes were actually laid in the preceding centuries, the initial time period of the book of Daniel's development. Ironically, cautious assimilationist tendencies found at the beginning of the book give way to visionary triumph of the scattered Israelites against their conquerors. Daniel acknowledges a debt to imperial education and religious institution (1:4), but finds the tools of political insight first imparted by the colonizer ultimately turned back against the conquerors.

Of course, reading Daniel has become a complicated affair among scholars. Daniel's veiled visions of the Seleucids (e.g., Daniel 2; 7; 8; 11), especially the dreaded Antiochus IV Epiphanes (175–164 B.C.E.), bear striking similarities to the more straightforward description of events given in 1–2 Maccabees, especially given our hindsight view of the successful Jewish rebellion against this same ruler (1 Maccabees 1—6; 2 Maccabees 4—9). The apparent second century B.C.E. setting for this book would seem to be confirmed by its rather correct depiction, albeit symbolic, of Alexander's conquest and the post-Alexander age (e.g., Daniel 2; 7). Likewise, the distortions one finds with respect to earlier rulers would tend to argue against a Persian period composition. Most glaring are the confusions about Nebuchadnezzar (whose madness would seem to be reflective of Nabonidus), Belshazzar (who was not the successor king to Nebuchadnezzar), Darius the Mede (who succeeded Cambyses and not a Belshazzar; neither was he the son of Ahasuerus, who actually reigned *after* Darius!). Though reference to Cyrus the Persian would seem to clarify matters (1:21; 10:1), the time spans covered through all these reigns would seem to be inordinately long. Moreover, Darius and Cyrus are referenced in the reverse order of their reigns (6:29). Needless to say, unless one were to argue, as Greenstein does for the confusions in Esther, that these historical distortions are deliberate, we must acknowledge that we are contending with a writer who shows little regard for the chronological stream between the exile and the second century B.C.E.[68]

The historic complexities are compounded by the obvious mythic overtones which dominate the book. On the one hand, the writer has adapted the hoary figure of the wise Daniel for theological purposes far different than his roots. Our earliest attestation of Daniel goes back to the Dan-el (*dn'l*) figure at Ugarit. This Dan-el, who like Abraham lacks and receives an heir (in Daniel's case, a son, Aqhat), is otherwise depicted as a wise and righteous judge who dispenses justice (*dn . . . ytpṭ*) for the widow (*'lmnt*) and the orphan (*ytm*).[69] Precisely when the ability to interpret dreams first became attached to the Israelite Daniel we cannot be sure, but it does seem clear that the language and tales of Daniel 1—6 undoubtedly stem from the centuries prior to the Maccabean revolt. In other words, the final form of the book of Daniel represents a powerful adaptation of an ancient mythic figure of wisdom stature, an adaptation made for purposes not originally connected with the Ugaritic presentation of the figure or presumably the earlier Israelite stories of Daniel the moral hero. Indeed, the earlier Israelite lore, as reflected in many of the stories in Daniel 1—6, would seem to make Daniel a counterpart to Mordecai, or even a male equivalent of Esther, that is, a loyal Jewish courtier who gains boons for his people via his loyal, upright conduct within the limits of his Jewish practice. The final form of the book, however, diminishes the obvious emphasis on assimilation/loyalty to bring out the potent and imaginative force latent in the posture of resistance.

Far from being a book on the margins, as apocalyptic writing is often depicted, the book of Daniel in its final form is a work that bespeaks the confidence of Jews who have gained enough political clout not only to imagine throwing back the danger of imperial assimilation but also to succeed in that attempt.[70] This visionary language is a *prophetic* language, at home in the post-Alexander age, as the Babylonian *Dynastic Prophecy*, for example, would seem to attest.[71] The *Dynastic Prophecy*, as Grayson indicates, "is a description, in prophetic terms, of the rise and fall of dynasties or empires, including the fall of Assyria and rise of Babylonia, the fall of Babylonia and rise of Persia, the fall of Persia and the rise of the Hellenistic monarchies."[72] These *vaticinia ex eventu*, or prophecies after the fact, carry a rather surreal aspect, especially in depicting the final triumph, through the assistance of Babylon's gods, of the Persians against the Greeks (events that did not occur). Certainly one must wonder to what extent nationalist forces were driven by flights of fancy. Yet this perspective that is shared with the final form of the book of Daniel, a work that takes shape as it must have through a successful period of Jewish rebirth under the Hasmoneans, would seem to situate such prophetic imaginings right at the heart of highly placed, influential movements on behalf of the Jewish cause. As such, we should see in the book of Daniel political reflections not of the disenfranchised few but of aspirants in a defense of the homeland, not unlike the failed Ionian rebellion or the successful Spartan-Athenian resistance to Persia.

Manifesto

Despite the historical and mythic complexities, in general we can look to Daniel as a manifesto for action during the Hellenistic Age, seeing in this work a symbolic investigation of questions of imperial authority vis-à-vis Jewish autonomy. Yet the disjuncture we have noted between chaps. 1—6 and 7—12 suggests that this "resistance theology" in Daniel grew in stages. Chapters 1—6, tales of Daniel as an influential and wise courtier in the courts of Nebuchadnezzar and Belshazzar, give way to visions under Belshazzar, Darius, and Cyrus that betray a reframed political content. By adapting chaps. 1—6, the writer of Daniel has set the action ideology of chaps. 7—12 against the backdrop of postexilic attempts to manage both life in the diaspora and the reconstruction of the homeland under imperial auspices. Daniel and his companions have successfully faced the challenges of such a life (chaps. 1—6), proving themselves ready to face a postimperial future (chaps. 7—12).

What is the sociopolitical tenor of chaps. 1—6? It would seem that the overall thrust of these chapters is summed up well at the end of chapter 6 when Darius issues his decree regarding Daniel's God:

> I have hereby given an order that throughout my royal domain men must tremble in fear before the God of Daniel, for He is the living God who endures forever; His kingdom is indestructible, and His dominion is to the end of time; He delivers and saves, and performs signs and wonders in heaven and on earth, for He delivered Daniel from the power of the lions. (Dan. 6:27–28 [26–27])

This passage indicates the twofold burden of these early chapters, namely, to demonstrate the ultimate role of Daniel's God in the workings of worldly power and to have the most powerful earthly sovereign acknowledge that power. Thus, in chap. 1, we not only see God favoring Daniel and company as they decline royal rations and wine to consume only legumes and water, but we also find the king turning to these youths for "wisdom," since he found them to be vastly more capable than his own entourage. In chap. 2, when an angry Nebuchadnezzar is forced to turn to Daniel as the only one who can possibly reveal and interpret the king's dream, Daniel himself indicates the writer's theological purpose:

Let the name of God be blessed forever and ever,
For wisdom and power are His.
He changes times and seasons,
Removes kings and installs kings;
He gives the wise their wisdom
And knowledge to those who know.
He reveals deep and hidden things,
Knows what is in the darkness,
And light dwells with Him.
I acknowledge and praise You,
O God of my fathers,
You who have given me wisdom and power,
For now You have let me know what we asked of You;
You have let us know what concerns the king.

Dan. 2:20–23

When Daniel, who relies on the "God in heaven who reveals mysteries" (2:28), successfully shows that Nebuchadnezzar's dream of the composite statue (gold, silver, bronze, iron, clay) is symbolic of the empires that follow upon Nebuchadnezzar's own, the king rightly accords Daniel various honors, including a government appointment. By this point, Nebuchadnezzar is openly acknowledging the God of Daniel: "Truly your God must be the God of gods and Lord of kings and the revealer of mysteries to have enabled you to reveal this mystery" (2:47).

This twofold purpose, that of elevating Daniel's God and doing so through the earthly king's acknowledgment, is played on through the rest of the stories in chaps. 3—6 with added twists and dilemmas. In chap. 3, the Chaldeans slander the Jews, as Mordecai was slandered in the book of Esther (Esth. 3:8–15). In Daniel's case, he is accused for not bowing down to a statue of Nebuchadnezzar. For this, Daniel and his companions find their lives in grave danger. This is the diaspora dilemma in a nutshell: When loyalty to one's own heritage is a costly matter, what will God's people do? To which Shadrach, Meshach, and Abednego affirm unswervingly:

O Nebuchadnezzar, we have no need to answer you in this matter, for if so it must be, our God whom we serve is able to save us from the burning fiery furnace, and He will save us from your power, O king. But even if He does not, be it known to you, O king, that we will not serve your god or worship the statue of gold that you have set up." (Dan. 3:16–18)

Once these three have been saved from the flaming furnace (the punishment for not bowing down to the statue), the king, who saw the angelic being protecting them inside the furnace, is forced to pay homage not only to the survivors but also to their God. As with the reversal in Esther, so also in Daniel, the punishment sought from Shadrach, Meshach, and Abednego reverts to their accusers:

> I hereby give an order that [anyone of] any people or nation of whatever language who blasphemes the God of Shadrach, Meshach, and Abed-nego shall be torn limb from limb, and his house confiscated, for there is no other God who is able to save in this way." (Dan. 3:29)

This notion that the pagan king himself will somehow come to acknowledge the role of God's sovereign power, despite the misguided efforts of antagonistic advisors, provides the grist for chaps. 4–6. In chap. 4, when Nebuchadnezzar has yet another uninterpretable dream about a tall tree ordered cut by a "holy watcher," Daniel makes it clear that this work of God will bring about Nebuchadnezzar's deranged wanderings for seven years but will lead to his deep acknowledgment of God. After the wandering, Nebuchadnezzar confesses,

> When the time had passed, I, Nebuchadnezzar, lifted my eyes to heaven, and my reason was restored to me. I blessed the Most High, and praised and glorified the Ever-Living One,
>
> > Whose dominion is an everlasting dominion
> > And whose kingdom endures throughout the generations.
> > All the inhabitants of the earth are of no account.
> > He does as He wishes with the host of heaven
> > And with the inhabitants of the earth.
> > There is none to stay His hand
> > Or say to Him, "What have You done?"
>
> There and then my reason was restored to me, and my majesty and splendor were restored to me for the glory of my kingdom. My companions and nobles sought me out, and I was reestablished over my kingdom, and added greatness was given me. So now I, Nebuchadnezzar, praise, exalt, and glorify the King of Heaven, all of whose works are just and whose ways are right, and who is able to humble those who behave arrogantly. (Dan. 4:31–34 [34–37])

This confession offers a political theology not unlike that of the Joseph story in Genesis. These works share the notion that a good ruler who can utilize his loyal Jewish subjects can thereby serve as positive tools in the hands of the God of Israel. As with Esther, chaps. 1—6 of Daniel recognize that a cautious participation in the political life of the empire can lead to the flourishing of the Jewish community. Indeed, these chapters would seem to encourage the leading of the double life, hence Daniel and his companions bear Jewish as well as pagan names (1:6–7).[73]

However, while Joseph, Esther, and Daniel laud the virtues of positive foreign rule, the writer of Daniel 1—6 joins with the first chapters of Exodus to acknowledge that there can be arrogant rulers who will do damage to God's people. In that situation, as with the midwives in Exodus, it is incumbent upon God's followers to speak the truth to the powers. Thus, whereas Nebuchadnezzar comes to see God as one who justly humbles the proud (Dan. 4:34 [37]), King Belshazzar who is (wrongly) said to be his successor, brazenly uses the Jerusalem temple vessels as drinking vessels at a royal banquet (5:1–4). The handwriting on the wall could only be revealed by Daniel, who is drawn to the attention of the king by the queen. In the mind of the writer, a just woman can, like Esther, destroy all the machinations of the wicked (Dan. 5:9–12), though in the queen's case her deed may have been unwitting. Ironically, Belshazzar remains true to his word and honors Daniel's interpretation even though he has learned that his reign is doomed due to his own arrogance (5:17–30).

Darius the Mede, posited (wrongly) as Belshazzar's successor, does not make the same mistake as Belshazzar. Drawn into a trap by his advisors to issue a decree against petitioning any man or god apart from Darius (6:1–10 [5:31–6:9]), the king's decree immediately finds a violator in the prayerful Daniel (6:11–14 [10–13]). Though Daniel is thrown into the lion's den (6:16–17a [6:15–16a]), Darius has learned the lesson that Nebuchadnezzar discovered the hard way and that Belshazzar discerned at the price of his life, namely, that a humble ruler who acknowledges the Jewish God can find miracles happening (6:15, 17b [14, 16b]). The king himself fasts (6:19[18]) and, though fearful, discovers Daniel fit in the morning (6:20–24 [19–23]). Again, the Esther-like reversal finds Daniel's penalty meted out to his adversaries (6:25 [24]). Chapter 6 concludes with the royal confession, quoted previously, that God's dominion is forever (6:27–28 [26–27]).

In these tales from chaps. 1—6, the consistent sociopolitical themes are clear: (1) total assimilation to pagan life is not an option, but cautious participation in the flourishing of the empire can lead to the success of the Jewish people (cf. Jeremiah 29); (2) positive imperial rule is not only desirable but it is possible, as Nehemiah and Ezra attest; (3) arrogant political power is an ever-present danger, but in times of conflict, loyalty to the Jewish community is a valued commodity. This is a diaspora political vision, in part. The writer of Daniel has moved into the larger world and acknowledges that the Jewish political future is largely dependant on the ebb and flow of imperial history. This is an imperial vision without blinders. As this vision moved into the community of Judaean reconstruction and lived itself out under the aegis of Hellenism, undoubtedly new tensions would emerge, leading to the sharper edge of chaps. 7—12.

Intensively, throughout chaps. 7—12 a postimperial vision emerges. While there is some superficial similarity between Nebuchadnezzar's dreams in chaps. 1—6 and 7—12, especially insofar as the composite statue of chapter 2 purports to reveal the course of "future" events, nonetheless the differences with respect to chaps. 7—12 are outstanding in terms of the person dreaming (in chaps. 7—12 the dreamer is Daniel) and in terms of the specificity of content in the dreams of chaps. 7—12. When these dreams in chaps. 7—12 are unpacked, we find ourselves well into the Seleucid era, in particular down to the time of Antiochus IV.

Daniel's first dream concerns four beasts (7:2–8: lionlike, bearlike, leopard-like, and monstrous with horns), representing a succession of kingdoms down to the reign of the "arrogant horn," Antiochus IV (7:11–12, 15–25). This latter ruler is put down by the power of "one like a human being" sent by the "Ancient of Days" (7:9–10, 13–14, 26–27). Thus, while chaps. 8—12 become ever more frightful, still a sense of triumph beyond the imperial age pervades these chapters.[74] The specificity continues in Daniel's second dream, in chapter 8, where a ram and he-goat bearing various horns function as symbols of the emergent Hellenistic kingdoms (8:20–26). The postimperial vision of this segment of Daniel posits that the political struggle for freedom from foreign control will be waged around the central symbol of Jewish life, the sanctuary and its sacred offerings (8:11–12, 14). This locus of the liberation fight is reiterated in a later vision, wherein Gabriel sets forth the timing and duration of the temple's cleansing (9:24–27). One cannot help but imagine that if the Maccabean revolt anchored itself in the temple as a national symbol, much as the Acropolis and Athena's temple were a focus for Greek resistance during the Persian wars, that in the post-Maccabean triumph, the Zadokites, who had previously run the temple and no doubt did so via collaboration with the empire builders, would have found themselves ousted by the revolutionary theology of resistance presented in Daniel.

The set of Daniel's visions concludes with yet another highly detailed vision of the future, relayed by a man of variegated features: "It was on the twenty-fourth day of the first month, when I was on the bank of the great river—the Tigris—that I looked and saw a man dressed in linen, his loins girt in fine gold" (10:4–5). This unusual personage, prompted by Daniel's prayers and slightly delayed by his battles against Persia, presents a nuanced account of the rise of the Ptolemid (Egypt) and Seleucid (Syria) empires and their costly conflicts (11:1–45). These north-south disputes, alliances, and open conflict will obviously pose serious problems for Judah and Jerusalem, leading to the desecration of the temple under Antiochus IV (11:31). This era will be remembered as a time of major conflict (11:40–41). Indeed, the writer labels the period, "a time of trouble, the like of which has never been since the nation came into being" (12:1).

How does the Jewish community ensure its survival through the tumult into the final vouchsafing of the heavenly kingdom to God's faithful? In part, the book of Daniel's program is predicated on a renewal of the Deuteronomic covenant (9:4–19). With conscious reference to the book of Jeremiah (9:2), the writer uses the "covenant" idea to underscore Judah's past sin and its experience of exilic shame and curse, offering a call to the exodus God for relief (9:4–19). While Schiffman may be correct to suppose that the Qumranites emerged out of religious elements disaffected and dislocated by the Maccabean program, we are thereby reminded that the Maccabean revolt encompassed both monarchic ideals and temple traditions.[75] As a renewal of the Deuteronomic ideal, the Maccabean revolt rekindled interest in political power and ritual particularity. Schiffman's disgruntled Zadokites may not have liked the theological developments that transpired as the revolt progressed, but the book of Daniel attests to the creative religiopolitical thinking that emerged with concrete acts of resistance.

Certainly the period of the canonical shaping of the book of Daniel must have been a creative time, affecting the final amalgamation of Genesis–Kings and other Deuteronomic-styled texts. The biblical scrolls will have finally been transformed from "documents of survival" into "documents of national distinctiveness." Ironically, a tradition that witnessed its initial codification under Persian auspices would receive its final stamp at the hands of those who would work to throw off such domination, those who through devotion to God knew how to "stand firm" (11:32–33). In so doing, they preserved for all time the sense that to invoke the exodus God is a profoundly political act (9:15). This is no surprise, for the exodus ideal ultimately works, in the biblical imagination, to deconstruct all "Pharaohs" who imagine their reigns are eternal.[76] Resurrection belongs only to those who give their lives for the sacred national struggle (12:2; cf. 2 Maccabees 7). In this sense, the postimperial vision of the book of Daniel is valid for the dead as well as the living. Rhetorically, those who succumb in battle and those who survive to carry on the tradition are equally sharers in the eternal dominion of God. The lasting cost and dangers of this political posture would only be seen in the later wars with Rome (66–70 C.E. and 135 C.E.). Revolutionary ideologies are, after all, only as potent as the weapons that implement them.

To conclude this chapter: Taken together, these five books reach into the heart of the debates of the Persian and Hellenistic periods both for those in Judah who were attending to the reconstruction under foreign domination as well as those living outside Judah who were wrestling with the dilemmas of diaspora. Careful attention to the growth of the Ezra-Nehemiah literary complex makes us aware of the changing shape of some of those debates. Whereas the historic Nehemiah may have been an architect-reformist, the theological and political debates shaped a literary figure who, along with Ezra, could speak to the ritual concerns and the broader opposition that threatened the community of the reconstruction. Still later, these figures would play a role in the crisis over intermarriage. Works such as Esther and Ruth reveal the integral character of women to the program envisioned in priestly circles. Granting the hierarchical and patriarchal cast of these texts, Esther and Ruth are nonetheless portrayed as active agents in the building up of a just commonwealth. In Ruth's case, the accent is on the assistance to the poor, a key theme for P, whereas in Esther's case, the emphasis is on personal integrity, loyalty to one's people, and support for the community's developing traditions. Both of these books shore up central aspects of this commonwealth's social structures. Ruth invests itself in nurturing law, while Esther sustains the importance of the community's ritual life. Finally, Daniel charts a postimperial political vision, one in which a person of integrity might support foreign rulers when they act justly, but does not shy from acts of resistance when the commonwealth's fundamental values and institutions come under foreign fire. It is true that Rome's military might would ultimately crush these structures, but the social visions of these five books continue to speak to the reforms and struggles that are integral to the construction of a more just society.

Notes

1. J. Bright, *A History of Israel*, 2d ed. (Philadelphia: Westminster Press, 1972), 362.
2. *ANET*, 315–16.
3. For a critical appraisal, see A. Kuhrt, "The Cyrus Cylinder and Achaemenid Imperial Policy," *JSOT* 25 (1983): 83–97.
4. Bright, *History of Israel*, 367.
5. Ibid., 369–70.
6. S. Japhet, "Sheshbazzar and Zerubbabel—Against the Background of the Historical and Religious Tendencies of Ezra-Nehemiah," *ZAW* 94 (1982): 66–98, explores the historical complexities and the tendentious character of Ezra-Nehemiah, which tends to deemphasize official titles and roles of the Judaean politicos in favor of Persian dominance and Judaean priestly authorities.
7. For the Persepolis materials, see D. M. Lewis, "The Persepolis Fortification Texts," *Achaemenid History*, vol. 4, *Centre and Periphery*, ed. H. Sancisi-Weerdenburg and A. Kuhrt (Leiden: Nederlands Institute voor het Nabije Oostan, 1990, 1–6, who surveys the state ration system as reflected in texts that stem from the reign of Darius I (522–486 B.C.E.); for economic texts toward the end of the reign of Darius I and into the subsequent decades, see G. G. Cameron, *The Persepolis Treasury Tablets*, Chicago: University of Chicago Press, 1948); idem, "New Tablets from the Persepolis Treasury," *JNES* 24 (1965): 167–92; and R. T. Hallock, *The Persepolis Fortification Tablets* (Chicago: University of Chicago Press, 1969); idem, "The Evidence of the Persepolis Tablets," *Cambridge History of Iran* (Cambridge: Cambridge University Press, 1968–1991) 2: 588–609. For the Nabonidus Chronicle, see *ANET*, 305–7. For the Murašu texts, see M. Stolper, *Entrepreneurs and Empire: The Murašu Archive, the Murašu Firm, and Persian Rule in Babylonia* (Leiden: E. J. Brill, 1985); and G. Van Driel, "The Murašus in Context," *JESHO* 32

(1989): 203–229. Regarding Jewish life in Nippur in light of the Murašu archive, see R. Zadok, *The Jews in Babylonia during the Chaldean and Achaemenian Periods: According to the Babylonian Sources* (Haifa: University of Haifa, 1979). Zadok gleans key details regarding Jewish life in Babylonia from the archives, namely that Jews generally did not sign business documents on Jewish holidays (82), did not use seal impressions with pagan iconography (82), and used Yahwistic names in percentages that mirror the records in Ezra-Nehemiah (81). Likewise, Zadok finds that Jews were small-landholders and agricultural tenants, fishermen, and shepherds (88). See also M. D. Coogan, "Life in the Diaspora: Jews at Nippur in the Fifth Century B.C.," *BA* 37 (1974): 6–12; and R. Zadok, "Some Jews in Babylonian Documents," *JQR* 74 (1984): 294–97. For the Elephantine texts, see B. Porten *Archives from Elephantine: The Life of an Ancient Jewish Military Colony* (Berkeley, Calif.: University of California Press, 1968); B. Porten and A. Yardini, eds., *Textbook of Aramaic Documents from Ancient Egypt*, vol. 1, *Letters* (Winona Lake, Ind.: Eisenbrauns, 1986).

8. These sources are conveniently surveyed by L. L. Grabbe, *Judaism from Cyrus to Hadrian*, vol. 1, *The Persian and Greek Periods* (Minneapolis: Fortress Press, 1992).

9. See A. D. Momigliano, "Eastern Elements in Post-Exilic Jewish and Greek Historiography" in *Essays in Ancient and Modern Historiography* (Middletown, Conn.: Wesleyan University Press, 1977), 25–35; H. Sancisi-Weerdenburg, "Decadence in the Empire or Decadence in the Sources? From Source to Synthesis: Ctesias," in *Achaemenid History*, vol. 1, *Sources, Structures and Synthesis* , ed. H. Sancisi-Weerdenburg (Leiden: Nederlands Instituut voor het Nabije Oosten, 1987); and idem. "The Fifth-Oriental Monarchy and Hellenocentrism," in *Achaemenid History*, vol. 2, *The Greek Sources*, ed. H. Sancisi-Weerdenburg and A. Kuhrt (Leiden: Nederlands Instituut voor het Nabije Oosten, 1987). It is clear that the Greek sources portray a Persia that is more often a literary fiction and an Orientalist projection than a well-understood and accurately described historical reality.

10. For key aspects of the general demographic, economic, and political situation, see K. Hoglund, "The Achaemenid Context," in *Second Temple Studies*, vol. 1, *Persian Period*, ed. P. R. Davies (Sheffield: JSOT Press, 1991), 54–72.

11. E. Stern, "The Province of Yehud: The Vision and the Reality," in *The Jerusalem Cathedra: Studies in the History, Archaeology, Geography and Ethnography of the Land of Israel*, ed. L. I. Levine (Jerusalem: Yad Izhak Ben-Zvi Institute, 1981), 9–21, esp. 21. See also C. E. Carter, "The Province of Yehud in the Post-Exilic Period: Soundings in Site Distribution and Demography," in *Second Temple Studies*, vol. 2, *Temple and Community in the Persian Period* (Sheffield: JSOT Press, 1994).

12. Stern, "Province of Yehud," 16–18.

13. Ibid., 21.

14. Cf. D. Graf, "Greek Tyrants and Achaemenid Politics" in *The Craft of the Ancient Historian: Essays in Honor of Chester G. Starr*, ed. J. W. Eadie and J. Ober (Lanham, Md.: University Press of America, 1985), 79–123; A. B. Lloyd, "The Inscription of Udjahorresnet: A Collaborator's Testament," *JEA* 68 (1982): 166–80; and M. Stolper, "The Governor of Babylon and Across-the-River in 486 B.C.," *JNES* 48 (1989): 283–305.

15. G. Widengren, "The Persian Period," in *Israelite and Judaean History*, ed. J. H. Hayes and J. M. Miller (Philadelphia: Westminster Press, 1977), 480–538. See also S. Japhet, "Composition and Chronology in the Book of Ezra-Nehemiah," in *Second Temple Studies*, vol. 2, *Temple and Community in the Persian Period* (Sheffield: JSOT Press, 1994), 189–215.

16. Certainly Momigliano, "Eastern Elements," is correct to suggest that Greek and Jewish historiographic writing was shaped in part as nationalist cultural explorations in response to the expansive "cosmopolitanism and tolerance" of Persian rule (25). Yet localizing the books of Ezra and Nehemiah more precisely in time is a rather guarded endeavor.

17. See J. Blenkinsopp, "The Mission of Udjahorresnet and Those of Ezra and Nehemiah," *JBL* 106 (1987): 409–21.

18. G. von Rad, "Die Nehemia-Denkschrift," *ZAW* 76 (1964): 176–87.

19. H. G. M. Williamson, *Ezra and Nehemiah* (Sheffield: Sheffield Academic Press, 1987), 18–19, 28.

20. This assumes that the ground stratum is not itself an expansion of some sort of official report to the Persian government by Nehemiah on the order of the Udjahorresne inscription noted below.

21. For the Themistocles connection, see Momigliano, "Eastern Elements," 25.

22. See Blenkinsopp, "Mission of Udjahorresnet."

23. "Statue Inscription of Udjahorresne," lines 31–41 M. Lichtheim, *Ancient Egyptian Literature*, vol. 3, *The Late Period* (Berkeley, Calif.: University of California Press, 1980) 39.

24. The "remember" motif is appropriately linked to Egyptian votive inscriptions by. von Rad, "Nehemia-Denkschrift."

25. Some of these complexities in the memoir seem to be recognized by Blenkinsopp, but their import is not fully elaborated. See Blenkinsopp, "Mission of Udjahorresnet, 416–17.

26. Udjhorresne's career follows a different set of phases: (1) expulsion of foreigners from the temple of Neith under Cambyses; (2) reestablishment of cult and festivals; and (3) under Darius, the reestablishment of a scholarly center for "medicine, theology, temple administration, and ritual" See Lichtheim, *Ancient Egyptian Literature*, 3:39.

27. Stern, "Province of Yehud," 16–17, sees the list in chap. 11 as an ancient relic in which the returnees place their hopes on restoring the ancient monarchic realm of Judah with borders far larger than the Persian province of Yehud.

28. On the broadening of the scope of Ezra to include the elders and the people by downplaying the leadership status of Sheshbazzar and Zerubbabel, see Japhet, "Sheshbazzar and Zerubbabel."

29. *ANET*, 315–16.

30. As observed by Blenkinsopp, "Mission of Udjahousenet," 412–13. For the *Demotic Chronicle*, see W. Spiegelberg, *Die Sogenannte Demotische Chronik des Pap. 215 der Bibliothèque Nationale zu Paris, Nebst den auf der Rückseite des Papyrus Stehenden Texten* (Leipzig, Germany: J. C. Hinrichs, 1914), esp. 30–32; and N. J. Reich, "The Codification of the Egyptian Laws by Darius and the Origin of the 'Demotic Chronicle,'" *Mizraim* 1 (1933): 178-85.

31. For important negative assessments of the Ezra materials, see L. Grabbe, "What Was Ezra's Mission," in Eskenzi and Richards, eds., *Second Temple Studies*, 2:286–99, and idem, "Reconstructing History from the Book of Ezra," in Davies, ed., *Second Temple Studies*, 1:98–106.

32. On the favoring of the elders and the public in Ezra, see Japhet, "Sheshbazzar and Zerubbabel."

33. Williamson, *Ezra and Nehemiah*, 20–26.

34. While biblical scholars have underscored the peasant character of the restiveness of Canaanite politics in the Amarna period, the letters attest to the *urban* rivalries that splintered the territory, a social process that was as much alive in the Late

Bronze Age as it was during the time of the Judaean restoration. The long-term perspective ought to make clear these recurrent sociopolitical issues and fault lines. See J. M. Halligan, "The Role of the Peasant in the Amarna Period," in *Palestine in Transition: The Emergence of Ancient Israel* ed. D. N. Freedman and D. F. Graf (Sheffield: Almond Press, 1983), 15–24, where one person's "peasant rebel" is another's "rebellious prince." Urban invective should not be confused with peasant–urban social processes. The Amarna letters hardly take us into the worlds of the average peasant or nomad. Clearly a nomadic reading of the Ezra text would completely misunderstand the social dynamics at work in a fractured urban environment.

35. See D. L. Smith-Christopher, "The Mixed Marriage Crisis in Ezra 9–10 and Nehemiah 13: A Study of the Sociology of the Post-Exilic Judaean Community," in Eskenazi and Richards, eds., *Second Temple Studies*, 2:243–65, esp. 257–58. Smith-Christopher's sociological instincts about this side of the Ezra text seem on target, although his restriction to the mixed marriage question overlooks the secondary aspects of the marriage question in the context of the total book of Ezra (see below).

36. See Graf, "Greek Tyrants," 79–123.

37. Graf, "Greek Tyrants," 82; cf. 95.

38. Ibid., 81–86.

39. Ibid., 91–92.

40. Ibid., 91.

41. Ibid., 92–93.

42. Ibid., 95.

43. Unfortunately the precise location of Ahava is unclear. See M. J. Fretz, "Ahava," *ABD* 1:105–6.

44. Blenkinsopp, "Mission of Udjahorresnet."

45. This phasing mirrors the text of Udjahorresne for whom cultic restoration (under Cambyses) preceded ritual and scholastic reforms (under Darius I). See Blenkinsopp, "Mission of Udjahorresnet," 413.

46. Smith-Christopher, "Mixed Marriage Crisis," sees the issue in Nehemiah as political (intermarriage fostered among the leadership of the community), whereas for Ezra the question is an intramural dispute defining who is a Jew. Smith-Christopher, however, overlooks the significance of the secondary character of these texts in the interpretation of both Ezra and Nehemiah.

47. Blenkinsopp, "Mission of Udjahorresnet," 421.

48. On the question of historical style, see J. D. Levenson, *Esther: A Commentary* (Louisville: Westminster John Knox Press, 1997), 11–12, 23–27. On the possible comic deliberateness of the text's fiction, see E. L. Greenstein, "A Jewish Reading of Esther," in *Judaic Perspectives on Ancient Israel*, ed. J. Neusner, B. A. Levine, and E. S. Frerichs (Philadelphia: Fortress Press, 1987), 225–43. The MT of Esther, the focus of this study, is significantly shorter than LXX's.

49. See V. Ehrenberg, "The Origins of Democracy," in *Polis und Imperium: Beiträge zur Alten Geschichte*, ed. K. F. Stroheker and A. J. Graham (Zurich: Artemis, 1965), 274–79.

50. R. Bergey, "Late Linguistic Features in Esther," *JQR* 75 (1984): 66–78, identifies five features that mark the Hebrew of Esther as a Late Biblical Hebrew source, with elements that especially anticipate Tannaitic Hebrew.

51. L. Klein, "Honor and Shame in Esther," in *A Feminist Companion to Esther, Judith, and Susanna* (Sheffield: Sheffield Academic Press, 1995), 149–75, esp. 155.

52. This reality contrasts markedly with the portrait the rulers liked to have of themselves as benevolent arbiters of a multicultural world. See, e.g., Herodotus 7.61–100 for the array of peoples comprising Xerxes' forces.

53. L. A. Rosenthal, "Die Josephgeschichte, mit den Büchern Ester und Daniel ver- glichen," *ZAW* 15 (1895): 278–84, demonstrates that the links with the Joseph story and Daniel are hardly only thematic. Linguistic ties would seem to indicate that Esther is built in light of the Joseph tale.

54. With respect to the conflict in virtues between Mordecai and Haman, one thinks of the profound contrast between Herodotus's portrayal of Cambyses' tyranny with Darius's nobility. With regard to the question of loyalty circumscribed by Jewish practice, see Greenstein, "Jewish Reading," 234–235.

55. Cf. Klein, "Honor and Shame," 167–68.

56. See K. D. Sakenfeld, "Feminist Uses of Biblical Materials," in *Feminist Interpreta- tion of the Bible*, ed. L. M. Russell (Philadelphia: Westminster Press, 1985); and J. C. Exum, "'Mother in Israel': A Familiar Figure Reconsidered," in the same volume.

57. E. Fuchs, "Who Is Hiding the Truth? Deceptive Women and Biblical Androcen- trism," in *Feminist Perspectives on Biblical Scholarship*, ed. A. Y. Collins (Chico, Calif.: Scholars Press, 1985), 137.

58. Klein, "Honor and Shame," 166.

59. Cf. ibid., 171–74.

60. One Greek variant (AT) would seem to suggest that Purim was not overtly con- nected with the story. See, e.g., Levenson, *Esther*, 33. As for its canonical reception as Jewish scripture, however, Purim's role is decisive. See Greenstein, "Jewish Reading," 226. Likewise, J. A. Loader, "Esther as a Novel with Different Levels of Meaning," *ZAW* 90 (1978): 417–21, shows that there is a strong religious dimen- sion throughout the Esther text despite the lack of explicit reference in MT to God.

61. Regarding the cultic marginalization of women, see P. Bird, *Missing Persons and Mistaken Identities: Women and Gender in Ancient Israel* (Minneapolis: Fortress Press, 1997), chap. 4.

62. Robert Scholes, *Structuralism in Literature: An Introduction* (New Haven, Conn.: Yale University Press, 1974), 47.

63. B. A. Levine, "In Praise of Israelite: Legal Themes in the Book of Ruth," in *The Quest for the Kingdom of God: Studies in Honor of George E. Mendenhall*, ed. H. B. Huffmon, F A. Spina, and A. R. W. Green (Winona Lake, Ind.: Eisenbrauns, 1983), 97.

64. J. Sasson, *Ruth: A New Translation with a Philological Commentary and a Formalist- Folkloristic Interpretation* (Sheffield: JSOT Press, 1989), 49.

65. Cf. Sasson, *Ruth*, 119–136, who ultimately disputes the levirate connections. Levine, "Israelite Mišpāḥâ," 102, observes that the situation created by the author is rather artificial and that real-life circumstances would not have called for "redemption."

66. Cf. Levine, "Israelite Mišpāḥâ," 104.

67. Sasson, *Ruth*, 124.

68. Greenstein, "Jewish Reading."

69. J. C. L. Gibson, *Canaanite Myths and Legends* (Edinburgh: T. & T. Clark, 1978), 107.

70. J. J. Collins, "Apocalyptic Genre and Mythic Allusions in Daniel," *JSOT* 21 (1981): 83-100, remains a valuable defense of the category.

71. A. K. Grayson, *Babylonian Historical-Literary Texts* (Toronto: University of Toronto Press, 1975), 24–37. See also A. K. Grayson and W. G. Lambert, "Akka- dian Prophecies," *JCS* 18 (1964): 7–30. R. D. Biggs, "More Babylonian 'Prophe- cies,'" *Iraq* 29 (1967): 117–32, argues for a mantic and astrological background for such texts. W. W. Hallo, "Akkadian Apocalypses," *IEJ* 16 (1966): 231–42, suggests

renaming these texts "apocalypses," both to distinguish them from the more classic Hebrew prophetic oracular collections and to highlight their obvious, though not altogether parallel, stylistic connections to biblical and extrabiblical apocalyptic materials. See also R. D. Biggs, "Babylonian Prophecies, Astrology, and a New Source for 'Prophecy Text B,'" in *Language, Literature, and History: Philological and Historical Studies Presented to Erica Reiner*, ed. F. Rochberg-Halton (New Haven, Conn.: American Oriental Society, 1987); H. Hunger and S. Kaufman, "A New Akkadian Prophecy Text," *JAOS* 95 (1975): 371–75; and P. Beaulieu, "The Historical Background of the Uruk Prophecy," in *The Tablet and the Scroll: Near Eastern Studies in Honor of William W. Hallo*, ed. M. Cohen et al. (Bethesda, Md.: CDL Press, 1993). Beaulieu discerns a Seleucid background to the shaping of the prophecy and suggests some general but definite links to Jewish apocalypticism.

72. Grayson, *Babylonian Historical-Literary Texts*, 24. See also A. Kuhrt, "Survey of Written Sources Available for the History of Babylonia under the Later Achaemenids (concentrating on the period from Artaxerxes II to Darius III)," in Sancisi-Weerdenburg and Kuhrt, eds. *Achaemenid History* 1:154–55.

73. On this phenomenon as attested among the Jews at Nippur, see Coogan," Life in the Diaspora," 10–11.

74. Grayson and Lambert, "Akkadian Prophecies," 10, draw specific attention to Daniel 8 and 11 in their discussion of Akkadian prophecies of the weal and woe of successive kingly reigns in the "future."

75. See L. H. Schiffman, *Reclaiming the Dead Sea Scrolls* (New York: Doubleday, 1995), part 2.

76. W. Brueggemann, *The Prophetic Imagination* (Philadelphia: Fortress Press, 1978), chap. 2.

Prophets

Chapter 6

The Ethics of Desolation and Hope

Isaiah

Early in the twentieth century, the study of social justice and poverty in the Hebrew Bible was dominated by etymological studies of Hebrew words such as *'ănāwîm*. More recent scholarship has come to recognize that etymology is of limited value in determining a word's meaning, even in cases where the study of cognate textual materials in related Near Eastern languages might offer some useful input toward understanding a term's range of meaning and history of usage within the overall context of the Semitic languages (see chapter 10). A contemporary approach to the social visions of the Hebrew Bible must be two-pronged: We will continue to study the language of oppression and justice employed in the biblical writings, doing so not in an abstract way but by asking precisely how the writers invoked such terms. In other words, when the prophets speak about the poor, in what situations is such vocabulary utilized? Can we gain an understanding of the social and economic situations the prophets confronted by contextualizing the language of these texts? Beyond language, however, we will want to draw on social-scientific analysis and historical data to provide insight into the various phases of development behind each of the prophetic texts, in particular in this chapter the book of

213

Isaiah. We will also want to explore the overall social vision of Isaiah, so as not to lose sight of the profound perspectives contributed by the final stages of the text. Taking these various dimensions together, we find that a contextually rooted sociological and historical analysis vastly supersedes the older etymological and cognate linguistic approach by sharply focusing our understanding of the social criticism and developing social vision of Isaiah.[1]

This chapter, which begins a four-chapter exploration of prophetic social ethics, opens with a consideration of a rather common characterization of the prophets. Theologians and biblical scholars, in particular under the lasting legacy of the social gospel movement, have come to treat Isaiah and the other prophets as "ethicists." We will want to explore some of the strengths and dangers of such a reading of the prophetic texts. We will then turn to discuss several of the social-scientific and historical perspectives that can be brought to bear on the interpretation of the prophetic literature. Following these broader considerations, we will begin an extended discussion of the prophetic texts (chapters 6—9), taking up first the complex book of Isaiah. While we will acknowledge the longstanding scholarly division of this book into three writers or traditions, our analysis of the social vision of the text will explore the conflict between desolation and hope that marks the entire book. In Isaiah, we will discover a God who meets God's people in the midst of their suffering, affliction, and oppression. We will find that through the exilic experience, however, the ancient justice message of the prophet became the springboard for renewed reflection by later writers who sought to reconfigure the theological and social possibilities surrounding Israel's release from exilic domination.

Prophets as Ethicists?

Recalling our discussion in chapter 1 of various "classic" sociological analyses of the social visions of the Hebrew Bible, we are reminded of W. B. Bizzell's characterization of the social criticism of prophets like Isaiah as "agrarian protests." Bizzell expressed ideas typical among those biblical scholars of his time who were seeking to read the Hebrew Bible in sociological terms: "The prophets, Micah and Isaiah, are good examples of great social reformers who reflect the sentiments of discontent of the peasants of their respective ages."[2]

To some extent, this sort of interpretation represents the logical outgrowth of the sociological approach to the Bible we examined in chapter 1. Yet there is a wider theological context in which this reading of the prophetic texts was taking place. The interest in a sociological approach to the biblical materials, such as we have seen in the work of Bizzell and Wallis, was complemented in the latter part of the nineteenth and the earlier part of the twentieth centuries by an interest in social concerns as generated by the social gospel movement in the United States. Wallis captured well the convergence of the sociological approach to the Bible and the movement for a social gospel:

> There can be no doubt how the struggle [for justice and democracy in the modern world] will end. The social gospel will triumph; and the Bible, as explained by scientific scholarship, will stand at the center of the greatest movement for justice and freedom that the world has ever seen.[3]

Certainly one of the leading speakers for this convergence of sociology, the scientific reading of the Bible, and a social justice message was Walter Rauschenbusch.[4] While Rauschenbusch often merely popularized scholarly ideas, his own reading demonstrated with particular aptness how a concern for social justice issues can illuminate one's interpretation of the Bible. When Rauschenbusch turned to write on the Hebrew Bible he had no qualms about limiting his study to a discussion of the prophets, those whom he termed "the beating heart of the Old Testament."[5] He felt free to do this because, he maintained, the prophetic materials provide the essential ground of a biblical view of justice. Rauschenbusch believed the prophetic perspective ran counter to the religious views and ideals that dominated Israelite society.

The prophets, in Rauschenbusch's view, used a religion steeped in ethical concerns to challenge popular faith in ritual forms. In describing the prophetic emphasis, Rauschenbusch wrote, "The prophets were the heralds of the fundamental truth that religion and ethics are inseparable, and that ethical conduct is the supreme and sufficient religious act."[6] Rauschenbusch claimed that for the prophets "morality…was not merely a prerequisite of effective ceremonial worship. They brushed sacrificial ritual aside altogether as trifling compared with righteousness, nay, as a harmful substitute and a hindrance for ethical religion."[7]

Since, according to Rauschenbusch, the prophets were concerned with matters of ethics rather than ritual (a view rightly challenged by many scholars today), it is not surprising that they took sides in matters of state. Rauschenbusch believed that the prophets were more concerned with public affairs than private morality: "The prophets were public men and their interest was in public affairs. Some of them were statesmen of the highest type."[8] They spoke out in the name of YHWH against the "twin-evil" of "injustice and oppression."[9] The prophetic condemnation was directed against a broad range of public misdeeds: "the land-hunger of the landed aristocracy," "capitalistic ruthlessness," and the "venality of the judges."[10]

For Rauschenbusch, prophetic ethics served both critical and affirmative functions. In its critical aspect, the prophetic critique "furnished a higher ideal standard by which to measure the present."[11] This standard served as the basis for the prophet's criticism of the state. It also provided the foundation for the prophetic predictions of "the doom of the nation."[12] But from a positive side prophetic ethics developed into a basis for national hope: "The less [the prophets] lived by sight, the more they had to live by faith in the future."[13] On the horizon was the eradication of social evils by an act of God. Rauschenbusch wrote that the "day of Jehovah was to the prophets what the social revolution is to modern radical reformers, but expressed in terms of fervent religious faith; therefore its real goal was moral justice rather than economic prosperity, and it was to come by divine help and not by mere social evolution."[14]

This understanding of YHWH's action in the social sphere offers a clear point of comparison between the position developed by social gospel advocates and the views currently suggested by liberation theologians in Latin America. For the social gospel writers, divine action in history serves as an impetus toward social reform, whereas for the practitioners of liberation theology divine action in history provides a basis to radically transform the existing socioeconomic order through social revolution (see chapter 4). Such widely divergent estimates of the prophetic view encourage us to seek to clarify what the prophets' purpose was in denouncing the contemporary social order, announcing its demise, and envisioning a renewed order inaugurated by YHWH.

The prophets took up a particular role in the public sector of their society as "champions of the poor." According to Rauschenbusch, "When the prophets conceived Jehovah as the special vindicator of these voiceless classes, it was another way of saying that it is the chief duty in religious morality to stand for the rights of the helpless."[15] This advocacy for the poor functioned to extend religiously rooted ethical commitments into the public domain. In the case of the "herdsman" Amos, such a posture was ascribed to the fact that this prophet "expressed the feelings of the agrarian class to which he belonged."[16] The prophetic role then, according to Rauschenbusch, was to give voice to the concerns of the lower classes—a group to which the prophets seem to have had close ties. Yet the exact ties between prophets and peasants that caused the prophets to raise the issue of poverty and oppression are not altogether clear and deserve further consideration (see especially chapter 9).

Another issue raised by Rauschenbusch was the relation of the prophets to other sectors of Israelite society and their traditions. Rauschenbusch did not think that prophetic criticism developed in a vacuum. Rather, the early "democratic" traditions of Israel (such as equal distribution of the land and lack of social stratification) and its religious teachings were taken up by the prophets to be applied to new political and economic circumstances in the life of Israel.[17] Rauschenbusch treated the establishment of the monarchy as the greatest challenge to prophetic values, for along with the rise of the monarchy and "the growth of luxury, tyranny, extortion, of court life and a feudal nobility," came values and practices that deviated sharply from the inherent equality of the agrarian-based communities.[18] Rauschenbusch viewed the prophets as individuals who gave expression to the anger that many in Israelite society must have felt over the loss of "primitive democracy" that took place with the rise of the tyranny of the kings.[19] In characterizing this anger Rauschenbusch wrote, "When a well-fed and independent people, with fresh memories of better days, are forced under the yoke, they are sure to protest."[20] It was the prophets who took up this protest. Is this, one wonders, the thrust of prophetic books such as Isaiah, namely, to lean against the excesses of the upper class by acting as advocates for the poor peasants in the name of ancient communal values?

Rauschenbusch also maintained that an intimate relationship existed between the prophetic utterances and the Law, recognizing that "the Law and the prophets are a deposit of the same strong current of historical life, related to each other as cause and effect."[21] In fact, Rauschenbusch believed that "the book of Deuteronomy was the outgrowth of prophetic ideas and agitation,"[22] a position initially suggested by Duhm and taken up by the Wellhausen school.[23] As evidence of the interrelatedness of the prophets and the legal traditions, Rauschenbusch pointed to their shared concern over justice for laborers and slaves, for those who hunger, and for those in debt.[24] Of prime importance to Rauschenbusch was the attempt in the legal tradition to "counteract the separation of the people from the land" by giving over all the land to YHWH.[25] He saw in this an effort to "prevent the growth of great estates and a landed aristocracy on the one side, and the growth of a landless proletariat on the other side" (cf. Leviticus 25).[26] In this way the "democratic," or egalitarian, values of the early Israelite community continued to find a place in Israelite society, both through the bearers of the legal traditions and by way of the teachings of the prophets. Unfortunately, Rauschenbusch did not specify the social context of these legal materials. Did Deuteronomy grow up in monarchic circles? And if so, how did it come to share a concern for poverty with the prophets? Furthermore, do prophetic texts such as Isaiah carry forward the legal tradition or do they operate as alternate traditions with their own sociopolitical perspectives and theological tendencies?

Rauschenbusch was sensitive to the fact that the prophetic tradition was not uniform in its approach to matters of social justice. On the contrary, he believed that there were important changes in religious thinking over time that altered the prophetic conception. The shift from a prophetic pessimism about the present social order toward a hopeful view of YHWH's action in the future, a shift that we find in Isaiah, marks one such change in the prophetic tradition. He also identified a broadening of the prophetic perspective in light of international events. The rise of Assyria and the consequent loss of the Northern

Kingdom to Assyrian imperial designs raised questions about YHWH's role in the affairs of the superpowers. The prophetic mind had to come to terms with these harsh international realities. Their solution, as Rauschenbusch saw it, was to develop a concept of God as one who "moves on the plane of universal and impartial ethical law. Assyria belongs to him as well as Israel."[27] This development meant that prophetic "religion became international in its horizon and more profoundly ethical."[28] Similarly, our consideration of the total book of Isaiah will make us aware that changing political circumstances in the Mesopotamian world affected the internal reshaping and development of the traditions we now label the book of Isaiah.

Finally, Rauschenbusch drew attention to the emphasis on individualism in the tradition. This development came about, he thought, with the destruction of Judah by the Babylonians and the subsequent deportation of the population to foreign centers. Until the exile "the nation had been the subject of prophecy, and now the nation as such was blotted out. How could the prophets any longer appeal for national righteousness, when it was not at the option of the people to be righteous?"[29] In light of this situation, Rauschenbusch suggests that the focus of religious conviction turned inward: "Thus all the religious passion and reflection which had formerly flowed into social and political channels was dammed up and turned back. Prayer and private devoutness in pious individuals and in groups of pious men was the only field left to the religious impulse."[30] And yet, even the growth of a more individually oriented religion was not without its social implications, for the call of the exilic prophets to "personal holiness" was the basis upon which national restoration would take place.[31] We may agree with Rauschenbusch that the exile stamped prophetic texts such as Isaiah and others, but we must also ask if the question of national justice altered as he suggests. Far from being an era of individualized piety, books such as Isaiah and Ezekiel would appear to bring forth social visions rooted in intense nationalistic fervor and a commitment to Israel as a *communal* enterprise.

Many lessons can be drawn from this consideration of Rauschenbusch and the social gospel approach to prophetic social criticism. If Rauschenbusch is correct, then the social criticism of the prophets must be seen as advocacy for the poor by individuals who came from agrarian communities or else had close ties to such communities. Were prophets the representatives of a broad cultural tradition that resisted exploitation and favored equality? Were the prophets "the voice of an untainted popular conscience, made bold by religious faith"?[32] Such are the questions that the social gospel movement continues to raise for us as we look more deeply into the social vision of the prophetic literature. The book of Isaiah, as we shall see, will defy a simple characterization of its wrestlings.

Prophecy: Sociocultural Considerations

While our word "prophet" goes back to the Greek, *prophetes*, "prophet, interpreter, declarer," this designation in its Greek cultural context fails to convey the full import of its ancient Near Eastern counterparts. It is true that the Greeks and Romans made distinctions regarding prophetic and oracular activities that bear resemblances to the Near Eastern realm. Plato's separation of divination from inspired madness—his contrast between the "rational investigation of futurity" and the more muse-like inspiration of prophecy— does find a counterpart in the Near Eastern distinction between diviners and ecstatics, as seen in the Mari texts.[33]

However, the Mesopotamian materials from the time of Mari through the Neo-Assyrian period reveal subtle gradations of oracle deliverers who exhibit a wide range of behaviors, whether ecstatic or not, and who bear varying degrees of connectedness to the central bureaucratic apparatus, as Wilson has so cogently delineated.[34] An awareness of this varied ancient Near Eastern matrix of behaviors and social locations can serve as a cultural guide when we turn to the biblical material, where a comparable range of behaviors and activities can be discerned.

While the preferred method for obtaining messages from the gods in ancient Mesopotamia was divination, in particular the reading of animal livers, the study of deformities in animals and humans, and the collection of notices of historical events linked to a variety of animals, it is also clear from texts that stem from various periods that prophetic activity was also a social reality of no small importance in this cultural setting.[35] Huffmon's study of prophecy at Mari, for example, draws together references to a number of prophetic agents who convey messages from the gods.[36] The *āpilu/āpiltu*, "answerer," whom Huffmon considers a peripheral figure, acts as a representative for gods outside of Mari. The *muḫḫū/muḫḫūtu*, "ecstatic," a figure that Huffmon regards as a dependant on the central cultic apparatus, fell into trances to receive divine communiques. Additional oracles come from otherwise untitled individuals. In most cases, perhaps not surprisingly given the context of the archaeological finds, the bulk of the prophetic messages deal with the king. Notably, however, the texts can be critical of the king, either with regard to state politics or the king's conduct with respect to the cult. By way of a succinct definition, Huffmon considers these prophetic figures at Mari to represent either a man or woman, "who through non-technical means receives a clear and immediate message from a deity for transmission to a third party."[37] Though distant in time from the Hebrew prophetic texts, the Mari materials present remarkable points of comparison to the social locations, cultic connections, and rhetorical forms of the Bible's prophets. Likewise, their ability to critique the monarch is certainly mirrored in the biblical texts, although the Hebrew prophets carry such a critique to greater depths than their Mesopotamian counterparts, at least as far as our records indicate.

From the Neo-Assyrian period, a variety of figures, the *raggimu/raggintu*, "shouter, caller," the *šabrû*, "seer, visionary," and the *šēlūtu* (a female figure) all offer oracular statements of assurance from the gods to kings Esarhaddon (680–669 B.C.E.) and Ashurbanipal (668–627 B.C.E.).[38] The Neo-Assyrian texts comprise 28 oracles delivered by 13 prophets (4 male, 9 female). In the case of Esarhaddon, messages come through the prophets from the gods Ishtar and Aššur, urging the king not to fear, announcing deliverance from the enemy, assuring the king of long life and an enduring kingdom, and promising enduring rule to the king's heirs. Some "oracles of salvation" play a role in the reinforcement of a covenant (*a-de-e*) and covenant meal with the god Aššur. Similarly, Ashurbanipal is assured of divine protection and a safe succession.

Taking into account these Near Eastern sociological complexities ought to lead us to be cautious about creating a monolithic image behind any of the Hebrew terms for prophet, whether *nābî*, "prophet," *ḥozeh*, "seer," *ro'eh*, "visionary," or the like. Among these words, *ro'eh* is by far the rarest. Occurring several times in 1 Samuel 9, the bulk of the occurrences, even there the term is treated as an archaic word for prophet (1 Sam. 9:9, 11, 18, 19). This is the text's designation for Samuel as one who answers inquiries that require special insight or knowledge. In Samuel's case this meant not merely the clairvoyance to locate Saul's lost donkeys (9:20) but also the ability to learn from God that Saul should be anointed the next one to deliver God's people and act as ruler (*nāgîd*) over Israel (cf. 9:16; 10:1). First Chronicles follows up on these references with further links to Samuel (1 Chron. 9:22; 26:28; 29:29). Apart from these passages, the term is extremely rare in the Hebrew Bible (2 Sam. 15:27; Isa. 30:10), perhaps confirming its archaic flavor. At the other end of the chronological spectrum is a word that is used almost exclusively in later materials, such as 1–2 Chronicles—the term *ḥozeh*, "seer" (1 Chron. 21:9; 25:5; 29:29; 2 Chron. 9:29; 12:15; 19:2; 29:25; 29:30; 33:18–19, 35:15). Here the Chronicler imports a word into its rendition of 1–2 Samuel and 1–2 Kings that appears only rarely in those books (2 Sam. 24:11; 2 Kings 17:13). Apart from these references, the term crops up in a few of the prophetic writings (Isa. 28:15; 30:10; 47:13; Ezek. 13:9, 16; 22:28; Amos 7:12; Micah 3:7). By far the most significant word for prophet in the Hebrew Bible is the term *nābî*. The biblical occurrences are numerous, though notable concentrations occur in 1–2 Kings and Jeremiah, giving the latter a different cast than its Greek equivalent, which uses the Greek word for prophet (*prophetes*) far less than its Hebrew counterpart. The term *nābî* is attested outside of the Hebrew Bible in an early sixth-century B.C.E. inscription from Lachish.[39] In this ostracon, which also notes the arrival of an army commander (*šr ḥṣb'*), there is a fragmented report regarding a letter that has arrived "from the prophet" (*m't ḥnb'*).[40] Although the report only indicates the first word of the prophet's letter, "Take care!" (*hšmr*), the military context and the phrasing are enough for us to concur with Barstad that this lost letter probably fulfilled the "prophetic task to give advice in times of war" (cf. 2 Kings 6:9).[41] That this is a role accorded the canonical prophets is certainly the case. The biblical text, however, is not uniform in its use of this word or in its understanding of prophecy. We might note, for example, that the E and P sources rarely invoke this word, and J not at all (Gen. 20:7 = E; Ex. 7:1 = P; Num. 11:29; 12:6 = E), leaving the book of Deuteronomy to worry over the issue of true and false prophecy (Deut. 13:2, 4, 6 [1, 3, 5]; 18:20, 22). Likewise, Deuteronomy shows an interest in the raising up of a significant prophet in the future (Deut. 18:15, 18). This emphasis in Deuteronomy is entirely appropriate, as the book inaugurates the keen interest in prophecy displayed in the rest of DH (see chapter 3). Likewise, as we shall see in this and the next several chapters, the prophetic texts themselves exhibit changing and conflicting understandings of prophecy and the role of the prophetic voice in Israel's debates over social ethics.

In a discussion of the sociohistorical background to the biblical prophetic materials, the importance of the prophetic phenomenon to the public life of the ancient Syro-Palestinian milieu cannot be underestimated. The public role of prophecy is evidenced for us particularly in texts such as the Wenamun autobiography, the Zakir inscription, and the Balaam texts.[42]

The *Report of Wenamun* offers an account of the economic mission of an Egyptian government official to Byblos during the reign of Rameses XI (1090–1080 B.C.E.).[43] While at Dor, Wenamun finds that he has been robbed by one of the men who had been on his ship. Complaints to the local prince lead him nowhere and even the prince of Byblos refuses to assist. On departure, Wenamun commandeers silver from a Tjeker ship and insists that he will not return these valuables until his own are returned. Immediately the Byblian prince banishes Wenamun from his harbor. However, the prince's order is rescinded when, while making offerings to the gods, a young ecstatic prophet delivers the divine order of the Egyptian god Amun to bring Wenamun back. While Wenamun argues for Egypt's influence in the world and for Amun's pervasiveness, the text makes it clear that Egypt's economic reach and political grandeur had fallen on hard times. Were it not for the intervention of a prophet defending the honor of the god Amun, Wenamun may have never succeeded in a land that had become troublesome to Egyptian hegemonic designs.

The *Zakir inscription*, which dates from the early eighth century B.C.E., lauds the military victory of Zakir, king of Hamath and Lu'ath, against a coalition headed by the king of Aram, Barhadad, the son of Hazael, a figure known from the Bible (2 Kings 8—13). When these armies lay seige against the town of Hadrach, the capital of Lu'ath, a town that Zakir had been given by the god Baalshamayn ("Lord of Heaven"), Zakir reports that he consulted this god in prayer: "I lifted up my hands to Baalshamayn."[44] The god's answer came in the form of a message sent by means of "seers" (*ḥzîn*) and "messengers" (*'ddn*). This message sounds very much like biblical prophetic announcements of comfort of the sort that we shall find so integral to Isaiah's presentation of hope: "Fear not, because it was I who made you king, [and I shall stand] with you, and I shall deliver you from all [these kings who] forced a siege upon you."[45]

The *Balaam text* from Tell Deir 'Alla in the eastern Jordan River valley, plaster inscriptional material dating perhaps to the late eighth or early seventh century B.C.E., offers a unique look at a figure known otherwise from the E texts in Numbers 22—24.[46] The biblical text presents Balaam as a powerful pagan seer (although the term is not used as such) who is called upon by Balak, the king of Moab, to curse Israel, a feat which YHWH does not permit Balaam to do. To the consternation of Balak, Balaam ends up blessing Israel in the course of four major oracles. While the content of both the biblical texts and the archaeological finds differ significantly, the archaeological discoveries present us with a record of Balaam (*bl'm*), son of Beor (*brb'r*), a "seer of the gods" (*ḥzh 'lhn*), a phrasing that bears resemblance to one of the terms used for "seer" in the Hebrew Bible (although not used specifically of Balaam in Numbers). In that part of the inscription that explicitly deals with Balaam, the seer, having received a distressing night vision that causes him to weep and be downcast, announces to the people a message of harsh judgment from the gods (*'lhn*) and the Shaddayin, a subgroup of the gods (a term which bears obvious relation to an epithet of God in the Bible, namely, *El Shaddai*). Whether the rest of the inscriptional material bears on the Balaam figure is unclear.

Taken together, these records not only alert us to the fact of prophetic activity in the more immediate region of the Bible but also make us aware of the need to analyze the complex relationships prophetic mediaries had to the power structures of their society. In other words, a comparative methodology will keep us from reducing the biblical prophets to a singular type or role vis-à-vis the political authorities of their day.

While the Near Eastern texts offer valuable points of illumination and comparison with the biblical texts, one great difference we ought to note between the biblical and Near Eastern texts is the preponderance of women as prophetic speakers and intermediaries in the Near Eastern materials, especially as attested at Mari. While it appears that ancient Israelite prophecy was largely a male preserve, there are hints here and there of female prophets (*nĕbî'āh*). Four of these figures appear in positive connections—namely, Miriam, the sister of Moses and leader of the early community together with

Aaron (Ex. 15:20); Deborah, one of the early "deliverers" in the premonarchic age (Judg. 4:4); Huldah, the prophetess who pronounces affirmatively on the veracity of a legal document found during the reign of Josiah, which sparks his religious reforms (2 Kings 22:14; 2 Chron. 34:22); and an anonymous figure (Isa. 8:3). An additional reference concerns Noadiah, a negative figure (Neh. 6:14). Yet the absence of substantive materials in this regard hampers any effort at giving a complete picture of Israelite prophecy as a historical phenomenon, in particular in relation to women.

Likewise, our lack of clarity concerning which canonical prophets ought better to be characterized as "central," as opposed to simply "peripheral," surely distorts our understanding of the historical development of Israelite prophecy.[47]

Given these complexities, we must be careful not to let our social-scientific models and interests dictate our "findings" in the regard. In many cases, as we shall see, the biblical textual evidence can be read quite differently and a final analysis might be impossible given the lack of contextual specificity in our sources. Carroll is particularly adamant about the problems involved in applying social-scientific models of prophecy to texts that have rather unclear historical and sociological connections.[48] Yet even Carroll's radical skepticism appears unwarranted when a judicious use of comparative Near Eastern materials and social-scientific perspectives are conjoined.[49] In other words, there is still much that we can say of a positive character regarding the social function and thrust of prophetic social criticism and the social visions of the prophetic literature.[50]

An Emergent Social Vision: Reading Isaiah as a Unity

With these more general considerations regarding the ethical side of biblical prophecy and the Near Eastern background in mind, let us turn to consider the book of Isaiah. Recent study of Isaiah in its final canonical form has caused scholars to pause and reassess the gains and weaknesses of the genetic schemes and varied divisions posited for the book since the identification in the eighteenth and nineteenth centuries of a Second Isaiah (originally chaps. 40—66 but now restricted to 40—55) by J. C. Döderlein, J. G. Eichhorn, and others, and the further refinement of this analysis through the identification of a Third Isaiah (chaps. 56—66) by B. Duhm.[51] To say that historically speaking the book of Isaiah has diverse origins, not only from an eighth-century B.C.E. prophet (First Isaiah) but also from the exilic and postexilic periods (Second and Third Isaiah), marked an incredibly important contribution to our understanding of the character and theological motivation of the various sections of the work. However, as scholars are well aware, the simple assignment of chaps. 1—39 to First Isaiah, 40—55 to Second Isaiah, and 55—66 to Third Isaiah, obscures the very real uncertainty about linking specific chapters to specific periods.[52] Upon further analysis, much of First Isaiah collapses as an eighth-century text, with a variety of segments clearly to be assigned to later periods or showing signs of having been shaped by the postexilic theological concerns raised in chaps. 40—66. While eighth-century Isaiah does not disappear entirely, as we shall see, there nonetheless remains great uncertainty about the assignment of material to this date and figure.[53] This is the case for even the most well-known of chapters. Why, for instance, should Isaiah 11 be seen as eighth-century material when its very outlook envisions a shoot growing out of the stump, an obvious reference to the exile?[54] On the other hand, Isaiah 58 echoes the very strongest social criticism voiced in First Isaiah. Given the redactional complexities of the text, we are led to observe that the tripartite division of the book of Isaiah, however powerful this scheme is in its own way, has not solved all our hermeneutical issues and has oversimplified the transmission history of the text.

One way out of this impasse has been provided by canonical criticism's insistence that we look at the final form of the text for guidance. Childs accents the resultant editorial unity of Isaiah that effectively subsumes the anonymous sixth-century B.C.E. origins of Second Isaiah under the larger rubric of "a prophetic word of promise offered to Israel by the eighth-century prophet, Isaiah of Jerusalem."[55] The canonical approach is not simply a clever trick to avoid dealing with transmission history issues. Childs's emphasis on the canonical shape of the Isaianic text is insightful. We are drawn to consider how the Second Isaiah material integrates with issues and questions already at work in First Isaiah.[56] Childs's analysis tilts in favor of a canonical reading that challenges the scholarly splintering of the text. Certainly, as Seitz has also forcefully argued, Isaiah 1—66 benefits from a unified reading, for the final text does indeed say something vital that is not picked up from the fragments that scholars have made out of the text.[57] However, rather than privileging an eighth-century construct for the entire book, a sound canonical approach ought to hold in tension the eighth-century Isaiah and the postexilic context of Second and Third Isaiah.[58] Acknowledging these two dimensions, we will reference the First-Second-Third Isaiah scheme, not so much as a key to the determination of the dating of the texts, but as a hermeneutic scheme to unlock the competing theological trajectories of the text, through which the authors, editors, and compilers offer *new* theological perspectives to the postexilic community—renewed social visions rooted in the ancient prophetic social critique—as a measure for the viability of postexilic political institutions, ritual structures, and community rebuilding projects.

Thus, we shall discuss the text in light of the text's canonical shape and purposive schemes:

Desolation vs. Hope: Which Will Triumph?   This struggle constitutes the warp and woof of Isaiah 1—35. These texts permit the very real differences of exile to percolate as theological matters. At the heart of the experience of exile is uncertainty, uncertainty about the future and skepticism about communal hope. This uncertainty arises out of the shifting sands of communal desolation, judgment, and despair. Thus, First Isaiah is neither a segment solely about desolation, judgment, renewal, or hope. Rather, like a dissonant symphony, all voices clash.

The Hiatus of Exile: Judgment Will Reign for a Time   Isaiah 36—39, set in an eighth-century context, anticipates future exile as a very real possibility. Our only confusion arises if we read this text as if it were about the Assyrians. This text, particularly in this rhetorical context, carries a transparent message about the Babylonian exile: It will endure for a time. Here First Isaiah closes on a note of doom, as if the tension between desolation and hope might end with judgment gaining the upper hand. For those who experienced the exile, this would seem to be a realistic appraisal of the people's condition.

The Community of Renewal: The Triumph of Hope over Desolation   Sensitive writers, knowing the shifting sands of political history, could see hope in the sweeping changes brought by Persian expansion under Cyrus. Second and Third Isaiah give expression to this national hope, albeit at times in qualified form.

The point to bear in mind here in a canonical analysis is that the rootedness of the message of chaps. 40—66 makes little sense or carries little persuasive value without chaps. 1—39. Whatever sorts of ancient collections of Isaianic materials there may have been, if any, most of this material has been obscured by the overarching editorial scheme that lets the desolation vs. hope motif of chaps. 1—35 and the hiatus of chaps. 36—39 give way to the brilliant announcement of hope in chaps. 40—55 and in a bit more qualified form in chaps. 56—66. Interpreters who slice away chaps. 1—39 as if they can be explained as having arisen at a different time or as if they are theologically dispensable miss the very important point made by W. Brueggemann in his work *Israel's Praise*, namely, that for the call to praise in biblical literature to be persuasive, it has to be rooted in *reasons* for praising, especially in relation to the constitutive memories and formative traditions of the people.[59] Praising without reasons and without cognizance of the people's struggles is not praise, but a manipulation of religious symbols and hence a violation of the worshiping community. As we look at each subblock of Isaiah we must do so with this larger theological project in mind, not allowing ourselves to become bogged down in an effort to extract the message of an eighth-century Isaiah, as if this fact were decisive to the interpretation of the entire work, but holding that ancient message in tension with later realities.

Isaiah 1—35: Desolation vs. Hope—Which Will Triumph?

Read as a unit, chaps. 1—35 lay out the basic issues that the entire compilation will seek to resolve. By way of framing these issues, we begin with a consideration of the major rhetorical resonance of these chapters, namely, the conflicting ideas of judgment and hope. Within this larger theological grid, the redactor has interspersed a number of oracles and pronouncements that bear on the issue of social ethics. We shall explore a number of justice matters in turn, culminating our discussion of chaps. 1—35 with yet another key theme that results from this theological encounter with conflictual notions of justice and compassion, namely, the anticipation of the future rectification of injustice. We shall find that the ancient prophet's call for justice for the oppressed is being transformed into the postexilic hope of national transformation.

The Word of Judgment

The words of Isaiah 1:2 provide the downbeat for the first half of the book: "I have reared children and brought them up—And they have rebelled against Me!" It is all the more startling then that chap. 40 gives way to comfort and hope. Yet, such is the unexpected conclusion of a national odyssey that witnessed not only destruction and exile but also restoration. By what intellectual turnings does the text of Isaiah manage to break open desolation to find hope? Do chaps. 40—66 emerge without precedent? Or are these latter chapters somehow organically related to the ebb and flow of chaps. 1—35? Even more so, has the message of chaps. 40—66 indelibly stamped the retro-shaping of chaps. 1—39? As we examine the themes of judgment and hope in chaps. 1—35, we shall see that while chaps. 40—66 certainly do add new ideas and motifs to the whole, they offer a fitting and structured engagement with the issues that arise in chaps. 1—35. Chapters 40—66 in the form that we now have them were constructed to present a measured response to the tension between judgment and hope played out in chaps. 1—35.

The judgment motif of Isaiah 1:2, which opens the initial section of oracles against Judah and Jerusalem (chaps. 1—5), is sounded repeatedly throughout chaps. 1—35. The land is "laid waste" (1:7) and the temple is scorned (1:11–17). An extensive section, interrupted only by the vision of peace in Isa. 2:1–4, castigates Israel's leadership: The rulers and the judges have filled the "faithful city" with murder and corruption (1:21–23). The once faithful city of Jerusalem is condemned as a whore. Land grabbing by the elite has become a way of life (1:29–31). Idol worship is flatly denounced (2:17–21) and the people face devastation: "As for idols, they shall vanish completely. And men shall enter caverns in the rock and hallows in the ground—before the terror of the

LORD and His dread majesty, when He comes forth to overawe the earth" (2:18–19). The leadership is named specifically: "Soldier and warrior, magistrate and prophet, augur and elder" (3:2; cf. 3:14), such that the leaders have become "misleaders" (3:12). The arrogance of unbounded wealth will be put to an end (3:16–24). This is prophetic social criticism at its best.

As Brueggemann observes, the prophetic imagination mourns the collapse of the old order as a way to permit newness to spring forth.[60] No passage mourns the reckless abandon of the wealthy elite more than Isaiah 5, which portrays Israel as a ruined, hopelessly exploited vineyard. The resulting picture of judgment here is terrifying:

> That is why
> The LORD's anger was roused
> Against His people,
> Why He stretched out His arm against it
> And struck it,
> So that the mountains quaked,
> And its corpses lay
> Like refuse in the streets.
> Yet his anger has not turned back,
> And His arm is outstretched still.
> He will raise an ensign to a nation afar,
> Whistle to one at the end of the earth.
> There it comes with lightning speed!
> In its ranks, none is weary or stumbles,
> They never sleep or slumber;
> The belts on their waists do not come loose,
> Nor do the thongs of their sandals break.
> Their arrows are sharpened,
> And all their bows are drawn.
> Their horses' hoofs are like flint,
> Their chariot wheels like the whirlwind.
> Their roaring is like a lion's,
> They roar like the great beasts;
> When they growl and seize a prey,
> They carry it off and none can recover it.
> Isa. 5:25–29

Chapters 6—8 establish a narrative setting for the prophet's activity as the bearer of this judgment message. Ostensibly, the prophet's work occurs under Uzziah and Ahaz, with the looming threat being Assyria. Chapters 6—8 are unusual in that they are couched as narrative, whereas prior to this point the oracles have taken a poetic form. The fact that chaps. 36—39 constitute the only other sizable narrative block in the entire book of Isaiah forces us to consider the functions of each narrative block and ponder their possible relation to one another. Chapters 6—8 and 36—39 are not literal accounts of events in Israel in the late eighth century B.C.E., but their placement in the Isaianic corpus urges us to read these texts against the backdrop of the Babylonian invasion and exile. These chapters are focused on judgment and destruction (6:11–12). Even so, the note of hope is far stronger in this narrative material than one might expect (see below). These chapters, therefore, carry an *aggadic* teaching function for the exilic situation. Given the overarching literary context, it is not strange that the book mentions Ahaz, Hezekiah, and Cyrus, while giving no apparent narrative counterpart to the actual invasion of Nebuchadnezzar. (Chapters 24—27 might give the poetic counterpart to this invasion.). If the rhetorical context is exilic, then the narrative materials can be read insightfully in relation to those devastating events. If so, then what are chaps. 6—8 saying? Perhaps that while threats loom, God's people can have confidence in a changing history that will yield the defeat of Israel's enemies. This confidence may explain why chaps. 6—8 offer more hope than judgment, already anticipating the turning of chap. 40.

The subsequent section, the oracles concerning Israel and the remnant (chaps. 9—12), again takes up the question of judgment. While chaps. 9 and 11 herald renewal, chap. 10 makes it clear that God's judgment remains in force, stymieing the process of renewal. We will consider the social justice aspects of this judgment below. Here we observe the role of Assyria. That by "Assyria" the text transparently means Babylon can be inferred from Isa. 10:11: "Shall I not do to Jerusalem and her images what I did to Samaria and her idols?" Our literary setting holds together the destruction of Samaria and the eve of the exile. The prophet adopts a view of divine action in history that was common throughout the ancient Near East, namely, that God (or the gods) can use the armies of one nation to execute the divine wrath against another.[61] While the prophet does not wrestle as acutely with the contradictions introduced by this view, the prophet does, like Habakkuk, seek to take into account the sheer arrogance of empire building. For a time, a nation can be used as the instrument of divine anger:

> But when my Lord has carried out all his purpose on Mount Zion and in Jerusalem, He will punish the majestic pride and overbearing arrogance of the king of Assyria. For he thought,

>> "By the might of my hand have I wrought it,
>> By my skill, for I am clever:
>> I have erased the borders of peoples;
>> I have plundered their treasures,
>> And exiled their vast populations.
>> I was able to seize, like a nest,

The wealth of peoples;
As one gathers abandoned eggs,
So *I* gathered all the earth:
Nothing so much as flapped a wing
Or opened a mouth to peep."

Does an ax boast over him who hews with it,
Or a saw magnify itself above him who wields it?
As though the rod raised him who lifts it,
As though the staff lifted the man!

                              Isa. 10:12–15

The restoration of the remnant, the survivors of exile, graphically demonstrates that God's judgment against the empire builders, Egypt and "Assyria," has been effected (10:20–27). The bridge with chap. 11 makes this view clear. It is God's felling of the top of the tree, the haughty empire builders spoken of in Isa. 10:33–34, that clears the way for the new growth of Israel as a just society (11:1–5). With chaps. 9 and 11 as frames, we already see the judgment announced in chap. 10 (and in the previous chapters) mitigated. Chapter 11, in particular, focuses our attention on the social justice character of the judgment, but also of Israel's restoration. This is to say that the struggle to wrestle hope out of desolation will be sterile to the extent that the community fails to address the structural social injustices that had come to characterize the monarchic and bureaucratic apparatus over the centuries. In other words, judgment is a force to be reckoned with in the divine economy, but justice can triumph over judgment. Indeed, justice is the only means to success in the vision of the prophet (12:1–2).

While the international character of judgment has already been anticipated by material devoted to the fall of empire builders, these texts hardly prepare us for the scope of the prophetic discourse found in chaps. 13—23, commonly termed oracles against foreign nations. At a glance, the range alone is impressive:

Babylon (13—14), includes Persia (13:17—22)
Assyria (14)
Philistia (14)
Moab (15—16)
Damascus (17)
Cush/Nubia (18)
Egypt (19—20)
Cush/Nubia (20)
Babylon (21)
Edom = Seir (21)
Arabia = Dedan and Tema (21)
Jerusalem in relation to Assyria (22)

Tyre and Sidon (23)
Tarshish (23)

Such oracles against the nations form a consistent element in the prophetic corpus. The prophetic social critique is grounded in a vision of international judgment. While in so many respects it may be difficult to define what it means to be prophetic, it is clear that one aspect of the prophetic task is to situate a vision and critique of Israel's and Judah's politics in a broader international context of divine action. Of course, since Israel and Judah were the conquered, rather than the conquerors, Israel's royal and prophetic literature views national success in terms of judgment and survival as opposed to conquest and expansion, unlike the Assyrian and Babylonian royal annals.

With a poetic eloquence that speaks of the stars, constellations, and the sun being darkened, the "day of the LORD" becomes the day when tyrants tumble, when the Medes bring Babylon to its knees (13:1–7). A link with the legends known also from Genesis sharpens the cosmic or mythical character of Babylon's defeat: "And Babylon, glory of kingdoms, proud splendor of the Chaldeans, shall become like Sodom and Gomorrah overturned by God" (13:19). The circumstance permits the oppressed to go free (14:4–5), a literary context that provides the final redactor an occasion to see in these events a moment when YHWH shows compassion to Jacob (14:1–3).

The convulsion of history, the collapse of tyrants, constitutes birth pangs of Israel's rebirth after exile. Babylon is the first to go:

You shall recite this song of scorn over the king of Babylon:

> How is the taskmaster vanished,
> How is oppression ended!
> The LORD has broken the staff of the wicked,
> The rod of tyrants,
> That smote peoples in wrath
> With stroke unceasing,
> That belabored nations in fury
> In relentless pursuit.

> All the earth is calm, untroubled;
> Loudly it cheers.
> Even pines rejoices at your fate,
> And cedars of Lebanon:
> "Now that you have lain down,
> None shall come up to fell us."

> Sheol below was astir
> To greet your coming—
> Rousing for you the shades

Of all earth's chieftains,
Raising from their thrones
All the kings of nations.

All speak up and say to you,
"So you have been stricken as we were,
You have become like us!
Your pomp is brought down to Sheol,
And the strains of your lutes!
Worms are to be your bed,
Maggots your blanket!"

Isa. 14:4–11

The earth is finally to be free of the convulsions of empire building. The empire, reduced to nothing, becomes an object of scorn:

Once you thought in your heart,
"I will climb to the sky;
Higher than the stars of God
I will set my throne.
I will sit in the mount of assembly,
On the summit of Zaphon:
I will mount the back of a cloud—
I will match the Most High."
Instead, you are brought down to Sheol,
To the bottom of the Pit.
They who behold you stare;
They peer at you closely:
"Is this the man
Who shook the earth,
Who made realms tremble?"

Isa. 14:13–16

The text's concern for national or tribal rivalries strikes closer to home with an assessment of Philistia (14:28–32) and Moab (15:1–16:14). Philistia, an oracle warns, ought not to see in the collapse of the tyrant an occasion for joy (i.e., an opportunity to return to conflict with Israel and Judah):

Rejoice not, all Philistia,
Because the staff of him that beat you is broken.
For from the stock of a snake there sprouts an asp,
A flying seraph branches out from it.
The first-born of the poor shall graze
And the destitute lie down secure.
I will kill your stock by famine,
And it shall slay the very last of you.

Isa. 14:29–30

And why should Philistia not rejoice? Simply because Zion exists for a purpose, namely, to serve as a refuge for the needy (14:32). This is the litmus test for Zion's successful mission among the nations. Whether we are speaking of a First, Second, or Third Isaiah, Israel's own treatment of the poor will remain the measure of its mission and rule in whatever form it takes after the exile.

Moab bears the brunt of the war refugees. The picture of wailing and strife is poignantly set out for us by the prophet:

> He went up to the temple to weep,
> Dibon [went] to the outdoor shrines.
> Over Nebo and Medeba
> Moab is wailing;
> On every head is baldness,
> Every beard is shorn.
> In its streets, they are girt with sackcloth;
> On its roofs, in its squares,
> Everyone is wailing,
> Streaming with tears.
> Heshbon and Elealeh cry out,
> Their voice carries to Jahaz.
> Therefore,
> The shock troops of Moab shout,
> His body is convulsed.
> My heart cries out for Moab—
> His fugitives flee down to Zoar,
> To Eglath-shelishiyah.
> For the ascent of Luhith
> They ascend with weeping;
> On the road to Horonaim
> They raise a cry of anguish.
>
> Isa. 15:2–5

Yet, unlike Philistia, the prophet's message concerning Moab extends that litmus test to these refugees. The "tent of David" must become a shelter for them:

> "Give advice,
> Offer counsel.
> At high noon make
> Your shadows like night:
> Conceal the outcasts,
> Betray not the fugitives.
> Let Moab's outcasts
> Find asylum in you;
> Be a shelter for them
> Against the despoiler."

For violence has vanished,
Rapine is ended,
And marauders have perished from this land.
And a throne shall be established in goodness
In the tent of David,
And on it shall sit in faithfulness
A ruler devoted to justice
And zealous for equity.

Isa. 16:3–5

Stunning in its poetic eloquence is the text's sympathy for kindred suffering:

Therefore,
As I weep for Jazer,
So I weep for Sibmah's vines;
O Heshbon and Elealeh,
I drench you with my tears.
Ended are the shouts
Over your fig and grain harvests.
Rejoicing and gladness
Are gone from the farm land;
In the vineyards no shouting
Or cheering is heard.
No more does the treader
Tread wine in the presses—
The shouts have been silenced.

Therefore,
Like a lyre my heart moans for Moab,
And my very soul for Kir-heres.

Isa. 16:9–11

This passage is perhaps less startling when we recall that wounded Israel's role is to be that of "a light of nations" (42:6; 49:6). Compassion to war refugees is the concrete form of Israel's role in the international arena.

The message here is essentially that of the Joseph narrative in Genesis, where reconciliation with Esau (i.e., Edom) constitutes the prelude to the successful reconciliation of the twelve tribes (see chapter 3). In viewing both Isaiah and Genesis in their final form as works addressing the postexilic situation, it is clear that there were thinkers, both prophetic and otherwise, who saw Israel's survival to be intimately connected to a successful outbreak of regional peace. Of course, it is Israel's remnant, not Moab's, that is central to the task of reconciliation (cf. Isa. 16:13–14). The ravages of war were to give way to intercommunal relief, support, and rebuilding. This is a profound, if precarious vision. Rooting such a hope in a sensitive awareness of the fragility of the exilic situation shows us that the vision of chaps. 40—66, far from being escapist fantasy, must have been seen by the redactor to be intimately linked to a credible reassessment of the community's mission in relation to the poor, the survivors, and the refugees. The door is open for legal reforms such as those seen in Nehemiah.

Agricultural imagery drives the picture of judgment in the Damascus pronouncement (Isaiah 17), where the city's destruction is proclaimed. Israel's fate and Damascus's fate are one:

> Fortresses shall cease from Ephraim,
> And sovereignty from Damascus;
> The remnant of Aram shall become
> Like the mass of Israelites
> 　　　—declares the LORD of Hosts
> 　　　　　　　　Isa. 17:3

Only gleanings remain (17:6) and the branches wither (17:10–11). Then, in a passage that resembles Psalm 2, the raging nations who plunder Israel are toppled by the God who is a Rock (17:10–14). The appended, commentary-like, prose section in the chapter draws out the concrete thrust of the text: The ritual apparatus of the urban centers and the very fortresses themselves will be abandoned. The devastation of judgment implicates the wealth and symbol systems of the bureaucratic establishment (17:7–9). As if to jar these centers of political "wisdom," the prophet uses a common wisdom referent to god as "Maker" to underscore the idea that future hope lies beyond the devastation wrought against the oppressive urban centers, whether in Israel or in Damascus.

The prophetic oracles against the nations open out at this point toward the distant lands of Nubia and Egypt. To Nubia, the announcement is that, after a time of "trimming," tribute will pour into Israel (Isaiah 18). Returning to the anti-idol theme of chap. 17, the pronouncement against Egypt casts in sharp relief the conflict between a resplendent YHWH, "mounted on a swift cloud" (i.e., as Baal once was depicted), and Egypt with its trembling idols (19:1). The conflict plunges Egypt into civil war, with idols and spirits providing no comfort or insight:

> Utter fools are the nobles of Tanis;
> The sagest of Pharaoh's advisers
> [Have made] absurd predictions.
> How can you say to Pharaoh,
> "I am a scion of sages,
> A scion of Kedemite kings"?
> Where, indeed, are your sages?
> Let them tell you, let them discover

What the LORD of Hosts has planned against Egypt.
The nobles of Tanis have been fools,
The nobles of Memphis deluded;
Egypt has been led astray
By the chiefs of her tribes.
The LORD has mixed within her
A spirit of distortion,
Which shall lead Egypt astray in all undertakings
As a vomiting drunkard goes astray;
Nothing shall be achieved in Egypt
By either head or tail,
Palm branch or reed.

Isa. 19:11–15

Since we know that divination was used throughout the Near East as part of the state's political forecasting and decision making network (see above), the prophet's critique exposes a critical weakness in the ritual and symbol system of the elite. The resultant judgment provokes a fundamental reversal in the religious symbol system that puts Judah squarely at the center of the international arena (19:16–24).

Isaiah 20 presents a narrative fragment from what appears to have once been a part of a separate collection of Isaiah narratives that has been interspersed throughout the book of Isaiah. Here the shocking defeat of Egypt and Nubia by Assyria, a theme apropos to this general section of Isaiah, throws open a poignant question for the coastland dwellers: "If this could happen to those we looked to, to whom we fled for help and rescue from the king of Assyria, how can we ourselves escape?" (20:6). Indeed, where in the international arena is there escape? Seen from the exilic perspective, relief comes only through a positive act of YHWH. The text reinforces an ardent nationalist hope, as do so many of the passages in Isaiah.

Amid these many oracles against the nations is set the exile's greatest hope: the fall of Babylon (chap. 21). The poem is cleverly written, for the subject nation is not named until verse 9. To be sure, the "harsh prophecy" that has come from the "Negeb" does call for Elam and Media to advance (v. 2), but against whom and for what purpose is not immediately clear. The bitter taste of the judgment is revealed in one of the most vivid passages in Isaiah:

Therefore my loins
Are seized with trembling;
I am gripped by pangs
Like a woman in travail,
Too anguished to hear,
Too frightened to see.
My mind is confused,

I shudder in panic.
My night of pleasure
He has turned to terror:
"Set the table!"
To "Let the watchman watch!"
"Eat and drink!"
To "Up, officers! grease the shields!"

For thus my LORD said to me:
"Go, set up a sentry;
Let him announce what he sees.
He will see mounted men,
Horsemen in pairs—
Riders on asses,
Riders on camels—
And he will listen closely,
Most attentively."
And [like] a lion he called out:
"On my LORD's lookout I stand
Ever by day,
And at my post I watch
Every night.
And there they come, mounted men—
Horsemen in pairs!"
Then he spoke up and said,
"Fallen, fallen is Babylon,
And all the images of her gods
Have crashed to the ground!"

                                        Isa. 21:3–9

Ultimately these are words of hope, but not one word of true release directed at Israel is spoken at this juncture, though certainly chaps. 40—66 will emerge directly out of wrestlings such as those of chap. 21. The passage's political hope is grounded in the collapse of particular empires that ruined Israel and Judah for their own sport. In the meantime, all the prophet can do is urge the surrounding peoples, such as those at Dedan and Tema, to accept the refugees with bread (21:13–15). The picture of a social consciousness rooted in the concrete struggles of the landless could hardly be more plain. Then, too, concrete hope lies beyond the reduction of Kedar's bows, an event to happen within a time that is "fixed like the years of a hired laborer" (21:16–17).

The international focus of this section of Isaiah briefly gives way to a reflection on Judah's judgment. In dark words, very much like the opening cries of the book of Lamentations, the horrible fate of Judah's executed victims and captives is bitterly exposed: "Your slain are not slain of the sword nor the dead of battle" (22:2). Again, the text anticipates the release of chaps. 40—66 but here only the grim side is arrayed before the reader: "I will weep bitterly. Press not to comfort me for the ruin of my poor people" (22:4). The words of comfort in chap. 40 will be heard more clearly in light of such a text. Thus, a portrait of devastation, in this case presumably authored during the Assyrian period, has been infused with new meaning by being recast in relation to the experience of devastation *and release* in the exilic period. Particular attention is paid to the destruction of Jerusalem and the devastation of its housing and water supply (22:10–11a). It is said to be a moment when the aggressor ignores the God who was the architect of Jerusalem and who demanded mourning rites in light of its destruction. Of course, the victor only celebrates, thereby angering Jerusalem's sovereign (22:11b–14). This passage hints at the royalist character of the Isaianic project, at least insofar as the text anticipates the rebuilding of Jerusalem as a political and religious center for the restoration community after the exile.

The so-called Tyre pronouncement in chap. 23, which actually concerns also Sidon, Tarshish, and Phoenicia, rounds out the oracles against the nations. Tyre, recognized for plying the sea with its travelers and merchants, is brought to an ignominious end by YHWH: "The LORD poised His arm o'er the sea and made kingdoms quake; It was He decreed destruction" (23:11).

The so-called "little apocalypse" of chaps. 24—27 presents us with a picture of devastation in Judah, with the horrors of judgment actualized. If hope arises out of the ashes of Judah's destruction, as the prophet announces in chaps. 40—66, then the "little apocalypse" portrays the ashes of that destruction. The grim, "Woe is me!" arises when YHWH "will strip the earth bare." It is a time where:

> Layman and priest shall fare alike,
> Slave and master,
> Handmaid and mistress,
> Buyer and seller,
> Lender and borrower,
> Creditor and debtor.
>
> Isa. 24:2

The betrayal of an "ancient covenant" has left the land defiled, awaiting judgment. A major focus of this wrath are the "kings of the earth" (24:21). Beyond their day of doom is YHWH's renewal (chap. 25). Yet the words of restoration in chap. 26 are set out as an unrealized hope from the dim confines of exile:

> Like a woman with child
> Approaching childbirth,
> Writhing and screaming in her pangs,
> So are we become because of You, O LORD.
> We are with child, we writhed—

It is as though we had given birth to wind;
We have won no victory on earth;
The inhabitants of the world have not come to life!
Oh, let Your dead revive!
Let corpses arise!
Awake and shout for joy,
You who dwell in the dust!—
For Your dew is like the dew on fresh growth;
You make the land of the shades come to life.

Isa. 26:17–19

Following the "little apocalypse," the next series of oracles (chaps. 28—33) constitute five major pronouncements of woe (as indicated by the use of *hôy*, "woe" in 28:1; 29:1; 30:1; 31:1; 33:1).[62] This "woe series," while taken up with pronouncements against Israel and Judah, makes full reference to the demise of "Assyria" and Egypt. The series begins with a jibe against "the proud crowns of the drunkards of Ephraim" (i.e., the leadership in Samaria, perhaps marking the passage out as quite ancient). Their injustice is built on their enjoyment of "rich food," a critique similar to that found in Amos 6, which is itself part of an ancient woe cycle (Amos 5:7, 18; 6:1). Both the Amos and Isaiah woe cycles offer extensive critiques of the lifestyle and political policies of the urban elite in ancient Israel and Judah. Here we are witnessing the clearest voice of an ancient prophetic tradition, which has been adapted by the redactor of Isaiah. Thus, the poet's critique goes out against priest and prophet (28:7; 29:10–11). The rulers in Jerusalem are under divine threats of wrath (28:14), the covenant in Jerusalem is termed a "covenant with death" (28:15, 18), and their worship has been false worship (29:13–14).

This critique extends as well to the sort of political alliances Israel and Judah pursued, primarily with Egypt. Some of the prophet's harshest words are reserved for this issue:

Oh, disloyal sons!
    —declares the LORD—
Making plans
Against My wishes,
Weaving schemes
Against My will,
Thereby piling
Guilt on guilt—
Who set out to go down to Egypt
Without asking Me,
To seek refuge with Pharaoh,
To seek shelter under the protection of Egypt.

The refuge with Pharaoh shall result in your shame;
The shelter under Egypt's protection, in your chagrin.
Though his officers are present in Zoan,
And his messengers reach as far as Hanes,
They shall come to shame
Because of a people that does not avail them,
That is of no help or avail,
But [brings] only chagrin and disgrace.
Isa. 30:1–5; cf. 30:12–14; 31:1–4

This past is to become a written record against the people (30:8). The record is to reveal to later generations that the word of prophecy was bitterly and deliberately falsified and unheeded (30:8–11). Here we are subtly made aware that the prophetic voice is actively seeking to gain a postexilic hearing by a rhetoric of persuasion. By convincing the hearers that a failure to heed prophetic warnings in the past led to disaster, this later writer is seeking thereby to gain adherents who will follow a program for restoration after the exile. The competing postexilic voices found in the Hebrew Bible assure us that there were many programs afoot hoping to gain a following at the end of the exile and during the period of the return and restoration. One difference we may note in the prophetic tone of the biblical materials is that while DH seeks to give itself a prophetic cast to make a similar case about Judah's demise, only Isaiah mines earlier prophetic social critique to push its program. Thus, Isaiah resembles Amos and Micah in terms of its talk about social justice, unlike DH.

Two passages in the woe-series concern YHWH's war on Assyria (30:27–33; 31:8–9). These passages either refer to the fall of the historic Assyria at the hands of Babylon or reveal in hidden phraseology or rhetorical use the collapse of Babylon with its conquest by Cyrus the Persian. One wonders if the fall "not by the sword of man" refers to Cyrus's apparently peaceful entry of Babylon and its open submission to him. Regardless, in the current context, these passages bring the reader down to the time period just prior to the exile or to the end of the exilic period and must be seen in light of these events. Once again, as with so much of Isaiah, a context later than that of an eighth-century B.C.E. prophet proves decisive for making sense of the total project of the book and not solely of chaps. 40—66.

The woe series forges ahead with Amos-like warnings to the carefree women of the capital city (32:7; cf. Amos 4:1–3). Palace and city, citadel and towers will all be abandoned and destroyed. It is an era when the rulers of Israel will be judged (33:1). At the hour of the devouring fire of judgment, the people will cry for help but not be delivered, for that is the wrong time to expect piety to save (33:2–14). The standards of justice are clearly laid out:

> He who walks in righteousness,
> Speaks uprightly,
> Spurns profit from fraudulent dealings,
> Waves away a bribe instead of grasping it,
> Stops his ears against listening to infamy,
> Shuts his eyes against looking at evil—
> Such a one shall dwell in lofty security,
> With inaccessible cliffs for his stronghold,
> With his food supplied
> And his drink assured.
>
> Isa. 33:15–16

But as with the inhabitants of Sodom in the time of Abraham (Gen. 18:22–33), presumably too few righteous were to be found in Jerusalem's palaces.

A final word of judgment rounds off First Isaiah in chap. 34. However, this is not the last word in the struggle between desolation and hope that dominates the construction of chaps. 1—35, for chapter 35 raises up an unmitigated hope. Thus, by the literary structuring of chaps. 34—35, we already anticipate the movement of the prose section in chaps. 36—39 to be dire yet not final. Even with chap. 34's word of desolation, hope is not over. Nevertheless, we await further articulation of chaps. 40—66, wherein the total book holds out the hope of chapter 35 as a hope of release from the prison of devastation, defeat, and dispersion.

To sum up: The picture of judgment in Isaiah 1—35 forms the dark underside to Israel's hope. That the fragile boat of ancient Israelite nationalism survived the turmoil is nothing short of miraculous. Chapters 40—66, severed from this chilling anchor of judgment, carry far less persuasive theological substance in isolation. Yet against the grim tableau of the judgment passages and the oracles against the nations in chaps. 1—35, chaps. 40—66 show themselves to be the product of a bitter struggle to find hope in the midst of the chaos of imperial expansion and national exile. In a sense, the deep probings of chaps. 1—35 win the prophetic voice the right to offer a concrete hope amid exile and beyond. Theologically speaking, hope can be wrestled out of desolation only if the desolation is authentically and genuinely confronted. The total work of Isaiah is a masterpiece in this regard. As we shall see, the centrality of the justice dimension to this wrestling allows the postexilic prophetic voice to fine tune the ancient prophetic social critique to speak to the changed social, material, and political conditions of the reconstruction period after the exile.

A Yearning for Communal Hope

For all the talk of desolation, Isaiah 1—35 also wrestles with the possibilities of survival, restoration, and hope. The initial oracles against Judah and Jerusalem (chaps. 1—5) herald this aspect: "Had not the LORD of Hosts left us some survivors, we should be like Sodom, another Gomorrah" (1:9). Indeed, the theology of rewards and punishments, a theology we normally identify with DH, is held out as the basis for hope: "Be your sins like crimson, they can turn snow-white" (1:18). If the people heed God's design, they will prosper; but if not, they "will be devoured [by] the sword" (1:19-20). The divine vengeance against Jerusalem will give way to the restoration of the city and its dignitaries (1:24–26). Thus, from the very first chapter of Isaiah, we see the redactor presenting the case that hope is to be wrestled out of judgment. Chapters 1—35 struggle with this tension without a permanent resolution.

Probably the most well-known statement of hope occurs in Isa. 2:1–4, a text that almost exactly corresponds to Micah 4:1–3. Here Zion emerges as the location of an international worship rooted in the peace that ends all war: "Thus He will judge among the nations and arbitrate for the many peoples, and they shall beat their swords into plowshares and their spears into pruning hooks: nation shall not take up sword against nation; they shall never again know war" (2:4). Elsewhere, in a passage that harkens back to the description of the divine protection of the people in the wilderness, Jerusalem will be restored for the survivors (4:2–6).

Chapters 6—8 offer a narrative setting concerning Isaiah situated during the reigns of Uzziah and Ahaz. The narratives point forward to that moment in time when the desolation will end and the restoration will begin:

> I asked, "How long, my Lord?" And He replied:
>
> > "Till towns lie waste without inhabitants
> > And houses without people,
> > And the ground lies waste and desolate—
> > For the LORD will banish the population—
> > And deserted sites are many
> > In the midst of the land.
>
> "But while a tenth part yet remains in it, it shall repent. It shall be ravaged like the terebinth and the oak, of which stumps are left even when they are felled: its stump shall be a holy seed." (Isa. 6:11–13)

The people, like trees, will be felled, but the stump will contain the seed of the remnant, those survivors of the destruction in whom resides the nation's hope. The stump obviously anticipates chap. 11.

In chap. 7, the message to Ahaz is not to despair: "And say to him: Be firm and be calm. Do not be afraid and do not lose heart on account of those two smoking stubs of firebrands, on account of the raging of Rezin and his Arameans and the son of Remaliah" (7:4). And why not? Wherein lies the prophet's confidence? Chapter 7 roots hope in the necessity of historical and political change: "For before the lad knows to reject the bad and choose the good, the ground whose two kings you dread shall be abandoned" (7:16). Kings who threaten will eventually disappear (cf. 8:4); Egypt and Assyria will pass. Of course, if, as suggested above, these texts are reflective of the exilic period, either in composition or at least in rhetorical usage, then the *aggadic* instructional thrust of the text is to highlight a moment when Egypt and *Babylon* no longer pose a threat. The renewal envisioned by this anticipation is as rich as anything imagined in chaps. 40—66 (cf. 7:18–25). The pledge for renewal rests in God's character and decree (8:8–16), a theme rejoined in chaps. 40—55 in response to the failed mission of the suffering servant.

The theme of restoration receives full expression in chaps. 9 and 11, texts that stand in direct tension with the judgment address of chap. 10 as part of the oracles concerning Israel and the remnant (chaps. 9—12). Chapter 9 acknowledges Israel's political defeat, blamed on faulty leadership (9:13–16 [14–17]), and finds solace in the hope sounded in vv. 1–6 (2–7), where a Davidic heir is trumpeted as Israel's release. Far from finding this heir literally in Hezekiah (stemming from an eighth-century B.C.E. prophet who operates with a Davidic theology), this talk of David is reflective of a postexilic interest, probably nostalgic, in the renewal of the Davidic throne, a theme expressed likewise in Jeremiah and Ezekiel. Scholars frequently fail to observe that an interest in David, in fact, binds the so-called First, Second, and Third Isaiahs *together*.[63] The interest in David can hardly be argued to be some unique interest of an eighth-century Isaiah. Indeed, failure to grasp the broad use of David throughout the book of Isaiah obscures what is actually contributed by chaps. 40—66, namely, a strong affirmation of Abraham, Sarah, and the idea of covenant (see below). Chapters 9 and 11 sound the note of a Davidic royal hope. Yet Isa. 9:11–12 makes it clear that without a national turning, the people's defection from God will keep God's judgment in force. The term of service does not end until chap. 40. Chapter 10 makes it clear that judgment threatens to hold the nation back.

While chap. 10 strongly trumpets judgment, it is also evident that Israel's judgment is not the end of the story:

> But when my Lord has carried out all his purpose on Mount Zion and in Jerusalem, He will punish the majestic pride and overbearing arrogance of the king of Assyria. For he thought,
>
>> "By the might of my hand have I wrought it,
>> By my skill, for I am clever:
>> I have erased the borders of peoples;
>> I have plundered their treasures,
>> And exiled their vast populations.
>> I was able to seize, like a nest,

> The wealth of peoples;
> As one gathers abandoned eggs,
> So *I* gathered all the earth:
> Nothing so much as flapped a wing
> Or opened a mouth to peep."
> Isa. 10:12–14

The superpower is used by God as an instrument of judgment. Yet the conqueror becomes arrogant in conquest and thus loses authority in the divine economy, a line of thought developed by another exilic period text, Habakkuk (see chapter 9). Hence, the conqueror is also overthrown: "Does an ax boast over him who hews with it, or a saw magnify itself above him who wields it? As though the rod raised him who lifts it, as though the staff lifted the man!" (Isa. 10:15). The moment of historic transformation thus arrives: "And in that day, the remnant of Israel and the escaped of the House of Jacob shall lean no more upon him that beats it, but shall lean sincerely on the LORD, the Holy One of Israel. Only a remnant shall return, only a remnant of Jacob, to Mighty God" (Isa. 10:20–21). The scattered, the remnant, are returned. While the tension in chaps. 1—35, therefore, is between judgment and restoration, restoration is breaking loose via the text's agonizing confrontation with judgment.

Now it should not be supposed that this pulse from judgment and desolation to the restoration of the remnant is unique to the Hebrew Bible. The Mesopotamian tale of Erra and Ishum exhibits the same thrust. Erra (Nergal), the war god, feels weakened and wishes to fight. Persuading the god Marduk to stand aside for a while, Erra devastates the world. Only the persuasive speeches of his adjutant, Ishum, cause Erra to cease, permitting a remnant of survivors to be restored. Note that the biblical prophet's role is analogous to Ishum. The prophet, like Ishum, points out the consequences of devastation both to God and to the people.[64] Persuasive speech, understood here as the rhetoric of stark consequences, permits a new order to emerge. The god Erra ceases destroying and the remnant can be restored. The unique element for the Bible is its insistence on the ethical dimension as a factor behind the turning from desolation to restoration (see further below). Thus, while vv. 24–26 undoubtedly constitute later prose commentary on the poetry of the rest of chap. 10, nevertheless, the sentiments expressed are organically related to and logically extend the basic pulse of the poetry in the context of Mesopotamian religious ideas:

> Assuredly, thus said my Lord GOD of Hosts: "O My people that dwells in Zion, have no fear of Assyria, who beats you with a rod and wields his staff over you as did the Egyptians. For very soon My wrath will have spent itself, and My anger that was bent on wasting them." (Isa. 10:24–25)

Hence, whereas Israel can rightly grieve that its leaders will be cut down and the populace will suffer (10:33–34), the people can also be reassured that the "shoot will grow out of the stump of Jesse" (11:1). In other words, through national renewal, a new and just society can emerge.

The hope theme emerges most strongly in chaps. 11 and 12 with a tone that graphically anticipates the announcement of chap. 40. The exile's survivors are the bearers of a new dawn: "In that day, the stock of Jesse that has remained standing shall become a standard to peoples—nations shall seek his counsel and his abode shall be honored" (11:10). And in what can only be an anticipatory summons to return from exile, we see in chaps. 11 and 12 the hope of a reassembly of the survivors:

> In that day, My Lord will apply His hand again to redeeming the other part of His people from Assyria—as also from Egypt, Pathros, Nubia, Elam, Shinar, Hamath, and the coastlands.

> > He will hold up a signal to the nations
> > And assemble the banished of Israel,
> > And gather the dispersed of Judah
> > From the four corners of the earth
> > Then Ephraim's envy shall cease
> > And Judah's harassment shall end;
> > Ephraim shall not envy Judah,
> > And Judah shall not harass Ephraim.
> > Isa. 11:11–13

Note the accent on *Judah's* dispersed, language that thinly veils the *Babylonian* exile. Thus, we must see in First Isaiah an *exilic* assessment of Judah's national hope beyond exile, to which one might compare the prose comment:

> The LORD will dry up the tongue of the Egyptian sea—He will raise His hand over the Euphrates with the might of His wind and break it into seven wadis, so that it can be trodden dry-shod. Thus there shall be a highway for the other part of His people out of Assyria, such as there was for Israel when it left the land of Egypt. (Isa. 11:15–16)

Chapter 12, which follows closely on these thoughts, anticipates fully chap. 40:

> > In that day, you shall say:
> > "I give thanks to you, O LORD!
> > Although You were wroth with me,
> > Your wrath has turned back and You comfort me,
> > Behold the God who gives me triumph!

I am confident, unafraid;
For Yah the LORD is my strength and might,
And he has been my deliverance."

Joyfully shall you draw water
From the fountains of triumph,
And you shall say on that day:
"Praise the LORD, proclaim His name.
Make His deeds known among the peoples;
Declare that His name is exalted.
Hymn the LORD,
For He has done gloriously;
Let this be made known
In all the world!
Oh, shout for joy,
You who dwell in Zion!
For great in your midst
Is the Holy One of Israel."

Isa. 12:1–6

Yet it is clear from the structural arrangement of the rest of Isaiah that this hope must still face the very real challenges of judgment.

The oracles against foreign nations (chaps. 13—23) have been discussed above in the context of judgment, but a clear message of hope for Israel, indeed for the world, results from that judgment. The first party addressed is that of Babylon (chaps. 13 and 14). In the context of Babylon's collapse, Israel is promised resettlement and release from hard service (14:1–3). The song that follows, a song of triumph at Babylon's demise, may be an old song, but its use now fully anticipates the release proclamation of chap. 40:

You shall recite this song of scorn over the king of Babylon:

How is the taskmaster vanished,
How is oppression ended!
The LORD has broken the staff of the wicked,
The rod of tyrants,
That smote peoples in wrath
With stroke unceasing,
That belabored nations in fury
In relentless pursuit.

All the earth is calm, untroubled;
Loudly it cheers.
Even pines rejoices at your fate,
And cedars of Lebanon:
"Now that you have lain down,
None shall come up to fell us."

Sheol below was astir
To greet your coming—
Rousing for you the shades
Of all earth's chieftains,
Raising from their thrones
All the kings of nations.

All speak up and say to you,
"So you have been stricken as we were,
You have become like us!
Your pomp is brought down to Sheol,
And the strains of your lutes!
Worms are to be your bed,
Maggots your blanket!

How are you fallen from heaven,
O Shining One, son of Dawn!
How are you felled to earth,
O vanquisher of nations!

Once you thought in your heart,
"I will climb to the sky;
Higher than the stars of God
I will set my throne.
I will sit in the mount of assembly,
On the summit of Zaphon:
I will mount the back of a cloud—
I will match the Most High."
Instead, you are brought down to Sheol,
To the bottom of the Pit.
They who behold you stare;
They peer at you closely:
"Is this the man
Who shook the earth,
Who made realms tremble,
Who made the world like a waste
And wrecked its towns,
Who never released his prisoners to their homes?"
All the kings of nations
Were laid, every one, in honor
Each in his tomb;
While you were left lying unburied,
Like loathsome carrion,
Like a trampled corpse
[In] the clothing of slain gashed by the sword
Who sink to the very stones of the Pit.
You shall not have a burial like them;
Because you destroyed your country,
Murdered your people.

Isa. 14:4–20a

It is worth quoting this remarkable passage at length. The nation that arrogantly thought it would plant its throne on Zaphon, the mountain of the divine assembly in Canaanite tradition, finds itself thrust instead down to Sheol, the netherworld. Here myth is used to read the nations' political history. Myth provides the key for unlocking the meaning and fate of Babylon's expansion. The host of Shaddai defeats Babylon, causing the nations to rejoice (cf. 14:22–23). It would seem that the reference to Assyria in v. 25 represents either a veiled reference to Babylon or the more ancient text out of which the critique of chaps. 13—14 is built. The portions devoted to Philistia (14:28–31) may argue for the latter view. However, it is clear from v. 32 that any ancient message of Zion as refuge is being appropriated in the context of the larger book of Isaiah to bolster a postexilic program of triumphal hope and restoration.

The somewhat disjointed Moab pronouncement would appear to indicate, at least in part, that a Davidic throne will provide shelter for a remnant of Moab, a remnant that will no longer, however, pose any political danger to Israel (16:2–5). Thus, the same processes of history that are at work in Israel are seen by the prophet to be operant in the foreign sphere as well. Isaiah's God is an international figure who dispenses justice in a consistent fashion without concern for or need of a covenant relationship to establish guidelines of royal conduct or national behavior. Since covenant plays so little a role in chaps. 1—39, this should come as no surprise. Yet more is at stake here than a covenant theme. By viewing the processes of history as predictable and international, the text's vision credibly paves the way for viewing Cyrus in as messianic a light as an actual Davidic bloodline dynast. Throughout the world, YHWH pulls nations down and installs rulers of YHWH's own choosing. It would seem that the insistence in Second Isaiah on Israel's status as a "light of nations" (42:6 and 49:6) represents, in part, an international acknowledgment of this cosmic, world-encompassing, dominion of YHWH. Such a view is consistent with the prophet's announcement to Nubia that after the time of "trimming," tribute will pour into YHWH's "calm" habitation on Mount Zion (chap. 18).

Envisioning the collapse of Egypt, the prose comment (19:16–24) on the poetic oracle of Egypt's judgment (19:1–15) eagerly anticipates the salvifically effective presence of Israel in Egypt (19:19). In this reversal of the exodus motif, the Egyptians, like the Babylonians, participate in the international rule of YHWH, but with a critical difference: The reversal of the exodus motif does not mean that Israel will be permitted to oppress Egypt. On the contrary, since YHWH's rules apply across the board internationally, the Egyptians will be able to cry out to YHWH against oppressors and receive divine aid (19:20–21; cf. Ex. 2:23–25; 3:7–10; 22:22 [23]). In and through Israel there is hope for the nations. When read in the exilic context, one must presume this means that Israel's exile in Babylon (cf. Jeremiah 29) and Egypt (cf. Jeremiah

42—44) will engender a message of hope for all suffering communities. The
Elephantine community and the Jewish community in Babylonia represent
the concrete realization of the struggle to remain a definable people over and
against a perceived environment of hostile paganism.[65] The experience of persecution and dispersion led to the creative theological response that Israel's
God travels with people into exile, overturning the common ancient Near
Eastern view that the capture of a people's idols or gods by an enemy was a disaster. This international rule of God is given an astonishing stamp in Isa.
19:24–25:

> In that day, Israel shall be a third partner with Egypt and Assyria as a
> blessing on earth; for the LORD of Hosts will bless them, saying, "Blessed
> be My people Egypt, My handiwork Assyria, and My very own Israel."

The hope of First Isaiah is given a decidedly political cast in Isa. 22:15–25.
This segment juxtaposes two very different sorts of administrators, Shebna
and Eliakim, figures who turn up again in chap. 36. Shebna, who is given the
technical term, "in charge of the palace" (22:15), a sign of his high official status, is condemned for hewing out a fine tomb. His end will be a death wrought
by divine judgment. The poetic passage concerning Shebna is followed by a
prose passage concerning, "My servant Eliakim son of Hilkiah" (22:20).
YHWH's judgment against Shebna is not complete until the divine sovereign
has given over Shebna's tunic, sash, and authority to Eliakim so that Eliakim
can be "a father to the inhabitants of Jerusalem and the men of Judah" (22:21).
The text explicitly references David as the source of this authority: "I will place
the keys of David's palace on his [Eliakim's] shoulders" (22:22). The movement from desolation to recovery involves a transferral of political authority
to a new generation of leaders who walk in the paths of David. This insight is
critical to understanding the fundamental flow of ideas in the whole of Isaiah.

The last of the pronouncements concerns Tyre. Here the similarity of
Tyre's seventy years of punishment to that of Judah's suffering (cf. Jer.
25:11–12; 29:10) is unmistakable. Certainly the final redaction, at least, of
Jeremiah, DH, and Isaiah are in related hands. Curiously, however, the end of
Tyre's seventy years only witnesses its return to politics as usual, with the proviso that its economic gains, its harlotry fees, will be turned over to Israel, perhaps as compensation (Isa. 23:17–18). Restoration means concrete economic
improvements for the people of Israel.

Before leaving these oracles and turning to the "little apocalypse" of chaps.
24—27, one general observation is in order concerning the oracles against the
nations. These oracles, spoken against a host of major and minor political
players, contain within themselves a more fundamental message of hope: The

collapse of each and every opponent of Israel means that there is one less source of oppression to contend with. Of course, all this judgment means bitterness for innocents abroad, a fact that Habakkuk and Job wrestle with, but in the context of Isaiah, the oracles, comprising chaps. 13—23, provide insight into a dominant prophetic view of history. The very processes that create and overturn the nations are at work in Israel's history, signaling a way through judgment and desolation to restoration and healing. It should be clear that these oracles are integral to the overall pattern of the book and the scope of the prophetic message. Chapters 13—23 reveal the general trajectory of history's movement in relation to Zion. Thus, even though chaps. 34—39 will leave us pitched poised on the precipice between healing and judgment, chaps. 13—23 have already created the sense, to be confirmed by chaps. 30, 31, and 33, that superpowers such as Egypt and Assyria (Babylon) are not the final shakers and movers of history. The text gives room to a judgment that will have its day, but opens the way to historic reversals that herald a much brighter future for an Israel beyond the ashes of exile.

As we have seen, the "little apocalypse" presents a frightening portrait of exilic destruction at the hands of the invading Babylonian troops. Yet even this grim picture has not toppled the hope that yearns to break free from this devastation to arise like a Phoenix from the ashes of destruction. This hope is at work in the "little apocalypse," bringing light to a darkened landscape (24:14–16). The prophet anticipates this as a time when YHWH will reign on Mount Zion, i.e., after the exile. Chapter 25 works to pull hope out of desolation by speaking to the plight of war's victims:

> O LORD, You are my God;
> I will extol You, I will praise Your name.
> For You planned graciousness of old,
> Counsels of steadfast faithfulness.
>
> For You have turned a city into a stone heap,
> A walled town into a ruin,
> The citadel of strangers into rubble,
> Never to be rebuilt.
> Therefore a fierce people must honor You.
> A city of cruel nations must fear You.
> For You have been a refuge for the poor man,
> A shelter for the needy man in his distress—
> Shelter from rainstorm, shade from heat.
> When the fury of tyrants was like a winter rainstorm,
> The rage of strangers like heat in the desert,
> You subdued the heat with the shade of clouds,
> The singing of the tyrants was vanquished.
>
> Isa. 25:1–5

Having faced war's brutality, the prophet envisions a time of reconstruction and prosperity:

> The LORD of Hosts will make on this mount
> For all the peoples
> A banquet of rich viands,
> A banquet of choice wines—
> Of rich viands seasoned with marrow,
> Of choice wines well refined.
>
> And He will destroy on this mount the shroud
> That is drawn over the faces of all the peoples
> And the covering that is spread
> Over all the nations:
> He will destroy death forever.
> My Lord GOD will wipe the tears away
> From all faces
> And will put an end to the reproach of His people
> Over all the earth—
> For it is the LORD who has spoken.
>
> In that day they shall say:
> This is our God;
> We trusted in Him, and He delivered us.
> This is the LORD, in whom we trusted;
> Let us rejoice and exult in His deliverance!
>   Isa. 25:6–9

Chapters that at first glance appear to be filled only with gloom have been cleft asunder by unmitigated triumph. The nationalist program of reconstruction is offered as a concrete way out of the paralysis of imperial politics:

> In that day, this song shall be sung
> In the land of Judah:
> Ours is a mighty city;
> He makes victory our inner and outer wall.
> Open the gates, and let
> A righteous nation enter,
> [A nation] that keeps faith.
> The confident mind You guard in safety,
> In safety because it trusts in You.
>
> Trust in the LORD for ever and ever,
> For in Yah the LORD you have an everlasting Rock.
> For He has brought low those who dwelt high up,
> Has humbled the secure city,
> Humbled it to the ground,
> Leveled it with the dust—

To be trampled underfoot,
By the feet of the needy,
By the soles of the poor.
The path is level for the righteous man;
O Just One, You make smooth the course of the righteous.

Isa. 26:1–7

Presumably here the "poor and needy" are the returning exiles who will lay claim to the seats of power. One does not imagine here a proletarian revolution of the Marxist variety. As will become clear in our discussion of chaps. 40—66, the exile has brought about an adaptation of the ancient prophetic call for justice to the poor. Where once this language may indeed have been spoken in relation to the concrete needs of Israel's oppressed, this language has, with the exile, been amalgamated, via prophetic recasting, into the political program of the displaced *elite* in ancient Israel. The experience of exile has elevated that group as the "poor and needy" through whom YHWH will raise a triumphant banner during the restoration under Cyrus. A chastened elite now boasts: "For when Your judgments are wrought on earth, the inhabitants of the world learn righteousness" (26:9).

Culling mythic language, as happens time and again in Isaiah, at this point the text invokes the ancient myth of the slaying of the sea monster by the deity of power.[66] As YHWH topples Pharaoh in Exodus, so also here the LORD destroys ancient enemies to plant a fruitful garden (27:1–6). Yet internal renewal is also required. The lifting of foreign domination must go hand in hand with the dismantling of the idolatrous system that accompanied the political system (27:9). The postexilic program of this prophet asserts national independence under the banner of an "uncontaminated" worship of YHWH. These are the conditions for regathering from exile, according to the expanded comments of Isa. 27:12–13.

The subsequent woe series (chaps. 28—33) likewise sets out a future restoration. This restoration occurs when Jerusalem's besiegers finally exhaust themselves and depart to leave Mount Zion free (29:1–8). The time is an era of total social transformation, wherein the excesses of the tyrant and the injustices in legal matters give way, for the redactor, to an Abrahamic tradition of honor and justice (29:17–24).

The issue of alliances with Egypt becomes an occasion for the prophet to hold out hope. The people's "victory" was to come from "stillness and quiet," not in the swift movement of war horses (30:15–17). But counterproductive national alliances are to give way to "pardon" (30:18). A prose commentary on renewal intrudes here (30:19–26). This remarkable passage presents a Jerusalem that heeds God's commands implicitly, that shuns idols as unclean, that sees economic renewal and the binding of the exile's wounds (cf. 31:5–7).

In such a passage we see a total mutation of the old prophetic social critique as the exiled elite has become the suffering remnant, a theme profoundly developed in chaps. 40—66.

At this juncture, the woe series permits the intrusion of a vision of royal justice that harks back to chap. 11:

> Behold, a king shall reign in righteousness,
> And ministers shall govern with justice;
> Every one of them shall be
> Like a refuge from gales,
> A shelter from rainstorms;
> Like brooks of water in a desert,
> Like the shade of a massive rock
> In a languishing land.
>
> Then the eyes of those who have sight shall not be sealed,
> And the ears of those who have hearing shall listen;
> And the minds of the thoughtless shall attend and note,
> And the tongues of mumblers shall speak with fluent eloquence.
>
> Isa. 32:1–4

Beyond the devastation is a renewal that brings a generalized "justice" and "security" (32:15–20). This is the work of a spirit poured out from above, bearing obvious kinship to the spirit of justice that emerges later in the text (33:15; cf. 61:1). Ultimately, Zion is to be the center where YHWH rules as king and prince (33:20–24).

Finally, chaps. 1—34 give way to a tremendous word of hope in chap. 35. While the narrative concerning desolation's threat awaits to be told in chaps. 36—39, nevertheless, the struggle between desolation and hope is given a temporary respite, with hope as the final word in chap. 35. This vision powerfully anticipates the news of chap. 40, which follows on the tensions that arise in chaps. 36—39:

> Then the eyes of the blind shall be opened,
> And the ears of the deaf shall be unstopped.
> Then the lame shall leap like a deer,
> And the tongue of the dumb shall shout aloud;
> For waters shall burst forth in the desert,
> Streams in the wilderness.
> Torrid earth shall become a pool;
> Parched land, fountains of water;
> The home of jackals, a pasture;
> The abode [of ostriches], reeds and rushes.
>
> And a highway shall appear there,
> Which shall be called the Sacred Way.

No one unclean shall pass along it,
But it shall be for them.
No traveler, not even fools, shall go astray.
No lion shall be there,
No ferocious beast shall set foot on it—
These shall not be found there.
But the redeemed shall walk it;
And the ransomed of the LORD shall return,
And come with shouting to Zion,
Crowned with joy everlasting.
They shall attain joy and gladness,
While sorrow and sighing flee.

Isa. 35:5–10

Such a vision sets Zion down as the spiritual center of national and even international renewal. All of chaps. 1—35 lead to this vision and hope. The exiles have begun to taste, however rhetorically, their freedom from Babylonian domination. They have become YHWH's redeemed, brought out of slavery to establish a just society in Judah, the land of their return. We shall not be surprised to find in chaps. 40—66 a renewal of the exodus motif, in all its mythic grandeur, functioning as a ground of appeal to energize this prophet's program of national restoration.

If we view chaps. 1—35 in its entirety, two clear strands run through the block at every step: judgment and hope for Zion.[67] Yet this is a hope that has not yet appeared. It is a hope, a restoration, that must break forth out of the desolation and judgment experienced by the community. It is a hope that only prophetic wrestling can accomplish.[68] This is the legacy of each subsection of chaps. 1—35 that pertains to the people of Israel, whether the oracles against Judah (chaps. 1—12), the "little apocalypse" (24—27), the oracles against Israel (28—33), or the vision of Zion (34—35). Throughout these sections, woe and restoration, judgment and survival contend for the final word. With the close of chap. 35, we might expect hope and healing to emerge victorious. However, chaps. 36–39 offer a sobering pause to any sort of theological triumphalism that roots hope solely in a restoration of the Judaean or Israelite monarchy.

Social Ethics and Judgment

It is arguable that at least some of the materials strewn throughout Isaiah 1—35 stem from a corpus of texts dating from the eighth century B.C.E. There are strands that bear a strong resemblance to the sorts of socioeconomic issues raised by Amos and Micah. However, while there is a good deal of overlap between the messages of these other prophets, there are also significant differences. In part, there is a difference in emphasis. The materials in First

Isaiah, for example, do not detail the situation of the poor to the same extent as Amos and Micah do. Rather, First Isaiah speaks much more about the *consequences* of unjust activity than Amos, with the fact of future judgment and the potential decimation of the land always in view. Another key difference is one of content. Many of the references to the poor in Isaiah look to a future rectification of that condition within history. This notion of a future amelioration of present evils infuses First Isaiah with a vision and a hope that is decidedly less prominent in the social critique of Amos or Micah. Thus, even if portions of Isaiah are contemporaneous with the earliest materials in Amos or Micah, the perspectives in Isaiah have been reframed by forces and factors from a later time. We will have to treat First Isaiah in a more general fashion with respect to its "chronological" origins as we consider the economic arrangements and political processes that stand in back of this material.

The early chapters of Isaiah depict the members of the urban establishment as exhausting the produce of the vineyard, God's people, and taking the property of the *'ānî* (3:13–14). The driving concern of the decadent upper classes is depicted as enhancing pleasure and increasing material prosperity: "Ah [better: "Woe to"], those who are so doughty—as drinkers of wine, and so valiant—as mixers of drink! Who vindicate him who is in the wrong in return for a bribe, and withhold vindication from him who is in the right" [better: "They take away the justice of the just."] (5:22–23; cf. 5:18–21).[69] The prophetic critique is clear: The prosperity of the wealthy is directly linked to injustices against other members of Israelite society.

The prophet specifies that the mode of exploitation adopted by the rich: "Ah ["Woe to"] those who add house to house and join field to field, till there is room for none but you to dwell in the land" (5:8). The rich were continually increasing their holdings by taking over the property of others, even resorting to bloodshed to attain these ends (5:7). The establishment and extension of the monarchy supplied the base for this economic development.[70] Although originally only "intended primarily to ensure a united military leadership in defensive warfare," the monarchy eventually became a "decisive factor" in shaping Israel's economic structures.[71] This socioeconomic context is what some scholars are inclined to term "*Frühkapitalismus*," or early capitalism (see further below).[72] The establishment of the monarchy in Israel under David and Solomon placed great demands on the populace. In the first place, there was a need for a complex bureaucracy to administer the realm (cf. 2 Sam. 8:15–18; 20:23–26).[73] This bureaucracy required support. In the narratives regarding King Solomon, it is reported that the land was divided into twelve administrative districts, divisions made with little regard for the previous tribal allotments (1 Kings 4:7–19; 5:7–8 [4:27–28]). Operating on a monthly rotation schedule, each district was to supply the central government in Jerusalem the goods and materials it required.[74] Undoubtedly such a system of redistribution was maintained by both the Northern and Southern King-doms throughout their existence. Similarly, the centralization of worship in Jerusalem and the subsequent influx of sacrifices, from which the priesthood gained their livelihood, placed further burdens on the peasant populace.[75] It is unfortunate that in the case of the temple we do not have a better picture of the material demands made by the religious hierarchy regarding the goods they would have extracted from the villages.

The rapid rise of such a complex bureaucracy over a village-based tribal confederation is best explained by the supposition that David and Solomon adapted Canaanite administrative structures from Jerusalem and other areas that were brought under Israelite control.[76] Beyond adapting structures, it would also have been the case that many of the actual bureaucrats and religious functionaries would have been brought over from the Canaanite city-states into David's realm.[77]

The monarchy increased the economic burdens of the populace in several *military* ways. As already mentioned, goods were supplied to the central government from the outlying districts. But labor was also supplied. The biblical record makes it quite clear that forced labor was imposed to conduct royal construction projects (2 Sam. 12:31; 20:24; 1 Kings 5:27–32 [13–18]; 9:22; 11:28; 1 Chron. 20:3).[78] Further, the monarchy found it necessary to establish a permanent standing army rather than rely on peasant levies to conduct its campaigns of expansion and tribute exaction.[79] Such a military apparatus would require support not only when stationed at home but also when engaged in military enterprises. From the populace, soldiers would have to be conscripted (1 Sam. 8:11–12), although as Wittenberg points out, "From David onwards kings relied more and more on mercenaries for their military campaigns."[80] Moreover, the populace would have to supply goods for the sustenance of the soldiers and military officials. In addition, the peasants would be called on to serve as forced laborers in the construction of military fortifications. The tendency would be for a military elite to develop, and this elite would acquire economic clout in the form of land given by the ruler as payment to military personnel for services rendered to the state (1 Sam 8:14–15).[81]

Perhaps the most significant effect of the monarchy, at least in the discussion *land* of poverty in Israel, is the development of crown property and the rise of large landowners. The establishment of crown property presumably goes back to the time of David's conquest of Jerusalem, a city that became, appropriately enough, the City of David, a domain outside tribal holdings (2 Sam. 5:6–9). From that time on, the kings of Israel held crown property (1 Sam. 8:14; 2 Sam. 14:30; 1 Kings 16:24; 2 Chron. 26:6).[82] Furthermore, the members of the royal elite sought to extend their land holdings. Davies suggests that the monarchy and its officials extended the crown's holdings through the purchase of land, the acquisition of property belonging to condemned criminals, and the takeover of abandoned property.[83] In addition, Davies contends that land acquisition was carried out by both creditors and royal officials.[84] This process would have undercut any premonarchic system of land tenure practiced among the villagers (1 Sam 22:7).[85] The tribal groupings in Israel represented small farming communities of independent, self-sufficient families who divided the land according to traditional inheritance patterns (*naḥălâ*). [86] With the establishment of the monarchy, the urban elite sought to displace these village claims to land, thereby allowing a cadre of landowners to emerge (1 Sam. 8:14–15; 1 Kings 21).[87] The injustices that resulted from these socioeconomic developments, in particular the high cost of land acquisition for the peasant populace, elicited prophetic protest. Citations by Schottroff concerning Israel's premonarchic period demonstrate that land acquisition among Israelites was not a Canaanite or "foreign" practice as Donner claims.[88] And yet it was with the monarchy that this process was accelerated, disrupting the land tenure structures of the villages to the benefit of the urban elite. This appears to be the situation reflected in Isa. 5:8.

It is misleading to characterize the conflicts that resulted from these political developments as conflicts between Canaanites and Israelites, as if there were some ethnic distinction involved, still worse to treat this as a confrontation between nomadic and civilized peoples (see the discussion in chapter 1). Most "Israelites" were doubtless simply native Canaanites who became adherents of Yahwism, there being very few who were actually descended from the exodus group (if even this group can be labeled "non-Canaanite" or if it ever existed). Likewise, many of "Israelite" background adopted the lifestyle and patterns of "Canaanite" society.[89] To avoid confusion here, it seems best to speak in terms of an urban-village complex and to place the injustices witnessed by the prophets against just such a background.[90] The rise of the bureaucracy must be seen as the incorporation of elements from the urban sphere, via Canaanite administrators, into the sphere of the Israelite tribal confederation. Urban structures were adopted by the Israelite rulers as part of the process of conquering the urban enclaves. This development allowed urban-based society once again to exert influence over the local village groups, but this time in the name of YHWH of Jerusalem. Viewed in this way, the economic injustices witnessed by Isaiah, Amos, or the other early Hebrew prophets should be understood as the product of the interaction between the urban and village societies. It should be borne in mind that the economic practices criticized by the prophets, namely, latifundization, were not exclusively "Canaanite" in any case, for such practices were current throughout the ancient Near East and the Roman Empire.[91]

The concentration of land in the hands of the few cannot be separated from other forms of domination by the elite. Dijkema correctly observes that the monarchy acted on its own, apart from the interests or will of the general populace.[92] The administration of the country as well as land ownership was taken over by a few families. Likewise, the administration of justice would be in the hands of the landowners, whether urban or rural, and with Jehoshaphat (c. 873–849 B.C.E.) the control of the practice of law was brought fully over into the control of royal officials (2 Chron. 19:8–11; on legal practices see further below).[93] Furthermore, the control of commerce was in the hands of the elite. This would include the merchants who abused the poor (see the discussion on Amos in chapter 9) as well as the crown itself, which controlled trade and trade routes.[94]

Many scholars tend to understand the economic development under the monarchy to be a form of rent capitalism. Lang, for example, argues for this model in the context of his discussion of Amos, but his thoughts apply here as well. In the first place, Lang maintains that "quite often the rich are townspeople, who indulge in drinking and lead a life of shameless luxury."[95] This lifestyle is made possible as a result of the exploitation of others, since the landowners take advantage of the "small tenants" who work land owned by the wealthy.[96] In applying this analysis to ancient Israel, Wittenberg suggests the relationship between the landowners and the peasant farmers was organized in such a way that the "wealthy landowners lived in the cities and had their *latifundia* worked by slaves or paid farm labourers."[97] Debts that result in this situation, Lang observes, force "peasants overburdened with debts…to sell themselves into bondage to work off their liabilities."[98] This is an essential feature of rent capitalism. As Lorentz states, "The absolute ideal of rent-capitalism appears to be to ensnare so many farmers in lasting debt that they cannot pay off the sharply mounting original debt with all their yearly payments."[99] A final feature Lang identifies as vital to this economic setup in Israel is grain trade.[100]

Lorentz notes that rent capitalism has several deleterious effects on societies in which it functions as an economic system. In the first place, the drive for profit among the landowners brings about the exhaustion of both the soil and livestock.[101] But more importantly, the human toll such an economic arrangement can take is quite high. The life of indebtedness is one of grueling oppression. The contrast between urban dwellers and village peasants is stark. While city culture flourishes, the population of the countryside is impoverished.[102] Thus, the ruining of the poor and the carefree existence of the power elite are often mentioned together in Isaiah because the prophet understood that the increased standard of urban living came at the expense of the village populations, the 'ebyôn and 'ānî [Q]/'ănāwîm [K] (32:7, 9). The situation is as Miranda observes: The continual acquisition of property "can only be explained by the exploitation and violence perpetrated by the rich upon the rest of the population."[103]

Isaiah's condemnation of Judah's judicial system is similar to Amos's critique. The text offers a stern warning to those who "decree iniquitous decrees"

(Isa. 10:1). The system of law and legal transaction was reinforced with laws that served to benefit the more influential members of society. The rulers did not take up the cause of disenfranchised individuals, such as the *dal* and the *'ānî* (10:2), the widow and the orphan (1:21–23). As Tamez observes, the widows and orphans were numbered "among the poor and helpless, because they had no one to defend them and no means of subsistence."[104] The same undoubtedly applies to the poor in general as well. The situation is clearly reminiscent of the legalized injustice "at the gate" that the book of Amos ascribes to the Northern Kingdom. Judah's political and economic structures were maintained by falsehoods and legal institutions, which did not rectify the imbalances of economic privilege that continually benefited the rich (cf. 32:7). False claims were made in court by the rich, who disregarded the innocence of the *'ebyôn* and *'ānî*. We can surmise that much injustice was tolerated by bending the laws to the advantage of the rich. In other cases, the judges interpreted the laws in favor of the rich because they were naturally inclined toward the people who shared the same values and came from the same backgrounds as they did.

Davies argues that the unjust decrees Isaiah has in mind were laws designed by court officials to facilitate the king's acquisition of property from the peasants and thereby insure "the continued existence of vast royal estates from which they themselves might hope to derive some benefit as a reward for their service and loyalty to the king."[105] However, although one concern is the unjust acquisition of property by the elite, the text does not mention this specific issue in the passage in question. Therefore, laws related to land acquisition must remain only one of the many plausible types of iniquitous decrees made by the government to the disadvantage of the poor.

Davies suggests that injustices in the legal system in Israel stemmed from two sources. In the first place, judicial officials were corrupt and accepted bribes from the rich.[106] This is evidenced by Isa. 5:23, which refers to those who "vindicate him who is in the wrong in return for a bribe, and withhold vindication from him who is in the right" [better: "acquit the guilty for a bribe, and deprive the innocent of his right"]. The bribes mentioned here are to be considered "gifts" (*šoḥad*), bribes in the true sense of the term, to be distinguished from the *koper* mentioned in Amos 5:12.[107] Next, Davies argues that the assembly of elders who would hear cases at the gate were undoubtedly the senior property owners in the community.[108] The interests of this group might easily take precedence over the rights of the disenfranchised, namely, those who lacked or had little property. As Dijkema points out, "It is evident that the law is not inviolable when its jurisdiction is in the hands of the large landowners and functionaries answerable to the king."[109] Davies contends that Isaiah's opposition to land grabbing was tied to the prophet's concern for justice:

> Isaiah's condemnation of those who acquire the property of others (Isa.
> 5:8–10) may be directly related to his passionate concern for justice in the
> assembly, since the judiciary could only function on a democratic basis as
> long as every man remained an independent, land-owning citizen.[110]

While one might criticize Davies for an anachronistic use of the term "democratic," nevertheless, it seems that a fair distribution of land lay at the base of the most ancient communal ideals of early Israel. In this, the prophet would seem to be a defender of the old patrimonial land distribution system of premonarchic Israel and hence of the villages.

We have already seen how integral the message of judgment is to Isaiah 1—35. In this context, we should take care to note the socioethical dimension of that judgment message, for, according to chap. 1—35, only the desolation of the oppressive urban elite, with its corrupt legal and economic structures, could pave the way for God's spirit to fall and true justice to reign (32:1–20). YHWH is judging the rulers of the land for their exploitation of the poor: "The LORD will bring this charge against the elders and officers of His people: 'It is you who have ravaged the vineyard; that which was robbed from the poor ['ānî] is in your houses'" (3:14). The land was to be judged. Since the elite prospered through the exploitation of others, the leaders were to lose their power and chaos was to ensue (3:1–5). Like Amos, the text issues a warning to the "carefree women" of the upper crust (32:9). The prophet proclaims to them that "the castle shall be abandoned, the noisy city forsaken" (32:14). Elsewhere, the prophet makes it clear that the demise of the social order was not without cause; it is a collapse that would come about because of the ruling elite's own policy choices (3:9). Specifically, the land's leaders, who were guilty of misleading the people (3:12), were to be judged for their oppression of the poor ('ānî ; 3:14–15). The high standard of living the rich obtained through exploitation would be destroyed in judgment and all the fine garments and jewels would be carted off by Assyria (3:25–26). The strong tone of a socioethical dimension to the message of judgment indicates the concrete character of the text's social analysis, offering a wide-ranging critique of the ideology and social practices of the ancient ruling elite.[111]

Anticipation of Future Rectification of the "Oppressed"

As with the message of judgment in chaps. 1—35, so also the message of hope carries with it a clearly discernable socioethical dimension. Several sections in chaps. 1—35 that deal with the poor do so with reference to a future relief of that condition. The texts envision for the poor a coming release from their present social and economic woes. One passage, for example, looks ahead to the day when the ruler of Israel, the "proud crown of the drunkards of Ephraim," will topple (28:1), and "Ariel," that is Jerusalem, will be surrounded by armies (29:2–3). Then the *'ebyôn* and *'ănāwîm* will exult in YHWH (29:19). The deaf and blind will be released from their afflictions. The slander and unjust legal practices of the ruthless and scoffers will come to an end (29:20–21).

Likewise, in the "little apocalypse" (chaps. 24—27), YHWH, the protector of the *'ebyôn*, "poor" (25:4), is depicted as the one who will judge both the host of heaven and the earthly kings. At that time the feet of the oppressed and poor (*'ānî* and *dal*) will trample the city (26:6). Then the political alliances by which Israel and Judah sought security will be broken and the grip of foreign ideologies, gods, and kings over God's people will end (26:13–14). The broad vision of renewal found in Isaiah is more developed than in Amos (cf. Amos 9:6–15).

Elsewhere, the prophet envisions this future rectification as the work of a ruler who will abandon the unjust ways of those who ruled previously, inaugurating a rule based on justice (11:1–4). Similarly, the text proclaims that the *'ebyôn* who has a just plea will find relief when the just king is enthroned (32:7; cf. 9:5–6). These passages offer a critique of the legal system of the writer's time. The expression of hope for a just order is a recognition that the existing structures were exploiting the poor and powerless. The prophet's vision of a transformed royal tradition is found in another text which states that the afflicted (*'ānî*) of Philistia will take refuge in Zion (14:32).

Finally, the text announces a future relief that extends to the oppressed outside of Israel. The prophet warns Philistia not to rejoice over Ahaz's death because the Philistines themselves will fall (14:31). As a result of the collapse of the governing authority in Philistia, the prophet states, "The first-born of the poor [*dal*] will feed, and the needy [*'ebyôn*] will lie down in safety" (14:30).

To sum up: First Isaiah is laden with a message of hope that is socioethical in character. To what extent this message is to be traced back to an eighth-century Isaiah is unclear. What is clear is that the compiler has capitalized on this message not only to anticipate the outcome in chaps. 40—66 but also to see that those chapters carry forward the socioethical dimensions of the Isaianic hope. Consequently, the community, when standing at the horizon of total destruction (chaps. 36—39), is called to seek its moorings both in its treatment of the poor and in its self-recognition as those who have been chastened by God.

Isaiah 36—39: The Hiatus of Exile— Judgment Will Reign for a Time

The bitter struggle between desolation and hope at work in Isaiah 1—35 does not directly give way to the glorious note of triumph sounded in chap. 40. Rather, the text sets down the largest narrative block in the entire book, chaps. 36—39, which serve to focus the flow of the book beyond the narrative intrusion made by chaps. 6—8. Positioned as they are before chap. 40, one must ask what the function is of this narrative block, apparently lifted from DH (2 Kings 18:13, 17–37; and chaps. 19—20), in the context of the larger book of Isaiah.[112] Do the chapters shape the desolation versus hope question? Do the chapters contribute to our understanding of the sociopolitical vision of our editor/redactor/author?

The *aggadah* is set during an invasion of the Assyrian king Sennacherib against Judah. That such an invasion took place is not doubted, but our text is doing more than simply reporting historical events. The text becomes the occasion for the development of a prophetic royal theology.

Sennacherib at Lachish sends ahead his official, the Rabshakeh, to threaten Hezekiah's position at Jerusalem (36:2). Present are Eliakim and Shebna, figures mentioned in chap. 22, the former signaling hope and the latter a representative of divine disfavor. The key theological question is posed by the Rabshakeh to Hezekiah: "Thus said the Great King, the king of Assyria: What makes you so confident?" (36:4). Hezekiah is castigated for relying on Egypt, that "splintered reed of a staff" (36:6). Curiously, the author pushes the critique further by having the Rabshakeh say, "And if you tell me that you are relying on the LORD your God, he is the very one whose shrines and altars Hezekiah did away with, telling Judah and Jerusalem, 'You must worship only at this altar!'" (36:7). Further, the Rabshakeh presents himself as YHWH's agent of judgment (36:10). He also presses home the point that King Hezekiah can offer no hope to his people (36:11–21).

This then is the prophetic critique prior to the exile in a nutshell: (1) In what rests a monarch's confidence? Is it in a foreign power like Egypt? Do the alliances matter or are they even effective? (2) Did the centralization program undermine the nation's religiosity? When Jerusalem is the only center, have the religious underpinnings of the nation actually been toppled? (3) If the foreign powers are agents of judgment, how ought one to regard them? Is rebellion or even rebuilding contrary to the divine will? (4) What is the place of the monarchy in Israel's social fabric? Did it serve them well in the past? Does monarchy have a future?

These questions are hardly the sort of things discussed by ancient combatants across the walls of Jerusalem. We confuse matters if we treat such a text as the record of Hezekiah's time. When read in light of the exile and in light of its rhetorical position in the total scope of the text of Isaiah, such questions emerge as some of the most profound issues with which an ancient theologian might struggle who wished to move the community beyond the paralysis of exile to the project of rebuilding. As the theological discussions take a new turn beyond the old questions, so the tradition itself is reinvented. Out of the confrontation between the Rabshakeh and Hezekiah, between looming desolation and unrealized hope, there emerges a new prophetic voice, a reconstituted

Isaiah, who will guide the community through the challenges of chaps. 36—39 toward the dramatic announcement of chap. 40.

What specifically does the prophet contribute in these chapters? What Isaiah does builds on the initial resolve of Hezekiah not to answer the Rabshakeh (36:21). For the exiles, this means a posture of noncooperation with the Babylonian political machine. Hezekiah's resolve is articulated concretely in the form of ritual mourning (37:1–4). The king has understood the nature of the hour: "The babes have reached the birthstool, but strength to give birth is lacking" (37:3). In this context, the messengers are sent to Isaiah to garner support for the "surviving remnant" (37:4). The prophet's response is insightful: "Thus said the LORD: Do not be frightened by the words of blasphemy against Me that you have heard from the minions of the king of Assyria" (37:6). The prophet is confident that a deluding rumor will drive the Assyrian king off (37:7).

Yet Hezekiah's encounter with the divine requires a deeper response. Thus, as the Rabshakeh again threatens with the bald force of Assyria's might (37:8–13), Hezekiah himself turns to the House of the LORD:

> O LORD of Hosts, enthroned on the Cherubim! You alone are God of all the kingdoms of the earth. You made the heavens and the earth. O LORD, incline Your ear and hear, open Your eye and see. Hear all the words that Sennacherib has sent to blaspheme the living God! True, O LORD, the kings of Assyria have annihilated all the nations and their lands and have committed their gods to the flames and have destroyed them; for they are not gods, but man's handiwork of wood and stone. But now, O LORD our God, deliver us from his hands, and let all the kingdoms of the earth know that You, O LORD, alone [are God]. (37:16–20)

Isaiah can now bring the reply of YHWH. Assyria in its arrogance may have assumed it was acting under its own power, but such judgment comes only from YHWH. Thus, it will be that YHWH's designs now also include shipping the Assyrians back from whence they came (37:21–29). In the collapse of the ruling power, the exile finds this hope: "And the survivors of the House of Judah that have escaped shall renew its trunk below and produce boughs above" (37:30–31). Rendered more poetically, the text offers this gem:

> For a remnant shall come forth from Jerusalem,
> Survivors from Mount Zion.
> The zeal of the LORD of Hosts
> Shall bring this to pass.
>
> Isa. 37:32

Hezekiah's renewed confidence in YHWH has yielded great fruit. The survivors, the remnant, will restock Jerusalem and give birth to a community that was nearly stillborn. The monarch, the temple, and the prophet converge as institutional forces in this program of renewal. The royal element at work in the Isaianic project is underscored by reference to YHWH's offer of protection, "for the sake of my servant David" (37:35). While the precise context of the compilation of Isaiah will probably always remain elusive, the persistent royal hope ought to at least make us consider the possibility that the larger text emerged from the circles surrounding the exiled King Jehoiachin in Babylon (2 Kings 24:8–17).

Hezekiah's troubles were far from over with the deliverance from Assyria, however. Drawing on a stock tradition known to us elsewhere in Canaanite tradition from the story of the illness of King Keret, Hezekiah falls terribly ill, such that his rule is mortally imperiled (38:1).[113] Again, Hezekiah's personal piety buys him a prophetic announcement from Isaiah that the king's life will get a fifteen-year extension (38:5). The reference here builds further on the royal connection by calling YHWH "the God of your father David." Furthermore, Isaiah announces rescue from the Assyrian king, which either means protection from future incursions or indicates that the chapter is out of order and should appear prior to the deliverance passage in chap. 37. By the end of chap. 38, Hezekiah is wondering when he can go back to the temple. Once again, the triangle of monarchy, temple, and prophet converge as joint forces in a successful program for Judah's future.

The final twist is given in chap. 39. All the lessons and warnings of chaps. 36—38 receive a sensible political and historic context. After some Babylonian messengers see Hezekiah's treasures and depart, the prophet Isaiah makes one last call to announce that in the future, "everything in your palace, which your ancestors have stored up to this day, will be carried off to Babylon; nothing will be left behind, said the LORD" (39:5–6). The exile shapes the received chapters and provides the key for unlocking the political lessons harbored by chaps. 36—39, both in terms of judgment and hope.

To sum up: The program of Isaiah is a decidedly nationalist political program. Chapters 36—39 bring out in a narrative fashion these tendencies and trajectories, which can assist us in assessing the so-called universalism of chaps. 40—66. But for the moment, it is clear with chaps. 36—39 that a crisis has been weathered. The predicted exile will be endured by means of a prophetic voice that is capable of breathing new life into the royalist program of the remnant. All that awaits is the announcement of deliverance from exile, for desolation has finally had its day.[114]

Isaiah 40—66: The Community of Renewal— The Triumph of Hope over Desolation

The latter half of the book of Isaiah is usually ascribed to prophetic voices of the exilic period, and is conveniently delineated as Second Isaiah (chaps. 40—55) and Third Isaiah (chaps. 56—66).[115] However, while segments of Third

Isaiah appear to stand out as later additions—for example, Isaiah 63 with its rather unique use of Moses—here we shall tend to group chaps. 40—66 together as a unit that is to be read against the backdrop of chaps. 1—39.[116] My thesis here is that the message of hope in chaps. 40—66 makes sense against the pitched struggle we have seen between desolation and hope in chaps. 1—35. The interlude of chaps. 36—39 now gives way to the announcement of chap. 40. Since so much of Second and Third Isaiah has already been anticipated by chaps. 1—39, it makes sense to see in the balance sheet of chaps. 40—66 a theological reckoning that is a deliberate step forward beyond the impasse of judgment.

This theological reckoning does not simply replicate First Isaiah, but builds on earlier themes while exploring new dimensions. Brueggemann insightfully sees a twofold contribution, with Second Isaiah offering a "public embrace of pain" and Third Isaiah presenting the resultant social imagination that emerges from that embrace.[117] In terms of what Brueggemann identifies as Israel's "memories," chaps. 40—66 continue to affirm David, but add a clear emphasis on Abraham, Sarah, and covenant, even as the exodus motif gains renewed significance.[118] For Sweeney, the texts in Third Isaiah transform First Isaiah's David and subtly displace Second Isaiah's Cyrus in favor of YHWH's sovereignty, thereby stamping the book as a whole with new theological perspectives on the ideal king and the place of Israel's priestly people as the bearers of the eternal covenant (building on chap. 55) in the realization of divine rule in Zion under Persian auspices.[119] These chapters, likewise, continue to speak of the poor, but focus on the *'ānî / 'ănāwîm* dimension as a way to reconceptualize the experience of Israel's dislocated elite. In other words, any First Isaiah materials have been grossly recast to follow the theological project of the postexilic author(s). This is not to categorically deny the presence of older materials in chaps. 1—39 but to suggest that the scholarly tendency to treat these texts in isolation has served to obscure the very real continuities and manipulations across the entire book with links and adaptations that allow chaps. 1—39 to rhetorically foreshadow and theologically undergird chaps. 40—66.

The context of chaps. 40—66 is certainly the exile of Judah in Babylonia (c. 587–539 B.C.E.) and the period that immediately follows. The texts address those taken into captivity and their heirs. Babylon is prominent as the nation used by YHWH to punish the people of Judah (47:6). However, since the prophet shows no knowledge of the actual manner in which Babylon fell to the Persians, the writing of Second Isaiah may need to be placed on the eve of 539 B.C.E. Cyrus is active on the political scene, but perhaps not yet ruler over Babylon (or only recently installed as ruler there). Part of the prophet's message of assurance to the people is that one day soon Babylon will no longer be a major power in the world (47:1–15). God merely used Babylon as an instrument to punish the nation of Judah, but a time was coming when YHWH would bring the nation of Babylon to its knees and its shame would finally be exposed (47:1–9). Then the sorcery and divination that Babylon counted on to keep its power intact would turn out to be impotent and the empire would collapse (47:9–15, cf. 48:26).

The prophet comforts a people who are in despair over the experience of the destruction of their homeland and their subsequent deportation to a foreign land, a land from which none of the original deportees might ever return; only their descendants might hope for release. The prophet casts the despair of the situation in a vivid manner in a text where *'ānî* is used in combination with *'ĕbyôn*. The prophet states,

> The poor [*'ānî*] and the needy [*'ĕbyôn*]
> Seek water, and there is none;
> Their tongue is parched with thirst.
> I the LORD will respond to them.
> I, the God of Israel, will not forsake them.
> I will open up streams on the bare hills
> And fountains amid the valleys;
> I will turn the desert into ponds,
> The arid land into springs of water.
>   Isa. 41:17–18

The prophet's mission was the proclamation of a message of hope to those who had given up hope and who had become like those who suffer thirst. The text presents a concrete hope of deliverance from the bondage of exile and encourages the hearers to prepare to return to their homeland. The message of the prophet provides a sudden but appropriate counterweight to the struggle of chaps. 1—35 and the impasse reached in chaps. 36—39. To the *'ānî* who is broken and afflicted by the trauma of exile the prophet declares, "The spirit of the Lord GOD is upon me, because the LORD has anointed me; He has sent me as a herald of joy to the humble [*'ănāwîm*], to bind up the wounded of heart, to proclaim release to the captives, liberation to the imprisoned" (61:1). Concretely this liberation signified escape from Babylon (48:20) and a life of relative freedom under Cyrus the Persian (45:1–5, 13). Most importantly, this release meant the rebuilding of the temple and a restoration of those cities in Israel that had fallen into ruin (44:28; 61:4).

The bulk of the material concerning the *'ānî* in Second and Third Isaiah centers around several major themes.[120] The first theme is that Judah was judged for a reason, namely, its sin (50:1; 59:1–4). Yet this prophet makes known to the captives that the wrath of God against Jerusalem was temporary:

> For the mountains may move
> And the hills be shaken,
> But my loyalty shall never move from you,
> Nor My covenant of friendship be shaken
>   —said the LORD, who takes you back in love.
> Unhappy ['ānî], storm-tossed one, uncomforted!
> I will lay carbuncles as your building stones
> And make your foundations of sapphires.
>
> Isa. 54:10–11

Though Judah was judged for its sins, the purpose of this judgment was not to obliterate the nation but to purify its inhabitants: "For the sake of My name I control My wrath; to My own glory, I am patient with you, and I will not destroy you. See, I refine you, but not as silver; I test you in the furnace of affliction ['onî]" (48:9–10). A similar line of thought is found in a later section where the prophet promises relief for the people now that the time of punishment has ended. The prophet addresses the exiles in this way:

> Therefore,
> Listen to this, unhappy one ['ānî],
> Who are drunk, but not with wine!
> Thus said the LORD, your Lord,
> Your God who champions His people:
> Herewith I take from your hand
> The cup of reeling,
> The bowl, the cup of My wrath;
> You shall never drink it again.
> I will put it in the hands of your tormentors.
>
> Isa. 51:21–23a

No longer would the wrath of God be poured out on the people of Judah; instead it would be turned toward those who had tormented the exiles. To earlier prophets, such as Amos, Israel was judged for its exploitation of others, for making others 'ānî, but the assessment in Second and Third Isaiah alters the theological conception underlying 'ānî by applying it to the people as a whole.[121] Through the experience of judgment for its sin and rebellion, the nation has become 'ānî. By this ideological shift, the prophet has turned the tradition of prophetic social criticism on its head. The elite has suffered, and in a way this vocabulary is descriptive and justified in that the elite has become the suffering servant of God, bringing redemption to God's people (42:1–4; 49:1–6; 50:4–9; 52:13–53:12).[122] Yet at another level we can see a marked ideological distortion of the vocabulary that permits the elite to appropriate a vocabulary of poverty to itself and thereby temper the raw criticism of the elite found in other parts of the prophetic tradition. We will observe this process again in our discussions of the books of Jeremiah and Micah (see chapters 7 and 9).

The second theme found in the *'ānî* texts is the encouragement to hope amid the debilitating circumstances of exile. Zion has indeed suffered, but YHWH will not abandon the people forever (49:14–18). Such were the thoughts that motivated the prophet to exclaim: "Shout, O heavens, and rejoice, O earth! Break into shouting, O hills! For the LORD has comforted His people, and has taken back His afflicted ones in love" (49:13). In this text, the terms *'ammô*, "his people," and *ănîyāw*, "afflicted ones," modify each other, serving as a reference to the entire exilic community in its suffering. The prophet's awareness of the comfort of YHWH in the midst of the nation's suffering allows him to boldly assert that the people should stand firm in the presence of the oppressor (*hammēṣîq*), namely, Babylon, for YHWH will soon free Israel from domination in a foreign land (51:12–14, 22–23).

The *'ānî* texts of Second and Third Isaiah are overwhelmingly concerned with the fate of the community in exile and hold out the hope of future relief. It is on this latter point of a future rectification of existing oppressive conditions that we find a clear movement beyond the struggle motif developed in chaps. 1—35. However, chaps. 1—35 already linked this approaching restoration to an extensive presentation of the oppressive social and political conditions that needed to be rectified. The data in chaps. 40—66 afford something of a significant contrast at this point because these chapters do not regularly speak about the *'ānî* against the backdrop of specific oppressive economic and political structures. While the matter of exile is a question of political significance, Second and Third Isaiah's concern with the beleaguered community does not come close to the sharp economic and political analysis provided in portions of chaps. 1—35. Perhaps herein lies a real difference between the earlier Isaianic texts (eighth century B.C.E.) and the exilic redaction and expansion of that material. Such a shift would appear to mimic that identified by Mosala for Micah, wherein an original prophetic critique of social injustice is later toned down into a message about abstract "justice," only to finally be commandeered by the elite as a message about its own predicament of judgment.[123] If so, then Second and Third Isaiah's major concern is to adapt and transform traditional themes and motifs with a view to adapting the ancient prophetic traditions to the situation of the elite as they faced the crisis of faith engendered by the exile. However, perhaps ironically, the exiled elite has forever transformed the ancient prophetic texts, turning them into a manifesto for their own nationalist agenda, now stamped with a divine imprimatur.

This is not to say that chaps. 40—66 totally deviate from the earlier prophetic understanding of oppression. On the contrary, there is much in these chapters that echoes the sociopolitical perspectives of earlier prophets, even as we note some shift in balance. Political powers are seen as impotent ephemeral entities in the presence of YHWH; they are like "a drop from a bucket and are accounted as the dust on the scales" (40:15). Third Isaiah understands that the nations maintain their might through a combination of violence and murder (59:1–4, 6–7). The text clearly observes that the profit motive was the driving force behind the actions of the "shepherds" of society—its kings, public officials, landowners, and business magnates (56:10–11). Second and Third Isaiah attest to the centrality of the system of idol worship to the workings of the nations, going so far as to say that God actively sought to frustrate the omens and diviners of the political powers (44:25; cf. 44:9–10; 45:20; 46:1–2; 57:13). The ideology of idol worship offered a value system that ran counter to that advocated in these chapters in the name of YHWH. Clearly the social critique of an eighth-century Isaiah has not been entirely lost, although we must acknowledge the notable differences that occur between chaps. 1—35 and 40—66 with regard to the poverty question and the use of the term *ʿānî* .

A keen awareness of economic and political oppression comes out most clearly in Third Isaiah (Isaiah 58). Here the writer depicts a people who try to curry divine favor by taking refuge in the religious ritual of fasting. But the text observes that this will be done to no purpose because "on your fast day you see to your business and oppress all your laborers!" (58:3b). This is not to draw a disjuncture between ritual and ethics. Sweeney rightly observes that Isaiah 58 falls in a section of Third Isaiah (chaps. 56—59) that is devoted to the "issue of proper observance of YHWH's covenant."[124] This observance is carried forward both by Sabbath observance as well as by acting in a socially responsible manner. Through unjust social practices, the members of society's most influential sectors were guilty of the kind of economic exploitation that the prophets had railed against for centuries. This state of affairs serves to indicate that economically not all the exiles suffered in the same manner; some actually took advantage of the disruptive situation for their own gain. The prophet points out that it is the duty of the true follower of YHWH to bring justice to the *ʿānî* who is victimized by the machinations of the rich:

> No, this is the fast I desire:
> To unlock fetters of wickedness,
> And untie the cords of the yoke
> To let the oppressed go free;
> To break off every yoke.
> It is to share your bread with the hungry,
> And to take the wretched poor [*ʿānî*] into your home;
> When you see the naked, to clothe him,
> And not to ignore your own kin.
>
> Isa. 58:6–7[125]

Such an understanding of *'ānî* would be at home among the prophet's pre-decessors, whether we mean the early material in Micah and Amos, or even a now obscure eighth-century Isaiah. For Third Isaiah, this "poetic act of social imagination" reaches a pinnacle in the announcement of a new jubilee:[126]

> The spirit of the Lord GOD is upon me,
> Because the LORD has anointed me;
> He has sent me as a herald of joy to the humble,
> To bind up the wounded of heart,
> To proclaim release to the captives,
> Liberation to the imprisoned;
> To proclaim a year of the LORD's favor
> And a day of vindication by our God;
> To comfort all who mourn—
> To provide for the mourners in Zion—
> To give them a turban instead of ashes,
> The festive ointment instead of mourning,
> A garment of splendor instead of a drooping spirit.
> They shall be called terebinths of victory,
> Planted by the LORD for His glory.
> And they shall build the ancient ruins,
> Raise up the desolations of old,
> And renew the ruined cities,
> The desolations of many ages.
>
> Isa. 61:1–4

To sum up our findings in this chapter: Positively we might say that the writers and compilers of Isaiah sought to understand the events of the exile within the categories and prophetic values passed on from preexilic times. Yet the philosophic and nationalistic wrestlings of this complex book press this heritage to develop new theological ideas, enabling the community of the exile to come to grips with its situation of dislocation. In offering reflections on the plight of the nation (i.e., its elite), the text broadens the scope of the term *'ānî*. The overall thrust of the prophet's message is that YHWH meets the chosen people in the midst of their suffering, affliction, and oppression. Just as YHWH sought out a people who were exploited in Egypt and led them out of that captivity, so YHWH seeks out those who are ensnared by circumstances beyond their control, exiles in foreign Babylon. Indeed, the exodus story becomes a key motif in this revisioning of the tradition, as renewed prophetic voices explore the possibilities of release from exilic domination.[127] Second and Third Isaiah emphasize that YHWH looks to all who are characterized as *'ānî*: "Yet to such a one I look: to the poor [*'ānî*] and brokenhearted, who is con-cerned about My word" (66:2b).

In looking forward to the end of the cycle of oppression, the final form of the Isaiah text argues that past economic practices must be transformed: "They shall not build for others to dwell in, or plant for others to enjoy" (65:22a). Prior to the exile only the exploited peasants who had given up their lifeblood to the rapacious desires of the ruling elite of society could appreciate the kind of relief the prophet promised. This was the source of desolation so clearly articulated in chaps. 1—35. But after the agony and suffering of the exile, the whole community came to understand the meaning of the ʿānî experience. In light of this experience, according to parts of chaps. 1—35 and throughout chaps. 40—66, the entire community could justifiably begin to yearn for release from oppression and reasonably expect YHWH to take note of their condition, for YHWH had long been known to be the protector of the poor and the liberator of the oppressed. The process of exile has made the entire nation ripe for release, readying a people to build a new and just national order. The scriptures themselves bear the marks of that collective dislocation and renewal, a fact that makes our next prophetic text, the book of Jeremiah, a rather cacophonous and jarring collection of communal struggles.

Notes

1. Yet even a contextual survey of the uses of a word can be disheartening where we lack sufficient data for establishing the precise nuances of the Hebrew terms for "poor." At best one can use the evidence to argue that the *dal* may have been a small farmer who was not in the most dire of poverty-stricken situations that are characterized by ʿānî and ʾebyôn. Nevertheless, as commentators such as Baudissin, Lurje, Munch, and Van der Ploeg have shown, a general attention to linguistic context is critical for our choice between a spiritualized understanding of poverty that one might glean from the psalter and a socioeconomic understanding of poverty when reading other portions of the biblical text, in particular the prophets. See the discussion in chapter 10 for Baudissin and Van der Ploeg. See also M. Lurje, *Studien zur Geschichte der Wirtschaftlichen und Sozialen Verhältnisse im Israelitisch-Jüdischen Reiche* (Giessen: Alfred Töpelmann, 1927); and P. Munch, "Einige Bemerkungen zu den ʿănāwîm und den rĕšaʿîm in den Psalmen," *Le Monde Oriental* 30 (1936): 13—26.
2. W. B. Bizzell, *The Green Rising: An Historical Survey of Agrarianism, with Special Reference to the Organized Efforts of the Farmers of the United States to Improve Their Economic and Social Status* (New York: Macmillan, 1926), 15.
3. L. Wallis, *The Struggle for Justice* (Chicago: University of Chicago Press, 1916), 57.
4. See, e.g., K. Cauthen, *The Impact of American Religious Liberalism* (New York: Harper & Row, 1962), 87–88.
5. W. Rauschenbusch, *Christianity and the Social Crisis* (New York: Macmillan, 1910), 3.
6. Ibid., 7.
7. Ibid., 5.
8. Ibid., 9.
9. Ibid., 8.
10. Ibid., 11–12.

11. Ibid., 32.
12. Ibid., 33.
13. Ibid., 33.
14. Ibid., 34.
15. Ibid., 11–12.
16. Ibid., 16.
17. cf. Ibid., 15–16.
18. Ibid., 14.
19. Ibid., 15–16.
20. Ibid., 16.
21. Ibid., 18.
22. Ibid., 18.
23. See, e.g., B. Duhm, *Israels Propheten*, 2d ed. (Tübingen: J.C.B. Mohr/Paul Siebeck, 1922), 201–26; and J. Rogerson, *Old Testament Criticism in the Nineteenth Century: England and Germany* (London: SPCK, 1984), 260.
24. Ibid., 19–20.
25. Ibid., 19.
26. Ibid., 19–20.
27. Ibid., 25.
28. Ibid., 26.
29. Ibid., 27.
30. Ibid.
31. Ibid., 29.
32. Ibid., 16.
33. H. Huffmon, "The Origins of Prophecy," in *Magnalia Dei: The Mighty Acts of God: Essays on the Bible and Archaeology in Memory of G. Ernest Wright*, ed. F. M. Cross, W. E. Lemke, and P. D. Miller (Garden City, N.Y.: Doubleday, 1976), 172.
34. R. R. Wilson, *Prophecy and Society in Ancient Israel* (Philadelphia: Fortress Press, 1980), chap. 3. See also Huffmon, "Origins of Prophecy"; and idem, "Prophecy in the Mari Letters," in *Biblical Archaeologist Reader III*, ed. E. F. Campbell and D. N. Freedman (Garden City, NY: Anchor Books, 1970), 199–224.
35. See A. L. Oppenheim, *Ancient Mesopotamia: Portrait of a Dead Civilization*, rev. ed. completed by Erica Reiner (Chicago: University of Chicago Press, 1977), 206–27. Regarding the attendant ritual practices, see I. Starr, *The Rituals of the Diviner* (Malibu: Undena, 1983).
36. Huffmon, "Origins of Prophecy" and "Mari Letters."
37. Huffmon, "Origins of Prophecy," 172.
38. Wilson, *Prophecy and Society*, 111–19.
39. See J. C. L. Gibson, *Textbook of Syrian Semitic Inscriptions*, vol. 1, *Hebrew and Moabite Inscriptions* (Oxford: Clarendon Press, 1971), 38–41.
40. H. M. Barstad, "Lachish Ostracon III and Ancient Israelite Prophecy," *Eretz Israel* 24 (1993): 8–12. Barstad makes the clear case for reading *m't* as "from" rather than "through" as has been done by many scholars who have thereby reduced the prophet to a mere conveyor of mail.
41. Barstad, "Lachish Ostracon III," 9.
42. See Wilson, *Prophecy and Society*, 129–33, for an assessment.
43. M. Lichtheim, *Ancient Egyptian Literature*, vol. 2, *The New Kingdom* (Berkeley, Calif.: University of California Press, 1976), 224–30.
44. J. C. L. Gibson, *Textbook of Syrian Semitic Inscriptions*, vol. 2, *Aramaic Inscriptions including Inscriptions in the Dialect of Zenjirli* (Oxford: Clarendon Press, 1975), 9.

45. Ibid., 9–10.

46. See J. Hoftijzer and G. van der Kooij, *Aramaic Texts from Deir 'Alla* (Leiden: E. J. Brill, 1976); and P. K. McCarter, "The Balaam Texts from Deir 'Alla: The First Combination," *BASOR* 239 (1980): 49–60.

47. These are among the categories elaborated by Wilson, *Prophecy and Society*, ch. 2.

48. R. P. Carroll, "Prophecy and Society," in *The World of Ancient Israel: Sociological, Anthropological and Political Perspectives*, ed. R. E. Clements (Cambridge: Cambridge University Press, 1989), 203–25.

49. See the compelling rejoinder offered by H. M. Barstad, "No Prophets? Recent Developments in Biblical Prophetic Research and Ancient Near Eastern Prophecy," *JSOT* 57 (1993): 39–60.

50. For a survey of some of the pathbreaking literature, see J. S. Kselman, "The Social World of the Israelite Prophets: A Review Article," *Religious Studies Review* 11/2 (1985): 120–29.

51. See C. R. Seitz, *Zion's Final Destiny: The Development of the Book of Isaiah: A Reassessment of Isaiah 36–39* (Minneapolis: Fortress Press, 1991), 1–14.

52. For a review of the major positions and trends in interpretation see Seitz, *Zion's Final Destiny*, chap. 1. As Seitz points out, Duhm regarded Isaiah 1—39 as a composite set of texts from diverse periods, with some material emanating from after the time of Second and Third Isaiah.

53. Contrast J. Hayes and S. Irvine, *Isaiah, the Eighth-Century Prophet: His Times and His Preaching* (Nashville: Abingdon Press, 1987), who begin with this presumption: "With the exception of Isaiah 34—35, practically all of the prophetic speech material in what is traditionally called First Isaiah—that is Isaiah 1—39—derives from the eighth-century B.C.E. prophet" (13). Their appendix offers a convenient summation of the history of the interpretation of chaps. 1—39.

54. At the very least, as Sweeney argues, we should not overlook the integral role of Isaiah 11 to the conceptual project of Third Isaiah. See M. A. Sweeney, "The Reconceptualization of the Davidic Covenant in Isaiah," in *Studies in the Book of Isaiah: Festschrift Willem A. M. Beuken*, ed. J. Van Ruiten and M. Vervenne (Louvain: Leuven University Press, 1997), 41–61, 54–58.

55. B. Childs, *Introduction to the Old Testament as Scripture* (Philadelphia: Fortress Press, 1979), 325.

56. To some extent, Clements's contention that Second Isaiah works consciously with First Isaiah materials makes a great deal of sense, provided we also make room for secondary expansions and additions to those materials. See R. E. Clements, "Beyond Tradition History: Deutero-Isaianic Development of First Isaiah's Themes," *JSOT* 81 (1985): 95–113; and "The Unity of the Book of Isaiah," *Int* 36 (1982): 117–29.

57. C. R. Seitz, *Reading and Preaching the Book of Isaiah* (Philadelphia: Fortress Press, 1988), chap. 6.

58. While recognizing the existence of pervasive themes and resonances in Isaiah, Carr's criticisms suggest that the composite character of the collection argues against unified purposes or overarching structures in Isaiah. See D. Carr, "Reaching for Unity in Isaiah," *JSOT* 57 (1993): 61–80. Seitz, by contrast, sees in the notion of unity a theologically productive paradigm, one that does not seek a "uniformity of perspective" but functions "to constrain emphasis on multiplicity of perspectives in a single work." See C. R. Seitz, *World without End: The Old Testament as Abiding Theological Witness* (Grand Rapids: Wm. B. Eerdmans Publishing Co., 1998), 128. Seitz joins many others in seeing thematic movement and rhetorical links across the old divisions of Isaiah into three segments.

59. W. Brueggemann, *Israel's Praise: Doxology against Idolatry and Ideology* (Philadelphia: Fortress Press, 1988), chap. 4.

60. W. Brueggemann, *The Prophetic Imagination* (Philadelphia: Fortress Press, 1981).

61. On divine judgment in Mesopotamia, see B. Albrektson, *History and the Gods: An Essay on the Idea of Historical Events as Divine Manifestations in the Ancient Near East and Israel* (Lund: Gleerup, 1967); and H. W. F. Saggs, *The Encounter with the Divine in Mesopotamia and Israel* (London: Athlone, 1978).

62. The *hôy* or "woe" theme is clearly a prophetic expression. The word occurs only once outside of the prophetic writings (1 Kings 13:30). Of all the prophetic occurrences, those in Isaiah predominate. This word binds First, Second, and Third Isaiah thematically in a striking fashion: 1:4, 24; 5:8, 11, 18, 20, 21, 22; 10:1, 5; 17:12; 18:1; 28:1, 15; 30:1; 31:1; 33:1; 45:9–10; 55:1. The prophetic propensities of the related interjection *'ôy* support this view.

63. References to David in Isaiah: 7:2, 13; 9:7; 16:5; 22:9, 22; 29:1; 37:35; 38:5; 55:3.

64. See, e.g., S. Dalley, *Myths from Mesopotamia: Creation, The Flood, Gilgamesh, and Others* (Oxford: Oxford University Press, 1989), 282–315.

65. B. Porter, *Archives from Elephantine: The Life of an Ancient Jewish Military Colony* (Berkeley and Los Angeles: University of California Press, 1968). See, also J. Neusner, *A History of the Jews in Babylonia* (Chico, Calif.: Scholars Press), 1984).

66. Cf. R. J. Clifford, "The Unity of the Book of Isaiah and Its Cosmogonic Language," *CBQ* 55 (1993): 1–17.

67. Seitz, *Reading and Preaching*, 112–19, notes the integrative role of the Zion idea to the entire book of Isaiah.

68. See Brueggemann, *Prophetic Imagination*, chaps. 3–4.

69. J. Kelly, "The Biblical Meaning of Poverty and Riches," *Bible Today* 33 (1967): 2284.

70. Cf., e.g., G. J. Botterweck, "Sie verkaufen den Unschuldigen um Geld," *Bibel und Leben* 12:218–19; E. W. Davies, *Prophecy and Ethics: Isaiah and the Ethical Traditions of Israel*, JSOT Supplement Series 16 (Sheffield: JSOT Press, 1981), 76ff.; and M. Fendler, "Zur Sozialkritik des Amos," *EvTh* 33 (1973): 34.

71. W. Schottroff, "The Prophet Amos: A Socio-Historical Assessment of His Ministry," in *God of the Lowly: Socio-Historical Interpretations of the Bible*, ed. W. Schottroff and W. Stegemann (Maryknoll, N. Y.: Orbis Books, 1984), 38.

72. H.-J. Kraus, "Die prophetische Botschaft gegen das soziale Unrecht Israels," *EvTh* 15 (1955): 304.

73. Fendler, "Sozialkritik des Amos," 34.

74. Cf. E. W. Heaton, *Solomon's New Men: The Emergence of Ancient Israel as a National State* (New York: Pica Press, 1974), 47–60; and Schottroff, "Prophet Amos," 38.

75. Schottroff, "Prophet Amos," 38.

76. Cf. J. Bright, "The Organization and Administration of the Israelite Empire," in Cross et al., eds., *Magnelia Dei*, 193–208; H. Donner, "Die soziale Botschaft der Propheten im Lichte der Gesellschaftsordnung in Israel," *Oriens Antiquus* 2 (1963): 494; and G. E. Mendenhall, "The Monarchy," *Int* 29 (1975): 155–70.

77. Schottroff, "Prophet Amos," 39.

78. Cf. Davies, *Prophecy and Ethics*, 76–77.

79. F. Dijkema, "Le Fond des Prophéties d'Amos," *Oudtestamentische Studiën* 2 (1943): 24; and Schottroff, "Prophet Amos," 38.

80. G. Wittenberg, "The Message of the O.T. Prophets during the Eighth Century B.C. concerning Affluence and Poverty," in *Affluence, Poverty and the Word of God*, ed. K. Nürnberger (Durban: Lutheran Publishing House, 1978), 144.

81. Botterweck, "Unschuldigen um Geld," 220; Donner, "Soziale Botschaft," 497–500; Wittenberg, "Message of the O. T. Prophets," 144.

82. J. Alberto Soggin, "The Davidic-Solomonic Kingdom," in J. H. Hayes and J. M. Miller, eds., *Israelite and Judaean History* (Philadelphia: Westminster Press, 1977), 353, 355.

83. Davies, *Prophecy and Ethics*, 78–79 with references.

84. Ibid., 66–69, 83, 88.

85. Wittenberg, "Message of the O. T. Prophets," 144.

86. Botterweck, "Unschuldigen um Geld," 218; Fendler, "Sozialkritik des Amos," 33; and Wittenberg, "Message of the O.T. Prophets," 143.

87. Cf. Fendler, "Sozialkritik des Amos," 33.

88. Donner, "Soziale Botschaft," 500; Schottroff, "Prophet Amos," 37–38 with references.

89. On the theoretical issues regarding Israelite origins, see, e.g., D. N. Freedman and D. F. Graf, eds., *Palestine in Transition: The Emergence of Ancient Israel* (Sheffield: Almond Press, 1983), esp. 25–90.

90. Cf. G. Herion, "The Role of Historical Narrative in Biblical Thought," *JSOT* 21 (1981): 25–57.

91. Cf. O. Lorentz, "Die Prophetische Kritik des Rentenkapitalsmus: Grundlagen-Probleme der Prophetenforschung," *Ugarit-Forschungen* 7 (1975): 277; and R. Macmullen, *Roman Social Relations: 50 B.C. to A.D. 284* (New Haven, Conn.: Yale University Press, 1974), 28–56.

92. Dijkema, "Le Fond d'Amos," 24–25.

93. Dijkema, "Le Fond d'Amos," 26.

94. Cf. Bright, "Israelite Empire," 210–12; M. Elat, "The Monarchy and the Development of Trade in Ancient Israel," in *State and Temple Economy in the Ancient Near East 2*, Orientialia Lovaniensia Analecta 6, ed. E. Lipinski (Louvain: Department Oriëntalistiek, 1979), 545–46; and idem, "Trade and Commerce," in *The Age of the Monarchies: Culture and Society*, The World History of the Jewish People 4, ed. A. Malamat (Jerusalem: Massada Press, 1979), 186.

95. B. Lang, *Monotheism and the Prophetic Minority: An Essay in Biblical History and Sociology* (Sheffield: Almond Press, 1983), 121.

96. Ibid., 124.

97. Wittenberg, "Message of the O. T. Prophets," 144.

98. Lang, *Monotheism and the Prophetic Minority*, 124.

99. Lorentz, "Prophetische Kritik des Rentenkapitalsmus," 275.

100. Lang, *Monotheism and the Prophetic Minority*, 126; cf. Lorentz, "Prophetische Kritik des Rentenkapitalsmus," 277.

101. Lorentz, "Prophetische Kritik des Rentenkapitalsmus," 275–76.

102. Ibid., 276.

103. J. Miranda, *Communism in the Bible*, trans. R. R. Barr (Maryknoll, N. Y.: Orbis Books, 1982), 37.

104. E. Tamez, *Bible of the Oppressed* (Maryknoll, N. Y.: Orbis Books, 1982), 71; cf. F. C. Fensham, "Widow, Orphan and the Poor in the Ancient Near Eastern Legal and Wisdom Literature," *JNES* 21 (1962): 129–39.

105. Davies, *Prophecy and Ethics*, 83.

106. Ibid., 92–94.

107. Cf. ibid., 108.

108. Ibid., 92, 100; cf. Fendler, "Sozialkritik des Amos," 44; and L. Köhler, *Hebrew Man*, trans. P. R. Ackroyd (Nashville: Abingdon Press, 1956), 142.

109. Dijkema, "Le Fond d'Amos," 26.

110. Davies, *Prophecy and Ethics*, 102.
111. W. Brueggemann, "Unity and Dynamic in Isaiah," *JSOT* 29 (1984): 89–107, esp. 94.
112. P. R. Ackroyd, "An Interpretation of the Babylonian Exile: A Study of 2 Kings 20, Isaiah 38—39," *SJT* 27 (1974): 329–52, argues strongly that the tales of Hezekiah's illness and the reception of the Babylonian ambassadors, together with the emphasis on the miraculous sign and the psalm of thanksgiving in Isaiah, attest to the reshaping of these narratives to bring out their significance for exilic judgment and hope. See also B. S. Childs, *Isaiah and the Assyrian Crisis* (Naperville, Ill.: Alec R. Allenson, 1967) and R. E. Clements, *Isaiah and the Deliverance of Jerusalem* (Sheffield: JSOT Press, 1980).
113. J. C. L. Gibson, *Canaanite Myths and Legends* (London: T. & T. Clark, 1977), 94–102.
114. Brueggemann, "Unity and Dynamic," 95–96, locates the "abyss" between chaps. 39 and 40, but rhetorically, chaps. 36—39 represent that abyss of exile and judgment.
115. See, e.g., R. Ackroyd, *Exile and Restoration* (Philadelphia: Westminster Press, 1968), 118–37; and M. D. Guinan, *Gospel Poverty: Witness to the Risen Christ* (New York: Paulist Press, 1981), 45 ff.
116. Brueggemann, "Unity and Dynamic," 99, is quite correct, however, to think that Third Isaiah builds on Second Isaiah.
117. Brueggemann, "Unity and Dynamic."
118. Brueggemann, "Unity and Dynamic," 97. For references to Abraham, covenant, and exodus in Isaiah, see the following citations. Abraham: 29:22; 41:8; 51:2; 63:16; covenant: 24:5; 28:15; 33:8; 42:6; 49:8; 54:10; 56:4, 6; 57:8; 59:21; 61:8; exodus: 43:16–21; 44:27; 63:11–14. See also B. W. Anderson, "Exodus and Covenant in Second Isaiah and Prophetic Tradition," in Cross, et al., eds., *Magnalia Dei*.
119. Sweeney, "Reconceptualization of the Davidic Covenant."
120. In examining the linguistic frequency and distribution of the terms for poor between chaps. 1—39 and 40—66, a marked contrast can be observed between the two halves. In chaps. 1—39, we find that all three terms (*'ānî*, *dal*, *'ebyôn*) are used in various combinations. However, chaps. 40—66 make exclusive use of *'ānî* in all but one passage (3:14, 15; 10:2, 30; 14:32; 26:6; 32:7; 41:17; 49:13; 51:21; 54:11; 58:7; 66:2), and even there *'ānî* is combined with *'ebyôn* (41:17). This extensive use of *'ānî* alone finds parallel only in the postexilic work of Zechariah, and is uncharacteristic of the earlier prophetic tradition. Perhaps this is evidence that older prophetic material appears in First Isaiah. It certainly marks a shift in focus for chaps. 40—66.
121. See W. Baudissin, "Die alttestamentliche Religion und die Armen," *Preussiche Jahrbücher* 149 (1912): 193–231 and the discussion of his contribution in chap. 10.
122. For a convenient review of the major interpretations, see R. N. Whybray, *The Second Isaiah* (Sheffield: JSOT Press, 1983), 66–78.
123. I. J. Mosala, *Biblical Hermeneutics and Black Theology in South Africa* (Grand Rapids: Wm. B. Eerdmans Publishing Co., 1989).
124. Sweeney, "Reconceptualization of the Davidic Covenant."
125. Cf. Tamez, *Bible of the Oppressed*, 51.
126. Brueggemann, "Unity and Dynamic," 100–101.
127. On the rootedness in communal memory of Second Isaiah's message, see W. Brueggemann, *Hopeful Imagination: Prophetic Voices in Exile* (Philadelphia: Fortress Press, 1986), chap. 5.

Chapter 7

Subverting the Message

Jeremiah

Ostensibly, it would seem that we know more about Jeremiah and his social justice message than we do of any prophetic figure in the Hebrew Bible. The book offers us numerous biographic details and presents a number of scenes decked with named actors. In particular, the demise of Judah in its final decades is vividly portrayed throughout the text. The invective against idolatry and injustice would seem to reflect the deep social commitments of this torn individual. The so-called confessions of Jeremiah, a series of lament poems, appear to take us inside the mind of the prophet himself. We even know the name of his scribe, Baruch, and some would go so far as to hazard that this scribe's own seal has been found amid the archaeological ruins of a devastated Judah.[1]

    Yet the editorial complexities and the variations between poetic and prose sections of the book of Jeremiah create interpretational challenges that are far more daunting than initial impressions allow, justifying Huffmon's observation:

"Jeremiah is the most accessible of the prophets; Jeremiah is the most hidden of the prophets."[2] The first series of texts (chaps. 2—25) afford us no clear scheme of organization, such that even if the materials emanate from Jeremiah himself, we cannot be sure of the precise historical moments many of these texts seek to address. While Jeremiah, like Isaiah, contains oracles against the nations (chaps. 46—51), the radical differences in order and placement of the materials that exist between the Hebrew MT and the Greek LXX make us very much aware of the fluidity of the Jeremiah tradition.[3] Furthermore, the fact that the LXX text of Jeremiah is roughly one-eighth shorter than the MT has led some to conclude that the LXX actually preserves an earlier version of the book.[4] In this discrepancy in length, we see more of the shifting sands of the Jeremiah traditions, for whereas Jeremiah is labeled a "prophet" in the LXX only four times, in the MT he is labeled a prophet thirty times.[5] Yet even here, as Carroll observes, the "LXX seems to know Jeremiah as a prophet only after the fall of Jerusalem."[6] Clearly the traditioning process has moved well beyond our historical figure, increasingly imbuing him with a greater air of prophetic authority. Jeremiah, by the time of the fuller MT, appears to have been received by his handlers as the exemplary prophetic voice.[7] Thus, the very treatment of Jeremiah as a prophetic figure carries with it a problematic aspect. In other words, in terms of the historical setting of the texts, the ordering of their presentation, and the manner of Jeremiah's portrayal as a prophet, the book of Jeremiah reveals beneath its prophet-hero veneer a starkly fragmented history of transmission, reflective of ancient Israel's debates over prophetic authority and questions of social justice.

Despite these complexities, there is a clear exilic focus to the overall text. A large portion of the book is devoted specifically to detailing through narrative texts the demise of Jerusalem and Judah (especially chaps. 37—45, 52), material that follows on a series of narratives and oracles, which in large part have King Zedekiah as the central figure (chaps. 26—35). Chapters 37—46 actually have as their lead-in King Jehoiakim's dramatic slashing and burning of the scroll of Jeremiah's words that had been read in the temple compound by Baruch, Jeremiah's scribe (chap. 36). This chapter sets up the literary pattern of the royal rejection of the prophet's pronouncements, a mode of behavior carried on by King Zedekiah in chap. 37. Zedekiah, however, is more ambivalent than Jehoiakim and thus at times courts Jeremiah's support in ways that Jehoiakim would not. Zedekiah's indecisiveness permits Jeremiah to become the volleyball in a dangerous debate that pitted those who would label Jeremiah a traitor against his would-be supporters (chaps. 37—38). Jeremiah's counsel to Zedekiah to surrender to the Babylonians goes unheeded, and a massive Babylonian invasion occurs, proving wrong Jeremiah's prophetic detractors (chap. 39). Turmoil continues in the land with the assassination of Gedaliah, the governor appointed by the Babylonians, but Jeremiah elects to accompany those Judaeans who fled to Egypt (chaps. 40—41). In Egypt, Jeremiah is portrayed as denouncing the idolatry of the Judaeans who fled there, indicating that most would die in Egypt as a result of their misdeeds (chap. 44).

Thus, the book of Jeremiah holds out the period of the Babylonian invasion as its ostensible context, even as the various subtexts introduced by later compilers and editors make use of the invasion as a foil for agendas reflective of specific postexilic developments and later circumstances that are now impossible for us to reconstruct with any degree of certainty. For example, the temple sermon is given something of a narrative historical context in chap. 26, whereas the undoubted precursor in Jer. 7:1–15 stands on its own.[8] The historicizing of the more ancient poetic text provides us with an "eve of the exile" framework in which to read the texts, as we seek to recover something of the social dynamics that originally provoked the prophet's words and led to a very different sort of reception and preservation of those traditions. In this way, the book itself invites us to hold its synchronic and diachronic dimensions in tension as we grapple with the social visions that are at work in this rich and complex record. Yet we will want to ascertain, to the extent that we are able, exactly what forces were behind this historicizing of the career and words of Jeremiah, especially insofar as the teachings of the prophet came to be altered in that process. By attending to both the text's synchronic and diachronic dimensions, we see the traditioning process in action, elaborating, adapting, and recasting the prophet's justice message to speak to the difficult questions of the era of postexilic reconstruction. The importance of such a message is central to the book of Jeremiah no matter how hard pressed we are to reconstruct the history of the Jeremiah traditions and no matter how much that message was subverted as the tradition was remapped for the needs and issues of subsequent handlers.

In this chapter, then, we shall explore the justice message of Jeremiah in terms of its ideological parameters and sociohistorical connections, insofar as this message crops up in the oracular texts concerning Judah's judgment. We will then turn to gauge the presence of that message in blocks devoted to the prophet's visions and parables. Since the "confessions" of Jeremiah constitute an integral feature in the book's portrayal of Jeremiah as a prophet, we will devote special attention to the manner in which they interface with the justice message of Jeremiah. Following this discussion, we will consider ideas of covenant in the book of Jeremiah and conclude with a study of the oracles against the nations as they appear in this text. Notwithstanding the transmission complexities of this text, we shall see that Jeremiah presents a powerful message that comes to be subtly subverted in the course of the book's development. We begin, however, with a view of the historical context presupposed by the vivid imagery of the book's oracles, namely, the Babylonian invasion of Judah.

The Babylonian Invasion: "A Whirling Storm"

Since the decades leading up to the period of the Babylonian invasion and the invasion itself are so pivotal to the text of Jeremiah (whether to the life of the prophet himself or to his later packagers), it is useful to review the salient details about this time period as presupposed by the book of Jeremiah and as reconstructed through other biblical, Mesopotamian, and archaeological materials. The developing understanding of the prophetic voice in Judaean tradition sprang from the traditionalists' continued wrestling with the meaning of these events. The justice message forms simply one aspect of this larger grappling with the disaster of the invasion, when the Lord went "forth in fury, a whirling storm" (Jer. 23:19).

The rise of the Neo-Babylonian dynasty came about under the leadership of Nabopolassar (625–605 B.C.E.) and his son Nebuchadnezzar II (604–562 B.C.E.). The successes of these dynasts occurred at the expense of an ever-weakening Assyrian empire, which was beginning to lose its grip on Near Eastern politics during the later years of Ashurbanipal (668–627 B.C.E.).[9] In the course of Nabopolassar's rule, the Assyrians saw their power ultimately eclipsed by a coalition of Medes and Neo-Babylonians, permitting a throne centered in Babylon to come to the fore as the leading power in Mesopotamia. The reforms of Josiah (640–609 B.C.E.) took place during this period of transition from Assyrian weakness to Neo-Babylonian hegemony.[10] But Josiah's bid for political independence for Judah was undone in 609 B.C.E. when he was killed in an effort to hold off the army of Pharaoh Neco (609–594 B.C.E.), who was on his way to aid the staggering Assyria (2 Kings 23:29–30). However, Egyptian influence in Palestine was soon squashed when Pharaoh's warriors received a decisive defeat at the hands of Nebuchadnezzar II in the battle of Carchemish (605 B.C.E.).[11] Because of this shift in the political climate, Judah's king Jehoiakim (609–598 B.C.E.), whom Neco had placed on the throne in 609 B.C.E., was forced to submit to the Neo-Babylonians (605/4 B.C.E., cf. 2 Kings 24:1).

When Nebuchadnezzar sought to go after Egypt in its own territory (601 B.C.E.), the results were not nearly so decisive. Babylonian records concerning this year report that their king "took the lead of his army and marched to Egypt. The king of Egypt heard (it) and mustered his army. In open battle they smote the breast (of) each other and inflicted great havoc on each other. The king of Akkad and his troops turned back and returned to Babylon."[12] Nebuchadnezzar's army, having been dealt a serious blow, was forced to remain at home during the following year. Although Egypt did oust the Babylonians from their immediate environs, they must have suffered badly too, because they do not appear to have attempted to reassert their authority in the Syro-Palestinian region in the years that followed.[13]

These events supplied Jehoiakim with a good opportunity to rebel against the Babylonian ruler (2 Kings 24:1). But it was only a matter of time before Nebuchadnezzar's troops recovered and returned to Palestine. In 598 B.C.E., Jehoiakim found these unlikely visitors perched outside the gates of Jerusalem. The Babylonian chronicles state, "In the seventh year, the month of Kislev, the king of Akkad mustered his troops, marched to the Hatti-land, and encamped against [i.e., besieged] the city of Judah and on the second day of the month of Adar he seized the city and captured the king."[14] The exact sequence of events at this point is not altogether clear because Jehoiakim apparently died at some time during the siege. It is probable that he died (or was murdered?) before the surrender came, and that his son Jehoiachin took it upon himself to draw the whole nasty affair to a close by submitting to the Neo-Babylonians.[15] Whatever the case, it was at this time that Nebuchadnezzar carried off the leading officials of Judah to exile in Babylonia, including King Jehoiachin, in what is known as the first deportation.[16] Zedekiah, another of Josiah's sons, was placed on the throne in Jehoiachin's stead (see 2 Kings 24:12ff; Jer. 13:18ff; 2 Chron. 36:9–10).

The reign of Zedekiah (598–587 B.C.E.) was dominated by political fragmentation and indecision, and Zedekiah was finally, whether willingly or not, pulled into a revolt against his Babylonian overlord. The rebellious act, which was led by the pro-Egyptian party in Judah, met with swift retribution from Nebuchadnezzar, who promptly sent his army against Jerusalem, destroying the temple, taking booty, and carrying off many of the officials and residents of the territory in and around Jerusalem (2 Kings 24:20b–25:2, 8–12). This resulted in a second deportation of people from Judah and it is this depopulation that is usually identified with the destruction layers found at several tells in the region dated to the early sixth century B.C.E.[17]

At this time, Gedaliah of Judah was appointed governor to oversee the poor peasant population that remained in the territory of Judah.[18] He located his administrative headquarters at Mizpah, just north of Jerusalem. Some time after this Gedaliah was assassinated. Those who remained in Judah either fled the inevitable consequences of such a flagrant violation of Babylonian authority or suffered some other fate (Jeremiah 40—43). That the Babylonians did react is indicated in Jer. 52:30: "in the twenty-third year of Nebuchaddrezzar, Nebuzaradan, the chief of the guards, exiled 785 Judeans" (c. 582 B.C.E.). This marks the third and final deportation of the population of Judah to Babylon.

Extrabiblical material bearing on the Neo-Babylonian treatment of Jehoiachin comes from cuneiform documents recording the distribution of food rations of oil, barley, dates, and spices by the central bureaucracy. These texts were discovered in the vaulted building near the Ishtar gate in Babylon.[19] Weidner places the texts between the tenth and thirty-fifth year of Neb-uchadnezzar II (c. 595/4 to 570/69 B.C.E.).[20] Two sources are sufficiently pre-served to indicate what Jehoiachin and some of those with him received. The texts read as follows:

> *Weidner text B*
> 10 *sila* for [Y]a'u-kinu, the king of the land of Yâ[hudu].
> 2½ *sila* for the 5 [son]s of the king of the land of Yâhudu . . .
> 4 *sila* for 8 people of the land of Yâhud, 1/2 [*sila*] . . .
>
> *Weidner text C*
> 10 *sila* for Yakû-kînu, the son of the king of Yakudu.
> 2½ *sila* for the 5 sons of the king of Yakudu at the hands of Qana'a[ma].

Here we see that the king of Judah was a recipient of state goods as part of the monthly outlays.[21] Albright observed that "this distribution of rations undoubtedly means that Jehoiachin was free to move about Babylon and was not in prison." Albright suggested that Jehoiachin's "imprisonment was then a later event, perhaps brought by an attempt to escape in connection with intrigues or actual revolt in Judah."[22] We might note that Jehoiachin was given royal designations. It is difficult to know how much significance to place on references to him as "king" and "son of the king." Such designations may have been used only for purposes of identification or might even indicate that the Neo-Babylonians did accord Jehoiachin some royal status. The interpretation of the statement about "5 sons" is more problematic. It is not inconceivable that Jehoiachin, who was childless at the time of the exile (Jer. 22:30), had five sons while in exile, but it must be remembered that he was only eighteen when taken into exile (2 Kings 24:8) and would only have been twenty-three when text C was recorded in the thirteenth year of Nebuchadnezzar II. This state of affairs has led some to suggest that the word "sons" here may simply refer to princes or brothers.[23]

That the people did settle in and pursue a life in Babylonia has been given support by documents unearthed in the Babylonian city of Nippur. These texts belonged to an important banking and commercial family known to us as "Murashu's sons," which was active during the reigns of Artaxerxes I (464–424 B.C.E.) and Darius II (424–404 B.C.E.). The content of the materials concern "payment of taxes on behalf of others, land management, and the granting of loans to be repaid at a higher rate of interest."[24] Although these texts come from a time after the exile, the information they give concerning the living situation in Babylonia during the period under consideration is consistent with the exhortation ascribed to the prophet to actively participate in the life of that people (Jer. 29:7–8). Among these cuneiform texts are found a number of names that are West Semitic in origin, such as Hanana (Hanan), Minahhimu (Menachem), Miniamini (Minyamin), and compounds with *ili* (el).[25] Care must be taken here when making use of the proper names as historical evidence. Names like these are common West Semitic names and do not necessarily refer to those who are of Israelite descent, since such names are not restricted to Israel proper.[26] More certain are those names formed from compounds with the divine name, such as Ahiyama (Ahijah, Ahiyyah), Yahulakim (Yeholanu), and Yuhunatanu (Jonathan).[27] From this kind of evidence, Coogan has developed lineages of the two largest families of Israelites in these texts.[28] The groupings run as follows:

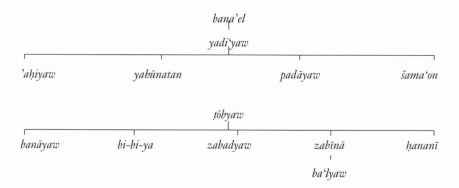

Of the names in list one, four are Yahwist and the other two have biblical parallels. The second list consists of four Yahwist names: Hanani is possibly abbreviated from *hananyaw*, and Zabina is an Aramaic name used by Jews.[29] Those Yahwist names, whether standing in isolation or bearing family associations, possibly reflect Israelite presence and influence in Babylonia. Such personages acted "as witnesses in documents dealing with taxes," worked as "tenants cultivating the land of others," lived as "landowners on whose half taxes are paid," and some seem to be have been "highly placed royal officials."[30] The types of occupations they held ranged from sheep and goat herding to date growing and fishing.[31] None of this is really surprising. Nebuchadnezzar himself did not conquer without a purpose. One reason for taking back people of a foreign land was so that the victor could make use of the skills and abilities of those he conquered to bolster his own economy and hence to enhance his political influence.[32]

Jeremiah: A Message of Justice

Given this tumultuous history, one may well wonder what word Jeremiah spoke to his times. Admittedly, the study of the social criticism of Jeremiah has suffered because this book stands in the shadows of Amos, Micah, and Isaiah. Fortunately, Wisser has worked hard to rectify this situation, in part, through an examination of Jeremiah's social orientation.[33] Nevertheless, further investigation is still required since Wisser tends to emphasize literary matters over socioeconomic questions. In general, we may say that the materials that bear on social justice and poverty in Jeremiah indicate a continuation of the kind of social critique initiated by Amos, Micah and early Isaiah, but also reveal a specificity of concepts not found in the earlier prophets, as seen in particular in the attack on King Jehoiakim (c. 609–598 B.C.E.) and in his forging a strong link between idol worship and the exploitation of the poor. In this section, we examine the socioeconomic conditions that are the focus of the social critique displayed in Jeremiah.

Acquisition of Wealth

Various oracles in Jeremiah warn that the economic corruption of the bureaucrats and merchants would lead to the downfall of the state. The prophet contended that the rich acquired their wealth through fraud (*mirmâ*): "As a cage is full of birds, so their houses are full of guile; that is why they have grown so wealthy. They have become fat and sleek" (5:27–28a). In the process of accumulating wealth, the rich consistently violated the legal claims of the poor. The text criticizes the wealthy elite for this: "They pass beyond the bounds of wickedness, and they prosper. They will not judge the case of the orphan, nor give a hearing to the plea of the needy" (5:28). The text draws a direct connection between the rich accumulating wealth and the legal injustices practiced against the poor.

The idea of legal injustice here is not necessarily limited to the courts. As Wisser notes, the notion of legal injustice can include a broad range of offenses: "The accusation, therefore, would relate not only to injustices committed in regular legal cases but also to those committed in the general conduct of community business, in particular, in meetings at the city gate, under the guidance of the elders (among whom the rich and influential would hold a key place)."[34]

Such texts in Jeremiah echo Amos and early Isaiah in announcing that judgment must come upon those who exploit the *'ebyôn*, "poor" and who engage in legal abuses in order to make material gains. Hence it comes as no surprise that following upon the prophet's indictment of the elite, words of judgment invariably follow: "Shall I not punish such deeds—says the LORD—Shall I not bring retribution on a nation such as this?" (5:29). The failure of the people of Judah to fulfill YHWH's desires for justice in society was the primary basis for judgment.[35] The prophet announced that this punishment was to take the form of invasion from the north, presumably by the Babylonians (4:5–6:30).[36]

A Just King?

The social critique of the text moves beyond merchants and landowners to directly address the king. In a passage set amid a group of texts devoted to criticisms of royal figures (21:11–23:8), the policies King Jehoiakim pursued to increase his wealth are severely criticized.[37] Wisser plausibly suggests that Jehoiakim engaged in these building projects in an effort to shore up his image since he was not the recognized successor to Josiah.[38] The text criticizes the king because the royal construction projects were done without paying the laborers just wages (22:13–14). As Wisser points out, the use of forced labor imitates the practice of earlier rulers in Israel; this was certainly not an uncommon form of "taxation" in the ancient world.[39] Compounding the injustice, the king's economic gains were maintained through a combination of systematic murder, oppression, and extortion (22:17). Jehoiakim's government kept itself solvent by torturing and censuring its critics as it fattened its purse. Because Jehoiakim had chosen to set his mind only on "ill-gotten gains" (i.e., the exploitative accumulation of wealth), the prophet announced that the fate of this king would be like the ignominious burial of an ass and that the leaders would go into exile (22:19, 22). Rhetorically, a contrast is drawn between the activities of Jehoiakim and those of his father, the reform-minded King Josiah (c. 640–609 B.C.E.). It is said of Josiah that "he upheld the rights of the poor ['ānî] and needy ['ĕbyôn]; then all was well" (22:16). The prophet's condemnation of Jehoiakim's labor practices and consequent appeal for justice do not draw on specific laws for support; rather, the prophet bases the call for justice on the ancient claims made by the kings of the Near East that they were the chosen protectors of the poor and powerless (see chap. 2). Such an open critique of monarchic exploitation is actually unique in the prophetic literature.[40] One might have expected that since the prophets felt no qualms about attacking the rulers and merchants, they would have directly addressed the king on such matters more often. But, in fact, they do not, and this situation deserves some discussion, for it is vital to understand the prophets' attitude toward the king in their social critique.

To begin with, it is possible that the prophets attributed responsibility for exploitation only to the officials and merchants, but did not think that the kings were directly implicated in any of these injustices. Davies, following Alt, suggests that the prophetic critique was leveled against the elite surrounding the king as the ones who "were the people primarily responsible for the grad-ual accumulation of property in the hands of the few."[41] However, our previ-ous discussion of crown property (see chapter 6) would seem to argue against a lack of prophetic awareness concerning royal involvement in the injustices perpetrated against the villages.

Yet there are examples of a prophetic understanding of the king's direct involvement in injustice. Both Jeremiah's criticisms of Jehoiakim noted above and the story of Naboth's vineyard clearly indict kings for economic exploita-tion and injustice. In the case of Naboth's vineyard, Elijah attacks Ahab for his involvement in unjust land acquisition (1 Kings 21:17–19). Such texts make it seem unlikely that the prophets were unaware of royal complicity in injustices against the peasant population. Thus, the general silence of the canonical prophets about the monarchs in this regard seems doubly strange.

One might suggest that the prophets were reluctant to directly attack the king because they recognized him as a divinely chosen representative. They may have regarded the king as one who stood apart from normal officials and hence was above criticism, whereas they felt free to criticize the king's officials since those serving under the king were not thought of as anointed by YHWH. Yet in the biblical narrative materials, prophetic figures do not fear to criticize the king when they deem it necessary, and, more importantly, in the prophetic literature, a number of texts show the prophets to be openly crit-ical in general ways of the kings and their policies: Amos opposes Jeroboam (Amos 7:11); Isaiah rebukes Ahaz (Isa.7:13–25); and Jeremiah speaks out against Zedekiah (Jer. 21:1–22:10), Jehoahaz (22:10–12), Jehoiakim (22:13–19), and Jehoiachin (22:20–30).[42] On the basis of this evidence, it is mistaken to maintain that the prophets feared making criticisms against the king as the "anointed" of YHWH, although Ezekiel reduces Zedekiah to a mere "prince in Jerusalem" (Ezek. 12:10).[43] However, apart from Jeremiah's critique of Jehoiakim (22:13–19), passages attributed to the prophets specifi-cally tying Israel's kings to injustices against the poor do not occur.

In explaining the prophetic silence toward the kings in matters of social jus-tice, Donner draws a distinction between criticism of a specific king and crit-icism of the institution of kingship itself. Donner maintains that the recognition of the legitimacy of kingship inevitably implied some acceptance of the monarch's acquisition of wealth and property, at least of amounts suffi-cient for the maintenance of the state bureaucracy.[44] Donner argues that only Hosea sought to undermine the monarchic institution itself, but that the other prophets did not offer fundamental criticisms in this regard, thereby tacitly indicating their basic acceptance of both the institution and some of the injus-tices that would have accompanied its existence (Hos. 3:4; 7:3; 8:4, 10; 13:10ff.).[45] In this acceptance, the prophets would have been political realists.

Donner claims that the prophetic critique was offered against state administrative officials and not the king, since the officials under the king bore only a secondary mandate from YHWH and had not been granted divine permission to extend their holdings at will.[46]

While plausible, Donner's view suffers from the absence in Jeremiah's oracles of a positive assessment of kingship as an institution, an omission not expected on the basis of Donner's analysis. Apart from the brief laudatory comments concerning Josiah (Jer. 22:15–16), the only positive portrayal of kingship in the book concerns the coming Davidic ruler, a king who has not yet been enthroned (the abortive efforts of Haggai and Zechariah to crown Zerubbabel as YHWH's anointed notwithstanding; cf. Hag. 2:4, 21–23; Zech. 3:8; 4:6–10; 6:12–13). However, it is clear that a number of the texts on David in Jeremiah are actually Deuteronomic reinterpretations of various oracles (e.g., Jer. 13:13; 17:25; 21:12; 22:2, 4). Several references to David are coordinated with hopes for the raising up of an ideal ruler and the restoration of Jerusalem (Jer. 23:5; 30:9; 33:15, 17, 21, 22, 26). Two such references occur as foils for critiques of Jehoiakim and Jehoiachin/Jeconiah (22:30; 36:30). The remaining reference to David occurs in the letter to the exiles and is used to invoke a notice of critique and judgment (29:16). These occurrences are highly isolable, with no crossover into the visions, parables, or confessions. The evidence would appear to assign most of these references to a later Deuteronomic redactional layer, wherein the oracles and initial collections of other texts were expanded in terms of a profound anticipation of a future renewal of royal rule in Judah.[47] Thus, tracing Davidic materials back to the historic Jeremiah is exceedingly problematic, and one should not conclude from the praiseworthy assessment of Josiah in the earlier strata that the institution of kingship was accorded central importance by this prophet; the king was praised for simply doing what all just people should do regardless of their status (7:6).[48] It was left to the Deuteronomic handlers to expand the monarchic thrust of the text.

Taking a different approach, one might suggest that the prophetic silence was simply an act of discretion. The prophets would have realized that continued condemnation of the monarchy would have ensured further conflict and probably produced a violent response from the king. Prophets were known to have been assassinated on occasion (26:20–23). Such caution may seem odd given the prophets' willingness to be highly critical of the ruling establishment. However, this possibility should not be ruled out completely and may serve at least as a partial explanation of the prophetic approach.

There is yet another line of thought that is suggested by the prophetic materials: The king and the elite are critiqued together as a unit. This possibility is clear from the section of Jeremiah devoted to criticisms of various monarchs

(21:1-22:30). Following the criticisms of specific kings is a text that contrasts the prophet's vision of a just ruler with the failures of the nation's kings (23:1–8). The just ruler is set against the "shepherds" of the people, a general reference to the rulers of the people (22:22; Ezek. 34:1–31, 37:24; Zech. 11:4–17). The juxtaposition of the "shepherds" text with the preceding critique of monarchic figures cannot be accidental. It would seem that the Deuteronomic handlers of the Jeremiah tradition and even the prophet himself treated the nation's king as simply one of the many leaders, "shepherds," who were guilty of injustice (2:5–8; 23:1–4). In their critique, the prophets would have accorded the kings no special status or responsibility for crimes against the poor. This would reflect the recognition that the prophets, after the time of Elisha at any rate, did not see the king to be the *sole* cause of the nation's problems. Instead, the entire ruling establishment centered on the capital cities of Jerusalem and Samaria, including the king, was considered responsible for the exploitation of the poor, and all would suffer national judgment.

Further, while the king is generally not given a central role in the nation's injustices by the prophets, neither is the king singled out by the prophets to be the sole protector of the poor (see chapter 2). Such may have been the role taken up by the kings of the Near East, as is well known from various ancient texts, but the canonical prophets do not appear to hope that the reigning monarch would actually try to solve the nation's problems.[49] We might argue, therefore, that the prophets offer criticisms of the bureaucratic establishment on a general basis (thereby including the king), and expect the entire ruling administration to see to the needs of the underprivileged. This did not stop Jeremiah from directly attacking Jehoiakim for the king's treatment of the poor when such criticism seemed singularly appropriate, but such a practice forms the exception rather than the rule in prophetic proclamations concerning poverty and injustice.

This relativizing of the status of the reigning king may be a sign that the prophets simply did not regard the land's kings as truly anointed by YHWH. This posture ironically opens the door for later editors to increasingly speak of the coming Davidic ruler, with Second Isaiah going so far as to treat Cyrus the Persian as YHWH's special designate, a foreign-born potentate (Isa. 11:1, 10; 16:5; 32:1–4; 44:28; 45:1; cf. Jer. 23:7–8; 30:8–9; 33:10–15; Ezek. 34:23–24; 37:22–24). The development of such a vision is certainly an open criticism of the existing monarchy. However, prophetic appeals to the kings on other matters would seem to rule against the view that the prophets accorded no legitimacy at all to the institution of kingship.

Finally, it is certainly possible that the prophets made attacks on kings which have not been preserved, and even that texts resembling Jeremiah's harsh critique of Jehoiakim may have been expunged from the record (cf. Jer.

36:23). However, such considerations must remain matters of speculation and do not seriously grapple with the prophets' apparent silence about the kings with respect to matters of exploitation and social injustice.

Idolatry and Ideology

Beyond institutional practices and political arrangements, the text of Jeremiah understands the plight of the poor to be greatly affected by the ideological base (i.e., the religion) of the monarchic establishment. One passage, for example, criticizes all of Judah's leadership for departing from the worship of YHWH and replacing it with idol worship:

> Like a thief chagrined when he is caught,
> So is the House of Israel chagrined—
> They, their kings, their officers,
> And their priests and prophets.
> They say to wood, "You are my father,"
> To stone, "You gave birth to me,"
> While to Me they turned their backs
> And not their faces."
>   Jer. 2:26–27; cf. 1:15–19; 2:5–8,
>   20–26; 4:1–9; 5:26–31; 8:8–12

Such a text argues that the actions of the ruling elite were guided by values that ran counter to Israel's commitment to the rule of YHWH. One of the most telling pieces of evidence for the deplorable nature of the elite's religion was that the "lifeblood of innocent poor ['ĕbyôn]" was found on the "garments" of the nation's leadership (2:34). Wisser comments that "in this passage, social injustice appears as a consequence of idolatry."[50] In the prophet's analysis, the exploitation of the poor went hand in hand with idol worship.

The sharpness of such a critique is best appreciated when idols are sociologically understood as the concrete representation of a religiously based value system that accorded the urban establishment the primary role as powerholders chosen by the divine to govern the nation.[51] The system of idol worship was drawn on to legitimize the existing social order, and thus this religious system lent support to the powerbrokers' desire to dominate and exploit the populace. Analyzed in this way, the critique in Jeremiah parallels the observation in Amos that the value structures of idol worship undergirded the economic and political excesses of the Northern Kingdom's bureaucratic establishment (Amos 8:4–8).[52] Knowing the bankruptcy of the elite's values, the prophet felt free to mock the state's gods as ineffective when social and political pressures increased: "And where are those gods that you made for yourself? Let them arise and save you, if they can, in your hour of calamity. For your gods have become, O Judah, as many as your towns!" (Jer. 2:28). At the heart of the prophetic critique stood fierce opposition to the cherished beliefs and ritual practices that functioned to support the exploitative lifestyle of the urban establishment. The distorted religious framework of the elite, from the point of view of the prophetic rhetoric, represented a betrayal of Israel's most ancient religious traditions and peasant institutions. Speaking for YHWH, the prophet states, "Can a maiden forget her jewels, a bride her adornments? Yet My people have forgotten Me—days without number" (Jer. 2:32).

The divergent religious values of the urban and village populations can be illustrated from a text that narrates YHWH's command to Jeremiah to search the streets of Jerusalem for someone who is just, in order that the city might be pardoned and escape judgment (5:1). Jeremiah began this search with the *dal*, "poor," but found them ignorant of the demands of YHWH (Jer 5:4). This evidence poignantly indicates that the formative religious traditions of the culture had lost much of their significance even among the peasant population by the time of the exile. Surprisingly, the text makes allowance for this ignorance because the *dal* did not claim to be the official bearers of the covenant tradition. But when the prophet turned to consider the temple officials who did claim to bear the Yahwist tradition, they had willfully abandoned the *derek*, "way," and *mišpaṭ*, "justice" of YHWH, i.e., the ethics and practices of the Yahwist tradition, while merely maintaining a facade of religious ritual (5:5). Ignorance of YHWH's demands for justice was widespread throughout the population. In this text, as Wisser observes, "One encounters the protest that all the members of the community are culpable, a protest expressed by the citation of two social extremes: the lesser people (*dallîm*) and the nobles (*gĕdôlîm*, literally, "the great")."[53]

However, the nature of this religious ignorance was not as evenly distributed among the people as Wisser implies. Jeremiah held the temple officials to be accountable in a way that the village peasants were not. To be sure, the text in no way romanticizes the life and ways of the poor, as if they were somehow nobler or more virtuous because of their poverty and hence closer to God. As Gelin observes, when the prophets bring the notions of poor and just together, "this does not mean that the poor as poor were pleasing to YHWH, but that God looked on the mistreatment of the poor as an affront to His sovereignty over Israel."[54] Instead, the text seeks to call to account the representatives of the official theology for supporting a state program that falsely promised prosperity and political success (cf. 28:1–11), but that actually led to the degradation and impoverishment of the masses.

International Relations

One passage in Jeremiah takes the prophetic analysis still further by looking beyond the land's own borders to tie the abuse of the *'ĕbyôn*, "poor," in the prophet's own land to the relationship Judah had developed with the superpowers Egypt and Babylon (2:34–36). The prophet rebukes Judah for seeking other "lovers" (2:25, 33), namely, the Egyptian and Babylonian kings. Judah sought foreign aid from other nations as a means of producing security at home, rather than placing corporate trust in YHWH. Consequently, Judah's rulers spent more effort on courting the superpowers than on doing justice to the poor within their own borders. The text declares that, in the end, Judah would be as disappointed by Egypt as it was with Assyria (2:36). As such passages widen the focus of the prophetic social critique, we come to see the poor caught in a vicious web of oppressive circumstances created by a variety of agents, a web that ranged from Judah's economic structures and its ideological foundations to the politics of international relations.

The Term *'ĕbyôn* as Self-Designation

A unique reference to poverty appears in one of Jeremiah's confessions. The text reveals the prophet's anguish over those who persecuted him. In the midst of painful struggle, the prophet exclaims, "Sing unto the LORD, praise the LORD, for He has rescued the needy [*'ĕbyôn*] from the hands of evildoers!" (20:13). This is apparently the only case where a prophetic figure uses the terminology of poverty as a self-designation. Though Jeremiah was not poor in origins or means (note the prophet's purchase of land in Jer. 32:6–25), it is perhaps significant that the passage presents the prophet in much the same situation as others who were victims of economic and political injustice in Israel and Judah. While the historical character of the evidence remains problematic (see below), nevertheless, the tradition presents us with a Jeremiah who suffered arrest and threats against his life (11:18–23; 20:2; 33:1–3; 37:13; 38:5–6), faced censorship (36:5, 17–31), encountered religious opposition (20:1–6; 26:7–9), and often lapsed into despair at the way the ruling elite dealt with him (15:10, 15–18; 20:7–18). The use of the term *'ĕbyôn* to characterize the prophet's condition lays stress on his unjust treatment vis-à-vis the elite.

Victims of Invasion: The Poor of the Land

A few of the references to the poor in Jeremiah make use of the term *dallat/ dallôt* (39:10: *hā-'ām haddallîm*; 40:7: *dallat hā-'āreṣ*; 52:15: *dallôt hā-'ām*; 52:16: *dallôt hā-'āreṣ*). These were the inhabitants of Judah left by the Babylonians after the rebellion of Zedekiah and the subsequent deportation of the urban leadership (c. 587 B.C.E.; cf. 2 Kings 24:14). The poor who were left behind did not own property prior to the exile, and were given vineyards and fields in Judah out of the vast holdings that the rich lost to the conquering Babylonians (Jer. 39:10). The "liberation" of the *dallat/dallôt* was short-lived, however, because they became farm laborers to provide subsistence for the Babylonians (52:16; 2 Kings 25:12).[55] The term *dal*, "poor," is placed in an agricultural context, as also occurs in the legal materials of the Pentateuch (see chap. 2).

To sum up: The social justice message of Jeremiah is sharp and articulate. Bitter accusations were leveled at the fraudulent manner in which the elite acquired its wealth at the expense of the poor, whose legal claims the rich consistently violated. In making these pronouncements, the prophet invariably proclaims a word of judgment against the callous and impertinent elite. Jeremiah's critique is spoken directly at the abusive policies and deeds of the king. This singling out of the king is particularly noteworthy insofar as the general practice of the prophets appears to have been to lump the king in with the elite when making their pronouncements of judgment. Jeremiah's justice message subtly engages not merely the surface economic and political conditions of the time but also the underlying ideology that drove the royal system, namely, idol worship. This religious link led the prophet to include the temple and its officials in his denunciation of the society's injustices against the poor. Throwing down the gauntlet, the prophet tied injustice at home to Judah's international relations. We also note that in one of the "confession" texts, the prophet is depicted not simply as an advocate for the poor but is also classed among them as one who has suffered similar abuses and hence can speak on their behalf. Finally, references to the toiling poor after the exile remind us that the issue of poverty and social injustice remains for Jeremiah a sad legacy of ancient empire building. This powerful justice message, though tempered as we shall see in other parts of the book of Jeremiah, was so strongly identified with the ancient figure of Jeremiah that the tradition was hard-pressed to ignore these words, even as it sought to adapt this message for a later time.

Jeremiah the Ecstatic?

In stark contrast to the depiction of the prophet in the book of Isaiah, the prophet in the book of Jeremiah is presented as a symbolist and a visionary. Some deeds border on the magical and leave one with the impression that comparative anthropology might better serve us in explaining and interpreting the social mechanisms at work in this behavior (see chapter 6).[56] We certainly must be cautious when moving beyond the written text to posit psychosocial realities behind the text.[57] Yet whether behind the book or in the book itself, depictions of shamanistic behavior, for want of a better term, draw our attention to a number of key interpretive moments for clarifying the stance of the texts. As we examine the visions and parables attributed to Jeremiah, we shall consider to what extent such texts contribute to the deepening of the social justice critique we have discovered thus far in the book of Jeremiah.

The Visions: Obscuring the Justice Message?

The vision texts in the book of Jeremiah comprise the following:

1:11–12	almond tree, watchman
1:13–19	boiling pot
13:1–7	loin cloth
24:1–10	baskets of figs
25:15–38	wine drinkers

The first and second texts are linked and follow immediately on the narrative of the prophet's call and commissioning (1:4–10). Presumably these initial visions carry forward aspects of the prophetic task of uprooting and tearing down nations outlined in the call narrative. The first vision plays on the Hebrew *šqd*, which means, depending on the vowels supplied, either "almond tree" or "watchful":

> The word of the LORD came to me: What do you see, Jeremiah? I replied: I see a branch of an almond tree.
>
> > The LORD said to me:
> > You have seen right,
> > For I am watchful to bring my word to pass.
> > > Jer. 1:11–12

The word that will come to pass is presumably one of judgment, as is laid out in the second vision:

> And the word of the LORD came to me a second time: What do you see? I replied:
>
> > I see a steaming pot,
> > Tipped away from the north.
> > And the LORD said to me:
> > From the north shall disaster break loose
> > Upon all the inhabitants of the land!
> > For I am summoning all the peoples
> > of the kingdoms of the north
> > > —declares the LORD.

They shall come and shall each set up a throne
Before the gates of Jerusalem,
Against its walls roundabout,
And against all the towns of Judah.
And I will argue My case against them
For all their wickedness:
They have forsaken Me
And sacrificed to other gods
And worshiped the works of their hands.

So you, gird up your loins,
Arise and speak to them
All that I command you.
Do not break down before them,
Lest I break you before them.
I make you this day
A fortified city,
And an iron pillar,
And bronze walls
Against the whole land—
Against Judah's kings and officers,
And against its priests and citizens.
They will attack you,
But they shall not overcome you;
For I am with you—declares the LORD—to save you.
                                         Jer. 1:13–19

This vision is clear and to the point. The message is one of judgment from the north. Here "north" simply refers to the direction from which the Babylonian army will come as it moves into Judah.[58] The invasion is read Deuteronomically as an event of divine wrath. God's "case" against the people concerns idol worship (1:16) and does not embrace matters of social injustice, even though it is directed against "kings and officers" and "priests and citizens" (1:18).

The third vision concerns a buried loincloth that is recovered and found to be ruined (13:1–7). This loincloth, buried and uncovered again by the prophet at YHWH's command, is interpreted to mean judgment will take place because of the "overweening pride of Judah and Jerusalem" (13:9). Judgment comes specifically because of idol worship and disobedience (13:10–11). This vision, as with the two preceding, does not invoke social justice concerns beyond idol worship.

The fourth vision depicts baskets of figs (24:1-10). This vision speaks of baskets of figs that stand in front of the temple, one good and one bad. We learn that the "good figs" are the Judaean exiles who will one day be restored in Judah, whereas the "bad figs" are King Zedekiah along with his courtiers, the remnant around Jerusalem, and those who went off to Egypt. We do not learn why this distinction is made. No basis, moral or otherwise, is presented for the choice. This vision, like the others, treats good and bad in general terms and no hint of a social justice critique is present. As we observed with the *'ānî* material in Isaiah (see chapter 6), there is a tendency in the biblical materials for originally caustic and highly specific social justice criticism against the elite to be coopted by the elite through the exile, as if the exilic suffering has transmuted the exiled elite into the poor once defended by the prophets (see chapters 6 and 9). The more generalized moral categories of these visions become a rhetorical means by which the exiles embrace the earlier Jeremiah tradition and make it their own.

The fifth and final vision regarding the wine drinkers (25:15–38) sustains these observations. There the cup of wrath proceeds not only against Jerusalem and Judah, but against the nations at large: Egypt, Philistia, Tyre, Sidon, Arabia, Zimri, Elam, Media, and Sheshach (i.e., Babylon). Once again, although the announcement of judgment is vivid and vitriolic, we are not informed of the reason for YHWH's "case against the nations" (25:31). The frenzy of war is seen as judgment, but the nature of that judgment remains largely a mystery in these passages.

The Parables: Coopting the Prophetic Voice

So if not in the visions, then perhaps we will find a social critique in the so-called parables. These texts are as follows:

16:1–4	no marriage or children
18:1–12	potter's house
19:1–20:6	broken pot
27:1–28:17	wooden yoke
32:6–44	field purchase
43:8–13	large stones
51:59–64	scroll thrown in river

In the first parable, the prophet is instructed not to marry or have sons and daughters (16:1–4). Those who are born will be fated to a gruesome death by judgment for unspecified actions.

The second parable (18:1–12) concerns the prophet's observations at the potter's house. Spoiled vessels are remade, providing occasion for a likening to YHWH's treatment of Israel:

> Then the word of the LORD came to me: O House of Israel, can I not deal with you like this potter?—says the LORD. Just like clay in the hands of the potter, so are you in My hands, O House of Israel! At one moment

> I may decree that a nation or a kingdom shall be uprooted and pulled
> down and destroyed; but if that nation against which I made the decree
> turns back from its wickedness, I change My mind concerning the pun-
> ishment I planned to bring on it. At another moment I may decree that
> a nation or a kingdom shall be built and planted; but if it does what is
> displeasing to Me and does not obey Me, then I change My mind con-
> cerning the good I planned to bestow upon it. (Jer. 18:5–10)

The theme of uprooting is reiterated and the disaster falls on those of
"wicked ways" (18:11). Obedience and repentance are key, yet nothing beyond
these more general notions guides us into an understanding of the reasons for
judgment.

The third parable, concerning the broken pot, is more insightful (19:1–20:6).
In a prophetic pronouncement and imitative action, the prophet announces
judgment for idol worship and proceeds to smash the pot to symbolize that judgment. The text speaks of having "filled this place with the blood of the innocent"
(19:4), though whether this means murdering the poor is less clear here than in
other texts. It is possible that v. 5 provides an alternate interpretation where child
sacrifice is in view. The judgment is specifically connected with the Babylonian
invasion and the loss of possessions that resulted (20:4–5).

The fourth parable, concerning the wooden yoke, breaks new ground
(27:1–28:17). In this scene, Jeremiah wears a yoke, symbolizing the pronouncement that Zedekiah and all the kings of the region ought to submit to
the rule of Nebuchadnezzar. This parabolic act provides the occasion for the
writer to have Jeremiah condemn the lying prophets who have called on the
rulers to resist Babylonian rule (27:9–11, 16–18). In particular, Jeremiah
denounces those prophets who announce that the cultic vessels of the temple
which have already been taken to Babylon will be returned. This scene moves,
in turn, to the altercation between Hananiah and Jeremiah (chap. 29). Hananiah breaks Jeremiah's yoke and proceeds to announce the return of the cult
vessels in two years time, together with the restoration of Jehoiachin and the
rest of the exiles (28:3–4). Here the writer presents a litmus test for prophecy:

> The prophets who lived before you and me from ancient times proph-
> esied war, disaster, and pestilence against many lands and great king-
> doms. So if a prophet prophesies good fortune, then only when the
> word of the prophet comes true can it be known that the LORD really
> sent him. (Jer. 28:8–9)

The latter pronouncement hardly deters Hananiah, who reaffirms his stance.
The only clue we have as to a sense of the historical context for this passage
appears in Jer. 27:22, where the hope of the return from exile is raised. Clearly
the notion of true versus false prophecy became an issue as the postexilic

community sought to reclaim the ancient prophetic tradition.[59] We have a case of cognitive dissonance here, not so much with respect to the failings of the classical prophets to always predict the future correctly, but with respect to the difficulty with which the community's exiled elite might have in embracing a prophetic voice that was once perceived to be a threat. By sublimating the more ancient prophetic social critique, the rhetoric of the parable's passages has effectively generalized the question of justice versus injustice and true prophecy versus false prophecy.

In a fifth parabolic action, the prophet Jeremiah redeems a piece of familial property while still in prison, as instructed by YHWH (36:6–44). The action is done as a sign that "Houses, fields, and vineyards shall again be purchased in this land" (36:15). The prophetic voice quite literally participates in the project of postexilic restoration. The contrast is drawn between this action of buying and the imminent destruction of Jerusalem, which is interpreted as judgment for having failed to heed the Torah and tradition, a tradition of the Ten Commandments and the exodus (32:16–25). The tradent's hand is clear. We are not looking at a prophetic voice concerned with covenant and social justice, but at a pentateuchal voice that seeks to reinvigorate stories found in Exodus and Deuteronomy. The sin? Idol worship and child sacrifice (32:29, 34–35) and wickedness (32:31). Renewal comes as an arbitrary act of divine regathering and through the institution of an everlasting covenant (32:37–44). The time of restoration will be a time of purchasing land. Judah's exiled elite envisions a return to the land, but this time with the support of a prophetic voice. Regarding the emphasis on holding the legal deed to the land (32:9–15), Carroll keenly observes, "Implicit in that ruling would be the view that those who had 'occupied' the land since the fall of Jerusalem were not the legitimate owners of that land. Only those who had come 'back' from foreign lands could claim by right of purchase an entitlement to the land."[60] This emphasis hardly stems from an imprisoned Jeremiah who is still free enough to make land purchases (32:8), a literary absurdity as Carroll rightly notes, but is strongly indicative of the ideological and political leanings of the composer of these narratives.

The sixth parable examined here concerns large stones that YHWH instructs Jeremiah to place at the entrance of Pharaoh's palace (43:8–13). The action signifies YHWH's intent to put Nebuchadnezzar's throne over the stones of Pharaoh (43:10). This passage carries forward a consistent theme in Jeremiah, namely, that Babylon's political interests are to be accepted as God-given. It is not too far-fetched to find the redactor of the Book of Jeremiah among the entourage of Jehoiachin taken into exile. The pro-Babylonian stance of the book stands out in a number of passages and contrasts sharply with the pro-Persian policy of the book of Isaiah. By the same token, the pro-Babylonian posture of

Jeremiah may simply be a foil for anti-Egyptian leanings. Yet these passages push support for Babylon to a far greater degree, and one suspects that the tradent has the security and welfare of the exiles to Babylon in mind.

The commitment to Babylon is not permanent, however, as seen in the final parable, concerning the scroll thrown in the river (51:59–64). In a fitting ending to the prophet's words, the prophet presents a scroll to one of Zedekiah's officials and instructs him to open and read it in exile as a sign that the prophet predicted the disaster would come to pass (51:61–62). The prophet then instructs the official to attach the scroll to a stone to throw it into the Euphrates, and, as it sinks, to announce that Babylon too will sink. It turns out that support for Babylon is a pragmatic device to ensure that some will survive and return to rebuild Jerusalem. Again, the text raises no issues of prophetic social critique to ground the renewal. Instead, the text seems designed to ensure a place for the prophetic voice, in a more generalized way, in a post-exilic community that requires an ancient anchor for its restoration program.

We cannot reconstruct the group out of which these sentiments emerge, but the project of this layer in Jeremiah seems more tentative than the strident and politically driven Isaiah or the priestly and institutionally engaged Ezekiel. The voice that finally emerges in Jeremiah is as ambiguous as that of an Elijah or an Elisha in DH. The general moral character of this program is clear, but it ran the risk of failure due to the lack of specificity, if by failure we mean translating the more serious dimensions of the ancient prophetic social critique into a powerful political program for the postexilic community. Our study of other passages shows us that materials with a more substantive prophetic social critique can be found in Jeremiah, but that the final redactors have sublimated those trajectories to a very different social and political agenda.

To sum up our findings regarding the visions and parables: While not wanting to claim a genre or form status for these texts concerning visions and parables or parabolic actions, it seems clear that, studied as a whole, they provide us with an insight into the traditioning of the social justice message of Jeremiah within a circle that both valued but also wished to adapt that prophetic voice during the exile and early second temple period. In the process, the political shifts and fragmentation of these periods came to indelibly stamp the Jeremiah tradition. What might once have been a prophetic voice focused on clear and specific social and economic matters, political alliances, and international empire building, has given way to a more generalized concern for justice, obedience, and true prophecy. Though somewhat muted, the elite nonetheless has also permitted the more strident prophetic voice to live side by side texts that have effectively coopted these oracles to create a veneer of prophetic support for the postexilic elite's claims over a rebuilt temple and urban establishment. An ironic development indeed!

The Confessions of a World-Weary Prophet

The five so-called confessions or laments of Jeremiah that intersperse chaps. 11—20 at irregular intervals offer another opportunity to test our suspicions about the layered character of the social justice message of Jeremiah. These five texts appear to take us inside the mind of the prophet, presenting to us a portrait of the inner psychological and spiritual struggles of Jeremiah. Their connection to the psalms of lament is obvious, but here the texts are given a quasi-historical literary context largely absent in the Psalter, except where the psalms provide oblique connections to scenes in the life of King David. Do these "confessions" betray a particular social agenda?

The first confession (11:18–20 and 12:1–6) offers complaints to YHWH concerning those who seek to cut the prophet down (11:19) and those who are the prosperous wicked (12:1), the latter echoing a motif found throughout Job. The call, "How long must the land languish" (12:4a), yields an assurance of judgment (12:7–13; cf. 11:21–23). In one case, the enemies of YHWH are personalized as the enemies of the prophet, namely, "the men of Anathoth who seek your life" (11:21).

The second confession (15:10–21) takes up the theme of the prophet's opponents. The prophet despairs over having become, "a man of conflict and strife with all the land" (15:10). His situation is so desperate that he cries out, "O LORD, You know—Remember me and take thought of me, avenge me on those who persecute me" (15:15). While the precise situation is not detailed, following the typical style of the psalms of lament, the juxtaposition of this passage amid texts that depict Jeremiah's trials at the hands of various rulers creates a vivid, imaginative use of the lament genre. The assurance of rescue is not unlike the hope of rescue expressed in psalms of lament:

> Assuredly, thus said the LORD:
> If you turn back, I shall take you back
> And you shall stand before Me;
> If you produce what is noble
> Out of the worthless,
> You shall be My spokesman.
> They shall come back to you,
> Not you to them.
> Against this people I will make you
> As a fortified wall of bronze:
> They will attack you,
> But they shall not overcome you,
> For I am with you to deliver and save you
> —declares the LORD.
>   Jer. 15:19–20

However, we must note that even though the juxtaposition of such poetry and the life of Jeremiah serves as an effective literary device, neither of these poetic blocks carries forward specific matters of social justice. Perhaps this is a function of the genre, or more likely the result of the ideological leanings of the compiler.

Not surprisingly, the third confession (17:14–18) focuses on the prophet's conflict with his persecutors, without reference to the nature of the conflict or the issues at stake beyond fulfillment of predictions:

> Heal me, O LORD, and let me be healed;
> Save me, and let me be saved;
> For You are my glory.
> See, they say to me:
> "Where is the prediction of the LORD?
> Let it come to pass!"
> But I have not evaded
> Being a shepherd in your service,
> Nor have I longed for the fatal day.
> You know the utterances of my lips,
> They were ever before You.
> Do not be a cause of dismay to me;
> You are my refuge in a day of calamity.
> Let my persecutors be shamed;
> And let not me be shamed
> Let them be dismayed,
> And let not me be dismayed.
> Bring on them the day of disaster,
> And shatter them with double destruction.
>
> Jer. 17:14–18

Likewise, in the fourth confession (18:18–23) the focus is on the prophet's conflict with those who devise "plots to kill me" (18:23). The call for judgment is harsh and precise:

> Oh, give their children over to famine,
> Mow them down by the sword.
> Let their wives be bereaved
> Of children and husbands,
> Let their men be struck down by the plague,
> And their young men be slain in battle by the sword.
> Let an outcry be heard from their houses
> When You bring sudden marauders against them;
> For they have dug a pit to trap me,
> And laid snares for my feet.
> O LORD, You know
> All their plots to kill me.

> Do not pardon their iniquity,
> Do not blot out their guilt from Your presence.
> Let them be made to stumble before You—
> Act against them in Your hour of wrath!
>
> Jer. 18:21–23

The prophet's message is reduced to that of intercession on behalf of the people to divert divine wrath (18:20)—hardly the scope of the broader justice message found elsewhere in Jeremiah!

The final confession (20:7–19) reproduces many of the same themes and factors already discussed. The conflict with the prophet's opponents is clear, as they seek to ensnare him (20:10). The call for judgment is similar to the other confessions (20:12). If we may note one difference, this text displays a greater degree of confidence in divine support for the prophet (20:11), although this comes as the uneasy result of wrestling with absolute abandonment (20:7–9). The confidence that YHWH "has rescued the needy," a curious self-identification with the poor discussed earlier, is an element that sits dissonantly beside a Job-like curse of the day of the prophet's birth:

> Accursed be the day
> That I was born!
> Let not the day be blessed
> When my mother bore me!
> Accursed be the man
> Who brought my father the news
> And said, "A boy
> Is born to you,"
> And gave him such joy!
> Let that man become like the cities
> Which the LORD overthrew without relenting!
> Let him hear shrieks in the morning
> And battle shouts at noontide—
> Because he did not kill me before birth
> So that my mother might be my grave,
> And her womb big [with me] for all time.
> Why did I ever issue from the womb,
> To see misery and woe,
> To spend all my days in shame!
>
> Jer. 20:14–18

Taking the confessions as a group, we are left with the impression that for all their depth and stridency, these passages function as stock and formulaic texts of a psalm-like character that have been attached to the larger book of Jeremiah to deepen the issue of prophetic conflict.[61] While this infusion of material may serve to indicate the postexilic ideological climate of controversy and strife that shaped the compilation of the larger work, the texts do not in and of themselves further the social justice message we have seen elsewhere in Jeremiah. Admittedly, such a conclusion is negative. Nevertheless, we still glimpse, however obscurely, something of the attendant issues at work in the later preservation of the earlier, concrete prophetic justice message in a community that vigorously debated the role and nature of that prophetic voice in society. It will be left to the writer of Job to more decisively connect the lament form with a concrete advocacy for the poor and oppressed, although the seeds for this creative literary mix are already present in Jeremiah.

Covenant and Justice: Recasting the Tradition

Even a cursory glance reveals that the concept of covenant is hardly integral to the book of Jeremiah. In fact, the references to covenant are largely concentrated in three sections—chaps. 3, 11, and 31—34. The effect, however, of the addition of these materials, which obviously form a later editorial layer, is striking, for this material transforms the prophet of judgment into a preacher of the covenant.

This new direction for the tradition of Jeremiah is presented boldly in the first reference to covenant in the book (3:16), specifically a reference to the ark of the covenant. This section (3:6–20) offers an extended discussion of Israel and Judah's adulterous rebellion, which fits well in its context among various poetic oracles of judgment. However, the covenant emphasis of the prose passage betrays an emergent concept of prophecy quite foreign to the wideranging tenor of the oracles that precede and follow the prose text. The sense of injustice is markedly reduced to superficial references to the nation's faithlessness and sin. The chord of hope is struck through references to a new covenant situation, where the exiles are regathered as adopted children.

The covenant idea is taken up again more extensively in chap. 11. In a Mosaic-like exhortation, echoing the best of Deuteronomy, this passage calls firmly for obedience to God's commands, predicating this obedience on a reminder of Israel's rebellion during the time of the exodus (11:2–8). The full passage, however, offers little hope, since the former rebellion is seen to be continued in the "conspiracy" at work in Judah to throw off the worship of YHWH in favor of Baal (11:9–13).

Apart from references to "covenant" in a psalm-like lament of divine rejection (14:19–22) and in a prose comment regarding the justification of God's wrath against Jerusalem (22:9), there is a large hiatus until the set of references in chaps. 31—34. Clearly the idea of covenant is not the theological engine that drives the heart of the book of Jeremiah. Neither is the notion of a covenant violation brought in tandem with any of the detailed social critiques found in the book, a state of affairs compounded by the fact that the only crossover to our selected genres of visions, parables, or confessions occurs rather loosely in connection with the parabolic action of the purchase of the land by Jeremiah (32:40).

In what remains, the references to covenant function to give theological depth to the chronicle-like narratives of chaps. 26—35, with covenant invoked most specifically in chaps. 31—34. The narratives, set in the reigns of Jehoiakim and Zedekiah, are largely concerned with the issue of true and false prophecy. In chap. 26, under Jehoiakim, the prophet warns that unless the people turn to God they will suffer the fate of Shiloh (26:6–9; cf. 7:12–14), namely, utter destruction. The people initially seize Jeremiah, but a debate arises over the fact that Jeremiah's words resemble those of the prophet Micah, who was not mistreated in his day. The chapter ends with the killing of the prophet Uriah, who spoke in terms much as Jeremiah, highlighting the dangers Jeremiah faced. Chapters 27—28 take up Jeremiah's conflict with other prophets during Zedekiah's reign, in particular against Hananiah, a prominent opponent who figures in the yoke parable discussed previously. At issue is Jeremiah's prediction that further invasions by Babylon are on the horizon. Thereupon follows Jeremiah's seemingly treasonous letter to the exiles (chap. 29), which encouraged the community to flourish during their stay in Babylon. This passage included the vision of the good and bad figs discussed earlier. Clearly these chapters help to explain how the prophet could possibly speak a positive message to the people that was not the false sort of message a Hananiah or one of the other court prophets might deliver. Having laid the rhetorical groundwork of doom, the Deuteronomic tradents present a Jeremiah who can see beyond the seventy years of exile to a time of hope (31:16–17).

What is the nature of the time of renewal as presented in chaps. 31—34? The old, broken covenant of the days of the exodus has given way to an interiorized commitment to the one God (31:31–34; cf. 50:5). Israel and Judah's final humiliation paves the way for this covenant to take the form of a restoration of the line of David (33:23–26), indeed, the recovery of the entire biblical narrative tradition from Abraham, Isaac, and Jacob. In this passage, we find the same sort of ambivalence to the royal tradition that we find in DH, where the text holds in tension the halcyon days of King David and the bitter years of collapse after Josiah. Yet the Jeremiah text urges us to see this as a creative tension, provided God can be relied on to reestablish the fragile line of David. Covenant here is being employed in a political program quite removed from the vigorous social critique of the earlier oracles of judgment. This program is far from certain about the nation's ascendancy, as the caustic verbiage of judgment in chap. 34 would seem to indicate (vv. 8, 10, 13, 15, and 18). Yet the text is clear that this renewal cannot be based on the rebuilding of the temple alone, but must hinge more deeply on heeding the prophetic call to return to God. Again, we find the justice message of the earlier oracles subsumed to a very different understanding of the prophetic voice, even as that voice is ostensibly incorporated by the writer. The covenant idea, however, sits uneasily as a partner in the book's overall conversation with the social justice oracles found elsewhere in the book.

To sum up: If we take these passages on covenant as our guide, the impression of an intrusive theological layer would seem assured. We are led by these considerations to suggest that there are at least three major phases to the composition of the book of Jeremiah: (1) an initial oracular phase with a vivid social critique dimension; (2) an intervening expansion with prose commentaries, parables, visions, and confessions, all of which temper this initial more radical vision of the book and recast the character of Jeremiah's prophetic voice; and (3) a "covenant" redaction, which incorporates the prophetic critique and other materials into a Deuteronomic narrative tradition. This latter narrative material does have the virtue of giving the prophet a positive and enduring voice, long after the demise of Jerusalem under Nebuchadnezzar. In fact, the figure of Jeremiah becomes the locus around which the community might gather beyond its crisis in leadership in the postexilic reconstruction phases. In this way, the earlier prophetic vocation of uprooting and planting has been transformed into a political vision of royalist reconstruction for the exilic survivors. Oracles that once were unable to see little hope for the people's future have been swept up into a vision of a new covenant that flourishes beyond catastrophe. The covenant idea becomes a lens for rereading, recasting, and reclaiming oracles that otherwise would have run their course with Judah's destruction. This creative rewriting may have muted the justice message, but in so doing permitted the postexilic community to adapt and address that justice message in terms of its collective responsibility to build a new sort of Israel and Judah.

The narratives in chaps. 26—35, however, close with a sense of hardened realism. Much as Deuteronomy and DH recognize that a covenant relationship with God involves choice, so also does the text recognize the possibility of disobedience. Thus, while Zedekiah oversees the only freeing of slaves reported in the Hebrew Bible (34:8–22), enacting the provisions of the law codes regarding debt slavery (see chapter 2), soon afterward the owners revert to their old ways by reenslaving the people, thereby abrogating the covenant. By contrast, the Rechabites, in their abstinence from wine and the giving up of a settled lifestyle in favor of nomadism, show the kind of singular obedience that the populace has not shown to the command not to worship other gods (chap. 35). Covenant here and throughout is understood in terms of laws known to us from Deuteronomy and elsewhere (see chap. 2). The Deuteronomist has not chosen, however, to

join this presentation of covenant with other social justice issues raised elsewhere in the oracles of Jeremiah.

Oracles against the Nations: A Universal Accounting

We find in each of the major canonical prophetic texts large sections
devoted to oracles against the nations. Thus, just as the book of Isaiah gains
an international focus from such texts, so also does the book of Jeremiah find
a reshaping of its message in light of the incorporation of such material. However, the picture for Jeremiah is a bit more complex and puzzling than for the
other prophetic books. We find significant differences between the LXX and
MT in this regard. To begin with, the position of the texts is different. In the
LXX, the texts are in the middle of the book, as they are in Isaiah (chaps. 13—
23) and Ezekiel (chaps. 25—32). However, in the MT, these chapters appear
at the end (chaps. 46—51). Furthermore, the ordering of the texts differs
markedly between the LXX and the MT.

MT	LXX
Egypt	Elam
Philistia	Egypt
Moab	Babylon
Ammon	Philistia
Edom	Edom
Damascus	Ammon
Kedar	Kedar
Elam	Damascus
Babylon	Moab

This anomalous state of affairs presents no clear explanation. We are left to
observe that this material has the imprint of a fluid transmission history. We
adopt here the ordering of the MT, without drawing conclusions from this
specific ordering. If the arrangement of the MT is closer to that of Jer.
25:11–26, this either indicates that the MT preserves the more original order
of the oracles or that the compilers of the Masoretic version reconstructed the
LXX to present a grouping that meshed more neatly with chap. 25. We cannot be more precise here.

The disjuncture between Jer. 25:19–26 and chaps. 46—51 in the MT must
somehow be bridged, since it is actually chap. 25 that opens us to the question
of the nations. After Judah's judgment by Babylon is complete and the seventy
years of exile are over, the divine "cup of wine—of wrath" will be forced on
the nations, starting with Babylon: "Let them drink and retch and act crazy,
because of the sword that I am sending among them" (25:15–16). This wrath

goes out first against Babylon and then against a host of opponents: Egypt, Philistia, Tyre and Sidon, Arabia, Zimri, Elam, Media, and Sheshach (i.e., Babylon). We have already analyzed this passage as a "vision" text. Now, however, we also see its character as a text that contextualizes the oracles against the nations:

> And I will bring upon that land all that I have decreed against it, all that is recorded in this book—that which Jeremiah prophesied against all the nations. For they too shall be enslaved by many nations and great kings; and I will requite them according to their acts and according to their conduct. (Jer. 25:13–14)

Presumably we are to read this text as a summation or an invocation of curses in a scroll devoted to oracles against the nations attributed to Jeremiah. The distinct and separate character of such a scroll might go a long way toward explaining the curious editorial history of these oracles as witnessed in the Masoretic and Septuagint traditions. This invocation might also suggest that the political program of the compilers of the book of Jeremiah was volatile and working at the margins, setting up a rhetoric sharply defensive in scope and tone. For this project, the collection of prophetic oracles against the nations was programmatically attractive and presumably predated chap. 25. We turn now to the oracles proper as received in the Masoretic tradition.

The first oracle concerns Egypt and is editorially set at the moment when Pharaoh Neco's army was defeated by Nebuchadnezzar II at Carchemish (46:1–2). The picture of battle is vivid:

> Get ready buckler and shield,
> And move forward to battle!
> Harness the horses;
> Mount, you horsemen!
> Fall in line, helmets on!
> Burnish the lances,
> Don your armor!
> Why do I see them dismayed,
> Yielding ground?
> Their fighters are crushed,
> They flee in haste
> And do not turn back—
> Terror all around!
> —declares the LORD.
> Jer. 46:3–5

Editorially, the poetry is presented as a day of retribution by YHWH Sebaoth (46:10). This figure, YHWH Sebaoth, is a dominant epithet for God in the prophetic literature. Outside of these texts we find YHWH Sebaoth connected with the ark of the covenant, Shiloh, Elijah, and Elisha in the DH. Strangely, DH links YHWH Sebaoth only with King David and not with any of the other kings of Israel or Judah. Curiously, too, this designation is not uniformly distributed throughout the prophetic literature. It is notably lacking in Ezekiel and Amos. Its dominance in Haggai, Zechariah, and Malachi is to be noted, but it is also absent from Third Isaiah. Micah, Nahum, Habakkuk, and Zephaniah witness only occasional occurrences. Only three psalms use this precise terminology (Psalms 24, 46, and 84), with variations found in other psalms (59, 69, 80, and 89). YHWH Sebaoth is the great warrior for Israel, at least in several of the prophetic writings.

Another segment of this oracle concerns Nebuchadnezzar II's attack on Egypt. The oracle turns YHWH into a warrior who charts the outcome of this confrontation:

> Declare in Egypt, proclaim in Migdol,
> Proclaim in Noph and Tahpanhes!
> Say: Take your posts and stand ready,
> For the sword has devoured all around you!
> Why are your stalwarts swept away?
> They did not stand firm,
> For the LORD thrust them down;
> He made many stumble,
> They fell over one another.
>   Jer. 46:14–16

Egypt's collapse is certain. The prophetic voice in these passages wrestles a word of divine intervention and judgment out of the incessant conflicts of the ancient Middle East (4:18–24). But beyond Egypt's shaming, the editors also provide a note of renewal:

> I will deliver them into the hands of those who seek to kill them, into the hands of King Nebuchadrezzar of Babylon and into the hands of his subjects. But afterward she shall be inhabited again as in former days, declares the LORD. (Jer. 46:26)

The poetry gives way to an announcement of renewal for Israel:

> But you,
> Have no fear, My servant Jacob,
> Be not dismayed, O Israel!
> I will deliver you from far away,
> Your folk from their land of captivity;
> And Jacob again shall have calm

And quiet, with none to trouble him.
But you, have no fear,
My servant Jacob
                    —declares the LORD—
For I am with you.
I will make an end of all the nations
Among which I have banished you,
But I will not make an end of you!
I will not leave you unpunished,
But I will chastise you in measure.

                              Jer. 46:27–28

Israel's renewal is predicated upon the final demise of her oppressors. It is plain to see that the rhetoric of the oracles serves the twofold purpose of agonizing over Judah's collapse and galvanizing some sort of resistance to Egyptian and Babylonian domination. We will find this posture elsewhere in these oracles, revealing a disjuncture between the pro-Babylonian policy of other parts of the book of Jeremiah and the decidedly anti-Babylonian sentiment of the oracles against the nations.

A brief oracle against Philistia (chap. 47), set on the eve of an invasion of Gaza by Pharaoh (47:1), again depicts YHWH as the executor of judgment. The poignant question goes forth:

"O sword of the LORD,
When will you be quiet at last?
Withdraw into your sheath,
Rest and be still!"

How can it be quiet
When the LORD has given it orders
Against Ashkelon and the seacoast,
Given it assignment there?

                              Jer. 47:6–7

A significantly long oracle concerns Moab (chap. 48). Moab's destruction is predicated on its false worship of Chemosh, a god known extrabiblically from the famous late ninth-century B.C.E. Moabite Stone inscription:

I am Mesha, son of Chemosh-yat, king of Moab, the Dibonite. My father was king over Moab for thirty years, and I became king after my father. I built this high place for Chemosh in [qarhō], a high place of salvation, because he delivered me from all assaults, and because he let me see my desire upon all my adversaries. Omri, king of Israel, had oppressed Moab many days, for Chemosh was angry with his land. . . .[62]

The Jeremiah oracle is quite explicit about the reasons for judgment:

> Surely, because of your trust
> In your wealth and in your treasures,
> You too shall be captured.
> And Chemosh shall go forth to exile,
> Together with his priests and attendants.
> The ravager shall come to every town;
> No town shall escape.
> The valley shall be devastated
> And the tableland laid waste
> —because the LORD has spoken.
>   (Jer. 48:7–8; cf. 48:12–13)

Moab is branded as one who has "vaunted himself against the LORD" (48:26). However, the nature of Moab's "insolence" remains largely unidentified (48:29–30; cf. 48:42), unless in each case we are to understand this as idol worship (cf. 48:35). The ensuing judgment by war is depicted in words echoing those of Isaiah:

> Terror, and pit, and trap
> Upon you who dwell in Moab!
>   —declares the LORD.
> He who flees from the terror
> Shall fall into the pit;
> And he who climbs out of the pit
> Shall be caught in the trap.
> For I will bring upon Moab
> The year of their doom
>   —declares the LORD.
>   Jer. 48:43–44; cf. Isa. 24:17–18

In a sense, the exile experience of Judah is to become a universalized experience of the nations. Moab too suffers its own exile (48:46). But the ensuing era, says the final redactor, is one of restoration: "But I will restore the fortunes of Moab in the days to come—declares the LORD" (48:47a).

The next oracle deals with another of Judah's immediate eastern neighbors, the Ammonites (49:1–6). Israel is to dispossess the Ammonites, who had attacked Israel (49:2). As with the Moab oracle, the main god of the opponent is in view: "For Milcom shall go into exile, together with his priests and attendants" (49:3c). Ammon is castigated for relying on its "treasures" (49:4). The prophetic program of such oracles again sees hope in the collapse of former oppressors, neighbors who had perhaps benefited from Assyrian and Babylonian involvement in the region. But this program, in the final form of the text, is mediated by a school akin to the final Isaiah, for the judgment-desolation theme is balanced with a restoration promise (49:6).

The southernmost of Judah's most immediate eastern neighbors, Edom, is the subject of the next oracle (49:7–22). The oracle is dotted with language more at home in Genesis and Exodus. Edom is referred to as Esau, whose doom is assured (49:8, 10). The capital, Bozrah, is to be destroyed (49:13), according to the prose editor. The editor draws a connection between this devastation and the overthrow of Sodom and Gomorrah (49:17), anticipating similar comments about the doom of Babylon (50:44ff.). The destruction of Bozrah is read against a backdrop of Sea of Reeds verbiage that treats the capital's demise as an event of mythic proportions.

A brief oracle concerns the Syrian territory (49:23–27). Damascus, as with the other territories, falls by the sword and its fortresses are destroyed. The oracle against Hazor's kingdom (49:28–33) invokes Nebuchadnezzar as the agent of judgment.

A prose oracle concerning Elam follows (49:34–39). Ostensibly set at the start of Zedekiah's reign, the oracle simply pronounces Elam's destruction. The text proclaims that God's throne will be established in Elam. The oracle concludes with an editorial comment promising the restoration of Elam's fortunes. By this point the theme of restoration has become rather formulaic in the oracles.

These last three rather abbreviated oracles give way to extensive pronouncements against Babylon (50:1–51:64). Babylon's empire building is treated as insolence against YHWH (50:29–32), and these pronouncements proclaim the demise of Babylon and call forth the exiles to flee before the arrival of Babylon's destroyer from the north (50:2–3, 8–16, 41–43; cf. 51:6, 45). The poetic phrasing is precise and vivid as it envisions the fall:

> Hark! War in the land
> And vast destruction!
> How the hammer of the whole earth
> Has been hacked and shattered!
> How Babylon has become
> An appallment among the nations!
> I set a snare for you, O Babylon,
> And you were trapped unawares;
> You were found and caught,
> Because you challenged the LORD.
> The LORD has opened His armory
> And brought out the weapons of His wrath;
> For that is the task
> Of my Lord GOD of Hosts
> In the land of the Chaldeans.

Come against her from every quarter,
Break open her granaries,
Pile her up like heaps of grain,
And destroy her, let her have no remnant!
Destroy all her bulls,
Let them go down to slaughter.
Alas for them, their day is come,
The hour of their doom!
Hark! fugitives are escaping
From the land of Babylon,
To tell in Zion of the vengeance of the LORD our God,
Vengeance for His Temple.

Jer. 50:22–28

The judgment is against the imperial elite and its idols: inhabitants of Babylon, officials, wise men, diviners, warriors, and the motley crowd in its midst (50:35–37; cf. 51:15–19).

The baldness of the imagery is summed up in a key passage:

You are My war club, [My] weapons of battle;
With you I clubbed nations,
With you I destroyed kingdoms;
With you I clubbed horse and rider,
With you I clubbed chariot and driver,
With you I clubbed man and woman,
With you I clubbed graybeard and boy,
With you I clubbed youth and maiden;
With you I clubbed shepherd and flock,
With you I clubbed plowman and team,
With you I clubbed governors and prefects.
But I will require Babylon and all the inhabitants of Chaldea
For all the wicked things they did to Zion before your eyes

—declares the LORD.

Jer. 51:20–24

We find here the theology of the oracles in a nutshell. God uses the world's political powers to judge but then seizes ascendancy over those same powers. This rhetoric implies that the Judaeans could confidently resist Babylon and all other imperial contenders. They could, in fact, rely on prophetic support for such a resistance whether in dispersion or on home soil that might be occupied by a foreign power. We cannot know the success of movements galvanized by such poetry, but we can be certain that movements of resistance based on Judaean ideological underpinnings during the exilic and postexilic period found in such literature the theological inspiration for resistance to repeated encroachments by a series of foreign powers seeking control of ancient Palestine. The later book of Daniel, the Qumran War Scroll, and the book of Revelation constitute enduring parts of this stream of resistance literature. Certainly such movements found that participation in external alliances to be of pragmatic necessity. Hence, references to the kings of Media dot the text here and there (51:11, 28). Yet such alliances do not drive the text and hardly present Cyrus as the LORD's anointed as in Isaiah.

We may wonder at the fount of this prophetic anger. Little in this text gives us a clue. We know, of course, that Babylonian occupation of a myriad of territories must have come at great price to the occupied. That such a situation is alluded to only briefly in the text nevertheless makes the following passage critical to our understanding of the whole of the oracles:

> "Nebuchadnezzar king of Babylon
> Devoured me and discomfited me;
> He swallowed me like a dragon,
> He filled his belly with my dainties,
> And set me down like an empty dish;
> Then he rinsed me out.
> Let the violence done me and my kindred
> Be upon Babylon,"
> Says the inhabitant of Zion;
> "And let my blood be upon the inhabitants of Chaldea,"
> Says Jerusalem.
>
> Jer. 51:34–35

The degradation at the hands of the occupier, the "violence done me and my kindred," elicits an anger and humiliation on the part of the colonized that logically finds hope only in the collapse of the imperial power:

> Yes, Babylon is to fall
> [For] the slain of Israel,
> As the slain of all the earth
> Have fallen through Babylon.
>
> Jer. 51:49

We may suspect that this oracular literature served to incite movements of resistance devoted to this end. The occupier often leaves the colonized no other choice. The project of political resistance is couched in terms of myth. This has become a war on a cosmic scale between YHWH and Babylon's main deity, Bel:

> And I will deal with Bel in Babylon,
> And make him disgorge what he has swallowed,
> And nations shall no more gaze on him with joy.
> Even the wall of Babylon shall fall.
> . . . .
> Assuredly, days are coming,
> When I will deal with Babylon's images;

> Her whole land shall be shamed,
> And all her slain shall fall in her midst.
> ·
> Assuredly, days are coming
>   —declares the LORD—
> When I will deal with her images,
> And throughout her land the dying shall groan.
>   Jer. 51:44, 47, 52

This Bel is the god Marduk, better known to us from the Babylonian creation epic.[63] In this story, Marduk successfully defeats the sea goddess Tiamat and her forces. He then proceeds to create the universe out of her corpse, builds the temple complex in Babylon, and fashions humankind out of the blood of her general, Qingu. Marduk is then proclaimed to be the supreme god by the divine assembly. While the writer of Jeremiah may or may not have known this myth, the oracles constitute a poetic response of mythic proportions to this haughty Bel:

> Though Babylon should climb to the skies,
> Though she fortify her strongholds up to heaven,
> The ravagers would come against her from Me
>   —declares the LORD.
> Hark! an outcry from Babylon,
> Great destruction from the land of the Chaldeans.
> For the LORD is ravaging Babylon;
> He will put an end to her great din,
> Whose roar is like waves of mighty waters,
> Whose tumultuous noise resounds.
> For a ravager is coming upon Babylon,
> Her warriors shall be captured, their bows shall be snapped.
> For the LORD is a God of requital,
> He deals retribution.
> I will make her officials and wise men drunk,
> Her governors and prefects and warriors;
> And they shall sleep an endless sleep,
> Never to awaken
>   —declares the King whose name is LORD of Hosts.
> Thus said the LORD of Hosts:
> Babylon's broad wall shall be knocked down,
> And her high gates set afire.
> Peoples shall labor for naught,
> And nations have wearied themselves for fire.
>   Jer. 51:53–58

Only once is this retributive act by YHWH spelled out as just recompense for the destruction of the temple:

You fugitives from the sword,
Go, don't delay!
Remember the LORD from afar,
And call Jerusalem to mind.
"We were shamed, we heard taunts;
Humiliation covered our faces,
When aliens entered
The sacred areas of the LORD's House."
                                    Jer. 51:50–51

This lack of focus on the temple may simply be because the exiles had the more immediate issue of survival in mind. The call to remember Jerusalem is taken up more effectively by the final redactor in passages that set out a hope for the restoration of the exiles to their homeland (50:4–7, 17–20, 33–34). The book of Jeremiah, however, ends on a grim note of the destruction of the temple (chap. 52; cf. 2 Kings 24:18–25:30). A slight glimmer of hope is provided by the release of Jehoiachin from prison in Babylon, perhaps the occasion for the compilation of an edition of the book of Jeremiah.

Can we generalize from these oracles against the nations? Justice in the prophetic imagination, as seen in these oracles, is a universal accounting and resettlement that is the product of conflict and war. The prophetic voice engages the brutalities of war with the shocking language of bitter poetry in an effort to jar open an expansive view of the judgment, with YHWH at the center of the processes of history rendering impotent those rulers and patron deities who vaunted their claims to be the final arbiters of human history. Their repeated and successive topplings announce through the oracles against the nations that only YHWH Sebaoth is the true sovereign in the forward march of human history.

To sum up our findings in this chapter: We are led to a mixed set of conclusions regarding the book of Jeremiah, conclusions that create a unique set of problems for a modern appropriation of the text. On one level, we may observe that all layers of the text regard a confrontation with the historical experience of Judah, particularly of its invasion, to be the essential ground for continuing theological discussion. But here is where commonalities would seem to end. What would appear to be the ground layer of Jeremiah, namely, the oracles of judgment, openly presents the invasion as a result of the intersection between idolatry and social injustice, where idolatry is understood as a rejection of Judah's right relationship with YHWH and where social injustice is defined in terms of concrete and vivid violations of the poor. This substantive message about the poor is theologically potent. For these oracles of judgment, the spirituality that nourishes prophetic advocacy for the poor is grounded in a direct engagement with the lived realities of the suffering of the poor as the exploited and disenfranchised members of society. This prophetic advocacy is profound and powerful. In these passages, we find a social vision that uproots and tears down the cherished beliefs and political arrangements of the elite. This is, and always has been, the dangerous side of the prophetic tradition.

However, we have also seen that this social critique has been embraced, transmuted, and at times subverted by other hands. At various junctures, prophetic oracles are subjected to appended prose commentaries that mollify the message by reinterpreting it for radically changed social and historical circumstances. We find in this process the hand of the former elite, which has embraced and recast the earlier oracles for new political ends, an agenda that has found the prophetic voice to be of great value in ways akin to its depiction in DH. Clear shifts take place in this commentary phase, not only by submerging the blistering social critique of Jeremiah but also in the elevation of the issue of true vs. false prophecy as a key theological trajectory. Obviously the later commentators became the medium through which "true" prophecy was to be found, a voice that is long on judgment but very short on advocacy for the poor. Ironically, this segment of the postexilic community came to be invested in a tradition it once largely disdained, unwittingly attesting to the power of the earlier prophetic voice.

A canonical approach to this text might leave us perplexed. If the overall transmission history has not obliterated the earlier layers, nevertheless the developing ideas of prophecy, of the new Davidic monarch, of covenant, and of literary forms such as vision, parable, and lament have clearly taken the prophetic oracular message in startlingly divergent directions. To the extent that we value the apparently more ancient message of justice, the final form of Jeremiah will leave us dismayed. We might argue, however, that far from being a complete subversion of the prophet's social critique, these developments are a sign of a living and vital tradition whose growth was inevitable, for the oracles have a fixed moment as their context, whereas commentary and expansion allows those sentiments to live anew in ever-changing social and political circumstances. To move forward, in other words, subsequent generations must answer to the voices that came before. Yet it is also clear that the transmission history of the book presents in stark and disturbing ways the modes by which a strong voice for social justice can be obscured, even as the tradition pays lip service to the prophet's social critique.

Ironically, an appreciation of the contours of the final form of the text of Jeremiah, unlike our study of Isaiah, stands more as a warning signal than a beacon of hope. We await the time when the passages devoted to the message of justice will begin to exert influence over the rest of the book such that the added layers are transformed by the critique they seem so well positioned to hide. In that context, talk of a "new" covenant will truly yield something more than politics as usual. The final form of the book, however, leaves the outcome of the debate very much unsettled. To that extent, there is room for continued reconfiguring of the tradition, as with the book of Isaiah, or for radically different voices, such as the book of Ezekiel, to which we now turn.

Notes

1. N. Avigad, "Baruch the Scribe and Jerahmeel the King's Son," *IEJ* 28 (1978): 52–56. Baruch is a rather enigmatic figure in Jeremiah and is strangely absent from chaps. 37–42.
2. H. B. Huffmon, "Jeremiah of Anathoth: A Prophet for All Israel," in *Ki Baruch Hu: Ancient Near Eastern, Biblical, and Judaic Studies in Honor of Baruch A. Levine*, ed. R. Chazan, W. W. Hallo, and L. H. Schiffman (Winona Lake, Ind.: Eisenbrauns, 1999), 261. For background on the numerous issues that continue to puzzle interpreters, see J. L. Crenshaw, "A Living Tradition: The Book of Jeremiah in Current Research," *Int* 37 (1983): 117–29; and L. G. Perdue, "Jeremiah in Modern Research: Approaches and Issues," in *A Prophet to the Nations: Essays in Jeremiah Studies*, ed. L. G. Perdue and B. W. Kovacs (Winona Lake, Inc.: Eisenbrauns, 1984), 1–32. On the poetic-prose subdivisions, see R. R. Wilson, "Poetry and Prose in the Book of Jeremiah," in Chazan, et al., ed., *Ki Baruch Hu*, Scholars generally distinguish between three classes of texts: (1) poetic oracles, (2) biographic texts, (3) exhortations or sermons. Varying degrees of Deuteronomic editing are regularly seen in the book.
3. See K. T. Aitken, "The Oracles against Babylon in Jeremiah 50—51: Structures and Perspectives," *Tyndale Bulletin* 35 (1984): 25–63; and J. H. Hayes, "The Usage of Oracles against Foreign Nations in Ancient Israel," *JBL* 87 (1968): 81–92.
4. Qumran does not offer much direction here, for whereas 4QJer[a] is protoMasoretic, 4QJer[b] resembles the LXX.
5. As observed by R. P. Carroll, *Jeremiah* (Sheffield: JSOT Press, 1989), 23.
6. Carroll, *Jeremiah*, 23.
7. J. G. Janzen, *Studies in the Text of Jeremiah* (Cambridge, Mass.: Harvard University Press, 1973), argues for the primacy of the LXX.
8. On the complex relations between poetic, biographic, and exhortation texts, see Wilson, "Poetry and Prose."
9. A. L. Oppenheim, *Ancient Mesopotamia* (Chicago: University of Chicago Press, 1977), 170.
10. The chronology followed throughout for the Judaean kings is that of Albright, but see the discussion in J. H. Hayes and J. M. Miller, eds., *Israelite and Judean History* (Philadelphia: Westminster Press, 1977), 678–81. For the Neo-Babylonian kings, see Oppenheim, *Ancient Mesopotamia*, 340; for the Egyptian kings, see W. W. Hallo and W. K. Simpson, *The Ancient Near East: A History* (New York: Harcourt Brace Jovanovich, 1971), 301.
11. D. J. Wiseman, *Chronicles of Chaldean Kings (626–556 B.C.E.) in the British Museum* (London: Trustees of the British Museum, 1956), 67.
12. Ibid., 71.
13. D. N. Freedman, "The Babylonian Chronicle," in G. E. Wright and D. N. Freeman, eds., *The Biblical Archaeological Reader*, Volume I, Missoula, Montana: Scholars Press, 1975, 119.
14. Wiseman, *Chronicles of Chaldean Kings*, 73.

15. A. R. Green, "The Fate of Jehoiakim," *Andrews University Seminary Studies* 20 (1982): 103–9, argues quite plausibly that Jehoiakim was assassinated. Cf. Leviticus Rabbah XIX: 6.

16. On the numbers of people exiled, see P. R. Ackroyd, *Israel under Babylon and Persia* (Oxford: Oxford University Press, 1970), 9; and B. Porten, "Exile, Babylonian," *Encyclopaedia Judaica* (New York: Macmillan, 1971), 1037; cf. Jeremiah 52.

17. The destruction sites are discussed in K. Kenyon, *Archaeology in the Holy Land*, 4th ed. (New York: W. W. Norton & Co. 1979), chap. 12; J. M. Myers, "Edom and Judah in the Sixth–Fifth Centuries B.C.," *Near Eastern Studies in Honor of William Foxwell Albright*, ed. Hans Goedicke (Baltimore: Johns Hopkins Press, 1971); and E. Stern, "Israel at the Close of the Period of the Monarchy: An Archaeological Survey," *Biblical Archaeologist* 38 (1975). Janssen develops a contrary view, arguing that many village peasants remained behind and that only the urban centers were destroyed and the elite exiled. See E. Janssen, *Juda in der Exilszeit: Ein Beitrag zur Frage der Enstehung des Judentums*, Forschungen zur Religion und Literatur des Alten und Neuen Testaments 69 (Göottingen: Vanderhoeck & Ruprecht, 1956).

18. Observe that Jeremiah was spared from death through the efforts of Ahikam the son of Shaphan (Jer. 26:24). This Ahikam is said to have been the father of Gedaliah (2 Kings 25:12), and is seen elsewhere as one of those sent by Josiah to Huldah the prophetess (2 Kings 22:12, 14).

19. W. F. Albright, "King Jehoiachin in Exile," in G. E. Wright and D. N. Freedman, eds., *The Biblical Archaeologist Reader*, Volume I (Missoula, Montana: Scholars Press 1975), 108; H. W. F. Saggs, "Babylon," *Archeology and Old Testament Study* (Oxford: Oxford University Press, 1969), 45.

20. E. F. Weidner, "Jojachin, König von Juda, in Babylonischen Keilschrifttexten," *Melanges Syriens Offerts a Monsieur Rene Dussaud*, vol. 2 (Paris: Librairie Orientaliste Paul Geuthner, 1939), 924. See also *ANET*, 308.

21. Ibid., 924.

22. Albright, "King Jehoiachin in Exile," 109.

23. Weidner, "Jojachin, König von Juda, 924; D. W. Thomas, "The Age of Jeremiah in the Light of Recent Archaeological Discovery," *Palestine Exploration Quarterly* (1950): 7.

24. D. B. Weisberg, "Murashu's Sons," *Encyclopedia Judaica* (New York: Macmillan, 1971), 529.

25. Weisberg, "Murashu's Sons," 529. For additional references to these materials see chapter 5.

26. B. Oded, *Mass Deportation and Deportees in the Neo-Assyrian Empire* (Wiesbaden: Dr. Judwig Reichert Verlag, 1979), 12.

27. Weisberg, "Murashu's Sons," 529.

28. M. D. Coogan, *West Semitic Personal Names in the Murašû Documents*, Harvard Semitic Monographs 7 (Missoula, Mont.: Scholars Press, 1976), 119.

29. Ibid., 119.

30. Weisberg, "Murashu's Sons," 529.

31. M. D. Coogan, "Life in the Diaspora: Jews at Nippur in the Fifth Century B.C.E.," *Biblical Archaeologist* 37/1 (1974): 10. Cf. J. H. Hayes and J. M. Miller, eds., *Israelite and Judean History* (Philadelphia: Westminster Press, 1977), 481ff.

32. Cf. Oded, *Mass Deportation*.

33. L. Wisser, *Jérémie: Critique de la Vie Sociale* (Geneva: Labor et Fides, 1982.)

34. Ibid., 59.

35. Cf. ibid., 64.
36. Ibid., 46–48 with references.
37. Ibid., 93.
38. Ibid., 98.
39. Ibid., 99.
40. J. K. de Geus, "Die Gesellschaftskritik der Propheten und die Archäologie," *Zeitschrift des Deutschen Palästina-Vereins* 98 (1982): 56.
41. Davies, *Prophecy and Ethics: Isaiah and the Ethical Traditions of Israel*, JSOT Supplement Series 16 (Sheffield: JSOT Press, 1981), 80; A. Alt, *Essays on Old Testament History and Religion*, trans. R. A. Wilson (Garden City, N. Y.: Doubleday, 1967).
42. Examples from the historical narratives include the following: Nathan's opposition to David's affair with Bathsheba (2 Sam. 12:1–14); Ahijah's announcement of Rehoboam's rejection by YHWH (1 Kings 11:29–39); Shemaiah's resistance to Rehoboam's military action (1 Kings 12:22–24); Jehu's criticism of Baasha (1 Kings 16:1–4); and Elijah's condemnation of Ahab (1 Kings 16:1–4).
43. H. Donner, "Die soziale Botschaft der Propheten in Lichte der Gesellschaftsordnung in Israel," *Oriens Antiques* 1 (1963): 512.
44. Ibid., 513.
45. Ibid.
46. Ibid., 514.
47. On the marked shift from the negative teaching of Jeremiah to the more positive Deuteronomic view, see R. P. Carroll, *From Chaos to Covenant: Prophecy in the Book of Jeremiah* (New York: Crossroad, 1981). For other aspects of the Deuteronomic handling of the traditions, see E. W. Nicholson, *Preaching to the Exiles* (Oxford: Basil Blackwell Publisher, 1970).
48. Cf., e.g., Wisser, *Jérémie*, 123, 125.
49. See O. Lorentz, "Die Prophetische Kritik des Rentenkapitalsmus: Grundlagen-Probleme der Prophetenforschung," *Ugarit-Forschungen* 7 (1975): 273–74; and F. C. Fensham, "Widow, Orphan and the Poor in the Ancient Near Eastern Legal and Wisdom Literature," *JNES* 21 (1962): 121–39.
50. Wisser, *Jérémie*, 74.
51. G. E. Mendenhall, "The Worship of Baal and Asherah: A Study of the Social Bonding Functions of Religious Systems," in *Biblical and Related Studies Presented to Samuel Iwry*, ed. A. Kort and S. Morschauser (Winona Lake, Ind.: Eisenbrauns, 1985), 147–58.
52. Cf. ibid.
53. Wisser, *Jérémie*, 33.; contrast Jer. 6:13 which links *qtn* "small" to *gdl* "great," as all guilty of unjust profiteering, a fact noted by Wisser, *Jérémie*, 38; see also Jer. 8:10, 31:34. In 8:10, at least, the oppressed are set off from the "smallest" and "greatest," perhaps indicating that for Jeremiah the "smallest" refers to lower level functionaries and not the "poor." In this way, 5:4, 6:13, and 8:10 might carry some inner consistency. On the other hand, if "smallest" and "poor" are equivalent, then the prophet sees the poor as likewise involved in injustices but not culpable in the same way the knowledgeable elite would be.
54. A. Gelin, *The Poor of Yahweh*, trans. K. Sullivan (Collegeville, Minn.: Liturgical Press, 1964), 19.
55. Cf. H. J. Fabry, "dal," *TDOT*, 3: 226.
56. See T. Overholt, *Cultural Anthropology and the Old Testament* (Minneapolis, Fortress, 1996), chap. 1.

57. See the criticisms raised by R. P. Carroll, "Prophecy and Society," in *The World of Ancient Israel*, ed. R. E. Clements (Cambridge: Cambridge University Press, 1989), chap. 10.

58. D. J. Reimer, "The 'Foe' and the 'North' in Jeremiah," *ZAW* 101 (1989): 223–32, explores the complexities regarding the northern foe in Jeremiah. Reimer's tendency to localize the "north" in YHWH's timeless realm does not do justice to the image's rather concrete character. Given the time period, there are few candidates for most of the references in Jeremiah. Given the historic circumstances, Babylon must be a factor in one way or another.

59. This analysis treats the figure of Jeremiah in these passages as an image within a tradition that is under construction, a theological effort that is reshaping the very nature of the prophetic for a particular community. Such an analysis broadens the focus beyond the more immediate reading of the text given by T. W. Overholt, *The Threat of Falsehood: A Study in the Theology of the Book of Jeremiah* (Naperville, Ill.: Alec R. Allenson, 1970).

60. R. P. Carroll, "Textual Strategies and Ideology in the Second Temple Period," in *Second Temple Studies*, vol. 1, *Persian Period*, ed. P. R. Davies (Sheffield: JSOT Press, 1991), 114.

61. See J. Vermeylen, "Essai de Redaktionsgeschichte des 'Confessions de Jérémie,'" in *Le Livre de Jérémie*, ed. P. M. Bogaert (Louvain: Leuven University Press, 1981). Vermeylen is correct to see in these confessions not *Jeremiah's* confessions but "*psalms* of the *book* of Jeremiah" (268). Vermeylen argues that genuine fragments of the prophet's oracles (not confessions) underlie the current confessions, which are complex documents that built up in stages and that include Deuteronomic material and phases of postexilic adaptation and expansion. One such phase concerned pious sufferers in distress (fifth century B.C.E.) and the other phase is attributed to a radicalization of the conflict between the pious and the impious (fourth century B.C.E.). While tantalizing as a theoretical construct, Vermeylen's phasing would seem to make too much out of the rather stylized lament language of these texts.

62. J. C. L. Gibson, *Textbook of Syrian Semitic Inscriptions, Volume I: Hebrew and Moabite Inscriptions* (Oxford: Clarendon Press, 1971), 75–76.

63. See, e.g., S. Dalley, *Myths from Mesopotamia: Creation, The Flood, Gilgamesh, and Others* (Oxford: Oxford University Press, 1989), 233–277.

Chapter 8

Territory and Temple

Ezekiel

The book of Ezekiel takes us into the whirlwind of the exile and beyond. In some ways, its highly structured character resembles the rhetorical purposiveness of Isaiah. Isaiah's desolation/restoration downbeat is matched by Ezekiel's judgment/revivification trajectory. However, Ezekiel structures its motif development quite differently, and is likewise decidedly different than the groping for new perspectives that we found in Jeremiah.[1] Whereas Isaiah carves a jostling path through desolation toward hope, and Jeremiah offers a many-paneled work that seeks to refurbish a more ancient structure, Ezekiel sets itself up as a highly ornamented triptych. On one side, the notion of divine judgment dominates the oracles against Judah (chaps. 4—24). On the other side, communal revivification dominates the oracles of renewal (chaps. 33—39). These two side panels of the prophetic text stand cheek by jowl with the inevitable and centrally placed oracles against the nations (chaps. 25—32). While there certainly is movement to the overall book, the triptych arrangement allows every historical moment to come under the scrutiny of judgment and bathe in the light of revivification.

In other words, the postexilic context of the book was one in which the national questions were far from settled even as the temple had been rebuilt in Jerusalem. Unlike Isaiah, which presents its social vision as the underpinnings

319

for a restoration that was only at its inception, Ezekiel offers a vision that would deepen the priestly institutions that had already been put into place during the early years of the restoration from exile; hence the comfort with which Ezekiel blends prophetic language with a priestly view rooted in purity code terminology.[2] Yet the urgency of Ezekiel would seem to indicate that, from the author's perspective at least, all was not well in Jerusalem. That the temple rebuilding project was only partly successful would seem to be indicated by the need for reforms, as evidenced by the books of Ezra and Nehemiah. The program of Ezekiel also stands apart rhetorically and institutionally from the expanded sections of Jeremiah, in particular with respect to the temple program (Ezekiel 8), again a sign that the postexilic community was in turmoil over the direction the reconstruction should take and over the social policies that should guide the people into their future as the commonwealth of God under foreign rule. Thus, while all three works, Isaiah, Jeremiah, and Ezekiel, are committed to a theological assessment of the exile, Ezekiel's vision of divine power, apportionment of political authority, sense of social justice, commitment to the poor, and understanding of the nations offers a stunning alternative to the views cultivated elsewhere in the prophetic tradition. Indeed, one wonders after reading Ezekiel whether we should even speak as if such a tradition existed except as a rhetorical construct.

We begin this chapter with an examination of the political dimensions of the symbolism of divine power with which the book opens. We then turn to a broad look at the social justice terrain covered by the exhortations and allegories that are found in the chapters devoted to the oracles against Judah (chaps. 4—24). After a brief discussion of the commitment to the poor advocated in these chapters, we next consider the text's oracles against the nations. This chapter ends with a discussion of the issues of territory and national hope as fielded in the latter chapters of Ezekiel, in particular by the stirring and elaborate vision of a new temple for Jerusalem (chaps. 40—47).

Vision of Divine Power: The Politics of God

The awe-inspiring vision of the divine presence that opens Ezekiel (chaps. 1—11) can now be understood against the iconography of the time. The vision of the winged creatures with composite faces and features of humans, lions, oxen, and eagles are abundantly represented for us in all manner of seals, carving, reliefs, and furnishings from the ancient Near East. The most remarkable examples come from the excavations of the palaces of the Assyrian kings, where numerous pairs of composite creatures decorate the palatial manors and governmental centers of the empire. The Assyrian versions have human heads, lion bodies, ox feet, and eagle wings.[3] In order to enter the presence of the king, one would have to pass by these rather startling and mysterious representations that root monarchic power in a far deeper metaphysical reality. The composite creatures are evocative of the transcendental mystery that impinges on and creates the world order, a mystery that is continually at work destroying and refashioning the fabric of history. In other words, the iconography and the divine vision presupposed by Ezekiel are ideological analogues to the structuring of human power in the polis throughout the ancient Near East. When an Assyrian king is present, the divine awe-inspiring Presence goes with him.[4] Likewise, when YHWH is present, Judah throbs with life. Yet Ezekiel probes the underside of this symbol system: When that Presence ascends out of the city, only oracles of judgment remain, in particular against Zedekiah, who is treated as the sum and substance of political arrogance (Ezek. 11:25).

The first eleven chapters of Ezekiel outline the charges: The relationship between the divine and earthly powers has broken down. The corruption of the human political authorities has become the measure of the success or failure of the city as an embodiment of the divine will. Ezekiel's is an urban-based program. At times the prophet's address is to the society in general, "that nation of rebels" and "the House of Israel" (2:3; 3:1, 4–7). At other times, the address is to the generalized "wicked" people (3:18–21). Yet the references can also be quite specific, as, for example, with regard to mercantile activity:

> Here is the day! See, the cycle has come round; it has appeared. The rod has blossomed; arrogance has budded, lawlessness has grown into a rod of wickedness. Nothing comes of them, nor of their abundance, nor of their wealth; nor is there preeminence among them. The time has come, the day has arrived. Let not the buyer rejoice nor the seller mourn—for divine wrath shall overtake all her multitude. For the seller shall not return to what he sold so long as they remain among the living. For the vision concerns all her multitude, it shall not be revoked. And because of his guilt, no man shall hold fast to his life. (Ezek. 7:10–13)

The nature of "lawlessness" remains unspecified. Wealth, however, "shall not avail to save them in the day of the LORD's wrath—to satisfy their hunger or to fill their stomachs" (7:19; cf. 7:11). While such a critique of wealth finds its counterpart in other portions of the prophetic corpus, the talk of "abominations" and "unclean things" places the text squarely within a priestly philosophic framework.[5] The text becomes most specific about the society's power holders, the elite of the city:

> Horror comes, and they shall seek safety, but there shall be none. Calamity shall follow calamity, and rumor follow rumor. Then they shall seek vision from the prophet in vain; instruction shall perish from

the priest, and counsel from the elders. The king shall mourn, the prince shall clothe himself with desolation, and the hands of the people of the land shall tremble. I will treat them in accordance with their own ways and judge them according to their deserts. And they shall know that I am the LORD. (Ezek. 7:25–27)

The judgment of the bureaucratic and religious elite could not be clearer. Indeed, two "leaders of the people" are named specifically, Jaazaniah son of Azzur and Pelatiah son of Benaiah (11:1). If the text is meant literally, murder and assassination filled the city with corruption, as in the other nations (11:5–12). This would seem to be the implication of the judgment meted out, for Jaazaniah and Pelatiah, receiving appropriate recompense, simply "dropped dead" (11:13).

For all its focus on the city, the first eleven chapters of Ezekiel also reveal an exilic program. The very first verse underscores the possibility of reorientation via divine power in exile:

In the thirtieth year, on the fifth day of the fourth month, when I was in the community of exiles by the Chebar Canal, the heavens opened and I saw visions of God. On the fifth day of the month—it was the fifth year of the exile of King Jehoiachin—the word of the LORD came to the priest Ezekiel son of Buzi, by the Chebar Canal, in the land of the Chaldeans. And the hand of the LORD came upon him there.

I looked, and lo, a stormy wind came sweeping out of the north—a huge cloud and flashing fire, surrounded by a radiance; and in the center of it, in the center of the fire, a gleam as of amber. (Ezek. 1:1–4)

The prophet's vision of divine power is connected to the fate of the exiles, but in particular with King Jehoiachin. Ezekiel fashions an iconographic portrayal of a divine power that is thought to stand behind Judah's royal apparatus in much the way that the Babylonian gods supported their chosen kings, but the twist here is that Judah's ruler is among the exiles. The question the book wrestles with is whether and to what extent the divine Presence remains committed to the old royal arrangements and ritual apparatus. Must the monarchy and the temple continue to stand together, or can the temple institution find an independent place in the divine economy? The theological creativity of Ezekiel's project is seen in its revitalization of the old royal symbols while seeking a political and sacral restoration of God's city that is predicated on a nonmonarchic basis. It remains to the survivors to carry forward this program (6:8–10). This political and religious interplay is driven home in these chapters through the blurring that so readily occurs between the vision of God in the Jerusalem temple and the vision of the divine Presence at the Chebar Canal in exile (chap. 10). The exiles who experience the divine Presence can hear the word of hope that their successful return to Judah will be predicated on a commitment to a priestly effort at restructuring the worship practices and political life of Judah's capital and land (11:14–21).

However, this urban project of renewal is not to be left entirely in the hands of the old establishment. The prophet is to be the architect of the awareness of a divine commitment to the political aspirations of Judah beyond judgment, beyond the temporary dismantling of Judah's state bureaucracy. How does the prophet bridge these two worlds, the worlds of temple and exile, of political loss and religious restoration? The prophetic role is couched, in part, as watchman. The prophet is the tower guard who sees devastation looming (3:16–21; 33:1–33). He is sent to speak to the populace, "whether they listen or not" (2:5, 7; 3:11). Unlike the dislocated people and the disenfranchised leadership who know only the loss of power and the collapse of the symbol system, the overwhelming sense of God's presence even in exile leaves the prophet sitting "stunned" for seven days (3:15). Silence gives way to prophetic speech, as Ezekiel assumes his watchman role (cf. 3:22–27). Speech and symbol go hand in hand throughout this section, and so we find omens of judgment enacted by the prophet. This array of symbolic actions includes (1) modeling a siege of Jerusalem (4:1–3), (2) lying for 390 days on one side as a term for judgment (4:4–6), (3) prophesying bare armed against Jerusalem (4:7), (4) being tied up with cords (4:8), (5) eating food while lying on one side (4:9–11), (6) baking cakes in excrement (4:12–15), and (7) and shaving head and beard (5:1). All these omen-like activities create a sense of uneasiness about Judah's judgment, while paving the way for a new configuration of God's relation to Judah's power structures.

The prophet's role, in part, is to mediate between exile and revitalization. Thus, theologically speaking, the gruesome horrors of the slaughter attendant upon the Babylonians' taking of the city of Jerusalem must be squared with the departure of God from the altar. The identification of the sanctuary as a place of abomination creates a space for YHWH to order its cleansing by war (9:1–11). The picture is horrifying and the concomitant theology, so fiercely dismantled in modern times by Auschwitz, manages to bind together war, judgment, divine absence, divine presence, and the hope of restoration. This latter hope was an emergent possibility for the exiled community only through the prophetic voice, according to Ezekiel.[6] By scattering coals about the city, the prophet permits the divine cloud to continue filling the temple, if only for a time. But soon after the announcement of a word of hope to the exiles, the divine Presence is removed from the city of Jerusalem, transporting the prophet into exile, departing ahead of the oracles of judgment that follow (11:22–24).

The vision of divine power in the first eleven chapters of Ezekiel specifically shows this urban movement to hinge on a temple program. Not only are general abominations denounced, using priestly language (5:5–9), but the defiling of the sanctuary is singled out as the most hideous of the populace's crimes:

> And He said to me, "O mortal, turn your eyes northward." I turned my eyes northward, and there, north of the gate of the altar, was that infuriating image on the approach. And He said to me, "Mortal, do you see what they are doing, the terrible abominations that the House of Israel is practicing here, to drive Me far from My Sanctuary? You shall yet see even greater abominations!" (Ezek. 8:5–6; cf. 5:11–17, 6:1–7, 13; 7:24)

Worshiping images, women bewailing Tammuz, people bowing to the sun as it arises—all these are seen as sources of judgment (8:7–18). While these activities have driven YHWH out of the city, the postexilic nature of the text attunes us to look to the balancing material in chaps. 34—37, where a new leadership is installed and a new sacrificial system is established with a revitalized temple containing the restored presence of God to the city. The program of Ezekiel is thoroughly urban in focus, centered on a priestly-prophetic capture of the reigns of power. The temple becomes the sacral symbol and the liturgical lynchpin of this rhetorical and political effort.

Sense of Social Justice: The Outrage of the Prophet

Already the initial chapters of Ezekiel have displayed a keen sense of moral outrage at the misdeeds committed by a wide array of members in the bureaucratic and religious elite. When measured against their "abominations," the divine Presence, unable to tolerate the uncleanness, is forced to depart. This removal opens the door to a broad series of oracles and allegories in chaps. 12—24 that deepen this sense of outrage, sharpening the prophet's broad critique.

Crimes of the People

Key to this critique is an impassioned attack against King Zedekiah, other prophets, and the general populace of Judah (chaps. 12—14). The prophet gathers his "gear" to dramatize the exile march, as if this might wake up his comrades (12:1–7). The real march is to be headed by "the prince among them" (12:12). The forced departure of the blinded Zedekiah (the one termed simply the "prince in Jerusalem") is in view (12:12–13; cf. 2 Kings 25:4–7). The prophet's diatribe strikes at the very heart of Judah's leadership. The army is then scattered, and so are the people (12:14–15). Those who survive become witnesses against themselves, able to "recount all their abominable deeds among the nations to which they come" (12:16). Zedekiah's demise is primary to the book's critique.

Since the state apparatus throughout the ancient world functioned in light of the omens and prophetic words gathered by its ritual experts, we might suggest that the book's critique extends to the prophetic sector, as also occurs in Jeremiah. The writer of Ezekiel imagines a reestablishment of the prophetic office on a new basis: Where a prophecy and its fulfillment were once separable in time, leading to confusion and conflict over true and false prophecy, the time lapse is to be obliterated and prophetic visions are to be fulfilled with regularity and immediacy (12:21–28). The rhetoric of this passage accents the struggle that has arisen in various circles over the character and scope of prophetic authority. This priestly-styled movement readily capitalized on this conflict to lay claim to only that sort of prophecy that unequivocally joined forces with the book's program. The verbiage is caustic:

> Assuredly, thus said the Lord GOD: Because you speak falsehood and prophesy lies, assuredly, I will deal with you—declares the Lord GOD. My hand will be against the prophets who prophesy falsehood and utter lying divination. They shall not remain in the assembly of My people, they shall not be inscribed in the lists of the House of Israel, and they shall not come back to the land of Israel. Thus shall you know that I am the Lord GOD (Ezek. 13:8–9; cf. 13:17–23)

Seemingly the entire prophetic establishment is written off as a flimsy wall (13:10–16). These are the prophets who are invested in an urban vision of unmitigated prosperity, a vision proven false by the exile (13:16).

Curiously, or perhaps conveniently, the priesthood as such does not come under attack here, but the defiling "fetishes" do (14:1–11). The entire house of Israel has been "estranged" from YHWH through these idols (14:5). The only response such worshipers can hope for from a prophet is a word of judgment (14:6–8). If the prophet speaks otherwise, YHWH punishes both the "inquirer" and the prophet (14:9–11). This passage reinforces the idea of the immediacy of judgment, found previously in Ezek. 12:21–28. We are beginning to see a pattern, exploited more fully in chap. 18, that stresses a factor that has been so often wrongly labeled as individual responsibility. The emphasis is rather on the immediacy both of prophecy and judgment, as opposed to long-term judgments that are delayed and thereby create confusion about the viability of prophecy. It would seem that an urgency must have undergirded the Ezekielian project as its architects sought to persuade the Judaean exiles to return to their initial postexilic agenda, a delay that becomes even more pronounced in the books of Ezra and Nehemiah.

This section of oracles closes by invoking the names of the great symbols of justice: Noah, Job, and Daniel (14:12–20). Not even these three paragons of virtue could save the city of Jerusalem from its destruction by famine, wild beasts, sword, and pestilence. Noah, the flood hero, found favor with God. Job, the innocent sufferer, had the merit to argue openly with God. Daniel (the traditional judge and hero Dan-el known from Ugarit and later recast as an Israelite exile in the book of Daniel) also could not avert the fate of invasion, judgment, and exile. These names encapsulate a sense of justice in Ezekiel that yearns for something higher and better for the prophet's society. The ancient wise become the measure of the society's degradation, but also the measure for the comfort and restoration assured by the book's program that envisions a restored city beyond the degradations of exile (14:21–23).

Allegories and Ethics

Symbols, visions, and allegories frame Ezekiel's theological imagination. Chapters 15—17 offer a series of three allegorical passages drawn from nature and marriage, which are used to measure the national soul of Ezekiel's people. The allegories provide occasion for reassessing Judah's ethical commitments, its political alliances, its faithfulness to the covenant tradition, its worship life, and its history.

Chapter 15 presents an allegory about the grapevine. The text dwells on the uselessness of such wood:

> Even when it was whole it could not be used for anything; how much less when fire has consumed it and it is charred! Can it still be used for anything?
> Assuredly, thus said the Lord GOD: Like the wood of the grapevine among the trees of the forest, which I have designated to be fuel for fire, so will I treat the inhabitants of Jerusalem. (Ezek. 15:5–6)

The dwellers of the capital city, so much a focus of the book, bear the weight of this allegory of judgment.

The allegory gives way, in chapter 16, to a birth discourse concerning the origin of Jerusalem. Unlike the story of conquest offered in Joshua, where the Israelites are external invaders to a pagan Canaanite landscape, for Ezekiel the Jerusalemites are products of Canaan:

> Thus said the Lord GOD to Jerusalem: By origin and birth you are from the land of the Canaanites—your father was an Amorite and your mother a Hittite. As for your birth, when you were born your navel cord was not cut, and you were not bathed in water to smooth you;

you were not rubbed with salt, nor were you swaddled. No one pitied you enough to do any one of these things for you out of compassion for you; on the day you were born, you were left lying, rejected, in the open field. (Ezek. 16:3–5)

The birth discourse then yields to a marriage scene:

When I passed by you and saw you wallowing in your blood, I said to you: "Live in spite of your blood." Yea, I said to you: "Live in spite of your blood." I let you grow like the plants of the field; and you continued to grow up until you attained to womanhood, until your breasts became firm and your hair sprouted.

You were still naked and bare when I passed by you [again] and saw that your time for love had arrived. So I spread My robe over you and covered your nakedness, and I entered into a covenant with you by oath—declares the Lord GOD; thus you became Mine. I bathed you in water, and washed the blood off you, and anointed you with oil. (Ezek. 16:6–9)

This marriage metaphor finds Jerusalem bedecked as a queen. However, the betrothed of God "played the harlot," flouting the covenant through image worship (16:15–24) and alliances with Egypt, Assyria, and Babylon (16:25–29). The critique of their idolatry is particularly pointed:

You even took some of your cloths and made yourself tapestried platforms and fornicated on them—not in the future; not in time to come. You took your beautiful things, made of the gold and silver that I had given you, and you made yourself phallic images and fornicated with them. You took your embroidered cloths to cover them; and you set My oil and My incense before them. The food that I had given you— the choice flour, the oil, and the honey, which I had provided for you to eat—you set it before them for a pleasing odor. And so it went— declares the Lord GOD. You even took the sons and daughters that you bore to Me and sacrificed them to those [images] as food—as if your harlotries were not enough, you slaughtered My children and presented them as offerings to them! In all your abominations and harlotries, you did not remember the days of your youth, when you were naked and bare, and lay wallowing in your blood. (Ezek. 16:16–22)

The denunciation of foreign alliances is couched in coarse sexual imagery:

You built your mound at every crossroad; and you sullied your beauty and spread your legs to every passerby, and you multiplied your harlotries. You played the whore with your neighbors, the lustful Egyptians—you multiplied your harlotries to anger Me. Now, I will stretch out My arm against you and withhold your maintenance; and I will surrender you to the will of your enemies, the Philistine women, who are shocked by your lewd behavior.

In your insatiable lust you also played the whore with the Assyrians; you played the whore with them, but were still unsated. You multiplied your harlotries with Chaldea, that land of traders; yet even with this you were not satisfied. (Ezek. 16:25–29)

This critique of idolatry and foreign alliances, prominent also in Isaiah and Jeremiah, is reflective of the general social critique of Israel's prophets. The prophetic rhetoric consistently forges a link between the crudeness of idol worship and the lust for international influence and support. As Uffenheimer points out, the rude sexual language overturns the long-standing belief that the people enjoyed an intimate relationship with their covenant God.[7] In the context of the birth discourse, the corruption of Jerusalem as an Amorite/Hittite-styled petty kingdom mimicking the political patterns and strategies of its neighbors is plain.

What is remarkable here is that the prophet does not perpetuate the ancient Israelite myth of invasion and conquest, so beloved of those gathered around the program of the Deuteronomic History. For the DH camp, the myth of external origins (i.e., Joshua's conquest of the Canaanites) became an excuse to dehumanize and devastate the Canaanite population, not in the period before the establishment of the monarchy (for this is after all an imaginative projection on Israel's mythic past) but against any who remained in the land after the exile, whether persons from the lower economic layers or of diverse various nationalities, who resisted the restoration to power of an elite that had been deposed and exiled. However, to Ezekiel, the Jerusalemite exiles could not be accorded this mythological luxury because their origins as native Canaanites were betrayed by the very mode of operation adopted by their temple and bureaucratic establishment. Jerusalem's politics and religion were obviously pagan in origin and direction. No myth of national origins and heroic invasion by the ancient tribes as perpetuated by Ezekiel's opponents could veil this reality. Herein we find hints of the priestly program's effort to encompass the land's disenfranchised in a way that the nostalgic royalist program of DH could not (see chapters 2—3).

The image of the adulterous prostitute climaxes with a shameful judgment of the "lovers"—Egypt, Assyria, and Babylon—stripping Jerusalem to destroy it:

I will assuredly assemble all the lovers to whom you gave your favors, along with everybody you accepted and everybody you rejected. I will assemble them against you from every quarter, and I will expose your nakedness to them, and they shall see all your nakedness. I will inflict upon you the punishment of women who commit adultery and murder, and I will direct bloody and impassioned fury against you. I will deliver you into their hands, and they shall tear down your eminence and level your mounds; and they shall strip you of your clothing and take away your dazzling jewels, leaving you naked and bare. Then they shall assemble a mob against you to pelt you with stones and pierce you with their swords. They shall put your houses to the flames and execute punishment upon you in the sight of many women; thus I will put a stop to your harlotry, and you shall pay no more fees. (Ezek. 16:37–41)

The language in this section draws rather obviously and heavily on ancient Near Eastern sexual and marital categories. The pattern of a woman's subordination to her husband in the context of a rigid pattern of sexual mores frames Ezekiel's discussion of YHWH's domination over Jerusalem. The image is pressed to its limits through a comparison between Jerusalem, Samaria, and Sodom as "sisters" who rejected their husbands and children (16:44–45). So bad is Jerusalem that Samaria and Sodom, "appear righteous in comparison" (16:52). The ancient Near Eastern anthropological categories of shame/honor play a decisive role in shaping the prophet's critique. Only at the end of the passage is this language linked to talk of covenant violation (16:59–63). Perhaps this dose of traditional family language ought to be considered a sign of the conservative nature of the prophet's political aspirations. To predicate a political movement in these terms is possibly indicative of an attempt on the part of a traditional priestly sector of the elite to exert control by invoking representative priestly categories—clean/unclean, sacred space/secular space, male/female, Jerusalem/countryside. Clearly Ezekiel reflects a priestly anthropological matrix, defining the territory of its power through language and categories integral to priestly thought (see chapter 2). Stated more bluntly, foreign alliances, in this view, are counterproductive because they drain the temple treasury. For all its negative tone, however, one must not overlook the emphasis on renewal envisioned in this passage. Once the harlot is punished, the divine wrath subsides (16:42). The fortunes of the wayward sisters, Sodom, Samaria, and Jerusalem, are to be restored (16:53–55).

These words of forgiveness are jarred by the allegory of the two eagles, which follows in chap. 17. Here one brilliant eagle plucks a cedar bough and plants it in Babylon where it grows. But another eagle, Egypt, seeks to dominate the plant. This domination is short-lived, however, for the first eagle returns to destroy the plant. The text itself supplies the interpretation, presenting the allegory as a rather transparent critique of Kings Zedekiah and Jehoiakim (17:11–21). The Babylonian king had carted Zedekiah off to Babylon, replacing him with Jehoiakim, who should have remained submissive to

Babylon. In turning to Egypt, however, Jehoiakim launched a foolish rebellion, which ended in disaster—invasion by the Babylonians. The writer seems to imagine that Jehoiakim was carted off to Babylon and was punished there, although the course of events is not clear either from 2 Kings 24:1–5 or later rabbinic tradition.[8] If these segments of Ezekiel are to be dated to the exile, then we must imagine the book to be the product of a movement among certain sectors of the priesthood who sought to develop a program beyond the immediate circles surrounding the exiled (or even deceased) Jehoiakim or the later incarcerated Jehoiachin. The royalist option is minimized here and elsewhere in the text, where the *nāśî'*, "prince," predominates rather than *melek*, "king." It is this priestly faction that would see itself as the "tender twig" clipped from the tree and is then replanted in Israel to regrow into a vast tree (i.e., as a successful restoration project). If, however, Ezekiel is to be set well into the Persian period, the talk of "Zedekiah" would simply be representative of all royalist aspirations to which some prophetic-priestly critic or group is offering a comprehensive and bold alternative.[9]

To conclude: The allegories of the useless grapevine, the Canaanite birth of Judah, and the destructive eagle all point beyond replicating the old royal house, with its corrupt politics. The book of Ezekiel, through these allegories, calls instead for a renewed priestly program for the constuction of a viable society. Ironically, even DH leads to this conclusion, for although pagan worship doomed Jerusalem's temple, this sort of worship was the result of kings who led the people astray. However, whereas DH might suggest that the solution is in having good kings, Ezekiel's group saw the future in priestly terms, which meant that the monarchy would have to be strictly limited if it was to be permitted to exist at all.

Theology and National Guilt

Chapters 18—20 present two major theological discourses and a funerary dirge, texts that highlight the issue of national guilt. These passages coincide with issues raised in preceding chapters, but extend them in terms of YHWH's sovereignty in that historical context, paving the way for the acceptance of a prophetic-priestly cadre that might lead the nation beyond the ills of judgment.

We have already anticipated our discussion of chap. 18. We observed earlier that certain elements of chaps. 12 and 13 appear to call into question the standard assessment of chap. 18. Frequently, chap. 18 is read as a shift away from a more ancient tradition of punishment meted out in terms of *corporate* responsibility. This interpretation holds that Ezekiel is introducing *individual* responsibility as an alternative to the more ancient conception and practices.[10] However, our analysis of chaps. 12 and 13 suggested that this distinction between the corporate and the individual is misleading. Chapter 18 is also similarly misconstrued.

In the first place, individuals can and were held responsible for their actions in the old law codes, such as Exodus 21—23 and Deuteronomy 12—26. Even the Ten Commandments are couched in the second person singular form, accenting each person's individual commitment to the corporate endeavor. Here the balance is struck between corporate and individual. Talk of an anthropologically grounded "corporate personality" tends to obscure the composite character of the corporate/individual matrix of biblical legal thought.[11]

In chapters 12 and 13 the writer is concerned that there no longer be a time lag between a prophetic pronouncement and its fulfillment. Likewise, for chapter 18, the prophet sees no time lag between sin and punishment. Hence the shift is not, as some think, from corporate guilt to individual responsibility; rather, the shift is from transgenerational punishment to the *immediate* punishment of the unjust.[12] By implication, there are to be immediate rewards for the just (Ezek. 18:5–19). With Ezekiel 18, the transgenerational pattern of punishment found in the Ten Commandments, where God visits the iniquities of the ancestors on their descendants, is mitigated (Exod. 20:5; cf. Deut. 5:9). Why does the prophet seek immediacy? This would seem to be a rhetorical device that permits the returning exiles to see themselves as the bearers of hope and not the victims of a curse that would still be in effect. Thus, even the unjust who repent will immediately be forgiven (18:21–28). The accent for those engaged in the project of the Judaean restoration is on repentance, forgiveness, and life.[13] The immediacy factor permits *all* the exiled to participate in the project of renewal. Thus, the prophet's message of repentance is addressed throughout chap. 18 to the corporate entity, the house of Israel, and to the individuals, good and evil, who constitute that national body.

Chap. 19 offers a dirge lamenting the demise of the Davidic house, a "lioness among the lions," as a result of the misguided policies of Jehoahaz and Zedekiah:

> Your mother was like a vine in your blood,
> Planted beside streams,
> With luxuriant boughs and branches
> Thanks to abundant waters.
> And she had a mighty rod
> Fit for a ruler's scepter.
> It towered highest among the leafy trees,
> It was conspicuous by its height,
> By the abundance of its boughs.
> But plucked up in a fury,
> She was hurled to the ground.
> The east wind withered her branches,

They broke apart and dried up;
And her mighty rod was consumed by fire.
Now she is planted in the desert,
In ground that is arid and parched.
Fire has issued from her twig-laden branch
And has consumed her boughs,
She is left without a mighty rod,
A scepter to rule with.

Ezek. 19:10–14

Following this dirge, chapter 20 offers the second extensive theological discourse of this section, a discourse that reinterprets the Exodus theme in light of the exilic disaster. YHWH makes himself known in Egypt: "I the LORD am your God" (20:5). Called on to abandon the "fetishes" of Egypt, the house of Jacob lapses into rebellion. The exodus becomes, for Ezekiel, a way for YHWH to save face by dragging the people out into the wilderness to punish them so that the nations might not see the rebellion of God's people, which threatened to dishonor YHWH's name (20:8–9). There, in the wilderness, the laws and the Sabbath were enjoined, but the desecration of the Sabbath led to punishment in the wilderness (20:10–17). The rebellion prohibited entry into the land flowing with milk and honey (20:15). Only YHWH's pity spared them (20:17). The "children," who were likewise warned about the iniquities of the "fathers," also rebelled against the laws and the Sabbath (20:21–24). The divine wrath was again somewhat tempered for the sake of God's honor in front of the nations, but a scattering among the nations is decreed (20:23). The defiling shrines in the land of promise and the "passing of children through the fire" in the diaspora becomes the final point of tension between God and Israel (20:27–32). This leads to a new "wilderness" judgment wherein the transgressors in the lands of exile are separated from those brought into the covenant (20:33–38). What ensues is a successful restoration of worship on God's mountain, a deed which the text ostensibly emphasizes is entirely God's own doing (20:39–42). However, the prophetic-priestly nature of the judgment/restoration discourse also requires a prophetic-priestly interpreter to articulate and enact God's triumph over the people's evil. Subtly the text paves the way for authorities such as the Zadokites to emerge as the bearers of the people's burdens and the executors of God's commonwealth (see below).

This remarkable discourse reassesses the traditional exodus story and turns it into a tale of YHWH's honor. Beyond the conduct of individuals and the community, the honor/shame factor governs God's activity. This anthropologically powerful category now serves as the ground for YHWH's revitalization of the covenant bond. Rebellion does not have the last word, at least for those inside the sacred territory. Perhaps we can see in this passage an answer to the conundrum of whether or not Ezekiel was written in Israel or in the dispersion. Everything is set for Jerusalem, but the sense of struggle dominates. The renewal of the exodus traditions, so akin to the pentateuchal and Second Isaiah materials, is subject to bitter setbacks, and yet the hope remains that God will act for the sake of God's name. When we consider the duration that separates Cyrus's triumph and the arrivals of Nehemiah and Ezra, we can well imagine that Ezekiel emerges as a text in Babylon well into the Persian period, marked by the woes and hopes of such factions as were sending forth their Nehemiahs and Ezras to reestablish "true" worship in Jerusalem. Hope rested on the children's children of the original returnees and their sponsors. The mid-fifth century B.C.E. provides a context for a prophetic-priestly amalgam such as we find in Ezekiel. The hope of the "pleasing odor" going forth to YHWH, the restoration of the Sabbath, and the cleansing of the sanctuary, so important to P and Ezekiel, gained further impetus in the political openings that permitted Nehemiah and Ezra to reassert the Babylonian community's interests in the "land of promise."

Death of the Old Order

The discourses in chaps. 21—24 take us to the edge of the oracles of judgment. These final discourses envision the collapse of Jerusalem, the city without whose demise the program of renewal and restoration could not proceed. As such, these texts carry forward YHWH's intent to act against the rebellion of the people, their idolatry, unproductive national alliances, mistreatment of the poor, desecration of shrines, and neglect of the Sabbath. There is, then, the principle of divine honor and a commitment to covenant that overrides the failings of the house of Israel.

Acknowledging the devastating character of the war, the Prophet sees that the just and unjust alike will fall by the sword (21:8–10 [3–5]). Yet this message of judgment is not a message of triumph but of deep prophetic grief and divine agony that such a fate should befall God's people and God's city (21:11–18 [6–13]). Uniquely, the Babylonian king learns via divination to set upon Jerusalem (21:23–27 [18–22]). The sword is to fall specifically against the "dishonored wicked prince of Israel," presumably Zedekiah.

The prophet elaborates one last time a catalogue of ethical, political, and religious crimes for which the people are to be judged. First on this list are the "fetishes," i.e., idol worship (22:1–5). In addition, the murderous princes have exploited strangers, orphans, and widows (22:6) and have profaned the Sabbath (22:8). Sexual perversity runs rampant (22:9–11). In economic dealings, bribes have been taken, interest exacted, and fraud committed (22:12–13). Even the priests come into severe condemnation:

> Her priests have violated My Teaching: they have profaned what is
> sacred to Me, they have not distinguished between the sacred and the
> profane, they have not taught the difference between the unclean and
> the clean, and they have closed their eyes to My sabbaths. I am pro-
> faned in their midst. (Ezek. 22:26)

By focusing on these practices, the prophetic voice of the book actually
works to restore the priestly order. As such, this priestly group would hold
sway over other agents brought under scrutiny in the text. The governing officials "are like wolves rending prey in her midst; they shed blood and destroy
lives to win ill-gotten gain" (22:27). The prophets are again singled out, as
they were in chap. 13, for specific criticism (22:28). Furthermore, the list is
rounded out with a condemnation of the landed elite: "And the people of the
land have practiced fraud and committed robbery; they have wronged the poor
and needy, have defrauded the stranger without redress" (22:29).

The catalogue of crimes gives way in chap. 23 to a final allegory about two
whoring daughters, Oholah (Samaria) and Oholibah (Jerusalem). Once again,
a traditional patriarchal family structure is put to the service of a political analysis and social critique of the capital cities, one fallen and the other assured of
collapse (although this is written in hindsight). Oholah, "Tent," is the city of
Samaria. This city is depicted as a woman who started her whoring with Egypt
in her youth and followed this with a lust for warlike Assyria. Her destruction
followed (23:5–10). Oholibah, "My Tent Is in Her," is the city of Jerusalem.
The progression from one to the other serves to accent the historical flow, with
Jerusalem's whoring beginning with Assyria and ending destructively with
Chaldea, i.e., the Babylonian war machine (23:11-21). The comparison is used
rhetorically by the writer to emphasize Jerusalem's greater crimes. The writer
roots this whoring ultimately back to Egypt, a theme introduced in chapter 20.
Jerusalem's destruction at the hands of her "lovers" is couched as yet in the
future (23:22-27). The judgment is depicted as drinking from the cup of divine
wrath, a theme that is perhaps better known from Jeremiah (23:32–34; cf. Jer.
25:15–29). The passage, remarkable in its historical depth and the severity of
its language, provides an occasion for a terse summation of Jerusalem's crimes,
according to the prophet: idol worship, child sacrifice, defilement of the sanctuary, and the profanation of the Sabbath (23:40–45). All these misdeeds engender divine wrath and punishment, with a view toward the people coming to
"know that I am the Lord GOD" (23:49). This latter idea of "knowing" God,
frequently in light of punishment, is a theme that weaves its way throughout
the bulk of Ezekiel (chaps. 6—39).

Chapter 24 takes us to the day of the Babylonian invasion "in the ninth year,
on the tenth day of the tenth month" (24:1). The poetic response envisions the
war as a cauldron cooking and purifying:

Assuredly, thus said the Lord GOD:
Woe to the city of blood!
I in turn will make a great blaze.
Pile on the logs,
Kindle the fire,
Cook the meat through
And stew it completely,
And let the bones be charred.
Let it stand empty on the coals,
Until it becomes so hot
That the copper glows.
Then its uncleanness shall melt away in it,
And its rust be consumed.
It has frustrated all effort,
Its thick scum will not leave it—
Into the fire with its scum!

Ezek. 24:9–12

The writer lets the death of the prophet's wife coincide with the evening of the day of invasion (24:18). But the order is given by God to the prophet *not* to mourn the loss. Likewise, the people are told, they will respond similarly at the desecration of the sanctuary (24:19–24). Only after the prophet hears the news of the temple's destruction will he be allowed to speak again (24:27). This moment of silence is one of three such moments that structure the intensity of the text. The first such moment occurs in Ezek. 3:22–27, when in seeing the divine Presence the prophet is told to lock himself away to await the time when the message denouncing Jerusalem's rebelliousness is permitted to be spoken. The final moment of silence occurs in Ezek. 33:21–22, which picks up on the silencing in chap. 24, for in chap. 33 the messenger arrives bringing news of Jerusalem's fall. With that, the prophet can begin the oracles of restoration and revivification. Once the city and the land is cleansed via judgment, the prophet is able to announce the new stages in the divine plan. Heightening the tension still further between the moments of silence in chaps. 24 and 33 is the placement of the oracles against the nations.

The oracles of chaps. 21—24, then, work an end to the old order. The ethical, political, and religious commitments of these passages are largely transparent. A conservative set of familial values and sexual attitudes is put to the service of a critique of the urban establishment as it once sought to weave its way amid the minefield of Egyptian, Assyrian, and Babylonian imperial projects. The allure of the war machines gave way to horrific destruction. So much is clear about the prophet's view and critique. What we are less clear about is precisely when this critique is elevated, yet it would seem that the book is compiled in hindsight and is invested with a P-like political and religious program. We must seriously entertain the idea that the period just prior to or during

Nehemiah's and Ezra's reforms is the likely context for the sort of rhetorical program envisioned by the book of Ezekiel. This would put the writer squarely inside one faction that sought to restore the Sabbath and to purge the temple as a ground for social renewal. The latter chapters (34—47) indicate that the program of return and restoration had probably been well underway by the time of the writing of Ezekiel. The social critique against the Jerusalem elite, then, while it looks like a contemporary social critique on the order of an Amos or Micah, is really largely a later set of rhetorical devices designed to persuade hearers to support the temple reform effort as conceived by this faction. The encouragement is put forward not to repeat the perceived errors of Jerusalem's past.

Commitment to the Poor

While Ezekiel does not offer an extended discussion of poverty in the course of this complex visionary treatise, what little material is found here fits snugly into the patterns of the earlier prophetic material; the text of Ezekiel allies itself with this tradition, by underscoring the prophetic critique against oppression and injustice. The writer of Ezekiel makes use of the terms *'ĕbyôn*, "poor" and *'ānî*, "oppressed," in contexts of injustice. The word *dal*, "poor," never appears in the book. This vocabulary reveals a commitment to the poor that serves at least as a rhetorical component of Ezekiel's social program, if not an indicator that beyond rhetoric this priestly-prophetic complex had gained adherents among the actual poor and among those committed to developing their political program in light of the older prophetic social critique. The abuse of the poor forms one item among several in lists of "crimes" the prophet levels against his society (see above).

In the chapter devoted to the issue of immediate judgment, the prophet contrasts the qualities of one who is just with one who is not just (chap. 18). The just person does not engage in idolatry and pagan religious practices, avoids sexual immorality, and practices justice; the latter restores to the debtor items given in pledge, does not rob, feeds the hungry, clothes the naked, and does not lend at interest (18:5–18; cf. 33:15). The oppression of the *'ĕbyôn* and *'ānî* is mentioned in Ezekiel's catalog of injustices as one of a number of crimes that benefited the few over against the many (18:12, 17). The just person, in contrast to the unjust, does not exploit for gain, but seeks to rectify the imbalances in society and bring "true justice between man and man" (18:8).

Another section in the book of Ezekiel presents a long catalog of Judah's offenses before YHWH, serving as the basis of judgment against the people of Judah (chap. 22). The crimes include idolatry (22:4), murder (22:6), neglect of one's father and mother (22:7), wronging of the fatherless and the widow

(22:7), rape and sexual misconduct (22:10–11), accepting bribes as payment for murder (22:12), taking interest (22:12), and, in general, exploiting one's fellows (22:22, 25). The misdeeds that Ezekiel thought deserved divine judgment again reflect the traditional social critique of prophets such as Amos, Micah, and early Isaiah. Also, Ezekiel's charges are consistent with what the books of Jeremiah and Zephaniah had already brought before the people of Judah in the exilic and postexilic context.

The prophet makes it clear who is the offending party in Judah: the ruling classes, the governing officials, and the religious leaders. The princes and officials are condemned for their economic gains, which have ruined some and made widows of others (22:25, 27). Ezekiel says that the princes were "like wolves rending prey . . . ; they shed blood and destroy lives to win ill-gotten gain" (22:27). Violence and profit making are closely linked in this connection, for as Tamez notes, "Murderous oppression has for its background the desire to increase one's wealth."[14] The prophet also criticizes the nation's religious practitioners. The priests are guilty of violating YHWH's torah by not distinguishing between pure and impure things (22:26). The prophets are attacked for giving words of divine legitimation to the society's unjust way of life (22:28). In identifying these agents of oppression, Ezekiel mirrors the scope of Amos and Micah in this regard.

Thus, in the midst of these corrupt activities of the urban establishment, Ezekiel saw the poor as the victims of economic oppression. One text states that, "the people of the land have practiced fraud and committed robbery; they have wronged the poor ['ānî] and needy ['ĕbyôn], have defrauded the stranger without redress" (22:29). YHWH would respond to the unjust gains that resulted from these crimes with deportation and exile (22:15).

The plight of the poor as depicted in Ezekiel offers a surprising counterpoint to the Genesis narrative concerning the city of Sodom (16:48–50; Gen. 19:1–29). In Genesis, the sins of Sodom appear to have been exclusively sexual in nature (Gen. 19:5, 8). However, for the writer of Ezekiel, the arrogance of Sodom lay in its hoarding of wealth and its life of ease built on injustice (Ezek. 16:49). The Ezekiel text singles Sodom's abusive treatment of the 'ĕbyôn and 'ānî, factors unknown from Genesis. This radical reassessment of these traditions reveals how powerful a rhetorical tool the social criticism of the ancient prophets could be in the hands of a skillful and insightful thinker. When the question of a city's collapse arose, this interpreter culled the experience of national upheaval, sifted the society's foundational lore, and engaged the critical legacy of earlier prophets to see in the people's dislocation an indictment against the society's unjust treatment of the poor. In the book of Ezekiel, the narrative tradition is combined with the prophetic voice to produce a social critique that is put at the service of the priestly reclamation of power in Judah. Ezekiel represents a potent rhetorical act of the political imagination on behalf of the poor and the oppressed who were not to be left behind in the priestly program of reconstruction. Not surprisingly, these issues remained on the table for Nehemiah (see chapter 5). For those who today would drive a wedge between the priestly and the prophetic, as if the prophets were the ethicists and the priestly group was simply power hungry, books such as Ezekiel and Nehemiah offer difficult counterexamples that complicate these far too simplistic readings of the history of ancient Israelite social thought.

View of the Nations: The Triumph of God

Seven oracles against the nations punctuate the central section of the book of Ezekiel. The first four are rather brief, against Ammon, Moab, Edom, and Philistia, the immediate neighbors and opponents of Judah. There is an extensive oracle against Tyre and a brief text devoted to Sidon. Theologically the most sophisticated of all the oracles is the final one devoted to Egypt.

The measure applied to Ammon, Moab, Edom and Philistia appears to arise out of the way these groups treated Judah at the time of the invasion. For having joined in rejoicing over the desecration of YHWH's sanctuary, Ammon is condemned to destruction:

> Assuredly, I will deliver you to the Kedemites as a possession. They shall set up their encampments among you and pitch their dwellings in your midst; they shall eat your produce and they shall drink your milk. (Ezek. 25:4–5)

Likewise, for having mocked Judah in its hour of need, Moab is to be blotted out (25:8–10). Edom is singled out for actively participating in the destruction of Judah; it too is promised divine wrath (25:12–14). This view of Edom bears strong resemblance to the book of Obadiah (see chapter 9). Similarly, Philistia, which also took "revenge" against Judah, is to be wiped out (25:15–17). Throughout the passage, YHWH's action against the participants and supporters of Judah's downfall is designed to produce a "knowledge" of the LORD (25:7, 11, 14, 17).

The Tyre oracle (26:1–28:19) is actually a series of prose and poetic pronouncements concerning this opponent of Judah. Fundamentally, the oracle is delivered for the same reason as the first four. Tyre is guilty of "gloating" over the demise of Jerusalem (26:2). However, this text offers an epic-like depiction of Nebuchadnezzar's invasion of Tyre:

> From the cloud raised by his horses
> Dust shall cover you;

From the clatter of horsemen
And wheels and chariots,
Your walls shall shake—
When he enters your gates
As men enter a breached city.
With the hoofs of his steeds
He shall trample all your streets.
He shall put your people to the sword,
And your mighty pillars shall crash to the ground.
                                        Ezek. 26:10–12

Acknowledging its character as a vital trade city, the prophet senses in its demise something greater than the fall of the other territories in the face of the Babylonian onslaught:

> Judah and the land of Israel were your merchants; they trafficked with you in wheat of Minnith and Pannag, honey, oil, and balm. Because of your wealth of merchandise, because of your great wealth, Damascus traded with you in Helbon wine and white wool. (Ezek. 27:17–18)

The picture of Tyre's demise invokes mythic language, with the "mighty waters" covering the city and its inhabitants descending to the murky underworld (27:19–21). We know from one of the tales appended to the end of the standard version of the epic of Gilgamesh (seventh century B.C.E.) that the underworld was considered an undesirable location.[15]

Such a horrible image contrasts sharply with the catalogues of Tyre's great wealth presented in Ezekiel (27:3–36). The downfall resounds throughout the region:

> They shall intone a dirge over you as they wail,
> And lament for you thus:
>
> Who was like Tyre when she was silenced
> In the midst of the sea?
> When your wares were unloaded from the seas,
> You satisfied many peoples;
> With your great wealth and merchandise
> You enriched the kings of the earth.
> But when you were wrecked on the seas,
> In the deep waters sank your merchandise
> And all the crew aboard you.
> All the inhabitants of the coastlands
> Are appalled over you;
> Their kings are aghast,
> Their faces contorted.
> The merchants among the peoples hissed at you;

> You have become a horror,
> And have ceased to be forever.
>
> Ezek. 27:32–36

This construction of a vast empire of wealth is treated as if Tyre was acting like a god. The destruction, then, is intended to bring Tyre back to its senses, to remind its inhabitants that they are human after all. This attack on human wisdom or "shrewdness in trade" (28:5) offers a sophisticated assessment of the ideology that underlies empire building. The prophet is aware that the accumulation of wealth, as such, is no sign of sound religious grounding or depth. In fact, the amount of accumulation becomes a sign of how far Tyre has strayed from Eden-like perfection (28:11–19). Insofar as corrupt trading practices can be considered to define Tyre's sanctuaries, the writer hints at a universalist philosophy and social critique that undergird this text. That YHWH would act against this desecration of a pagan sanctuary is nothing short of remarkable as a theological concept in the context of an Israelite literature that often tends toward purely nationalistic preoccupations. In such an oracle, we find the broadening out of a prophetic theology that expands the justice question into a free floating idea, applicable in Judah or throughout the world.

After a brief pronouncement against Sidon (28:20–24) and an assurance concerning the house of Israel's return from exile (28:25–26), the text develops an extensive set of pronouncements concerning Egypt (29:1–32:32). Whereas Tyre's arrogance lay in its wealth, Egypt's source of downfall is in the Nile River:

> Thus said the Lord GOD:
> I am going to deal with you, O Pharaoh king of Egypt,
> Mighty monster, sprawling in your channels,
> Who said,
> My Nile is my own;
> I made it for myself.
> I will put hooks in your jaws,
> And make the fish of your channels
> Cling to your scales;
> I will haul you up from your channels
> With all the fish of your channels
> Clinging to your scales.
> And I will fling you into the desert,
> With all the fish of your channels.
> You shall be left lying in the open,
> Ungathered and unburied:
> I have given you as food
> To the beasts of the earth
> And the birds of the sky.

> Then all the inhabitants of Egypt shall know
> That I am the LORD.
>
> Ezek. 29:3–6a

The prose commentary that follows envisions a forty-year exile for Egypt (29:11–12). Again we see a universalizing principle at work in these oracles. Here the Israelite experience of dispersion is applied to Egypt, to be followed up by a promise of Egypt's restoration, though with a sharp reduction in its power (29:13–16). The dispersion results from Nebuchadnezzar's invasion, which is depicted as a reward for Babylon's demolition of Tyre (29:17–21; 30:1–26). Yet this invasion by Babylon is treated as YHWH's war:

> Thus said the Lord GOD: I will destroy the fetishes and make an end of the idols in Noph; and no longer shall there be a prince in the land of Egypt; and I will strike the land of Egypt with fear...
>
> Thus I will execute judgment on Egypt;
> And they shall know that I am the LORD.
>
> Ezek. 30:13, 19

The Babylonian battle for Egypt is soon waged (30:20–26). The exact years and days of the month frame the time question throughout this book, with the greatest number of dates apportioned throughout these oracles against the nations.[16] The judgment of Judah's opponents constitutes the inexorable logic of the entire book of Ezekiel. In their demise is Judah's rebirth.   *again*

Once again the Eden image is invoked to compare Egypt to the tall tree of Assyria (chap. 31). This tree was the envy of all the trees in the "garden of God" (31:8–9). But Assyria was pulled down from its arrogant height, smashed by the Lord GOD. Its collapse to Sheol shook the earth, particularly grieving Lebanon. Thus, Egypt is warned of its doom.

To sum up: The use of mythic imagery to create a political critique is noteworthy and follows a regular pattern throughout the book, but especially in these oracles of judgment.[17] There is consistent interest in pressing the old myths and received historical traditions into a higher level of critique, whether this critique invokes Eden, Sodom, the exodus, Samaria, or figures such as Noah, Job, and Daniel. Finding new political import in the old myths permits the writer of Ezekiel to freshly ground a social critique, weaving the oracles against the nations into a theological framework that is richly textured and incisive. We see a similar interest in recasting the old materials in Second Isaiah, though with decidedly different purpose and effects. Ezekiel's interest in divine battle imagery sends the critique in a more militant direction (cf. chap. 32). Thus, YHWH's successful campaign thrusts the powers to the netherworld:

Assyria, Elam, Meshech, Tubal, Edom, princes of the North, Sidonians, and Pharaoh (32:21–32). YHWH's triumph is nearly complete. The central frame of the triptych reveals the power by which a God who can judge Judah may also revive the people given over to calamity who seemed all but lost to history. Ezekiel's initial triptych frame concerning Judah's demise, therefore, does not tell the entire story.

Territory, Temple, and National Hope

With the literary centerpiece of the oracles against the nations concluded, the text returns to address Ezekiel's "fellow countrymen" (33:2). Several themes are revisited at this point: the characterization of Ezekiel as watchman (33:2–9), the notion of immediacy of punishment (33:10–20), the call for all to repent and the promise of renewal that comes with that turning (33:15–16), the arrival of the messenger announcing the fall of the city (33:21), and the speechlessness of the prophet that now becomes speech (33:22). In one sense, the story of Judah has not missed a beat. In another sense, in the interim, the entire order of the empire and the universe has begun to change unalterably. For Judah and the world it can no longer be politics as usual, at least in the social vision of Ezekiel.

Here we find one of the most straightforward references to the swirl of ancient Israelite narrative traditions in use at the time of Ezekiel's writing over which groups debated as they framed their theological discourse:

> The word of the LORD came to me: O mortal, those who live in these ruins in the land of Israel argue, "Abraham was but one man, yet he was granted possession of the land. We are many; surely, the land has been given as a possession to us." Therefore say to them: Thus said the Lord GOD: You eat with the blood, you raise your eyes to your fetishes, and you shed blood—yet you expect to possess the land! You have relied on your sword, you have committed abominations, you have all defiled other men's wives—yet you expect to possess the land! (Ezek. 33:23–26)

At this point in the text, Judah's judgment is on the horizon. Bearing in mind the postexilic setting of the actual writing of the book, we see the author attempting to take a stand amid the debates over the meaning and direction of traditions, especially as known to us elsewhere from Genesis (see chapter 3). The old promise materials were being recast to undergird a variety of projects and programs that were vying with others for a slice of the political pie. This passage in Ezekiel rather self-consciously acknowledges the fact of this debate.

The book of Ezekiel, however, does not cast its lot with the deposed political class, whom it views as the deceptive shepherds who led Judah down the path of destruction:

> The word of the LORD came to me: O mortal, prophesy against the shepherds of Israel. Prophesy, and say to them:
> To the shepherds: Thus said the Lord GOD: Ah, you shepherds of Israel, who have been tending yourselves! Is it not the flock that the shepherds ought to tend? You partake of the fat, you clothe yourselves with the wool, and you slaughter the fatlings; but you do not tend the flock. You have not sustained the weak, healed the sick, or bandaged the injured; you have not brought back the strayed, or looked for the lost; but you have driven them with harsh rigor, and they have been scattered for want of anyone to tend them; scattered, they have become prey for every wild beast. (Ezek. 34:1–5)

In fact, the prophetic-priestly program of Ezekiel rips away the old monarchic propaganda from its former moorings among the elite, commandeering the royal legends for a new agenda. Ezekiel holds out hope for a new David (34:22–24; cf. 37:24–26), yet we must not think of this David as the equivalent of the royal figure found in Isaiah. In Isaiah, the just ruler is an image elevated to sustain a decidedly royalist project, of the sort that finds expression in Haggai and Zechariah. That postexilic royalist movement was nostalgic, reflecting an elite agenda stemming from the time of the ancient monarchy itself. This agenda is critically mediated to us via the Deuteronomic History and finds a postexilic strain that runs through the later royalist efforts of the Maccabees and the much later Bar Kokhba. By contrast, Ezekiel's "David" is more akin to his portrayal in Chronicles, where David is the disembowelled figurehead whose sole function is to affirm a temple-based program of political power.[18] Hence, after another castigation of Edom for its role in Judah's demise (chap. 35), we find the book of Ezekiel turning its attention to its primary focus, namely, territory (chap. 36) and temple (chaps. 40—47).

The commitment to territory is directed specifically to the "mountains of Israel" (36:4). The "ancient heights" that the nations "gloated over," having, like Edom, been treated as a conquered possession, will be restored to grandeur in the postexilic context:

> Yes, prophesy about the land of Israel, and say to the mountains and the hills, to the watercourses and to the valleys, Thus said the Lord GOD: Behold, I declare in My blazing wrath: Because you have suffered the taunting of the nations, thus said the Lord GOD: I hereby swear that the nations which surround you shall, in their turn, suffer disgrace. But you, O mountains of Israel, shall yield your produce and bear your fruit for My people Israel, for their return is near. For I will

> care for you: I will turn to you, and you shall be tilled and sown. I will
> settle a large population on you, the whole House of Israel; the towns
> shall be resettled, and the ruined sites rebuilt. (Ezek. 36:6–10)

The land question is a key dimension throughout the biblical text. Davies'
study amply attests the key role accorded YHWH's commitment to the land
in each of the Bible's traditions.[19] The divine charter motif, once the prerogative of the ancient Near Eastern kings who gave grants of lands to their more
prized subjects, is subtly transformed in Ezekiel and elsewhere into a grant of
land by God to the people of Israel.[20] Most importantly for the writer of
Ezekiel, this land is under the care of the temple priests, who are assisted by a
figure who is quite simply designated a "ruler" (nāśî') and not the "king"
(melek). Thus, in chap. 36, the focus is on the land's restoration in the wake of
the people's return from exile, not the restoration of the monarchy:

> I will multiply men and beasts upon you, and they shall increase and
> be fertile, and I will resettle you as you were formerly, and will make
> you more prosperous than you were at first. And you shall know that
> I am the LORD. I will lead men—My people Israel—to you, and they
> shall possess you. You shall be their heritage, and you shall not again
> cause them to be bereaved. (Ezek. 36:11–12)

Theologically, the land restoration motif is clarified in Ezek. 36:16–23. The
defilement of the land led to the scattering of God's people. Yet the restoration is not predicated upon Israel's behavior in exile, for even there the divine
name was profaned (36:20). The initiative for the restoration is solely on the
side of the divine: Israel is restored for the sake of the divine name (36:23; cf.
39:22–29). This pattern of divine initiative is buried deep in covenant thought.
As Mendenhall has argued, such an initiative on the part of any sovereign,
human or divine, creates a situation of obligation on the part of the recipient
to heed the directives of the sovereign.[21] Yet even the will to obedience in the
postexilic renewal is said in Ezekiel to be supplied by God:

> I will take you from among the nations and gather you from all the
> countries, and I will bring you back to your own land. I will sprinkle
> clean water upon you, and you shall be clean: I will cleanse you from
> all your uncleanness and from all your fetishes. And I will give you a
> new heart and put a new spirit into you: I will remove the heart of
> stone from your body and give you a heart of flesh; and I will put My
> spirit into you. Thus I will cause you to follow My laws and faithfully
> to observe My rules. Then you shall dwell in the land which I gave to
> your fathers, and you shall be My people and I will be your God.
> (Ezek. 36:24–28)

Here the divine charter, or grant of land, is from beginning to end a divine program:

> Thus said the Lord GOD: When I have cleansed you of all your iniquities, I will people your settlements, and the ruined places shall be rebuilt; and the desolate land, after lying waste in the sight of every passerby, shall again be tilled. And men shall say, "That land, once desolate, has become like the garden of Eden; and the cities, once ruined, desolate, and ravaged, are now populated and fortified." And the nations that are left around you shall know that I the LORD have rebuilt the ravaged places and replanted the desolate land. I the LORD have spoken and will act. (Ezek. 36:33–36)

Yet, ideologically speaking, we see in this appeal to the divine initiative an attempt on the part of the writer to recover an exodus-style mentality about divine action, wherein YHWH becomes the impetus and legitimizing factor for a nationalist, or in this case, sacerdotal, political program. The Ezekielian movement will rebuild the land of Eden.

The revivification project does not come without trauma or struggle.[22] This is at least tacitly acknowledged by the character of chaps. 37—39. Chapter 37 provides us with the famous vision in the valley of bones. Yet the vision, so often treated simply as a comforting metaphor, is a product of the horrific conditions of exile. The revived, after all, are the slain (37:9). However, without this revival, the presence of God cannot return to a rebuilt sanctuary. In this sequencing, we notice the pattern so vital to the Torah: (1) exodus-departure, (2) defeat of Pharaonic army, (3) entry to promised land, (4) construction of shrine/temple. In Ezekiel, however, elements two and three are reversed.

The return to the land, "your own soil," is the goal of the raising of Israel's dead (exiles) from the graves (37:13–14). This is, in other words, an exodus act, if by this we mean the creation of a new people brought from one land to another (promised) land for the purpose of building the sanctuary of God. While some have argued that chaps. 40—48 concerning the temple are later texts, the vital character of this exodus act pattern *requires* the sanctuary to be the *goal* of the creation of a new people of God. Having read J, E, and P from the vantage point of the exile in chapters 3 and 4, we found that their social programs were fundamentally situated within the historical and theological debates of the postexilic period. Likewise, we also find that at some point in the course of these debates the Ezekiel text offered a significant contribution. Thus, reference to Joseph and Ephraim as players in Ezekiel's program comes as no surprise, for Ezekiel's appeal straddles E's effort to draw all parties under the restorative Judaean umbrella (37:15–23; see chapter 3). Joseph and

Ephraim had become the requisite ciphers in this debate. In Ezekiel's interpretation, there shall be continued Davidic rule, yet with the one sanctuary serving as the driving force in the revitalization of the community after the exile (37:22–27). We have seen this Davidic theme at work elsewhere in Ezekiel, to much the same effect of coopting the royalist ideology for a very different political effort against others who might claim this same royal banner.

Another aspect of the mythic struggle or trauma attendant on Judah's renewal is framed as the battle against the mysterious Gog of the land of Magog. To unlock this text would be helpful toward situating Ezekiel in the historical stream. Perhaps this is another reference to Babylon. Yet if Ezekiel was composed well into the Persian period, a requiem over Babylon would serve rather unclear rhetorical purposes. With Persia as an actor in Ezek. 38:5, it would nevertheless seem as if Babylon is in view. The text envisions as the period of Gog's invasion a time when Israel is secure (38:14–16). Again, given the period of writing, the purposes of this characterization of Israel's situation are not certain. Unless we decide to locate Ezekiel in the period of Alexander the Great and his generals, which hardly seems likely, perhaps we should simply see in chaps. 38 and 39 an early manifestation of the sort of literature that in its later manifestations we label "apocalyptic." In other words, these chapters transport us to a time of Judah's establishment beyond all wars. We term this "fantasy" only in hindsight. To the writer, this vision undoubtedly seemed the inevitable outcome of empire building and large-scale war making. The picture of the seven-month period of burials after this war is horrifying in its scale (39:11–16). Despite these complexities in interpretation, the defeat of Gog plays a role similar to the defeat of Pharaoh (at the sea) in Exodus. Gog's defeat is simply another mutation of the age-old divine combat/creation myth, but cast onto a metahistorical plane.[23] This battle to end all battles yields a Noahic-like promise: "I will never again hide My face from them, for I will pour out My spirit upon the House of Israel—declares the Lord GOD" (39:29).

With the defeat of the cosmic enemy, we are readied for the fulfillment of the "exodus act" pattern, namely, the construction of the sanctuary. Yet in Ezekiel, at least in the final form of the tradition, the temple is already present![24] In other words, unlike P's tabernacle project—which required the entire community's collaboration, both men and women (Exodus 35)—the work of restoration in Ezekiel is God's work through and through, a view that is consistent with the opening chapters of Ezekiel.

The prophet is given a tour of the temple simply to measure the structure in all its details, particulars that are surely reminiscent of P's concern for the wilderness tabernacle. Does the apportionment of space tell us anything about the politics of this commonwealth that God is building according to Ezekiel?[25] Chapters 40—42 are devoted to the measurements of the temple and its precincts. The northern chamber is under the authority of "the descendants of Zadok, who alone of the descendants of Levi may approach the LORD to minister to Him" (40:46). The Zadokites, together with the priests of the southern chamber "who perform the duties of the temple" are the only temple actors mentioned in chaps. 40—42. The prophet and the angelic figure thereby mediate a Zadokite-priestly political and social vision—the program of a tightly organized and influential faction among the priestly group in ancient Israel.

Having completed the measurements of the gates, walls, and chambers, the Presence of God can now enter through the east gate (43:1–3). The entry of the Presence of God leads to a temple speech with a decidedly anti-royalist sentiment:

> O mortal, this is the place of My throne and the place for the soles of My feet, where I will dwell in the midst of the people Israel forever. The House of Israel and their kings must not again defile My holy name by their apostasy and by the corpses of their kings at their death. When they placed their threshold next to My threshold and their doorposts next to My doorposts with only a wall between Me and them, they would defile My holy name by the abominations that they committed, and I consumed them in My anger. Therefore, let them put their apostasy and the corpses of their kings far from Me, and I will dwell among them forever. (Ezek. 43:7–9; cf. 44:4)

The author proceeds to describe the temple itself but does so with a continued underscoring of the people's "iniquities" (43:10–12). The altar is described in relation to the Zadokite priests (43:18–21). They are the ones who can offer the young bull as a sin offering (43:18–27). It would seem that the temple program and the royal limitations are key to the author, for relief from the weight of shame comes by a renewal of the sacrificial system as encoded in the controlled and detailed knowledge of the temple, which is embodied in these visionary texts. One must, of course, separate this knowledge from any physical temple in Jerusalem. The movement of Ezekiel is built around an ideology of the temple and not simply the building itself. We should probably see in these texts the marks of a priestly faction seeking influence over the postexilic sacrificial setup. Ezekiel's group, the Zadokite priesthood, wishes to claim sole authority over this system, in opposition to other priests or politicos. Similar tendencies govern the P source, on which Ezekiel would seem to be building.

The regulation of the sacred by the Zadokites (north gate) and their priestly cohorts (south gate) is driven home by the permanent closure of the eastern gate through which YHWH has reentered the temple (44:1–2). Likewise, the

limitations on the prince's (nāśî') movement into the divine presence in relation to this gate is regulated by the text (44:3). The regulation concerning
access to the presence of God also invokes the prohibition of entry. In this
priestly scheme, the sanctuary can no longer be polluted if the community will
abide by the guidelines established by the priests. This is reinforced in Ezek.
44:5–14, especially with respect to the uncircumcised and the foreigner. Any
Levitical priest or priestly group suspected of past rebellion is placed squarely
under Zadokite domination, serving in more menial temple labors (44:10–14).
Those Zadokites in power are deemed to be those who maintained the true
priestly tradition during the preexilic era of apostasy (44:15). Subject to
renewed regulation regarding alcohol, marriage, and the dead, these priests,
"shall declare to My people what is sacred and what is profane, and inform
them what is clean and what is unclean" (44:23).

The apportionment of Zadokite power is further reinforced by the land distribution scheme around the temple in chap. 45. Here are the allotments:

> Sanctuary: 500 x 500 cubits
> Open space around sanctuary: 50 cubits
> Housing for priests: 25,000 x 10,000 cubits
> Levites: 25,000 x 10,000 cubits
> City land: 25,000 x 5,000 cubits
> Prince: special tribal size allotment

The housing space for the priests contains the sacred sanctuary. In other
words, priestly power displaces princely power and does so with an ethical end
in mind:

> And to the prince shall belong, on both sides of the sacred reserve and
> the property of the city and alongside the sacred reserve and the prop-
> erty of the city, on the west extending westward and on the east
> extending eastward, a portion corresponding to one of the [tribal] por-
> tions that extend from the western border to the eastern border of the
> land. That shall be his property in Israel; and My princes shall no more
> defraud My people, but shall leave the rest of the land to the several
> tribes of the House of Israel.
>   Thus said the Lord GOD: Enough, princes of Israel! Make an end
> of lawlessness and rapine, and do what is right and just! Put a stop to
> your evictions of My people—declares the Lord GOD. Have honest
> balances, an honest ephah, and an honest bath. (Ezek. 45:7–10)

In this system, many of the abuses identified in prophetic social criticism find
institutional regulation and redress. This emphasis fits in with the sort of institutional adjustments and advocacy for the poor found in the P material (see

chapter 2). Our findings earlier for P were twofold and continue to hold here in Ezekiel: (1) the P system has stronger ethical content than some suppose who tend to focus on the prophetic texts for inspiration; (2) the P tradition offers a persuasive rhetorical pitch that must have garnered adherents among the poorer groups for whom the texts appear to advocate. In the latter case, Ezekiel likewise stands out as a credible priestly voice for prophetic justice.

That the Ezekielian group is antiroyalist is plain from its statements that undercut monarchic practice and authority. Here, for example, the temple regulates commerce, exercising royal authority. Furthermore, the temple freely sets its allotments for sacrifices to be offered by the prince for festivals, including Passover and the seventh month (45:24–25). The tremendous power exerted by the temple in relation to the palace is the sort we find elsewhere in the ancient Near East. One is reminded of the Babylonian New Year festival of the month of Nisan, where the chastened king is struck by the high priest to elicit submission of the king before the god. In Ezekiel's vision, the humbled prince follows prescribed rules to conduct Sabbath and freewill sacrifices (46:1–7, 12). At other times, the prince moves through the sacred space in ways prescribed for ordinary folk (46:9–10).

As for royal property, a sharp distinction emerges between the property the prince may pass on to his heirs and other property. Again, the regulation has strong ethical content:

> Thus said the Lord GOD: If the prince makes a gift to any of his sons, it shall become the latter's inheritance; it shall pass on to his sons; it is their holding by inheritance. But if he makes a gift from his inheritance to any of his subjects, it shall only belong to the latter until the year of release. Then it shall revert to the prince; his inheritance must by all means pass on to his sons.
>
> But the prince shall not take property away from any of the people and rob them of their holdings. Only out of his own holdings shall he endow his sons, in order that My people may not be dispossessed of their holdings. (Ezek. 46:16–18)

To this one may compare the distinctions at work in Lev. 25:29–31.[26] The Holiness Code's year of jubilee is at least arguably comparable to Ezekiel's year of "release" (*děrôr*), with the latter term being shared in both contexts (Lev. 25:10; Ezek. 46:17). Likewise, both texts are concerned with property transfers, whether related to the urban sphere (Leviticus) or the royal context (Ezekiel). In other words, Ezekiel makes explicit what could only be implicit for Leviticus: Where Leviticus, as a "desert" text, can only rather oddly speak to life within walled cities (*'îr 'ăšer lō'ḥōmâ*), Ezekiel is able to go further to apply these regulations more overtly to royal hopefuls. Thus, jubilee regulations are not simply to be exemptions proclaimed by the king for the land's subjects, as would have been the case in Mesopotamian tradition (see chapter 2). Rather, Israel's "release" is to extend right to the top of the social pyramid. Any future prince's acquisitions and land ownership is not be exploitative either at the time of the release or in any other year.

This theme of land proprietorship continues as the vision of the temple closes with a depiction of it as a source of communal water and new growth (47:1–12; 48:1–8). The ancient tribes receive land allotments, with Joseph having a double allotment (47:13–14). This invocation of Joseph (i.e., the Northern Kingdom) is, as we have seen, a key subtheme in Ezekiel and runs parallel to E's interest in embracing the North (see above and chapter 3), a political yearning that would appear to be part of the postexilic reconstruction effort of the priestly group and others. Resident aliens do get their allotment after the twelve tribes (47:22–23). There is no stated ethical motivation for the latter pronouncement. The apportionment to Judah becomes the occasion for a reiteration of the central role of Zadok in this priestly political economy (48:8–14). In the final estimation, Ezekiel's program is predicated on the triangulation between the sanctuary, its priests, and the tribal workers in the city who tend the land (48:15–22). In short, Ezekiel's social vision culminates in a postmonarchic society ruled by God's Zadokite elect.

To sum up our findings in this chapter: We cannot know to what extent the book of Ezekiel emanated from established temple circles or from some fringe group. To know this elusive fact would clarify the ideological intentions and historical motivations of the book's adherents. Our discussion has tended toward the view that this work arose from a writer or group vying with others for control of the priestly political program sometime during the Persian period, prior to the time of Ezra and Nehemiah. We have seen that there are tendencies in E and P that resemble Ezekiel's efforts, in particular E's embrace of the North and P's efforts at forging a link between the sanctuary's laws and the poor. Whether or not Ezekiel was written by a central player, the book's rhetorical appeal displays a persuasive power that would set it logically far into the period of reconstruction after the exile. The voice of Ezekiel is a prophetic-priestly voice that has found a way to balance, on the one hand, claims for the restored temple and priestly authority with, on the other hand, a prophetic-styled social criticism. Yet unlike other parts of the prophetic tradition, the book of Ezekiel has also found a mechanism to contain the abuses of the monarchy by bringing the prince (*nāśî*) into a reduced role vis-à-vis the temple, while still bearing the Davidic flag. As an urban program, Ezekiel's social vision begins from the heart of Jerusalem, its temple, and works to transform the entire social order. Clearly, Ezekiel represents only one end of the prophetic spectrum on these matters. That prophetic continuum includes a variety of village and urban voices with competing social visions, as we shall see in the next chapter.

Notes

1. L. Boadt, "Ezekiel, Book of," *ABD* 2:711-22.
2. W. Zimmerli, *Ezekiel 1: A Commentary on the Book of the Prophet Ezekiel, Chapters 1—24*, trans. R. E. Clements (Philadelphia: Fortress Press, 1979), 23, 46–52, acknowledges vocables unique to Ezekiel, while also noting numerous links to the Holiness Code in Leviticus. The explanation for these apparent links remains much disputed.
3. See, e.g., J. Reade, *Assyrian Sculpture* (Cambridge, Mass.: Harvard University Press, 1983), 7.
4. A phenomenon detailed by G. E. Mendenhall, *The Tenth Generation: The Origins of the Biblical Tradition* (Baltimore: Johns Hopkins, 1973), chap. 2.
5. On the grounding of Ezekiel's message in the utter holiness of God, see W. Brueggemann, *Hopeful Imagination: Prophetic Voices in Exile* (Philadelphia: Fortress Press, 1986), chap. 3.
6. On wrestling with Auschwitz theologically, see E. Fackenheim, *What Is Judaism? An Interpretation for the Present Age* (New York: Collier/Macmillan, 1987), chap. 14.
7. B. Uffenheimer, "Theodicy and Ethics in the Prophecy of Ezekiel," in *Justice and Righteousness: Biblical Themes and Their Influence*, ed. H. G. Reventlow and Y. Hoffman (Sheffield: JSOT Press, 1992), 209–15. Uffenheimer argues that Ezekiel even contradicts Hosea and Jeremiah, who use relational terminology to speak positively of a connection between God and God's people.
8. See Leviticus Rabbah XIX: 6.
9. Zimmerli, *Ezekiel 1*, sets the text squarely in the early sixth century B.C.E. The past century has seen considerable disputes over the dating of the text. See H. McKeating, *Ezekiel* (Sheffield: JSOT Press, 1993), chaps. 4–5.
10. For a review of the arguments, with some subtle nuancing of the integration of individual and corporate elements, see J. S. Kaminsky, *Corporate Responsibility in the Hebrew Bible* (Sheffield: Sheffield Academic Press, 1995), esp. chap. 7.
11. Kaminsky, *Corporate Responsibility*, chap. 1.
12. Something of this sensibility is gauged by P. Joyce, "Ezekiel and Individual Responsibility," in *Ezekiel and His Book: Textual and Literary Criticism and Their Interrelation*, ed. J. Lust (Lowain: Leuven: University Press, 1986), who speaks of "imminent and thorough judgement" (320).
13. Uffenheimer, "Theodicy and Ethics," offers a constrasting analysis in which the book of Ezekiel falls into contradictions when holding up both the inexorability of judgment and the opportunity for repentance. Uffenheimer is correct to point out that the accent on repentance is what keeps hope alive for the later exiles and the community of the reconstruction (222–23).
14. E. Tamez, *Bible of the Oppressed* (Maryknoll, N.Y.: Orbis Books, 1982), 52.
15. S. Dalley, *Myths from Mesopotamia: Creation, The Flood, Gilgamesh, and Others* (Oxford: Oxford University Press, 1989), 123–24.
16. Ezek 1:1; 3:16; 8:1; 20:1; 24:1; 26:1; 29:1; 29:17; 30:20; 31:1; 32:1, 17; 33:21; 40:1; see the discussion in H. McKeating, *Ezekiel* (Sheffield: JSOT Press, 1993), chap. 6.
17. Concerning both the mythic trajectory and the unifying structures of the book, see L. Boadt, "Rhetorical Strategies in Ezekiel's Oracles of Judgment," in J. Lust, ed., *Ezekiel and His Book*, 182-200.

18. For a positive discussion, see W. Brueggemann, *David's Truth: In Israel's Imagination and Memory* (Philadelphia: Fortress Press, 1985), 99–109.
19. Succinctly discussed in W. D. Davies, *The Territorial Dimension of Judaism* (Berkeley: University of California Press, 1982), chap. 1.
20. For a general discussion of the ancient Near Eastern motif, see M. Weinfeld, "The Covenant of Grant in the Old Testament and in the Ancient Near East," *JAOS* 90 (1970): 184–203.
21. G. E. Mendenhall, "Covenant Forms in Israelite Tradition," *BA* 17 (1954): 50–76.
22. In this segment we read chaps. 37—38 as intimately connected to chaps. 1—36, following the analysis of L. Boadt, "Mythological Themes and the Unity of Ezekiel," *Literary Structure and Rhetorical Strategies in the Hebrew Bible*, ed., L. J. de Regt, J. de Waard, and J. P. Fokkelman (Assen: Van Gorcum, 1996), 210–31.
23. As discussed by B. F. Batto, *Slaying the Dragon: Mythmaking in the Biblical Tradition* (Louisville, Ky.: Westminster/John Knox Press, 1992), chap. 6.
24. While some will argue that the temple vision is a later addition, its integral character to the mythic pattern would seem to argue for the integrity of these chapters to the original work. Of course, the explicit emphasis on the Zadokites in chaps. 40—47 is without parallel in the rest of the book. However, the specificity of the vision is quite compatible with and balances uniformly the descriptions of God and the divine messengers that open the book. See, e.g., L. Boadt, "Ezekiel, Book of," *ABD* 2:721.
25. J. Z. Smith, *To Take Place: Toward Theory in Ritual* (Chicago: University of Chicago Press, 1987), chap. 3.
26. Zimmerli, *Ezekiel 1*, 50, however, draws contrasts between these passages.

Chapter 9

The Voice of the People

Hosea–Malachi

If Amos's call was for justice to "well up like water" and for righteousness to roar like an "unfailing stream" (Amos 5:24), then the Book of the Twelve, the so-called "minor" prophets, can certainly be said to constitute the tributaries of that river of justice. Though spanning several centuries in terms of composition, editing, and transmission, when taken together these texts, which round out our study of the social ethics of the prophetic literature, attest to the continuing effort of key figures in Israel and Judah and their followers to raise hard

353

questions about the social structures, religious practices, and ideological commitments of their society.[1]

More than this, however, we witness in the Twelve a growing self-awareness about the prophetic task. Where the individual oracles of a Hosea, Amos, Micah, or Haggai might be situated in particular historical circumstances, after the exile there is a developing consciousness that prophecy functions beyond its given historical moment. Prophecy becomes, in other words, a *tradition* that can be tapped to measure social praxis, long after the prophet's words have been conveyed. This traditioning of prophecy is not restricted, then, to the Deuteronomic History, where tales of shaman-like figures, seers, and oracle deliverers bring a prophetic underpinning to DH's understanding of power politics and ritual norms in the Israelite and Judaean monarchies (see chapter 3). Likewise, we find a prophetic tradition-making trajectory also at work in the compendia of oracles that constitute the Twelve.

The stringing together of oracles from various time periods and the creation of oracle collections serves the purpose of continuing to raise the justice question. Each generation, in other words, seeks to redefine how it understands the call of Micah to do "what the LORD requires of you: Only to do justice and to love goodness, and to walk modestly with your God" (Micah 6:8). In the ebb and flow of the waters of this righteous stream, we hear some provocative answers regarding how to live out that collective call to justice. We also hear words of warning spoken to the society that fails to heed this call. Furthermore, in the writing, transmission, and reading of these words, we see this tradition-under-construction offering a hermeneutical model for bringing past prophecies into active dialogue with radically changed social circumstances and institutional realities.

We turn now to consider each member of the Twelve. By the time we reach Malachi, we will realize that, far from coming to an end, prophecy continued to flourish in the second temple period. This flourishing may have been something less than the sociological phenomenon of public performance attested for preexilic prophecy, but the postexilic acts of literary imagination, ritual dramatization, and theological reflection were no less powerful social forces in their own way.[2] Indeed, given the lasting importance of these oracular collections, sayings that reflect a variety of village and urban voices for justice, one may say that the pen of prophetic prophecy has proven its mettle against the sword on many occasions, past and present.

Hosea: The Measure of Justice

Hosea, which stands at the head of the Twelve, is in many ways more of a counterpart to Jeremiah, in terms of style and subject matter, than it is to Ezekiel, the book it now follows. By the same token, however, the image of

Samaria's demise plays a significant role in both Hosea and Ezekiel. If, as many believe, much of Hosea dates from the mid-eighth century B.C.E., then content and themes more fully realized in Jeremiah and Ezekiel find their initial packaging in a precursor that frames its vision of justice in terms that are strikingly different than that of supposed contemporary texts such as Amos and Micah. Whereas the latter provide us with strong clues regarding the shape of peasant life in ancient Israel and Judah, Hosea focuses more profoundly on the idolatry of the bureaucratic establishment. The strong sense of social justice that pervades the text of Hosea has reverberated down through the later prophetic tradition. Hosea's position as the first of the Book of the Twelve helps to place the social critique of the rest of the Twelve within a wider theological and philosophic framework.

While Hosea argues in broad terms that the guilt of a "rotting" Ephraim (Hos. 4:3) is "withering" the earth (7:1, 8), the text does not leave its talk of crimes to generalities:

> Hear the word of the LORD
> O people of Israel!
> For the LORD has a case
> Against the inhabitants of this land,
> Because there is no honesty and no goodness
> And no obedience to God in the land.
> [False] swearing, dishonesty, and murder,
> And theft and adultery are rife;
> Crime follows upon crime!
>
> Hos. 4:1–2; cf. 10:4

Neither is Hosea afraid to name names. A wide range of social actors come under intense scrutiny in the prophet's diatribe. Strong statements are offered against priests:

> "Let no man rebuke, let no man protest!"
> For this your people has a grievance against [you], O priest!
> So you shall stumble by day,
> And by night a prophet shall stumble as well,
> And I will destroy your kindred.
> My people is destroyed because of [your] disobedience!
> Because you have rejected obedience,
> I reject you as My priest;
> Because you have spurned the teaching of your God,
> I, in turn, will spurn your children.
> The more they increased, the more they sinned against Me:
> I will change their dignity to dishonor.
> They feed on My people's sin offerings,

And so they desire its iniquity.
Therefore, the people shall fare like the priests:
I will punish it for its conduct,
I will requite it for its deeds.
Truly, they shall eat, but not be sated;
They shall swill, but not be satisfied,
Because they have forsaken the LORD
To practice lechery.

Hos. 4:4–11a; cf. 5:1; 6–9

Likewise, rival court prophets find a measure of trenchant critique:

That is why I have hewn down the prophets,
Have slain them with the words of My mouth:
And the day that dawned [brought on] your punishment.

Hos. 6:5; cf. 4:5

However, the lion's share of the prophet's social criticism is reserved for the royal house and its military officers:

Hear this, O priests,
Attend, O House of Israel,
And give ear, O royal house;
For right conduct is your responsibility!
But you have been a snare to Mizpah
And a net spread out over Tabor.

Hos. 5:1

Charging the political leadership with lacking divine sanction (8:4) and being a "burden" to the populace, presumably through overtaxation (8:10), Hosea accuses the populace's rulers of engaging in power plays and coups that have destabilized the nation as a whole (7:3–7). Repeatedly, unruly military figures bear the brunt of the prophet's scorn (5:9b–10; 7:16; 9:15).

On the horizon, the prophet sees the final collapse of this political system:

Where now is your king?
Let him save you!
Where are the chieftains in all your towns
Whom you demanded:
"Give me a king and officers"?
I give you kings in my ire,
And take them away in My wrath.

Hos. 13:10–11; cf. 14:1 [13:16]

There are three major changes Hosea levels against the bureaucratic establishment, the first of which is that they have established foreign alliances that have led the people astray from their loyalty to Israel's God:

In that their mother has played the harlot,
She that conceived them has acted shamelessly—
Because she thought,
"I will go after my lovers,
Who supply my bread and my water,
My wool and my linen,
My oil and my drink."

Assuredly,
I will hedge up her roads with thorns
And raise walls against her,
And she shall not find her paths.
Pursue her lovers as she will,
She shall not overtake them;
And seek them as she may,
She shall never find them.
Then she will say,
"I will go and return
To my first husband,
For then I fared better than now."

Hos. 2:7–9 [5–7]; cf. 2:14 [12]

On the one hand, the leadership has trotted off like a "lonely wild ass" (8:9) to an Assyria that offers no lasting assistance:

Yet when Ephraim became aware of his sickness,
Judah of his sores,
Ephraim repaired to Assyria—
He sent envoys to a patron king!
He will never be able to cure you,
Will not heal you of your sores.

Hos. 5:13; cf. 14:4 [3]

Likewise, the nation's repeated appeals for economic and military assistance from Egypt gain a similar response from the prophet:

Instead, Ephraim has acted
Like a silly dove with no mind:
They have appealed to Egypt!
They have gone to Assyria!
When they go, I will spread
My net over them,
I will bring them down
Like birds of the sky;
I will chastise them
When I hear their bargaining.
Woe to them
For straying from Me;

> Destruction to them
> For rebelling against Me!
> For I was their Redeemer;
> Yet they have plotted treason against Me.
>   Hos. 7:11–13; cf. 7:16; 11:5; 12:2 [1]

The second major charge Hosea levels against the bureaucratic establishment concerns idol worship. They are guilty of drawing away the populace through the worship of various gods, termed collectively the Baalim:

> Thus will I punish her
> For the days of the Baalim,
> On which she brought them offerings;
> When, decked with earrings and jewels,
> She would go after her lovers,
> Forgetting Me
>   —declares the LORD
>   Hos. 2:15 [13]

The worship of the Baalim appears to involve the use of "carved images" (11:2; 13:1–2; cf. 14:4, 9 [3, 8]), "sacrifice in the mountaintops" (4:13), and the building of various "temples" (8:14). All of these items represent the accouterments of Canaanite religion, whose variety and form is better known from ancient Ugarit.[3] The prophet would seem to have in mind a thoroughgoing attack on the standard theology and religious life fostered by the urban elite throughout Canaan's history.[4]

Yet the prophet specifically appears to target his invective against that religious systems engendered by the house of Israel under Jeroboam II (786–746 B.C.E.) and his successors, referring rather pointedly to Bethel ("house of God") as Beth-aven ("house of Iniquity"; 4:15; cf. Amos 4:4). Likewise, reference is made in passing to the "calf" of Samaria, better known to us from the Deuteronomic History and which receives a similarly harsh critique there (Hos. 8:5–6; cf. 10:5; 1 Kings 12:25; 13:5). In this connection, we might take note of Hosea's condemnation of the sacrifice of oxen, which must have formed part of the rites of northern religious practice (Hos. 12:11–12 [10–11]). The critique of the prophet is so harsh precisely because it is this religious system that the urban elite turns to as they make their alliances and seek to increase their prosperity through "altars aplenty" (10:1).

However, the ensuing political and economic stability may have been more apparent than real, as the prophet observes in this compelling allusion to social turmoil:

> Israel is a ravaged vine
> And its fruit is like it.
> When his fruit was plentiful,

> He made altars aplenty;
> When his land was bountiful,
> Cult pillars abounded.
> Now that his boughs are broken up,
> He feels his guilt;
> He himself pulls apart his altars,
> Smashes his pillars.
>
> Truly, now they say,
> "We have no king;
> For, since we do not fear the LORD,
> What can a king do to us?"
> So they conclude agreements and make covenants
> With false oaths,
> And justice degenerates into poison weeds,
> Breaking out on the furrows of the fields.
>
> Hos. 10:1–4

One may wonder what the prophet proposes as a religious system if the standard fertility cult apparatus is to be removed as a viable option. Put more crudely, if phallic worship is out (4:12), then upon what sort of devotional practice is the nation to be established?[5]

This brings us to the third charge the prophet levels against the bureaucratic elite, namely, that they have caused the populace to defect from the religion of YHWH:

> For Ephraim has multiplied altars—for guilt;
> His altars have redounded to his guilt:
> The many teachings I wrote for him
> Have been treated as something alien.
> When they present sacrifices to Me,
> It is but flesh for them to eat:
> The LORD has not accepted them.
> Behold, He remembers their iniquity,
> He will punish their sins:
> Back to Egypt with them!
> Israel has ignored his Maker
> And built temples
> (And Judah has fortified many cities).
> So I will set fire to his cities,
> And it shall consume their fortresses.
>
> Hos. 8:11–14

The link between the altars and the fortresses is explicit, plainly indicating that it is the religion of the urban establishment that is in view here.[6] Yet one may ask what these "teachings" are that the prophet wishes to defend. While not in the form that we now have them in the Torah and the DH, surely Hosea has in mind a variety of ancestral traditions, fostered among the village tribes and in urban settings, at times at odds with the Samarian establishment, which have come to stamp the Hebrew Bible.[7] Hosea's god is primarily the God of the exodus who has liberated the people from Egypt and brought them through the wilderness (11:1; 12:10 [9]; 13:4–6). Indeed, a new wilderness wandering will put an end to the dominance of the Baalim:

> Assuredly,
> I will speak coaxingly to her
> And lead her through the wilderness
> And speak to her tenderly.
> I will give her her vineyards from there,
> And the Valley of Achor as a plowland of hope.
> There she shall respond as in the days of her youth,
> When she came up from the land of Egypt.
>
> Hos. 2:16–17 [14–16]

Likewise, Hosea's god is the God of Jacob, who is mentioned with reference to the story of the struggle in the womb and for his flight to Aram (12:3–5, 13–15 [2–4, 12–14]; cf. Genesis 27—31). Oddly, there are no references to Abraham or Isaac, possibly indicating the fragmented origins of traditions that were amalgamated more extensively in the postexilic period. In any case, Hosea's antimonarchic use of such traditions runs counter to the monarchic appropriation of the Abrahamic stories, as evidenced in Genesis (see chapter 3).[8] Further links to traditions known from Hebrew narrative are found in the brief reference to the defection at Baal-Peor (9:10; cf. Num. 25:1–3) and the "days of Gibeah" (9:9; cf. Judges 19—20). Less clear are the allusions to the "misfortune at Gilgal" (9:15) or the ravings of Beth-arbel (10:14–15).

The pervasive role in Hosea of traditions preserved elsewhere in the Hebrew Bible makes it clear that in Hosea's day there existed a set of ancestral traditions that many perceived running counter to the religious traditions, rites, and practices nurtured by the elite inside their urban complexes and fortresses. These counter traditions elevated by the prophet became the ground both for a critique of the prospering urban elite and for a call toward the work of justice under the banner of the exodus God, however much the urban establishment might seek to lay claim to those very traditions (12:6–7 [5–6]). Having defected from these traditions, the elite were threatened with shame (2:11–12 [9–10]), punishment (8:7; 9:7), war (11:7), the collapse of the monarchy (10:14–15), and exile to Assyria (10:6) at the hands of a God who remembers wickedness (7:2) and who devours like a lion despite the promising start of the exodus from Egypt (13:6–8; cf. 5:14). Ultimately, this devastation would bring down the ritual system the elite believed sustained their hold on power (2:13–14 [11-13]).

Since this defection and punishment is couched at times in terms of a broken "covenant," we may well wonder to what extent Hosea's appeal for justice reflects the Mosaic covenantal and legal tradition as found in the Torah. Clearly, fragments of the Ten Commandments seem to have worked their way into various passages (3:1; 4:1–2, 12:10 [9]; 13:4; see discussion in chapter 2 above). Unfortunately, Hosea's other references to "covenant" (6:7; 8:1–3) and to "my teaching" and "teachings" (8:1, 12) are only of the vaguest sort and offer no guide to the content of the covenantal tradition as envisioned by this prophet. Surely, the prophet's measure of justice in terms of obedience and not sacrifice (6:6; 7:14) cannot be reconciled with the priestly materials of the Torah. Indeed, insofar as sacrifice is an issue, Hosea would seem only to find a counterpart in the anticalf passages ascribed undoubtedly to E in the Pentateuch. Beyond this, it is difficult to specify the precise nature, if any, of Hosea's understanding of the traditions ascribed to Moses. Apparently, Hosea's exodus God stands alone, without a Mosaic figure to serve as a focal point for the covenant or the escape from Egypt. Yet the call for obedience, pursued so vigorously in Deuteronomy, does find a strong counterpart in Hosea's vision of renewal based on obedience (6:1–3; 7:10; 14:3–8 [2–7]). This renewal, which is a veritable rescue from Sheol (13:14), in concrete terms means a rescue from exile in Egypt and Assyria (11:8–11). Again, the content of the renewal is less than clear. However, the sense is plain that a new exodus will create a new covenant situation wherein the old monarchy will be replaced with a people who are committed to the building of a just community, obedient to YHWH, and invigorated by the traditions of the ancestors. Such an impulse points the way toward survival following the demise of Samaria in 721 B.C.E. and ultimately lights the logical path to be taken by the prophetic voices after the exile into Babylon in 587 B.C.E.

To this point, we have discussed Hosea without reference to the well-known tale of the prophet's marriage to the prostitute. This story, as well as the misogynist leanings such a story reflects, is not cast in the same fashion in the poetic and prose passages of Hosea.[9] In the prose passages, images of marriage (chap. 1) and even friendship with women (chap. 3) are invoked, whereas in the poetic oracles, the accent is on the rejection of the marital image in favor of a deeper sort of relationship:

> And in that day
>   —declares the LORD—
> You will call [Me] Ishi,
> And no more will you call Me Baali.
> For I will remove the names of the Baalim from her mouth,
> And they shall nevermore be mentioned by name.
>   Hos. 2:18–19 [16–17]

The prose texts are patent additions to the text that serve to obscure and even supplant the vigorous voice for social justice evident in the oracles (cf. 2:21–22 [19–20]). It is true that the prose passages construct a critique of the monarchy, but they do so in terms and in a tone that diverges from the oracles. Whatever the source, it is apparent that the vision of power, new covenant (2:20 [18]), and Davidic renewal (3:5) at work in the prose segments is, in part, predicated on a view of women as marginal actors, an image congenial to particular partisans in a turf war between establishment figures and imaginary upstart prophetic figures. It is hard not to see the Deuteronomic hand at work here, where a similar constellation of views about prophets and attitudes towards women find their way into the DH corpus, most notably throughout the book of Judges (see chapter 3).[10]

The poetic or oracular segment, on the other hand, is not couched as a marriage between God and a prostitute. Rather, the images employed, while no less potentially misogynist, speak of the "mother who has played the harlot" who is *not* YHWH's wife (2:4–7 [2–5]). This mother has gone after other "lovers," political powers such as Egypt and Assyria for aid, later to return to her "first husband," namely, Baal (2:7–12 [5–10]). The oracular speaker is at pains not to have the relationship between God and God's people portrayed on a par with a marriage to Baal. The logic may be a bit contorted and the image stretched, but the poetic vision of YHWH's relationship with Israel is not construed in the same manner as in the prose portrait. We might also note that Israel is treated as the beloved "son" elsewhere in the oracles (11:1), indicating that the poetic text could work with a variety of kin relationships when seeking to image God's connection to Israel, again, in marked contrast to the prose passages.

Curiously, the book ends with a "wisdom" reflection:

> He who is wise will consider these words,
> He who is prudent will take note of them.
> For the paths of the LORD are smooth;
> The righteous can walk on them,
> While sinners stumble on them.
>
> Hos. 14:10 [9]

This voice is undoubtedly akin to that of the framers of the Psalter, who are responsible for introducing Psalm 1 into the Psalms corpus, thereby shifting the accent of the Psalter in the direction of wisdom and meditation. The effect of such wisdom prologues and appendices is to transform the nature of the psalms and prophetic materials away from liturgical and chanted oracular texts, turning them into texts for reflection in locales far removed from their original historical context. Hosea, in other words, has entered the wider stream of tradition, where the text may exert a continual push for justice beyond the apparatus of ritual life. Wittingly or not, this wisdom gnomic verse contributes to the construction of a tradition where rites of sacrifice and calls for justice remain in dialogue with one another, not in opposition as the earlier oracles seem to suggest.

Joel: Worship amid the Storm of Judgment

The current canonical positioning of the book of Joel as second in the Twelve, while not the only position held by the book in the history of the transmission of this collection, nonetheless makes a great deal of sense with respect to the unfolding of the justice message of the Twelve in the wake of Hosea's opening salvos.[11] Very simply, Joel may be seen, from the point of view of the Hebrew canon, as the realization of the message of judgment and hope presented in Hosea.

Where Hosea offers stern warnings of the punishment to come as a result of injustice and idolatry, Joel witnesses the storm of judgment raining down on the populace:

> For a nation has invaded my land,
> Vast beyond counting,
> With teeth like the teeth of a lion,
> With the fangs of a lion's breed.
> They have laid my vines waste.
> And splintered my fig trees:
> They have stripped off their bark and thrown [it] away;
> Their runners have turned white.
>
> Joel 1:6–7[12]

Beyond judgment, however, Joel also represents the concretization of the hope that remained only a potentiality in Hosea's vision. In words strikingly reminiscent of Hosea, Joel sees the anticipated hope coming to pass:

> Then the LORD was roused
> On behalf of His land
> And had compassion
> Upon His people.
> In response to His people
> The LORD declared:
> "I will grant you the new grain,
> The new wine, and the new oil,
> And you shall have them in abundance.
> Nevermore will I let you be
> A mockery among the nations."
> (Joel 2:18–19; cf. Hos. 2:10–11 [8–9])

Yet the book of Joel does far more than simply concretize and realize the judgment and hope themes of Hosea; it also provides a liturgical process (whether real or imagined is disputed among scholars) for moving from judgment to hope.[13] The marriage to YHWH must involve nothing short of a divorce from Baal; thus, "mourning" precedes the new dawn:

> Gird yourselves and lament, O priests,
> Wail, O ministers of the altar;
> Come, spend the night in sackcloth,
> O ministers of my God
> For offering and libation are withheld
> From the House of your God.
> Solemnize a fast,
> Proclaim an assembly;
> Gather the elders—all the inhabitants of the land—
> In the House of the LORD your God,
> And cry out to the LORD.
>
> Joel 1:13–14

This mourning picks up on two of the pillars of judgment anticipated in Hosea, namely, the marriage and nature images. Just as Hosea is inflamed with anger over Israel's veritable marriage to Baal, so also Joel takes up the need to bewail the loss of YHWH as the nation's true spouse: "Lament—like a maiden girt with sackcloth for the husband of her youth!" (Joel 1:8).[14]

The second theme of judgment, echoing Hosea, concerns the need to restore the natural order.[15] In words again reminiscent of Hosea, the prophet points to the pervasiveness of crop and harvest failures as a sign of judgment for this "marital" faithlessness:

> The country is ravaged,
> The ground must mourn;
> For the new grain is ravaged,
> The new wine is dried up,
> The new oil has failed.
> Farmers are dismayed
> And vine dressers wail
> Over wheat and barley;
> For the crops of the field are lost.
> The vine has dried up,
> The fig tree withers,
> Pomegranate, palm, and apple—
> All the trees of the field are sear.
> And joy has dried up
> Among men.
>
> Joel 1:10–2; cf. 1:15–20

While it is true that the reference to *ba 'al* in Joel 1:8 can simply be translated "husband," we should not overlook the roles the very term *ba 'al* and the death of nature theme play in Canaanite mythic literature.[16] The demise of the god Baal at the hands of Mot, "Death," produces similar consequences as the judgment of God in Hosea and Joel.[17]

Thus, the liturgical process envisioned here transfers the powers of Baal and his priests into the hands of the priest and altar of YHWH via the mediation of a prophet. In the prophetic voice, this worship scene becomes a stage in the prophetic drama of the announcement of the coming "day of YHWH" (Joel 1:15; 2:1–2, 11; 3:3–4 [2:30–32]; 4:14 [3:14]; 4:18 [3:18]).[18] However, unlike Hosea, which stands more as a precursor to these dire events, Joel resides at the cusp, virtually enacting the moment of transition from Baal-like death to life. Thus, the enemy's invasion occurs as a liturgical, if not historical, reality (2:3–16; cf. 4:9–16a [3:9–16b]).[19] Yet it is YHWH's doing:

> And the LORD roars aloud
> At the head of His army;
> For vast indeed is His host,
> Numberless are those that do His bidding.
> For great is the day of the LORD,
> Most terrible—who can endure it?
>
> Joel 2:11

Rhetorically, in the wake of the exilic invasion (even if the book dates from a much later time), the prophet creates a religious crisis to sever the ties between YHWH's altars and Baal's altars.[20] In the process, the old Canaanite mythology is submerged, but not so much that we cannot see the pagan roots of Israelite belief.[21] Still, there is a philosophic or theological difference we can observe between these religious systems, with respect to the recovery of a sense of divine compassion, so important also to many tales in the Pentateuch. However, again, the classic Canaanite categories are not far behind, for where the revival of Baal occurs as a result of the goddess Anat's intervention, in the Israelite variant, the nation of Israel plays both the role of the dying-rising goddess *and* that of the goddess who embodies her mourning in a ritual of lamentation:

> (Then) Anat also went to and fro and scoured
> every rock to the heart of the earth. . . .
> She [happened upon] Baal; he had fallen [to] the ground.
> [For clothing] she covered herself with sackcloth;
> she scraped (her) skin with a stone,
> with a flint [for a razor]
> she shaved (her) side-whiskers and beard;

> [she harrowed] her collar-bone,
> she ploughed (her) chest like a garden,
> she harrowed (her) waist like a valley, (saying)
> "Baal is dead!
> "What (will become) of the people of Dagon's son,
> "what of his multitudes?"[22]

However, whereas Anat gashes her body, the people of Israel must strike deeper, returning, not to a god who has died, but to a God who calls a dead people to return:

> "Yet even now"—says the LORD—
> "Turn back to Me with all your hearts,
> And with fasting, weeping, and lamenting."
> Rend your hearts
> Rather than your garments,
> And turn back to the LORD your God.
> For He is gracious and compassionate,
> Slow to anger, abounding in kindness,
> And renouncing punishment.
> Who knows but He may turn and relent,
> And leave a blessing behind
> For meal offering and drink offering
> To the LORD your God?
> . . . .
> Between the portico and the altar,
> Let the priests, the LORD'S ministers, weep
> And say:
> "Oh, spare Your people, LORD!
> Let not Your possession become a mockery,
> To be taunted by nations!
> Let not the peoples say,
> 'Where is their God?'"
>
>   Joel 2:12–14, 17; cf. 1:8[23]

Through the mourning process, the people play the part of the bride, the goddess, becoming linked once again to the power of the groom, that is, YHWH. Yet who governs this process? Sociologically speaking, we observe that priestly action is decisive, although the text implicitly argues for the addition of prophetic mediation as an element integral to the effort of national recovery, agricultural flourishing, and future military triumph, what Ogden terms the "theme of 'reversing'" (cf. Joel 4:16b–21 [3:16b–21]).[24] Clearly the prophetic voice, in seeking to become a participant in the national lament recovery process, is, to use Wilson's categories, that of a figure at the periphery of a power apparatus now under the control of a priesthood.[25] Perhaps the priesthood has yet to establish full sway over the community. This is the sort of prophetic marginalization known also from the Mari texts where prophetic figures serve as advocates for various gods and their shrines, but not central figures in the sacerdotal system.[26]

The absence of any reference to Israelite kings would seem to situate this text squarely in the rivalries of the Persian period, which events we have seen from our study of the shaping of the Pentateuch.[27] The prophetic voice is seeking, albeit within limitations, to play a role in the larger political, social, and religious developments of the period. In other words, the writer of Joel puts prophetic support behind a priestly program of social restoration focused on Zion/Jerusalem and Judah. The future prosperity of the society rests, in the mind of the author, firmly in a conjunction of priestly and prophetic efforts:

> Fear not, O soil, rejoice and be glad;
> For the LORD has wrought great deeds.
> Fear not, O beasts of the field,
> For the pastures in the wilderness
> Are clothed with grass.
> The trees have borne their fruit;
> Fig tree and vine
> Have yielded their strength.
> O children of Zion, be glad,
> Rejoice in the LORD your God.
> For He has given you the early rain in [His] kindness,
> Now He makes the rain fall [as] formerly—
> The early rain and the late—
> And threshing floors shall be piled with grain,
> And vats shall overflow with new wine and oil.
> Joel 2:21–24; cf. 2:18–20; 2:25–27

The revival imagery makes use of "new grain," "new wine," and "new oil" motifs found also in Hosea (cf. Hos. 2:10–11). Hence, the prophetic-priestly program of Joel is ultimately a readaptation of the mythic imagery known from Hosea, and perhaps ultimately the Baal cycle. [28]

That the integral character of prophetic voice is at the heart of Joel's prophetic-priestly collaborative vision is made clear by perhaps the most well-known passage of this brief book:

> After that,
> I will pour out My spirit on all flesh;
> Your sons and daughters shall prophesy;
> Your old men shall dream dreams,
> And your young men shall see visions.
> I will even pour out My spirit
> Upon male and female slaves in those days
> (Joel 3:1–2 [2:28-29])

Notably, the classic categories of the poor are entirely absent from Joel's vision. No reference is made to the alien, widow, orphan, or the poor as such. The writer is attempting to latch onto and shore up a political program that has not set the poor at the center of its agenda. For those who want to see the prophets as advocates for the poor, this might seem to be an unsettling observation. However, our attentiveness to the probable marginal social location of this book and its support of priestly aims makes us aware that the prophetic tradition, if tradition is even an appropriate designation, is diverse with respect to matters of social justice and national restoration. Joel's vision is more at home with the tendencies of the so-called Second Isaiah than it is with prophetic texts such as Micah or even Amos, which follow Joel in the Hebrew canon.[29]

Amos: The Structures of Poverty

Insofar as we can reconstruct the earliest phases of the book of Amos, the prophet Amos was acutely aware that questionable economic interests dominated Israelite society, displacing ethical values rooted in the Yahwist faith. While later editorial additions and expansions recast the message, these modifications do not displace the prophet's ancient ringing cry.[30] Amos's mission to the Northern Kingdom (c. 760 B.C.E.) exposed the pervasive decay of moral sensibilities throughout Israel that accompanied the economic prosperity experienced under Jeroboam II (c. 786–746 B.C.E.).[31]

Prosperity, Politics, and Prophecy

Paving the way for the economic and political developments of the eighth century were the significant trade efforts and construction projects of the Omride dynasty.[32] Setbacks were undoubtedly felt as a result of the revolution under Jehu (c. 842 B.C.E.), including a shift in land ownership; nevertheless, the economic development experienced under the Omrides must be seen as an important legacy for the later kings.[33] In terms of more contemporaneous factors, however, the enhanced way of life of Amos's contemporaries was tied to the expansion of territory under both Joash (c. 801–786 B.C.E.; cf. 2 Kings 13:25; 2 Chron. 25:5–24) and Jeroboam II (cf. 2 Kings 14:25, 28). This prosperity was facilitated by the decline of the Aramean kingdom of Damascus in the face of the expansionist policies of the Assyrian ruler Adad-Nirari III (c. 809–782 B.C.E.).[34]

In the political window created thereby, Israel was opened to pursue its own political advantage, free from the tribute demands of its rivals. However, Amos "was not blinded by the prosperous reign of Jeroboam or by his victories."[35]

The prophet points out quite clearly that Israel's success story included in its cast of characters a host of peoples victimized by the rise to the top of a few urban dwellers. With Amos we obtain our first insight into the plight of the poor in the biblical world: The poor are "at mercy of the arbitrary expectations and demands of the rich."[36] The structures of poverty revealed in this brief text give us an unusual insight into the material conditions of the time, giving substance to the prophet's call for justice.

Creditors and Debts

Many found themselves sold into service because they lacked the means to stay out of debt. Becoming a debt slave was permitted in Israel as a way to pay off one's financial obligations (cf. Ex. 21:2–6; Lev. 25:39–43; Deut. 15:12–15), but injustices had crept into the system.[37] These injustices put increased burdens on those who had fallen into debt. Amos raised the outcry in opposition to the unjust ways the ruling elite of Israelite society used this institution to their advantage. One key passage states, "Thus said the LORD: For three transgressions of Israel, for four, I will not revoke it [the punishment]: because they have sold for silver those whose cause was just, and the needy ['ĕbyôn] for a pair of sandals" (Amos 2:6). Elsewhere the prophet puts into the mouths of the merchants these words: "We will buy the poor [dal] for silver, the needy ['ĕbyôn] for a pair of sandals" (Amos 8:6). The buying and selling of the 'ĕbyôn, "beggarly poor," and 'ānî, "oppressed," refers to their falling into debt-servitude as a result of their failure or inability to pay off their debts.

The interpretation of Amos 2:6 and 8:6 has posed some problems for commentators, concerning, in particular, the precise meaning of the phrases bakke-sep, "for silver," and ba'ăbûr na'ălāyim, "for a pair of sandals." Fendler suggests that the text presents a difference in emphasis toward the ṣaddîq and the 'ebyôn. In Fendler's analysis, the silver mentioned in relation to the ṣaddîq refers to the proceeds received by the creditor for the sale of one indebted, whereas the pair of sandals characterizes the specific item involved and not the quoted price.[38] Lang, in contrast, takes the reference to "silver" to signify "debts of money."[39] He also considers the reference to the "pair of sandals" to be an idiomatic expression used to refer to some type of legal obligation. To this, Lang compares the situation described in the book of Ruth wherein the giving of a sandal to another party attests to a business transaction (Ruth 4:7–8). By transferral of meaning, Lang contends, na'ălāyim comes to stand for the obligation itself. Therefore, for someone to be sold into debt slavery "for a pair of sandals" would indicate that the indebted person was unable to fulfill certain obligations and was therefore forced into debt slavery. Yet it seems that an analysis such as Lang's is, as Vesco claims, "too elliptical."[40]

We might suggest, based on the poetic structure of the passage, that the silver is the value of the sandals and thus represents the amount of debt involved, namely, only a few days' wages. Amos is incensed that the creditors were so greedy that they sold debtors into slavery for even minor debts. [41]

Whatever the precise interpretation of the text may be, it is clear from the passages under consideration that the *'ĕbyôn* and *'ānî* were pawns bought and sold over debts, however small. The poor were taken advantage of because the social elite failed to fulfill their obligations toward the poor. Once caught in the web of indebtedness, the abused *'ānî* and the destitute *'ĕbyôn* became the prey of the wealthy. It should be stressed here that the opposition Amos raised was not against the system of debt servitude per se; rather, Amos maintained that the grounds upon which many found themselves sold into slavery were illegitimate because they "had only incurred debt for some minor necessity of life."[42] The problem was not the fault of the poor, who were in this instance blameless.

Fendler attempts to differentiate between Amos 2:6 and 8:6 on the basis of the identity of the buyers and sellers. For 2:6, Fendler suggests that here the creditor is in view.[43] The application of this text to creditors would seem to fit in with the context in which lending is involved (2:8). For 8:6, Fendler identifies the landowners as the purchasers of laborers to work their land, noting that the reference's context includes wheat sales, a concern of these landowners (8:5).[44]

In addition to the abuse of debt slavery, those who turned over their garments as loan collateral were defrauded when lenders disregarded laws designed to protect the destitute (Ex. 22:25–26 [26–27]; Deut. 24:12–13).[45] Israel's laws, as preserved in legal traditions that appear to stem back to the premonarchic period, state that if the lender takes a "neighbor's garment in pledge," then the lender is to "return it to him before the sun sets; it is his only clothing, the sole covering for his skin. In what else shall he sleep?" (Ex. 22:25–26 [26–27]). In the case of a widow, no pledge was to be taken at all (Deut. 24:17). But in Amos's day the garments of the poor were not returned: "They recline by every altar on garments taken in pledge" (Amos 2:8a). Garments given in pledge were kept by the lender, ignoring the fact that without them these poor people might suffer or die from harsh weather conditions. Such an act at a cultic site represented a flagrant flouting of the Israelite community's ancient religious principles. As Botterweck points out, if the creditors thought that they need not return the garments because they were put to a cultic use, then they were sorely mistaken.[46] The prophet carefully juxtaposes the oppression of the poor with the intense religiosity of the elite to emphasize that a religiosity without a concern for economic justice is hollow.[47]

Fendler contends that these creditors themselves could not have been terribly rich if they needed the clothing of the poor, preferring Rudolph's suggestion that those who were taking the garments of the poor were merely the overseers of the agricultural laborers.[48] Yet the text does not imply that the creditors and wealthy wore these garments but that they were used as part of some sort of incubation rite. The economic status of those taking these garments is not at all clear from the text; thus, one need not assume, as Fendler does, that the offenders in this case are creditors who stand barely above the poverty line. The garments in question had value, and could be bought or sold. Further, the creditors involved were in a position to lend to those in need. Fendler's view that the creditors were nearly as poor as their clients would seem implausible.

The oracles also link the increased wealth of the rich to the taxation of the poor. The prophet says, "you impose a tax on the poor [*dal*] and exact from him a levy of grain, you have built houses of hewn stone . . .; you have planted delightful vineyards" (5:11). The fact that the poor mentioned here were able to pay the necessary amounts of wheat demanded by the rich indicates that the victims in this case were small farmers,[49] perhaps even full citizens.[50] Miranda suggests in this connection that the reference to the exactions should not be restricted to taxation, but be construed as a reference to the "underpayment of the workers, the short measure to the consumer through high prices, and the take of the businessman, who buys the underpriced harvest which small farmers are able to sell only by refraining from consuming it."[51] Whether the reference incorporates all these elements is unclear; nonetheless, Miranda does alert us to the levels at which injustice may take place in an agrarian-based economy. More specifically, the exactions mentioned would seem to be the accumulated rents of landowners from tenant farmers. As Botterweck observes, "The unjust economic set up favored the affluent large landowners, so that they continually were enriched through rents and taxes on produce, all the while the small farmers had hardly enough left over from the harvest."[52]

The statement in Amos 5:11 shows that the prophet also drew a direct connection between the impoverishment of the poor, in this case the *dal*, and capital gains of housing and land made by the elite. It was on the basis of the exactions that the rich could extend their holdings and build a prosperous life of ease. Several passages in Amos attest to the life of luxury enjoyed by the elite.[53] As Amos 5:11 indicates, the houses of the elite were built of ashlar blocks. The ruling class was able to enjoy the benefits of winter and summer residences (3:15a; cf. Jer. 36:22). Interiors of the houses were adorned with ivory (3:15b; cf. 1 Kings 22:39) and contained costly furnishings, including couches made with ivory panels (3:12; 6:4).[54] As Fendler rightly notes, to Amos the houses of the rich "were considered representations of self assuredness and pride, as symbols of social injustice."[55]

The reference to exactions in Amos 5:11 may be further illuminated by the statement that the rich trample on the *dal*. The Hebrew verb *bôšaskem*, which JPS reads as "impose a tax" and which is commonly rendered "your trampling," is difficult to interpret. It has been suggested that the verb should be related to the Akkadian *šabāšu*, "collect, gather" (used of grain duty),[56] which Torczyner applies to the verb in Amos with the meaning "to levy rent."[57] Chirichigno, citing Dearman, argues for a separation of the ideas of rent and taxation, favoring the latter as the practice under consideration in this phrase.[58] However, the Hebrew text may be explained more simply as a scribal error based on *bos*, "to trample underfoot," in which "the correction has crept into the text alongside of the corrigendums."[59] It is even possible that this is an example of Amos's village dialect. In any case, according to the structure of the passage, the notion of "trampling" would refer to the general exploitation of the *dal*, with the reference to exaction of a "levy of grain" supplying the specific mode of injustice.

A similar situation may stand behind the statement that the rich drank wine taken as "fines" (2:8). In some contexts, the verb *'nš* is rendered by "to fine" (cf. 2 Kings 23:33; 2 Chron. 36:3) and is also linked to certain crimes in the biblical text (cf. Ex. 21:22; Deut. 22:19). Fendler, however, suggests that in Amos the meaning of the term is "exacting," a sense that finds support in the LXX (*oî'non ek sukophantiōn*) and the Targum (*hĕmar 'onāsā'*).[60] Fendler seeks, moreover, to identify the group perpetrating this injustice, arguing that those responsible in this case were creditors who took over the wine harvest as compensation for unpaid debts.[61] The notion of penalties imposed on debts approaches that of a fine, although here the context is economic as opposed to the juridical setting found elsewhere in the biblical text.[62] However, it must be conceded that this interpretation goes beyond the text. While creditors are the object of Amos's accusation in the first half of (Amos 2:8), they need not necessarily be seen as the focus of the second half of the verse. Hence, the latter part of Amos 2:8 probably admits no more than Wolff's interpretation that "fines were meant to make restitution for damages and not to finance drinking bouts," regardless of whatever group was taking advantage of the situation.[63]

Market Practices

The poor were victims of artificially high prices. Amos gives us a glimpse into the common business practices found in the marketplaces of Israel. The prophet offers a stern warning to the merchants of Israel, those who "devour the needy [*'ebyôn*], annihilating the poor [Q = *'ānî*; K = *'ănāwîm*] of the land" (8:4). The text mockingly portrays these merchants as saying, "If only the new moon were over, so that we could sell grain; the sabbath, so that we could offer wheat for sale, using an *ephah* that is too small, and a shekel that is too big, tilting a dishonest scale" (8:5). In everyday market transactions, the merchants and traders were engaged in deceptive practices. They would decrease the amount of wheat sold and even sell the grain refuse (8:6). The increase of the shekel mentioned here functions as an artificial increase in prices. Fendler explains the practice as follows: The shekel serves as the weight on the scale to which the consumer must offer silver as a counterbalance in making payment for goods purchased. The increase of the weight of the shekel would force the consumer to pay more in silver than was legitimately required.[64] Furthermore, the prophet accuses the merchants of tampering with the scales as well. It would appear from the prophet's perspective that in the marketplace the exploitation of the poor was the rule, not the exception. What the prophet has in view here is domestic commerce and not transit or foreign trade, which were royal monopolies.[65] Moreover, the references to religious days in this passage, such as the new moon and Sabbath, serve to show that such disreputable commercial activity took precedence over the facade of ritual religion, which undoubtedly gave credence to the society's social arrangements.

In general, the prophet speaks out against existing economic practices, which were bleeding the life out of the peasant population. By these business practices and economic structures the members of the upper classes were guilty of taking property that rightfully belonged to others, whether land, grain, or clothing. As Vesco succinctly characterizes the context, "The social arrangements in Samaria terrorized and increased victims. The rich piled up violence (Amos 6:3), a blow struck at people's lives (*ḥāmās*) through plundering (Amos 5:9) and a crime perpetrated against property (*šod*)."[66] Miranda describes this process as well: "Amos analyzes, with perfect perspicacity, the source of differentiating wealth: it is accumulated by continuously depriving the poor of a small portion of their income."[67] According to Wittenberg, this is a conscious process: "This dispossession of the peasant population is not merely the result of natural economic developments but is actively pushed by the ruling class."[68] Since it was virtually impossible to increase one's wealth without taking the possessions of someone else, the rich turned to oppression in order to increase their wealth. In the process they impoverished those they exploited.

Legal Practices

The *'ebyôn* was taken advantage of at the city gate, the economic and legal hub of the city. The prophet states, "For I have noted how many are your crimes, and how countless your sins—you enemies of the righteous, you takers of bribes, you who subvert in the gate the cause of the needy ['*ebyôn*]!" (5:12).

The gate was the hub of unjust activity because this was the place where business decisions were finalized, products were sold, and the legal claims of the poor went unheard.[69] The term "subvert" would seem to be clarified by Job 24:4, which reads, "They chase the needy off the roads." The text in Amos would therefore be better translated as, "They thrust aside the poor from the gate" (however, see below on Amos 2:7). The term for bribe (*koper*) here more specifically refers to the payment of money in lieu of suffering physical punishment for crimes (cf. Ex. 21:30; 30:12; Num. 35:31–32).[70] Apparently the judges were using a legitimate institution as a means to provide loopholes for the rich. As Davies states, "What lies at the basis of Amos's indictment (Amos 5:12) is not simply the giving of a bribe in order to influence a decision, but rather the placid acceptance by the legal assemblies of monetary compensation for crimes which should have incurred the death penalty."[71] In contrast to all this unjust activity the prophet calls for the establishment of justice at the gate (Amos 5:15).

Many also place in a legal context the text's statement that the people of Israel are guilty because they "trample the heads of the poor [*dal*] into the dust of the ground, and make the humble [*'ănāwîm*] walk a twisted course" (2:7). The RSV rendering of the latter part of this line ("turn aside the way of the afflicted") is clearly false, if for no other reason than the rendering, like the common translation of Amos 5:12, makes no intelligible sense out of the passage. Vesco examines several possibilities: The term *derek*, "way," might be taken literally and thus the reference might mean that the rich put obstacles in the path of the poor or that they stood in front of the poor on the road. Vesco finds this interpretation "not probable." Alternately, the term *derek* could be taken as an abstraction, referring to moral conduct. In this sense, the statement in Amos would indicate that the rich force "those of modest means to live in a mode different than that which they would prefer to follow."[72] Vesco appears to prefer this latter explanation. Further, one might suggest that this means that justice is not dispensed to the poor. This is how the NIV understands the text: The people of Israel, "deny justice to the oppressed [*'ănāwîm*]." The latter interpretation would seem preferable on the basis of Ex. 23:6, where the full phrase uses the verb *nṭh* in the Hiphil with the noun *mišpaṭ* to mean "divert judgment" (i.e., "pervert justice").

Judgment of God

To be sure, these oracles are not offering a bare bones portrait of the economics of monarchic Israel. The text is thoroughly imbued with theological assessments and overtones. Specifically, the oracles urgently sound the warning of judgment against those who engendered economic and legal injustices.

To the prophet, the immediate future cast dark shadows on Israel's ability to survive, with death and devastation on the horizon (8:2). The ruling elite bore the guilt, since they were the ones to "store up lawlessness and rapine in their fortresses" (3:10). Those "fortresses" (*'armĕnôt*) were the "symbols of the prosperity and power of the ruling class."[73] Since the strongholds were built through the labor and exploitation of the poor, the elite were to be judged.[74] The linkage between injustice and judgment is rather straightforward.

The prophet's most gruesome announcement of judgment is directed toward the women of Samaria, whom the prophet mockingly portrays as "cows of Bashan" (4:1). As "the wives of the court officials (Amos 3:9), of the wealthy proprietors of large estates (Amos 5:11–12), and of the merchants (Amos 8:4–6)," they enjoyed a life of luxury at the expense of the *'ĕbyôn* and *dal* (4:1).[75] This life of luxury involved carousing, excessive feasting, and drinking (4:1; cf. 2:8; 5:11; 6:4–7; 9:14). Coote reminds us of the institutionalized and ritual character of drinking clubs in the ancient world, as attested in the *mrzḥ* associations at Ugarit in ancient Syria and elsewhere.[76] Coote also points to a Ugaritic text in which the god El, the main god of the Ugaritic pantheon, keels over drunk at one of these feasts.[77] Whatever the precise extent of the women's involvement in their husbands' business, legal, and social activities, Amos warns that the women too would be swept away on the fish-hooks of judgment (4:1–2).[78] The guilt was equally distributed: the entire body of merchants, landowners, and bureaucrats, men and women alike, was culpable before the God of judgment.

Thus we find that the prophet's sweeping analysis constantly refers to religious categories and values. To the prophet, the maintenance of a high standard of living through exploitative structures and activities constituted a rejection of the community's obligations to YHWH (2:4, 9–10). The problem of poverty was more than an economic problem. For Amos, the issue was one of basic religious values. Israelite society, built as it was on practices that violated the deepest traditions of the community, could not expect to endure, as Schottroff notes:

> The God of Amos is not the defender of the political and social system, as the Israel of that age thought him to be, or of its questionable "achievements." Rather he refuses it any permanence and even any right to permanence. The God of Amos is the God of the lowly, the victims who were crushed without pity in the economic machinery of the Israel of that age."[79]

At a fundamental level, firm theological perspectives frame the conviction that the "existence of a rich upper stratum runs contrary to God's will, since it destroys the people which God had created in salvation history."[80] Israel had become the oppressor like the Amorites before it, and like the Amorites, Israel would be destroyed (2:10–16).[81] To the prophet's mind, YHWH's judgment of Israelite society would be total, not only against the economic and legal institutions that dominated it, but also the pagan value structures that guided those repressive activities.[82]

Certainly the values of Canaanite urban society continued to have a strong influence on the life and institutions of Israel and Judah through the monarchic complexes that the Israelites erected.[83] The Israelite and Judaean kings came to use, to one extent or another, the religion of Yahwism to legitimize their position as rulers (if the preponderance of Yahwistic names in the inscriptional materials is any guide to the belief system of the ancient Israelite population).[84] Through this system, the elite established the ideological base that undergirded the lifestyle and economic practices the prophet attacks. However, there was no safety for the monarchies in Yahwism, since, for the peasants at least, covenant language had become a measuring stick for monarchic ways, not simply the point of its legitimation.

Yet how comprehensive is this prophetic social critique? Amos's message of judgment may seem like the propaganda of a revolutionary who wants to overthrow the existing social order. Many today would argue, as Lucal does, that figures like Amos "might be called revolutionaries in that they announce the destruction of the existing institutions."[85] But Amos does not work for the overthrow of the state.[86]

As Kraus observes, the prophet is simply announcing the nation's inevitable demise, not presenting a social manifesto.[87] Amos, in offering a concise critique of the social order, is warning in advance of its overthrow at the hands of YHWH. In so doing, "Prophecy reveals the hidden connection between social injustice and historical catastrophe."[88] As such, the prophet's critique of abuses in the social order must not be confused with a thorough "systemic analysis" of injustice, as Lorentz has cogently observed.[89] In the prophetic view, an economic, political, and legal order that has as its victim the *'ānî*, *dal*, and the *'ebyôn* is subject to the judgment of YHWH. The society that tolerates such behavior inevitably will collapse. The specific abuses and the underlying ideology of their society remained the focus of the prophets' social critique. The notion that Amos attacks the "entire system" is a modern conception.

We must, however, not overstate this critique of the systemic character of the prophet's analysis, for there is an ancient tradition that reports that the priest at Bethel, Amaziah, viewed Amos's call for integrity to be a threat to the state (7:10–17). This editorial layer is cognizant of the historical experience of Samaria and would understand that the prophet's "judgment" took the form of the Assyrian campaign against Samaria under Shalmaneser V (c. 726–722

B.C.E.) and Sargon II (c. 721–705 B.C.E.), a campaign that led to the collapse of Samaria, the deportation of Israel's leadership, and the fall of the Northern Kingdom (2 Kings 17: 1–6). Vesco is perhaps right to see in the book's description of judgment a bitter irony, for in the hour of judgment so many rich died that they were forced to call on the poor peasants to attend and mourn at their funerals (Amos 5:16).[90]

Is there no alternative to judgment? The only real hope for Israelite society rested, it would seem, in a return to the foundational values of the covenant tradition (cf. 5:21–25), since it was out of this perspective that Amos issued a call for integrity in the marketplace and the courts. Such an emphasis, as Wittenberg argues, saves the prophetic critique from functioning as a nostalgic desire for the restoration of the old premonarchic social order. One would have to agree with Wittenberg that, "the simple restoration of a by-gone order under completely new and different circumstances does not solve the problems."[91] Rather, the traditions preserved in the book of Amos urge a return to the Yahwist ethic upon which Israel was founded (5:14–15) and for the people to seek God (5:4–6).[92] Yet at some level it was left to later redactors to fully enflesh the view that it was this past covenant with Moses, together with a glimpse of YHWH's future restoration of society, that might transform words of judgment into words of hope for Israel. Such hope, however, did not rest in humanly initiated political activism in the vein of an Elijah (e.g., 1 Kings 18:40–45) or Elisha (e.g., 2 Kings 9:1–3), still less the "enthusiasm of positive social manifestos."[93] The creation of a just society is, after all, a divine grace.

Obadiah: Liberty, Equality, Fraternity

The rather brief text ascribed to Obadiah, styled as an oracle against Edom (Obad. 1:1), presents a portrait of justice in terms of divine vengeance of the most straightforward variety. We are familiar with the motif of God's triumph over arrogant powers from other prophetic writings, though often greater powers than Edom are in view, such as Egypt, Assyria, or even Tyre.[94] However, while Edom may be treated as something of a secondary actor, one should bear in mind that the territory is extensive and the archaeological remains attest to a vigorous cultural sphere with numerous forts and towns that flourished along the trade routes between Damascus, Aqaba, and Gaza.[95]

Thus, Edom's status as an important political neighbor who "betrayed" Judah during the Babylonian invasion is a historically plausible image that looms large in the mind of the prophet (Obad. 1:11). With poetic punch, the prophet charges Edom with base callousness on Judah's day of "calamity," "ruin," "anguish," and "disaster" (Obad. 1:12–14). The arrogant one that God will pull down in this case is Edom itself, in total destruction (Obad. 1:4–5, 9–10; cf. Jer 49:7–16).

The kinship between Obadiah and other oracles against the nations in the prophetic literature is rather obvious (see especially Jer. 49:7–22; Ezek. 25:12–14; 35:1–15), although whether or not Obadiah's oracles constituted performances within the cult is hardly certain, much less whether Obadiah was a "cult prophet" as many contend.[96] What is unique, however, is the "brother" language that infuses the text. The writer repeatedly charges that Edom/Esau has betrayed "brother Jacob" (Obad. 1:6, 8–9, 12, 17–18, 21). This preponderance of brother language is analogous to the characterization in the E source, which likewise portrays Jacob and Esau as two estranged brothers (Gen. 25:21–34; 27:1–45). However, whereas the Genesis materials opt for the message of hegemonic reconciliation, Obadiah looks forward to Edom/Esau's complete destruction as the just recompense for its actions during the siege, a sentiment that finds currency elsewhere in the biblical text (cf. Ezekiel 35; Mal. 1:2–5; and Ps. 137:7). In other words, the politics of Obadiah thoroughly diverges from that of the Jacob-Esau story in Genesis.[97]

This is, however, not the only instance where we find prophetic oracles at odds with narrative literature. As we shall see, Nahum's thoroughgoing pronouncement of judgment against Nineveh by a God who shows no mercy runs counter to the narrative of Jonah, a text that holds out as very real the possibility that Nineveh's tyrant might actually discover the fruits of repentance and reconciliation. We must see in this split between the prophetic literature and narrative materials, even when they are prophetic narratives, one of the key horizons of biblical social ethics: political militancy versus social remediation. This split constituted the fault line of the ancient Judaean discussion over how to face a future of political and social uncertainty when confronting the larger powers. Given the high stakes, there is little wonder that the positions were held so fiercely or that the divisions ran so deeply.

However, it is the narrative writers, not the prophets, who appear to be the keener political ethicists. The rather uncompromising prophetic view could not generate the sort of regional stabilization needed for both Judah and Edom to prosper well into the Persian and Hellenistic ages. A reading of Haggai and Zechariah will show that prophetic agitation was actually rather short-lived and that time would be on the side of the Ezras and Nehemiahs in Judah's midst. Obadiah, therefore, must be seen as a member of those forces after the exile who longed for the forceful restoration of Judaean power. This posture is underscored by the later redactor of the prose segment in Obad.1:19–20, where the exilic return and Zion's dominion are seen as logical outgrowths of Obadiah's initial oracles, building, in turn, on the Zion "remnant" motif found in the poetic expansion in vv. 15–18.[98] The reconciliation program of the E source, on the other hand, played both to the postexilic prophetic literature's tendency toward militant isolationism as well as to the narrative literature's theme of hegemonic reconciliation, ironically paving the way for the prophetic voice to yield to the social ideas expressed in works such as Ezra-Nehemiah, Esther, Jonah, and the early Daniel, works that envisioned cooperative imperial political efforts as the only hope for the community's survival.

These temperate voices would not have the last word, for the harsher prophetic nationalistic rhetoric of independent sovereignty and the all-encompassing reach of narrative's hegemonic politics would reconfigure themselves to spark the later Hasmonaean bid for nativist Judaean political power to be exerted once again from Jerusalem.

Jonah: Universal Redemption from Injustice

What is the scope of God's justice? How far does the compassion of God extend? Does God's care reach beyond the people of Israel to touch the unwitting pagans of the earth? These are issues that charged the theological imagination of parts of the postexilic intellectual community, in particular those elements that were seeking in one way or another to reach an accommodation with their diasporic environment while at the same time working to preserve something of the substance of the faith of ancient Israel.

The book of Jonah reflects several facets of this theological development. While little is known from the book of Kings about the prophet's namesake (cf. 2 Kings 14:25), Jonah itself fleshes out the story of an eighth-century B.C.E. figure, who, much like Elijah and Elisha, receives a commission from God to carry a message to the people. Unlike Elijah and Elisha, however, whose dramas are largely cast against the backdrop of Israelite politics (though foreign figures like the Sidonian woman of Zarephath and Naaman the Aramaean commander should not be overlooked), the story of Jonah is set thoroughly in the pagan context of Nineveh during the height of Assyrian rule. While Assyria had long since met its demise by the time of the book's writing, the literary distance provided the writer an occasion to reflect on theological questions of the sort raised in Esther and early Daniel regarding the tension between assimilation and religious distinctiveness under imperial rule.

The parallels to Esther and Daniel are instructive. Where we find in these books non-Israelites affirming the power of the God of Israel, so also in Jonah the pagan sailors not only call on Jonah to worship this God but they also take up the performance of sacrifices to Jonah's God (Jonah 1:9–16). Likewise, the Ninevite king, when he hears the prophetic announcement of Nineveh's doom for wickedness, participates in the mourning and fasting that evokes God's compassionate relenting of judgment (3:4–10, cf. 1:2).

The book of Jonah is hardly satire, as some have tried to characterize it.[99] On the contrary, the figure of Jonah is representative of every exilic victim who has felt the need to hide his or her identity from the outside world. As with the books of Esther or early Daniel, the exilic experience is, in theological terms, a moment of self-examination: Jonah is called to account by the pagans and he must now squarely face his identity as a Hebrew when confronting the demands and dangers of exile (1:7–9). The practice of Judaism survived precisely because the Esthers, Daniels, and Jonahs learned to navigate between the Scylla of veiled orthodoxy and the Charybdis of pagan presence.

Likewise, to imagine a faith that transforms empires is the work of the books of Jonah, Esther, and at least the first half of Daniel. In each case, too, the question of justice is central to the theological reflection of the writers. In part, this is a question of justice toward the Jewish people. Esther and early Daniel, in particular, point the way for benevolent monarchs to rule in light of a recognition of the God of Israel. The Assyrian ruler in Jonah is a precise counterpart to this hope. The book of Jonah frames the justice question in terms of divine compassion. The writer is at pains to have Jonah confess the profound implications of a belief in a "compassionate and gracious God, slow to anger, abounding in kindness, renouncing punishment" (4:2). Although some, like Jonah, might have been grieved at the prospects that God's love could extend to the conqueror (a view roundly countered, for example, by Nahum), nevertheless, the author joins the voices of the book of Esther and the early materials in Daniel to argue that the construction of a just future for Israel will include divine compassion toward Israel's conquerors. This is not, however, an easy task. The future requires a new theological response which Israel, in its wrenching experience of having been "swallowed," must prepare itself to fashion, namely, a theology and a liturgy of repentance: "Let everyone turn back from his evil ways and from the injustice (*ḥāmās*) of which he is guilty. Who knows but that God may turn and relent? He may turn back from His wrath, so that we do not perish" (3:8b–10).

In this theology for the whole world, we see the seeds of liturgical movement that could successfully press beyond the limits of the political-theological horizon. Whereas the writer of Habakkuk could envision only the collapse of the empire as the solution to the dilemmas of domestic and global injustice, the texts of Esther, early Daniel, and Jonah forge a justice theology for living and worshiping in between times, for living in the diasporic interim between the more tumultuous times when empires rise and fall, and for worshiping the God of Israel in a pagan environment. This "in-between" ethic envisions not the demise of the empire but its redemption through an active Jewish presence.

Of course, Jonah's continued grief (4:5–11) reflects a tacit acknowledgment of the degree to which texts like Esther, early Daniel, and Jonah have departed from the prophetic claims about the inevitable demise of evil empires. Historically, this grief, which could never be fully submerged by the cautious assimilationist tendencies reflected in Jonah, Esther, and early Daniel, resurfaces in the later Daniel materials and the Hasmonaean rebellion. While the theological musings of the writer of Jonah must have been tantalizing, it would seem that history itself belies the possibility of universal imperial redemption.

Micah: Village with a View

The seven chapters of this sixth Book of the Twelve poses a series of enigmas for interpreters wishing to recover the social justice teaching of the prophets. The seeming pervasiveness of a harsh social critique throughout the book is complicated by the more recent scholarly proposals that identify distinctive stages or layers in the editorial history of the work. Furthermore, the probable social location of Micah himself holds profound implications not only for the analysis of this short work but also for our understanding of the prophetic tradition as a whole with respect to the overall development of the prophetic social critique.

The stern warnings of judgment against both Israel and Judah that open the book, specifically concerning the capital cities of Samaria and Jerusalem, are leveled ostensibly against their shrines and idolatry (Micah 1:5–7; 5:9–14 [10–15]). Yet the call to mourn the disastrous judgment presses the prophet beyond simple idolatry to address a wide range of social and economic practices that incur divine wrath:

> Ah, those who plan iniquity
> And design evil on their beds;
> When morning dawns, they do it,
> For they have the power.
> They covet fields, and seize them;
> Houses, and take them away.
> They defraud men of their homes,
> And people of their land.
>
> Micah 2:1–2

A consistent strain of this short work argues that the powerholders amass their wealth through exploitation. The taking of the clothing of those in need is criticized, calling to mind the laws of the Torah (see chapter 2), though admittedly the Micah reference is itself somewhat obscure (2:8). More clear is the condemnation of the taking of homes from women, presumably widows (2:9). Likewise, corruption in the legal system comes under strict scrutiny (3:9–10; 6–16; 7:2–3). No more harsh a picture of the severity of the exploitation in ancient Israel and Judah has ever been rendered into words than this statement of the prophet:

You have devoured My people's flesh;
You have flayed the skin off them,
And their flesh off their bones.
And after tearing their skins off them,
And their flesh off their bones,
And breaking their bones to bits,
You have cut it up as into a pot,
Like meat in a caldron.
Someday they shall cry out to the LORD,
But He will not answer them;
At that time He will hide His face from them,
In accordance with the wrongs they have done.

Micah 3:3–4

Given the severity of this critique, it is not surprising to find words of opposition leveled against the bearers of the sacred traditions of the land as well, namely, other prophets and the priests. The general picture is presented in this way:

Her rulers judge for gifts,
Her priests give rulings for a fee,
And her prophets divine for pay;
Yet they rely upon the LORD, saying,
"The LORD is in our midst;
No calamity shall overtake us."

Micah 3:11

When the prophet condemns the shrines, anticipates the destruction of the temple, or defines justice as a quality beyond sacrifices, certainly the priests are in view (1:5; 3:12; 6:6–8). However, while priests come under some measure of scrutiny, it is the prophets who receive the most vigorous attack. A frontal assault is launched against prophetic figures who are seen to be presenting false teachings, doing so for pay, and who, because they have been bought off, mislead the people, risking the loss of their prophetic powers (2:11; 3:5–8).

This strident portrait provokes a notice of confrontation between Micah and his opponents:

"Stop preaching!" they preach.
"That's no way to preach;
Shame shall not overtake [us].
Is the House of Jacob condemned?
Is the LORD's patience short?
Is such His practice?"

Micah 2:6–7

This confrontation, whether real or rhetorical, indicates the status of the prophetic voice of Micah and its reception into the tradition: To accept Micah as canonical meant reevaluating the religious and theological experience of the monarchy. The rhetoric of the text is compelled to cast prophets, priests, and rulers in a bad light. On the one hand, this brings a unifying aspect to the book: Both the original prophetic figure and those who preserved the Micah tradition, found varying degrees of value in harnessing images of opposition to the social cry of the prophets against injustice. As we shall see, however, the transmission history of Micah is complex and has ultimately led to a tempering of the original prophetic social critique. In other words, the image of the prophet and his message are adapted to different agendas even as they are "preserved."

Before we turn to a discussion of the editorial stages of the work, some observations about the book's views of judgment and restoration are in order. Specific segments of the judgment/renewal motif are bound together with a message of social injustice. Most notably, the book's famous vision of future renewal is spelled out in terms of economic rectitude and a regathering of the outcast:

> In the days to come,
> The Mount of the LORD's House shall stand
> Firm above the mountains;
> And it shall tower above the hills.
> The peoples shall gaze on it with joy,
> And the many nations shall go and shall say:
> "Come,
> Let us go up to the Mount of the LORD,
> To the House of the God of Jacob;
> That He may instruct us in His ways,
> And that we may walk in His paths."
> For instruction shall come forth from Zion,
> The word of the LORD from Jerusalem.
> Thus He will judge among the many peoples,
> And arbitrate for the multitude of nations,
> However distant;
> And they shall beat their swords into plowshares
> And their spears into pruning hooks.
> Nation shall not take up
> Sword against nation;
> They shall never again know war;
> But every man shall sit
> Under his grapevine or fig tree
> With no one to disturb him.
> For it was the LORD of hosts who spoke.
> Though all the peoples walk
> Each in the names of its gods,

We will walk
In the name of the LORD our God
Forever and ever.

Micah 4:1–5

One of the more unusual passages about judgment/renewal is the *rîb*-law-suit text, where the prophet's covenant lawsuit against the people is predicated on the historical basis that YHWH acted through the exodus for God's people:

Hear what the LORD is saying:
Come, present [My] case before the mountains,
And let the hills hear you pleading.

Hear, you mountains, the case of the LORD—
You firm foundations of the earth!
For the LORD has a case against His people,
He has a suit against Israel.

"My people!
What wrong have I done you?
What hardship have I caused you?
Testify against Me.
In fact,
I brought you up from the land of Egypt,
I redeemed you from the house of bondage,
And I sent before you
Moses, Aaron, and Miriam.

"My people,
Remember what Balak king of Moab
Plotted against you,
And how Balaam son of Beor
Responded to him.
[Recall your passage]
From Shittim to Gilgal—
And you will recognize
The gracious acts of the LORD."

Micah 6:1–5

This act of YHWH in the past created a covenantal obligation for succeeding generations, not, however in conjunction with ritual activity as in the P source but for works of justice, specifically the use of just weights and measures:

With what shall I approach the LORD,
Do homage to God on high?
Shall I approach Him with burnt offerings,
With calves a year old?
Would the LORD be pleased with thousands of rams,

With myriads of streams of oil?
Shall I give my first-born for my transgression,
The fruit of my body for my sins?

"He has told you, O man, what is good,
And what the LORD requires of you:
Only to do justice
And to love goodness,
And to walk modestly with your God;
Then will your name achieve wisdom."

Hark! The LORD
Summons the city:
Hear, O scepter;
For who can direct her but you?
Will I overlook, in the wicked man's house,
The granaries of wickedness
And the accursed short *ephah*?
Shall he be acquitted despite wicked balances
And a bag of fraudulent weights?—
Whose rich men are full of lawlessness,
And whose inhabitants speak treachery,
With tongues of deceit in their mouths.

Micah 6:6–12

The covenantal grounding of Micah 6, together with its call for justice, would seem to situate this chapter squarely within the legal stream of the Torah, with its concern for just weights and measures, though whether the passage is reflective of Deuteronomy or Leviticus could be debated.[100] Blenkinsopp may be right about the immediate motivation of this text:

> It must also be borne in mind that the strain of resentment expressed by Micah and others against the endless round of animal sacrifice (6:6) probably had less to do with liberal religious convictions, as assumed by so many scholars during the nineteenth and early twentieth century, than with the economic burden that the sacrificial system represented for the agrarian class.[101]

Yet it must be understood that the book frames its critique in covenant terms that, while not liberal categories, do provide a perspective from which to measure urban/rural relations.

Blenkinsopp's emphasis on the concrete character of the injustices remind us that, for this passage in Micah, future renewal means the renewal of a covenant that generates a just set of social practices. There is a strong sense, in other words, that a recovery of the e xodus tradition would induce a social embodiment of God's exodus intentions: This view finds its counterpart in modern liberation thinking about the exodus God.[102]

Yet the interpreter cannot ignore the fact that most of the passages concerning judgment and renewal do not have in view either past social injustices or the creation of a just society. Rather, we find the bulk of these texts caught up in one way or another with the exile and the restoration of the Judaean monarchy (Micah 4:8, 9–13; 5:1–5 [2–6]; 7:8–20). Even among these texts there are significant subdivisions. While we find a simple anticipation of a future ruler (4:8; 5:1–3 [2–4]), we also find liberation from Assyrian and Babylonian rule (4:9–13; 5:4–5 [5–6]). Freedom from Assyria involves multiple rulers and not one single monarch, a conception that seems to have arisen in the struggles of the postexile period. Portraits of renewal in Micah, therefore, have been heavily shaped by the tendencies and trends of the postexilic age (7:8–19), to be stamped ultimately with the imprimatur of Abraham and Jacob at the very end of the book (7:20). The patriarchal figures demarcate the final reception of the book into the postprophetic canon of the larger set of traditions found in Genesis–Kings, traditions unimportant to the inception and initial shaping of the book.

Having noted tangentially the presence of pre- and postexilic phases to the book, we must now turn to examine the extent to which this transmission history affected the social justice message of the book. Drawing on Coote's work on the layering of Amos, I. Mosala, a South African liberation proponent, has dissected the book of Micah, unearthing its editorial layers a la Coote, but also exposing the ideological and class categories that govern the distinct layers.[103] For Mosala, the initial layer of Micah, the level A texts, are those passages which are "specific about the class of people A addresses."[104] In other words, agents in society are named and charged with concrete social injustices in a harsh indictment of the social practices of the ruling elite:

> Ah, those who plan iniquity
> And design evil on their beds;
> When morning dawns, they do it,
> For they have the power.
> They covet fields, and seize them;
> Houses, and take them away.
> They defraud men of their homes,
> And people of their land.

> Assuredly, thus said the LORD: I am planning such a misfortune against this clan that you will not be able to free your necks from it. You will not be able to walk erect; it will be such a time of disaster. (Micah 2:1–3)

By contrast, Mosala's B level texts, which form the subsequent layer, tend to speak in more generalized terms about actors or agents of injustice and even about the topic of justice itself:

Woe is me!
I am become like leavings of a fig harvest,
Like gleanings when the vintage is over,
There is not a cluster to eat,
Not a ripe fig I could desire.
The pious are vanished from the land,
None upright are left among men;
All lie in wait to commit crimes,
One traps the other in his net.
They are eager to do evil:
The magistrate makes demands,
And the judge [judges] for a fee;
The rich man makes his crooked plea,
And they grant it.
The best of them is like a prickly shrub;
The [most] upright, worse than a barrier of thorns.
On the day you waited for, your doom has come—
Now their confusion shall come to pass.
Trust no friend,
Rely on no intimate;
Be guarded in speech
With her who lies in your bosom.

                              (Micah 7:1–5)[105]

Mosala sees in this layer evidence of an ideological posture that represents a "historically marginal but spiritually central class position."[106] Specifically, he treats the open-ended call for justice in B level texts as "largely the product of a scribe or scribes who are at the service of the ruling elite."[107] Mosala identifies the key weakness of B level texts when he writes,

> They are eloquent by their silence on the struggles of the poor and exploited peasants in the Israelite monarchy. Although these oracles condemn evil and injustice and exhort people to good and justice, they do not name the actual actions of oppressors, except vaguely, and the resistance of the oppressed is present only by its absence.[108]

Given his typology, we shall not be surprised to find Mosala's C layer texts, the final adaptations, to be even more detached from the concrete situation of the poor.[109]

Though all the peoples walk
Each in the names of its gods,
We will walk
In the name of the LORD our God
Forever and ever.
In that day
            —declares the LORD—

I will assemble the lame [sheep]
And will gather the outcast
And those I have treated harshly;
And I will turn the lame into a remnant
And the expelled into a populous nation.
And the LORD will reign over them on Mount Zion
Now and for evermore.

And you, O Migdal-eder,
Outpost of Fair Zion,
It shall come to you:
The former monarchy shall return—
The kingship of Fair Jerusalem.

Now why do you utter such cries?
Is there no king in you,
Have your advisors perished,
That you have been seized by writhing
Like a woman in travail?
Writhe and scream, Fair Zion,
Like a woman in travail!
For now you must leave the city
And dwell in the country—
And you will reach Babylon.
There you shall be saved,
There the LORD will redeem you
From the hands of your foes.
Indeed, many nations
Have assembled against you
Who think, "Let our eye
Obscenely gaze on Zion."
But they do not know
The design of the LORD,
They do not divine His intent:
He has gathered them
Like cut grain to the threshing floor.
Up and thresh, Fair Zion!
For I will give you horns of iron
And provide you with hoofs of bronze,
And you will crush the many peoples.
You will devote their riches to the LORD,
Their wealth to the LORD of all the earth.

                                        Micah 4:5–13

Since this editorial layer is a result of the Babylonian exile and the postexilic reconstruction process, we find a curious ideological reversal of the A level texts. Where once the prophet of old cried out from the midst of the situation of the concrete exploitation of the poor by the ruling elite, by twists and turns the C level presents the former elite as the truly exploited!

The former oppressors of peasants and casual laborers and underclasses in Judah are now seeing themselves as the oppressed in relation
to their captors. More importantly, they rewrite the traditions of
struggle of ancient Israel to apply to their situation. Thus, instead of
the rich and the powerful, it is the nations and the pagans who become
targets of Yahweh's judgment. [110]

As the "exploited," the elite develops a theology built around the triumph
of David and Zion, melded in a transformed way with the older prophetic outcry against injustice. As we have seen, this process governs other prophetic
texts, most strikingly the final shaping of Isaiah. To find the elite appropriating the ancient critique against them is an irony of the transmission process
and Mosala is absolutely correct to observe that the ideological distortions
between layers inevitably complicate modern efforts at a liberation appropriation of an entire biblical text such as Micah, Amos, or Isaiah.

Nevertheless, we should not minimize the harsh reality of the exilic experience. The destruction of the elite through exile would have been a devastating experience, and we owe the preservation of the biblical texts to this crowd
who saw in their own dislocation a kinship with the lot of the poor during the
time of the Israelite and Judaean monarchies. While it may be true, as Mosala
argues, that the C layer promotes a postexilic project of domination and control, it may also be the case that the nationalist recovery program could have
worked by means of a reconciliation of social actors, poor and elite, as they
engaged in a common struggle to create a "state," to define and preserve a cultural heritage in the face of Babylonian and Persian assimilation. [111]

Having identified an A layer to Micah, can we locate this speaker in the context of the eighth century B.C.E., the date to which such material is generally
set by most scholars? If so, what is the social location of the prophet? What
are his origins and his agenda? Is he an isolated figure or does he represent a
particular group, specific class interests, or segment of the tradition?

We have already discussed the land and labor context of the eighth century
B.C.E. in relation to Amos. It is clear that Mosala's A layer texts speak unam-
biguously about the downside of the economic and political developments in
the post-Omri/Ahab century. Yet Mosala keenly observes that even the A layer,
while "radical" to an extent, is not "revolutionary." [112] To posit that a "fundamental disruption of the status quo" as "the only solution to the violence and
corruption of the ruling classes" is not, however, to call to take up arms against
the ruling elite. [113] We know that at least as far back as the Amarna letters, such
civil unrest was possible in Canaan.[114] Yet for the prophet to give over the
action to YHWH would seem to fall far short of a revolutionary program. In
a sense, we may have in this reading a confirmation of the suggestion by H. W.
Wolff that the prophet Micah was an "elder" of the small town of Moresheth,

a location that was ever alert to the encroachment of the royal house insofar as "the Judaean kings maintained five fortress cities within a radius of less than six miles about Moresheth."[115] As an elder, Micah takes up the defense of the peasantry, standing in opposition to the greed and expansionism of the capital city and its inhabitants. This figure's proclamation is powerful but ineffectual in terms of actual implementation.

Curiously, as the prophet frames his advocacy, he does not do so in precisely the terms of Amos or other prophetic writings. The standard Hebrew terms for "poor" used regularly in the prophetic literature, namely, 'ĕbyôn, dal and ănî/'ănāwîm, never find a place in Micah's diction. Rather, the prophet speaks of "my people" (2:9; 3:3). Wolff is probably correct to suggest that Micah "has in mind the 'man' capable of military service (gbr), the 'citizen' who possesses full legal right and obligations ('yš), whose rights and freedoms have been violated."[116]

Thus, while there is overlap in terms of content between Amos and Micah, differences in language regarding poverty and in specific views about the socioeconomic situation of that time serve to undermine the idea that there was a singular prophetic tradition about social justice. Unlike Amos, who is bedecked with prophetic calls and visions, the Micah of the A layer would seem to have been a town elder and poet driven by the political and social circumstances of the time to defend the cause of the residents of the countryside, both villagers and farmers.[117] Comparisons with Amos or any other prophetic text ought not to obscure the uniqueness of this little book among the Twelve.

Nahum: Taunting the Tyrants

The taunt song of Nahum comprises a rather brief but significant set of oracles that celebrate the triumph over the Assyrians by YHWH, who takes the form of El Qanoh and Noqem, "God of Passion and Vengeance," and Baal Hemah, "Lord Wrath" (Nahum 1:2). Historically, the Assyrian empire fell to Cyaxares of Persia and Nabopolassar of Babylon in 612 B.C.E. Theologically, the empire fell, according to Nahum, to the God of Israel, whose exercise of cosmic power brings tyrants to their knees. It becomes the task of the prophet to articulate these developments in light of the received liturgical and theological traditions of the community.

Whether or not these oracles have their specific roots or location inside the Israelite cultus remains the disputed question among scholars.[118] Nevertheless, the complete book would appear to represent the historicization of mythic themes that would have once been thoroughly at home in the Canaanite royal cultus. Presumably these themes remained central to the preexilic cultus of the Judaean monarchy. The mythic component is supplied by chap. 1, where

YHWH, who "takes vengeance on His enemies," is displayed in martial splendor. The opening verses of this chapter do not immediately tie in to a specific portrayal of Assyria. Rather, we find in vv. 2–10 a depiction of YHWH as the avenging God, who, like Baal in his conquest of the sea god Yam, "rebukes the sea and dries it up," and "makes all rivers fail" (1:4).[119] These words are embedded in an acrostic poem that reads like an ancient mythic epic text. Yet the tendency in ancient Israel was for these mythic complexes to be more overtly historicized in relation to foreign powers than their Canaanite or Mesopotamian counterparts. In the case of Exodus 15, for example, the figure is Pharaoh. For the Nahum compiler, Assyria becomes the object of mythic deconstruction. Nevertheless, we should be aware that the prophetic speaker appears to be thoroughly at home in the mythic liturgical milieu and that language shapes the prophet's response to the Assyrian crisis.

The historicization element is provided concretely by the rest of the book, where the brutal onslaught against Assyria is depicted in vivid, eyewitness-like terms. Such historicization was spurred on by the larger prophetic tradition of oracles against the nations, texts that celebrate the demise of specific worldly foes of God and Israel (noted above under Obadiah). In part, Nahum represents one example of this type of prophetic utterance. Yet with its explicit invocation of the Canaanite mythic tradition, perhaps via the Jerusalem cultus, the book of Nahum, in its final form, comprises a unique amalgam of historicized myth and oracular materials. In other words, the response of Nahum to the Assyrian crisis answers simultaneously to the temple and prophetic traditions. If the cultus is an active social location of this prophet, then every effort is being made to articulate a timely prophetic rhetoric about empires within that context. Of course, we cannot rule out the possibility that Israel's cultus itself adapted the mythic traditions of Canaan to celebrate and endorse the palace's posturing militarily over against the rival superpowers. The mythic collapse of Pharaoh must have been very old in the monarch's liturgical repertoire by the time of Nahum. As such, the prophet may have been the oracular speaker on liturgical occasions that were devoted to this theme. One need not go so far as to restrict this event to a New Year's festival, and yet the paradigmatic Babylonian New Year's Festival, with its celebration of Marduk's celestial triumph over his foes, must certainly have carried a clear political message for its Babylonian celebrants.[120] If such a liturgical tradition existed, and the Psalms would seem to give evidence of such a tradition (see chapter 10), then Nahum more specifically represents the voice of the moment that articulates the nation's crisis in terms of the long-standing view that Israel's God is to be celebrated as the God who defeats Israel's adversaries.

There is no mistaking the justice message of Nahum. The empire of the Assyrians is depicted as a lion who has fallen (2:12–13 [11–12]). Specifically,

Assyria is brought low for its "killings" (*trp*, literally "prey") and for having been a "city of crime [*dāmîm*, literally "blood, murder"], utterly treacherous, full of violence, where killing [*trp*] never stops" (2:14 [13]; 3:1). The nation's imperialism is likened to "harlotries" and Assyria's reversal is viewed as "shame" (*qālôn*), invoking blatant sexual terminology akin to Hosea (3:4–6; on Hosea see above). The devastation Assyria experiences extends from its children to its nobles and troops (3:10–13). The book makes a point of mentioning Assyria's forts, traders, and shepherds, both as a way to indicate its wealth as well as to demonstrate the staggering price of its fall before the God of vengeance (3:12, 16–18).

Curiously, the book of Nahum would seem to stand as a prophetic answer to the Book of Jonah. While this is the opposite order in which they were composed (Nahum is certainly far older), nevertheless, both works touch on the themes of God's forbearance in the face of evil (Nahum 1:3; Jonah 4:2). Whereas the writer of Jonah holds out hope of imperial redemption through Jewish presence, when set side by side with Nahum, it is clear that Jonah represents a decisive departure from the prophetic viewpoint, presented so forcefully in Nahum, that the God of vengeance "does not remit all punishment" (Nahum 1:3). Nahum stands poles apart from Jonah on this score. In actuality, Nahum pushes forward the theology found also in Habakkuk and other prophetic texts that God's justice is a universal reality only in the sense that God's action in the world leads to the universal judgment of injustice. There is no room for compromise in this prophetic voice. Nahum is not cowed into theological submission as Jonah is. Certainly if Nahum is a cultic voice, his influence would have functioned to shore up the tendencies toward rebellion against the imperial powers that ultimately brought down the Judaean royal house, as it sought in one way or another to maneuver in opposition to Egypt and Babylon. That later Persian-Hellenistic writings such as Jonah adopt a very different course is not surprising, in particular where the question of communal survival in an imperial structure became a pressing concern.

For long-term survival, the prophetic voice of resistance may not always have been the better path. On the other hand, since foreign intervention persisted long after Nahum's time, it is also not surprising to find the book of Nahum providing insights into ruthless political power amid the documents of Qumran.[121] The second century B.C.E brought forward a successful application of the motif of the God of vengeance in the form of the Hasmonaean rebellion. By virtually juxtaposing Nahum and Jonah in the canon, however, the overall tradition reminds us that no single theological response to imperialism is possible. When national survival and the question of justice constitute the matter at hand, the thoughtful observer of history will need to show discretion regarding which side of the tradition to invoke in that particular historical moment.

Habakkuk: Shaking the Pillars of the Empire

The work of Habakkuk is generally set on the eve of Judah's conquest by the Babylonians, although the precise dating of the work depends in large part on the acceptance of the originality of the reference to the Babylonians, *kasdîm*, found in Hab. 1:6.[122] It is probably safe to place the work around 600 B.C.E. The precise connection between the oracles in the first two chapters of the book and the hymn in chap. 3 is vigorously disputed by scholars. While they are clearly two separate compositions, they probably stem from the same prophetic figure. The texts are treated together here because themes of justice and judgment bind these materials.

From the outset Habakkuk's concern is about national injustice: "How long, O LORD, shall I cry out and You not listen, shall I shout to You 'Violence!' and You not save?" (1:2). The prophet searches for YHWH's judgment against the evils perpetrated by his own people and fails to grasp any purpose in YHWH's silence: "Why do You make me see iniquity[?] [Why] do You look upon wrong?" (1:3). The prophet had seen enough. To him there was no justification for permitting further domestic strife and oppression, and there was no reason to delay judging the nation. Habakkuk waits for YHWH's reply. At long last the silence is shattered by a word of judgment. YHWH reassures Habakkuk that this ill-fated chapter of Judah's history is about to close:

> "Look among the nations,
> Observe well and be utterly astounded;
> For a work is being wrought in your days
> Which you would not believe if it were told
> For lo, I am raising up the Chaldeans
> That fierce, impetuous nation."
>
> Hab. 1:5–6a

And then the prophet is given a description of the horrible machinery of Babylonian domination, the conquering army (1:6–11). Yet the atrocities of the conqueror grieve the prophet as much as, if not more than, the injustices found among the prophet's people (1:12-17). Then, in a series of five woe pronouncements, the prophet condemns the manifold injustices that go into building an empire: plunder and bloodshed (2:6–8); unjust gain and plotting the ruin of others (2:9–11); murder, crime, and worthless endeavors (2:12–14); deception and violence (2:15–17); and image worship (2:18–20).

In the hymn found in chap. 3, which follows these reflections on national and international injustice, the prophet weathers a crisis period in the nation's history, still waiting for YHWH's deliverance (3:2, 16–18). It is difficult to decide from the text if the prophet intends to portray YHWH's warring as directed against Judah (e.g., by means of the Babylonian army raised up by YHWH to judge the people of Judah) or against the nation that YHWH used to judge Judah (e.g., the routing of the Babylonian army or even the fall of the Babylonian empire.) Perhaps the prophet intends to convey to those who hear the prophet's word that though the nation of Judah is under attack, still YHWH would not allow the fierceness of war to go unchecked. In any case, reference to 'ānî, "oppressed," is made in the context of the activity of the army, which opposes the people of Judah. The warriors were those "whose delight is to crush me suddenly, to devour a poor man ['ānî] in an ambush" (3:14b). Besieged and in hiding, the situation of the 'ānî (possibly a self-designation of the prophet, but more likely a reference to the entire people of Judah) is one of utter distress. But YHWH's action brings about the release of the 'ānî from these desperate straits: "You will crack [his] skull with Your bludgeon; blown away shall be his warriors" (3:14a).

chap. 3 may reflect an ancient mythic tradition that depicts YHWH as the divine warrior who struggles against primordial chaos. But in the hands of the prophet, the subject matter is the concrete historical experience of Judah's struggle with Babylon; the victory over chaos becomes the release of the 'ānî from the anguish of battle. In the context of the entire book, the prophet's message rings out loud and clear: Israel's God shakes the pillars of empire.

Zephaniah: A Triptych of Judgment

The few words of hope offered to the poor in Zephaniah arise as slivers of light in a sea of darkness. The dominant motif of Zephaniah is that of judgment, against Judah and against the nations. If, however, we can gain a sense of the context of Zephaniah's words to the oppressed, we will find in this work significant insights concerning social ethics in the prophetic writings.

Set in the reign of Josiah by the book's Deuteronomic handlers, these oracles anticipate an invasion of judgment, on the order of the Assyrian and Babylonian incursions into the region. With God as the warrior who will "sweep everything away from the face of the earth" (Zeph. 1:2), the first target in Zephaniah is Judah and Jerusalem (1:4a; cf. 3:1). The judgment here is twofold, akin to the perspective of Jeremiah against both idolatry (1:4b–15) and the luxuriant, presumably exploitative, lifestyle of the elite (1:12–14; cf. 1–18).

Likewise, the naming of concrete social actors and institutions is central to the text: officials and the king's sons (1:8; cf. 3:3), the palace (1:9), traders and merchants (1:11), judges, prophets, and priests (3:3–4). In this sense, Zephaniah adopts the tone of early Jeremiah or the A layer of Micah, offering, in other words, a clear social critique that frames its message as a blistering attack on the social elite. The day of YHWH's judgment against this populace is as stark as anything in the book of Joel (1:14–18). Yet, whereas Joel serves a mediating function between the prophetic and priestly groups, Zephaniah shows no such social location or rhetorical orientation.

Zephaniah is a veritable triptych of judgment. Where chaps. 1 and 3 are devoted to Judah and Jerusalem, chap. 2 opens out to threaten the surrounding powers. These oracles against the nations present in miniature form the same themes and motifs known to us elsewhere in the prophetic literature. God's judgment extends to the Philistine cities, though the crimes are never specified (2:4–6). Likewise, Ammon and Moab are judged, but here there is some specification of their wrongdoing, namely, insulting Judah, presumably a reference to Judah's weakness during the Babylonian invasions (2:8–11; cf. Obadiah). Farther flung are the references to Cush (2:12) and Assyria (2:13–14), the latter due to its imperial arrogance (2:15). Yet these pronouncements of judgment are not designed as news notices to the powers so much as words of consolation to Judah. In the announcement of Judah's future plundering of its enemies (2:7, 9–10), the process of reconstruction after the invasion or exile has begun. This sentiment is shared with Second Isaiah.

Thus, along with warnings of judgment, the prophet does hold out hope for the oppressed. In the book of Zephaniah, this hope takes the form of a call to abide in the ways of YHWH: "Seek righteousness, seek humility ['ănawâ]. Perhaps you will find shelter on the day of the LORD's anger" (2:3). The call, interestingly enough, goes out to the "humble of the land," the 'anwê hā'āreṣ, those who carry out YHWH's commands (mišpaṭô; 2:3). Clearly the term 'ănāwîm in this case bears a religious sensibility. Even the mention of 'ānî and dal in Zephaniah tends toward a spiritual connotation, for the people so designated are further defined as those who will "find refuge in the name of the LORD" (3:12). Yet humility in this sense is not divorced from economic realities, rather "humility is the state of the poor and afflicted . . . , whose situation is one in which they must acknowledge their own helplessness and utter dependence upon God."[123] In turn, God becomes the champion of the oppressed.

It would seem, however, that in the hands of its later handlers, the oracles of judgment are transmuted to some extent by the interpretational displacement found in a more detailed form in Second Isaiah and Micah, namely, that the elite, humbled by exile, will reemerge triumphant to plunder the spoils of the enemy. In part, this theme builds upon the more ancient prophetic idea that a remnant will survive the judgment (2:1–3; 3:8–13), an idea found elsewhere in the Mesopotamian epic of Ezra.[124] That a remnant would survive was undoubtedly a fact of ancient life in many postwar situations. Where the biblical tradition strikes a new chord is in having the displaced elite become the "poor," who, having been humbled, have earned the theological right to triumph over the enemy in the name of God:

In that day,
This shall be said to Jersusalem:
Have no fear, O Zion;
Let not your hands droop!
Your God the LORD is in your midst,
A warrior who brings triumph.
He will rejoice over you and be glad,
He will shout over you with jubilation.
He will soothe with His love
Those long disconsolate.
I will take away from you the woe
Over which you endured mockery.
At that time I will make [an end]
Of all who afflicted you.
And I will rescue the lame [sheep]
And gather the strayed;
And I will exchange their disgrace
For fame and renown in all the earth.
At that time I will gather you,
And at [that] time I will bring you [home];
For I will make you renowned and famous
Among all the peoples on earth,
When I restore your fortunes
Before your very eyes
                    —said the LORD (3:16–20)

In this passage, so transparently replete with postexilic ideas, we find traces of a profound shift in the handling of the prophetic tradition. The very elite that once was critiqued by Zephaniah has commandeered the oracles to shore up its own claims to power. This layer of the book of Zephaniah is equivalent to Mosala's C layer identified in Micah (see above), where the specific language about social actors and injustices becomes tempered and vague. This layering is remarkable insofar as it does not entirely obliterate the received prophetic words. In their starkness, the prophet's social critique must have carried weight. Then again, we will want to be careful not to treat this elite as being entirely disingenuous with regard to the tradition, for their uprooting was doubtless a horrific experience. In that sense, then, we can learn much theologically from the text's history of transmission and development. The transmission history attests to the vital character of the prophet's words even as its exegesis draws out a revised signification for later social and political circumstances.

It will remain for others, such as Haggai, Zechariah, Ezra, and Nehemiah, to point in very different ways toward new directions for the tradition, ensuring thereby the tradition's successful venture into an uncharted future. Yet

Zephaniah, like Second Isaiah and the later layers of Micah, has taken major steps in the reconstruction scenario.

Haggai: Overturned Kingdoms and Fallen Soldiers

Though brief, the book of Haggai opens up several key considerations regarding the political and ideological developments in ancient Israelite thought for the period between Cyrus's taking of Babylon and the later reform efforts of Nehemiah, Ezra, and their congeners. In fact, were it not for works such as Haggai and Zechariah, we should be terribly uninformed, or rather misinformed, concerning the tumultuous first decades after the return from exile. The book of Ezra's attempt to marshal the "original documents" issued by the Persian rulers serves to expunge from the record the vying for position that took place among prophets, governors, and priests during the early period, as evidenced plainly by Haggai and Zechariah. Undoubtedly, it would not have served the interests of the writers and compilers of Ezra and Nehemiah to remind their overlords about this interim period with its prophetic enthusiasms and political ferment.

To be sure, Haggai shares with Ezra and Nehemiah the perspective that the initial reconstruction phase after the exile was slow and ineffectual, in particular with respect to the rebuilding of the temple. Haggai capitalizes on this delay to insert a prophetic critique against the establishment. This critique, while directed at members of the elite, is not a social critique on the order of an Amos or a Micah, where social injustice is under scrutiny, a critique also found in the earliest phase of the Nehemiah text (see chap. 5). Rather, Haggai's critique reflects the oldest sort of prophetic pronouncement known to us from the Mari texts. In such a pronouncement, the prophet arises to defend the honor and interests of the local deity before a neglectful king.[125] Echoing a theme found in Hosea, the prophet contends that the failure to attend to the nation's God has left the entire community in relative poverty:

> Now thus said the LORD of Hosts: Consider how you have been faring! You have sowed much and brought in little; you eat without being satisfied; you drink without getting your fill; you clothe yourselves, but no one gets warm; and he who earns anything earns it for a leaky purse. (Hag. 1:5–6)

Specifically, their failure to rebuild the temple of YHWH has led, so the prophet contends, to drought and famine (1:10–11). This linkage between the god's possession of a house (temple) and recovery from drought are old themes in Canaanite religion, as attested by the texts from Ugarit, where Baal's successes and failures against the sea god and with his acquisition of a house serve as grist for the mythic mill.[126] Yet, rather than construct a myth of divine triumph (as at Ugarit) or even a liturgical process for mourning (as in Joel), Haggai channels these ideological energies into a political calling to account of the governor (Zerubbabel), the high priest (Joshua), and the people (1:12).

Much as in the E source, the people begin to fear YHWH (1:12). Likewise, Haggai also reflects E's caution with regard to the priesthood. We may surmise that E and Haggai overlap somewhat in terms of political tendencies and relative positioning in relation to the main reconstruction efforts, namely, that both are outsiders to the overall process.[127] The priests are necessarily consulted for a ritual determination (2:12–13). They are, after all, central to the power distribution in the postexilic community. But from the point of view of the text, the consultation of the priests is rhetorically designed to accent the prophet's apocalyptic-styled announcement of a future splendor that goes far beyond the achievements, however real, of the current politicos (2:6–9, 14–19). In other words, for the writer of Haggai, only prophetic intervention could ensure religious stability and domestic prosperity, a view shared with E.

This link with E is not surprising insofar as Haggai offers a covenant renewal formula as the basis of a successful reconstruction effort. The exodus experience is invoked directly: "For I am with you—says the LORD of Hosts. So I promised you when you came out of Egypt, and My spirit is still in your midst. Fear not!" (2:4b–5). Here "fear" and the exodus are the twin pillars of Haggai's program, as in E. Likewise, the plundering of Egypt motif, known from E's cycle in Exodus, runs parallel to Haggai's view that the nations shall be shaken to release tribute to Israel, specifically, for both silver and gold (2:6–9; cf. Ex. 12:35–36). While this shaking undoubtedly feeds into later developments in apocalyptic thought, this image is actually derived from exodus traditions where Pharaoh's army is overturned and defeated by an act of God, an image universalized at the end of Haggai (2:21–22; Exodus 15). In a sense, the book of Haggai assists us greatly in contextualizing the covenantal, theological, and political perspectives dominant in the E source. We find the prophet decisively in support of a particular political figure, namely, the governor Zerubbabel, just as E supports Moses, and detracting from the priests, much as E turns the tables on Aaron and sons. E is certainly a prophetic viewpoint with an overt political purpose, bearing a kindred spirit to Haggai and Zechariah 1—8.

Unfortunately, Zerubbabel disappears from history without a trace, and we may suspect that the messianic fervor expressed in Haggai and Zechariah (Hag. 2:23) led to the sorts of periodic rebellions—such as the rebellions in Babylon, Elam, Egypt, Ionia, and elsewhere—that the Persian ruler Darius I found so necessary to put down.[128] The Persian rulers adopted a largely collaborative policy, which meant that they saw fit to work as much as possible with the existing dominant families. However, it is apparent that they were more careful later when selecting figures such as Nehemiah and Ezra (to the extent that these are historical personages), who worked more firmly within Persian parameters. The overall tendency of the book of Haggai, however, makes us very much aware that during the initial restoration period more militant voices were at work laying claim to the Yahwistic traditions than Ezra and Nehemiah would have us believe. Such voices as E and Haggai may have stirred up the political cauldron a bit, though E's message of reconciliation with Edom surely played to a different crowd than Obadiah's denunciation of the same. In any case, Haggai and E's wranglings with the priesthood only make us more aware that in the early period of the restoration, the priesthood was, politically speaking, the more dominant social actor. Ironically, perhaps, the priestly trajectory could make room for self-critique, and it found a way to incorporate perspectives such as E's and Haggai's into the final shaping of the canon of scripture. A commonwealth might not be able to be built on fear and covenant alone, but the final priestly compilers of the canon recognized the strength of being able to incorporate diverse perspectives as a way to build that commonwealth, so long as the priestly group remained the dominant voice. Laws and rulings are needed, as even Haggai tacitly acknowledges (2:12–13).

The times, however, required an Ezra, not a Zerubbabel, if the tradition was going to have any hope of survival (see chapter 5). One might look for the temporary overturning of the enemies as do Haggai and later Esther. Yet the reality would soon set in that appeals to the conqueror might be the only way to completely restore the temple and the city of Jerusalem. It is this unsettling compromise that leaves its tense mark on the final compilation of scripture, indelibly marking biblical social thought with both centripetal and centrifugal tendencies, as Ateek has so keenly observed.[129]

Zechariah: A Tradition for Seeking Justice

As with many of the prophetic books, Zechariah has undergone a series of developments that provide us with a clear example of a tradition in the making. What is unusual about the work, however, is its rather self-conscious character with respect to these developments. Particularly important for our analysis of biblical social ethics are the ways in which this book overtly constructs a prophetic tradition about justice matters in order to update that tradition for the issues of the writer's day. Zechariah, in other words, is truly a shining example of a tradition seeking to elaborate the justice question. The book's development appears to follow several distinct phases, with the composition of the oracles in chaps. 1—8 and their redaction with Haggai preceding the composition and addition of chaps. 9—14. The dating of these materials and possible subdevelopments has been the subject of much discussion, but, broadly speaking, the Persian period would seem to be in view, both at its beginning and throughout the time of Persian domination.

Zechariah 1—8: The Prophetic Message of Justice

Zechariah 1—8 represents a conscious readaptation of the prophetic tradition. Unfortunately for the modern interpreter, these chapters reveal complexities that are difficult to unravel insofar as this segment exhibits not only different layers but different understandings of prophecy.

Chapter 1 immediately throws open the question by focusing on the notion of divine wrath and on a call for repentance, and not, initially, on a message of social justice as such (1:1–16; cf. 6:15). As an adaptation of the idea of prophecy, the writer of chap. 1 finds need to invoke a reduced form of the prophetic tradition. In this emphasis, chaps. 1—6 are predicated on a Deuteronomic view of prophecy. This framing of the prophetic message is in contrast to Haggai's consistent call to "fear God," a factor that is shared only with Zechariah 8. One might presume that this chapter was framed to tie in to Haggai's program. However, the handlers of chaps. 1—6 wished to stamp the amalgam with a more distinctively Deuteronomic view.

Nonetheless, the writer/compiler of Zechariah 1—8 shares with Haggai a keen interest in the temple rebuilding process (an interest comparable to DH's focus on the Solomonic temple). God's energetic activities on behalf of Judah and Jerusalem are evident in the book. Yet even here there are differences. Whereas Haggai faulted the high leadership and the people for the delay in building the temple, Zechariah sees the fault lying with the nations who "overdid the punishment against Israel" (Zech. 1:15). Thus, Zechariah can be even more enthusiastic than Haggai in endorsing Zerubbabel's leadership, for divine protections surround the exiles' return and Zerubbabel's time in power (2:8, 15–17 [4, 11–13]). Jerusalem's prosperity is assured, with the locale booming as a "city without walls" (2:8b [4]) and with God dwelling triumphant in the people's midst (2:14–17 [10–13]).

We note also the same sort of ambivalence to priestly authority in Zechariah 1—8 that we sensed in Haggai.[130] Rhetorically, we find the writer trying to carve a place for a rejuvenated prophetic voice in the restoration community. In the case of Zechariah, the high priest Joshua needs to have his "filthy garments" of guilt removed and replaced with attire suited to the dignity of his office (3:4–5). This figure is exhorted to follow the Deuteronomic proviso:

> And the angel of the LORD charged Joshua as follows: "Thus said the LORD of Hosts: If you walk in My paths and keep My charge, you in

turn will rule My House and guard My courts, and I will permit you to move about among these attendants. Hearken well, O High Priest Joshua, you and your fellow priests sitting before you! For those men are a sign that I am going to bring My servant the Branch. (Zech. 3:6–8)

In this way, the high priest is readied by prophetic intervention to stand beside the "Branch," the divinely chosen earthly sovereign, namely, Zerubbabel. Acknowledging the old prophetic message of anger, the framework of fear adopted by Haggai was not sufficient to the writer of Zechariah 1—6, who seeks a more active prophetic endorsement of the commonwealth's political and religious leadership, a tendency displayed by the DH in similar tales concerning Elijah and Elisha's political involvements (see chapter 3). Thus, in heavily symbolic language, the prophet dresses Zerubbabel's administration with the power of God's spirit:

This is the word of the LORD to Zerubbabel: Not by might, nor by power, but by My spirit—said the LORD of Hosts. Whoever you are, O great mountain in the path of Zerubbabel, turn into level ground! For he shall produce that excellent stone; it shall be greeted with shouts of "Beautiful! Beautiful!" (Zech. 4:6b–7)

The visible sign of Zerubbabel's success is, of course, his completion of the rebuilding of the temple (4:9). The writer's social vision, in other words, offers a coordinated triangulation between prophetic endorsement, priestly cooperation, and, most importantly, royal presence (6:9–15; 8:9). Given the Deuteronomic orientation of the prophetic message in chaps. 1—6, one might be surprised at the portrait of the message ascribed to the earlier prophets in chap. 7. Here in a nutshell is the classic social justice message of the canonical prophets:

And the word of the LORD to Zechariah continued: Thus said the LORD of Hosts: Execute true justice; deal loyally and compassionately with one another. Do not defraud the widow, the orphan, the stranger, and the poor; and do not plot evil against one another—But they refused to pay heed. They presented a balky back and turned a deaf ear. They hardened their hearts like adamant against heeding the instruction and admonition that the LORD of Hosts sent to them by His spirit through the earlier prophets; and a terrible wrath issued from the LORD of Hosts. Even as He called and they would not listen, "So," said the LORD of Hosts, "let them call and I will not listen." I dispersed them among all those nations which they had not known, and the land was left behind them desolate, without any who came and went. They caused a delightful land to be turned into a desolation. (Zech. 7:8–14)

While the message is placed in Deuteronomic packaging, the contents are remarkably akin to the messages that we have seen ascribed to the earlier Amos, the earlier Jeremiah, and the A layer of Micah, texts which also undergo a Deuteronomic adjustment. That is to say, the Deuteronomic view of prophecy and ethics, even though it went in its own direction concerning political power and justice, still found it rhetorically and ideologically useful to preserve the earlier prophetic tradition even as it expanded that tradition. In the case of the larger context of chap. 7, the writer finds it useful to invoke the prophetic tradition, a construct that the Deuteronomist has in fact created, to counter the claims of the regnant priesthood concerning the people's fasting (7:7). In this stance, we discover the Deuteronomic handler's view that the prophetic tradition be treated as a fixed entity that can be referenced and reinterpreted to speak to later questions and issues. In so doing, the writer/compiler of chap. 7 treats the earlier prophetic oracles as a tradition or heritage with a message of judgment for injustice that critiques liturgical practices and hence priestly structures, but apparently not contemporary social injustices. This is a rather ironic side to the development of the so-called prophetic tradition, but it is one that canonical interpreters must confront as they try to bring all sides of the tradition, diachronic as well as synchronic, into contemporary discussions of theological issues.[131]

The vividness of Zechariah's restatement of the prophetic message speaks volumes about the currents unleashed in the postexilic period. In Zechariah, we find a voice that is coming to terms with the Deuteronomic critique of the monarchy on the one hand, and the prophetic message of justice on the other. This twofold dynamic does not arise out of a simple nostalgia for Israel's lost political glories. It is true that in claiming Zerubbabel as the "Branch," the writer is making an obvious invocation of the Davidic royal line. Nevertheless, the work of the writer/compiler of Zechariah is part of a creative effort that leans on the rhetorical power of prophetic language as the text pits the past against Judah's uncertain political future. Most sectors of the literary tradition have come to be stamped by this theological trajectory.

These creative processes are at work likewise in chap. 8, which takes the prophetic justice message much further, linking it to the temple reconstruction program, the flourishing of Jerusalem, the growth of the land's crops, and the flocking of the nations to Jerusalem. Chapter 8 represents the most advanced stage of the 1—8 chapter complex. This chapter has taken over Haggai's use of the term "fear" (8:13, 15), but ultimately predicates the forward movement of the reconstruction era on the basis of heeding the message of the prophets, although in the more tempered Deuteronomic tones of a generalized call for justice, typical of the B layer identified in the Micah text (see above). In the broader view, the currents behind the E source and Haggai are giving way to and are being subsumed by those of the DH.

Zechariah 9—14: No More Oppression!

The apocalyptic voice, more familiar perhaps from the later sections of Daniel and works outside the Hebrew canon, is a boldly militant voice.[132] Whereas Zechariah 1—8 envisions the internal machinery needed for a divinely sanctioned governance, Zechariah 9—14 anticipates the trouncing of Judah's enemies as the ferocity of the invasion of Judah turns against the perpetrators themselves. This militant voice, with a vision that is eschatological though hardly otherworldly, becomes increasingly important in the centuries that follow the mixed results obtained through attempts to collaborate with Persian overlords. Of course, such militancy offered its own mixed blessings in the later Hellenistic and Roman periods, as the Maccabean successes gave way to the dismal failures of the later Jewish revolts of 66–70 C.E. and 135 C.E. Nonetheless, chaps. 9—14 inform us that the impetus to such militant rhetoric and action, namely, the desire for an end to foreign military domination and oppression, grew as Persian rule persisted.

Chapter 9 offers a startling picture of the ruler who will emerge from the chaos of foreign intervention. Termed *'ānî* , once a classic prophetic term for the oppressed, this king, though "humble," enters Jerusalem in triumph. Zechariah here follows a usage of the term *'ānî* better known from Second Isaiah. In Second Isaiah, the term has shifted away from the prophetic social critique that treated the *'ānî* as the victims of Israel and Judah's own injustices. In Zechariah, the anticipated ruler is to personify the experience of humiliation and triumphal restoration, the latter notion representing a likely borrowing from the royal ideology of the so-called First Isaiah (see, e.g., Isaiah 11).

With the reframing of the term *'ānî* in Second Isaiah and Zechariah 9—14, Judah's former elite comes to apply to itself terms once reserved for the truly downtrodden, doing so as a way to demarcate the boundary between external powers and Judah's postexilic royalist hopefuls. By making this rhetorical move, the former elite is empowered through prophetic language to play the part of the "wretched of the earth," to adopt Fanon's phrase.[133] The language becomes a tool for the former elite to reassert its own political autonomy, for the prophets in some sense opened the door for the poor to defend themselves in the face of injustice.

Curiously, chaps. 9—14 attach the elite to the prophetic tradition in a far deeper way than the overt connections made in chaps. 1—8, for in the latter, the elite were still presented as being under the scrutiny of God's judgment for having perpetrated oppression. With Zechariah 9—14, Second Isaiah, and the

C layer of Micah, the elite themselves take their stand as the oppressed who wish to take charge of their own destiny. The older prophetic rhetoric is put into the service of the nationalist cause with a vengeance. The hope is held out that wealthy Tyre and grand Philistia, even Egypt and Assyria (meaning Persia?), will tumble like the Egyptians of old when God defeated them at the sea (9:4; 10:11; 11:1–3; cf. Exodus 15), reminding us that the postexilic framing of the exodus story undoubtedly reflects this nationalist elite climate and is hardly a statement on behalf of the poor as such (see chapter 4).

Yet Zechariah 9—14, in both its poetic and prose segments, presents this hope as if on the cusp of the dawn of the new age. Acknowledging Judah's judgment for bad rule and injustice (11:4–17), chaps. 9—14 read as if they were a call to arms during the time of the invasion and foreign occupation:

> My anger is roused against the shepherds,
> And I will punish the he-goats.
> For the LORD of Hosts has taken thought
> In behalf of His flock, the House of Judah;
> He will make them like majestic chargers in battle.
> From them shall come cornerstones,
> From them tent pegs,
> From them bows of combat,
> And every captain shall also arise from them.
> And together they shall be like warriors in battle,
> Tramping in the dirt of the streets;
> They shall fight, for the LORD shall be with them,
> And they shall put horsemen to shame.
> I will give victory to the House of Judah,
> And triumph to the House of Joseph.
> I will restore them, for I have pardoned them,
> And they shall be as though I had never disowned them;
> For I the LORD am their God,
> And I will answer their prayers.
> Zech. 10:3–6; cf. 9:10a, 13–15; 12:2–14; 13:7–9

In the editorial additions to the oracles, this battle marks the great reversal in which Judah, under seemingly angelic empowerment, emerges triumphant:

> The LORD will give victory to the tents of Judah first, so that the glory of the House of David and the glory of the inhabitants of Jerusalem may not be too great for Judah. In that day, the LORD will shield the inhabitants of Jerusalem; and the feeblest of them shall be in that day like David, and the House of David like a divine being—like an angel of the LORD—at their head. (Zech. 12:7–10; cf. 14:1–21)

The disemboweled elite is revitalized militarily to take up the cause of God. The writer faces the harsh reality that divine mandates are not enough. The only way for Judah to reestablish itself as a people in its own right is by brute force, for that is the only language the surrounding powers understand. Herein, for the writer of Zechariah, lies the genesis of the future dominion of God. The old royal ideology of the Judaean monarchy returns in this phase of the development of Zechariah in terms that are far more than nostalgic. Undoubtedly, members of the once displaced elite found in this rhetoric and ideology a rallying point for stepping decisively beyond foreign domination.

While such oracles may have originally been secondary to the process of reconstruction, they certainly must have stirred the embers of resistance as the compilation expanded over time. If, as we imagine, this resistance manifested itself throughout the Persian period, then we have evidence that not all were content to collaborate with the overlord as were those behind Ezra-Nehemiah, Esther, and the early Daniel materials. Zechariah 9—14 would seem to provide an insight into the sociological process and ideological developments concurrent with rebellions elsewhere against the Persians, perhaps most notably that in Ionia (see chapter 5).

In any event, the complete work of Zechariah preserves for us vital trajectories in ancient Israelite thought about prophecy, politics, religion, and society. In a sense, these developments point to the final chapters of ancient Israelite prophecy, insofar as Zechariah anticipates the emergence of full-blown apocalyptic works and the stilling of the voice of classical prophecy (13:2–6). This latter development will have significant import for the ongoing use of the biblical prophets as points of reference rather than as living embodiments of the message of God. Yet even here Zechariah has already begun to point the way. Where the collecting of the psalms under the rubric of wisdom might suggest the path of meditative reflection as the locus of future revelation, Zechariah points to exegesis and interpretation as the way to discover God's will for society.[134] In the end, it is this work of the informed scholar that will develop into rabbinic Judaism, allowing the tradition to survive the destruction of the priestly apparatus. In a very real sense, then, Zechariah's intellectual influence has lasted far longer than its more militant side. Zechariah not only assisted in the construction of the prophetic tradition, it created the hermeneutical framework needed to ensure that this tradition endured.

Malachi: Where Is the God of Justice?

The book of Malachi is staged as an imaginary dialogue between a lethargic worshiping community and a prophet committed to covenant values. While the priestly apparatus is up and running, hence placing us squarely in the Persian period, it is clear that, from the prophet's point of view at least, the fundamental claims of the Mosaic tradition are in the process of being undermined by a lackadaisical approach to the covenant's legal and ethical demands. While not systematically reflective of the torah traditions as we know them from the Pentateuch, nevertheless the book of Malachi presents us with considerations which indicate that the basic pentateuchal traditions were operant, serving as content and focus for postexilic debates about worship and society. In other words, the issues surrounding social justice, worship, and intermarriage that drive the early Nehemiah materials and the later Ezra-Nehemiah amalgam, find an incisive prophetic counterpart in Malachi. While the prophetic and priestly voices have not entirely merged, with Malachi, the prophetic voice continues to seek a direct role in relation to the people's cultic and liturgical life.[135]

The "dialogue" between the prophet and the worshiping community begins with a discussion of God's love. The skeptical community wonders about the reality of that love. Whereas Second Isaiah turned to the exodus story for postexilic hope, the opening of Malachi mines the Esau-Jacob rivalry for insight. However, unlike the writer of Genesis, who discerns hope in reconciliation of the two figures, Malachi constructs a rivalry based on divine favoritism: God's love for God's people is shown in the rejection of Esau and the acceptance of Jacob. Sharing sentiments with Obadiah, the writer of Malachi attaches overt political significance to this reading of the tale by drawing out implications for the future status of Edom:

> After all—declares the LORD—Esau is Jacob's brother; yet I have accepted Jacob and have rejected Esau. I have made his hills a desolation, his territory a home for beasts of the desert. If Edom thinks, "Though crushed, we can build the ruins again," thus said the LORD of Hosts: They may build, but I will tear down. And so they shall be known as the region of wickedness, the people damned forever of the LORD. Your eyes shall behold it, and you shall declare, "Great is the LORD beyond the borders of Israel!" (Mal. 1:2b–5)

In a sense, this admission confirms our suspicion that the Genesis story itself carries political weight (see chapter 3). That the writer of Malachi can predicate hope on the basis of Edom's destruction is a sign that the prophet operates in different circles than the compilers of Genesis. In any case, both strands of the tradition do find in this story a more positive outcome for God's people, despite the tensions of the moment created by Edom/Esau's past actions toward the land of Judah.

As the dialogue continues, however, the focus is fully on Judah's priesthood, which is castigated for having neglected the ritual offerings in a manner that has brought humiliation to God:

> When you present a blind animal for sacrifice—it doesn't matter! When you present a lame or sick one—it doesn't matter! Just offer it

to your governor: Will he accept you? Will he show you favor?—said the LORD of Hosts. And now implore the favor of God! Will He be gracious to us? That is what you have done—will He accept any of you? (Mal. 1:8–9)

The prophet's measuring stick for these excesses is torah itself, the "Teaching of My servant Moses" (3:22 [4:4]). Enough allusions occur for us to at least suggest that pentateuchal traditions in one form or another are in view, with the sacrifice of the blind animal in Mal. 1:8 being akin to Deut. 15:21, with the reference to the Levitical priesthood in Mal. 2:4 being comparable to Lev. 10:8–11 and Deut. 33:8, 20, and with the discussion of tithing in Mal. 3:8–12 being shared with Num. 18:21.[136]

In this way, Malachi's concept of covenant gains refinement in light of the amalgamation of pentateuchal traditions during the Persian period. In a sense, Malachi does for the Torah what Zechariah does for the prophets. Both set up theological constructs surrounding tradition and invoke the concept to critique ritual and social practices in their own day. This dynamic of interaction between tradition-as-construct and tradition-in-the-making provides modern users of the tradition with a method of engaging the prophetic and legal materials as creative forces out of which new insights can be drawn for contemporary social questions (see chapter 13).

In this framework, the prophet plays the role of accuser (*'ēd*; 3:5), bringing to light the nation's injustices:

> But [first] I will step forward to contend against you, and I will act as a relentless accuser against those who have no fear of Me: Who practice sorcery, who commit adultery, who swear falsely, who cheat laborers of their hire, and who subvert [the cause of] the widow, orphan, and [those who unjustly abuse the] stranger, said the LORD of Hosts. (Mal. 3:5–6)[137]

The prophetic tradition has become rather truncated in Malachi's hands, following a process similar to that of the layering and adapting of the prophetic message in Zechariah. Part of this accusatory role includes the charge of having broken the "covenant of our fathers" (Mal. 2:10), an apparent reference to Deut. 24:14–18 (laborer, alien, orphan, and widow) that is perhaps conflated with Ex. 22:20–23 (alien, widow, orphan). In Malachi, the charge invokes the covenant lawsuit motif better known from Micah 6, but adding the language of the covenant of fear so important to the E source and to Haggai. Such a lawsuit of God against the people involves the putting into force of the covenant's curse provisions (Mal. 2:1–3), which for Malachi becomes enshrined as the judgment of God on the day of the divine messenger's coming (3:1–3; cf. 3:19 [4:1]).[138]

In addition to the question of sacrifice, the prophet raises the issue of corrupting the legal norms of the covenant through the priests' showing partiality in their rulings (nośîm pānîm ba-tôrâ; 2:9), a matter that is handled similarly to Ex. 30:15, where both rich and poor must give the same shekel offering, and Lev. 19:15, where virtually the same terminology is used (unlike Lev. 14:21 which does make distinctions between rich and poor). However, since the triangulation of fear, nonpartiality (Deut. 10:17), and obedient love form the fabric of Deut. 10:12–11:23 (in the face of the threat of curse), one must not dismiss the possibility of some sort of interaction with the so-called Deuteronomic materials on this score ("so-called" because Deut. 10:12–11:23, together with the superfluous reference to the Levitical inheritance in Deut. 10:6–9, constitute later additions to Deuteronomy, reflective of the debates found in Malachi).

What Hosea handled more metaphorically, namely the breakup of the people's "marriage" with God, becomes in Malachi's hands an attack on intermarriage with idol-worshiping pagans and the proliferation of divorces (2:11–16). Perhaps we have here an example of an intermediate stage between the early Nehemiah material, with its focus on social injustices, and the later Ezra-Nehemiah complex, with its focus on the problem of intermarriage. If so, then in Malachi we have an example of a prophetic voice that has to some extent succeeded in shaping the Ezra-period reforms of the priestly structure.

Malachi's role as accuser is not thoroughly negative. Here the prophetic voice is conceived as one that faces those who argue that it is useless to worship God (3:13) or to look for the God of justice (2:17). In response, the prophet champions the judgment of God over their skepticism (3:1–3; 3:19, 23 [4:1, 5]). Thus, for all its harshness, the book of Malachi envisions triumph and blessings from the hand of this God, triumph for the just (3:16–18) and blessing for the land (3:10–12).

In leveling the accusations, Malachi acts as a prophet of old. In refocusing the early prophetic message, however, Malachi functions as a Joel, defending God's honor and securing the prosperity of the land. Paganism may present challenges, but the ethical voice of the Mosaic covenant under prophetic mediation becomes a locus for the community to refine its ritual and reassert its commitment to the laborers, widows, orphans, and strangers. The comparisons with early Nehemiah are striking (see chapter 5).

While Malachi marks the end of the book of the Twelve, the end of classical prophecy, and for Christians the terminus of the Old Testament, it is clear that this little book encourages continued dialogue between priestly and prophetic voices in an age of questions and uncertainties.

To conclude this chapter: The sweep of time and range of issues covered by these twelve short books is rather staggering. Hence, we find a variety of perspectives on the social ethics questions that plagued their peoples. Nonetheless, the Deuteronomic editor's message that God calls on God's people to "execute true justice" (Zech. 7:8–14) continues to ring loudly through the corridors traversed by these writings, in their initial formulation and subsequent compilation. In a very real sense, we are watching the prophetic justice tradition under construction. In particular, the study of the social visions in these texts reveals that many of these figures had a clear understanding of the nature and origins of poverty and injustice in their society. A number of texts observe that the poor were continually assailed by the power of the influential. Exploitation by the rich regularly deprived the poor of life's essentials, namely, "wages, clothing, food and housing."[139] The overriding concern of the urban elite was the accumulation of possessions, and because of this they ignored the cost of their activities to the masses and ultimately to the society itself. This accumulation of wealth came about through a network of structures in society—political, economic, and legal—by which the goods of those who were disenfranchised came into the hands of the wealthy. Such economic and social institutions perpetuated injustices that were affronts to YHWH. In terms of religious ideology, the rich legitimized their authority, and thus their hold over the populace, through the practice of idol worship, which to the prophetic mind ensured YHWH's judgment of both Israel and Judah.

The Book of the Twelve, then, presents us with articulate prophetic statements on their social world. We find that the wide-ranging prophetic critique of society was not the rumbling of a few backward peasant folk who could not face the upward progress of civilization.[140] Rather, these stalwart village and urban voices for justice offer clear perspectives on power politics, ritual commitment, social oppression, and the advance of the elite in society. Throughout the postexilic period, these ideas were tailored to changing audiences and a host of conflicting agendas. Nonetheless, a concern for justice, albeit at times coopted by the leadership of the reconstruction movements, came to define the ground upon which the prophetic voice in the book of the Twelve remained a vital component in new moments that demanded vigorous theological reflection on pressing social matters.

Notes

1. On the relative merits and demerits of treating the Book of the Twelve not merely as twelve isolated historical strands but also as a theologically fruitful whole, see J. Barton, "The Canonical Meaning of the Book of the Twelve," in *After the Exile: Essays in Honour of Rex Mason*, ed J. Barton and D. J. Reimer (Macon, Ga., Mercer University Press, 1996), 59–73. Some may detect a "Deuteronomic" hand at work weaving the books together in light of new theological considerations and societal demands. Others find additional postexilic expansions. Certainly the Book of the Twelve underwent several stages of development, and the evidence of Qumran and the LXX would indicate that while an initial core developed earlier on, several books remained rather unstable in their relation to the whole, especially Joel, Obadiah, and Jonah. Our arguments here are based on the MT tradition. For a review and analysis see the proposals of B. A. Jones, *The Formation of the Book of the Twelve: A Study in Text and Canon*, SBL Dissertation Series 149 (Atlanta: Scholars Press, 1995).

2. See T. W. Overholt, "The End of Prophecy: No Players without a Program," *JSOT* 42 (1988): 103–15.
3. A succinct discussion of the relation between Ugarit and the Bible is offered by P. C. Craigie, *Ugarit and the Old Testament* (Grand Rapids: Wm. B. Eerdmans Publishing Co., 1983). On the iconography, see A. Caquot and M. Sznycer, *Ugaritic Religion* (Leiden: E. J. Brill, 1980).
4. Regarding the social functions of the Canaanite mythic system, see G. Mendenhall, "The Worship of Baal and Asherah: A Study in the Social Bonding Functions of Religious Systems," in *Biblical and Related Studies Presented to Samuel Iwry*, ed. A. Kort and S. Morschauser (Winona Lake, Ind.: Eisenbrauns, 1985).
5. On the overt character of ancient sexuality and its attendant iconography, so often censored from museum collections, see E. C. Keuls, *The Reign of the Phallus* (New York: Harper & Row, 1985) and L. Manniche, *Sexual Life in Ancient Egypt* (London: KPI, 1987).
6. This view is contrary to E. K. Holt, *Prophesying the Past: The Use of Israel's History in the Book of Isaiah*, JSOT Supplement Series 194 (Sheffield: Sheffield Academic Press, 1995), 82, who, like others, sees Hosea's attack to be directed against *popular* religiosity.
7. For a full study see Holt, *Prophesying the Past*.
8. See D. R. Hillers, *Covenant: The History of a Biblical Idea* (Baltimore: Johns Hopkins, 1969), chap. 5.
9. See T. D. Setel, "Prophets and Pornography: Female Sexual Imagery in Hosea" in *Feminist Interpretation of the Bible*, ed. L. M. Russell (Philadelphia: Fortress Press, 1985), 86–95, who mistakenly conflates the Gomer figure with the mother figure of the oracles. See also A. Brenner, "Pornoprophetics Revisited: Some Additional Reflections," *JSOT* 70 (1996): 63–86. Neither author posits reading the prose texts as from a later, divergent hand.
10. See G. Yee, *Composition and Tradition: Redaction Critical Investigations*, SBL Dissertation Series 102 (Atlanta: Scholars Press, 1987).
11. The LXX differs in this regard, placing the book fourth in the set.
12. The enemy is treated as the foe from the north, a classic category of prophetic analysis (cf. Joel 2:20). See, e.g., B. S. Childs, "The Enemy from the North and Chaos Tradition," *JBL* 78 (1959): 187–198, who treats Joel as an example of an apocalyptic-styled, mythological use of the chaos tradition to expand the image of the once purely historical image of the enemy from the north.
13. On the use of the lament form in Joel and its much disputed liturgical links, see, G. W. Ahlström, *Joel and the Temple Cult of Jerusalem*, VTS 21 (Leiden: E. J. Brill, 1971), 130–37; A. S. Kapelrud, *Joel Studies* (Uppsala: A. B. Lundequistka Bokhandeln, 1948), 179; and G. S. Ogden, "Joel 4 and Prophetic Responses to National Laments," *JSOT* 26 (1983): 97–106, who sees Joel 4 as a prophetic oracular response to the lament ritual developed in Joel 1—3. In fact, Ogden demonstrates the intimate connection of the language of Joel 4 to various psalms of lament. By accenting the literary character or lament style of the ritual in Joel, both G. W. Ahlström and H. W. Wolff perhaps underplay the place of the prophetic voice in postexilic liturgical enactments. See Ahlström, *Joel and the Temple Cult*, 130–31; and H. W. Wolff, *Joel and Amos* (Philadelphia: Fortress Press, 1977), 9.
14. Ogden, "Joel 4 and Prophetic Responses," 104–5 argues that Joel is not calling for repentance but simply to turn to God as deliverer. Yet the context and links with Hosea would seem to suggest that Joel's call is to repent or mourn past injustices as a way to induce a new act of God on behalf of the people.

15. War and not drought, however, is the context of the oracles. The nature references provide the imagery but not the situation for the poetry. Contrast Kapelrud, *Joel Studies*, 177–78; and S. Bergler, *Joel als Schriftinterpret*, BEATA 16 (Frankfurt am Main: Peter Lang, 1988). To treat Joel as a text about an actual drought is to distort the character of such imagery as reflections of social and national dislocation.

16. For the Canaanite background, see F. F. Hvidberg, *Weeping and Laughter in the Old Testament* (Leiden: E. J. Brill, 1962), chap. 2; O. Loretz, *Regenritual und Jahwetag im Joelbuch*, UBL 4 (Altenberge: CIS-Verlag, 1986), 70, 122, 142–43, reads Joel more basically as a postexilic adaptation of drought texts and rain rituals (collapsed together with "day of YHWH" texts having astronomical aspects) reflective of Canaanite mythic belief and religious practice. To be sure, Canaanite and Near Eastern myth provides the language for much of the Bible, but political collapse, economic distress, and war provide the material context for this specific realization of that language (contrast Loretz, 76).

17. For the Ugaritic text, see J. C. L. Gibson, *Canaanite Myths and Legends* (Edinburgh: T. & T. Clark, 1977), 68–81.

18. On Joel as a literary theology, see F. E. Deist, "Parallels and Reinterpretation in the Book of Joel: A Theology of the Yom Yahweh, in *Text and Context : Old Testament and Semitic Studies for F. C. Fensham*, ed. W. Classen, JSOT Supplement Series 48 (Sheffield: JSOT Press, 1988), 63–79. Studies of the "day of YHWH" are offered in Y. Hoffman, "The Day of the Lord as a Concept and a Term in the Prophetic Literature," ZAW 93 (1981): 37-50; and K. D. Schunck, "Strukturlinien in der Entwicklung der Vorstellung vom 'Tag Jahwes,'" *VT* 14 (1964): 319–30. The idea would seem to have originated in the prophetic tradition through Amos (see Amos 5:18–20), although the concept developed over time. Hoffman's argument that the concept was originally of a divine visitation and not an eschatological event would seem to be correct. The eschatological dimensions would have been framed by Zephaniah. See Hoffman, 46–47. This stands in opposition to Plöger's view that Amos was eschatological and that Joel developed a kind of liturgical realized eschatology. See O. Plöger, *Theocracy and Eschatology*, trans. S. Rudman (Richmond: John Knox Press, 1968), 101–102.

19. Deist, "Parallels and Reinterpretation," 66–67, highlights the connectedness at Ugarit between locust and military imagery in the Keret and Anat texts. See also the later postexilic addendum in Joel 4:4–8 (3:4–8).

20. The dating of this book is notoriously difficult. Some reasonable considerations for a date for the bulk of the text from the period between 445 and 343 B.C.E. are offered by Wolff, *Joel and Amos*, 4–5.

21. See, e.g., Hvidberg, *Weeping and Laughter*, chap. 3.

22. Gibson, *Canaanite Myths and Legends*, 74.

23. For reference to the Canaanite cultic background, see Ahlström, *Joel and the Temple Cult*, 23–34; and Hvidberg, *Weeping and Laughter*, 140–42.

24. Ogden, "Joel 4 and Prophetic Responses," 98.

25. R. R. Wilson, *Prophecy and Society in Ancient Israel* (Philadelphia: Fortress Press, 1980), chap. 2. The distinction and role of Joel as prophet vis-à-vis the priests is more weakly captured by Kapelrud, *Joel Studies*, 182-87.

26. H. B. Huffmon, "The Origins of Prophecy," in *Magnalia Dei:The Mighty Acts of God: Essays on the Bible and Archaeology in Memory of G. Ernest Wright*, ed. F. M. Cross, W. E. Lemke, and P. D. Miller (Garden City, N. Y.: Doubleday, 1976), 171–86.

27. J. L. Crenshaw, *Joel: A New Translation with Introduction and Commentary* (New York: Doubleday, 1995), 23–29, puts forward compelling arguments for a fifth-century B.C.E. date.

28. For the Baal cycle, which is caught up in a renewal of rain, plow land, oil, wine, and honey, see Gibson, *Canaanite Myths and Legends*, 77–78.
29. Rhetorical links with Amos include Joel 4:16a (3:16a), which parallels Amos 1:2 as anticipation and fulfillment respectively. Likewise, Joel 4:18 (3:18) shares some fragmentary elements with Amos 9:13.
30. For a study of the transmission history of Amos that takes into account the changing shape of the justice message of the prophet, see R. B. Coote, *Amos among the Prophets: Composition and Theology* (Philadelphia: Fortress Press, 1981). Essentially, Coote sees three broad phases of development: (1) An eighth-century B.C.E. set of oral oracles with a harsh social critique is gathered by the book's main editor in the seventh century. (2) Under the main editor, the original focus against Samaria shifts to an anti-Bethel and pro-Jerusalem theme. (3) The final stage, at the end of the exile, incorporates the notion of a reversal of bad fortunes and essentially subverts the original critique of Amos.
31. See, e.g., S. Cohen, "The Political Background of the Words of Amos," *Hebrew Union College Annual* 36 (1965): 153; and W. Schottroff, "The Prophet Amos: A Socio-Historical Assessment of His Ministry" in *God of the Lowly: Socio-Historical Interpretations of the Bible*, ed. W. Schottroff and W. Stegemann (Maryknoll, N.Y.: Orbis Books, 1984), 28.
32. See J. K. de Geus, "Die Gesellschaftskritik der Propheten und die Archäologie," *ZDPV* 98 (1982): 50–59, esp. 54–55; and J-L. Vesco, "Amos de Teqoa, Dèfenseur de l'Homme," *RB* 87 (1980): 481–482.
33. De Geus, "Gesellschaftskritik der Propheten," 54; M. Elat, "The Monarchy and the Development of Trade in Ancient Israel" in *State and Temple Economy in the Ancient Near East*, vol. 2, ed. Edward Lipinski (Louvain: Department Oriëntalistiek, 1979), 541–45; and idem, "Trade and Commerce" in *The Age of the Monarchies: Culture and Society*, ed. Abraham Malamat (Jerusalem: Masada Press, 1979), 181–85.
34. See, e.g., G. J. Botterweck, "Sie verkaufen den Unschuldigen um Geld," *Bibel und Leben* 12 (1971): 216–18; F. Dijkema, "Le Fond des Prophéties d'Amos," *OTS* 2 (1943): 32; J. H. Hayes and J. M. Miller, *Israelite and Judaean History* (Philadelphia: Westminster Press, 1977), 414; and W. Schottroff, "Prophet Amos," 34.
35. Dijkema, "Fond des Prophéties," 31, my translation.
36. H. W. Wolff, *Joel and Amos*, 104.
37. On the biblical and related Near Eastern materials, see G. C. Chirichingno, *Debt-Slavery in Israel and the Ancient Near East* (Sheffield: JSOT Press, 1993).
38. M. Fendler, "Zur Sozialkritik des Amos," *EvTh* 33 (1973): 38.
39. B. Lang, *Monotheism and the Prophetic Minority: An Essay in Biblical History and Sociology* (Sheffield: Almond Press), 125.
40. Vesco, "Amos de Teqoa," 490, my translation.
41. Botterweck, *op. cit.*, 226; and Vesco, *op. cit.*, 490.
42. Wolff, *Joel and Amos*, 165; cf. Botterweck, "Unschuldigen um Geld," 226.
43. Fendler, "Zur Sozialkritik des Amos," 49; cf. Botterweck, "Unschuldigen um Geld," 226.
44. Fendler, "Zur Sozialkritik des Amos," 49–50.
45. Wolff, *Joel and Amos*, 167.
46. Botterweck, "Unschuldigen um Geld," 227–228.
47. Cf. Dijkema, "Fond des Prophéties," 30–31.
48. Fendler, "Zur Sozialkritik des Amos," 36.
49. Cf. H. J. Fabry, "dal," *TDOT* 3: 219; K. Koch, "Die Entstehung der Sozialen Kritik bei den Propheten," in *Probleme biblischer Theologie: Gerhard von Rad zum 70 Gerburtstag* (Munich: C. Kaiser, 1971), 575; and G. Wittenberg, "The Message of the O.T. Prophets during the Eighth Century B.C. concerning Affluence and

Poverty," in *Affluence, Poverty and the Word of God*, ed. Nürnberger, (Durban: Lutheran Publishing House, 1978), 146.

50. Fendler, "Zur Sozialkritik des Amos," 37, 50–51.
51. J. Miranda, *Communism in the Bible* (Maryknoll, N.Y.: Orbis Books, 1982), 36.
52. Botterweck, "Unschuldigen um Geld," 228, my translation.
53. Cf. Schottroff, "Prophet Amos," 34; and Wittenberg, "Message of the O. T. Prophets," 141–142.
54. Cf. Wolff, *Joel and Amos*, 202.
55. Fendler, "Zur Sozialkritik des Amos," 45, my translation.
56. W. von Soden, *Akkadisches Handwörterbuch* (Wiesbaden: Harrassowitz, 1959), 1119, my translation.
57. H. Torczyner, "Presidential Address," *Journal of the Palestine Oriental Society* 16 (1936): 6–7; cf. Vesco, "Amos de Teqoa," 498; Wolff, *Joel and Amos*, 230.
58. Chirichigno, *Debt-Slavery in Israel*, 126.
59. W. Gesenius and E. Kautzsch, *Gesenius' Hebrew Grammar* (Oxford: Clarendon Press, 1910), 61e.
60. Fendler, "Zur Sozialkritik des Amos," 36, note 10, my translation.
61. Cf. Vesco, "Amos de Teqoa," 493.
62. Fendler, "Zur Sozialkritik des Amos," 36 note 10.
63. Wolff, *Joel and Amos*,168.
64. Fendler, "Zur Sozialkritik des Amos," 41.
65. Cf. Elat, "Monarchy and the Development of Trade," 545–46; idem, "Trade and Commerce," 186; and Fendler, "Zur Sozialkritik des Amos," 42.
66. Vesco, "Amos de Teqoa," 494–95. We may also add Amos 3:10.
67. Miranda, *Communism in the Bible*, 35.
68. Wittenberg, "Message of the O. T. Prophets," 146.
69. Cf. A. L. Oppenheim, *Ancient Mesopotamia: Portrait of a Dead Civilization* (Chicago: University of Chicago Press, 1977), 115, 128; Elat, "Trade and Commerce," 175; and L. Köhler, *Hebrew Man*, trans. P. R. Ackroyd (Nashville: Abingdon Press, 1956), 127–150.
70. Botterweck, "Unschuldigen um Geld," 224–25; and Vesco, "Amos de Teqoa," 500.
71. E. W. Davies, *Prophecy and Ethics: Isaiah and the Ethical Traditions of Israel*, JSOT Supplement Series 16 (Sheffield: JSOT Press, 1981), 109.
72. Vesco, "Amos de Teqoa," 491, my translation.
73. Wittenberg, "Message of the O. T. Prophets," 142.
74. Cf. Botterweck, "Unschuldigen um Geld," 223.
75. Wolff, *Joel and Amos*, 205.
76. Coote, *Amos among the Prophets*, 37–38. For representative background information, see M. Smith, *The Ugaritic Baal Cycle*, vol. 1, *Introduction with Text, Translation and Commentary of KTU* 1.1–2 (Leiden: E. J. Brill, 1994), 140–44.
77. Coote, *Amos among the Prophets*, 38. See also N. Wyatt, *Religious Texts from Ugarit: The Words of Ilimilku and His Colleagues* (Sheffield: Sheffield Academic Press, 1998), 404–13. The text in question is a medical cure for drunkenness.
78. Cf. Fendler, "Zur Sozialkritik des Amos," 47.
79. Schottroff, "Prophet Amos," 40.
80. F. Hauck and W. Kasch, "Ploutos," in 6:324. G. Friedrich, ed., *Theological Dictionary of the New Testament*, trans. G. W. Bromiley (Grand Rapids: Eerdmans, 1968), vol. 6, 324.
81. Cf. Vesco, "Amos de Teqoa," 493.
82. Cf. M. D. Guinan, *Gospel Poverty: Witness to the Risen Christ* (New York: Paulist Press, 1981), 40.

83. Cf. G. Mendenhall, "The Monarchy," *Int* 29 (1975): 155–70.
84. See the study of J. H. Tigay, *You Shall Have No Other Gods: Israelite Religion in the Light of Hebrew Inscriptions* (Atlanta: Scholars Press, 1986).
85. J. A. Lucal, "God of Justice: The Prophets as Social Reformers," *Bible Today* 32 (1967): 2223.
86. Cf. Fendler, "Zur Sozialkritik des Amos," 53.
87. H. J. Kraus, "Die prophetische Botschaft gegen das soziale Unrecht Israels," *EvTh* 15 (1955): 298, my translation.
88. Ibid., 299–300, my translation.
89. O. Loretz, "Die Prophetische Kritik des Rentenkapitalsmus: Grundlagen Probleme der Prophetenforschung," *UF* 7 (1975): 273.
90. Vesco, "Amos de Teqoa," 500, my translation.
91. Wittenberg, "Message of the O. T. Prophets," 148.
92. Kraus, "Prophetische Botschaft," 300.
93. Ibid., my translation.
94. I cannot accept Bič's thesis that Obadiah be restricted to an enthronement drama. See M. Bič, "Zur Problematik des Buches Obadja," *VTS* 1 (1953): 11–25.
95. As documented in P. Bienkowski, ed., *Early Edom and Moab: The Beginning of the Iron Age in Southern Jordan*, Sheffield Archaeological Monographs 7 (Sheffield: J. R. Collis, 1992).
96. Such oracles are found in Isaiah 13—23, Jeremiah 46—51, Ezekiel 25—32, as well as in Amos 1:1–2:16, Nahum (against Nineveh), Habakkuk (on Babylon), Zephaniah 2, and Zechariah 9. Concerning Obadiah as cult prophet, see H. W. Wolff, "Obadja—ein Kultprophet als Interpret," *EvTh* 37 (1977): 273–84, where he argues that the prophet, in the liturgical context, updates an older prophetic pronouncement concerning Edom (vv. 1b–4).
97. B. C. Cresson, "The Condemnation of Edom in Postexilic Judaism," in *The Use of the Old Testament in the New and Other Essays: Studies in Honor of William Franklin Stinespring*, ed. J. M. Efird (Durham, N. C.: Duke University Press, 1972), offers a useful survey of the "Damn Edom theology" of the Hebrew Bible. Cresson overlooks, however, the possibility that Genesis represents an alternate view on this point.
98. W. Rudolf, *Joel—Amos—Obadja—Jona* (Gerd Mohn: Gütersloher Verlagshaus, 1971), 314–18, offers a mediating view of this passage. R. Mason, *Micah, Nahum, Obadiah* (Sheffield: JSOT Press, 1991), 104, plausibly argues from the similarities between Obad. 1:19–21 and Zechariah 14 that these texts both stem from similar (later) circles who liked to expound earlier prophecy and relate it to the circumstances and hopes of their times.
99. See the defense of J. C. Holbert, "'Deliverance Belongs to Yahweh!' Satire in the Book of Jonah," *JSOT* 21 (1981): 59–81, for whom the presence of satirical elements is extensive and obvious.
100. Hillers, *Covenant*, chap. 6. Similar concerns over just weights and measures are found in the legal traditions of the Pentateuch in Deut. 25:13–15 and Lev. 19:35–36.
101. J. Blenkinsopp, *A History of Prophecy in Israel* (Philadelphia: Westminster Press, 1983), 94.
102. A. A. Boesak, *Farewell to Innocence: A Socio-Ethical Study on Black Theology and Power* (Maryknoll, N.Y.: Orbis Books, 1977), 17–20.
103. I. Mosala, *Biblical Hermeneutics and Black Theology in South Africa* (Grand Rapids: Wm. B. Eerdmans Publishing Co., 1989).
104. Ibid., 146; texts include Micah 1:10–15a; 2:1–5, 8–9; 3:8–12; 5:11–14 (10–15); 6:9–15.

105. B layer texts include Micah 1:5b–9; 2:6–7, 10–11; 3:1–7; 5:1, 4–6 (2, 5–7); 6:1–8, 16; 7:1–5. I have to agree with Blenkinsopp that 7:1–10 is a Persian period cultic lament text thoroughly out of character with the rest of the book. See Blenkinsopp, *History of Prophecy*, 93.

106. Mosala, *Biblical Hermeneutics*, 139.

107. Ibid., 141.

108. Ibid.

109. C layer texts include Micah 1:1–5a; 2:12–13; 4:1–2; 5; 5:4–5 (3–4), 8–9; 7:8–20.

110. Mosala, *Biblical Hermeneutics*, 132.

111. Ibid., 134.

112. Ibid., 149. Cf. G. V. Pixley, "Micah—A Revolutionary" in *The Bible and the Politics of Exegesis: Essays in Honor of Norman K. Gottwald on His Sixty-Fifth Birthday*, ed. D. J. Jobling et al. (Cleveland: Pilgrim Press, 1991), 53–60, whose reading, while imaginative, finds peasant insurrection in passages fraught with so many translation difficulties that his provocative thesis is rendered far from certain.

113. Ibid., 148–149.

114. See, e.g., J. M. Halligan, "The Role of the Peasant in the Amarna Period," in *Palestine in Transition: The Emergence of Ancient Israel*, ed. D. N. Freedman and D. F. Graf (Sheffield: Almond Press, 1983).

115. H. W. Wolff, *Micah the Prophet* (Philadelphia: Fortress Press, 1978), 4; cf. 18–25; Wolff identifies the fortresses as Adullum, Azekah, Lachosh, Moresheth, and Mareshah. See his *Micah: A Commentary* (Minneapolis: Augsburg, 1990), 30.

116. Wolff, *Micah: A Commentary*, 78.

117. Curiously, Micah's memory is invoked by a later group of elders in defense of Jeremiah's outspokenness (Jer. 26:17–19). A useful assessment of Mosala's thesis in light of the South African political question is offered by F. S. Frick, "Sociological Criticism and Its Relation to Political and Social Hermeneutics, with a Special Look at Biblical Hermeneutics in South African Liberation Theology in Jobling et al., eds., *Bible and the Politics*, 225–238.

118. J. Jeremias, *Kultprophetie und Gerichtsverkündigung in der späten Königszeit Israels* (Neukirchen-Vluyn: Neukirchener Verlag, 1970), develops the view that a core of Nahum stems from a noncultic prophetic figure and that later cultic prophets transformed these oracles into liturgical materials, a view that seems less likely than simply positing a cultic role for the work from its inception. Similarly, R. J. Coggins does not regard Nahum as a cultic figure, suggesting only that the literary usage of Nahum may often imply an indebtedness to the language of the cult. See R. J. Coggins and S. P. Reemi, *Israel among the Nations: A Commentary on the Books of Nahum and Obadiah and Esther* (Grand Rapids: Wm. B. Eerdmans Publishing Co., 1985), 10.

119. For the Canaanite text, see Gibson, *Canaanite Myths and Legends*, 44–45.

120. A. Haldar, *Studies in the Book of Nahum* (Uppsala: A. B. Lundequistska, 1947), 88–154, argues for close links between the deeds of YHWH in the book of Nahum and the portrayal of Marduk in the Babylonian creation epic. Whereas Haldar sees Nahum to be reflective of the "political propaganda of the cultic circles" and hence imbued with ritual motifs (153), P. Humbert treats the book as a liturgical libretto celebrating YHWH's New Year's enthronement in light of the collapse of the Assyrian empire. See P. Humbert, "Le problème du livre de Nahoum," *RHPhR* 12 (1932): 1–15. See also P. Humbert, "Essai d'analyse de Nahoum 1:2–2:3," *ZAW* 44 (1926): 266–80. In any event, the cultic and mythic character of the text is plain.

121. See, e.g., F. García Martínez, *The Dead Sea Scrolls Translated: The Qumran Texts in English*, 2d ed., trans. W. G. E. Watson (Leiden: E. J. Brill, 1994), 195–97.

122. Cf. J. Blenkinsopp, *A History of Prophecy in Israel*, 2d ed. (Louisville, Ky. Westminster John Knox Press, 1996), 150.

123. G. E. Mendenhall, "Humility," in *Interpreter's Dictionary of the Bible*, ed. G.A. Buttrick (Nashville: Abingdon Press, 1962), 3:659.

124. For a translation, see S. Dalley, *Myths from Mesopotamia: Creation, The Flood, Gilgamesh, and Others* (Oxford: Oxford University Press, 1989), 282–315.

125. Huffmon, "Origins of Prophecy."

126. See Gibson, *Canaanite Myths and Legends*, 37–67.

127. Cf. P. Hanson, *The Dawn of Apocalyptic* (Philadelphia: Fortress Press, 1975), 240–62.

128. The Bisitun (Behistun) Inscription of Darius I is concerned with rebellions faced in Persia's more immediate environs. For the Aramaic version, see B. Porten and A. Yardeni, *Textbook of Aramaic Documents from Ancient Egypt*, vol. 3, *Literature, Accounts, and Lists* (Jerusalem: Hebrew University Press, 1993), pp. 60–71.

129. N. Ateek, *Justice and Only Justice: A Palestinian Theology of Liberation* (Maryknoll: Orbis Books, 1989), 104-14.

130. Cf. Hanson, *Dawn of Apocalyptic*, 251-52.

131. See B. S. Childs, *Introduction to the Old Testament as Scripture* (Philadelphia: Fortress Press, 1979), 482-485, where the often overlooked link between chaps. 1, 8 and 9-14 suggest that the conjunction of the materials is not as incongruous as one might think. In Childs's estimation, the conjunction opens up new theological possibilities for the community's understanding of the times between the return from exile and the end of time. Likewise, for Childs, the preservation of chaps. 1-8 affected the community's awareness concerning the sort of ethics that were appropriate to this new stage in the history of salvation.

132. Hanson, *Dawn of Apocalyptic*, 284-86.

133. See F. Fanon, *The Wretched of the Earth*, trans. C. Farrington (New York: Grove Press, 1963), esp. 148-205, in which the misdeeds of the usurping native middle class, in the process of decolonizing, as shown to reflect historical processes that are remarkably similar to the elite's commandeering of the prophetic images of poverty and suffering.

134. On the various understandings of the means of Torah revelation in this creative period, see J. D. Levenson, "The Sources of Torah: Psalm 119 and the Modes of Revelation in Second Temple Judaism," in *Ancient Israelite Religion: Essays in Honor of Frank Moore Cross* P. D. Miller, P. D. Hanson, and S. D. McBride ed. (Philadelphia: Fortress Press, 1987).

135. Whether the Book of Malachi results from displaced Levitical circles is one possibility raised by P. D. Hanson, *The People Called: The Growth of Community in the Bible* (New York: Harper & Row, 1986), 276-290.

136. See A. Hill, "The Book of Malachi," *ABD* 4:479.

137. The JPS translation omits *ûmaṭṭê* before "stranger," but the parallelism with "who subvert" is rather clear and the translation suggests itself from the Hiphil's more basic sense of "to stretch out."

138. For a discussion of the covenant lawsuit or *rîb* pattern, see Hillers, *Covenant*, chap. 6. Curiously, however, Hillers does not discuss the Malachi material in this connection.

139. E. Tamez, *Bible of the Oppressed*, 47.

140. C. Miranda, *Communism in the Bible*, 39.

Poetry and Wisdom

Chapter 10

Poetic Imagination

Psalms, Song of Songs, Lamentations

In the corpus of materials from Egypt and Mesopotamia we find works of poetry akin to the Psalms, the Song of Songs, and Lamentations. Throughout the ancient Near East, the sacred poets composed texts that made appeals to the gods for divine assistance from suffering, offered thanks for the beneficent deeds of the gods, extolled the virtues of love, and praised the attributes of the gods.[1] Significant portions of the biblical record carry on these poetic traditions, echoing the themes and the mythic elements common to the poetry of Egypt and ancient Mesopotamia.

Of course, there is a specifically Israelite stamp to the biblical materials. The council of the ancient pantheon has largely, though not entirely, been displaced by the one God. But more importantly for our purposes here, the Israelite texts, as a canonical complex, are stamped by the experience of the exile. While certainly the Mesopotamian laments over the destruction of major cities stand in the distant background to Israel's community laments, Israel's exilic dislocation and subsequent efforts at renewal mark many of the biblical poetic texts well beyond the infrequent communal laments of the psalms.[2] Indeed, if recent studies on the canonical shape of the Psalter as a whole can serve as our guide, the Psalter in its entirety purposively responds to the crisis of the collapse of the Davidic monarchy through a body of texts that is in the end committed to survival and hope.[3] Of course, we do not want to lose track of the monarchic period stamp that indelibly undergirds the ideological structures of various texts. Yet our analysis must equally not lose track of the human dimensions of these texts that appear to break out of these pre-exilic ideological constraints to give expression to a quest for social equity, a critique of wealth, a call for judgment, a reflection on gender relations, and an elevation of YHWH as the God of justice who hears the cry of the oppressed.

In this chapter, then, we explore Israel's poetic imagination, treating in turn the Psalms, the Song of Songs, and Lamentations. With regard to the Psalms, we will explore the issue of the material character of the poverty described there, the question of divine rule, the image of the "enemy," and the role of wealth in the psalms. Song of Songs will enable us to raise questions of gender, while Lamentations will take us inside a liturgy of destruction. In short, Israel's poetic and liturgical imagination grapples with the emotive side, creating pictures that reach into the deepest aspects of human yearnings for justice and life.

Toward a Materialist Reading of Poverty in the Psalter

Marking a new direction in the interpretation of the Bible, a number of studies appeared during the latter part of the nineteenth and the early part of the twentieth century that approached the question of poverty in the Bible with special reference to the Psalms.[4] The modern discussion of poverty in the Bible was initially generated by Grätz and Loeb.[5] The latter, in his work *La littérature des pauvres dans la Bible*, sought to develop an understanding of the poor in the Psalms in light of ideas originated by Grätz, raising questions regarding the reality of the suffering of the poor as an underclass and their sociological relation to the "wicked."[6] Scholarly research on this question was put on firmer footing by Rahlfs in his work *'ānî und 'ānāw in den Psalmen*.[7] Subsequently a number of studies appeared that adapted and sometimes extended the work of Loeb and Rahlfs. Most noteworthy are the treatments of Baudissin, Birkeland, Kittel, Kuschke, Bruppacher, and Van der Ploeg.[8] Though in varying ways, for each of these scholars one key question arose: Are the Psalms simply concerned about the "humble" or do they raise deeper and more concrete socioeconomic concerns? Generally, the various discussions turn on the meaning and usage of the Hebrew terms *'ānî* and *anaw* in the Psalms, and on the possible roles of the *'ănāwîm* in Israelite society.

Poverty as Humbleness: Baudissin

Baudissin's concern was to place the evaluation of the poor found in the Psalms, especially with regard to its religious dimension, within the larger context of the religion of the Hebrew Bible. Fully half of Baudissin's comments are addressed to the preexilic and related materials that deal with poverty: the prophets, the Covenant Code and Deuteronomic legislation, and the Priestly code. In all these groups, Baudissin sees a negative stance toward poverty. At issue for Baudissin is how the more positive estimate of poverty found in the Psalms arose.

According to Baudissin, the exile brought a dramatic shift in the biblical understanding of poverty, a change reflected in the meaning and usage of *'ānî*.[9] From his study of the prophetic texts, Baudissin understands the preexilic view to be that poverty is not fitting to God's ways.[10] Four critical themes emerge in these writings: (1) the prophets depict poverty as evil; (2) the people must spare no effort to remove it from the community of God, and those who caught the prophetic vision would try to enact reforms and legislation to achieve this end; (3) poverty will eventually be eliminated by God, but this awaits an act of God at some point in the future; and (4) God has a special concern for the poor. However, after the exile, Baudissin argues, poverty came to be treated as a mark of honor before God.

Specifically, the experience of the exile allowed the entire population of Judah to feel as if it had joined the ranks of the poor and oppressed. The repeated invasions on the part of the Babylonian army, the deportation of the populace, and the ravaging of the cities of Palestine all contributed to the sense of humiliation that the people carried into exile. Though in many ways akin to the poverty known by the lower classes prior to the exile, this was a humiliation borne by the entire nation. References to the entire nation as poor and suffering were rare before the exile, but now the notion was legitimately applied to the group because the exiles found themselves in an enduring poverty-stricken condition.[11]

The path to this renewed understanding of poverty was paved, Baudissin argues, by the exilic writer known as Deutero-Isaiah or Second Isiah.[12] On Baudissin's analysis, the earlier Isaiah could not have characterized the entire people as poor in any positive sense because First Isaiah, like the other preexilic prophets, would have adhered to the view that poverty was evil, temporary in nature, and had to be removed.[13] If the earlier Isaiah ever characterized the entire group as oppressed, it would only have been in relation to a brief social crisis that affected the whole society.[14] By contrast, Second Isaiah can say that the people will find God's compassion because they now stand in the appropriate relation to God:

> Since the Israelites in Exile now saw and felt themselves oppressed and
> humbled under the Babylonian yoke, they or Deutero-Isaiah, who was
> addressing the exiles, found comfort in this humbled situation because
> it appeared to place the people in the right position in relation to God.[15]

The material in the Psalms, Baudissin argues, carries forward the understanding of poverty inaugurated by Second Isaiah. Baudissin observes that in
many places the Psalms make a close link between terms for poverty and terms
for piety.[16] This is not to say that all who are poor are pious but that the humiliating experiences of poverty and suffering can produce an inner humbling and
openness before God.[17] The pious poor are those, "who through the experience of being brought low allow themselves to bend inwardly."[18] This development is an expansion on the earlier prophetic notion that God has a special
concern for the poor. The psalmist believed that, "when God scans heaven and
earth, [God] looks down upon the lowly" (cf. Ps. 113:5).[19] Aware of God's favor
toward the lowly, the people were able to boast in being humbled by God's
guidance.[20]

This is not to say that, according to Baudissin, poverty was desired for its
own sake by postexilic writers.[21] Indeed, the poor do await compensation for
their submissiveness in their present sufferings, namely, that God will hear
them.[22] Rather than treating poverty as an end in itself, Baudissin suggests that
these writers see the condition of poverty as a means to God. Poverty becomes
one stage of the spiritual life.[23]

Poverty as a Negative Circumstance: Bruppacher

Bruppacher directs his criticism against two scholars, Causse and Loeb,
who maintained, much like Baudissin, that poverty and piety were linked in
the Psalms, and that a more positive regard for poverty developed in the postexilic period. In opposition, Bruppacher contends that, in fact, there is no ideal
of poverty anywhere in the Bible, nor is it exalted. Bruppacher claims, for
example, that Causse sustained his positive assessment of poverty only by
diminishing and neglecting the prophetic critique of injustice and poverty.
The prophets, as we have seen, reveal a negative evaluation of poverty which
Bruppacher thinks is characteristic of the entire biblical tradition. Bruppacher
argues that the prophetic concern for the poor results from a sense of compassion and opposition to poverty as such, and not out of value structures that
idealize poverty.[24] He adds that while this compassion may have been generated from a nomadic ideal as Causse claims (see ch. 1), it is an oversimplification to connect the nomadic ideal to an elevation of poverty.[25] In any case, the
negative evaluation of poverty that Bruppacher finds in the prophets and else-

where in the biblical materials mitigates the contention that one can find in the Psalms an idealization of poverty.[26] In the Bible, "an ascetic valuation of poverty is not demonstrated."[27]

Likewise, Bruppacher believes that the evidence for a religious or political movement built around the pious poor is weak. In particular, he criticizes Loeb's position that the poor of the Psalms are the pious Israelites of the post-exilic period who had come together as "the party of the poor."[28] It is Bruppacher's contention that "the literary sources offer us no handle for the proof that the 'miserable and poor' of the Old Testament were a more or less tightly organized community."[29] Poverty may invoke a religious attitude, but not more than this. Were this the case, Bruppacher insists, one would have to argue that the "wicked" in the Psalms constitute a specific organization as well.[30] Of course, while the poor may not have been a political party in Israel, this need not discount the view that the biblical materials, in particular the prophets, see the poor as a *group* victimized by another group, namely, the urban elite. It may be that both the wicked rich and the victimized poor were distinguishable elements of the society.

Poverty as a Concrete Reality: Van der Ploeg

Perhaps the most damaging set of criticisms against the early interpretations of poverty in the Psalms has been offered by Van der Ploeg. After surveying the positions of other scholars who maintained that the *'ănāwîm* constitute either a party of the pious poor or at least a religious movement in Israel, Van der Ploeg offered his own brief but telling review of the materials on poverty in the biblical text.

The prophetic literature brings out more readily the concrete nature of the poverty question, as Van der Ploeg observes. In Amos, the poor cannot pay off economic debts and are consequently hounded by creditors. Likewise, they lose grain to those who oppress them.[31] Van der Ploeg claims that the *dallat hā-'āreṣ* found in Jeremiah (e.g., Jer. 40:7) were the "poor *fellahîn* whom the Babylonians had not deported and whom they had left in the country to cultivate it."[32] These and other examples from the prophetic writings demonstrate for Van der Ploeg that the poverty which is of concern to the prophets is not some spiritual phenomenon; rather, it is social and economic oppression:

> From these prophetic texts, it clearly appears that, for the pre-exilic prophets, the *aniyim, ebyonim,* and *dallim,* etc., were the poor, the wretched (in the proper sense of the word) . . . who possessed nothing and who were unable to defend themselves against the rich, the powerful, and the strong.[33]

The prophetic materials foreground the socioeconomic ties that held sway in ancient Israelite society, both in the countryside and in the city.[34] Van der Ploeg comments, "In Israel there were poor people not only among the small merchants and artisans but also among those who had to make their livelihood through laboring in the fields."[35] In this context, the poor are those who are oppressed by the rich.[36] Van der Ploeg takes great pains to show that there is no positive estimate given to poverty in the biblical material, neither in the prophetic literature, the Pentateuch, nor in the wisdom literature.[37]

Such an overwhelmingly negative evaluation of poverty leads Van der Ploeg to suggest that scholars have misunderstood the nature and role of poverty in the Psalter. Van der Ploeg, therefore, offers a revised assessment of the 'ănāwîm. In the first place, he separates the 'ănāwîm from the poor on the basis of Psalms 10, 22, and 69, where the 'ănāwîm are said to rejoice in the salvation of the 'ănîyyîm and the 'ĕbyônîm.[38] Poverty ('ănîyyîm) and piety ('ănāwîm) are not to be connected on his estimation. For Van der Ploeg, the term 'ănāwîm does not denote any form of poverty, rather, it brings out the general stance of submission before God on the part of the believer.[39] This attitude of submission applies to believers no matter what their social status or condition may be, whether rich or poor: "Thus, we believe that the *anawim* were Israel's humble and pious, stemming from every social level, possibly especially among those who were not rich in worldly goods, without for this reason being poor in the material sense of the word."[40]

To sum up: Previous lexical analysis has left scholars divided over the nature and scope of the Psalter's approach to the poor. Clearly, lexical analysis alone is not a sufficient means for us to open up the justice dimension of the Psalms. While the prophets offer deep insights into the exploitative structures of their own society, their views cannot be invoked with certainty as a tool for the interpretation of the Psalms. Consequently, to make progress in our theological investigation of the social ethics of the Psalms, we must ask very different questions of these texts. Rather than looking at the poor, then, let us turn to consider pertinent aspects of the Psalter. In so doing, we will open up the contours and contexts of the justice question for the Psalms.

Divine Enthronement and Justice: God's Reign in the Psalms

The notion that a god achieves supremacy by triumphing over enemies appears integral to the mythological constructs of various ancient Near Eastern societies. The Babylonian myth of Marduk's defeat of Tiamat and the Canaanite story of Baal's conquest of the sea god Yam provide us with pertinent examples of this pattern. Since we know that the tale of Marduk was recited as part of the elaborate rituals of the Babylonian New Year's festival, the question naturally arises as to whether such a mythic tale was celebrated in ancient Israel. A number of scholars have "discovered" such evidence in the Psalter. A review of the evidence will enable us to raise questions about Israel's ritualization of justice matters. Does liturgy contemporize or defer the justice question?

Among Scandinavian scholars, in particular, the notion of a festival for the enthronement of YHWH gained notoriety.[41] The initial connection between the Babylonian festival and YHWH was offered by H. Gressmann.[42] This idea was extensively expounded by S. Mowinckel.[43] Mowinckel argued that the Psalms retain the flotsam and jetsam, the fractured libretti as it were, of the ancient Israelite autumnal festival that functioned with the same dramatic structure and according to the same sort of rituals as the Babylonian counterpart.

Adopting this festival as a lens, there is no doubt that we can discern among the Psalms a strong sense of the liturgical affirmation of the kingship of God. Eight psalms, specifically, are so taken up with the establishment of God's reign that they are commonly grouped together under the rubric "psalms of God as king," namely, Psalms 29, 47, 93, and 95—99 though Psalm 68 could also be added to round out this category and give definition to the liturgical possibilities in ancient Israel. When read against the backdrop of the Marduk and Baal tales, various features stand out. We notice, for example, the acclamation that God reigns (Pss. 93:1; 96:10; 97:1; 99:1; cf. 47:9 [8]). More importantly, we observe that several texts clearly invoke the mythical language of divine combat to shore up YHWH's claims to the throne of justice.[44] This language serves to underscore YHWH's authority and just rule, much as other tales of combat function to highlight the god's hold on supreme power and executive authority.

Another aspect of the Psalms that appears to be illuminated by comparison with other texts is YHWH's relationship to the earthly king. The Babylonian New Year's festival materials afford a vivid connection in this regard.[45] The king has the duty to fetch the god Nabu, Marduk's firstborn son, from Borsippa to ensure this god's presence at the ceremony. More significantly, on day five, the king is divested of his accouterments of office, namely, his staff, ring, mace, and crown, and is led into the presence of the god to confess his integrity. Twice during this ceremony the king is slapped by the high priest to signify the king's humble submission before the god. This ritual humiliation reinforces the intimate bond between the king and the god. The act also highlights the integral role of the temple in effecting this mediation.

Certainly one can examine the Psalms in light of the Babylonian ritual to ask whether or not such a festival ritually explored the relationship between YHWH and the monarch of Judah on David's throne.[46] The ambiguous position of the monarch in the Psalter, who is spoken of both as God's son (Psalm 2) and as a humiliated sovereign (Psalm 89), can perhaps find illumination against the backdrop of the enthronement festival thesis. A. R. Johnson has fully explored the position.[47] Perhaps such a festival in Israel rekindled the bonds between YHWH and the monarchy, serving as a demonstration of palace-temple authority before the populace. Such a theoretical construct might help contextualize references to the autumn dedication of the temple by Solomon, where royal prayers and priestly rituals combine to powerfully present the exodus God under the aegis of monarchic authority (1 Kings 8). Yet labored speculations over a probable Israelite autumnal festival must not cause us to lose sight of the mythopolitical quality of the spring festival, which truly and overtly celebrates YHWH's combat triumph over Pharaoh. Rather than speculate about the fall festival and about the various psalms of God as king, we observe Psalm 68 where the liturgical celebration of the God of exodus power is clearly in view (vv. 8–11, 25–28 [7–10, 24–27]). This God casts off the enemies (v. 2 [1]), defending orphans, widows, and prisoners (vv. 6-7 [5–6]). This spring festival, celebrated also poetically in Exodus 15, most clearly taps the strains of the Babylonian New Year's festival, which likewise accents blood purification, divine enthronement, defeat of enemies, creation of a new order, and the proper configuration of human political authority.

Thus, we see that the reconstruction of Israelite parallels to the Babylonian New Year's festival is fraught with speculation and tantalizing insights. With respect to a possible fall festival of YHWH's enthronement, we are left largely in the dark. The Psalms offer only hints and no sure guide. The spring festival would seem to put us on far safer ground. Yet even here we are left puzzled by this notice in 2 Kings 23:21–23:

> The king commanded all the people, "Offer the passover sacrifice to the LORD your God as prescribed in this scroll of the covenant." Now the passover sacrifice had not been offered in that manner in the days of the chieftains who ruled Israel, or during the days of the kings of Israel and the kings of Judah. Only in the eighteenth year of King Josiah was such a passover sacrifice offered in that manner to the LORD in Jerusalem.

Does this passage imply that no Passover was ever held during the time of the monarchy? On the face of it, this would seem to be the meaning of the text and not simply that no Passover quite like Josiah's grand celebration was ever held in Israel. This is an odd state of affairs, but might indicate that whereas under the monarchy the fall season may have held prime position (as seen in Solomon's dedication of the temple) in the late preexilic period and on into the second temple era, the community would come to place greater emphasis on YHWH's spring triumph, a victory that not only brought relief from foreign oppression but that more importantly foregrounded priestly authority vis-à-vis a chastened monarchy.

Whatever else we may find in the psalms about monarchy, it seems clear that in the total Psalter there is a new function for liturgy. No longer will there be bold affirmations of monarchic power, as with, in particular, Psalms 2, 18, 21, 45, 72, 110, and 144. Rather, in the tempered climate of the postexilic period, the reformist policies of a Josiah together with a more vigorous priestly voice will be the only political arrangement permitted. As Psalms 89 and 132 make painfully apparent, liturgy's revitalized role will be to mourn the failure of the old political institutions. Such mourning, as Brueggemann notes for the prophetic context, permits social newness and revitalization.[48] Here we find the potential coopting of the prophetic voice for liturgical purposes noted in our discussion of the prophetic literature. Such rhetoric is powerful in its adaptation toward postexilic reconstruction efforts. In any case, the die is cast. The priestly work of worship will become, through the spring festival and regular acts of worship, the potent voice for justice in the postexilic community. Hence, the Psalter will come to embrace the voices of the individual sufferer, the suffering community, and the prophetic call for judgment by placing all under an umbrella that boasts praises for God and for God's abode in Zion.[49] Indeed, those who take charge of Israel's worship life mediate the meaning of Israel's past for this new historic movement.[50] As in Chronicles, the Davidic image, so prevalent in the Psalms, becomes the vehicle of postexilic liturgical imagination.[51]

The implications of this liturgical development for our justice analysis are enormous. No longer does the monarchy serve as the locus of the political institutionalization of future social reconstruction. However, the monarchic past becomes a banner and wellspring for imaging a more just future. It is as if the old Near Eastern ideals regarding the monarch's duties to the disenfranchised have become detached from their original moorings to gain currency in a discussion to be carried on by priests, prophets, landowners, and teachers operating in a nonmonarchic milieu. We should not underestimate the political potency of royalist imagery in the postexilic context even in the absence of a viable royal claimant or a credible royalist movement. The priestly coopting of the Davidic rhetoric ensured that any such royalist nostalgia or hopes would come to be articulated more vibrantly in the sort of priestly-prophetic voice we have seen in Ezekiel. Perhaps we should see in DH and Jeremiah an effort to hold open the Davidic construct, but we should see in P's successful embrace of the spring festival the final triumph of the Priestly voice as the mediating point for the justice question as an institutional endeavor of the postexilic period. David the king becomes David the liturgical

emblem for a priestly program that has commandeered the categories of suffering, thanksgiving, and justice.

Suffering and Justice: Enemies in the Psalms

While it is true that much of the suffering discussed in the Psalter is of a
personal nature, with the psalms serving a potentially "therapeutic" function,
and while it is also conceivable that the "wicked" in the psalms may be, as
Mowinckel argued, sorcerers who send curses and illness, nevertheless, Birkeland's contention that much of the suffering evidenced in the Psalter is of a
national and political character deserves special consideration here in a materialist reading of the text.[52] Birkeland forcefully argues that, sociologically
speaking, various enemies alluded to in the Psalter must be understood to be
foreign enemies. My own study of the psalms of lament suggests that three
types of enemies can be distinguished, further nuancing Birkeland's analysis:
(1) domestic oppressors, (2) foreign conquerors of Israel, and (3) opponents of
Israel's exiles.[53] Birkeland is correct to point to Israel's national enemies, especially those who have wrought the destruction of the exile, a deed so vividly
captured by Psalms 74, 79, and 137. In a more general way, the entrapment of
Israel by foreign powers speaks to the enduring realities of national subjugation (see, e.g., Psalms 44, 60, 80, 83, 108, and 129). Out of the depths of political humiliation, the psalms allow the community to vent its anger at God by
asking, "How long, O LORD, will You be angry forever, will Your indignation
blaze like fire?" (Ps. 79:5).

With this as a plausible sociological context for the background of so many
psalms, we are left to ponder whether the Psalms speak not only to national
oppression but also to oppression within the body politic. Certainly the so-
called prophetic oracles of judgment explicitly address such concerns. Wealth
and exploitation, disenfranchisement of the poor, extortion, and idolatry all
find a bitter critique in these psalms (see, e.g., Psalms 50, 52, 75, 81, and 82;
cf. Psalms 15, 24, and 146). Perhaps the more problematic question remains
our inability to gauge the extent to which any of the individual psalms of
lament reflect domestic abuses and political injustice. Does the writing of a
psalm serve as a safety valve short of revolutionary action or rioting against the
elite? We will probably never know, but the sorcerer hypothesis undoubtedly
does not cover all references to unjust suffering depicted in the Psalter. Our
task is complicated further by the admittedly stock character of much of the
phrasing in such psalms. We know from Mesopotamian laments that many of
the psalmic images and formulas are traditional in character, serving to mask
the sociological realities behind the texts. G. T. Sheppard tries to rescue the
enemies from the oblivion of stylized forms by suggesting a social matrix in

which the psalms were intended for the hearing of the enemy.[54] While intriguing, this analysis fails to do justice to the cultic character of such texts. There is an internal communal dimension to the Psalms that one must not overlook when assessing the Psalter's form and social function.

The plight of the victim has been drawn into the rhetoric of the worship tradition concerning the enemies, regardless of whether or not the elite heeds the genuine outcry of the poor. This slant is characteristic of the priestly program, which, as we saw in our discussions of both law and narrative (in chapters 2 and 3), has made a strong pitch for being the voice of the oppressed. We may thus observe that the stock character of the texts does not negate a reality of unjust suffering brought about not merely by foreign conquerors but by the domestic leadership. More than illness, disease, and death, marginalization and exploitation were the undoubted concomitant socioeconomic by-products of the mode of production pursued by the petty monarchies and empires of the ancient Near East throughout the region's history. Stock phrases characterize this situation and remain in use precisely because the conditions they denote endure. That the priestly group has styled itself as the caretakers of such language does not thereby negate the attendant realities behind such texts. If only in a slightly rhetorical sense, the Psalms preserve for us the universal cry of the poor. In this sense, then, they continue to hold out poverty and justice as key issues for their community and any group that seeks to take up the Psalter to frame its liturgical life. Coopted by the religious sector or not, the Psalter nevertheless ensures that issues of both domestic oppression or international injustice remain on the community's agenda, perhaps even influencing the policies of chastened rulers and conscientized religious leaders. By the same token, the admittedly effusive language of the Psalms is malleable to the same sort of transformation we have seen in the concept of the *'ănî* in Second Isaiah.

Obedience and Justice: Psalmic Wisdom on Wealth

In the search for the wisdom genre of the Psalms, one cannot help but be a bit dismayed at the many and quite varied lists of so-called wisdom psalms. In an attempt to bring order out of the earlier chaos of this century, Roland Murphy offered some pointers beyond the impasse in his article, "A Consideration of the Classification 'Wisdom Psalms,'" an essay that has served as something of a benchmark in this area of study.[55] Murphy argued that literary factors such as style, theme, and content, together with a reconsideration of the question of the *Sitz im Leben*, could facilitate a clearer delimitation of this category of psalms.[56] To be sure, Murphy's was not the final word. Kuntz, Perdue, Scott, and others have brought to bear similar stylistic and thematic considerations, with the result that subsequent lists have continued to vary, offering further support for the category, but tending toward a greater degree of inclusion, especially with regard to torah Psalms 1, 19, and 119.[57]

Among the more recent interpreters, Kuntz, Scott, and now Hurvitz have, in particular, drawn our attention to the importance of linguistic criteria for gauging the wisdom stamp on the Psalter.[58] On Hurvitz's assessment, for example, the use of *ḥôn* for wealth in Psalms 112 and 119 as well as the use of *sûr mē-rāʿ*, "turn from evil," in Psalms 34 and 37 function to bring these texts inside the sphere of wisdom. In the case of Psalms 34, 37, and 112, Hurvitz helps to confirm Murphy's list, but does so on independent linguistic grounds. However, Hurvitz's addition of Psalm 119 to the category based on linguistic criteria serves to sustain the suspicions of others who would argue for an expansion of Murphy's list by keeping wisdom and torah psalms together as a single instructional unit.[59]

Admittedly, the wisdom category continues to pose something of a conundrum. Are these really texts in need of a genre? Or has the genre become a little too desperate in its search for unsuspecting texts? Before we give up entirely, leaving several psalms as orphans without a literary parent, I want to venture yet another attempt at a wisdom psalms genre. Partly my analysis rests on the sort of criteria offered by Murphy, Hurvitz, and others.[60] We will linger in particular over Psalms 37, 49, and 73. Psalms 37 and 49 are on Murphy's list, while 73 returns us to one of Gunkel's inclusions. The topic of wealth will serve as a partial clue to the delimitation of this genre.

Discipline, Obedience, and Success

The study of the book of Proverbs, in particular, reveals that the ancient Israelites shared with their Near Eastern counterparts the common wisdom views concerning poverty and laziness, hard work and wealth, success and rewards, obedience and loyalty, generosity and wickedness (see chapter 11).[61] In this tradition is a conscious social philosophy and public etiquette that breeds individuals who are adept at bureaucratic maneuvering and skillful discourse (see chapter 11).[62] This is made clear, for example, in the introduction to Proverbs (1:2–6).[63] Likewise, behind the many sections of admonition and collection of sentences in Proverbs stands a compelling vision of human reflection and action. Most notably for our purposes, the wisdom teachers show a great concern for diligence and offer strong warnings against laziness (Prov. 10:4; 19:15, 24; 21:5). Poverty, the wisdom instructions warn, results from too much sleep. The industrious ant becomes wisdom's model of success and prosperity (Prov. 6:6–11). Such a work ethic and ascription of poverty to laziness is cultivated throughout the text of Proverbs.[64] In addition to hard work, knowing one's place on the social ladder is essential to wisdom teaching.[65] In particular, obedience and loyalty to the king is key to the worldview of Proverbs.[66] As Bryce says, the king "is to be feared as God."[67] This attitude extends to all behavior in royal circles. Conduct at dinner with a ruler, for example, is to be circumscribed with respect and austerity (Prov. 23:1-3; cf. 25:15; 28:2).[68]

If hard work and obedience are the twin pillars of the wisdom philosophy of action, to what extent are these ideals represented in the wisdom and torah psalms? In the conscious pursuit of *tôrâ*, "instruction," the psalmists stand squarely within the wisdom tradition by affirming that loyalty and obedience yield rewards.[69] Primary obedience is shown to the decrees and judgments of the Lord: "Your servant is warned by them. In observing them there is great reward" (Ps. 19:12 [11]). This issue of obedience is dealt with most fully in Psalms 37 and 119.

In Psalm 119, the fact of the speaker's commitment to education and diligent study is used as the basis of an appeal to God to bring relief from persecution (Ps. 119:20–23, 84–87; cf. 119:58). Furthermore, the hard work of worship, rooted in love for and obedience to God's decrees, produces prosperity according to the psalmist (Ps. 119:164–165).

How concrete is this well-being engendered by obedience to God's decrees? In Psalm 37, such obedience becomes a precondition for dwelling and remaining in the land

> Look to the LORD and keep to His way,
>   And He will raise you high that you may inherit the land;
>   when the wicked are cut off, you shall see it.
>   Ps. 37:34

Human labor within the land is given renewed focus in Ps. 127:1–2. One significant reward, says this psalmist, is God's provision of children (Ps. 127:3–5). Similarly, Psalm 128 points to additional concrete benefits of loyalty to God:

> Happy are all who fear the LORD,
>   who follow His ways.
> You shall enjoy the fruits of your labors;
>   you shall be happy and you shall prosper;
> Your wife shall be like a fruitful vine within your house;
>   your sons, like olive saplings around your table.
> So shall the man who fears the LORD be blessed.
>   Ps. 128:1–4

To some extent, these passages display a connection to the larger wisdom tradition on matters of obedience, self-discipline, loyalty, and fruitfulness. · However, we must also note a significant point of divergence: The wisdom and

torah psalms are not concerned about hard work in general—only with diligence in studying and adhering to the ethical instruction, to *tôrâ*. Loyalty and
obedience, then, are categories invoked in these psalms to explicate one's relation to God. Here the standard wisdom categories, if such they are, receive
adaptation and refinement. In contrast to Proverbs, therefore, we find that the
wisdom and torah psalms contain nothing about obedience to earthly superi-
ors, in particular the king.

Most notably, the wisdom and torah psalms do not discuss the standard wisdom views of hard work and indigence, in particular, the view that poverty's
main cause is laziness. In this omission, writers of the wisdom and torah psalms
avoid promoting Proverbs's typical understanding of the origins of poverty,
thereby preserving the dignity of all human labor.[70]

Certainly the more substantive challenges to the prevailing wisdom view
linking work to rewards are found in Job, Qohelet, and the prophetic writings.
Yet, in kernel form, the wisdom and torah psalms open up an alternate understanding of obedience and success from that generated by Proverbs.

Poverty and Wealth

What are the attitudes toward poverty and wealth in the wisdom tradition?[71] Again, Proverbs serves as our guide. Poverty, according to the wise,
consigns the poor to a miserable, beggarly condition that leaves them poor at
the mercy of the whims of the rich and in slavery to lenders (Prov. 18:23; 22:7).
Socially and economically brutalizing, poverty is also physically destructive.
Drunkenness, for example, is connected with poverty (Prov. 31:7). These
observations that the wise make are stark and educationally instructive. Such
images strengthen Proverbs's view that poverty is essentially, in Van Leeuwen's
words, "a punishment that one brings upon oneself."[72]

Wealth, likewise, finds a prominent place in Proverbs. The extended sections
of instruction in Proverbs 1—9 take up such issues as the use of wealth (3:9–10)
and the problem of unjust gain (1:10–19). Elsewhere in the sentence literature
of Proverbs, we find wealth and poverty contrasted as two separate domains
(10:15; 13:7–8; 19:4). To have wealth is to have friends, observe the wise (14:20;
19:4), unlike the condition of poverty. Wealth creates security and stability for
those who possess it (10:15; 18:11). Wealth places one in a position of authority
or domination over the poor (18:23; 22:7). The contrast between the rich and
poor is made frequently in Proverbs 28.[73] Overall, as Malchow observes, we find
three attitudes toward wealth in Proverbs: (1) a respect for wealth, (2) an urging
to enjoy abundance, and (3) the suggestion that the rich deserve their wealth.[74]
This does not mean that the wise promote a hedonistic lifestyle. Indeed, they
emphasize the transitory character of wealth.[75] Further, they acknowledge the

need to exercise restraint in the use of one's wealth, noting that an excessive concern for wealth or the squandering of it can enslave and even lead to poverty.[76] Moreover, the wise counsel using wealth in charity toward the poor.[77]

The wisdom and torah psalms offer us some startling points of departure from the standard wisdom views about poverty and wealth, philosophic divergences that we might tend to overlook if we simply sought to explain these psalms under the rubric of "wisdom influence." Bearing in mind that there are passages that root prosperity in obedience and other passages that use the wisdom comparative style to state, for example, "Better the little that the righteous man has than the great abundance of the wicked" (Ps. 37:16), nevertheless, some of these psalms, in particular Psalms 49 and 73, provide striking critical statements regarding the vanity of wealth, statements that outstrip any of the discussions of the fleeting character of wealth found in Proverbs.

Consciously addressing the world—rich and poor alike—in a song concerning wisdom, Psalm 49 asks:

> Why should I fear evil times,
> When iniquity at my heels surrounds me?
> —those who trust in their wealth,
> boasting in their abundant riches.
> One person cannot redeem a brother.
> He does not give to God his ransom.
> The redemption of their Selves is costly.
> Ps. 49:6–9a [5–8a], my translation[78]

With sentiments that approach Qohelet's sense that death levels the differences between rich and poor, the wise and the ignorant, this psalmist states:

> He ceases forever—ever living again.
> He does not see the grave,
> But (only) sees wise people dying.
> Together the fool and the ignorant perish,
> leaving their wealth to others.
> Ps. 49:10–11 [9–10], my translation;
> cf. Qoh. 2:11–12, 18, 21

Reflection on the ultimate fate of the rich is mined to counter the fear that the rich instill in those who live beneath them:

> Do not fear when someone gets richer,
> or when the wealth (kĕbôd) of his house increases.
> For at his death he will not take anything.
> His wealth (kĕbôdô) will not go down after him.
> For he blessed his Self during his lifetime.

> And they praised you*, for it‡ improved you.
> He will go to the generation of his fathers.
> Never again will he see light.
> > Ps. 49:17–20 [16–19], my translation
> > *[= you were praised] ‡(i.e., the Self)

This text, although not without parallel to Proverbs's recognition of the fleeting character of wealth, powerfully moves beyond Proverbs in the direction of Qohelet's skepticism (see chapter 12).

We should observe, against Alexander, Gross, Kuntz, Lang, Ramaroson, and many others, that Psalm 49 does not offer the first glimpses of the afterlife.[79] Linguistically, Psalm 49's palindromic structure, partially misanalyzed by Casetti, clearly sets vv. 12–13 (11–12) at the text's center and establishes the text's original overarching unity from vv. 2–21 (1–20). This essential palindromic structural unity, which unfortunately cannot be detailed here, argues against Casetti's view that Psalm 49 is the product of a two-stage editorial development, wherein his second stage moves beyond the skepticism of his proposed initial phase (vv. 11–15, 21 [10–14, 20]) by positing a hope beyond death (vv. 6–10, 16–20 [5–9, 15–20]).[80] On the basis of content and palindromic structure, I would argue that for the author of Psalm 49, the wise person is one who recognizes (on this side of the grave) that what endures beyond death is one's reputation and not one's wealth. This realization is to govern one's conduct in this life, tempering one's attitude toward worldly wealth.[81] If these present observations hold, then clearly this psalm is in step with Proverbs's warnings about the elusive character of wealth. However, the text's overt mockery of the rich shares something of the skepticism of Job, Qohelet, and even the prophetic critique of the social elite's accumulation of wealth.

The most powerful critique of wealth appears in Psalm 73, a text that rather harshly assesses the dangers of amassing wealth. The poet begins by acknowledging a feeling of envy at the ease of the lifestyle of the wealthy and the health they enjoy:

> [F]or I envied the wanton;
> > I saw the wicked at ease.
> Death has no pangs for them;
> > their body is healthy.
> They have no part in the travail of men;
> > they are not afflicted like the rest of mankind.
> > > Ps. 73:3–5

The poet proceeds to draw a clear connection between this enviable way of life and the harsh realities of injustice this lifestyle entails, depicting the connection to a degree not found in Proverbs:

> So pride adorns their necks,
>> lawlessness enwraps them as a mantle.
> Fat shuts out their eyes;
>> their fancies are extravagant.
> They scoff and plan evil;
>> from their eminence they plan wrongdoing.
> They set their mouths against heaven,
>> and their tongues range over the earth.
> ·
> Then they say, "How could God know?
>> Is there knowledge with the Most High?"
> Such are the wicked;
>> ever tranquil, they amass wealth.
>> Ps. 73:6–9; 11–12

The last line is perhaps the most powerful. The term "wicked" contains no element of ambiguity in this poet's writing. Sociologically speaking, the text draws the connection, known more clearly from the prophets, to an amassing of wealth that is dangerously bound up with social injustices in ancient Israel.[82] In order to come to terms with wealth and the consequent attitudes wealth engenders, the psalmist turns, like Qohelet, to conscious reflection on the fate of the rich as a source of equalization and comfort:

> So I applied myself to understand this,
>> but it seemed a hopeless task
>> till I entered God's sanctuary
>> and reflected on their fate.
> You surround them with flattery;
> You make them fall through blandishments.
> How suddenly are they ruined,
> wholly swept away by terrors.
>> Ps. 73:16–19; cf. Qoh. 1:2–3; 2:1, 3–9;
>> 4:7–8; 5:9–12 [10–13]; 6:2

In the end, the poet affirms a commitment to the God who is a refuge to those who lack wealth, resources, and health (73:23–28). Psalm 73 is best considered a noteworthy inclusion among the wisdom and torah psalms, arguing against Murphy's and Kuntz's exclusion of this psalm from the genre.[83] We are led by this inclusion not to expect one specific view of poverty in the wisdom and torah psalms. By raising fundamental questions about wealth, Psalms 49 and 73 underscore the fact that there is much room for debate over the problem of poverty within the rubric of wisdom and torah psalms. Differences in attitude, even polarities, do not, however, constitute a basis for omitting particular texts from the genre.

Solidarity with the Poor or Charity?

Likewise, the category gives evidence of a debate over solutions to the poverty question. Psalm 112, for example, speaks of acts of giving to those in need (charity), invoking in the course of the first part of the text the proverbial wisdom motivation of personal reward as the basis for such generosity (Ps. 112:1–6, 9).[84] By contrast, Psalm 37 offers a perspective that rises above mere charity, namely, the view that God takes action to vindicate those innocents who are in need (Ps. 37:6–7, 11, 18–19, 25-26; cf. Prov. 22:22–29).

Of course, as Gutiérrez and Brueggemann have shown, the book of Job offers an even stronger statement of solidarity with those who are innocent yet who suffer.[85] Nevertheless, in Psalm 37, we have some of the seeds of the line of thought carried out in Job. It is fair to say that the writer in Psalm 37 offers a mediating position somewhere between the standard wisdom line of Proverbs and the critique of Job. The psalmist's words carry something of the conviction of the speaker Elihu in Job 32—37, who argues that God does indeed act in the world on behalf of those who are in need.[86] Insofar as we take seriously the more strident passages in Job, even the most radical of wisdom and torah psalms will be found to offer only a partial foundation for a critical discussion of wealth and poverty. Yet there is a striking kinship here that ought not to be overlooked as we seek to delimit the corpus of wisdom and torah psalms. This kinship with Job is highlighted, for example, by the sociological specificity in the use of the term "wicked" throughout Psalm 37, in contrast to the sociologically vague and philosophically stylized usage found in Psalms 1, 112, and 119.[87] The content of Psalm 37 clearly emerges out of a wisdom philosophic framework, but the text's solidarity with the cause of the poor borders on the prophetic.

Wisdom in the Psalter: An Ambiguous Trajectory?

A closer look at the topics of wealth and the wicked as they arise in the wisdom and torah psalms sustains the view that at some level these psalms are not exactly at home in the wisdom tradition represented by Proverbs. Sensing the dangers of the unbridled amassing of wealth, hearing the cries of the poor who are oppressed by the wicked, the writers of the wisdom and torah psalms are forced beyond the parochial endeavors of the wisdom tradition as represented by Proverbs. Where the wisdom and torah psalms depart from the standard wisdom view of wealth, poverty, and the wicked—and those passages are significant in range and depth—in those places we discover an alternate agenda for the pursuit of wisdom and instruction. In several of these psalms, the pursuit of wisdom and *tôrâ* comes to be directed toward a transformative ethical end, a vision that is keenly open to the plight of the poor in their oppression. Consequently, the wisdom and torah psalms consciously refuse to perpetuate the veritable attack on the poor that infuses Proverbs. The class motives that made the elite think it necessary to launch such an attack in order to establish its proverbial views on work, wealth, authority, poverty, and charity, were fundamentally undermined in the context of the wisdom and torah psalms debate. Where the wisdom and torah psalms capitalize on wisdom's ambiguousness about poverty and wickedness, we catch the glimpses of a social vision that comes to be more fully enshrined in Job, in Qohelet, and in parts of the prophetic tradition.

If these psalms were composed and collected in a priestly milieu, then we have yet another example of the priestly voice tailoring itself as one of advocacy for the poor (see chapter 2). In this regard, it may be helpful to adapt the framework outlined by Beyerlin in his study of Psalms 67 and 115, where he argues that a convergence of priestly and prophetic trajectories occurs in some postexilic psalms.[88] Similarly, we might suggest that wisdom had an impact on cultic poetry. Yet, much like a meteor spreading its debris over the landscape, the impact of wisdom is more strongly felt in specific texts. This impact is something more than can be accounted for by positing simple wisdom influence, for in some texts we appear to have a collision between torah, prophetic, and wisdom trajectories. Still, the priestly voice, with its program of justice for the poor, appears to have left its mark on the shape of the called wisdom and torah psalms. In any event, a sensitive reading of such psalms on the topic of wealth calls us to reexamine the wisdom and torah psalms against the geography of a broad wisdom-prophetic-priestly debate over pressing postexilic social concerns.

Engendering a Courtly Imagination: The Song of Songs

At the risk of sounding like one of Harold Bloom's "resenters," that is, those practitioners of a sociological-materialist analysis of literature whom Bloom contends "resent literature, or are ashamed of it, or are just not all that fond of reading it," I would like to render this socialethics study of the Bible complete by including the Song of Songs.[89] I do this not despite its greatness as a literary work (which it is) nor to turn it into a tract for justice (which it is not) but because, in the present context, the various literary motifs and forms of the text invite a reading that engages the seemingly open-ended gender relations implied by the text. The poetic pieces actually conspire to raise questions about the inclusion of sensuality in the construction of a common social life. Indeed, the work is the only book of the Bible that celebrates this integral element of our collective human experience.

Of course, we must contend with traditional Jewish and Christian readings that read the text as emblematic of God carrying Israel through calamity or the like.[90] Yet from earliest times there were those whose attitude was that of Origen's, namely, that in the study of scripture, "this book of the Song of Songs—should be reserved for study till the last."[91] In this, these interpreters tacitly acknowledge that a materialist reading, that is, a reading that takes seriously the character of the book as human love poetry, more naturally suggests itself as one encounters this "scandalous" inclusion in the canon of scripture.

While one need not dismiss the canonical and theological reception of this book in the tradition, nonetheless its literary shape has come more fully into focus in the light of a number of Egyptian love poems that bear striking similarities to the Song of Songs.[92] The various texts of Papyrus Chester Beatty I offer us the same balance of voices (male-female), the same rich body language and nature-linked descriptions, the same motifs of longing and quest, the same sickness and pining over love, the same sorts of euphemisms about locks and doors, and the same "brother" and "sister" language that we find throughout the Song of Songs.[93] Likewise, the collections found in Papyrus Harris 500 and the Cairo vases 1266 and 25218 afford comparable phrases about the unity of the lovers, the concern over what to tell "mother," the search for the beloved, the snare of love, and again the verbiage about "brother" and "sister."[94] While some of these themes may simply be a product of the universal character of love poetry, still their assemblage and concentration are too close to the Song of Songs not to suggest that the Song is an imitation of the court (not secular!) poetry of ancient Egypt. To be sure, the date of the current Song of Songs may be uncertain, but the Egyptian imperial contacts in Canaan are long lived, suggesting that precursors to the Song of Songs must have been part of the royal life of ancient Israel and Judah (cf. Cant. 1:1–5, 12; 3:7–11; 7:6 [5]; 8:11–12).

As a courtly work, the Song of Songs imposes on lived reality a grid for what is imaginable from an androcentric perspective and in terms of celebratable sensual relations, doing so under the literary guise of idealized types and forms. Sasson's distinction is worth noting in this regard: "I would argue that love poetry ordinarily ignores gender differences, focusing instead on sexual equality and that, written mostly by males, erotic poetry indulges a male fantasy, wherein females are made to seek out lovers with the determination that is supposed to be stereotypical of the male."[95] In other words, the egalitarianism of the lovers is only apparent and is not inconsistent with the distribution of social power and roles accorded women elsewhere in the biblical text.[96] Indeed, this poetry would normally reinforce a conservative social structure, as do the wasf poems in Syria often linked to the Song of Songs.[97]

The urban character of the texts is also more simply reflected in the shift of locales from Jerusalem and city to the countryside (1:5; 3:2, 5, 10; 5:7–8, 16; 6:4), and in the preponderance of royal allusions and military images (1:12; 3:7–8; 4:4; 6:10, 12; 7:5–6 [4–5]; 8:10). Most importantly, however, the urban character of this literature is betrayed by its idealization of the garden motif (1:6; 2:15; 4:12–15, 16; 5:1; 6:11; 7:13 [12]; 8:11–12). Such a tradition of agricultural idealization is no doubt shared with the Mesopotamian texts regarding the goddess Ishtar's relationship to the shepherd Dumuzi (Tammuz), poetry that undergirded the *hieros gamos* (sacred marriage) rituals of the royal court in the very ancient period of the region's history and that carry on in later settings apart from the Ishtar-Dumuzi theme.[98] While not wanting to turn the Song of Songs into such a set of sacred marriage texts, we cannot help but notice that these motifs are integral to the movement of the collection in a way not found in the Egyptian materials (1:1, 4–5, 8; 3:7, 9, 11; 7:6 [5]; 8:11–12).[99]

Jewish tradition has always been right in its celebration of this text, a use that Christian tradition could learn from in its general liturgical neglect of the Song of Songs. In a positive sense, keeping this side of the ancient poetic tradition alive is a much needed corrective or supplement to the psalms that speak to other aspects of human experience. Yet for all that, the modern reader cannot help but notice that such poetry provides the capstone to the "androcentric theater" that Ackerman warns us about, where the image of the feminine only expands to the limits dictated by the needs and imaginings of the males of ancient society.[100]

When the City Topples: Lamentations on Justice

The book of Lamentations mourns the death of an old theology and sows the seeds for the birth of a new vision of Israel as a postexilic people. These five stark chapters, set as they are in the hours of Jerusalem's destruction, focus the poetic imagination on the very eye of the storm to test the old theology of punishment and take the first steps toward a theology of survival. For the writer of Lamentations, the measure of God's justice can no longer be spoken of simply in terms of divine wrath, for the experience of the nation as victim and as oppressed proved to be the cracks in the theological wall that, through later writings such as Second Isaiah and Job, would burst through to radically different understandings of the issue of theodicy. Without the initial wrestlings in Lamentations, however, this philosophic opening regarding the justice question would not have been possible.

Lamentations is a relatively late example of a literary form known to us from ancient Sumer, namely, laments over the destruction of cities and their temples.[101] While texts for the cities of Eridu, Nippur, Sumer, and Uruk are also represented, the best known is the "Lamentation Over the Destruction of Ur."[102] This text offers a theopolitical reflection on the destruction of the city, an event that marked the end of the Ur III period (c. 2100–2000 B.C.E.). As the god Enlil abandons Ur and as the other gods abandon their various cities and shrines, a bitter lament is entoned over Ur's destruction. The text reads as if the city itself, its temples, shrines, and walls, grieve over this destruction. Not even the goddess Ningal, wife of Nanna the moon god, could, through her imploring, avert the disaster. The sky god Anu and the god Enlil are credited with the act of destruction. The text recounts in vivid terms the invasion, replete with corpses, wounded people, a collapsed government, and the temple's destruction. In that moment, the goddess Ningal leaves the city. While the gods "send" the "storm," the actual invaders are named: the Subarians and Elamites. There follows an elegant speech by Ningal, recounting the losses in terms of wealth, prisoners, and the destruction of the goddess's "house." The writer observes that, with this destruction, the feasting and offerings had come to an end, leaving the question lingering: "How long, pray, wilt thou stand aside in the city like an enemy? O Mother Ningal, (how long) wilt thou hurl challenges in the city like an enemy?"[103] The lament, which is really a song cycle, ends with the people turning to the moon god Nanna for assistance in this time of trial, anticipating the restoration of the city.

Another text that offers insight into Mesopotamian thinking on these matters is the ancient Sumerian "Curse of Agade."[104] The text opens by recounting the proud rise of Sargon (c. 2334–2279 B.C.E.) from his center in Agade throughout ancient Iraq's southern territory. The prosperity of Sargon's reign did not last, according to the text, as one of Sargon's successors, Naram-Sin (2254–2218 B.C.E.), sensing the goddess Inanna's abandonment of the city, sought unsuccessfully to force the gods to keep in place his hold on power. When divination did not produce the answers Naram-Sin wanted, he simply plundered and destroyed the city's temple. The text, reading as a politically charged, religious response to Naram-Sin's troubles, finds in the invasion of the Gutians a symbol of divine punishment for Naram-Sin's abuses. As with the Lamentation over the Destruction of Ur, this text also provides a vivid picture of the economic and social chaos, hunger, and death that accompanied this invasion. Likewise, words of lament go up to the gods. However, no matter how much the gods seek to appease Enlil in his wrath, the text concludes with a severe curse against the city. Lamentation does not, it would seem, automatically lead to hope.

Reading these texts with the book of Lamentations in view is rather enlightening. So removed in time, nonetheless, we find strong similarities in terms of the theological possibilities governing the shape of these texts, possibilities that go far beyond mere formal similarities in terms of subject matter.[105] With regard to Lamentations, a number of elements are noteworthy. Yet, as we shall see, what is outstanding in the case of the biblical text is that Lamentations seeks to take its own community, via this language, to a new theological horizon. The elite who once were the oppressors becomes defined through this text as the oppressed. Consequently, while they might not have all the philosophic answers about the God who is hidden (Lam. 3:44), the text allows its handlers to cross the divide of the exile's dislocation, leading to a reappraisal of all the old political and theological traditions.

One element in Lamentations' effort is the text's willingness to confront the destruction head on. Thus, as with the Mesopotamian city laments, the devastation of the city of Jerusalem and its temple get full play. The strongholds and the citadels, the walls and the gates, are all gone (see, e.g., 2:2–9). In good Mesopotamian style, the text sums up the situation with reference to the central shrine's destruction. With no temple (1:10), the festivals cease (1:4). Likewise, Lamentations goes on to detail the brutal situation of a people once prosperous (4:5) who have fallen into shameful degradation, where the city's inhabitants search for food (1:11, 19), infants starve (2:19), and children beg for bread (2:11–12; 4:1–2, 4). Most shocking of all, mothers devour their own babies to survive (2:20; 4:10). The brutality of the war is all too apparent as priests and prophets, men and women, young and old, find their respective ends at the edge of the sword (2:20–21). The aftermath for the survivors is equally brutal: princes are hanged, women are raped, and young men are sent into harsh slave labor (5:11–13). The poet's poignant pain is captured well when the text observes, "Better off were the slain of the sword than those slain by famine" (4:9).

When the poet queries, "Is there any agony like mine?" (1:12), the door is opened not only to an expression of a grief that knows no consolation (1:2, 9, 16–17; 2:13, 21) but also to the accusation that God is the one who has done this to God's own people (1:5, 8–9, 12–15, 17, 21; 2:1, 17, 20–21; 3:1; 4:11). Thus, at one level, while the text consistently acknowledges, "We have transgressed" (3:42; cf. 1:18, 20; 4:13; 5:7, 16) and thereby merit some form of retribution, the very circumstances and the brutality of the aggressor warrant asking, "Why have You forgotten us utterly, Forsaken us for all time?" (5:20). In essence, the punishment, if that is what the invasion of Jerusalem was, has far exceeded the crime (2:1–9).

This poetic expression of grief and questioning is, of course, good liturgical language in ancient Israel and Mesopotamia.[106] It is the language of lament known better from the Psalms, as we have seen.[107] Such language is consonant specifically with psalms devoted to the temple's destruction (Psalms 74 and 79). This language, while frequently stock in character, captures liturgically the dislocation of the community as it begins to confront a God who has become the enemy. Even the appeals to God for help fall into this rather stock rhetorical shape, using phraseology reminiscent of the Psalms (1:20; 2:20;

3:55–66; 5:1, 19–22). This language emerges, in part, from the honor-shame axis in ancient Israelite culture. The underlying issue, in this anthropological matrix, is the extent to which Israel's shame has become a sufficient punishment and the extent to which God's honor might be tarnished in a retribution process that has exceeded its appropriate frame (1:8–9; 2:15; 3:14, 42; 5:1–4). In the tension between God's honor and the people's shame is the opening beyond the dissonance created by the collision between the theological tradition and the experience of the exile.

Thus, for all its "stock" character, Lamentations presses through to a new level of the justice discussion. While this book has not reached the level of questioning present in Job, nevertheless, a philosophic opening has been made to measure theodicy by means of the treatment of the innocent. In Lamentations, this innocence stands in tension with the acknowledged sinfulness of the people. Yet the suffering of the innocent, so vividly depicted throughout Lamentations, will become the talking point in the continuing dialogue between the community and God over matters of divine governance.

For the writer of the poetic cycle of Lamentations, the exile raised new questions as the community's experience of suffering became a theological datum that refused to go away or be submerged under the Deuteronomic system of rewards and punishments. Imaginatively, this realization served to root the stubborn hope that begins to emerge in the text. Like Elihu's speeches in Job, this hope does not answer all the questions raised by the reality of the suffering of the innocent. Nevertheless, this belief in a God who does justice is a conviction woven into the tradition, a conviction that inserts itself into the discussion as necessarily as the accusations against God (3:21–39). Clearly, the exile unleashes the questions tackled by Job, but Lamentations points the way by highlighting the need to creatively mine the liturgical tradition for language that might move the community beyond mute suffering toward an engagement with the God of judgment.[108]

Yet the tendencies unleashed by Lamentations have consequences for our understanding of the sociological dimensions of this text. In seeing the tradition literally renew itself, we have a profound example of the way in which the elite, the carriers of the old liturgical voice, became the standard-bearers of the prophetic voice in a new way. As with Second Isaiah, Lamentations allows the elite to own its exilic experience not only as God's punishment of the "unjust" but also as God's ground for revitalizing the "just" who have been unjustly treated (3:31–37). In other words, by knowing affliction (3:1), the former oppressive elite becomes one, rhetorically and in human experience, with those who had been oppressed in former times. By its suffering, this chastened elite is readied to be the harbingers of God's hope. Sociologically, therefore, if, as Clines reminds us, we cannot find the writer of Job among the lower classes of the "oppressed," neither will the writer of Lamentations reside there.[109] Instead, we should see in such works part of the vital stream that enabled the preservation of many old Israelite traditions about law, prophecy, liturgy, and justice by an elite that sought to appropriate—not unjustifiably—those traditions through new theological filters. As the poet reconfigured the terrain of the tradition, new insights were forged that have become permanent markers in the discussion of the suffering of the innocent and in the construction of liturgies that seek justice.

To sum up our findings in this chapter: Ancient Israel's poetic imagination is alive with evocative texts that concretely raise questions of poverty, justice, gender, and divine presence. The Psalter's celebration of God's continued rule permitted both the mourning of failed institutions as well as the anticipation of a reinvigorated reign of God in Zion. This cultic consciousness encouraged the examination of such issues as personal and communal dislocation, the acquisition of wealth, and solidarity with the poor. The retention of a royal trajectory in the Psalms, within the postexilic context, functioned to underscore the need for a corporate embodiment of justice, as opposed to the pietistic isolation of individual believers. Similarly, the Song of Songs is reflective of the royal stamp that cast its shadow over the Psalter. Yet the preservation and reuse of royal love poetry in the postexilic setting speaks to the desire to have the community celebrate the whole of life, albeit within an androcentric framework. Finally, the book of Lamentations explores the liminal character of so much of Israel's cultic imagination, jarred as it was by bitter loss and dislocating destruction, though not without great gains: For at the very edge of the abyss the community finds the courage to fiercely interrogate the God of judgment. This is also one of the visionary discoveries of the wisdom writings, a side of the biblical tradition we now turn to in the following two chapters.

Notes

1. Examples of praise and lament poetry can be found in B. R. Foster, *Before the Muses: An Anthology of Akkadian Literature*, 2 vols. (Bethesda, Md. CDL Press, 1993), esp. 2:545–689.
2. For an example of the Mesopotamian material, see P. Michalowski, *The Lamentation over the Destruction of Sumer and Ur* (Winona Lake, Ind.: Eisenbrauns, 1989). See also *ANET*, 455–63, 611–19.
3. See J. C. McCann, ed., *The Shape and Shaping of the Psalter* (Sheffield: JSOT Press, 1993). McCann's defense of the view that the total Psalter ought to be viewed as instruction is fully detailed in his book, *A Theological Introduction to the Book of Psalms: The Psalms as Torah* (Nashville: Abingdon Press, 1993), esp. 13–40, although the very different arrangement and composition of the Psalms scroll at Qumran might make us a bit cautious in this regard. See J. A. Sanders, *The Dead Sea Psalms Scroll* (Ithaca, N. Y.: Cornell University Press, 1967). For a different approach see N. Whybray, *Reading the Psalms as a Book* (Sheffield: Sheffield Academic Press, 1996).

4. For a comprehensive survey, see N. Lohfink, "Von der 'Anawim-Partei' zur 'Kirche der Armen': Die bibelwissenschaftliche Ahnentafel eines Hauptbegriffs der 'Theologie der Befreiung,'" *Biblica* 67 (1986): 153–76.

5. Grätz, *Kritischer Commentar zu den Psalmen: Nebst Text und Übersetzung* (Breslau: S. Schottlaender, 1882–1883); and I. Loeb, *La littérature des pauvres dans la Bible* (Paris: L. Cerf, 1892).

6. For a general overview of the issues see Van der Ploeg, "Les Pauvres d'Israel et Leur Piété," *Oudtestamentische Studiën* 7 (1950): 236–270.

7. A. Rahlfs, *'ānî und 'ānāw in den Psalmen* (Leipzig: August Press, 1891.)

8. W. W. G. Baudissin, "Die alttestamentliche Religion und die Armen," *Preussische Jahrbücher* 149: 193-231; H. Birkeland, *'ānî und 'ānāw in den Psalmen*, Skrifter utgitt av det Norske Videnskaps-Akademi i Oslo II, klasse 1932, no. 4 (Oslo: J. Dybwad, 1933); R. Kittel, "Exhurs: Die Armen und Elenden im Psalter," in *Die Psalmen* (Leipzig: A. Deichertsche Verlagsbuchhandlung, 1914), 314–18; A. Kuschke, "Arm und Reich im Alten Testament mit besonderer Berücksichtigung der nachexilischen Zeit," *ZAW* 57 (1939): 31–57. For Bruppacher and Van der Ploeg "Les Pauvres," see below.

9. Baudissin, "Alttestamentliche Religion und die Armen," 210

10. Ibid., 209–10.

11. Ibid., 212.

12. Ibid., 211.

13. Ibid., 213.

14. Ibid., 213.

15. Ibid., 214, cf. 213.

16. Ibid., 216.

17. Ibid., 215–16.

18. Ibid., 216.

19. Ibid., 221.

20. Ibid., 218.

21. Ibid., 214–15.

22. Ibid., 220.

23. Ibid., 214–15. In his analysis, Baudissin wishes to distance himself from those who would identify the pious poor of the Psalms as a specific party or movement that emerged in Israel during and after the exile. On this score, Baudissin departs sharply from Loeb and Rahlfs, following a line of interpretation picked up by Kittel, Causse, and Birkeland. See Kittel, "Exhurs"; A. Causse, *Les "Pauvres" d'Israel* (Paris: Librairie Istra, 1922); idem, *Du Groupe Ethnique à la Communauté Religieuse: Le Problème Sociologique de la Religion d'Israel* (Paris: Librairie Félix Alcan, 1937); and Birkeland, *"'ānî und 'ānāw."* Baudissin identifies the notions of poverty and piety as tendencies, which logically emerged out of the national experience of the exile, building on ideas that were already found in rudimentary form in the prophets. According to Baudissin, the combination of piety and poverty finds expression in terms of a party only later in Jewish history in the Hasidim, who, in their humble reluctance to seek salvation in the present life, through revolutionary action are thought to carry on the pious poor tradition of the Psalms.

24. Bruppacher, *Die Beurteilung der Armut im Alten Testament (Zürich: Seldwyla, 1924)*. xi.

25. Ibid., xi–xii.

26. See, e.g., ibid., 2–24.

27. Ibid., 91.

28. Ibid., xii, 89; cf. Loeb, *Littérature des pauvres*, 147.

29. Ibid., 90.
30. Ibid., 91.
31. Van der Ploeg, "Les Pauvres," 244.
32. Ibid., 247.
33. Ibid., 250.
34. Ibid., 267.
35. Ibid., 245.
36. Ibid., 244, 246.
37. Ibid., 251–59.
38. Ibid., 263.
39. Ibid., 264.
40. Ibid., 265.
41. For the Scandinavian discussion and related studies, see the following: H. Gottlieb, "Myth in the Psalms," *Myths in the Old Testament*, ed. B. Otzen, H. Gottlieb, and K. Jeppesen (London: SCM Press, 1980); 62–93; A. R. Johnson, *Sacral Kingship in Ancient Israel*, 2d ed. (Cardiff: University of Wales Press), 1967; T. N. D. Mettinger, *The Dethronement of Sabaoth: Studies in the Shem and Kabod Theologies* (Lund: CWK Gleerup, 1982); J. C. de Moor, *New Year with Canaanites and Israelites, Part One: Description, Part Two: The Canaanite Sources* (Netherlands: Kamper Cahiers, 1972); idem, *The Seasonal Pattern in the Ugaritic Myth of Ba'alu: According to the Version of Ilimilku*, AOAT 16 (Neukirchen-Vluyn: Neukirchener Verlag, 1971); B. C. Ollenburger, *Zion, the City of the Great King: A Theological Symbol of the Jerusalem Cult* (Sheffield: JSOT Press, 1987), esp. 24–28. See also N. H. Snaith, *The Jewish New Year Festival* (London: SPCK, 1947); and C. Westermann, *Praise and Lament in the Psalms*, trans. K. R. Crim and R. N. Soulen (Atlanta: John Knox Press, 1981), 146–51.
42. H. Gressmann, *Der Ursprung der israelitisch-jüdischen Eschatologie* (Göttingen: Vandenhoeck & Ruprecht, 1905), 297.
43. See S. Mowinckel, *The Psalms in Israel's Worship*, vol. 1 (Nashville: Abingdon Press, 1962), chap. 5.
44. See F. M. Cross, *Canaanite Myth and Hebrew Epic: Essays in the History of the Religion of Israel* (Cambridge, Mass.: Harvard University Press, 1973), 147–86; and J. Day, *God's Conflict with the Dragon and the Sea: Echoes of a Canaanite Myth in the Old Testament* (Cambridge: Cambridge University Press, 1985), chap. 1.
45. For clarification from the Mesopotamian side, see J. A. Black, "The New Year Ceremonies in Ancient Babylon: 'Taking Bel by the Hand' and a Cultic Picnic," *Religion* 11 (1981): 39–59; and K. Van der Toorn "The Babylonian New Year Festival: New Insights from the Cuneiform Texts and Their Bearing on Old Testament Study," in *Congress Volume: Leuven 1989*, ed. J. A. Emerton (Leiden: E. J. Brill, 1991), 331–44.
46. For a full discussion, see W. Brueggemann, *Israel's Praise: Doxology against Idolatry and Ideology* (Philadelphia: Fortress Press, 1988).
47. See Johnson, *Sacral Kingship in Ancient Israel*, esp. 134–36, where he summarizes his oft misconstrued position.
48. W. Brueggemann, *The Prophetic Imagination* (Philadelphia: Fortress Press, 1978), chap. 3.
49. For a genre-based analysis of the psalter, see J. D. Pleins, *The Psalms: Songs of Tragedy, Hope, and Justice* (Maryknoll, N. Y.: Orbis Books, 1993).
50. This process is demonstrated in Psalms 78, 105, 106, 114, 136. See W. Brueggemann, *Abiding Astonishment: Psalms, Modernity, and the Making of History* (Louisville, Ky.: Westminster John Knox Press, 1991).

51. W. Brueggemann, *David's Truth: In Israel's Imagination and Memory* (Philadelphia: Fortress Press, 1985), chap. 4.

52. On the psychological function of the Psalms, see Athanasius, "The Letter to Marcellinus" in *Athanasius: The Life of Antony and the Letter to Marcellinus*, trans. Robert C. Gregg (New York: Paulist Press, 1980) 101-47. On the question of the enemies, see H. Birkeland, *The Evildoers in the Book of Psalms* (Oslo: J. Dyband, 1955); T. R. Hobbs and P. K. Jackson, "The Enemy in the Psalms," *Biblical Theology Bulletin* 21/1 (1991): 22-29; G. T. Sheppard, "'Enemies' and the Politics of Prayer in the Book of Psalms,'"in *The Bible and the Politics of Exegesis: Essays in Honor of Norman K. Gottwald on His Sixty-Fifth Birthday*, ed. D. Jobling, P. L. Day, and G. T. Sheppard (Cleveland: Pilgrim Press, 1991), 61-82.

53. Pleins, *Psalms*, chaps. 1 and 2.

54. Sheppard, "'Enemies' and the Politics of Prayer."

55. R. E. Murphy, "A Consideration of the Classification 'Wisdom Psalms'" in *Congress Volume: Bonn*, VTS 9 (Leiden: E. J. Brill, 1963), 156–67, reprinted in *Studies in Ancient Israelite Wisdom*, ed. J. L. Crenshaw (New York: KTAV, 1976), 456-57.

56. Murphy is aware that the *Sitz im Leben* question is complex and fraught with vagaries. Certainly scholars are much more cautious in their assessment than Mowinckel was when he sought to definitively place what he termed "learned psalmography" into a specific cultural milieu. See S. Mowinckel, *The Psalms in Israel's Worship*, vol. 2 (Nashville: Abingdon Press, 1962), 104-14. For a more cautious assessment, see. J. K. Kuntz, "The Canonical Wisdom Psalms of Ancient Israel— Their Rhetorical, Thematic, and Formal Dimensions" in *Rhetorical Criticism: Essays in Honor of J. Muilenburg*, PTMS 1, ed. J. J. Jackson and M. Kessler (Pittsburgh: Pickwick Press, 1974), esp. 221-22, where he endorses a cultic setting for Psalms 32, 34, and 49, but suggests that the public or domestic settings are also plausible.

57. See Kuntz, "Canonical Wisdom Psalms." L. G. Perdue, *Wisdom and Cult: A Critical Analysis of the Views of Cult in the Wisdom Literatures of Israel and the Ancient Near East*, SBL Dissertation Series 30 (Missoula, Mont.: Scholars Press, 1977); and R. B. Y. Scott, *The Way of Wisdom in the Old Testament* (New York: Macmillan, 1971), 192–201.

58. Kuntz, "Canonical Wisdom Psalsm," 199–211; Scott, *Way of Wisdom*, 121–22, 193–94; A. Hurvitz, "Wisdom Vocabulary in the Hebrew Psalter: A Contribution to the Study of 'Wisdom Psalms,'" *VT* 38 (1988): 41–51. Kuntz reckons with the limitations of this approach more readily than Hurvitz.

59. See, e.g., A. Deissler, *Psalm 119 (118) und seine Theologie*, MthSt 11 (Munich: Karl Zink Verlag, 1955), 269ff.; Perdue, *Wisdom and Cult*, 303–12, 323–24; A. Robert, "Le Psaume CXIX et les sapientiaux," *RB* 48 (1939): 5–20; and Scott, *Ways of Wisdom*, 199.

60. A useful introduction to the wisdom tradition is provided by R. E. Murphy, *The Tree of Life: An Exploration of Biblical Wisdom Literature* (New York: Doubleday, 1990). On the complex issue of the delimitation of the wisdom genre in the Psalter, see also Perdue, *Wisdom and Cult*, chap. 5.

61. For further discussion of the biblical wisdom writings within the context of the international ancient Near Eastern wisdom tradition, see the following: G. E. Bryce, *A Legacy of Wisdom: The Egyptian Contribution to the Wisdom of Israel* (Lewisburg, Pa.: Bucknell University Press, 1979); J. L. Crenshaw, "Education in Wisdom," *JBL* 104 (1985): 601–15; T. Donald, "The Semantic Field of Rich and Poor in the Wisdom Literature of Hebrew and Accadian," *Oriens antiquus* 2 (1964): 27–41; R. Gordis, *Poets, Prophets, and Sages: Essays in Biblical Interpretation* (Bloomington, Ind.: Indiana University Press, 1971); H.-J. Hermisson, *Studien zur*

israelitischen Spruchweisheit, WMANT 28 (Neukirchen-Vluyn: Neukirchener Verlag, 1968); A. Lemaire, "Sagesse et Ecoles," *VT* 34 (1984): 270–81; T. N. D. Mettinger, *Solomonic State Officials: A Study of the Civil Government Officials of the Israelite Monarchy* (Lund: CWK Gleerup, 1971); J. P. J. Oliver, "Schools and Wisdom Literature," *Journal of Northwest Semitic Languages,* Stellenbosch 4 (1975): 49–60; J. D. Pleins, "Poverty in the Social World of the Wise," *JSOT* 37 (1987): 61–78. For translations of representative texts, consult W. G. Lambert, *Babylonian Wisdom Literature* (Oxford: Clarendon Press, 1960), and M. Lichtheim, *Ancient Egyptian Literature,* vol. 1, *The Old and Middle Kingdoms* (Berkeley: University of California Press, 1973); idem, *Ancient Egyptian Literature,* vol. 2, *The New Kingdom* (Berkeley: University of California Press, 1976); idem, *Ancient Egyptian Literature,* vol. 3, *The Late Period* (Berkeley: University of California Press, 1980); idem, *Late Egyptian Wisdom Literature in the International Context: Study of Demotic Instructions,* Orbis Biblicus et Orientalis 52 (Göttingen: Vandenhoeck & Ruprecht, 1983).

62. The administrative and royal connections of the wisdom tradition are discussed in chapter 6. Against the royal analysis of the wisdom traditions, some, such as R. E. Clements, *Prophecy and Tradition* (Oxford: Basil Blackwell Publisher, 1975), 74, 81, have argued that the materials evidence a "popular, and often rural, background." Cf. J. A. Emerton, "Wisdom," in *Tradition and Interpretation,* ed. G. W. Anderson (Oxford: Clarendon Press, 1979), 214-37, esp. 221–27; P. J. Nel, *The Structure and Ethos of the Wisdom Admonitions in Proverbs,* BZAW 158 (Berlin: Walter de Gruyter, 1982), 79–81. What I am arguing is not that wisdom materials did not have a function (or origin) in the family or village; rather, my view is that the traditions we possess in Proverbs represent the educated urban-based wisdom tradition. As Lemaire, "Sagesse et Ecoles," 272, incisively observes, "The *written* transmission of *collections* of proverbs presupposes a cultural milieu different than that of the oral transmission of isolated proverbs used occasionally in daily life or in traditional palavers" (my translation) That setting, I argue, is the urban educational context, the *bêt midraŝî,* "my school," of Ben Sirach (Sir. 51:23). The view I develop runs somewhat counter to the analysis offered by R. N. Whybray, *The Intellectual Tradition in the Old Testament,.* BZAW 135 (Berlin: Walter de Gruyter, 1974), who, while he sustains an intellectual tradition as the ethos for the wisdom texts, does not envision the institutional background suggested here. Whybray's views find additional elaboration in *Wealth and Poverty in the Book of Proverbs,* JSOT Supplement Series 99 (Sheffield: JSOT Press, 1990), 45–59, 68–72, where he challenges the view that there is a royal ethos to the sentence literature of Prov. 10:1–22:16 and chaps. 25—29. On the other hand, Whybray does place the instruction literature of Proverbs 1—9 and 22:17–24:22 in the urban-royal educational context (Whybray, *Wealth and Poverty,* sections C and D).

63. Cf. the opening to the *Instruction of Amenemope*;

> Beginning of the teaching for life,
> The instructions for well-being,
> Every rule for relations with elders,
> For conduct toward magistrates;
> Knowing how to answer one who speaks,
> To reply to one who sends a message.
> So as to direct him on the paths of life,
> To make him prosper upon earth,
> Steering him clear of evil. (I, 1–10)
> (Translation of Lichtheim,
> *Ancient Egyptian Literature,* 1:148)

64. See, e.g., Prov. 10:4; 14:23; 19:15, 24; 21:5; 24:34.

65. The more skeptical and sociologically observant writer of Qohelet recognizes that the poor are victims of a system of hierarchical control; hence, the social ladder is one with powerholders and officials dominating and oppressing those who stand below them (Qoh. 5:7–8 [8–9]). The language used in this passage is striking, since the writer adopts the term *rāš* for "poor," the very term that Proverbs uses to speak of the poor as lazy. J. Kugel, "Qohelet and Money," *CBQ* 51/1 (1989): 35–38, offers the following nonstandard but intriguing translation of Qohelet 5:7 (8): "If you see the oppression of the poor and the perversion of justice and right in the place of judgment, do not be astonished at the matter; for one payment-taker upon another is at watch, and other payment-takers upon them." His argument sustains the view that the writer of Qohelet is brutally clear about the fact of oppression, but Kugel's translation alters the hierarchical dimension of standard translations of the text.

66. See, e.g., Prov. 16:12, 15; 20:28; 24:21–22; 25:2–6; 30:31.

67. Bryce, *Legacy of Wisdom*, 201. Cf. Prov. 14:35; 16:10, 14; 19:12; 20:2, 8; 24:21.

68. Likewise, God is also to be feared (Prov. 1:7, 29; 2:5; 3:7; 9:10; 10:27; 14:26–27; 15:16, 33; 19:23; 22:4; 23:17; 24:21).

69. On the pursuit of wisdom, see Ps. 1:2; 19:8–9, 11 [7–8, 10]; 37:34; 112:1; 119:1–16.

70. Cf. John Paul II, *On Human Work: Encyclical Laborum Exercens* (Washington, D.C.: United States Catholic Conference, 1981), esp. sections 9–10, 21–22.

71. For a survey discussion of poverty in the biblical tradition, see J. D. Pleins, "Poor, Poverty (Old Testament)," ABD 5: 402–14; and T. Hanks, "Poor, Poverty (New Testament)," ibid., 5:414-24. For studies specific to the wisdom tradition, see N. Habel, "Wisdom, Wealth and Poverty Paradigms in the Book of Proverbs," *Bible Bhashayam* 14 (1988): 26–49; Kugel, "Qohelet and Money," 32–49; Whybray, *Intellectual Tradition*, 14–22; and G. H. Wittenberg, "The Lexical Context of the Terminology for 'Poor' in the Book of Proverbs," *Scriptura: Tydskrif vir bybelkunde*, Stellenbosch 2 (1986): 40–85.

72. C. Van Leeuwen, *Le développement du sens social en Israël avant l'ère chrétienne*. Studia Semitica Neerlandica 1 (Assen: Van Gorcum, 1955), 153.

73. Prov. 28:6, 8, 11, 19, 20, 22, 25, 27. Cf. W. McKane, *Proverbs: A New Approach* (Philadelphia: Westminster Press, 1970), 621. Bryce maintains that Proverbs 28–29 is more favorable to the poor than the rich, thereby indicating a late date for this passage (cf. Bryce, *Legacy of Wisdom*, 118).

74. B. V. Malchow, "Social Justice in the Wisdom Literature," *Biblical Theology Bulletin* 12 (1982): 121.

75. Prov. 11:28; 20:17, 21; 23:4–5; 23:23–27; 28:22; 29:3. The Egyptian wisdom writings exhibit a clear awareness of the transitory character of wealth (cf. Ptahhotep §6, 30; Any 8:5–10; Amenemope 9:10–10:5, 18:12–13, 19:11–15, 24:15–17; Ankhsheshonq 9:11, 18:17; Papyrus Insinger 18:5).

76. Prov. 1:19; 10:2; 11:4, 28; 13:8, 11; 16:8; 17:1; 20:17, 21; 21:17; 23:20; 28:20; 29:3; 30:7–10. The Egyptian wisdom literature likewise counsels restraint in the use of wealth (cf. Ankhsheshonq 6:10; 7:7; 9:11, 24–25; 12:3; 25:6; Papyrus Insinger 6:17, 24; 15:7; 26:16).

77. Students are expressly told not to despise or mock the poor (Prov. 14:31; 17:5; 22:22). Similar counsel obtains in the Egyptian wisdom materials (Amenemope 4:4–7; 14:5–8; 15:6–7; 26:9; Papyrus Insinger 33:16). Charity toward the poor is enjoined as a virtue in the wisdom tradition (Prov. 21:13; 22:9, 16; 29:7, 14; cf. the Egyptian Any 8; Amenemope 16:5–10, 26:13–14, 27:4–5; Ankhsheshonq 15:6; Papyrus Insinger 15:22; 16:12–14' 25:6). I disagree with Malchow, "Social Justice," 122, when he argues that wisdom charity is an active posture deserving the label "social justice." In failing to separate the more activist posture of Job from

the charity solution of Proverbs, Malchow has overlooked an important debate within the wisdom tradition. Cf. J. D. Pleins, "Poverty in the Social World of the Wise," *JSOT* (1987): 70–71. The motivations provided in Proverbs for charitable giving do not exhibit a sense of social justice. One gives to the poor (1) to avoid falling into poverty (22:16), (2) to avoid being mistreated should one become poor (21:13; 28:27), or (3) to obtain blessings and rewards from God (11:24; 14:21; 19:17).

78. For a complete study of Psalm 49, see J. D. Pleins, "Death and Endurance: Reassessing the Literary Structure and Theology of Psalm 49," *JSOT* 69 (1996): 19–27.

79. See T. D. Alexander, "The Psalms and the Afterlife," *IBS* 9 (1987): 2–17; H. Gross, "Bei Ihm ist Erlösung in Fülle," BK (Stuttgart) 42 (1987): 104–8; idem, "Selbst-oder Fremderlösung: Überlegungen zu Psalm 49, 8–10," in *Wort, Lied und Gottesspruch: Beiträge zu Psalmen und Propheten*, ed. J. Schreiner (Würzburg: EchterVerlag, 1972); E. Haag, "Seele und Unsterblichkeit in biblischer Sicht," in *Seele: Problembegriff Christlicher Eschatologie*, ed. W. Breuning (Quaestiones Disputatae 106 (Freiburg: Herder, 1986), esp. 45–49; J. K. Kuntz, "The Retribution Motif in Psalmic Wisdom," *ZAW* 89 (1977): 223–33; B. Lang, "Afterlife," *Bible Review* 4/1 (1988): 12–23; T. Long, "Life after Death: The Biblical View," *Bible Today* 20 (1982): 347–53; O. Loretz, "Ugaritisches und Jüdisches Weisheit und Tod in Psalm 49: Stil contra parallelismus membrorum," *Ugarit Forschungen* 17 (1986): 189–212; F. Meyer, "The Science of Literature Method of Professor Weiss in Confrontation with Form Criticism, Exemplified on the Basis of Ps. 49," *Bijdragen: Tijdschrift voor Filosofie en Theologie* 41 (1979): 152–68; J. A. Mindling, "Hope for a Felicitous Afterlife," *Laurentianum* 32 (1991): 305–69; L. Ramaroson, "Immortalité et résurrection dans les Psaumes," *Science et Esprit* 36 (1984): 287–95; and F. Stolz, *Psalmen im nachkultischen Raum*, Theologische Studien 129 (Zürich: Theologischer Verlag, 1983), esp. 57–60.

80. See Casetti, *Gibt es ein Leben vor dem Tod? Eine Auslegung von Psalm 49*, OBO 44 (Freiburg/Göttingen: Universitätsverlag/Vandenhoeck & Ruprecht, 1982), 210–31. Likewise, my analysis would argue against Loretz, who sees the text not in terms of editorial stages but as text plus commentary. See Loretz, "Ugaritisches und Jüdisches Weisheit und Tod, 212.

81. This interpretation is in keeping with that of Craigie, who, however, does not review the previous discussions of the supposed afterlife dimensions of this psalm. See P. C. Craigie, *Psalms 1—50* (Waco: Word, 1983), 356–61.

82. See J. A. Dearman, *Property Rights in the Eighth-Century Prophets*, SBL Dissertation Series 106 (Atlanta: Scholars Press, 1988); and L. Epsztein, *Social Justice in the Ancient Near East and the People of the Bible*, trans. J. Bowden (London: SCM Press, 1986), chap. 7.

83. Murphy, *Tree of Life*, 164; J. K. Kuntz, "The Retribution Motif in Psalmic Wisdom," *ZAW* 89 (1977): 225.

84. Contrast this passage with the more complex Deut. 15:4–18, which combines the wisdom notion of rewards for generosity/loyalty with the additional covenantal/historical motivation to act because "you were slaves in the land of Egypt" (Deut 15:15). In the mind of the Deuteronomist, instruction (*tôrâ*) alone is not a sufficient catalyst for action apart from the recreative reality of the exodus liberation and the contractual obligations of the Sinaitic covenant. Within the wisdom tradition represented by Proverbs, however, the story of God's dealings with Israel plays no role as a basis for right action.

85. See W. Brueggemann, "Theodicy in a Social Dimension," *JSOT* 33 (1985): 3–25; and G. Gutiérrez, *On Job: God-Talk and the Suffering of the Innocent*, trans. M. J. O'Connell (Maryknoll, N.Y.: Orbis Books, 1987), esp. chaps. 5 and 6.

86. Cf. J. D. Pleins, " 'Why do you hide your face?' Divine Silence and Speech in the Book of Job," *Int* 48/3 (1994): 229–38.

87. The Hebrew term *rāšā'*, "wicked," for example, appears 76 times in the book of Proverbs, more than in the entire Psalter (74). The same word occurs regularly in the text of Job (25) and in Qohelet (6), in contrast to its rarity in the Pentateuch and DH. Generally the term is rare in the prophetic literature, appearing most frequently in Isaiah and concentrated in specific chapters of Ezekiel (3; 18; 21; 33). Virtually the same comments apply to the distribution of the term *ṣaddîq*, "just," with the exception that this word is noticeably less frequent in Job. With regard to the distinction between wise and fool, consult J. L. Crenshaw, *Old Testament Wisdom: An Introduction* (Atlanta: John Knox Press, 1981), 80; and W. O. E. Oesterley, *The Book of Proverbs* (London: Methuen, 1929), lxxxiv–lxxxvii. Cf. Prov. 11:4–5; 12:15; 13:6; 14:9; 14:24; 15:5; 16:14; 17:10.

88. W. Beyerlin, *Im Licht der Traditionen: Psalm LXVII & CXV, Ein Entwicklungszusammenhang* (Leiden: E. J. Brill, 1992).

89. H. Bloom, *The Western Canon: The Books and School of the Ages* (New York: Harcourt, Brace & Co., 1994), 521.

90. M. Pope, *Song of Songs: A New Translation with Introduction and Commentary* (New York: Doubleday, 1977), 102–3.

91. Ibid., 117.

92. For the comparative material, see M. V. Fox, *The Song of Songs and the Ancient Egyptian Love Songs* (Madison: University of Wisconsin Press, 1985); and M. Lichtheim, *Ancient Egyptian Literature*, 2:181–93.

93. Lichtheim, *Ancient Egyptian Literature*, 2:182–89.

94. Ibid., 2:190–93. For a full study of the poetic motifs, see M. Falk, *Love Lyrics from the Bible: A Translation and Literary Study of the Song of Songs* (Sheffield: Almond Press, 1982).

95. J. Sasson, "A Major Contribution to Song of Songs Scholarship," *JAOS* 107 (1987): 735.

96. Thus, I would argue against the apparent "mutual fulfillment" that Bergant finds in the text. See D. Bergant, "'My Beloved Is Mine and I Am His' (Song 2:16): The Song of Songs and Honor and Shame," *Semeia* 68 (1996): 23–40, esp. 29. Bergant's essay, nonetheless, remains insightful and provocative.

97. Pope, *Song of Songs*, 56–57.

98. See, e.g., S. N. Kramer, *The Sacred Marriage Rite: Aspects of Faith, Myth, and Ritual in Ancient Sumer* (Bloomington, Ind.: Indiana University Press, 1969), chap. 5.

99. For criticisms on attempts to tie the Song of Songs to a sacred marriage ritual, see Fox, *Song of Songs*, 239–43. While Fox's observations are well taken, his suggestion that such poetry was simply for entertainment hardly does justice to the courtly character of the texts, whether Israelite or Egyptian (244). For additional background, see J. S. Cooper, "Sacred Marriage and Popular Cult in Early Mesopotamia," in *Official Cult and Popular Religion in the Ancient Near East*, ed. E. Matsushima (Heidelberg: Universitätsverlag C. Winter, 1993); E. Matsushima, "Les Rituels du Mariage Divin dans les Documents Accadiens," *Acta Sumerologica* 10 (1988): 95–128; and D. Reisman, "Iddin-Dagan's Sacred Marriage Hymn," *JCS* 25 (1973): 185–202.

100. S. Ackerman, *Warrior, Dancer, Seductress, Queen: Women in Judges and Biblical Israel* (New York: Doubleday, 1998), 1.
101. Composed in the Isin-Larsa period (1950–1700 B.C.E.) and transmitted in the later scribal schools, any parallels between these texts and the biblical record may only be apparent rather than reflecting any later Mesopotamian practices. See D. R. Hillers, "Lamentations, Book of," *ABD* 4:140.
102. Michalowski, *Destruction of Sumer and Ur*; see also *ANET* 455–63; 611–19. For other background texts, consult M. Green, "The Eridu Lament," *JCS* 30 (1978): 127–169; and idem, "The Uruk Lament," *JAOS* 104 (1984): 253–79.
103. *ANET*, 462.
104. Ibid., 646-51. For a complete analysis, see J. S. Cooper, *The Curse of Agade* (Baltimore: Johns Hopkins, 1983).
105. Contrast T. McDaniel, "The Alleged Sumerian Influence upon Lamentations," *VT* 18 (1968): 198–209.
106. Regarding the Mesopotamian materials, see M. Cohen, *The Canonical Lamentations of Mesopotamia* (Potomac: Capital Decisions, 1988); and R. Kutscher, *Oh Angry Sea (a-ab-ba hu-luh-ha): The History of a Sumerian Congregational Lament* (New Haven, Conn.: Yale University Press, 1975).
107. Pleins, *The Psalms*, chaps. 1–2.
108. This is essentially the thesis of D. Soelle, *Suffering* (Philadelphia: Fortress Press, 1975).
109. D. J. A. Clines, *Job 1—20* (Dallas: Word Books, 1989), lii–liv.

Chapter 11

The Poverty Debate

Proverbs

Does a divine hand shape the ebb and flow of justice in the world? Does the punishment fit the crime on life's stage of ethical decision making? Can the poor ever hope for a fair shake this side of the grave? Sharing a deep kinship with the educational traditions of Egypt and Mesopotamia, the ancient Israelites also produced texts to address such questions. In the Hebrew Bible, three such works command our attention—Proverbs, Job, and Qohelet (Ecclesiastes). As we shall see in this chapter, Proverbs most closely resembles the collections of sentences and exhortations that are most well known from Egypt (though also represented in Mesopotamian tradition) texts that cull insight from an array of human deeds, desires, and distractions. On the other hand, the works of Job and Qohelet, studied in the next chapter, represent a variant literary type, the dispute text, known especially from Mesopotamia, in which common wisdom themes are subjected to further examination: The text of Job represents a disputation regarding the justice of God's judgments, while the book of Qohelet carefully scrutinizes the utility of wisdom in a world of unpredictability and death. Yet, whether in the form of collected "insight" or reexamined "wisdom," these three books offer a critical look at key matters of ethics and divine governance in ancient Israel's ongoing debates about justice.

    This chapter opens with a discussion of the social world of wisdom literature. While others have tried to place Proverbs in a folkish or familial context,

I will argue that, following kindred Egyptian and Mesopotamian wisdom texts, the book of Proverbs strongly reflects the amalgamated wisdom teaching predominant among the educated elite of ancient society. Having laid this historical foundation, we shall next turn to a discussion of Proverbs, detailing its social philosophy and exploring the text's treatment of the topic of poverty. As we unpack the Proverbs material we will begin to uncover significant disparities in language between Proverbs, Job, and Qohelet, thereby exposing divergent ideological outlooks, social locations, and ethical frames within the broader wisdom tradition.

Sociohistorical Background of the Book of Proverbs

Can we reconstruct the social world of Proverbs? In order for us to effectively compare this work to other biblical materials, in particular the prophetic texts, it is necessary to understand the sociopolitical context in which the wisdom writings arose. What views of the world drove the insights of the ancient wisdom outlook? What ethical modes of discourse governed their views of the just and the good? Studying the Israelite proverbial literature in light of its Mesopotamian and, in particular, its Egyptian parallels offers beneficial clues concerning this background.[1]

Many argue that the materials in Proverbs have their origins in the life and needs of the royal court, the "work of the literati," as Fox aptly observes.[2] Several scholars see evidence for this in the fact that the Egyptian and Mesopotamian wisdom writings were produced by the court schools, handing on the texts as an integral part of the elite's literary and educational training.[3] The Egyptian wisdom instructions in particular are often connected with kings or royal officials, and thus naturally have their place in the life of the court. We note the major Egyptian texts here, leaving the relevant Mesopotamian records for the next chapter.

The earliest example of such literature from Egypt's Old Kingdom (c. 2686–2181 B.C.E.) is a work from crown prince Hardjedef directed to his son.[4] Another text from this period was composed by an anonymous vizier for his son Kagemni, after whom the piece is named and who was eventually elevated to a prominent governing post.[5] The high-born status of the writers of such literature in the Old Kingdom is attested in the more extensive text ascribed to Ptahhotep, a crown prince and a governing official.[6] In the First Intermediate Period (c. 2181–2040 B.C.E.), the court associations of Egyptian wisdom writings were heightened. It was then that wisdom texts were assigned to the pens of the kings themselves. The *Instruction to Merikare* is that of an elder king to his son, the heir apparent.[7] These royal associations were carried on in the Middle Kingdom (c. 2040–1786 B.C.E.) in the form of the *Instruction of King*

Amenemhet I for his son Sesostris I.[8] A document from the same period, *The Satire of the Trades,*[9] has professional connections. This text contains admonition material and purports to be the sage advice of a scribe to his son, a would-be scribe. Such professional associations for the wisdom writings are found as well in the New Kingdom (c. 1558–1085 B.C.E.). The *Instruction of Any* is the writing of a scribe directed to his son,[10] the *Instruction of Amennakhte* offers teachings to the scribal apprentice Ḥarmin, and the *Instruction of Amenemope* is the work of a royal agricultural overseer.[11] The aristocratic locus of the wisdom material persists in the late period. The *Instruction of Ankhsheshonq* is ascribed to a priest of the sun god Re at Heliopolis.[12] A final example, *Papyrus Insinger*, unfortunately lacks its initial portion and does not explicitly identify either its author or recipient elsewhere in the text. However, the instructional character is clear from the content of the text and from its division into twenty-five lessons, which detail various aspects of proper conduct.[13]

The educational nature of the Egyptian materials as well as their court associations are well established.[14] It has been argued by some scholars, however, that such a background cannot be postulated for biblical wisdom texts since no evidence is available of either a textual or archaeological nature that can be used to substantiate the presence of a royal education system in Israel during the period of the monarchy.[15] For such scholars, the point of origin of the wisdom material is to be sought elsewhere, namely, in popular and clan settings.[16] An effective rejoinder to this approach has been offered by Lemaire, who observes that Israel would have needed centers of learning to educate its officials.[17] Lang offers a more cautious reassessment, though still sees Proverbs as an education text.[18] So while it is the case that such a center, the *bet midrasi*, "my study house," is only explicitly mentioned by Ben Sirach (Sir. 51:23), the needs of an administrative elite *required* training centers, whether in the form of "schools," classes held at the city gate (the "forum"), or some other manner of formalized instruction, such as apprentice programs.[19] These considerations in and of themselves do not prove that Proverbs served as an instructional text for court officials, but the apparent archaeological silence concerning schools in Israel does not thereby undermine the supposition that material in Proverbs most likely served as educational subject matter for members of the governing corps.[20] One must bear in mind that even the vast Egyptian wisdom literature rarely betrays a specific instructional setting, but its royal and scribal associations speak for the literature's elite educational and ideological purposes.[21] Further considerations can secure such a social background for the biblical wisdom writings as well.

The royal associations of Proverbs are not to be denied.[22] Kings, such as Solomon and Hezekiah, are expressly connected with the text (Prov. 1:1; 25:1).

Thus, on the surface at least, royal patronage, rather than popular culture, infuses the text of Proverbs, a fact that even Clements stresses.[23] Solomon, in particular, is portrayed as the wise ruler in the biblical tradition (1 Kings 3:7–14, 16–28; 5:9–14 [4:29–34]; 5:21, 26 [7, 12]; 10:1–9). The royal background of the wisdom literature may help to explain why the office of the king plays an important role in Proverbs.[24] The king is important to the maintenance of order and justice in society (Prov. 8:15–16; 16:12; 20:8, 26; 22:11; 29:4, 14; 30:22).[25] In particular, he is the protector of the weak (29:14).[26] The king has special access to the divine, and therefore has extraordinary knowledge and powers of judgment (16:10; 21:1; 25:2–3; cf. 1 Kings 3:4–14).[27] As Bryce indicates, for Proverbs, the king "is to be feared as God" (14:35; 16:10, 14; 19:12; 20:2, 8; 24:21).[28] The text repeatedly urges loyalty and respect for the king (16:12, 15; 20:28; 24:21–22; 25:2–6; 30:31).[29] The urban landscape, with kings, nobles, city gates, streets, and public squares, infuses the instructions of chaps. 1—9 (1:20–21; 8:2–3, 15–16; 9:3).[30] These themes and emphases are quite proper for those receiving an education in royal society.

Yet there is dissent on this matter, with some arguing that the biblical text of Proverbs reflects the traditions and attitudes of popular culture.[31] What is meant by this view is that the proverbial literature has its roots in the nonroyal village society of the premonarchic period, with the wisdom traditions being shaped and fostered in later periods in contexts, such as the family, largely separate from the royal court or an elite educational context.[32] However, Lemaire argues that written collections such as Proverbs would not have had their setting in popular culture: "The written transmission of collections of proverbs presupposes a different cultural setting than that of the oral transmission of isolated proverbs used occasionally in daily life or in traditional verbal parleys."[33] As a written text, therefore, the admonitions and sentence collections that comprise Proverbs would have served the needs of those who knew how to read and write and who were employed for scribal purposes. Thus, while it may be the case that some of the proverbial material derives from the popular culture, its transferral into writing and its subsequent transmission in written form is an indicator of the functional distinctions of this material as text for training the future educated elite. As Nel observes, "One can hardly conceive of a fixed wisdom tradition before the monarchy with its official administration."[34] Invoking the Egyptian and Mesopotamian parallels, Kovacs decisively negates the popular culture analysis: "The counter-inference is not plausible, that the sophisticated writings of the learned in one society [Egypt and Mesopotamia] should so closely resemble the popular wisdom of another [Israel] . . . especially when the two societies are closely affiliated socially and intellectually."[35]

The possible direct influence of Egyptian wisdom on the Israelite tradition strengthens this consideration. In particular, the instructional style, common to the Egyptian tradition, was also important to the Israelite scribal tradition (Prov. 1—9; 31:1–9).[36] Moreover, the royal and educational background of the Egyptian wisdom writings helps to place Prov. 22:17–24:34 and other texts in Proverbs in an intelligible context. It has been argued, for example, that Prov. 22:17–24:34, especially 22:17–23:11, exhibits close connections to the Egyptian text of Amenemope.[37] Furthermore, Bryce contends that Prov. 25:2–27 forms a book of instructions intended for the education of courtiers.[38] An appropriate setting for this literature, or at least the origins of such a tradition in Israel, would be the court of Solomon.[39] Solomon's connections with Egypt are known (1 Kings 3:1; 7:8; 9:16; 9:24; 11:11; 2 Chron. 8:11), and some have argued that the type of administrative structure adopted by Solomon has its roots in Egyptian models.[40] One may suppose, therefore, that these Israelite texts, like their Egyptian counterparts, would have been designed for the instruction of aspiring court scribes and officials.[41] The production of wisdom literature for the instruction of Solomon's civil service based on Egyptian literary styles and patterns would not be a surprising development in this setting.[42] The nascent Israelite bureaucratic structure grew so rapidly because it was able to take advantage of Egypt's vast cultural experience, either through direct borrowing, as appears to be the case for Amenemope, or else as mediated through the Canaanite city-states that had long been under Egyptian influence.[43] Solomon's court was, in fact, Canaanite and would have had access to these traditions.

On this reading, those who convey these traditions, the wise, are to be regarded as professional functionaries in the monarchic establishment.[44] The prophetic writings provide evidence that the wise were a distinct group of no small importance to the administrative bureaucracy.[45] The prophets group the wise among the other members of the ruling elite, namely the priests, diviners, prophets, governing officials, and warriors (Isa. 19:11–12; 44:25; Jer. 8:8–9; 9:22 [23]; 10:7; 18:8; 50:35; 51:57; Ezek. 27:8; Obad. 1:8).[46] On the basis of this evidence, Bryce rightly terms the wise a "professional class."[47] Similar views are propounded by McKane, who contends that the wise were high political advisors in the employ of the state.[48]

The prophets stood in opposition to the wise. Yet we must ask why the two groups were in conflict at all. The wisdom literature makes clear the basis for the strong opposition of the prophets toward the wise: The wisdom teachers take no account of the values and beliefs framed by Israel's covenant tradition.[49] While YHWH and the "Maker" (Prov. 14:31; 17:5) find a place in Proverbs, the elements of covenant history and (more important to the prophets) covenant-breaking are entirely absent.[50] This prophecy/wisdom conflict throws into sharp relief the question of the nature and role of religiously based values and norms in the wisdom literature.[51] Given its intimate connections to the prevailing political authority, many have suggested that the wisdom material is more secular or humanistic in its orientation.[52] Gordis, for example, depicts the morality of the wisdom literature to be a reflection of the universal cosmopolitan tendencies of the elite.[53] He considers the morality advocated in this literature to be utilitarian in its thrust, urging industry in one's labors and "submissiveness to authority."[54] However, it is clear that the biblical wisdom writings do give a place to the reality of the divine in human affairs. Moreover, this is not a late development in the biblical wisdom literature, for the religious dimension was long a vital element in the Egyptian wisdom material. Furthermore, the divine permeated ancient court life and thought; kingship in the ancient Near East was not a secular institution.[55] Kingship was infused with a sacral ideology even in Israel (Ps. 2:7; 45:7–8 [6–7]; 89:20–38 [19–37]; 2 Sam. 7:13–16; 1 Kings 8:22–26; 9:3–5).[56] Such considerations render implausible the view that Israelite wisdom literature emerged in a secular atmosphere, only to be recast in light of Yahwism. On the contrary, such literature would have had a role for YHWH and the divine from the beginning. Wisdom texts such as Proverbs actively cultivate a personal and social ethic within the parameters of a religiophilosophic frame of reference.

A divergence in their religious ground, not Proverbs's supposed secularity, is the most telling distinction between the thought forms of the wise and the value structures advocated by the prophets. The conflict, in other words, is over basic value orientations.[57] Whereas both the prophets and the wise operate within religiously structured value systems, from the prophetic standpoint the wise have failed to comprehend the demands of the Yahwist tradition. These ideological differences, in conjunction with differences in socioeconomic status between the wise and many of the prophets, help to clarify the social vision cultivated by the writers of Proverbs. More specifically, as we shall see later in this chapter, their conflicting understandings of the roots of poverty offer keen insight into the conflict between the wisdom and prophetic trajectories.

To sum up: One of the implications of the royal background of wisdom writing in Israel is that this literature is a product of the ruling elite, a sector of the society that, as Gordis observes, "had little in common with the poorer peasants clinging desperately to their holdings, or with the petty tradesmen and the artisans in the cities, who suffered their own discontents and were evolving new values in their religious tradition."[58] It is to be expected, then, that the values and practices advocated in the wisdom tradition are in accord with the political and economic leanings of the ruling classes.[59] It will be of interest to see if the wisdom teaching on poverty betrays the values and attitudes of the educated elite.

"Creed" and Rhetoric: Framing a Wisdom Social Ethics

With this data before us, how might we characterize the wisdom creed? For the purposes of this discussion, the wisdom creed will be defined as the social agenda and normative philosophy of the text of Proverbs. The reason for separating this text from the other so-called wisdom writings, Job and Qohelet, will become apparent in the next chapter, where the latter texts' alternative rhetorical forms will carry forward strikingly different ethical analyses. For the purpose of defining the wisdom creed, it will suffice to let Proverbs stand on its own. If our discussion of the social world of Proverbs is accurate, then, as with the Egyptian royal instructional literature, Proverbs reflects an ethical philosophy appropriate to the bureaucratic families of the more elite or up-and-coming elements of ancient society.

An Underlying Philosophy? The Educational Form

In our earlier discussion of the prophetic literature, we saw how integral the prophetic rhetoric regarding the poor was to the establishment of the prophetic social vision. Indeed, the ideological tempering of that vision at various stages in Israelite history and at various levels in Israel's society created competing and overlapping social visions within the prophetic tradition itself. In studying Proverbs, we find a rhetoric that is very different from the polarizing critique of the prophets. The rhetoric of Proverbs is educational, instructional, and traditional.

We can easily carve up Proverbs according to sections because its teaching rhetoric is so transparent. The first nine chapters of Proverbs constitute a distinctive body of instruction and exhortation built, in part, around a feminine personification of the figure of Wisdom (see further below).[60] The extended sections of instruction are clearly concerned with molding individual behavior (from a male student's perspective), covering such diverse topics as avoiding sexual misconduct (2:16; 5:3–23; 6:23–35; 7:5–27; 9:13–18), rightly using wealth (3:9, 27–29), controlling anger (3:30), shunning criminal activity (1:10–19; 4:14–19), working diligently (6:6–15), exercising right speech (6:16–19), and developing self-discipline (8:33).[61] Likewise, vast collections of sentence proverbs (chaps. 10—22; 25—29) teach by way of example and pithy reflection.[62] These sentences press the student to reexamine diligence, lawlessness, justice, wickedness, speech, and a hundred other "teachable moments" that life presents. Another section of extended instruction is found in Prov. 22:17–24:34 (perhaps subdivided as 22:17–23:11; 23:12–25; 23:26–24:22; 24:23–24:34), the so-called "Words of the Sages."[63] This segment, or more properly subsections thereof, has frequently been linked to Egyptian texts of this genre, in particular the Amenemope text, and succinctly offers rather dramatic exhortations on poverty, property, wealth, and the administration of justice (as we shall see below).[64] An additional abbreviated example of the instructional genre is found in Prov. 31:1–9.

Some may balk at the idea that there is anything like a coherent "philosophy" behind Proverbs, especially since the many proverbial statements of the book can hardly escape exhibiting contradictory elements.[65] Nevertheless, when surveying the vast reams of material from the Egyptian wisdom tradition,[66] not to mention the many Mesopotamian texts akin to this material,[67] one cannot help but sense that behind the collections of sentences and exhortations stand some deeply honed ideals.[68] Indeed, these writings are attempting to inculcate in their students a carefully considered philosophy of personal character and social comportment on the order of kindred Taoist, Confucian, Epicurean, and Stoic texts.[69] If this is the case, then we should also expect there to be some kind of integrated social vision in the rhetorical teaching forms adopted by Proverbs. As we look, we will see that our expectations are not unfounded. On the strength of the fact that Proverbs is part of a larger and far older educational tradition, I believe that Proverbs gives evidence for a creed, a normative social philosophy, that the prophets opposed when they stood against the wise.

Literary Devices Frame a Social Philosophy: Mastering the Contingent

The overarching educational form of Proverbs is linked to its more specific contents via intervening literary devices. These mediating units shape the isolated insights of Proverbs into organic wholes that have strong persuasive value. In other words, the sentence construction of Proverbs carries forward in a transfixing way its social philosophy. By exploring these mediating devices, we encounter the social vision of the wise.

The rhetoric of what are termed the instructional sections (Proverbs 1—9; 22:17–24:34; 31:1–9) provides one of the major literary devices in Proverbs.[70] The instructional genre relies heavily on the elements of authority ("my son"), command, example, and persuasion to achieve its aims. The rhetorical posture of this literature is summed up well when the writer says,

> My son, heed the discipline of your father,
> And do not forsake the instruction of your mother;
> For they are a graceful wreath upon your head,
> A necklace about your throat.
> Prov. 1:8–9

By linking terse couplets across thematic sections, the writer rivets the student's attention, establishing a literary hedge that circumscribes a cautious code of personal conduct:

> My son, if sinners entice you, do not yield;
> If they say, "Come with us,
> Let us set an ambush to shed blood,
> Let us lie in wait for the innocent
> (Without cause!)
> Like Sheol, let us swallow them alive;
> Whole, like those who go down into the Pit.
> We shall obtain every precious treasure;
> We shall fill our homes with loot.
> Throw in your lot with us;
> We shall all have a common purse."
> My son, do not set out with them;
> Keep your feet from their path.
> For their feet run to evil;
> They hurry to shed blood.
>
> Prov. 1:10–16

This persuasive rhetoric can offer positive inducements for wisdom-based action, invoking even a "religious" claim on the student's conduct:

> Do not be wise in your own eyes;
> Fear the LORD and shun evil.
> It will be a cure for your body,
> A tonic for your bones.
> Honor the LORD with your wealth,
> With the best of all your income,
> And your barns will be filled with grain,
> Your vats will burst with new wine.
> Do not reject the discipline of the LORD, my son;
> Do not abhor His rebuke.
> For whom the LORD loves, He rebukes,
> As a father the son whom he favors.
>
> Prov. 3:7–16; cf. 9:10

However, as is typical of Near Eastern wisdom, biblical wisdom does not invoke the standard elements of ancient Israel's exodus-Sinai credo to make these claims. Rather, wisdom itself is offered as its own aim and reward (a view undermined by Qohelet):

> Wisdom cries aloud in the streets,
> Raises her voice in the squares.
> At the head of the busy streets she calls;

At the entrance of the gates, in the city, she speaks out:
"How long will you simple ones love simplicity,
You scoffers be eager to scoff,
You dullards hate knowledge?
You are indifferent to my rebuke;
I will now speak my mind to you,
And let you know my thoughts."

Prov. 1:20–23

Although personified and feminized in Proverbs (1:20–33; 3:13–20; 7:4–27; 8:1–36), Wisdom is but a pale reflection of the "goddess" that some have argued "Wisdom" was so hypostatized prior to the postexilic monotheistic purging of such beliefs, at least in particular religious circles.[71] As Lang rightly observes, "she leads a miserable life in the textbook of postexilic apprentice scribes."[72] In any case, Wisdom hardly serves a liberating function for women in this rhetorical setting, where the feminine figure is the object of male devotion and education: Wisdom is "sister" to the "son" who heeds his "father's" advice (7:4–5). Rhetorically, the voice of the patriarch, the teacher, and that of wisdom are the same (cf. 8:32–36). Even the sage instruction of a "mother" is recorded for the benefit of the "son" and not a hypothetical "daughter" (31:1–9). Furthermore, if Perdue is right, the Persian period's sages were putting the image of Wisdom to work legitimating a hierocratic program for rebuilding the community after the exile.[73]

For the other major literary device used in Proverbs, we must turn to consider the collection of sentences found in chaps. 10—22 and 25—29. The sentence literature of Proverbs offers strong inducements toward wisdom conduct, although in the abbreviated form of sentence couplets.[74] The many sentences seek to present slices of human experience, offering them to us as empirical examples of the ways the world works and does not work, so that the student can mold his (and I mean "his"!) comportment accordingly. A few quotations will have to suffice here:

A wise son brings joy to his father;
A dull son is his mother's sorrow.

Prov. 10:1

He who lays in stores during the summer is a capable son,
But he who sleeps during the harvest is an incompetent.

Prov. 10:5

Like a gold ring in the snout of a pig
Is a beautiful woman bereft of sense

Prov. 11:22

Sinful speech is a trap for the evil man,
But the righteous escapes from trouble.
                                        Prov. 12:13

A healing tongue is a tree of life,
But a devious one makes for a broken spirit.
                                        Prov. 15:14

He whose ear heeds the discipline of life
Lodges among the wise.
                                        Prov. 15:31

He who loves pleasure comes to want;
he who loves wine and oil does not grow rich.
                                        Prov. 21:17

He who strives to do good and kind deeds
Attains life, success, and honor.
                                        Prov. 21:21

This type of collection, well known from Egyptian and Mesopotamian tradition, is a seemingly random amalgam of sayings, covering many aspects of human interaction. The range of behaviors, thoughts, and actions covered and inculcated by these sentences, though rather endless in scope and variety, actually comprise the philosophic palette that is typical of wisdom sentential collections. However, even though the many sentences are random in organization, this does not mean that their collection was without some overall purpose. Whybray, for example, traces verbal and other links down through the many chapters, presenting us with a carefully and subtly woven garment.[75] Moreover, the very process of collection imbues the text with a philosophic and educative character that individual sentences do not possess, or possess to a lesser degree.[76]

What is the underlying sensibility of these sentence collections? Confronting the "contradictions in social life," as Von Rad so aptly observes, these many sentences lead the practitioner to the "mastering of the contingent."[77] While falling far short of an abstract theory of existence, the works appear to have been collected with a view toward cultivating a reasoned approach to the seeming imponderables of life, organizing the world into a manageable whole, at least for the one schooled in its inner workings. Yet the rhetoric of Proverbs, regardless of how much it is couched to introduce the student to the successful management of the vicissitudes of life, serves equally to construct the very reality the wise seek to inhabit.

In addition to the instructional genre and the sentential literature, Proverbs also makes use of three other noteworthy literary devices, though these fea-

tures are not as common to the text as are the first two literary forms we have
mentioned. The first of these is what Crenshaw labels "a dialogue between a
skeptic and a believer," found in Prov. 30:1–9.[78] Such philosophic dialogues,
whether real or imagined, are found elsewhere in the ancient literary traditions (see chapter 13).[79]

The second additional literary device to note is the use of numerical sayings, as seen best in Prov. 30:15–28. To take but one example, wherein an
orderly rhetoric "creates" an ordered society:

> The earth shudders at three things,
> At four which it cannot bear:
> A slave who becomes king;
> A scoundrel sated with food;
> A loathsome woman who gets married;
> A slave-girl who supplants her mistress.
> Prov. 30:21–23[80]

The final literary device of note is the use of the acrostic form of poetry as
found in Prov. 31:10–31. In this text, which concerns placing the "ideal wife"
into a fitting cultural matrix, each sentence begins with a successive letter of
the Hebrew alphabet. While it is useful to note these additional devices, it is
not to these that the wise regularly turn to make the case for their creed. For
a real insight into their social vision we must confront, as we have seen, the
instructional and sentential bodies of material in Proverbs.

The wise in Israel relied on these specific modes of instruction to establish
their creed. Yet form alone does not explain the social power of this literature.
The various educative rhetorical strategies, especially the instructional and
sentential, have the weight of tradition behind them. As we saw earlier in this
chapter, the pursuit of wisdom was a time-honored international tradition
standing back of its Israelite expression in Proverbs. Yet this observation
means more than simply saying that education by means of instruction and
sentences had been used for a long time in the ancient Near East. To say that
wisdom instruction has the weight of tradition behind it means that the literary tradition itself becomes its own authority on matters of truth and human
action, which undergirds the teacher as the one directly responsible for passing on those insights.[81]

However, we should not be misled on this point. There is more going on
in the social vision of the text than an appeal to traditional modes of expression can possibly secure. The extensive use of persuasion in both the instructional and sentential sections indicates that the wisdom creed was not entirely
fixed in the minds and hearts of all of society's members. While the stated aim
was a deportment that made fathers show pride, kings confer honor, and

employers give respectable salaries, the sages felt themselves under attack. Whether the perceived threat is external or internal to the wisdom tradition is a matter we must now consider.

Drawing Boundaries and Defining Ethics

From Proverbs's persuasive rhetoric we are beginning to see that this creed is conscious that it is a creed in competition. Indeed, if we look just below the surface of these seemingly self-confident traditional texts, we find that the record exhibits a philosophic nervousness, expressed in the need, not unlike that of the prophetic, to name opponents as its writers seek to establish their personal and social visions. However, in the case of wisdom texts, the opponents are not so clearly defined sociologically as they are in the prophetic literature (though, as we have seen, the prophetic "sociology" is rhetorical in its own right). Nevertheless, a rhetoric of opposition does find its place in Proverbs and functions as one means by which the wise shape and define their creed. They do this not so much to advance their creed as a new set of ideas that deserve a hearing, as the prophets were often forced to do (though admittedly their ideas were not necessarily new), rather, the wise develop their own brand of opposition rhetoric in order to reinforce their claims to "knowledge" and justify their reading of the social order in the face of a sociologically ill-defined opposition.

So who are the opponents? In a number of sections of the text, the boundary line between those inside the creed and those outside is demarcated by the terms "just" and "wicked." In Proverbs, the primary term for "just" as an adjective, *ṣaddîq*, occurs 66 times, with only 4 of these occurrences in chaps. 1—9. (By contrast, the noun "just," *ṣedeq*, occurs only 8 times.) The term for "wicked," *rāšā‘*, is found in Proverbs 77 times (7 occurrences in chaps. 1—9 and 70 in chaps. 10—29.) Only the Psalter, a much larger text than Proverbs, has as many occurrences. The entire book of Psalms uses the adjective *ṣaddîq* 51 times and the noun *ṣedeq* 49; *rāšā‘* is used 82 times. For the most part, the other parts of the Hebrew Bible use these terms more sparingly, the notable exceptions being Job, Second Isaiah, and Ezekiel.[82] Clearly, then, the opposition between the "wicked" and the "righteous" defines the plot line in the wisdom drama of life lived in the pursuit of wisdom. Of the many sentences contrasting the "wicked" and the "upright," the following is typical:

> The wicked man is felled by his own evil;
> The righteous man finds security in his death.
> Prov. 14:32

Broadening the categories, Crenshaw also suggests that the rhetoric of Proverbs is shaped by a contrast between the "wise" and the "foolish."[83] Drawing on Oesterley's work, Crenshaw points out that Proverbs makes use of eight different Hebrew terms for "fool."[84] The contrast between the wise and the foolish is much the same as the contrast between the just and the wicked, both rhetorically and in terms of content. Whether wicked versus just, or wise versus foolish, the rhetoric serves to subtly undergird the vision of Proverbs.[85]

Yet in light of our consideration of the aims of prophetic rhetoric, we are struck by all the things that are not present in this rhetoric of the wise. Certainly this rhetoric lacks the sociologically overt boundary-line drawing that we find in the prophets. It is hard to place the wicked and the just, the wise and the foolish, into any definable societal landscape. In fact, what is so startling about a comparison between the prophetic texts and Proverbs is that the prophetic material concerns itself with false prophets, oppressive rulers, and the priesthood in a way that Proverbs decidedly does not. The wisdom creed finds no need to delineate the power groups and attack them in order to make its case. This is a crucial observation, which I take to be one piece of evidence that the prophets were largely powerless to enact their ideas. On the other hand, the lack of sociologically polarizing rhetoric in Proverbs suggests that the wise were defending ideas that had gained some currency among the elite in ancient Israelite society and served as an apparently legitimate expression of many of the society's basic values. No greater contrast exists between the rhetoric of the prophets and the wise than this: The prophetic rhetoric demands opposition toward the powerholders to establish it as a competitive social creed, whereas wisdom decidedly does not require that sort of opposition rhetoric to defend and establish itself as a competitive set of ideas. Yet wisdom rhetoric is not entirely governed by rhetorical straw men. There remains another, more definable, group—the poor.

An Attack on the Poor in Proverbs?

For our purposes, the most important locus of the opposition rhetoric in Proverbs is a direct product of its social analysis: The opponents are the poor. There are no bad words spoken in Proverbs against prophets or priests, and few against kings (in fact, loyalty to the state is a virtue). In Proverbs, beyond the urban prostitutes (7:5–27; cf. 2:16–19; 6:26; 9:13–18), the poor as such are the only sociologically defined objects of the wisdom creed's ethical landscape.

To Champion Their Cause: A Prophetic Voice in Proverbs?

To speak of the poor in the Psalms or the Prophets is to invoke the stock phrase 'ānî wĕ'ebyôn, "poor and needy." This traditional paralleling of 'ānî with 'ebyôn also occurs in Proverbs, but in restricted contexts.[86] Curiously, this pair is absent from the bulk of the material in Proverbs and appears only and repeatedly in chaps. 30—31, a section of Proverbs assigned to the sage Agur son of Jakeh (30:1), and to Lemuel's mother (31:1), although the exact authorship of the entire material remains uncertain.[87] The peculiarity of these texts is heightened further by the fact that *'ebyôn* and *'ānî* individually appear only rarely outside of chaps. 30—31 (*'ebyôn* in 14:31; *'ānî* in 3:34; 14:21; 15:15; and 16:19).[88] Moreover, the terms *dal*, *rāš*, and *maḥsôr*, common to chaps. 10—29, are not found at all in chaps. 30—31. This state of affairs suggests a different editorial history and authorship for chaps. 30—31, if not a different social background for this material.

In the sayings of Agur (30:1–14), the *'ebyôn* and *'ānî* are placed in the context of exploitation. The writer observes that there is "a breed whose teeth are swords, whose jaws are knives, ready to devour the poor [*'ānî*] of the land, the needy [*'ebyôn*] among men" (30:14). If the prophets offer any clue to the interpretation of this material, the agents of the suffering envisioned in the text are the ruling elite. Here the wisdom writer approaches the evaluation of the prophets using traditional phrasing shared with the prophets, though lacking the fuller advocacy posture of the prophetic texts. The sayings of Agur are intriguing in that the speaker requests not only freedom from the dangers of poverty but also from wealth (30:8–9), a view that, though not unparalleled in Proverbs, may reflect a "more consciously theological milieu" akin to Job.[89]

Next, the pair *'ebyôn* and *'ānî* is found in chap. 31, where King Lemuel passes on the instruction of his mother on the "ideal king."[90] He was exhorted to "speak up, judge righteously, champion the poor [*'ānî*] and the needy [*'ebyôn*]" (31:9). A concern for justice surrounds these terms for the poor, a concern connected with the king, who is treated, in typical ancient Near Eastern fashion, as the protector of the poor. To this one might compare Jeremiah's exhortations to King Jehoiakim (22:16). Strangely, however, as Whybray observes, the king is exhorted to use strong drink to help the poor forget their condition (31:6–7).[91] To protect the poor does not seem to mean radically altering their economic and political circumstance according to this text.

Finally, in the acrostic poem concerning the wise and capable wife (31:10-31), this woman's just character is demonstrated by the fact that "she gives generously to the poor [*'ānî*]; her hands are stretched out to the needy [*'ebyôn*]" (31:20). She is, in other words, to use her higher economic and social status to be charitable to the poor, a virtue cultivated by the wisdom texts (see below).[92]

In these chapters, we would seem to have a genuine case of prophetic influence on the shaping of the final form of Proverbs. However, prophetic advocacy and activism are not the typical postures for the wise according to the rest of the book. The bulk of the chapters adopt a more cautious line that reflects an understanding of poverty comparable to the Egyptian wisdom writings. In these other chapters of Proverbs, poverty is marshalled rhetorically as a warning sign on the road of character development. Far from the pages of prophetic protest, the bulk of Proverbs latches onto the poor as convenient ciphers in a curriculum geared toward personal conduct.[93]

The Burdensome Fate of the Poor

Language choice stands at the heart of rhetoric. Thus, we linger over the fact that these few references to *'ĕbyôn* and *'ānî* are entirely overshadowed by the use of terms such as *dal*, *rāš*, and *maḥsôr* in the rest of the book of Proverbs.[94] These latter terms are the markers by which we can identify the core wisdom voice in Proverbs. To reinforce the unique direction of the rhetoric, we also observe that the terms *rāš*, "be in want, poor," and *maḥsôr*, "need, thing needed, poverty," are rarely found outside the wisdom literature, and are not used at all by the prophets.[95] These clear divergences in word choice between the prophets and the bulk of Proverbs should be considered the sign that a different dialect is at work, in this case the specialized language of the wisdom teachers. In other words, the terms *dal*, *rāš*, and *maḥsôr* characterize the value system adhered to by the wise, one which differs substantially from that of the prophets. Through these words, the wise come to characterize a particular vision of the poor.

The terms *dal*, *rāš*, and *maḥsôr* occur several times in the sentence literature of chaps. 10—22. If the wisdom literature is concerned with schooling the student in how to respond to life's many circumstances and exegencies, then these sentences offer practical guidelines for meeting the challenges of life, and reveal what principles the wise thought governed the world. The wisdom material in this section cultivates the virtues of wealth, by warning of the hard realities of poverty. Many of the verses present the stark contrast between wealth and poverty in an effort to steer the student away from a lifestyle that would lead to indigence.

Poverty by its very nature consigns the poor to a miserable fate, one not to be sought or cherished. In Prov. 8:23 the *rāš* is presented as one who begs ("speaks beseechingly"). The response the poor person receives from the rich, however, is harsh. This observation does not thereby condone the attitude of the rich toward the poor. In fact, there are many exhortations from the wise that the poor are not to be mocked (see below). What this passage does indicate, however, is that poverty is an ugly situation, leaving one at the mercy of the often unsympathetic whims of the rich. The wise also know that the rich rule the *rāš* and that the borrower is a slave to the lender (22:7). This too serves as a solemn warning to the student to avoid falling into poverty if it is at all possible to do so. Wealth and poverty are contrasted in 10:15: "The wealth of

a rich man is his fortress; the poverty of the poor is his ruin." McKane comments that "wealth is an insurance against the chanciness of existence, and
whoever has it is not naked and defenseless before its vicissitudes."[96] There is
no virtue or refuge in poverty from the perspective of the wise.

The terrible condition of poverty is stressed through its friendless character: "A pauper [*rāš*] is despised even by his peers, but a rich man has many
friends" (14:20). The friendless character of poverty is stressed in Prov. 19:7:
"All the brothers of a poor man [*rāš*] despise him; how much more is he
shunned by his friends!" Friendship is also the concern of Prov. 19:4. There it
is observed that "wealth makes many friends, but a poor man [*dal*] loses his last
friend." The desertion of the *dal* has been explained on the basis that the term
dal indicates one who was once rich, but has been reduced in means.[97] On
Kennedy's analysis, this person, when wealthy, had friends, but when that
wealth was lost, this same person lost his friends as well. However, while it is
possible that the term *dal* denotes one who possesses a small amount of property (see chapter 2), Kennedy's contention that this person was once wealthy
is not supported by Prov. 19:4, where *dal* simply stands as an antithetic parallel to *hon*, "wealth." Furthermore, the close parallels to this verse noted above
(Prov 14:20; 19:7) use a different word for poor, *rāš*, to express the same idea
of the loss of friends, and no one supposes that the *rāš* was at one time rich!
The friendless character of poverty is stressed even further in a sentence which
suggests that the very worst situation to be found among the poor is when one
who is poor [*rāš*] oppresses the poor [*dal*] (28:3).[98] Gordis comments:

> But what an irony to see a poor man making life miserable for his fel-
> lows and gaining nothing thereby! The observation comes with espe-
> cial aptness from a perspicacious son of the upper classes, who was
> tired perhaps of the perpetual accusations levelled against wealthy
> malefactors by prophets, lawgivers and sages.[99]

The terms *rāš* and *mahsôr* are often connected with "laziness" ('*āṣēl* and
related forms) in Proverbs.[100] The wisdom teachers show a great concern for
diligence and offer strong warnings against laziness.[101] In the admonitions and
instructions in chaps. 1—9, *mahsôr* appears as the result of too much sleep and
not enough attentiveness to one's labors. The wise hold up the ant as the model
of success:

> Lazybones, go to the ant;
> Study its ways and learn.
> Without leaders, officers, or rulers,
> It lays up its stores during the summer,
> Gathers in its food at the harvest.

> How long will you lie there, lazybones;
> When will you wake from your sleep?
> A bit more sleep, a bit more slumber,
> A bit more hugging yourself in bed,
> And poverty [*maḥsôr*] will come calling upon you
> And want, like a man with a shield.
>
> Prov. 6:6–11

Invoking an agricultural context and diligence with respect to land owner-ship, another admonition text elsewhere in Proverbs raises similar concerns:

> Put your external affairs in order,
> Get ready what you have in the field,
> Then build yourself a home
> . . . .
> I passed by the field of a lazy man,
> By the vineyard of a man lacking sense.
> It was all overgrown with thorns;
> Its surface was covered with chickweed,
> And its stone fence lay in ruins,
> I observed and took it to heart;
> I saw it and learned a lesson.
> A bit more sleep. . . .
>
> Prov. 24:27, 30–33

The admonition ends with the same concern for oversleeping as the pre-ceding quote from chap. 6. The work ethic is enjoined. The wise see poverty's origins in a lack of commitment to the labors at hand.

The sentence literature of Proverbs trumpets the same theme. Diligence and laziness are also the concern of Prov. 10:4: "Negligent hands cause poverty [*rāš*], but diligent hands enrich." Work ('*eṣeb*) brings profit (*môtār*), but mere talk breeds want (*maḥsôr*; 14:23; cf. 19:15, 24; 21:5). Drunkenness is associated with *rîš*, "poverty," in Prov. 31:7. The connection with laziness may suggest that *rāš* could well be translated "bum."

The attempt to locate the roots of poverty in laziness is entirely absent from the prophetic literature. As C. Van Leeuwen observes, the perspective in Proverbs is that of one who has not known poverty: "Poverty can only be eval-uated in this way by someone who has never been a victim himself and who, as a result, has never felt the difficult problem." For the wise, poverty is merely "a punishment that one brings upon oneself through one's own fault."[102] It is the deserved result of drunkenness and lack of industry (10:4; 12:11; 19:15; 20:4, 13; 21:17; 23:20).[103] Such an understanding of the cause of poverty might have been congenial to the well-to-do, but the prophets argued that it was the socioeconomic structures of the society that produced poverty. Herein lies a major point of contention between the prophets and the wise.[104] In the prophetic analysis, the plight of the poor was not something for which the poor were themselves responsible. Indeed, the poor were "the victims of terrible social circumstances, swindled by oppression and by the thirst for possessions on the part of the great."[105]

For the wise, poverty is a reality to be avoided, but is rarely protested against. Whybray rightly observes that "despite the widely differing points of view expressed in the different parts of Proverbs, the book nowhere gives any hint of a changing situation or of a pressing need for change. What we see here is a self-portrait of a society on the whole uncritical of the status quo."[106] Unlike the prophetic social critique, the proverbial texts draw only the vaguest connections between the poverty of the poor and the wealth of the rich. Statements such as that found in Prov. 28:15 may be suggestive but hardly speak to endemic social conditions: "A roaring lion and a prowling bear is a wicked man ruling a helpless [dal] people." Thus, Proverbs fails to recognize that the poor as a group are poor because they have been wronged by the ruling elite, as the prophets consistently proclaim. Rather, the wise advise that taking from the dal is as pointless as giving to the rich. In the end, one comes to naught (22:16). How different are the prophetic texts, which consistently and extensively contend that much gain is made by those who take from the poor! For the wise, poverty, like wealth, was accepted as one of the givens of existence with which the student must learn to cope. One presumes that the student, who comes from an elite background, would be able to avoid a lapse into poverty if only the advice of the wise were followed.

Assistance for the Poor: The Virtue of Charity

Even though the poor are considered a despised and lazy lot in the proverbial literature, the mistreatment of the poor is discouraged as behavior inappropriate to the truly wise person. The student must learn what the proper posture toward the poor should be. In the first place, the text states that one should not despise or mock the rāš, for this is an affront to the Creator. In Prov. 14:31 the oppression ('šq) of the dal is condemned as an affront to God, whereas kindness to the 'ebyôn is lauded. The basis for this posture toward the poor rests on the belief that the Lord makes both the rich and the poor. Both poverty and wealth are given by God or fate (Prov. 22:2; 29:13).[107]

Similar sentiments are expressed a bit more strongly in the "Words of the Sages" (22:17–24:34), a text that has clear connections to the Egyptian instruction of Amenemope (as noted above). The writer states, "Do not rob the wretched [dal] because he is wretched [dal]; do not crush the poor man ['ānî] in the gate" (22:22). The close paralleling of dal and 'ānî is unusual in Proverbs.

The subject matter is even more striking because of the concern for the gate, another item unusual in the text. The motivation against oppression is largely unparalleled in Proverbs (cf. chaps. 30—31, discussed above). In this case, one must not rob the poor because "the LORD will take up their cause and despoil those who despoil them of life" (22:23; cf. Ex. 22:21–23 [22–24]). McKane draws attention to the parallel in Amenemope chapter 2: "Beware of robbing a wretch, of attacking a cripple."[108] This text reveals how ancient the concern about robbing the poor was in wisdom circles.[109] Yet, as McKane points out, the Egyptian text of Amenemope differs from the Hebrew injunction in that it lacks a religious motivation to encourage the support of the poor. In the Hebrew text, YHWH is presented as a God who defends the poor, and for that reason one should not mistreat the poor. Yet it must be observed that this passage is not typical for the wisdom of Proverbs. If this text could be dated more securely, one might have evidence for an important development in the biblical wisdom tradition or of evidence for prophetic influence in Proverbs. However, the writers of Proverbs are generally unconcerned with the notion of YHWH as the bringer of justice. It was the prophets who felt compelled to elevate the ancient values ignored by the wise, or to which the urban elite's educators only paid lip service. Proverbs 22:22 would seem to be a classic case of the exception that proves the rule. We must look to the prophets for a group that consistently champions the cause of the poor in the gate and elsewhere in society.

Assisting the poor through giving, charity, was the more important concern to the wise. The student is warned against neglecting the poor (*dal*; 21:13). It may be that one day the student might be in distress and the neglect of others would rebound to leave the student naked before disaster, with no one to assist. The wise person shares food with the poor (22:9). In chaps. 28—29, a section concerned with contrasting the wicked and the righteous (and subsets of these two groups), the defining feature of just rulers is their treatment of the poor (*dal*) in legal contexts (29:14). Similarly, the character of righteousness is defined in Prov. 29:7 as showing concern for justice to the poor (*dal*).[110] It is not the case as McKane claims that this verse is "another . . . of the few examples of a wisdom sentence which is an instrument of prophetic teaching."[111] Such an attitude is not foreign to wisdom thought, but the type of social justice envisioned here differs from that found in the prophetic literature (see discussion below). Nevertheless, the just treatment of the poor is a mark of righteousness to the wise.

Malchow argues that the wisdom literature's general approach to the poor extends beyond charity. He believes the writings advocate an active posture toward the poor, a posture that deserves the label of "social justice."[112] Against this I would argue, first, that Malchow has failed to separate the attitudes found in Proverbs from those in Job. As we shall see, the understanding of

poverty and the usage for the terms for poor in Job differ markedly from
Proverbs. Job overlaps with the prophetic materials, and hence the understanding of poverty found in Job might be termed "social justice." By contrast,
Proverbs rarely moves beyond charity.[113] The concern found in Proverbs over
false weights and measures (11:1; 16:11; 20:10, 23) and its call for the respect
for property lines (23:10–11) reflect elite interests and are ancient in the wisdom tradition, but this hardly qualifies as a comprehensive concern for social
justice such as that found in the prophetic literature.[114] As Fox observes of
Proverbs, "Laziness and folly cause poverty, though not all poverty comes
from these defects. Some poverty just *is*, but it requires mercy and mitigation,
not reform."[115] Moreover, the text of Proverbs exhibits no consciousness that
the wealth of the cities was obtained at the expense of the peasant population,
as the prophets so tellingly indicate was the case. There is no awareness on the
 part of the wise that there are institutionalized evils that need to be addressed.
Such an awareness, it would seem, constitutes the prerequisite for labeling a
perspective one of social justice rather than one of simply charity. By contrast,
the wise focus on the charitable care of individuals and seem oblivious to the
plight of the poor as a group. In general, the wise treated poverty as one of
life's inevitable though at times unpredictable misfortunes brought about by
the mysterious ways of YHWH. All that the wise person could do was work
diligently in the hopes of avoiding such a fate. One showed concern for the
poor only to avoid mistreatment should one also happen to fall into poverty.

The motivation for charity is perhaps not from the noblest sources. Nega-
tively, it is said that "to profit by oppressing the poor [*dal*] is like giving to the
rich—pure loss [*mahsôr*]" (22:16, JPS, with modifications); and elsewhere:
"Who stops his ears at the cry of the wretched, he too will call and not be
answered" (21:13). The practice of usury is condemned for similar reasons.
The student is warned that wealth gained in such a manner will pass on to one
who is generous to the poor (*dal*; 28:8; cf. Lev. 25:36; Ex. 22:24 [25]; Deut.
23:20 [19]).[116] Thus, the failure to help the poor and the attempt to make gains
at their expense can lead to poverty, the wise warn.

The inducement offered by the wise for assisting the poor is that blessings
and rewards from God are promised in return for charitable giving: "One man
gives generously and ends with more; another stints on doing the right thing
and incurs a loss [*mahsôr*]" (11:24). In Prov. 19:17, kindness to the *dal* is treated
as lending to YHWH (cf. 14:21). Note that one is not exhorted to aid the poor
in order to aright injustice, following the prophetic call; rather, one aids the
dal with material reward in mind. When one lends to YHWH, "He [i.e.,
YHWH] will repay him [i.e., the lender] his due" (19:17). Similarly, Prov.
28:27 states, "He who gives to the poor [*rāš*] will not be in want [*mahsôr*], but
he who shuts his eyes will be roundly cursed." According to the wise, the way

one overcomes society's inequities is through a reliance on the generosity of the rich, who will in turn benefit from their giving. This view is very different from prophetic and biblical legal thought, where assistance to the poor is done to fulfill covenant obligations or to extend God's dominion of justice.

Ambivalence about Poverty?

Attitudes toward poverty are merely the flip side of attitudes toward wealth.[117] An important role of the wisdom literature in the royal context would have been to instruct members of the court in the proper handling of wealth.[118] The wisdom writings contain material that is concerned with the virtues and limits of wealth, as well as observations about poverty and the proper response of a wise person to those who are poor. Malchow observes that the attitude toward wealth in the wisdom materials (1) reveals a respect for wealth, (2) encourages the enjoyment of abundance, and (3) suggests that the rich deserve their wealth.[119] It is true that the limits of wealth are known to the wisdom teachers, but it must be remembered that these statements are made by those who are, after all, well off. The wisdom texts seek to refine an understanding of wealth and poverty from the standpoint of one who has possessions, that is, as one who is fully and integrally involved in the life of royal society. Indeed, it must be admitted that such refinement often appears to be no more than enlightened self-interest. Thus, while bribes are sometimes condemned in Proverbs (15:23; 17:15, 23), they are also seen to be useful upon occasion (17:8; 18:16; 19:6; 21:14).[120]

Against this backdrop regarding wealth, poverty becomes a powerful rhetorical mediating device for evading the exploitation problem. Thus, the wisdom teachers feel free to use the notion of poverty to remind their audience that there are things in the world worse than poverty.[121] One would be better off poor (*rāš*) than be a liar (19:1, 22). Similarly, one would be better off poor (*rāš*) than be perverse in one's deeds (28:6).[122]

The poverty-wealth nexus becomes a lens for studying and managing the vicissitudes of wealth. Like poverty, wealth also has its dangers, according to the wise.[123] Wealth is transitory (see, e.g., 11:28; 20:17; 21; 23:4–5, 23–27; 28:22; 29:3).[124] Since wealth can cloud one's self-esteem, the wise state that it is better to have the perspective of the poor person: "A rich man is clever in his own eyes, but a perceptive poor man can see through him" (28:11). The wise warn that excessive concern for wealth can lead to poverty (*maḥsôr*; 21:17). Finally, the sages maintain that wealth can enslave (13:8). McKane suggests that the intent of this verse is to warn that the wealthy can be the subjects of threats and blackmail.[125] The poor, according to this understanding, have little or no property that can be extorted.

To the wise, the poor are insignificant elements in the social order from which nothing can be gained, except perhaps insight. In its instructional use of poverty, however, the wisdom literature appears to reveal an ambivalence in its attitude toward the poor, at times elevating them and at times disdaining them.[126] But in this, the wisdom text is only concerned to make the student aware of the need to limit one's enjoyment of wealth, and for this purpose references to poverty constitute a useful teaching device.[127] Nevertheless, this does not mean that the wisdom teachers took vows of poverty! Poverty is called upon for its heuristic value, enabling the student to grasp the proper attitude toward wealth and wisdom.[128] There is no attempt to elevate the condition of the poor or to treat poverty as a desirable existence.[129] Neither is there any awareness that, in fact, the urban population was making great gains from its exploitation of the poor.

In conclusion, we may ask why the wisdom creed requires this view of poverty to establish its ideas. It would seem that this particular understanding of the poor was useful for protecting the creed's views of wealth and status, establishing in this way its own peculiar social ethic. Thus, when Proverbs labels the poor as lazy, lacking in diligence, morally obtuse, and socially inferior, the text has defined the poor as a negative force in the body politic, thereby legitimating wisdom's claims regarding actors and processes in the social order. Any other kind of poverty would require a reassessment of this doctrine. For example, if poverty were consistently defined as the product of exploitation, the creed would have to call for a redistribution of wealth to meet the demands of justice. As it stands, Proverbs's rhetoric on poverty is a powerful link holding together the wisdom creed's chain of ideas about human conduct and action. Of course, Prov. 22:22 and chaps. 30—31 show us that there were prophetic chinks in the proverbial armor. But we must turn to another side of the wisdom tradition to find the strenuous voices of protest that will challenge the settled commitments and vision of Proverbs. In Job and Qohelet, we find radically conflicted voices that throw open the justice question at the deepest philosophic levels.

Notes

1. For Mesopotamian examples, see W. G. Lambert, *Babylonian Wisdom Literature* (Oxford: Clarendon Press, 1960), chaps. 4, 9. Also, a key source known from Elephantine is *Ahiqar*. See J. M. Lindenberger, *The Aramaic Proverbs of Ahiqar* (Baltimore: Johns Hopkins, 1983). As the story goes, the sage Ahiqar was apparently an authentic wisdom teacher among the court scholars (*ummānū*) of the Assyrian ruler Esarhaddon. The lore surrounding Ahiqar is diverse and eclectic.
2. M. V. Fox, "The Social Location of the Book of Proverbs," in *Texts, Temples, and Traditions: A Tribute to Menahem Haran*, ed. M. V. Fox et al. (Winona Lake, Ind. Eisenbrauns, 1996), 238. However, Fox does make the distinction that wisdom

texts were not written for schools but did embody the views of the "king's men." See also B. W. Kovacs, "Is There a Class-Ethic in Proverbs?" in *Essays in Old Testament Ethics: J. Philip Hyatt, In Memoriam*, ed. J. L. Crenshaw and J. T. Willis (New York: KTAV, 1974), who argues that the ethic of Proverbs is "a professional ethic of administrators or officials" (186).

3. See R. Gordis, *Poets, Prophets, and Sages: Essays in Biblical Interpretation* (Bloomington, Ind.: Indiana University Press, 1971), 163; B. V. Malchow, "Social Justice in the Wisdom Literature," *Biblical Theological Bulletin* 12 (1982): 121; T. N. D. Mettinger, *Solomonic State Officials: A Study of the Civil Government Officials of the Israelite Monarchy* (Lund: CWK Gleerups, 1971), 143–144; and J. P. J. Olivier, "Schools and Wisdom Literature," *Journal of Northwest Semitic Languages* 4 (1975): 49–60.

4. M. Lichtheim, *Ancient Egyptian Literature*, vol. 1, *The Old and Middle Kingdoms* (Berkeley and Los Angeles: University of California Press, 1973), 58–59.

5. Ibid., 1:59–60.

6. Ibid., 1:61–80; and E. W. Heaton, *Solomon's New Men: The Emergence of Ancient Israel as a National State* (New York: Pica Press, 1974), 117.

7. Lichtheim, *Ancient Egyptian Literature*, 1:97–109.

8. Ibid., 135–45.

9. Ibid., 184–92.

10. M. Lichtheim, *Ancient Egyptian Literature*, vol. 2, *The New Kingdom* (Berkeley and Los Angeles: University of California Press, 1976), 135–46; and Heaton, *Solomon's New Men*, 118.

11. Lichtheim, *Ancient Egyptian Literature*, 2:146–163; and Heaton, *Solomon's New Men*, 119–120.

12. M. Lichtheim, *Ancient Egyptian Literature*, vol. 3, *The Late Period* (Berkeley and Los Angeles: University of California Press, 1980) 159–84.

13. Ibid., 184–217.

14. See, e.g., R. J. Williams, "Scribal Training in Ancient Egypt," *JAOS* 92 (1972): 214–21.

15. Cf. W. F. Albright, "A Teacher to a Man of Shechem about 1400 B.C.," *BASOR* 86 (1942): 28–31.

16. Cf. J. A. Emerton, "Wisdom," in *Tradition and Interpretation*, ed. G. W. Anderson (Oxford: Clarendon Press, 1979), 221–27; and R. E. Clements, *Prophecy and Tradition* (Oxford: Basil Blackwell Publisher, 1975), 73.

17. A. Lemaire, "Sagesse et Ecoles," *VT* 26 (1984): 277; idem, "The Sage in School and Temple," in *The Sage in Israel and the Ancient Near East*, ed. J. G., Gammie and L. G. Perdue (Winona Lake, Ind.: Eisenbrauns, 1990), 165–81. Cf. J. L. Crenshaw, "Education in Wisdom," *JBL* 104 (1985): 607. Crenshaw offers a "minimalist" view based on the circumstantial nature of the evidence. Cf. Mettinger, *Solomonic State Officials*, 143–44; and Olivier, "Schools and Wisdom Literature," 56–59. See also N. Shupak, "The 'Sitz im Leben' of the Book of Proverbs in the Light of a Comparison of Biblical and Egyptian Wisdom Literature," *RB* 94 (1987): 98–119, who discerns Egyptian vocabulary equivalents and a consequent historical connection behind the Hebrew wisdom writings, in particular Proverbs.

18. B. Lang, *Wisdom and the Book of Proverbs: An Israelite Goddess Redefined* (New York: Pilgrim Press, 1986), 7–12. For more cautious assessments, see J. Crenshaw, *Education in Ancient Israel: Across the Deadening Silence* (New York: Doubleday, 1998) and G. I. Davies, "Were There Schools in Ancient Israel?" in *Wisdom in Ancient Israel* ed. J. Day, R. P. Gordon, and H. G. M. Williams (Cambridge: Cambridge University Press, 1995), 199-211.

19. With tablet houses (Mesopotamia) and temple schools (Egypt) standing as ancient institutions in the region, one is hard pressed to accept Crenshaw's view that schools were a late development in Israel. Schools and sages (philosophers) were hardly Hellenistic inventions in the ancient Near East. See J. Crenshaw, *Old Testament Wisdom: An Introduction*, rev. and enlarged (Louisville, Ky.: Westminster Press, 1998), 45.

20. To sever governance, the "middle class," and landowners from the royal court distorts the realities of the ancient social pyramid. These groups represent a very small percentage of the ancient population and taken together form the "ruling elite." Cf. N. Whybray, *Wealth and Poverty in the Book of Proverbs* (Sheffield: JSOT Press, 1990), 45 n. 1.

21. The Egyptian wisdom texts seldom refer to an educational setting in the course of the material but see "Satire of the Trades," in Lichtheim, *Ancient Egyptian Literature*, 1:185, and the text of Any, in ibid., 2:140. See also Heaton, *Solomon's New Men*, 103–14; cf. Mettinger, *Solomonic State Officials*, 140–43.

22. While Whybray plays down this evidence, the picture is really no different from that found in the Egyptian wisdom texts, indicating the more plausible elite and royal background for the biblical literature. See Whybray, *Wealth and Poverty*, 45–52. It is hard to imagine what Whybray means by a "readership of modest status" for texts written in the complex Demotic script (59 n. 1).

23. Clements, *Prophecy and Tradition*, 80–81. Cf. Fox, "Social Location," 234-39.

24. Cf. *Ahiqar*, sayings 17–21, 23, 25–26.

25. Cf. G. E. Bryce, *A Legacy of Wisdom: The Egyptian Contribution to the Wisdom of Israel* (Lewisburg, Pa.: Bucknell University Press, 1979), 189–210.

26. Cf. F. C. Fensham, "Widow, Orphan and the Poor in the Ancient Near Eastern Legal and Wisdom Literature," *JNES* 21 (1962): 138.

27. Bryce, *Legacy of Wisdom*, 201.

28. Ibid.

29. Cf. Bryce, *Legacy of Wisdom*, 141ff.

30. See Lang, *Wisdom and the Book of Proverbs*, chap. 3.

31. Downplaying any royal, elite, court, or educational connections, Whybray is left with the "ordinary citizen," the "*petit peuple*," "oral literature," and a "common stock of common sense" as mechanisms for Israelite wisdom. See Whybray, *Wealth and Poverty*, 45–74.

32. Cf., e.g, R. E. Murphy, "Wisdom—Theses and Hypotheses," in *Israelite Wisdom: Theological and Literary Essays in Honor of Samuel Terrien*, ed. J. G. Gammie et al. (Missoula, Mont.: Scholars Press, 1978), 37; idem, *Wisdom Literature and Psalms* (Nashville: Abingdon Press, 1983), 17–19; and P. J. Nel, *The Structure and Ethos of the Wisdom Admonitions in Proverbs*, BZAW 158 (Berlin: Walter de Gruyter, 1982), 14–15. Claims such as Crenshaw's, that "biblical proverbs arose as folk sayings and were transmitted in a family setting" or arose "initially among ordinary people in small villages" rest on sheer assertion (*Old Testament Wisdom*, 45). The existence of a centuries-old urban curriculum that included wisdom instruction elsewhere in the ancient Near East argues against such views. Israel is merely imitating its imperial overlords and cultural neighbors.

33. Lemaire, "Sagesse et Ecoles," 272, my translation.

34. Nel, *Structure and Ethos*, 1. Nel argues that while the court is associated with wisdom literature in Israel, one cannot ascribe all the material to a single ethos. Nel offers a variety of settings for the material: family, school, court, priestly, prophetic, and individual (79–81). However, while Nel contends that the city encompasses all these categories, it would seem that the city has simply been sub-

stituted for "court." There is no reason why the various materials would not be appropriate subject matter in a well-rounded elite education. This educational context has displaced any alternate ethos for Proverbs.

35. Kovacs, "Is There a Class Ethic?" 177.

36. Mettinger, *Solomonic State Officials*, 145.

37. See, e.g., W. McKane, *Proverbs: A New Approach* (Philadelphia: Westminster Press, 1970), 371. The extent of the connection, however, is widely disputed. Cf. Bryce, *Legacy of Wisdom*, chaps. 1–4. See also R. N. Whybray, *The Composition of the Book of Proverbs* (Sheffield: JSOT, Press, 1994), chap. 3. Whybray seriously understates Bryce's arguments. (Cf. Whybray, *Wealth and Poverty*, 85–98). J. Ruffle, "The Teaching of Amenemope and Its Connection with the Book of Proverbs," *Tyndale Bulletin* 28 (1977): 29–68, argues for a looser sort of connection. An alternate approach is taken by H. C. Washington, *Wealth and Poverty in the Instruction of Amenemope and The Hebrew Proverbs*, SBL Diss. 142 (Atlanta: Scholars Press, 1994). On the one hand, Washington does see Amenemope's lasting influence in Proverbs. However, he disputes the elite background posited by my own analysis. For Washington, Amenemope and the postexilic Proverbs reflect democratizing tendencies in relation to the poor not found in more ancient wisdom texts.

38. Bryce, *Legacy of Wisdom*, 148–49, 203–04.

39. Cf. Mettinger, *Solomonic State Officials*, 146-55.

40. J. Bright, "The Organization and Administration of the Israelite Empire," in *Magnelia Dei: The Mighty Acts of God*, ed. F. M. Cross, W. E. Lemke, and P. D. Miller (Garden City: Doubleday, 1976), 193–208; Heaton, *Solomon's New Men*, 47–60; and Mettinger, *Solomonic State Officials*, chaps. 4—6.

41. Bryce, *Legacy of Wisdom*, 154.

42. Ibid., 31; cf. Gordis, *Poets, Prophets, and Sages*, 160, 196; Heaton, *Solomon's New Men*, 126.

43. Crenshaw, "Education in Wisdom," 609–13; and Lemaire, "Sagesse et Ecoles," 275–77.

44. Cf. Clements, *Prophecy and Tradition*, 81.

45. For discussions on the phenomenon of the sage and some of the complexities locating the wise in the social matrix, see R. C. Van Leeuwen, "The Sage in the Prophetic Literature," in *The Sage in Israel and the Ancient Near East*, ed. J. G. Gammie and L. G. Perdue (Winona Lake, Ind.: Eisenbrauns, 1990). Also in the same volume, see J. L. Crenshaw, "The Sage in Proverbs," 205–16; and A. Lemaire, "The Sage in School and Temple," 165–81.

46. Cf. Bryce, *Legacy of Wisdom*, 150–51.

47. Bryce, *Legacy of Wisdom*, 151. This view is opposed by Lang, *Wisdom and the Book of Proverbs*, 12–13, although everything else he says speaks for the elite educational role of the text. Though cautious, Crenshaw does favor the view that there were professional sages in Israel (*Old Testament Wisdom*, chap. 1).

48. W. McKane, *Prophets and Wise Men* (Naperville, Ill.: Alec R. Allenson, 1965), 17–18, 38–47; cf. Bryce, *Legacy of Wisdom*, 196.

49. Cf. e.g., Heaton, *Solomon's New Men*, 122. The isolated reference to the covenant of the foreign woman is at best ambiguous in Prov. 2:17 and pertains to the forsaking of the covenant she has made with her own deity. See McKane, *Proverbs*, 286.

50. Cf. Bryce, *Legacy of Wisdom*, 206–7.

51. Regarding wisdom influence in Amos, I argue that the text is mocking, not endorsing, that mode of discourse. See chapter 10.

52. Bryce, *Legacy of Wisdom*, 154; Emerton, "Wisdom," 215–21; Gordis, *Poets, Prophets, and Sages*, 167; and McKane, *Prophets and Wise Men*, 15–16, 47, 96.

53. Gordis, *Poets, Prophets, and Sages*, 168.

54. Ibid., 169–170.

55. Cf. H. Frankfort et al., *Before Philosophy: The Intellectual Adventure of Ancient Man* (Baltimore: Penguin Books, 1949), 71–101, 200–216.

56. Cf., e.g., Bryce, *Legacy of Wisdom*, 200.

57. Lang, *Wisdom and the Book of Proverbs*, 12–13, overlooks this source of conflict.

58. Gordis, *Poets, Prophets, and Sages*, 162.

59. Cf. Gordis, *Poets, Prophets, and Sages*, 169.

60. For a full study, see Lang, *Wisdom and the Book of Proverbs*, R. C. Van Leeuwen, "Liminality and Worldview in Proverbs 1—9," *Semeia* 50 (1990): 111–44, is correct, however, to point out that the feminine image of wisdom is not the singular "root metaphor" for Proverbs 1—9.

61. On the delimitation into segments, see Whybray, *Composition of the Book of Proverbs*, 12–61. Whybray argues that ten instructions were supplemented by the personification of wisdom sections.

62. Whybray's attempt to situate the admonitions in an urban setting while distancing the sentences from this context is not convincing. Both forms, admonition and sentence collection, are well known from Egypt and Mesopotamia, where no such sociological or contextual distinction is warranted. In addition to the Egyptian texts referenced elsewhere in this chapter, see also B. Alster, *Proverbs of Ancient Sumer: The World's Earliest Proverb Collections*, 2 vols. (Bethesda, Md.: CDL Press, 1997); and Lambert, *Babylonian Wisdom Literature*, chap. 9.

63. On the subdivisions, see Whybray, *Wealth and Poverty*, 88.

64. Cf. Bryce, *Legacy of Wisdom*, chaps. 1—4.

65. See Whybray, *Wealth and Poverty*, 63–64.

66. Cf. M. Lichtheim, *Late Egyptian Wisdom Literature in the International Context: A Study of Demotic Instructions* (Freiburg: Universitatsverlag, 1983), in addition to her three-volume *Ancient Egyptian Literature*, cited above.

67. See W. G. Lambert, *Babylonian Wisdom Literature*.

68. On wisdom values, see, e.g., Whybray, *Wealth and Poverty*, 23—44.

69. Cf. G. von Rad, *Wisdom in Israel* (Nashville: Abingdon Press, 1972); J. L. Crenshaw, *Old Testament Wisdom: An Introduction* (Atlanta: John Knox Press, 1981), 10–15, 68–76. On the broader traditions, see J. Eaton, *The Contemplative Face of Old Testament Wisdom in the Context of World Religions* (London: SCM Press, 1989), chap. 1.

70. Purdue's suggestion that Proverbs 1—9 is a product of sapiential efforts in support of a hierocratic program is tantalizing. See L. G. Perdue, "Wisdom Theology and Social History in Proverbs 1—9," in *Wisdom, You Are My Sister: Studies in Honor of Roland E. Murphy, O. Carm., On the Occasion of his Eightieth Birthday*, ed. M. L. Barré (Washington, D.C.: Catholic Biblical Association of America, 1997) 78–101. Unfortunately, the themes and style of such texts are well known throughout Egyptian history and can be placed at any point in the history of Israel's monarchies. They are not simply to be restricted to the Persian phase. Even the biblical figure of Wisdom is paralleled by the Egyptian goddess Ma'at, as Perdue acknowledges (99).

71. For a full discussion see Lang, *Wisdom and the Book of Proverbs*.

72. Lang, *Wisdom and the Book of Proverbs*, 130.

73. Perdue, "Wisdom Theology."

74. See Crenshaw, *Old Testament Wisdom*, 55—59, for a discussion of the use of parallelism in these sections as a literary device.

75. Whybray, *Composition of the Book of Proverbs*, chap. 2.

76. Ibid., 129, although my own analysis sees deeper purposes than Whybray suggests.

77. G. von Rad, *Wisdom in Israel*, pp. 115, 124.

78. Crenshaw, *Old Testament Wisdom*, 63.

79. Lambert, *Babylonian Wisdom Literature*, chap. 6. One might also compare to this the "contest literature," where various plants and animals spar verbally with one another to vaunt their virtues. See ibid., chap. 7. It is undoubtedly significant that the book of Job chooses the dialogue format to make its case rather than the instructional or sentential forms common to Proverbs. This observation leads us to suspect that Job's difference in rhetorical form may be matched by a difference in social ideas; we will need to keep this consideration in mind when we take up the social critique of Job in the next section of this chapter.

80. Despite Whybray's protests to the contrary, it would seem that Van Leeuwen is correct to suggest that such a rhetorical configuration of society works to "quash revolutionary thoughts." In the case of the woman, Van Leeuwen insightfully translates the passage more exactly as "a despised wife when she rules," citing Near Eastern analogues that depict the chaos of an upside-down social and cosmic order. The social function of the text, in other words, is to "maintain respect for right order at all levels of society"—right order, that is , as defined by the wisdom writers. See R. C. Van Leeuwen, "Proverbs 30:21–23 and the Biblical World Upside Down," *JBL* 105 (1986): 599–610, esp. 602–3, 610. See also Whybray, *Composition of the Book of Proverbs*, 152; idem, *Wealth and Poverty*, 43–44. Proverbs 19:10 would seem to function similarly.

81. See Lang, *Wisdom and the Book of Proverbs*, 36–39.

82. The use of the terms for "just" and "wicked" in the Hebrew Scriptures:

	ṣaddîq	ṣedeq	rāšā'
Torah	16	12	11
Deuteronomic History	8	0	6
Ezra/Nehemiah	3	0	0
Psalms	51	49	82
Proverbs 1—9	4	4	7
Proverbs 10—29	62	4	70
Job	7	7	26
Qohelet	8	3	7
Isaiah 1—39	6	8	6
Isaiah 40—66	9	17	5
Jeremiah	3	6	5
Ezekiel	15	4	26
Minor Prophets	10	4	9

83. Crenshaw, *Old Testament Wisdom*, 67–68.

84. Cf. W. O. E. Oesterley, *The Book of Proverbs* (London: Methuen & Co., 1929), lxxxiv–lxxxvii.

85. Van Leeuwen, "Proverbs 30:21–23," takes the analysis further to argue that Proverbs social distinctions and limits are grounded in its understanding of the cosmic order.

86. G. H. Wittenberg, "The Lexical Context of the Terminology for 'Poor' in the Book of Proverbs," *Scriptura: Tydskrif vir bybelkunde* (Stellenbosch) 2 (1986): 40–85, argues from a nuanced awareness of the ways in which these texts vary from the rest of Proverbs. The failure to isolate such chapters in Proverbs can lead to confusion about the nature of the book as a whole.

87. Cf. W. McKane, *Proverbs*, 643.
88. The term *'ānî* is found once in the instructions on wisdom collected in Proverbs 1—9. This in itself is unusual since neither *'ebyôn* nor *dal* appear at all in Proverbs 1—9; only *maḥsor* is also found in the section in question (see below). In a series of antithetic pairs, Prov. 3:32–34 reveals the divergent responses YHWH makes to the wicked and the upright. The devious man is loathed, the wicked man's house is cursed, and the scoffer receives scorn. By contrast, the upright are taken into YHWH's confidence, and the righteous man's house is blessed. The *'ānî/'ānāw* are grouped among the upright and righteous as people who are favored by God. The link between *'ānāw* and piety has been argued by some in relation to the Psalms (see the preceding chapter) and may find a counterpart in this text. Here the writer uses the link to good effect, contrasting YHWH's attitude toward the upright/righteous/humble and the devious/wicked/scoffer. Altering the parallelism, the writer concludes in v. 3:35 by stating, "The wise shall obtain honor, but dullards get disgrace." It is difficult to know if the writer intends this statement to be treated as simply another example of YHWH's just ways or if through parallelism the writer seeks to identify the holders of wisdom with the humble and just, that is, those who are in YHWH's confidence, and thus blessed and favored. In so doing the wise would be numbered among the ranks of the *'ānî/'ānāw*.

The term *'ānî* occurs three times in the sentence literature of Proverbs 10—22. In the first instance, Prov. 14:21, those who show kindness to the *'ānî /'ānāw* are considered "happy," while those who despise friends are treated as "sinners." Kindness to the poor is, as shall be seen, a common exhortation in the wisdom literature, with charity being a mark of the truly wise. The lot of the *'ānî* is presented as a continual struggle in 15:15. Their plight is the opposite of a "feast without end," although the exact circumstances are not specified. McKane suggests that the "contentment" that produces this feast is "an inner resilience which is invulnerable to the whims of fortune." He adds that "whoever has it will not allow himself to be broken by the assaults of poverty. He will withstand them with unconquerable courage, with dignity and composure, and will not permit poverty to contaminate him. He will endure poverty without suffering degradation." See McKane, *Proverbs*, 481.

Finally, Prov. 16:19 states: "Better to be humble and among the lowly [*'ānî/ 'ānāw*] than to share spoils with the proud [better: ruthless/arrogant]." While wealth is seen as good in the wisdom literature, the wise often temper and limit the conditions under which it is to be enjoyed. Here the sage seeks to distance the student from associations with the proud, arguing that a place among the *'ānî* would be preferable. The notions that surround *'ānî* are not different from the rest of the terms for poor in Proverbs 10—22. Unlike the prophetic materials, however, even though Proverbs knows the word *'ānî* , the text does not link the term to the socioeconomic oppression of the poor by the ruling elite.

89. Whybray, *Wealth and Poverty*, 81.
90. See ibid., 107–8.
91. Ibid., 108.
92. Ibid., 111. Whybray's view that this text's "setting is neither royal nor aristocratic" is odd given his admission that the woman lives on an "estate." Clearly, she is no ordinary village dweller.
93. On this contrast, see E. W. Davies, "Schools in Ancient Israel," 106–7.
94. For discussions of *rāš* and *maḥsor*, see H. J. Fabry, *TDOT* 3: 208–30, *TDOT* 4: 80–90; A. George, "Pauvre," *DBSup* 7 (Paris: Letouzey et Ané, 1966), cols. 387–406; idem, "La pauvreté dan l'Ancien Testament," in *La Pauvreté Evangélique*, ed. C.

Koser (Paris: Cerf, 1971), 13–35; idem, "Poverty in the Old Testament," in *Gospel Poverty: Essays in Biblical Theology*, ed. M. D. Guinan (Chicago: Franciscan Herald Press, 1977), 2–21; *THAT* 2:347–48; J. Van der Ploeg, "Les pauvres d'Israël et leur piété," *OTS* 7 (1950): 236–70; C. Van Leeuwen, *Le développement du sens social en Israël avant l'ère chrétienne*, Studia Semitica Neerlandica 1 (Assen: Van Gorcum, 1955), 17. A. Kuschke, "Arm und Reich im Alten Testament mit besonderer Berüchsichtigung der nachexilischen Zeit," *ZAW* 57 (1939): 31–57, argues that the terms for poor can be separated into two groups. On one side he places 'ĕbyôn, dal, and 'ānî, and on the other he groups together rûš (and its derivatives), ḥsr, and miskēn (53). Kuschke claims that the two groupings reflect different mentalities concerning poverty, perhaps the mentalities of two opposing social classes. He suggests that rûš, ḥsr, and miskēn are used in the wisdom literature when poverty is subjected to scorn, but that 'ĕbyôn, dal, and 'ānî are used "when an inner sympathy (on religious grounds) with the fate of the poor is to be expressed and a call is made for just and brotherly deeds on their behalf" (45). Kuschke is correct to assert that different mentalities concerning poverty are present in the biblical literature. However, I believe that his division is oversimplified and misses the fact that the prophets and the wise infused radically different estimations of poverty into terms they shared, such as dal. See also T. Donald, "The Semantic Field of Rich and Poor in the Wisdom Literature of Hebrew and Accadian," *OrAnt* 2 (1964): 27–41.

95. F. Brown, S. R. Driver, and C. A. Briggs, *A Hebrew and English Lexicon of the Old Testament, with an appendix containing the Biblical Aramaic, based on the lexicon of William Gesenius as translated by Edward Robinson* (Oxford: Clarendon Press, 1952), 930, 341. The distribution of the terms rāš and maḥsôr in the Hebrew Bible is as follows: For rāš, *Historical Narrative*: 1 Sam. 18:23; 2 Sam. 12:1, 3, 4; *Poetry*: Ps. 82:3; *Wisdom Literature*: Prov. 10:4; 13:8, 23; 14:20; 17:5; 18:23; 19:1, 7, 22; 22:2, 7; 28:3, 6, 27; 29:13; Qoh. 4:14; 5:7. For maḥsôr, *Pentateuch*: Deut. 15:8; *Historical Narrative*: Judg. 18:10; 19:19, 20; *Poetry*: Ps. 34:10 (9); *Wisdom Literature*: Prov. 6:11; 11:24; 14:23; 21:5, 17; 22:16; 24:34; 28:27.

96. McKane, *Proverbs*, 417.

97. J. Kennedy, *Studies in Hebrew Synonyms* (London: Williams & Norgate, 1898), 84, 86.

98. C. Van Leeuwen, *Développement du sens social*, 160, notes that some emend rāš in Prov. 28:3 to read raša', rôš, or even 'ašîr. The only one of these suggestions that has any possible textual support at all is raša', but this reading requires a contorted derivation from the LXX's *en asebeiais*, "with impieties," an analysis disputed by McKane, *Proverbs*, 629. McKane contends that the MT reading be accepted, but that the translation be rendered by "powerful" or the like on the basis of cognate evidence. However, this rendering seems forced, especially in light of the frequent use of rāš in Proverbs. None of the proposed emendations improves upon the Hebrew text as it stands, and the meaning "poor" figures sensibly in the text.

99. Gordis, *Poets, Prophets, and Sages*, 172.

100. R. C. Van Leeuwen, "Wealth and Poverty: System and Contradiction in Proverbs," *Hebrew Studies* 33 (1992): 25–36, is correct to observe that Proverbs recognizes complicating factors, but the "act-consequence" scheme tends to be the organizing norm of proverbial thought. The contradictions and exceptions reinforce the norm, unlike Job and Qohelet, where clearly the contradictions organize new ways of thinking about wisdom. Job, in particular, must draw on *prophetic* vocabulary to grapple with these contradictions in an effective manner.

101. On the praise of hard work, see also *Ahiqar*, sayings 40, 42.

102. C. Van Leeuwen, *Développement du sens social*, 153, my translation.

103. Cf. E. W. Davies, *Prophecy and Ethics: Isaiah and the Ethical Traditions of Israel*, JSOT Supplement Series 16 (Sheffield: JSOT Press, 1981), 106.
104. C. Van Leeuwen, *Développement du sens social*, 153.
105. Ibid., my translation.
106. Whybray, *Wealth and Poverty*, 10.
107. T. Donald, "Semantic Field of Rich and Poor," 29. Poverty can come by fate and the hand of God according to Egyptian wisdom literature (Ptahhotep §10; Amenemope 7:1–6; 21:15–16; Ankhsheshonq 12:3; 22:25; 26:8, 14; P. Insinger 7:18; 17:2; 28:4; 30:15). Cf. *Ahiqar*, sayings 37, 39, 41.
108. McKane, *Proverbs*, 377; see also Lichtheim, *Ancient Egyptian Literature*, 150.
109. The wisdom writings often counsel against mistreating the weak (Ptahhotep §4; Merikare [Lichtheim, *Ancient Egyptian Literature* 1:100]; Amenemope 4:4–7; 14:5–8; 15:6–7; 26:9; P. Insinger 33:16). People are to aid the poor (Amenemhet [ibid., 1:136], Any [ibid., 2:141–42]; Amenemope 16:5–10; 26:13–14; 27:4–5; Ankhsheshonq 15:6; P. Insinger 15:22; 16:12–14; 25:6).
110. Bryce, *Legacy of Wisdom*, 118, thinks chaps. 28–29 are more favorable to the poor than the rich, treating this as an indication of a late date for the passage. The contrast between rich and poor is frequent in chap. 28 (vv. 6, 8, 11, 19, 20, 22, 25, 27); cf. McKane, *Proverbs*, 621.
111. McKane, *Proverbs*, 641.
112. Malchow, "Social Justice," 122. Malchow develops further this line of argument in *Social Justice in the Hebrew Bible* (Collegeville, Minn.: Liturgical Press, 1996), chap. 7.
113. Whybray, *Wealth and Poverty*, 113, also makes this observation. I feel the need to stress here that though some of our views on various matters are similar, my own position was developed previously in J. D. Pleins, "Poverty in the Social World of the Wise," *JSOT* 37 (1987): 61–78. This is an article of which Whybray was not aware.
114. The Egyptian wisdom materials exhibit a concern, however rare, for measures and property lines. For weights and measures, see Amenemope 17:18–19; 18:4; 18:15–19:7; for property lines, see Merikare (Lichtheim, *Ancient Egyptian Literature* 1:100); Amenemope 7:11–8:4; 8:11–12. Cf. Wittenberg, "*Lexical Context*, 78–81. The citation of a few exceptions here and there hardly overcomes the fact that Proverbs most consistently blames the poor for their predicament and not the rich. Contrast R. C. Van Leeuwen, "Wealth and Poverty," 29–30.
115. Fox, "Social Location," 238.
116. McKane, *Proverbs*, 626.
117. Whybray counts 120 out of 513 verses in the sentence literature devoted to wealth, with 70 dedicated to poverty. Given some overlap, there are by his count 158 that deal with wealth and poverty. In other words, nearly a third of the sentence literature is taken up with these concerns. See Whybray, *Wealth and Poverty*, 11–15.
118. Malchow, "Social Justice," 121.
119. Ibid.
120. Cf. E. W. Davies, *Prophecy and Ethics*, 107.
121. It is doubtful that this material was used to console the poor in their poverty as C. Van Leeuwen maintains (*Développement du sens social*, 161, 164). Awareness of wealth's unstable nature is meant to refine the attitude of the student toward fate and the use of wealth. One is warned not to waste wealth (cf. Prov. 22:22).
122. The Egyptian wisdom writings indicate that there are things worse than poverty, stressing the importance of a life of happiness and integrity (Amenemope 8:19–20; 9:5–6, 7–8; Ankhsheshonq 21:22; 23:8, 9; P. Insinger 27:9).

123. Prov. 1:19; 10:2; 11:28; 16:8; 17:1; 20:17, 21; 23:20; 28:20. The Egyptian wisdom literature counsels restraint in the use of wealth (Ankhsheshonq 6:10; 7:7; 9:11, 24–25; 12:3; 25:6; P. Insinger 6:17, 24; 15:7; 26:16). Gluttony is to be avoided (Kagemni [Lichtheim, *Ancient Egyptian Literature* 60]; Satire of the Trades [ibid., 1:191]; Ankhsheshonq 15:20; 24:12; P. Insinger 5:12). Greed brings strife and want, and is often condemned (Ptahhotep §19; Merikare [ibid., 1:100]; Amenemope 6:14–15; 10:10; Ankhsheshonq 9:22; 12:18; 14:7, 20; 15:7; 21:15; P. Insinger 4:7, 8; 15:7).

124. The Egyptian wisdom writings show an acute awareness of the transitory nature of wealth (Ptahhotep §6; §30; Any [Lichtheim, *Ancient Egyptian Literature*, 2:142]; Amenemope 9:10–10:5; 18:12–13; 19:11–15; 24:15–17; Ankhsheshonq 9:11; 18:17; P. Insinger 18:5).

125. McKane, *Proverbs*, 458.

126. See R. C. Van Leeuwen, "Wealth and Poverty."

127. The bottom line is reflected in *Aḥiqar*, saying 22, which observes that "there is nothing more bitter than poverty (*'nwh*)." See Lindenberger, *Aramaic Proverbs of Aḥiqar*, 89.

128. Cf. *Aḥiqar*, saying 43.

129. Whybray, *Wealth and Poverty*, 34.

Chapter 12

Questioning Prevailing Wisdom

Job, Qohelet

Job: Windbags and Whirlwinds
    Dialogue and Lament Forms in Mesopotamian Tradition
    Dialogue Form and the Book of Job
    The Speeches of Job's Friends
    God in the Book of Job: The Problem of Theodicy
    The Social Justice Vision of the Book of Job
    The Centrality of Poverty in the Book of Job
    Job: The Articulation of Grief

Qohelet: A System of Futility

Given the orientation of Proverbs, the books of Job and Qohelet (Ecclesiastes) deserve separate treatment. This is true for two reasons. In part, these books should not be lumped in with Proverbs because their rhetoric is quite different. For example, Job's choice of a dialogue format is obviously different from Proverbs's instructional or sentential style. Likewise, Qohelet reads like the skeptical and caustic philosophic musings of a king. In each case, the writers adopt a literary form and posture markedly different from that of Proverbs. Moreover, this difference in literary style is of interest precisely because the diverging discourses of Job and Qohelet frame social visions that contrast sharply with the views we have seen in Proverbs. The combination of an alternative literary style and a divergent social vision in both Job and Qohelet appears to have produced a conflicting creed or a competing faith, leading to the fragmentation of Israel's wisdom tradition. As we progress through these trenchant works, we shall find that Job and, to a lesser degree, Qohelet represent a social vision that is moving in the direction of the prophetic voice, pushing Job and Qohelet toward new horizons in wisdom thought. The more assured system of Proverbs had some acknowledged wrinkles in its philosophy, but with Job and Qohelet, as Crenshaw observes, "Once the sages acknowledged exceptions, their entire scheme became problematic."[1] The wrinkles become the objects of investigation in their own right in Job and Qohelet. Job, in particular, stands out because of its fundamental disagreement with the basic wisdom view concerning the poor. Qohelet wrestles with the value of wisdom as such. Both works build on still more ancient philosophic literary forms that permitted the critical exploration of accepted beliefs. Job and Qohelet, however, are not simply carbon copies of these genres, marking instead serious advances in thinking within the larger ancient Near Eastern educational tradition. Let us consider the argumentative Job and the bombastic Qohelet in turn.

Job: Windbags and Whirlwinds

The tale of the wealthy Job who loses all of his children and possessions over a wager between God and the Adversary is tersely told in the first two chapters of Job. This mythic recasting of the Job legend is tantalizing in its own right but our focus here concerns the multitextured poetic material that follows on these chapters. The central portion of the book of Job (chaps. 3—31) is quite consciously a dialogue—a dialogue among "friends."[2] This literary feature is key to this section's overall rhetorical thrust and movement. Such a form is not unique to ancient Israel. Whereas our reading of Proverbs is informed by a comparison with the exhortation and sentential texts from Egypt (forms not unknown from Mesopotamia), our reading of Job must take into account the dispute and dialogue texts known from Egypt and especially Mesopotamia.

Dialogue and Lament Forms in Mesopotamian Tradition

It is true that the dialogue form is not unknown in Egypt, as witnessed in the so-called "Dispute of a Man with His Ba ['soul']," and the "Tale of the Eloquent Peasant"; however, the more extensive texts of dialogue and dispute are those of Mesopotamian origin.[3] We may note in passing the Akkadian text, "The Dispute between the Tamarisk and the Date Palm," which, though concerned with trees and not persons, does frame itself as a dialogue in which each tree vaunts its own virtues.[4] Perhaps a bit closer to Job is the "Dialogue of Pessimism," in which a master proposes various activities and finds his servant's support in each endeavor—namely riding to the palace, dining, riding in the countryside, having children, acting dishonestly, making love, offering sacrifices, making loans, and doing a great deed. However, in each case the master then elects not to do the stated activity, whereupon the servant offers a pessimistic portrayal of each act so as to support his master's determination to avoid each deed. The dialogue leads to deeper insight regarding a range of human involvements, pointing up the potential gains and inevitable futility of existence.[5] Such probing is relevant to the book of Job and is taken further by

Qohelet. More relevant still is "The Babylonian Theodicy," a work that sets a sufferer in dialogue with a friend. The sufferer, in anguish, turns to the friend for insight. The friend, depicted as a wise person, cajoles the sufferer to see the workings of God in the world. The sufferer's posture resembles that of Job insofar as the sufferer insists on his own piety and innocence, questioning the friend's account of suffering. The topic of the accumulation of wealth is key as the friend argues that the apparently wicked rich will not endure forever.[6] The dialogue format drives home these reflections on the vicissitudes of human experience.

The prevalence of the dialogue between persons schema in Job ought not to cause us to overlook the other central literary dimension of Job, namely, dialogue with God. Here dispute texts are not our guide. Rather, we must look to the complaint prayers (lament poems) for comparative texts. Such forms are likewise well known both from Mesopotamia and the Psalms.[7] These texts, which frequently present poignant cries from the place of divine abandonment, offer rather stark, if not at times somewhat stylized, pictures of physical and psychological suffering.[8]

However, an even better counterpart is found in *Ludlul bēl nēmeqi*, "I Will Praise the Lord of Wisdom."[9] In this text, we find a sufferer, speaking in the first person, who details extensively the indignities of his suffering. A sense of divine abandonment pervades the text. The problem of innocent suffering and its complexities captivates the reader. A series of dreams transform the turmoil of the sufferer into a condition of healing. Finally, the sufferer's restoration is accredited to the god Marduk and the goddess Sarpanitum. Similarly, the Babylonian prayer, "Man and His God," speaks of a reversal of the suffering speaker's misfortunes, although in this case the sufferer acknowledges guilt, whereas the speaker in *Ludlul bēl nēmeqi* is innocent.[10]

Dialogue Form and the Book of Job

The uniqueness of the core of Job lies in its combination of these two forms, the dialogue and complaint genres. This brilliant move allows the writer to consider the sufferer's plight both as a communal issue and a theological problem.[11] That the complaint form can find a resolution through dreams and visions likewise provides the author with a productive framework that strives toward some sort of termination to the sufferer's dilemma. This combination, therefore, allows the writer of Job to make progress on the question of suffering. Were this not the case, Job would simply represent a variation on old genre schemes. However, as we shall see, Job moves the justice discussion forward to a new level of insight. Thus, although Job's dialogical rhetoric of opposition is rather distinctive when compared with Proverbs (yet common enough in wisdom circles), this format becomes, in the ancient writer's hands, a powerful tool for reevaluating wisdom teaching about matters of social justice in ancient Israel.

To be fair, bearing in mind the prevalence of dialogue and dispute as an ancient Near Eastern form, we should not presume that the raising of questions automatically indicates opposition to standard wisdom teachings as found in Proverbs. Indeed, many ancient Near Eastern dispute texts would seem to reflect efforts designed to return to and reinforce accepted views of the gods, even when human experience raises theological complications. However, on closer inspection, we find that for the writer of Job, the dialogue style, with its two levels of opposition, namely, against other wisdom teachers and against God, leads the writer in radically new theological directions that challenge the views we find in Proverbs. Against the standard wisdom tradition reflected in Proverbs, Job counters the essential wisdom teachings concerning the causes of poverty. Job, in this sense, represents a direct assault on the wisdom creed. In raising this challenge, the writer moves far afield from Proverbs, both in analysis and in language used to make the analysis. When the text moves against God, the challenge actually leads to a meeting of two worlds, what Gutiérrez calls the "mysterious meeting of two freedoms,"[12] namely, the encounter between the human responsibility and divine inactivity.[13]

The Speeches of Job's Friends

Since the author of Job utilizes dialogue and divine speeches as a device for inquiry, we turn to a rhetorical analysis of these speeches to see precisely how the writer pushes through the speeches toward new insight regarding the justice question. Beginning with the speeches of Job and his friends, we note Clines's assessment in which he argues that each speaker takes a distinctive posture over against a Job who makes creative philosophical progress.[14] While Clines's attentiveness here is instructive, one drawback to his analysis is the failure to ask how the interaction between Job and his interlocutors serves to frame the movement of Job's own thoughts. Let us consider the structuring of these rounds.

With Eliphaz, the initial suggestion is that since all suffer, it must be Job's turn to suffer. Eliphaz is concerned to explain the rationale for Job's "turn" and suggests that God does heed the cry of those who are in need (chaps. 4—5). Given this rather benign starting point, Job's own opening salvo is rather striking. In making God the enemy, Job offers a most radical point of departure for his theological exploration (chaps. 6—7). Job's posture is only partly in dialogue with Eliphaz, for Job already seeks to move the discussion beyond the circle of friends to the God who is the "Watcher of Humankind."

As Eliphaz proceeds, his argument turns to a consideration of the wise man as a knower (chap. 15). For Eliphaz, Job is not wise like the friends; consequently, Job cannot perceive what the wise know, namely, that the wicked suffer torment because of their rebellion. While Eliphaz begins to make progress (his line of argument is hardly static), Job simply refines his own argument: Whereas God was the enemy in Job's initial statement, God is now the hunter, with Job as the target (chap. 16). Job's argument only subtly shifts from "watcher" to "witness" (i.e., to one in heaven who will judge). By setting Eliphaz and Job side by side, we see that rhetorically Job has yet to make progress. Failure to find an anchor will lead to his entrapment, as we feel the vise of Eliphaz's argument begin to grip Job.

By chap. 22, Eliphaz has taken up Zophar's charge of chap. 20, namely, that wealth is the issue. Eliphaz blisteringly applies the analysis to Job. Eliphaz has been hunting for an explanation to Job's "turn" at suffering, and with the topic of wealth, he now has the key to unlock Job's dilemma. Job, by contrast, has made progress insofar as he can sort out his personal status vis-à-vis the wicked rich. Thus, he argues that God knows him to be innocent and that the wicked rich are not punished (chaps. 23—24). God is still the object of Job's queries as he responds to Eliphaz. However, now God is depicted as seeing nothing while killers are loose on the prowl.

Similarly, Job's response to Bildad, when read together with Bildad's speeches, provide the author with a structured movement for Job's reflection. Bildad offers a straightforward wisdom analysis by suggesting that the house of the unrighteous falls but that the just blossom (chap. 8). Here is the classic reward-punishment scheme known to us from Proverbs. Not to leave any stone unturned, Bildad also supposes that Job's children were evil. Since God sustains the innocent, Bildad, like Eliphaz, initially believes (correctly but rather ironically) that Job will be blessed. Job's response, quite statically, carries forward his claims of entrapment by God. God is the one who kills the just and the unjust. God is all powerful. Job cannot prove his innocence, but insists on taking his complaint about God directly to God (chaps. 9—10). Rhetorically, Bildad's initial move makes progress for the wisdom voice over against a rather static Job. Clearly, Job's line of thought has potential force. Yet without the catalyst of the wealth question as supplied by the wise interlocutors, Job's own approach is threatened with failure. Ironically, it is the "bad theology" of the friends that paves the way for Job's insight!

When Bildad raises the question of whether the world ought to be changed for Job's sake, he is simply refining the wisdom view of the universe's operations, laying bare their law-like character (chap. 18). Job's response, again rather statically, reasserts the hunt motif well known by this point. However,

Job is refining his level of appeal, for now he seeks to write a complaint that could be championed by his witness and avenger (chap. 19).

The few verses given over to Bildad in chap. 25 take his views to their logical conclusion, for if the world is governed by unbreakable moral principles, then universal rule must be in the hands of a divine sovereign. The analysis of Job's response at this juncture is rendered difficult by our uncertainty about the ascription of chaps. 26—27 to Job. Not all of these words seem to fit his character and might represent a displacement from the words of one of the three friends. When we resume with the Job of chaps. 29—31, we find Job carrying forward the wealth question raised by Zophar and decisively applied to Job by Eliphaz. Here Job has moved well beyond Bildad's views of universal moral principles, for Job seeks to ground his case in a far deeper moral element at work in the world, namely, justice. If it can be argued that Job is not merely innocent but that he has shown justice to the poor, then the confidence of Bildad and the others falls to the ground. The rhetorical juxtaposition of Job and Bildad shows us that Job has moved onto the wisdom turf to argue for a new understanding of the principles that govern the world. At the very moment when Eliphaz and Bildad seem to have clinched their case, Job capitalizes on one of their key concerns, that of wealth, to render a new verdict on the wisdom view of the world and on the friends' assessment of his situation.

How did Job achieve this insight? The key is provided by Zophar. Unlike the other friends, Zophar initially charged Job with guilt (chap. 11). God's ways might be beyond ours (as Job would contend) but God is in a position to know that Job has done wrong, even if the friends are not clear what Job has done to deserve his suffering. Zophar's only advice is to repent. At this juncture, we see from Job's response that his discussion is not so much with the friends as it is with God. Rhetorically, the friends are pushing Job down the road to insight, but his speeches in reply are really meant for God. After all, Job wants clarity about God, not about his friends. Hence, in chaps. 12—13 we gain an initial glimpse of the God who topples kings, a God of power encountered later in the divine speeches.

Zophar's second speech rather graphically underscores Bildad's clockwork view of the universe (chap. 20). Zophar argues that the sinner may briefly enjoy life, but soon perishes, vomiting up all the wealth he has accumulated. Zophar has taken his initial charge of guilt against Job and refined the issue in a way that links the opening chapter of the book of Job to the poetic segment. Ironically, by raising the wealth issue, Zophar has unwittingly provided Job with the means to launch a frontal assault on the increasingly encircling arguments of the friends. With his rejoinder that the wicked prosper and with his observation that the rich die in comfort, Job has a powerful line of argument that unravels and undermines the analysis the friends have sought to apply to him (chap. 21).

To reiterate, the friends' arguments are hardly static. Rather, at the point where their success seems assured, where Job seems hopelessly trapped, the friends provide Job with a way of escape that deconstructs their entire system of thought.[15] The friends are exposed as the liars. If we fail to keenly observe the juxtaposition and movement of these speeches, we risk missing the question of wealth as the turning point. By introducing solidarity with the poor as a way out of the trap, the writer of the book of Job, as Gutiérrez so persuasively observes, has achieved a real breakthrough on the question of human suffering.[16]

God in the Book of Job: The Problem of Theodicy

To this encounter, the writer sees God bringing various seemingly contradictory postures: While the prose prologue of Job turns the affair into a rather nasty divine chess game, the early part of the poetic segment is dominated by God's apparent silence in the face of injustice.[17] In the dialogue of the friends, only the "topic" of God finds expression. Eliphaz assumes that he knows the mind of God when he says, "As I have seen, those who plow evil and sow mischief reap them. They perish by a blast from God, are gone at the breath of His nostrils" (4:8–9). In the face of human grief, the figures are free to speculate about the activity of God and the meaning of suffering, but they are never granted the certainty of knowing the whys and wherefores of that suffering.[18] Eliphaz can cruelly tell Job, "See how happy is the man whom God reproves; do not reject the discipline of the Almighty" (5:17). But how does he know that this is the reason for Job's suffering? Dialogue in the midst of suffering only permits a rarefied understanding of suffering. When God is a topic, the danger is that "God" can become a fabricated logical construct that seeks to cover over suffering, a justification for the status quo, or a foil for the theological mystification of concrete horrors. The friends' speeches created a God of their own liking, a God who fits human conceptions of blessing and curse, hard work and laziness, wealth and poverty, piety and perversity.

Yet there is a virtue to human dialogue. Through the dialogue, and pressing beyond it, Job learns how to articulate his grief (see further below). This alone is what God offers Job—not answers, but the opportunity to grieve; not divine speeches, but the dark reality of God's silent presence:

> What is man, that You make much of him,
> That You fix Your attention upon him?
> You inspect him every morning,

> Examine him every minute.
> Will You not look away from me for a while,
> Let me be, till I swallow my spittle?
> If I have sinned, what have I done to You,
> Watcher of men?
> Why make of me Your target,
> And a burden to myself?
> Why do You not pardon my transgression
> And forgive my iniquity?
> For soon I shall lie down in the dust;
> When You seek me, I shall be gone.
>
> Job 7:17–21

Of course, the problem here is that the realm of human dialogue never brings answers to the painful questions about God's intention in that suffering. This is not something that God chooses to extend to Job in these chapters, indicating that human dialogue cannot penetrate God's inscrutable character. The uncertainties of human dialogue in the midst of suffering are far removed from the assurances of the fairy tale world of chaps. 1—2, where God battles the Adversary, creating a book that is, as Penchansky so perceptively observes, at odds with itself.[19]

Unlike the prologue and the epilogue, the chapters devoted to Job's dialogue with his friends are fraught with uncertainty—an uncertainty created by the incongruities of the clash between his innocence and his suffering, an uncertainty compounded by the very unwillingness of God to speak to the situation and right it:

> If indeed I have erred,
> My error remains with me.
> Though you are overbearing toward me,
> Reproaching me with my disgrace,
> Yet know that God has wronged me;
> He has thrown up siege works around me.
> I cry, "Violence!" but am not answered;
> I shout, but can get no justice.
>
> Job 19:4–7

Job's pain is increased because God chooses not to speak in the world of human dialogue and debate. The paradox of the book is that the debate about God appears to have left God out of the debate. The author does not permit God to speak in such a setting. Indeed, it seems that God has been rendered incapable of speech.

We need to be careful here not to confuse God's silence with God's absence from the human dialogue. God is far from absent. While it is true that God is often reduced to a theological topic in the friends' debate, God is far more than a topic for Job. God is a presence, however silent:

> With Him are wisdom and courage;
> His are counsel and understanding.
> Whatever He tears down cannot be rebuilt;
> Whomever He imprisons cannot be set free.
> When He holds back the waters, they dry up;
> When He lets them loose, they tear up the land.
> With Him are strength and resourcefulness;
> Erring and causing to err are from Him.
>
> Job 12:13–16

Beyond justifications, rationalizations, and mystifications, Job comes to artic-ulate a vision of a God who is painfully present (cf. 9:3–14). Job sets the tragedy of his suffering firmly beside the agonizing reality of a God who tears down and destroys (9:24; 10:8–18; 12:17–25). This is a God who can cast kings from their thrones, but who glaringly fails to take action in Job's case. The incon-gruities of divine action perplex the book's author. Yet, instead of offering sim-plistic answers, the writer prefers to confront rather than circumvent the pain endured when the sufferer refuses to detach suffering from the inscrutable power of God.

Against the backdrop of the discussion with the friends, Job is engaged in dialogue with God in the fullest sense of the word. He is even in communion with the divine.[20] Job may say, "Indeed, I would speak to the Almighty; I insist on arguing with God" (13:3). Yet we know that he is already in dialogue with God. This is evidenced, in particular, by the fact that frequently in his speeches Job turns from talking to his friends to speak directly with God:

> How many are my iniquities and sins?
> Advise me of my transgression and sin.
> Why do You hide Your face,
> And treat me like an enemy?
>
> Job 13:23–24

However exasperatingly silent God may be, God is still a conversation part-ner. Who else but God permits Job to lay bare his innermost fears and frus-trations with impunity?

> O that You would hide me in Sheol,
> Conceal me until Your anger passes,
> Set me a fixed time to attend to me.
> If a man dies, can he live again?
> All the time of my service I wait

Until my [relief] comes.
You would call and I would answer You;
You would set Your heart on Your handiwork
Job 14:13–15,
JPS, with slight adaptation

Job's friends do not allow this freedom to speak in this manner to or about God. In fact, Eliphaz censures Job's talk:

Does a wise man answer with windy opinions,
And fill his belly with the east wind?
Should he argue with useless talk,
With words that are of no worth?
You subvert piety
And restrain prayer to God.
Job 15:2–4

Job's friends try to short-circuit the grieving process. Their intervention stifles creative communion with God in the midst of suffering. It would seem, then, that God alone gives Job the room to have his say.

If we listen carefully to Job's speeches, we know that the problem rests not in God's absence but in the conjunction of God's presence with God's silence in the face of unjust suffering.[21] Job's grief does not arise simply from his suffering, but out of the encounter between that suffering and God's stony silence:

He regarded me as clay,
I have become like dust and ashes.

I cry out to You, but You do not answer me;
I wait, but You do [not] consider me;
You have become cruel to me;
With Your powerful hand You harass me.
Job 30:19–21

Job struggles to continue to speak well of God in the face of this suffering. Yet he cannot help but feel that God is somehow to blame for his suffering:

But He knows the way I take;
Would He assay me, I should emerge pure as gold.
I have followed in His tracks,
Kept His way without swerving,
I have not deviated from what His lips commanded;
I have treasured His words more than my daily bread.
He is one; who can dissuade Him?

> Whatever He desires, He does.
> For He will bring my term to an end,
> But He has many more such at His disposal.
> Therefore I am terrified at His presence;
> When I consider, I dread Him.
>
> Job 23:10–15

When Job's innocent suffering stares into the dark silence of God, no words of comfort can fill the emptiness he feels. Job must console himself with the knowledge that he has assisted others who have been in great need, which, as we have begun to sense and shall see, is a key theological turning point in the book. Yet, frequently the very knowledge that permits Job to know that he stands innocent before God only serves to increase his pain in the midst of the dialogue with the friends (Job 29:12–17; 30:25; 31:13–25, 32).

The subject of God's silence is tackled straightforwardly by the figure of Elihu. Most scholars separate the speeches of Elihu from the rest of the book of Job, treating them as the product of a later hand. Nevertheless, when we consider these speeches within the context of the movement of the entire book, they introduce another vital perspective into the dialogue, one directly relevant to our present discussion.[22] Elihu represents a mediating voice between the perspective of Job's friends and the views that emerge in the speeches of God. If we listen to Elihu carefully, we hear the "liturgical voice." This voice, more fully articulated in the Psalms, is open to human grief, but does not acquiesce in God's silence.

The liturgical voice operates firmly under the conviction that God chooses to listen to human grief and at times will intervene to aright injustice:

> See, God is mighty; He is not contemptuous;
> He is mighty in strength and mind.
> He does not let the wicked live;
> He grants justice to the lowly.
> He does not withdraw His eyes from the righteous;
> With kings on thrones
> He seats them forever, and they are exalted.
>
> Job 36:5–7

Thus far the book has not raised the language of praise and creation as a possible response to suffering and social injustice. Yet now the writer, through the figure of Elihu, directs us beyond suffering to such language:

> Remember, then, to magnify His work,
> Of which men have sung,
> Which all men have beheld,

Men have seen, from a distance.
See, God is greater than we can know;
The number of His years cannot be counted.
He forms the droplets of water,
Which cluster into rain, from His mist.
The skies rain;
They pour down on all mankind.
Can one, indeed, contemplate the expanse of clouds,
The thunderings from His pavilion?
See, He spreads His lightning over it;
It fills the bed of the sea.

Job 36:24–30

Elihu uses the language of worship to challenge Job, who has said, "I am right; God has deprived me of justice" (34:5). The writer challenges the reader to ask if praise and creation can enshroud (but not conceal) the experience of suffering to produce consolation and insight.

Through Elihu, the writer directly ties the language of praise and creation to concrete statements about God's governance of the world political order:

Would one who hates justice govern?
Would you condemn the Just Mighty One?
. . . .
He is not partial to princes;
The noble are not preferred to the wretched;
For all of them are the work of His hands.
. . . .
He shatters mighty men without number
And sets others in their place.
Truly, He knows their deeds;
Night is over, and they are crushed.

Job 34:17, 19, 24-25

In connecting praise and politics, the writer does not overlook the realities of social injustice:

He strikes down [the mighty] with the wicked
Where people can see,
Because they have been disloyal to Him
And have not understood any of His ways;
Thus He lets the cry of the poor come before Him;
He listens to the cry of the needy.

Job 34:26–28,
JPS, with slight adaptation

For the writer, the language of praise can reach into the world of suffering and social injustice. The cry of the poor does elicit a response from God.

But what about the silence of God? On the one hand, the writer reminds us that there are situations in which God does speak and act. The language of praise and creation continually calls to mind situations of relief and rescue. In cases where God does not act, the writer asks, "When He is silent, who will condemn? If He hides His face, who will see Him, be it nation or man?" (34:29). The language of praise and creation permits crying out to God for justice, but it does not permit condemning God for inaction. Worship can never go this far because worship remains conscious of the grandeur and power of the Mighty One who governs the world order. On the other hand, the liturgical voice places between humanity and God an ineluctable tension. Hence, the language of worship does not supply an "answer" or a "reason" for suffering. Instead, worship molds a posture toward that suffering and toward God in the midst of suffering, the posture of anxious waiting:

> Surely it is false that God does not listen,
> That Shaddai does not take note of it.
> Though you say, "You do not take note of it,"
> The case is before Him;
> So wait for Him.
>
> Job 35:13–14

This posture of anxious waiting can derive some benefit and insight from even the worst kind of suffering. This is not to acquiesce in suffering. The language of worship is not antithetical to the protest of the prophet (as we shall see). But the language of worship can assist the sufferer to look beyond that suffering to long openly for the reality of the God who consoles through might and splendor:

> Because of this, too, my heart quakes,
> And leaps from its place.
> Just listen to the noise of His rumbling,
> To the sound that comes out of His mouth.
> He lets it loose beneath the entire heavens—
> His lightning, to the ends of the earth.
> After it, He lets out a roar;
> He thunders in His majestic voice.
> No one can find a trace of it by the time His voice is heard.
> God thunders marvelously with His voice;
> He works wonders that we cannot understand.
>
> Job 37:1–5

The tongue that can cry out to God for justice can also marvel at the power of God. The language of praise and creation, liturgical language, does not negate suffering and pain, but gives tragedy a way to speak to a God who seems aloof.

When God finally speaks in the final chapters of the poetic section of Job, all topics and debates come to an end. The silence of God gives way to the terrifying reality of God's presence. We hear the language of praise and creation coming from the very mouth of God. God's "silence" yields to God's "speech." Rhetorically, God's speech dominates the interaction between God and Job to overwhelm Job in much the same way that the speeches of Job and his friends had earlier pushed God aside. Ironically, God brings all discussion to an end by asking for still further dialogue:

> Who is this who darkens counsel,
> Speaking without knowledge?
> Gird your loins like a man;
> I will ask and you will inform Me.
> Job 38:2–3

God now speaks after remaining silent for so long and through so much human pain and contentious debate about God's intentions. God is clearly provoked, but not by Job's grieving. God responds, but not on account of Job's suffering. God reacts to the presumption of Job and his friends that they really understand God. Job is on the verge of letting his suffering squelch his ability to speak well of God, to see the power of God, to praise the wonders of creation. The depth of despair expressed in chapters 29—31 demands the speeches of God in chaps. 38–41. Here Job is not disappointed.

The speeches tell of creation in all its freedom and power. The author passes before our eyes creation's waters and morning, the depths of the ocean, light and darkness, snow and thunderstorms:

> Who cut a channel for the torrents
> And a path for the thunderstorms,
> To rain down on uninhabited land,
> On the wilderness where no man is,
> To saturate the desolate wasteland,
> And make the crop of grass sprout forth?
> Job 38:25–27

Animals are paraded before us who run wild, virtually untamed by humans, beholden only to the whims of the divine: lioness, antelope, wild ass, wild ox, ostrich, horse, hawk and vulture, behemoth and Leviathan (38:39–39:30; 40:15–41:26 [34]).

The centerpiece of God's freedom and creative power in all these lists is God's judgment and justice. Again, praise and politics merge in the book of Job to bring a response toward creation into dialogue with humanity's longings for a just social order. At every turn in Job, whether the concern is God's silence or God's speech, the book consciously addresses the realities of political injustice and economic exploitation. But here the question is whether or not the justice demanded by those who suffer, when enacted, will produce utopia:

> Would you impugn My justice?
> Would you condemn Me that you may be right?
> Have you an arm like God's?
> Can you thunder with a voice like His?
> Deck yourself now with grandeur and eminence;
> Clothe yourself in glory and majesty.
> Scatter wide your raging anger;
> See every proud man and bring him low.
> See every proud man and humble him,
> And bring them down where they stand.
> Bury them all in the earth;
> Hide their faces in obscurity.
> Then even I would praise you
> For the triumph your right hand won you.
> Job 40:8–14

If the human demand for vengeance were unleashed, what would remain of society? Would justice really emerge as the architect of the state? God's query gets rather pointed. For God to ask, "Would you condemn Me that you may be right?" is to say that Job has gone too far. In demanding justice, Job was quite right to point to his own innocence and be perplexed. But in using his innocence to make a case against God, Job ran the risk of closing himself off from the only one who could bring him consolation.

The speeches of God in the final chapters of the book balance and answer the silence of God that reigned during Job's debate with his friends. Job's response to God accents the element of silence:

> See, I am of small worth; what can I answer You?
> I clap my hand to my mouth.
> I have spoken once, and will not reply;
> Twice, and will do no more.
> Job 40:4-5

The silence of Job balances the endless diatribes of the preceding chapters. It was in Job's cry for justice that he could sense God's silence. However, only after the cry had spent itself was Job prepared to hear God speak. The cry for justice is not muted by God's speech. This is the cry that must dominate human debates about suffering and injustice; this cry energizes the language of worship. But this cry must not deafen the worshiping community to the realities of God's freedom and creative presence. In the end, God speaks to a Job who has called out for justice.

God may not right things as Job would wish, but God provides sources of comfort amid grief and tragedy. Like Elihu, the figure of God in the book provides a vocabulary to grapple with injustice: God's playfulness and terror. This is enough for Job to confess,

> I know that You can do everything,
> That nothing you propose is impossible for You.
> *Who is this who obscures counsel without knowledge?* *
> Indeed, I spoke without understanding
> Of things beyond me, which I did not know.
> *Hear now, and I will speak;* *
> *I will ask, and You will inform me.* *
> I had heard You with my ears,
> But now I see You with my eyes;
> Therefore, I recant and relent,
> Being but dust and ashes.
>
> Job 42:2–6
>
> *emphasis added to indicate quotes from God's previous speeches

This encounter between the very human pain of Job and the unsettling possibilities of divine silence and action transforms the social vision of the book of Job. The writer urges us to look for God in the realities of suffering, grief, and painful silence. There God will be present, there God will speak. God is not necessarily heard in abstract, time-honored theological systems, but can be found in the struggles of grief beyond words. Since the book of Job most likely reflects Israel's postexilic dislocations, Penchansky is correct to suggest that "Job depicts the unease felt where ideology and experience have fallen into open combat."[23]

However, this final poetic frame ought not to lull us into thinking that the writer is concerned to provide the one solution to the very modern philosophic "problem of evil." For this wisdom writer, the rhetorical device of dialogue with the friends and the divine sovereign functions to adumbrate the many possible postures of God toward evil. In other words, as a creative educational work built around dialogue, the book of Job explores numerous possible explanations for suffering, treating suffering as the product of a divine contest (chaps. 1—2), a built-in aspect of the human condition (4:1–5; 5:6–7; 7:1–6; 15:14–16; 25:4–6), the result of impiety or wrongdoing (4:6–11; 8:11–13; 11:5–6, 13–16; 15:25–35; 18; 20:15–22; 22:5–11; 27:13–23), the outcome of divine plans and lessons (5:17–27; 11:7–12; 40:8–14; 42:1–6), the evil fruit of God's vicious ways (7:17–21;

9:1–14; 12:12–25; 19:6–14; 26:5–14; 30:19–31), or simply punishment for bad theologizing (13:1–12; 42:7–8). By entertaining many possible explanations and not just one, the writer is deliberately drawing the reader into an encounter with God by exploring the many ways God might see this situation.[24] No one "solution" commands assent. By this design, the reader is not absolved of the responsibility of seeking further answers for Job, for the community, and for oneself.

no one solution (margin note)

The Social Justice Vision of the Book of Job

This encounter between the very human pain of Job and the terrible possibilities behind divine action undergirds the social vision of the text. In a penetrating analysis of the role of social evil in Job and other biblical texts, Brueggemann has observed, "It is an important fact of the sociology of our scholarship that the enormous concern of Israel for social power and social goods is characteristically bracketed out when we come to the question of theodicy."[25] What Brueggemann offers is not simply a semantic updating of the problem of evil in terms of a trendy interest in social justice. On the contrary, he argues quite convincingly that matters of social power, social access, and land distribution are at the heart of Job. Consequently, any theologically engaging reading of the text must take into account these concrete elements. As Brueggemann aptly states, "the subject of God-justice (i.e., theodicy) requires a 'materialist' reading of text and experience."[26] We need to explore the social vision of Job that emerges from the dialogue, for this social vision is truly the heart of the text. We can characterize this vision along three related lines: the exploitation of the poor, the process of the accumulation of wealth in society, and solidarity with the poor.

The first trajectory concerns the exploitation of the poor. Of all the accusations Job's friends make against Job as they argue that he must indeed have done something to deserve his suffering, nothing could be more biting or trenchant than the accusation that Job has exploited the poor. Eliphaz the Temanite offers the most direct accusations against Job:

accusation: Job exploited the poor (margin note)

> You know that your wickedness is great,
> And that your iniquities have no limit.
> You exact pledges from your fellows without reason,
> And leave them naked, stripped of their clothes;
> You do not give the thirsty water to drink;
> You deny bread to the hungry.
> . . . .
> You have sent away widows empty-handed;
> The strength of the fatherless is broken.
> Therefore snares are all around you,
> And sudden terrors frighten you,

Or darkness, so you cannot see;
A flood of waters covers you.
Job 22:5–7, 9–11

Likewise, Zophar the Namathite, in an angry response to Job, explains the sinner's loss of wealth, meaning Job's losses, as follows:

The riches he swallows he vomits;
God empties it out of his stomach.
. . . .
He will give back the goods unswallowed;
The value of the riches, undigested.
Because he crushed and tortured the poor,
He will not build up the house he took by force.
He will not see his children tranquil;
He will not preserve one of his dear ones.
With no survivor to enjoy it,
His fortune will not prosper.
When he has all he wants, trouble will come;
Misfortunes of all kinds will batter him.
Let that fill his belly.
Job 20:15, 18–23a

Similar sentiments are expressed in Job 27:13–23 presumably by Zophar the Namathite, although precisely who is speaking in this passage is not clear from the Hebrew text and is debated by scholars.[27]

It is appropriate for representatives of the wisdom tradition to make a charge of abusing the poor. Proverbs, as we saw in chapter 11, shows us that the mistreatment of the poor is an object of reflection and concern to the practitioners of the wisdom school of thought. However, as this theme of the mistreatment of the poor crops up in Job, new theological moves have been made. Surprisingly, Job's friends go beyond the typical point of view in Proverbs when they sing their litany of mistreatment and exploitation. When we consider that the standard wisdom explanation for poverty, as evidenced by Proverbs, is that it results from laziness, it is rather noteworthy that the book of Job focuses on poverty as the product of exploitation, even if by this the friends mean the exploitative misdeeds of Job. While this approach to the poverty question is not entirely foreign to wisdom thought, it is far more at home in the world of the prophetic, where exploitation is the first explanation for the situation of the poor. Strangely, Job's friends, therefore, are using _prophetic_ language here to make their _wisdom_ arguments. Defining the key issue in terms of the mistreatment and exploitation of the poor, minus any allusion to the favorite wisdom scapegoat—the lazy poor—appears to be absolutely essential to the argument and the social vision of the core section of the book of Job. The rhetoric of the poetic chapters of Job has isolated out this social question as the ground for the establishment of its social vision, and it does this by imagining a dialogue with wisdom teachers over the question of the exploited poor. Certainly such a dialogue may not have taken place in the halls of the wisdom academies, but the writer of Job finds it absolutely essential to imagine just such a dialogue.[28] Comparisons with Proverbs should not mislead us; as we read Job, we need to bear in mind that even though the general line of thought carried out by Job's friends resembles ideas contained in Proverbs, this does not mean that the thoughts expressed by Job's friends are at all points the same as the views found in Proverbs. The author appears willing to fragment wisdom's most cherished views to probe more deeply the nature of social evil.

The second trajectory that Job takes up as it fleshes out its social vision concerns the process of the accumulation of wealth in society: How does this accumulation happen? The social vision of the dialogues in Job hinges on the answer to this question. For the writer, it is not the case that only those who are industrious prosper, as Proverbs teaches. It is also not the case that poverty is simply the result of laziness. The writer of Job sees a topsy-turvy world in which those who are wicked can accumulate wealth and live to enjoy it because God does not destroy them. This is obviously not the focus of Proverbs, and rips apart the logic of wisdom thought.[29] In confronting the contradictions the world economic order presents, the poet offers a jarring picture of the prosperity the wicked enjoy:

> Why do the wicked live on,
> Prosper and grow wealthy?
> Their children are with them always,
> And they see their children's children.
> Their homes are secure, without fear;
> They do not feel the rod of God.
> Their bull breeds and does not fail;
> Their cow calves and never miscarries;
> They let their infants run loose like sheep,
> And their children skip about.
> They sing to the music of timbrel and lute,
> And revel to the tune of the pipe;
> They spend their days in happiness,
> And go down to Sheol in peace.
>
> Job 21:7–13

The picture given here is instructive. We can imagine the wealth of the more prominent citizens of ancient Israel, those who made the agricultural and pastoral community work to their advantage. They have accumulated their fortunes and go on to enjoy what they have. What are we to make of this accumulation of wealth? Our assessment of Job must proceed with caution here, for the danger is not simply the fact of the accumulation of massive wealth, although this is an important question that any productive society must face because of the gross imbalances in distribution that inevitably occur (a reality the legal tradition tried to face, as we saw in chap. 2). The writer of Job seems primarily concerned with the methods the wicked use to accumulate that wealth:

> Why are times for judgment not reserved by Shaddai?
> Even those close to Him cannot foresee His actions.
> People remove boundary-stones;
> They carry off flocks and pasture them;
> They lead away the donkeys of the fatherless,
> And seize the widow's bull as a pledge;
> They chase the needy off the roads;
> All the poor of the land are forced into hiding.
>
> Job 24:1–4

To get their wealth, the wicked take over the land and property of others. As we would say, they oppress and exploit to amass their wealth. By defining the wicked in this way, the writer of Job puts some sociological meat on the flimsy skeleton that Proverbs terms "wicked." We can see here how the rhetoric of Job operates. The writer finds it absolutely necessary to redefine what "wicked" means in order to bring the dialogue around to matters of social justice. The writer has turned a basic category of Proverbs on its head, so that now the concepts of wicked and poverty can be discussed together under the rubric of exploitation, not industry versus laziness. In this way, the book of Job stands at the horizon of wisdom thought. The rhetoric has defined an alternative way of understanding the process of the accumulation of wealth. In so doing, the poetic dialogue breaks open a new social vision.

The final trajectory in Job's social vision brings us face to face with the book's only real solution to the so-called problem of evil, namely, the need for solidarity with the poor as the human response to those exploited by the social order. This line of thought, the critical step forward we have seen in the understanding of the book of Job, was ferreted out by Gutiérrez in his study of the book. While Gutiérrez rightly sees key philosophic advances when the author presses the edges of the old retributive justice scheme by raising the counterexample of innocent suffering, Gutiérrez's identification of commitment to the poor as a viable path out of the old conundrum concerning the justice of human suffering marks a major advance in our interpretation of Job.[30] The writer's particular articulation of solidarity is characterized by Gutiérrez as prophetic language, by which he means that the author of Job reflects the sort of social critique and advocacy found in the biblical prophetic texts.[31] In a similar vein, Brueggemann, speaking of Job 21:1, perceptively observes, "The problem thus is not some speculative theological argument, or an existential anguish about an intimate relation, but the problem is the distribution of social goods."[32] What, for Brueggemann, is talk of the "distribution of social goods" carries the label "prophetic" for Gutiérrez. In honing his observation, Gutiérrez is making more than an impressionistic claim, for this insight is bolstered in no small measure by an analysis of the very vocabulary for poverty utilized in Job, which, for all its other wisdom trappings, turns out to be prophetic terminology, not wisdom language.

The Centrality of Poverty in the Book of Job

Since rhetoric is, in part, a function of vocabulary choice, it is instructive to examine the poverty vocabulary of the text of Job. The contrast between Job and Proverbs in their respective uses of the terms for "poor" could not be more striking. Unlike Proverbs, the book of Job shows no special preference for the term *dal*. The words *'ebyôn* and *'ānî* are paired several times, and pairings with the term *dal* occur as well. Most significantly, *rāš* and *maḥsôr* are not used at all. This would initially suggest that a different perspective is found in Job that is more akin to the sentiments of the prophets. This suspicion is, in fact, confirmed upon closer examination.

As we have seen, there is a strong sense in Job that the poor are poor because they are exploited. The specific vocabulary carries forward the prophetic understanding. From one of Zophar's speeches the observation is made that since the wealth of the rich has been obtained through wrongdoing, it must be returned to the poor (*dal*; Job 20:10). While in Proverbs the *dal* suffers oppression, in Job, unlike Proverbs, the specific mode of injustice is the confiscation of housing (Job 20:19), a topic of concern to Isaiah (see discussion in chapter 6; cf. Hab. 1:6). Presumably, the implication of Zophar's speech is that Job had gained his wealth unjustly and therefore suffered the kind of judgment once proclaimed by the prophets. Job himself reveals an awareness of the tie between wealth and oppression. In one passage Job waits, much like Habakkuk (Hab. 2:1), for God's judgment against a host of injustices: moving boundary stones and stealing flocks (24:2), misuse of animals and pledges (v. 3; cf. 22:6–9),[33] abusing the *'ebyôn* "poor" and the *'ānî*, "oppressed" (v. 4), and forcing the poor to suffer in unbearable living conditions (vv. 5–8). Job is sensitive to the injustices bound up in the removal of the children of the poor (*dal*) because of debts, however legal the practice may have been (v. 9). The *'ebyôn* and *'ānî* are murdered, and yet God remains silent (v. 14). This conception of poverty and injustice found in Job is highly prophetic in character and is without parallel in the text of Proverbs. The difference in the distribution of terms between these texts is accompanied by a divergent understanding of the roots of poverty. In Job, the terms for "poor" are placed in contexts of exploitation, oppression, and unjust judgments against the poor.

In a later section, Job defends his actions, giving an example of his just behavior. He claims he rescued the *'ānî* and the fatherless (29:12). The context is the public gate (29:7–10), and so one can assume that Job depicts himself as a just member of the council of elders, one who brought legal justice to those in need. This is confirmed in Job 29:16: "I was a father to the needy [*'ĕbyôn*], and I looked into the case of the stranger." Once honored for civic virtue, Job had fallen into disrepute, yet he claims true compassion for the poor: "Did I not grieve for the *'ĕbyôn*" (30:25)? In fact, Job makes his treatment of the disenfranchised the litmus test of his righteousness:

> Did I deny the poor [*dal*] their needs,
> Or let a widow pine away,
> I never saw an unclad wretch,
> A needy man [*'ĕbyôn*] without clothing,
> · · · · · · · · · · · · · · · · · ·
> If I raised my hand against the fatherless,
> Looking to my supporters in the gate,
> May my arm drop off my shoulder;
> My forearm break off at the elbow.
> Job 31:16, 19, 21–22

As we have seen, one of the crucial issues in Job concerns God's silence in the face of unjust exploitation and suffering. At one point in the dialogue Elihu defends the actions of God. He argues that God is not one to favor the rulers and rich over the *dal* (34:19). The deeds of the wicked and mighty (34:24–25) cause the *dal* and the *'ānî* to cry out, an act that does elicit a response from God (34:28). Elsewhere, God is affirmed as the one who saves the *'ĕbyôn* from those rulers who seek to do them harm (5:15). By stopping injustice in its tracks, God supplies the *dal* with hope (5:16). The notion that God is the defender of the disenfranchised is strongly reminiscent of the prophetic perspective. Such an active conception of God toward the poor stands virtually without parallel in Proverbs (cf. Prov. 22:22). Elihu's claim is that God can and does take up the cause of the poor. Therefore, when God is silent, there should be no complaint or skepticism. Frankly, this is as close as the tradition comes to answering Job's questions about God's silence in the face of the suffering of the innocent (unless one adopts the less likely view that the bestowal of rewards in the epilogue is part of the original text). The writer of Job is all too aware of the painful injustice of the plight of the poor, a position starkly different from that found in Proverbs.

The analysis of injustice in the dialogues of Job is similar to the prophets: the powerful are seen to be preying on the poor. Yet there is no announcement of judgment, a factor that seemed almost inevitable from the prophetic viewpoint. Here a key difference between the prophets and Job is that the writer of the dialogues in Job was striving to grapple with one of the stark realities of social evil, namely, the fact that injustice often persists without relief. However, such concerns are not foreign to the prophetic tradition. There is a close kinship here, especially with the probings of Habakkuk. Yet unlike Habakkuk, who foresaw eventual judgment (Habakkuk 2—3), the writer of Job struggles with continual silence. Nevertheless, the Elihu speeches recognize that God at times does indeed judge injustice: "He does not let the wicked live; he grants justice to the lowly ['ānî]" (36:6). Furthermore, God "rescues the lowly ['ānî] from their affliction" (36:15). Both Habakkuk and the writers of Job struggled with the question of the suffering of the innocent. Habakkuk grew concerned over the plight of those who had to suffer when armies invaded, bringing about the deaths of innocent members of the populace. Habakkuk took comfort in the promise that one day even the Babylonian conqueror would topple. Job, likewise, wrestles over needless suffering, but, throughout the dialogues at least, neither justice nor release is immediately in sight.

With regard to the question of poverty, the perspective and vocabulary of Job is not that of the elite's wisdom writers, as fossilized in Proverbs. In fact, it appears that the dialogues in Job represent a challenge to their thinking. It is true that Job shares concerns with the wisdom tradition, such as over boundary markers (24:2), but the analysis of the socioeconomic condition of the poor is more akin to that of the prophetic writers both in its thrust and in its use of the terms for poor. Exploitation is clearly the consistent mark of poverty for Job, a sentiment largely unshared with Proverbs.

Job: The Articulation of Grief

Thus far it should be clear that social justice is the essential ground of the text. However, there is more: Job's posture of pain takes us ever deeper into the burden of the text, for rather than speaking merely as a prophetic advocate of the poor, he speaks, in the prologue, out of the ash heap of impoverished suffering (2:8). In the poetic debates, the theological articulation probes ever more deeply so that the rhetoric of dialogue embraces the reality of Job's grief. Rhetoric always points beyond itself to articulate a reality, whether this reality is imagined or existential in its scope. A text's rhetoric performs a powerful world-defining function. The rhetoric of the prophets and of Proverbs both seek to define a social world and to draw us into their ongoing discussion of poverty and justice. Similarly, the rhetoric of Job draws us into ancient Israel's debates over social ethics. As the Job traditions expand and accumulate, "the text becomes the site for conflicting strategies of interpretation which often correspond to the various groups that engage in a power struggle in the non-textual world."[34] More than this, however, the very intimate nature of the conversation opens us to a dimension of human experience that is totally absent from Proverbs, namely, human grief. It is this element of vulnerability to the harshness of the human condition, "the scars of the journey" that "impress themselves on the text," that gives the book its perennial character, a feature captured so well in the poet's opening gambit:[35]

> Perish the day on which I was born,
> And the night it was announced,
> "A male has been conceived!"
> May that day be darkness;
> May God above have no concern for it;
> May light not shine on it.
>
> Job 3:3–4

This vocabulary of grief finds a counterpart in the prophetic and psalmic laments. Such statements, whether in Job, the Prophets, or the Psalms, bring us close to the world of those who suffer under the weight of the silence of God, but who still hear God at work in the cosmos.

Significantly, it is at the meeting point of God's silence and God's presence that Job is free to express his grief. Of course, Job's grief can never fully contain either God's silence or the weight of God's presence, and so he continually staggers before each. But this is the place where Job can grieve, where he can challenge the theologies of his friends, where he can rail against God, and where new social visions can be born. Why does Job feel free to speak so with God? Because the element of dialogue permits conversation with God. This is one of the most intriguing and clever outcomes of this choice of rhetoric for the book. Unlike Proverbs, where God's presence all too often seems like an afterthought in the traditionally styled lore, the book of Job's dialogical rhetoric necessitates, even demands, God's ultimate participation in the justice discussion. Job is free to challenge the divine wisdom precisely because Job chooses not to leave God out of the discussion.

To sum up: Step by step through this dialogue with self, friends, and even God, Job is empowered to articulate his grief, to be open to his brokenness, to see in that brokenness a window into the world of the oppressed, and to encounter the whirlwind of the divine. In this articulation of grief, the book of Job goes beyond prophetic language, for where the prophets were far too confident about God's readiness to judge society, the writer of the dialogues of Job lays bare the sufferer's resentment at God's inaction in the face of massive injustices. Ultimately, however, the book, especially in its final form, draws on the prophet's language to recover the vocabulary of lament, thereby constructing a deeper social vision. This theological quest does not necessarily lead to philosophic answers or clarity so much as it does to commitment and protest.

Qohelet: A System of Futility

While scholars debate the central message of Qohelet, this enigmatic work is at the very least focused on skepticism about the utility of wisdom.[36] As such, like the book of Job, it challenges a fundamental tenet of the wisdom tradition. However, whereas the writer of Job successfully undermined the standard view of rewards and punishment, the net effect of Qohelet's probing of wisdom's value would seem to tend toward a more chastened view of wisdom itself, while nevertheless embracing the path of wisdom for guiding one's behavior.[37]

There is little doubt that Qohelet's quest is one of wisdom, framed in the traditional mode as a royal quest (Qoh. 1:1, 12–14; 7:23–25, 27; 8:16; 12:10). In confronting the harsh realities of folly, the writer raises the question of the advantage of wisdom (4:13; 6:8; 10:10–11). Folly and wisdom stand in stark contrast. Dangers ensue when wisdom goes unrecognized or when folly outweighs wisdom (7:2–5, 15–16; 9:14–16; 10:1, 6–7, 14). The writer seems to despair over a world in which justice and wickedness both find a home without the final triumph of good (3:16; 4:1; 5:7 [8]; 8:9–11). These observations open the writer to view the world as a restrictive, wearisome order (1:4–9; 3:1–11). At times, it is disturbingly apparent that the wise and the fool share the same fate (2:13–15; 3:17–21; 5:14–15 [15–16]; 8:5–7; 9:1–6, 10–12; 11:1–6; 12:3–8). This is not to say that the writer thoroughly abandons the way of wisdom, but the considerations are greatly reduced to (1) the enjoyment of simple pleasures in the here and now (2:24–25; 3:13, 22; 4:9–12; 5:17 [18]; 7:13–14; 8:15; 9:7–9; 11:7–12:2) and (2) a not overly excessive reverence for God and the king (3:14; 4:17–5: 6 [5:1–5:7]; 8:2–5; 10:17–20; 12:13–14).

In this context, the writer examines the frustrations and futilities of the amassing of wealth, in particular its slippery character (1:2–3; 2:1, 3–9; 4:7–8; 5:9-12 [10–13]; 6:2) and the inevitable loss of wealth to a successor (2:11–12, 18, 21). Certainly, Seow's suggestion that Qohelet is to be dated to c. 450–350 B.C.E. based on linguistic considerations is plausible.[38] If so, then he is correct to observe that Achaemenid taxation and coinage stood behind the writer's concerns over money.[39] In this social-political context, Seow observes, "While Qohelet clearly draws on timeless wisdom teachings, he also addresses people facing a new world of money and finance."[40] If Seow's analysis is correct, then something of the harshness of the times may be reflected in a passage that starkly depicts the brutalities of oppression:

I further observed all the oppression that goes on under the sun: the tears of the oppressed, with none to comfort them; and the power of their oppressors—with none to comfort them. Then I accounted those who died long since more fortunate than those who are still living; and happier than either are those who have not yet come into being and have never witnessed the miseries that go on under the sun.

I have also noted that all labor and skillful enterprise come from men's envy of each other—another futility and pursuit of wind! (Qoh. 4:1–4)

Notably, Qohelet offers yet another patterning of the terms for "poor" in the wisdom literature. The terms *'ebyôn*, *dal*, and *mahsor* are not found at all in this text. The book does make use of *rāš*, one of the terms common to Proverbs, making the absence of *dal* all the more peculiar. The term *'ānî* is found once. Perhaps the most significant feature of Qohelet in this context is that the book introduces yet another term into the vocabulary of poverty, namely, *miskēn*, "poor." What one becomes aware of in this comparison of the wisdom and prophetic traditions is how fragmented the wisdom tradition became in its understanding and articulation of the notion of poverty, at least in the hands of the creative thinkers behind the books of Job and Qohelet.

In our discussion of Proverbs, we found that one of the instruction techniques of the wisdom teachers was to argue that there are activities and conditions worse than poverty. Their intent in making these observations was to steer students away from pursuits that would jeopardize their status as members of the educated elite. Similarly, the writer of Qohelet suggests that it is better to be a *miskēn*, "poor person," than a foolish king, "for the former can emerge from a dungeon to become king; while the latter, even if born to kingship, can become a pauper [*rāš*]" (4:13–14). However, whereas Proverbs's injunction serves as a clear guide and warning, it is harder to gauge the thrust of the writer of Qohelet on this point. At the very least, a good measure of cynicism has crept into the writer's thinking in this and other matters.

The writer portrays the *'ānî*, "oppressed," as those who find no benefit in this world even when they themselves have acquired the ability to manage their own affairs. Pondering the fact that God gives wealth only to deny the enjoyment of it (6:1–7), the writer asks, "What advantage then has the wise man over the fool, what advantage has the pauper [*'ānî*] who knows how to get on in life?" (6:8). Though no answer is given, it is to be assumed that since the wise and the poor encounter the same fate in the end—namely, extinction—there is no advantage to wisdom no matter what one's status may be. The theme that the gods give both prosperity and misfortune is, as we have seen, an ancient perspective in the wisdom tradition. The writer of Qohelet is schooled in this perspective but seems to have focused entirely on its negative side.

The vanity of the life of the *'ānî* finds a counterpart in the author's musings on the fate of the *miskēn*. The writer speaks of a besieged city in which lived a wise *miskēn* who held the key to the town's deliverance in his hands (9:15). Unfortunately, the townspeople ignored this person. The lesson the writer draws from this is that "a poor man's [*miskēn*] wisdom is scorned" (9:16). The wisdom that may be possessed by the *'ānî* and the *miskēn* is in the end worthless, according to this teacher.

For the most part, Qohelet stands apart from the prophetic writings. However, in one place there is a degree of overlap. The writer observes that the oppression of the poor should not be treated as something surprising or unusual. Such people are simply victims of a system of hierarchical control, a system of powerholders and officials who live by dominating those who stand below them on the social ladder (5:7–8 [8–9]). Such an analysis bears striking similarities to the sentiments of the prophets and does have a counterpart in the perspectives adopted in Job. What is unusual, however, is the author's choice of words to express this notion. One might expect *'ānî* , *dal*, or *'ebyôn*. Instead, the writer chooses *rāš*, a term that in Proverbs often signified those who were poor due to their own lack of diligence; that is, they deserved to be poor. Selecting the term *rāš* to discuss oppression serves to turn the cherished wisdom analysis on its head. The thought that the *rāš* was poor because of oppression would have been unthinkable to the sages of Proverbs.

To conclude: It is extremely difficult to know how to assess the writing of Qohelet. The text stands firmly within the wisdom tradition, but seems to focus on the dark side of this style of reflection. The poor, whether *miskēn*, *'ānî*, or *rāš*, are all victims of the vast system of futility that the writer of Qohelet sees at work undermining the best of human plans and deeds. This awareness is strong but does not lead to the radical solidarity with the poor expressed so strikingly in the philosophic probings of the book of Job. Not being galvanized by this commitment to the poor, the writer of Qohelet notes their situation, taking refuge in what few goods and pleasures a more tempered wisdom might bring. Thus, if we seek a breakthrough on the question of justice, we must look to Job rather than the skeptical efforts of Qohelet for the richer insights.

Notes

1. J. L. Crenshaw, "Poverty and Punishment in the Book of Proverbs," *Quarterly Review* 9 (1989): 30–43.
2. While not wishing to overlook the framework of the book supplied by the prose tale (chaps. 1—2; 42), we focus here on the philosophic chapters of the book. The prose frame raises, perhaps, more questions than it solves. For my part, I read chap. 42 as deliberate irony. Rewards go to the winner of the philosophic game, the one willing to raise the questions and dispute with God. For further consid-

erations, see D. J. A. Clines, "Deconstructing the Book of Job," in *What Does Eve Do to Help? and Other Readerly Questions to the Old Testament* (Sheffield: JSOT Press, 1990), 106-23.

3. For translations of the Egyptian texts, see W. K. Simpson, *The Literature of Ancient Egypt: An Anthology of Stories, Instructions, and Poetry* (New Haven, Conn.: Yale University Press, 1972), 31–49, 201–9. For the Mesopotamian background, see K. van der Toorn, "The Ancient Near Eastern Literary Dialogue as a Vehicle of Critical Reflection," in *Dispute Poems and Dialogues in the Ancient and Medieval Near East: Forms and Types of Literary Debates in Semitic and Related Literatures*, ed. G. J. Reinink and H. L. J. Vanstiphout (Louvain: Peeters, 1991) 59–75; and M. E. Vogelzang, "Some Questions about the Akkadian Disputes," in ibid., 47-57. These two studies actually cover a different range of texts, with van der Toorn investigating the pessimistic dialogues and Vogelzang exploring the "contest literature," texts in which plants and animals verbally spar with one another regarding their respective virtues.

4. *ANET*, 592–93.

5. *ANET*, 600–91; see also W. G. Lambert, *Babylonian Wisdom Literature* (Oxford: Clarendon Press, 1960), 139–49.

6. Lambert, *Babylonian Wisdom Literature*, 63–89.

7. The biblical materials are discussed in J. D. Pleins, *The Psalms: Songs of Tragedy, Hope, and Justice* (Maryknoll, N.Y.: Orbis Books, 1993), chaps. 1–2. A number of relevant Mesopotamian examples can be found in B. R. Foster, *Before the Muses: An Anthology of Akkadian Literature*, vol. 2, *Mature, Late* (Bethesda, Md.: CDL Press, 1993), 491–689.

8. Failure to note this Mesopotamian background leads Penchansky to the false conclusion that the core of Job is later than the prose prologue and epilogue. The opposite would seem to be the case. D. Penchansky, *The Betrayal of God: Ideological Conflict in Job* (Louisville, Ky.: Westminster/John Knox Press, 1990). In the main, however, his deconstructionist study is rather provocative and stimulating.

9. *ANET*, 569–600; Lambert, *Babylonian Wisdom Literature*, 21–56.

10. W. G. Lambert, "A Further Attempt at the Babylonian 'Man and His God,'" in *Language, Literature, and History: Philological and Historical Studies Presented to Erica Reiner*, ed. F. Rochberg-Halton (New Haven, Conn.: American Oriental Society, 1987).

11. Penchansky is correct to see in Job a reflection of postexilic struggles. See Penchansky, *Betrayal of God*, 33, 56, 68.

12. G. Gutiérrez, *On Job: God-talk and the Suffering of the Innocent*, trans. M. J. O'Connell (Maryknoll, N. Y.: Orbis Books, 1987), 67.

13. While dissonance is a deep structural feature of the core, Penchansky, *Betrayal of God*, underplays the directionality of the core segment's overall movement and argument.

14. See D. J. A. Clines, "The Arguments of Job's Three Friends," in *Art and Meaning: Rhetoric in Biblical Literature*, in D. J. A. Clines, D. M. Gunn, and A. J. Hauser (Sheffield: JSOT Press, 1982). See also C. R. Seitz, "Job: Full-Structure, Movement, and Interpretation," *Int* 43 (1989): 5–17, esp. 11–16.

15. While Job may be "angst-ridden and tormented," there *is* a pivot to the dialogue's movement. Cf. Penchansky, *Betrayal of God*, 80.

16. Gutiérrez, *On Job*, chaps. 5-6.

17. This structural dissonance is thoughtfully explored in Penchansky, *Betrayal of God*, chap. 3.

18. Thus, in a sense, Penchansky is correct to say that the book supplies no answers. See Penchansky, *Betrayal of God*, 71.
19. Penchansky, *Betrayal of God*, chap. 3.
20. Whether Job is to be seen as "saint" or "sinner" has been hotly contested over the centuries. See N. N. Glatzer, "The Book of Job and Its Interpreters," in *The Dimensions of Job: A Study and Selected Readings*, ed. N. N. Glatzer (New York: Schocken Books, 1969), 197–220.
21. S. Terrien, *The Elusive Presence: The Heart of Biblical Theology* (San Francisco: Harper & Row, 1978), 361–73, explores several dimensions of this troubling presence in the book of Job.
22. In taking the total work into consideration, I do not accept Penchansky's view that such "harmonization" works to subvert the radicality of the core. In other words, the speeches of Elihu have a real contribution to make in the context of the overall arguments of the book of Job. See Penchansky, *Betrayal of God*, 18. N. C. Habel, "The Role of Elihu in the Design of the Book of Job," in *In the Shelter of Elyon: Essays on Ancient Palestinian Life and Literature in Honor of G. W. Ahlström*, ed. W. B. Barrick and J. R. Spencer (Sheffield: JSOT Press, 1984), 81–98, rightly argues that "Elihu provides the civil trial which Job had demanded" (87). However, I do not agree with his contention that Elihu is a "brash but intelligent young fool" (90), whose simplistic orthodoxy is dismantled by the "unexpected" speeches of God (93) who "upstages Elihu" (94). Whether original to the book or by later design, the speeches of Elihu are well positioned as a theological bridge to the speeches of God and are in no way "unexpected" in the flow of the final form of the book's overall argument.
23. Penchansky, *Betrayal of God*, 61, cf. 72.
24. While Penchansky is correct to find various layers of "dissonance" in Job, at least one layer is educative, reflecting the discourse of critical reflection that was an early part of the wisdom tradition in the ancient Near East. See K. van der Toorn, "Ancient Near Eastern Literary Dialogue."
25. W. Brueggemann, "Theodicy in a Social Dimension," *JSOT* 33 (1985): 5.
26. Ibid., 4.
27. See, e.g., M. H. Pope, *Job: Introduction, Translation, and Notes*, AB 15 (Garden City: Doubleday, 1965), 187, 191.
28. If Penchansky, *Betrayal of God*, is right that, "the book of Job is 'about' dissonance" (69), then the writer of the dialogues seeks to provoke some of that dissonance.
29. On this aspect of the logic of Proverbs, see R. C. van Leeuwen, "Proverbs 30:21–23 and the Biblical World Upside Down," *JBL* 105 (1986): 599–610.
30. Gutiérrez, *On Job*, 23–27, 31–38.
31. For S. Lasine, "Bird's-Eye and Worm's-Eye Views of Justice in the Book of Job," *JSOT* 42 (1988): 47, this prophetic view mediates the tension between the human-earthly and cosmic-divine viewpoints that collide in the book of Job.
32. Brueggemann, "Theodicy in a Social Dimension," 12.
33. Pope, *Job*, 175.
34. Penchansky, *Betrayal of God*, 72.
35. Ibid., 42.
36. On the diverse assessments of the contradictory aspects of Qohelet, see J. L. Crenshaw, "Qoheleth in Current Research," *Hebrew Annual Review* 7 (1983): 41–56.
37. That this rhetorical strategy and critical exploration are not wholly unique to Qohelet is indicated by two 14th–12th century B.C.E. texts from Emar discussed by A. Gianto, "Human Destiny in Emar and Qohelet," in *Qohelet in the Context of*

Wisdom, ed. A. Schoors (Louvain: Leuven University Press, 1998), 473–79. The connection had already been noted in the case of Emar VI.4: 767 by W. G. Lambert, "Some New Babylonian Wisdom Literature," *Wisdom in Ancient Israel*, ed., J. Day et al. (Cambridge: Cambridge University Press, 1995), 30–42.

38. C. L. Seow, *Ecclesiastes: A New Translation with Introduction and Commentary* (New York: Doubleday, 1997), 20–21. Admittedly, the philosophic underpinnings of the book would also be quite at home in the Hellenistic period. Nonetheless, one ought not to overlook the fact that 450–350 B.C.E. also demarcates the flourishing of diverse Greek philosophic systems. Surely the eastern Mediterranean was not entirely untouched by these earlier currents, at least among the more cosmopolitan and well-traveled teachers in the region.

39. Seow, *Ecclesiastes*, 21.

40. Ibid., 22.

Conclusion

Chapter 13

Diverse Visions in a
Canonical Context

Aggadah, Halakhah, and Torah: A Community of Story or a Tradition of Instruction?

Diversity as a Theological Norm

Trajectories of Biblical Ethics Debates
    Spiritualized vs. Concrete Views of Poverty
    Rights vs. Duties
    Poverty vs. Politics as a Framework
    Competing Views vs. a Monolithic View of Poverty

Biblical Ethics: La Longue Durée

Checks and Balances in Biblical Ethics

We arrive at what one of my social ethicist colleagues might call the "So what?" chapter. While kernels of a more comprehensive view concerning the appropriation of scripture can be ferreted out by the discerning reader from all the chapters that precede, still my colleagues are justified in asking what place a more historically oriented discussion of the biblical text can play in the continuing discussion of scripture and ethics. To put it bluntly: Does the biblical tradition have anything to offer of lasting significance in this regard? This chapter seeks to address that question in a more straightforward fashion. Remaining cognizant of the sweep of biblical texts in front of us, and wishing to avoid siding with this block of texts over against another or of supporting this particular theme as opposed to some other, can we find in the biblical record, or in our engagement of that record, perspectives that might inform our continued reflection on ethics in the contemporary context? In seeking to respond to my colleagues, I would like to offer up as a ground for ethical reflection the very tensions that infused the communities whose insights are extended to us in the pages of the Hebrew scriptures.[1]

Aggadah, Halakhah, and Torah:
A Community of Story or a Tradition of Instruction?

In his studies of scripture's integral role in Christian ethics, S. Hauerwas places strong emphasis on the church as a story-formed community.[2] Hauerwas argues that the larger biblical narrative or "story" (and consequently the Bible's ethics), only makes sense as that story takes up residence in a community committed to remembering and embodying that story.[3] In other words, a study of biblical ethics in the abstract or as a historical investigation cannot suffice as the basis of a Christian ethics. Rather, the ethical use of scripture in the church requires that the community that carries the scriptures be a community of interpretation, a community that understands that "interpretation is the constant adjustment that is required if the current community is to stay in continuity with tradition."[4] This is not to say that the community's appropriation of biblical ethics is a simplistic replication of the past; in fact, for Hauerwas the contemporary church may find itself at odds with its venerable "guides."[5] Reappropriation means a *new* appropriation. Yet scripture's place is such, indeed the very quest for truth is such, that for Hauerwas, "truth is known only by the conversation initiated by the tradition and carried out through political means."[6] By "political," Hauerwas does not have a liberation reading of scripture's ethics in mind; rather, he means something on the order of "polity"—an ethic that emerges in the great conversation between a remembering community and its community-sustaining biblical traditions.[7] Since this reappropriation is decidedly not mere replication, each generation is afforded the opportunity to ask "what kind of a community we must be to be faithful to Yahweh and his purposes for us."[8]

Hauerwas's insistence on placing scriptural ethics within the context of the remembering community makes a good deal of sense. How else could a communal tradition, which itself constitutes a "history of a community's sharing of such judgments as they have been tested through generations," hope to survive otherwise? Yet for all my enthusiasm for various aspects of Hauerwas's analysis, there are places where Hauerwas does not go far enough in his assessment of the bibilical tradition. Or should I say "traditions"? Although Hauerwas acknowledges, with Blenkinsopp, that creative tension is a dynamic at work in scripture, he does not rigorously or comprehensively grapple with the wide-ranging discourses and the plethora of ethical postures presented in the scriptures themselves.[9] To adopt Hauerwas's language, we would have to speak of a multiplicity of communities in scripture, which reflect a variety of interpretive contexts. To lump them all under the canonical umbrella as Hauerwas does tends to obscure the conflictual realities that have given rise to the received biblical record. Hauerwas is quite correct to suggest that "only through the means of a canon can the church adequately manifest the kind of tension with which it must live," but the fact is that it is only over time that the disparate struggles of the various groups, pockets, and movements that we term so loosely "ancient Israel" have come to be amalgamated as a "tradition."[10] Perhaps Hauerwas sees the church's unity to be the primary factor, over against its diversity. If so, I would argue conversely that the church's unity is a function of its diversity. *NB* Whether we decide to speak of tradition or multiple traditions will profoundly alter our appropriation of scripture today. Thus, whereas Hauerwas only seems to recognize controversy and diversity within *one* community, I would argue that the biblical record exposes us to the vital character of controversies and debates between competing communities that appear to claim the same banner. In this way, the very notion of a singular tradition or a singular community can hardly be anything more than a fiction when speaking of the biblical texts. Contrary to Hauerwas, the biblical dynamic is such that the biblical record becomes a "tradition" precisely at the very moment when a particular remembering community chooses to define itself within the history of tension reflected throughout the scriptures. By turns, this would seem to imply that any given remembering community ought not to be afraid of embracing its diversity in the modern situation. Yet this rarely occurs. More often a particular community will set itself up as the only authentic community, resting the group's views on a select portion of the biblical record. We have arrived at a time in our history, however, when the embrace of the Bible's diversity and a reappraisal of our own diversity have become global imperatives. Fortunately, the Bible itself refuses the reduction of its contents to either conservative or liberal agendas, to either right or left politics, to either premodern or postmodern views. By presenting us with a disjointed tableau from Israel's past, rather than a sanitized and systematized diatessaron, the so-called tradition has itself exposed the soil of Israel's survival, where, to borrow a Christian Testament image, weeds and wheat grow up together in God's enduring garden. Specifi- *NB* cally, in terms of a biblical ethics, therefore, the diversity of the biblical tradition's past must serve as a catalyst for wide-ranging discussions and debates in the present. Unless we want to relegate our reading of the tradition to a theological ghetto, scripture's overarching diversity must become a critical element in our reappropriation of the biblical tradition. Anything less will only serve to fragment the tradition and church or synagogue today. We will return to the subject of diversity below.

Beyond these comments, I would also add that I find Hauerwas's notion of the "biblical story" at times rather fuzzy. Having accented the narrative character of that story, Hauerwas runs the risk of overlooking or distorting biblical texts for which the notion of a national story or a story of salvation can only be of minor or marginal importance. One thinks of Proverbs, which is empirical in its approach and is hardly rooted in a story of any sort. Likewise, only in the most general terms or only in rare instances does Israel's national "story" play a part in the psalms. While one might argue that biblical law (*halakhah*) insists on the exodus story (*aggadah*, or narrative) as its locus of meaning or its context of interpretation, nevertheless, lawmaking in the Torah is much more than an expression of that story. One could argue that lawmaking in ancient Israel is more definitively oriented to the specific questions raised by the Ten Commandments, namely, of how to create an authentic worshiping community and a just society. Here the story creates the mandate to build such a community, but the hard work of lawmaking only rarely turns to the exodus story for its orientation. More often the laws seem to arise as a response to the great commandments. To name the entire biblical record "story" might appear akin to Jewish tradition's looser labeling of that same record as "Torah." Yet the term Torah strikes a different chord, for its basic meaning is "instruction." This difference is noteworthy, for we see that the story accompanied the rise of a tradition of instruction to which later communities were answerable if they ever hoped to embody the scripture's ethical traditions. That Christians have opted for story as the predominant pattern for ethical discourse perhaps says much more about the Christian Testament than it does the traditions of the Hebrew Bible. In other words, the "story" is only half the story when it comes to relating the Hebrew scriptures to contemporary questions of social ethics.

In breaking free of the story model, biblical ethicists would do well to recover the diversity of discourse at work in scripture. Beyond narrative, the discourse of "principle" finds equal weight in the Torah. The canon of the Hebrew Bible is likewise heavily invested in prophetic pronouncement, psalmic liturgy, and wisdom observation. The privileging of narrative over these other forms of discourse hardly does justice to the rich ways the tradition has sought to nourish communities that wrestle with the many ways to be a people of God. It is this distinctive variety of discourse that allows the traditions the flexibility they need to be reappropriated and revitalized through subsequent generations. Story by itself is not a sufficient category for this project. The fact that biblical narrative finds itself intermingling with these other discourses is sign enough that *sola scriptura* need not now be replaced with "story alone."

One final area of critique deserves our attention, namely, the rather short shrift that Hauerwas seems to give to the social-scientific recovery of Israel's past or of "higher criticism" as a part of the contemporary biblical ethicist's labors.[11] While the interpretive setting for scripture may very well be the community, it is by no means clear that "the narratives of scripture were not meant to describe our world . . . but to change the world."[12] Only a recovery of Israel's past will illuminate for us what these scriptures were about. At times, the subsequent carriers of the tradition have recast the scriptures in ways that diverge markedly from their earliest forms and contexts. One thinks, for example, of the later messianic readings of the early royal psalms or of the reappropriation by the elite of prophetic texts that were once in opposition to that very same elite. As the context changed so radically from a monarchic to a postmonarchic situation, the readings invariably changed. Yet we have found throughout our study that the social-scientific and historical recovery of the text has opened numerous vistas, sharpening our appreciation for the conflicts and hopes that drove the struggles evidenced across the biblical corpus. While postmoderns may be correct that we cannot recover the author's intent, the social-scientific and historical reading of texts such as the Psalms and the Prophets alerts us to the more probable meanings of the biblical texts for the periods in which they were originally written and warn us against an oversimplified use of these materials when attempting to address the contemporary situation.

One might well argue that these reconstructed readings of the texts' earlier history ought not to carry greater weight than later interpretations. Yet to ignore scripture's historical character and development is akin to reducing the gene pool; the range of images and perspectives for our discourse about justice issues in the religious context would invariably be diminished. There is also a downside to the squandering of this past. By ignoring the conflictual character of the shaping of the biblical record, we run the risk of unwittingly passing on Iron Age patterns of thinking, governance, and morality without asking to what extent these traditions deserve continued appropriation or what form this reappropriation ought to take. In other words, the social-scientific approach, by opening us to cultural patterns and the layers of meaning of so many texts, will hold in check the tendency to simply regard segments of scripture as "ethically useful" or "morally perverse" by not asking how our contemporary judgments might actually be getting ahead of a sound, historically informed reading of the text. Even if we come to regard the text's violence as chronic and irredeemable, a historically sensitized rhetorical strategy, such as Trible's brilliant rereadings of narratives of violence against women as texts *in memoriam*, will allow us to fruitfully confront the biblical record as a text that can carry continued moral weight for communities that need to openly wrestle with similar questions today.[13] A social-scientific and historical approach, far from being an overlay or a diversion, can serve to highlight the need for a hermeneutic that goes beyond the Bible as story to be treated more vigorously as a tradition of instruction.

Diversity as a Theological Norm

Thus, one of the strengths of the Hebrew Bible is that it develops its overarching ethical discourses by a variety of methods and in a diversity of contexts. Yet biblical diversity extends well beyond the fact that the Bible addresses a number of different issues and problems. The more important observation we can make is that this diversity is foundational to the biblical text. The biblical writers quite often diverge in their agendas, and this gives rise to significant differences in opinion and analysis within the biblical text itself. Theirs, too, was an age of pluralism, though their pluralism and philosophic diversity have often been obscured by *our* need to systematize and bring the Bible under a uniform ideological umbrella, whether we are conservatives or liberals, moral majority advocates or liberation activists. I believe that we need to rediscover the Hebrew Bible's diversity that shatters all our efforts to make the sacred text conform to our expectations and agendas. Adapting Anderson and Pickering's contention that the civil rights era witnessed "American creeds in competition," I would argue that ancient Israel saw a number of faiths and civic creeds collide as the community pursued (or evaded) the demands of justice, and that this diversity is attested throughout the Hebrew Bible—indeed, it is a fundamental feature of the text.[14]

In part, what I mean by diversity is that major blocks of biblical material—from the prophets, the wise, the legal writers, the historians, and the hymnists—are all vying for our attention, offering different and at times radically conflicting approaches to the social questions of their day. Furthermore, not only do these major blocks offer divergent outlooks, but it is clear that there are significant differences *within* each camp. We have seen, for example, that there is not one prophetic perspective nor one wisdom view. Since this diversity and conflict of creeds is endemic to all sides of the biblical tradition, it should be painfully clear that we cannot leaf through the Hebrew Bible hoping to find a unified directive on questions of peace, justice, family, or economics.

To some, the thought of a diversity of opinion inside sacred scripture will be disconcerting and even frightening. Positively, however, I would contend that the elements of dialogue, debate, and diversity are essential elements for grounding a vital contemporary biblical ethics and theology. Thus, while liberation thinking has rejuvenated our interest in the social justice dimensions of the biblical tradition, we have yet to grapple with theological tensions arising from within the biblical text that demonstrate that the Hebrew Bible does not automatically support one particular economic or liberation analysis of poverty. Certainly this reality disrupts our search for an adequate approach to the use of the whole of scripture in the context of a contemporary discussion of social ethics.[15]

Trajectories of Biblical Ethics Debates

While biblical diversity—and by this my focus is primarily on the diversity of the Hebrew Bible—may indeed complicate the use of the biblical text for contemporary socioeconomic and moral discussions, I would maintain that the Hebrew Bible's moral strength and enduring challenge rests precisely in its diversity of views on poverty and justice. Framed in this fashion, there are several perspectives that emerge which can guide us in our modern moral calculus. I offer here four considerations toward a reappropriation of the Hebrew Bible for contemporary discussions of religiously grounded ethics. I will draw on some of the results found in the preceding chapters as a way to illustrate a method of appropriation that I find more compelling for the contemporary discussion than is typical of many social ethics and liberation texts.

Spiritualized vs. Concrete Views of Poverty

Christian churches over the centuries have pursued a number of views of the poor. The study of the history of this question is a study in theological contrasts.[16] The traditional view of the poor—that the poor are the humble before God who deserve alms—later became institutionalized in the view that poverty is a virtue best pursued in a communal or monastic setting. The rise of the mercantilist-capitalist society reinforced the view that poverty is a result of laziness. Most radically, especially in the past century, the social gospel movement and liberation theology have redirected our theological attention, arguing that the Bible is concerned with transforming the social structures that oppress the poor. Proponents of these divergent analyses can invoke competing statements in the Christian Testament as support: Matthew's more spiritualized statement, "Blessed are the poor in spirit" (Matt. 5:3) is set against the more concrete Lukan sayings, "Blessed are you poor" (Luke 6:20) and "Woe to you that are rich" (Luke 6:24).[17] Examined in this simple manner, these statements present a bald contrast between a beatific and a materialist view of poverty.

The documents from Qumran give us Hebrew equivalents for Matthew's poor in spirit—" *'ānwē rûaḥ* " and " *rûaḥ 'ānāw* "—providing a precedent for the spiritualized reading of the Hebrew Bible's *'ānāwîm* as the "humble."[18] Following Qumran's lead, the Israelite *'ānāwîm* (and Matthew's Greek congeners) would be defined as any pious humble followers of God, regardless of economic status.[19] In this view, the poor in spirit are not the economically deprived. Yet this is but one possible analysis of the Hebrew term *'ānāwîm*. Over the past century, as we observed in chapter 10, the socioeconomic and theological interpretation of the term *'ānāwîm* has been the subject of serious debate.[20] Some in the late 19th century discovered in the *'ānāwîm* a party of the pious in ancient Israel. Early in this century, one scholar saw in this term a "humility" born of the severe economic deprivation of the Babylonian exile. This poverty was the precondition for experiencing God's compassion. In the ninteen-twenties and thirties a few scholars began to apply a class analysis to the texts and transformed the party of the pious into a class of the oppressed. By the mid-twentieth century, although many scholars returned to defining *'ănāwîm* as simple humility, scholarly attention began to make room for other Hebrew words that characterize poverty in terms of socioeconomic oppression.

With liberation theology's recovery of prophetic texts such as Amos and Micah, we have experienced an increased interest in the prophetic critique of social structures that oppress and crush the poor to the benefit of the rich— the poverty that Gutiérrez terms a "scandalous condition."[21] Of course, the Hebrew prophets were far better at the denunciation of oppression than they were at positing satisfying solutions to the question of poverty. Despite this caveat, the recovery of the socioeconomic dimension of poverty as the unjust result of oppression has revitalized our appreciation for ancient Israel's prophets, law codes, and the text of Job.

One way to think about poverty, therefore, is to consider its spiritual versus its economic dimensions. Our study of the biblical text does not easily settle on one dimension over the other. Instead, we are pressed by the biblical text and by the scholarly debate to attend to various aspects of the social question.[22] In other words, there is ample biblical precedent to induce us to reflect on poverty as humility, virtue, the result of laziness, and as the product of oppressive social structures. A contemporary ethic that wishes to ground its discussion in scripture will have to critically weigh and assess the relevance of each of these categories when seeking a normative, biblically grounded understanding of poverty and social justice.

Rights vs. Duties

Emerging as it does out of ancient Mesopotamian cultural traditions, the biblical text does not speak in terms of human rights. This issue raises serious questions about a modern use of the tradition, especially when translators introduce notions of "rights" into the biblical text. Translations that have God defending the "rights" of the poor, for example, are translations that reflect Enlightenment notions. In making this observation, we should be clear not to appear to say that since the Bible does not speak about "rights," we must therefore avoid speaking in such terms. On the contrary, "rights" language is *our* contribution to the theological debate about justice. However, we should also consider what we might gain by taking into account the biblical tradition's emphasis on *duties* toward the poor.

At a bare minimum, the biblical tradition supports charitable giving to the poor. Proverbs, which tends not to have the highest estimation of the poor, viewing them as victims of their own laziness, nevertheless endorses charity both for the rewards it accrues and because the poor are, after all, created by God.[23] Yet Proverbs provides us with the minimalist view.

More important for us is the ancient Israelite legal tradition as reflected in the law codes of Exodus 21—23 and Deuteronomy 12—26. Here there are numerous injunctions not merely to give to the poor, but to open the edges of fields for gleaning (Deut. 24:19–22; cf. Lev. 19:9–10; 23:22), to lend without taking interest (Ex. 22:24–26 [25–27]; Deut. 24:10–13, 17), to release slaves after six years of service (Ex. 21:2–6; Deut. 15:1–2, 12–18), to pay a day laborer on the day of labor (Deut. 24:14), and to restore land to the original owners after forty-nine years (Lev. 25:8–55).

The biblical law codes call for structured solutions to the situation of the hungry, the wage laborer, the landless, the debt slave, and the poor. Society as a whole has an obligation to the poor. Such provisions stand in marked contrast to ancient Mesopotamian law codes, which contain few laws governing the concrete situation of the poor (mainly laws governing debt slavery).[24] How ought we to think about poverty? The biblical legal tradition would urge structured social practices to ease the situation of those in need, going beyond mere almsgiving.

While the legal tradition places strong emphasis on the development of specific social structures to provide assistance to the poor, we are reminded that this same tradition does not simply provide a static response to the problem of poverty. In fact, as we have seen, the laws in the so-called Covenant Code in Exodus 21—23 are refined and expanded in (the later) Deuteronomy 12—26. Most significantly, the provisions for lending given in Ex. 22:24–26 (25–27) were emended in Deut. 24:10–15 to further characterize the poor ('ānî) as the day laborer (śākîr), and to restructure the question around wages as opposed to the issue of the garment taken in pledge. This updating of the ancient code indicates that, over many centuries of legal development, the legal tradition acknowledged that laws have to shift to accommodate changes in rural-urban relations.

This flexibility is likewise reflected in the later rabbinic tradition. The Mishnaic tractate *Peah*, for example, elaborates, extends, and nuances the access the hungry poor had to the corners of fields.[25] Bear in mind that this rabbinic tractate emerged after the Roman destruction of Judea and represents part of a comprehensive effort to establish a Judaism that could survive catastrophe.[26] This emergent Jewish attitude toward those in need is comparable to the Christian Testament's narratives in the book of Acts that state that the early Christians shared their property—narratives that place special emphasis on *chreia*, "need," as a baseline measure for assistance and communal restructuring (Acts 2:42–47; 4:32–37). I presume that the Acts narrative, although set before 70 C.E., actually arose afterward and reflects some of the same spirit that infused the early rabbinic tradition's concern to build a society that was institutionally structured to care for those in need and to survive catastrophe.

The rabbinic and early Christian interest in institutionalized structures for social justice represents a logical outgrowth of the Hebrew tradition concerning duties, specifically as adumbrated in the biblical legal tradition. Our modern debate over human rights, while not entirely a stranger to the concept of social duty—especially as realized in institutional structures—can nevertheless benefit from a rehearing of the Hebrew Bible's struggles with the question of social obligation, those social acts of reform on behalf of the poor that are bound up with the persistent biblical concern for *mišpāṭ ûṣĕdāqâ*, "justice and righteousness."[27]

Poverty vs. Politics as a Framework

In contemporary philosophic discussions, the issue of poverty tends to be displaced by the more general discussion of justice.[28] While we might not wish to separate these matters in this way, our choice of starting points for ethical analysis does have a profound effect on our consequent theological perspectives and human commitments. The debates over whether or not an "option for the poor" stands at the heart of the biblical tradition turn on precisely such a point. I would suggest that a similar state of affairs arises when we consider the social analysis that apparently obtained in the milieu of ancient Israel's "historians"—the compilers of Genesis, Exodus, Samuel–Kings, and Chronicles. For these writers and chroniclers, the question of poverty is of relatively little concern. Instead, the issue of monarchic political power dominates their narratives, providing us with a credible challenge to those who wish to make the question of poverty the center of contemporary theological ethics. Israel's "historians" carved up the social question in ways that diverge markedly from the prophets, Proverbs, and the legal tradition. When the biblical chroniclers critically appraised ancient Israel's economic and political structures, their criticisms tended to center on specific abuses of royal power and did not call into question the monarchic institution as such. Remarkably, Samuel's critique of kingship (1 Samuel 8), Solomon's use of forced labor (1 Kings 5:27–32 [13–18]; 9:15–22; 12:1–7), and Ahab's taking of Naboth's vineyard (1 Kings 21) are all narrated without invoking the vocabulary of poverty so important to the prophets, Psalms, Proverbs, Job, and the lawmakers. The distinct social analysis of the biblical historians could not be more striking.

Read in this light, even the exodus story does not fundamentally critique the institution of monarchy, as liberation theologians might have us believe from their specific focus on Exodus.[29] Joseph was able to work quite well under a previous pharaoh in Genesis 41. The problem rested with the recalcitrant pharaoh who knew not Joseph (Ex. 1:8). Presumably in the historian's economy there was room enough for good pharaohs and good King Davids. The problem for the historians was that too many bad kings engender rebellion, civil division, and ultimately foreign conquests that produce exile. Kings like David, Hezekiah, and Josiah were, for the historians, far too few in number.[30]

On the matter of poverty and injustice, the biblical historians would have us shift our framework away from poverty to a discussion of the uses and abuses of monarchic power. Whether our framework is defined by poverty or by political power is significant, for the consequent theological and social insights depend in large measure on what we define as the central concern of the biblical canon. We cannot readily dismiss the overwhelming silence of major tracks of the biblical text when it comes to the question of poverty. At the very least, we are challenged to reconsider the composition of our overall framework when offering a biblical grounding to a contemporary social ethic.

In the end, we may indeed choose to affirm poverty as a fundamental organizing principle for our modern theological commitments, but in so doing we must recognize that the biblical tradition as a whole offers conflicting views regarding overarching ethical frameworks and points of reference. We must likewise not force the entire biblical tradition into a straitjacket around the option for the poor or constrict ourselves through oversimplified notions of God as the Exodus "Liberator."[31] Moreover, if we choose to defend the liberation model, we will do well to face all the problems that are entailed when we create a "canon within the canon."

Competing Views vs. a Monolithic View of Poverty

Thus, if the biblical tradition entertains competing views regarding poverty and its solutions, then one way we ought to think about theological ethics is to continue to use the biblical texts to open up the debate about poverty and economic justice.[32] What I am proposing is an approach to the biblical text that differs considerably from that which commonly appears in church social documents, where a rather uniform, even monolithic, presentation of a biblical understanding of social and economic justice tends to be the norm.[33] Moving from the ground of biblical diversity, I would contend that a more incisive use of the biblical tradition would lead us to debate ethics questions in terms of their economic, legal, moral, social, political, and theological complexities.

From the foregoing, we would observe that, although the biblical tradition deals with poverty, power, and justice in radically different ways, no contemporary discussion of a biblically informed social ethics should proceed without making poverty a salient, though perhaps not solitary, issue in the debate generated by the scriptures. This commitment would not predetermine the outcome of the discussion about poverty. I would add, therefore, that the insistence on debating the questions, together with a wide-ranging consideration of divergent solutions, is one of the decisive contributions of the biblical tradition to our contemporary use of the scriptures in discussions of ethics and social justice.

Biblical Ethics: La Longue Durée

The identification of overarching trajectories and recurrent tensions in the biblical tradition can go a long way toward eliminating the cul-de-sac of so much discussion of biblical ethics, namely, the endless effort at identifying the one defining issue, the dominant perspective, or the key tract of scripture as privileged within the canon and our contemporary appropriation of that canon. Indeed, it is the text's very diversity over such matters as the implementation of law, the meaning of the exodus and kingship, and the nature of prophecy and wisdom that constitute the parameters of the ethics discussions in ancient Israel. Viewing the biblical text as a tradition under construction is perhaps more beneficial for a contemporary theological ethics than the attempt to piecemeal that tradition in the hopes of identifying that solitary view of justice or politics that we should imitate today.

In saying that the Hebrew Scriptures are a tradition under construction, I mean to indicate that we must also take seriously not simply the diversity *between* blocks but also the diversity *within* blocks of the biblical text. Certainly there is no singular prophetic social critique or one decisive reading of Israel's past, neither is there one fixed set of laws to abide by, nor one wisdom outlook on the nature of human existence.

Yet this diversity within various blocks of material points us toward another observation of this tradition under construction: we cannot ignore the continual and purposive layering of the tradition. We observe not merely texts juxtaposed like so many pieces of fruit on a plate. Rather, we have witnessed the active and repeated reworking and sifting of the received tradition. The scriptures as we now have them evidence continual expansion via what we might term "commentary" or "inner-biblical exegesis."[34] However, the entanglement of sources and commentary is so diffuse that in many cases the amalgam cannot be sensibly extracted without destroying the character of the text qua received tradition. While the identification of inner-biblical exegesis is quite valuable for lending insight into the process of scripture's development, for the purposes of the appropriation of scripture for contemporary discussions of theological ethics, we would want to accent the reality of traditioning, the continual process of expansion and elaboration that is part and parcel of the diverse character of scripture, marking the long-term trends in ancient Israel's ethical discussions. Each generation, in other words, has made a contribution to the ongoing discussion. Likewise, each generation must answer to what has gone before. The very openness of scripture in this regard will militate against any effort to freeze the tradition under the assumption that a contemporary ethical system need only mimic some particular moment of the biblical past as a moral golden age or turn to a particular text or set of texts as an ethical blueprint for our times. Yet this process of tradition formation is not merely additive, with new texts and visions simply being set alongside one another. Rather, this openness of scripture demands a contemporary theological ethics that is aggressively informed by all sides of the tradition, though not one that is a slave to these traditions.

If we remain aware of this dialectic between text as tradition and the subsequent need to engage that tradition, while formulating a revised set of ethical principles and stances, we might ask if such a use of scripture cannot be systematized, if not in the details, at least in the broad brush strokes. In fact, L. Cahill has supplied us with a plausible structure for seriously engaging scripture in the development of a substantive ethical system, while at the same time respecting the other resources we must likewise engage in this effort:

> [T]here are four complementary reference points for Christian ethics: the foundational texts or "scriptures" of the faith community—the Bible; the community's "tradition" of faith, theology, and practice; philosophical accounts of essential or ideal humanity ("normative" accounts of the human); and descriptions of what actually is and has been the case in human lives and societies ("descriptive" accounts of the human).[35]

[handwritten margin note: Catholic moral theology]

Agreeing with J. Gustafson that "Scripture *alone* is never the final court of appeal for Christian ethics,"[36] Cahill recognizes that the very fact of scripture as a record stamped by "interpretative reconstruction of foundational events" of necessity propels us into a dialogue between scripture, the subsequent tradition, and other philosophic and social-scientific tools, resources that together must be employed in the task of developing a contemporary theological ethics.[37]

To this multifaceted dialogue, scripture can bring not simply this or that isolated injunction regarding justice, power, or poverty. Rather, scripture as a totality can provide us with a working analogy of the need to tap the received tradition as a partner, sometimes congenial and sometimes cantankerous, in a long-term conversation to which we are all invited. The compelling authenticity of our own contribution to the next phase of this ongoing tradition will not be measured by how carefully we replicate scripture but in how broadly we will allow scripture to frame and instigate ongoing debates regarding a wide range of ethical questions. The checkered Talmud of Jewish tradition can serve as our guide, for we are only authentic to the biblical tradition to the extent that we give full vent to the wide-ranging construals possible as our own contribution to a modern engagement of this most ancient conversation.

Checks and Balances in Biblical Ethics

If we are prepared to acknowledge the polyvalent character of each strand or block of the biblical tradition, then we will be in a credible position to assess the sorts of contributions each block makes to the overall discussion. In the context of the entire canon of scripture, we find that an encounter with one part of the biblical tradition necessitates the involvement of the other sides of that tradition.[38]

The legal material points the way toward an ethics of obligation. At its best, such a system works from a positive perception of the past benefits of God, benefits that elicit dutiful devotion to the divine directives. At its worst, such ethics are totalitarian in scope and subject to lip service rather than heartfelt obedience. The virtue of the legal tradition is an attentiveness to detail, together with its recognition that a concrete realization of the grand principles is always required, no matter how far short that concretization may fall from the ideals of justice and community engendered by the exodus encounter with YHWH. The legal tradition has its own built-in corrective to ossification, namely, constant revision, a dimension strongly evidenced by the significant changes observable between the Covenant Code of Exodus 21—23 and the code of Deuteronomy 12—26. Yet the biblical tradition as a whole looks farther afield for correctives, not wishing to rely on the system to police itself. Recognizing that the legal system may narrow its focus to tangential matters, the tradition looks, for example, to prophetic voices to foster an ethics of conscience and advocacy for society in its brokenness. This is not to return to the tired notion of nineteenth-century scholars that the prophets somehow cornered the ethical market in ancient Israel, but it is to acknowledge that vis-à-vis their societies, the prophetic voices do often serve as voices of ethical sanity in troubled times.

The narrative voice, in turn, can be mined for an ethics of scrutiny. As the story of the institution of monarchy unfolds, we test, via concrete outcomes, the vitality and viciousness of a mode of social organization that ancient Israel experimented with, both to its greatness and its peril. These "historical" images and theological evaluations complement the biblical legal tradition by contextualizing for us the social processes that must be sharply evaluated when assessing the health and viability of any political system. The stresses and successes of Israel's monarchic experiment can supply us with images and issues for continued discussion of *our* history as people who are fashioning a sweeping new global village.

The wisdom voice, by contrast, offers an ethics of consequence in which the deeds of the day are measured by both the shape of the outcome and the character of the actor. The wisdom voice conjoins both "results" and "character development."[39] Despite their considerable differences, works such as Proverbs, Job, and Qohelet stand ready to protest whenever the cultivation of a virtuous character yields to the ruinous quest for worldly goods, the temptations of lust, or the abuses of power. Likewise, in one way or another, the wisdom books situate this sensibility, this ethics of consequence, in the context of a divine dimension, whether as "fear of God" (Proverbs), as vision of divine presence (Job), or even divine inscrutibility (Qohelet). As Spohn has shown, the crippling diversions of worldly pursuits are most fully seen to be devoid of positive attitudinal and moral significance when measured against the character-transforming encounter between the devout disciple and the God of love and justice.[40]

The voice of worship provides us with an ethics of disposition, a voice that through spiritual practice nurtures the sensitivities and qualities needed to do the hard work of lawmaking, to raise the prophetic voice, to develop the imagination for rereading *our* hour in history, and to nurture the virtues that will guide us to act justly. The voice of worship operates from the depths of suffering to the heights of praise. Worship at its best incorporates all the community's needs, wants, failings, hopes, and dreams, while through attentiveness to God draws individuals out of themselves toward the communal project of building the city of God on earth. The voice of worship, like the legal voice, has the resources to update itself, provided all liturgical forms and psalm genres are given free reign in the sanctuary. Of course, as with the legal voice, the prophets must push us if worship becomes too stylized and loses contact with life. Then too the wisdom voice can offer critique if worship fails to nurture right conduct or to heed the cry of the suffering of the innocent. Yet for all the strengths of the prophetic and wisdom strands, we have come to recognize that much of their power arises out of their direct mining of the ritual language of ancient Israel, as Elihu's speeches in Job (chaps. 32—37) or the book of Joel make abundantly clear. Liturgical language, in other words, is essential for shaping a people who do justice.

In dissecting the various layers and strands of the biblical record, we have tried to remain cognizant of the entire canon with its wider trajectories and visions. As we take in the broader sweep, we encounter the moral capital of the biblical tradition—the tradition's capacity for expansion and accretion that results from the fact that subsequent generations have culled fresh insights and added new readings to the social-political dimensions of the text. We need only think of the exodus story. As M. Walzer observes, "Wherever people know the Bible, and experience oppression, the Exodus has sustained their spirits and (sometimes) inspired their resistance."[41] Walzer's reading, which is less ideological and hence encourages the community to be more self-critical than his book's rather transparent (and mechanically Marxist) predecessor, L. Steffens's *Moses in Red*, enables us to see that the very Bible that we thought we had under cross-examination has turned the tables and begun to examine us.[42] It is this flexibility of the biblical tradition, this ability to draw the biblical record into dialogue with the present, that not only illumines our understanding of the political depths of the biblical materials but also urges us to unpack the theological depths of the contemporary political moment. Of course, cheaply imitating the past, treating the biblical text as the product of some theological golden age, will not solve contemporary problems, but neither will we squarely address pressing contemporary questions if we fail to probe the human and divine sides of these issues, as the Bible bids us to do. If the Bible's diversity stands out as a critical factor in this continuing endeavor, then perhaps Walzer is correct to suggest that God "intends all the meanings that [God] has made us capable of discovering."[43]

Biblical polyvalence remains ancient Israel's lasting legacy to humankind.[44] The flexibility of the traditions, on the one hand, and their inevitable stubbornness, on the other, work to present us with one of the most interesting case studies of ethical thought from the ancient world. More than a case study however, this ancient dialogue continues to have a place wherever thinking people and people of faith wish to wrestle with the moral imperative to build a better world. We have much to learn. The ancient Israelites have much to teach. The continuing dialogue between scripture, tradition, and the present holds great promise for our collective future. Where the social ethics of the Hebrew Bible is concerned, we are called to bring the text's rich insights to bear on our continued efforts to establish a more just society. This is the burden of torah study, but also its joy.

Notes

1. For a discussion of the broader questions regarding scripture and ethics beyond the Hebrew Bible, see W. Spohn, *What Are They Saying about Scripture and Ethics?* (New York: Paulist Press, 1995).
2. A useful study and critique of Hauerwas's ideas beyond what might be applicable to an analysis of the Hebrew Bible is offered by J. S. Siker, *Scripture and Ethics: Twentieth-Century Portraits* (New York: Oxford University Press, 1997), 97—125.
3. S. Hauerwas, *A Community of Character: Toward a Constructive Christian Social Ethic* (Notre Dame, Ind: University of Notre Dame, 53–54.
4. Ibid., 61.

5. Ibid., 62.

6. Ibid.

7. S. Hauerwas and S. Long, "Interpreting the Bible as a Political Act," *Religion and Intellectual Life* 6 (1989): 134–42.

8. Hauerwas, *Community of Character,* 67.

9. Ibid., 63.

10. S. Hauerwas, *Community of Character,* 66. See P. R. Davies, *In Search of "Ancient Israel"* (Sheffield: JSOT Press, 1992). While one need not argue for such an extreme disjuncture between the preexilic and postexilic periods, as if no preinvasion continuities inform the later traditions, still Davies' awareness of the character of the term "Israel" as an ideological football in the postexilic era is instructive.

11. Hauerwas and Long, "Interpreting the Bible," 134.

12. Hauerwas, *Community of Character,* 55.

13. P. Trible, *Texts of Terror: Literary-Feminist Readings of Biblical Narratives* (Philadelphia: Fortress Press, 1984).

14. A. B. Anderson and G. W. Pickering, *Confronting the Color Line: The Broken Promise of the Civil Rights Movement in Chicago* (Athens, Ga.: University of Georgia Press, 1986), 389–410.

15. T. W. Ogletree, *The Use of the Bible in Christian Ethics* (Philadelphia: Fortress Press, 1983), for example, is aware of the varying textures of ancient Israel's ethics discourse, yet he seems to see in these tradents, not many disparate voices, but contributors to an overall Israelite and early church "moral vision." This tendency toward a systematization of the "vision" can lead to a profound lack of appreciation for the element of biblical diversity. By opening up diversity, we are aware not only of diverse textures of discourse, but we become profoundly aware of the fact that the biblical tradition offers competing ethical voices and divergent analyses concerning the present social order.

16. For further discussions, see L. Brummel, "Luther and the Biblical Language of Poverty," *Ecumenical Review* 32 (1980): 40–58; D. Flood, "Gospel Poverty and the Poor," in *Option for the Poor: Challenge to the Rich Countries,* ed. L. Boff and V. Elizondo, Concilium 187: "Third World Theology" (Edinburgh: T. & T. Clark, 1986); B. Gordon, *The Economic Problem in Biblical and Patristic Thought* (Leiden: E. J. Brill, 1989); B. Ramsey, "Almsgiving in the Latin Church: The Late Fourth and Early Fifth Centuries," *Theological Studies* 43 (1982): 226–59; J. St. John, "God and Mammon: Responses in English Christianity," in *The Many Faces of Religion and Society,* ed. M. D. Bryant and R. H. Mataragnon (New York: Paragon House, 1985), 105–21.

17. See, e.g., R. J. Cassidy, *Jesus, Politics, and Society: A Study of Luke's Gospel* (Maryknoll, N. Y.: Orbis Books, 1978), 22–23.

18. See 1QM 14:7; 1QH 14:3; 1QS 3:8; 4:3. Cf. D. G. Flusser, "Blessed Are the Poor in Spirit . . . ," *Israel Exploration Journal* 10/1 (1960): 1–13; D. G. Flusser, "The Social Message from Qumran," *Journal of World History* 11 (1968): 107–115, and K. Murphy, "The Disposition of Wealth in the *Damascus Document* Tradition," *Revue de Qumran* 19 (1999): 83-129.

19. By way of comparison, see S. B. Dawes, " '*ănāwâ* in Translation and Tradition," *VT* 41/1 (1991): 38–48. See also J. M. Ford, "Three Ancient Jewish Attitudes towards Poverty," in *The New Way of Jesus: Essays Presented to Howard Charles,* ed. W. Klassen (Newton, Kans.: Faith & Life Press, 1980), 39-55, esp. 44–45.

20. For a full discussion of this and other terms for poverty in the Hebrew Bible, see J. D. Pleins, "Poor, Poverty (Old Testament)," in *ABD* 5: 402–414.

21. G. Gutiérrez, *A Theology of Liberation: History, Politics, and Salvation* (Maryknoll, N.Y.: Orbis Books, 1973), 291.

22. The following article series could serve as something of a model for continued scholarly sifting and discussion of relevant biblical matters: R. J. Coggins, "The Old Testament and the Poor," *Expository Times* 99 (1987–88): 11–14; J. E. Weir, "The Poor Are Powerless: A Response to R. J. Coggins, *Expository Times* 100 (1988–89): 13–15; S. Gillingham, "The Poor in the Psalms," ibid., 15–19; R. N. Whybray, "Poverty, Wealth, and Point of View in Proverbs," ibid., 332–36.

23. For a fuller discussion of views of poverty in Proverbs, see J. D. Pleins, "Poverty in the Social World of the Wise," *JSOT* 37 (1987): 61–78.

24. A more suggestive parallel between biblical and ancient Near Eastern sources may be found in the Mesopotamian edicts of royal release in which loans were cancelled, tax payments were reassessed, debt slaves were released, etc. The similarities between such an edict and the biblical jubilee is noteworthy. For a general discussion of the Mesopotamian context, see M. Weinfeld, "'Justice and Righteousness' in Ancient Israel against the Background of 'Social Reforms' in the Ancient Near East," in *Berliner Beiträge zum Vorderen Orient*, vol. 1, ed. H. Kühne, H.-J. Nissen, and J. Renger (Berlin: Dietrich Reimer Verlag, 1982), 491–519.

25. See R. Brooks, *Support for the Poor in the Mishnaic Law of Agriculture: Tractate Peah*, Brown Judaic Studies 43 (Chico, Calif.: Scholars Press, 1983). See also Ford, "Three Ancient Jewish Attitudes," 46–53.

26. This point is succinctly delineated by J. Neusner, *Ancient Israel after Catastrophe: The Religious World View of the Mishnah* (Charlottesville, Va.: University of Virginia, 1983).

27. See M. Weinfeld, "'Justice and Righteousness'—The Expression and Its Meaning," in *Justice and Righteousness: Biblical Themes and Their Influence*, ed. H. G. Reventlow and Y. Hoffman (Sheffield: Sheffield Academic Press, 1992), 228–46.

28. See, e.g., J. Reiman, *Justice and Modern Moral Philosophy* (New Haven, Conn.: Yale University Press, 1990). While topics such as fairness, the social contract, inequality, wealth, and even economic justice find their way into his dissection of the concepts of justice and social justice, poverty as such never becomes a measure of the question.

29. See J. S. Croatto, *Exodus: A Hermeneutics of Freedom*, trans. S. Attanasio (Maryknoll, N. Y.: Orbis Books, 1981), esp. chap. 2.

30. See, e.g., F. L. Moriarty, "The Chronicler's Account of Hezekiah's Reform," *CBQ* 27 (1965): 399–406.

31. As does, for example, A. A. Boesak, *Farewell to Innocence: A Socio-Ethical Study on Black Theology and Power* (Maryknoll, N. Y.: Orbis Books, 1976), 17–20. For a stringent critique from within the parameters of a liberation theology methodology, see I. J. Mosala, *Black Hermeneutics and Black Theology in South Africa* (Grand Rapids: Wm. B. Eerdmans Publishing Co., 1989), chap. 1.

32. See R. Nysse, "Moral Discourse on Economic Justice: Considerations from the Old Testament," *Word and World* 12 (1992): 337–44.

33. Consider, for example, the U.S. Bishops' Pastoral Message and Letter, "Economic Justice for All: Catholic Social Teaching and the U.S. Economy," *Origins* 16/24 (1986): 409–455. While not wishing to slight this important document, I would argue that its section on biblical perspectives (chap. 2, sec. A) would mesh better with its economic discussion had this section stressed biblical diversity rather than present a homogeneous view of the Bible on poverty and justice.

34. The phenomenon is detailed extensively by M. Fishbane, *Biblical Interpretation in Ancient Israel* (Oxford: Clarendon Press, 1985).

35. L. S. Cahill, *Between the Sexes: Foundations for a Christian Ethic of Sexuality* (Philadelphia: Fortress Press, 1985), 38.

36. J. Gustafson, *Theology and Christian Ethics* (New York: Pilgrim Press, 1974), 145.
37. Cahill, *Between the Sexes*, 38. See also D. Patrick, "Political Exegesis," in *Encounter with the Text: Form and History in the Hebrew Bible*, ed. M. J. Buss (Philadelphia: Fortress Press, 1979), 139–51.
38. In what follows, I am indebted to the style of analysis and the sort of categories adopted by W. C. Spohn, *Go and Do Likewise: Jesus and Ethics* (New York: Continuum, 1999).
39. G. von Rad, *Wisdom in Israel* (Nashville: Abingdon Press, 1972), 94–95.
40. Spohn, *Go and Do Likewise*, chap. 4.
41. M. Walzer, *Exodus and Revolution* (New York: Basic Books, 1985), 4.
42. L. Steffens, *Moses in Red: The Revolt of Israel as a Typical Revolution* (Philadelphia: Dorrance, 1926). The mechanical character of his Marxist analysis is evident throughout, but page 21 provides a succinct example. On the whole, Steffens eschews higher criticism entirely, thus leaving unchecked his rather monolithic reading of the text. The danger of such an approach becomes evident as Steffens draws on the stories of the deaths of the majority during the Sinai wanderings in Numbers to positively justify the hellish purges that seem to invariably accompany the revolutionist's bid for total control (44). Steffens's analysis makes the revolution an absolute at the expense of human life, and he seeks to find a biblical warrant for such a posture.
43. Walzer, *Exodus and Revolution*, 8.
44. See S. H. Blank, "The Hebrew Scriptures as a Source for Moral Guidance," in *Scripture in the Jewish and Christian Traditions: Authority, Interpretation, Relevance*, ed. F. E. Greenspahn (Nashville: Abingdon Press, 1982).

Subject/Author Index

537

Index of Ancient Sources